College Accounting

Third Edition 1-29

Douglas J. McQuaig

Wenatchee Valley College

Houghton Mifflin Company   Boston

Dallas   Geneva, Illinois   Lawrenceville, New Jersey   Palo Alto

This text and its related materials are dedicated to the students who will use them.

Printed in the U.S.A.

Library of Congress Catalog Card No.: 84-80982

ISBN: 0-395-35679-2

FGHIJ-RM-898

Contents

Preface

College Accounting provides students with a sound basic knowledge of accounting concepts and procedures, always taking into consideration the widely varying objectives students have. It offers:

- Vocational preparation for students entering the job market in accounting.
- A practical background in accounting for students embarking on other careers, such as clerical, secretarial, technical, sales, and managerial positions.
- Preparation and background for students planning more advanced studies in accounting.

Being a "chalk-in-hand" classroom teacher, I see the need for teachable accounting books, logically organized, liberally illustrated, and written in language that students can understand. In every way, I have endeavored to satisfy this need. In revising the text and its related materials, I have not departed from my original approach. However, since I am actively teaching the course, the material is continually reviewed and updated to reflect the latest developments and terminology affecting basic accounting. The accounting principles described are those endorsed by the Financial Accounting Standards Board and its predecessor, the Accounting Principles Board.

The fundamentals of accounting are presented in a practical, easy-to-understand manner. I believe in teaching by example. Consequently, each concept is well illustrated with specific business documents and report forms. An appropriate amount of repetition establishes fundamental concepts clearly in the minds of the students and enables them to develop confidence in handling more complex material. Each chapter relates new topics to the examples, concepts, and procedures presented in previous chapters. Even with computer-assisted accounting, entries for transactions must still be formulated, and the text will prepare students to make this transition.

College Accounting is designed primarily for use in a course extending two or three quarters or two semesters. The text may be divided into modules: Chapters 1–6 cover the full accounting cycle for a sole-proprietorship service business. Chapters 7–10 cover bank accounts and payroll accounting. Chapters 11–15 cover the full accounting cycle for a merchandising firm. Chapters 16–20 cover notes payable and receivable and, as well, the valuation of receivables, inventories, and plant assets. Chapters 21–25 cover vouchers, partnerships, and corporations. Chapters 26–29 cover analysis of financial statements and the statement of changes in financial position as well as departmental and manufacturing accounting.

In regard to the appendices listed below, note that two of them (Appendices A and C) are expanded and presented as full chapters in the second half of the text. However, a number of instructors recognize that some of their students will in fact take only one quarter or one semester of accounting; for these students the appendices offer a brief exposure to the rudiments of depreciation and financial statement analysis.

- **Appendix A: Methods of Depreciation** (after Chapter 5) Briefly describes methods of depreciation, including the Accelerated Cost Recovery System.
- **Appendix B: Computers and Accounting** (after Chapter 6) Surveys computer hardware, software, and accounting applications.
- **Appendix C: Financial Statement Analysis** (after Chapter 15) Briefly describes percentages and ratios used to interpret information in financial statements.
- **Appendix D: Estimating the Value of Inventories** (after Chapter 19) Describes the retail and gross profit methods.
- **Appendix E: Accelerated Cost Recovery System of Depreciation** (after Chapter 20) Details this government-mandated method.
- **Appendix F: COD, Layaway, and Installment Sales** (after Chapter 26) Portrays journal entries for these kinds of transactions.

Chapter Organization

- **Learning Objectives** Objectives state precisely what the students should be able to do when they complete the chapter. Each objective is also printed in the margin beside the relevant text discussion.
- **Examples** Each description of a concept is followed by an example.
- **Glossary** In addition to defining terms as they are introduced in the body of a chapter, the text presents the definitions again in the glossary at the end of the chapter.
- **Questions** Seven discussion questions, based on the main points, are included at the end of each chapter.
- **Classroom Exercises** For practice in applying concepts, eight exercises are provided with each chapter.
- **Problems** Each chapter contains four A problems and four B problems. The A and B problems are parallel in content and level of difficulty. They are arranged in order of difficulty, with Problems 1A and 1B in each chapter being the simplest and the last problem in each series being the most comprehensive.

Special Features

- **Extended Example** NuWay Cleaners, a fictional company, is used throughout Chapters 1–6 to illustrate accounting concepts.
- **Accounting Cycle Review Problem** This mini–practice set, following Chapter 6, involves the full accounting cycle for a fictional company called The Gamerama.
- **Representative T Accounts and Transactions** Simple charts organize this information for Chapters 1–6, 7–10, 11–15, 16–20, and 21–25.
- **Chapter 7: Accounting for Professional Enterprises** This is an optional chapter emphasizing the combined journal. (If the chapter is not used, an alternative set of achievement tests is available that omits the combined journal.)

Supplementary Learning Aids

- **Working Papers** Contain self-study review questions, an extended demonstration problem and solution for each chapter (new to this edition), forms for A and B problems and for the Accounting Cycle Review Problem, and answers to the self-study review questions. The Working Papers also include a Review of Business Mathematics and a list of check figures.
- **After Chapter 6** Sounds Abound, a computer practice set for one month in the life of a sole proprietorship service business. It requires only two hours of computer time or may be done manually.
- **Also after Chapter 6** A computer job simulation for a General Ledger Clerk at Lawson's Supply Center. Five computer job simulations are offered for use with *College Accounting*, Third Edition. All offer detailed and realistic training in specific accounting tasks.
- **After Chapter 10** Three practice sets are available. Each covers the basic accounting cycle, cash management, and payroll for one month in the life of a sole proprietorship service business. All three are published in a business papers format for the sake of realism.
  - Skate-O-Rama permits instructors to choose either a combined journal or a general journal.
  - C. W. Hale, M.D., has medical forms and business papers. A combined journal is used.
  - M. T. Chandler, Attorney at Law, has legal forms and business papers. A combined journal is used.
- **Also after Chapter 10** A computer job simulation for Payroll Clerk at Lawson's Supply Center.

- **After Chapter 11** A computer job simulation for Accounts Receivable Clerk at Lawson's Supply Center.
- **After Chapter 12** A computer job simulation for Accounts Payable Clerk at Lawson's Supply Center.
- **After Chapter 13** A computer job simulation for Cash Clerk at Lawson's Supply Center.
- **After Chapter 15** Sinclair Electronics, a practice set featuring business papers and special journals. It covers a one-month accounting cycle for a merchandising firm.
- **Also after Chapter 15** Denton Appliance and Air Conditioning, a computer practice set for a merchandising firm. Students first complete the set fully by hand, using a general journal; they then key the entries into the computer.
- **Also after Chapter 15** Cook's Solar Energy Systems, a computer practice set for one month in the life of a sole proprietorship merchandising firm.
- **After Chapter 22** Cloverton Outdoor Store, a one-month practice set utilizing a voucher system for a partnership merchandising business.

Instructional Aids

- **Instructor's Manual** Includes teaching suggestions for each chapter as well as solutions to questions and exercises. Solutions to all A and B problems are filled in on replicas of the Working Papers.
- **Transparencies** Provide transparencies for solutions to all exercises and all A and B problems. Several teaching transparencies are also provided (new to this edition and supplementary to the figures in the text).
- **Test Bank** New to this edition. Includes objective questions (true-false and multiple-choice) for each group of chapters (Chapters 1–6, 7–10, 11–15, 16–20, 21–25, and 26–29). Also provides final examinations in two versions (covering Chapters 1–10, Chapters 1–15, and Chapters 16–29). These are printed in a format suitable for copying and distributing to classes.
- **Achievement Tests** Preprinted tests ready for class use. Each test covers two or three chapters in the text. Series A, which covers Chapters 1–15 and Chapters 16–29, provides 32 copies of each test. Series B is an alternative set of tests covering the same material.
- **Computer Test Bank** This is a computerized version of the objective questions in the Test Bank. We can provide software for your use or a printed test based on your selections from the Test Bank.

Acknowledgments

Again, I would sincerely like to thank the editorial staff of Houghton Mifflin for their continuous support. I am still deeply appreciative of the assistance given to me during the preparation of the first edition of this text by Professors Hobart Adams, University of Akron, and Joseph Goodman, Chicago State University. The cooperation of my colleagues, Professors Audrey Chan-Nui, Geneva Knutson, and John Wisen, has been most helpful. Especially, I want to thank my many students at Wenatchee Valley College for their observations and my former students Esther Loranger and Elizabeth Frack for their diligent proofreading of the text.

During the writing of the third edition, I visited many users of the text throughout the country. Their constructive suggestions are reflected in the changes that have been made. Unfortunately, space does not permit mention of all those who have contributed to this volume. Some of those, however, who have been supportive and have influenced my efforts are:

Joseph Adamo, Cazenovia College
Stanley Augustine, Santa Rosa Junior College
Harry Baggett, Diablo Valley College
Pat Bille, Highline Community College
Linda Block, Babson College
Kenneth Brown, University of Houston
Carmela C. Caputo, Empire State College
Clairmont P. Carter, University of Lowell
John Chestnutt, Allan Hancock Joint Community College
Trudy Chiaravalli, Lansing Community College
Howard West Clark, Polk Community College
Edward Coda, Leeward Community College
Lyle Couse, Chemeketa Community College
Martha J. Curry, Huston-Tillotson College
Leonard Delury, Portland Community College
Fred Fitz-Randolph, American Business Institute, New York
Mary Foster, Illinois Central College
William French, Albuquerque Vocational and Technical College
Stuart Fukushige, Leeward Community College
A. Steven Graham, Vincennes University
Marie Gressel, Santa Barbara City College
Barbara Hall, Wabash Valley College
Robert Hellmer, Milwaukee Area Technical College
Thomas Hilgeman, Meramec Community College
Donald L. Holloway, Long Beach City College
James Howe, Oakland Community College
Eugene Janner, Blinn College
Van Johnson, Midland College
Edward H. Julius, California Lutheran University

Andre E. Kelton, American Business Institute, New York
Donna L. Randall Lacey, Bunker Hill Community College
Elliott S. Levy, Bentley College
Lorraine Lombardi, Katherine Gibbs School, Boston
Loren Long, Elgin Community College
Joyce Loudder, Houston Community College
Donald MacGilvra, Shoreline Community College
Libby Miller, Columbus Technical Institute
V. Eva Molnar, Riverside Community College District
Robert Nash, Henry Ford Community College
M. Salah Negm, Prince George's Community College
Dolores Osborne, Central Washington University
Frank Patterman, Shoreline Community College
Vincent Pelletier, College of DuPage
Bernard Piwkiewicz, Laney Community College
William Rodgers, Saint Paul's College, Concordia, Missouri
Frances Rubicek, Kalamazoo Valley Community College
Paul T. Ryan, Jackson State Community College
Viola Sauer-Singer, American Business Institute, New York
Lee H. Schlorff, Bentley College
Steve Schmidt, Butte College
Nelda Shelton, Tarrant County Junior College
Sharon Smith, Texas Southmost College
Mary Steffens, Crafton Hills College
Harold Steinhauser, Rock Valley Community College
Joseph Stella, New Hampshire College
Tom Vannaman, Midland College
William G. Vendemia, Youngstown State University
Russell Vermillion, Prince George's Community College
Florence G. Waldman, Kilgore College
Robert Weaver, Malcolm X College
Stan Weikert, College of the Canyons
Penny Westerfeld, North Harris County College
Maxine Wilson, Los Angeles City College
Theresa Wood, North Harris County College

As always, I would like to thank my family for their understanding and cooperation. Without their support, this book would never have balanced. Pertinent suggestions for updating the material were given by my daughter, Judith Britton, C.P.A., of Price Waterhouse; my son-in-law, Christopher Britton, C.P.A., of Touche Ross; and my son, John McQuaig, C.P.A., of McQuaig and Associates.

Douglas J. McQuaig

1 Analyzing Business Transactions: Asset, Liability, and Owner's Equity Accounts

Learning Objectives

After you have completed this chapter, you will be able to do the following:

1. Define accounting.

2. Record a group of business transactions, in columnar form, involving changes in assets, liabilities, and owner's equity.

3. Prepare a balance sheet.

Accounting is often called the language of business, because when confronted with events of a business nature, all people in society—owners, managers, creditors, employees, attorneys, engineers, and so forth—must use accounting terms and concepts in order to describe these events. Examples of accounting terms are *net, gross, yield, valuation, accrued, deferred*—the list could go on and on. So it is logical that anyone entering the business world should know enough of the "language" to communicate with others and to understand their communications.

The meanings of some terms used in accounting differ from the meanings of the same words used in a nonbusiness situation. If you have studied a foreign language, you undoubtedly found that as you became more familiar with the language, you also became better acquainted with the country in which it is spoken, as well as with the customs of the people. Similarly, as you acquire a knowledge of accounting, you will gain an understanding of the way businesses operate and the reasoning involved in the making of business decisions. Even if you are not involved directly in accounting activities, most assuredly you will need to be sufficiently acquainted with the "language" to be able to understand the meaning of accounting information, how it is compiled, how it can be used, and what its limitations are.

DEFINITION OF ACCOUNTING

Accounting is the process of analyzing, classifying, recording, summarizing, and interpreting business transactions in financial or monetary terms. A business **transaction** is an event that has a direct effect on the operation of the economic unit and can be expressed in terms of money. Examples of business transactions are buying or selling goods, renting a building, paying employees, buying insurance, or any other activity of a business nature.

Objective 1

Define accounting.

The accountant is the person who keeps the financial history of an economic unit in written form. The term **economic unit** includes not only business enterprises, but also nonprofit entities, such as government bodies, churches, clubs, and fraternal organizations. All these require some type of accounting records. The primary purpose of accounting is to provide the financial information needed for the efficient operation of the economic unit and to make the information available in usable forms to the interested parties, such as owners, members, taxpayers, creditors, and so on.

Accountants follow rules in carrying out the various phases of the accounting process. In the United States, these rules or guidelines have been determined by an independent body called the Financial Accounting Standards Board (FASB) and its predecessors. The Financial Accounting

Standards Board is composed of seven highly skilled accountants who are experienced in various areas of accounting.

FIELDS IN WHICH ACCOUNTING IS NEEDED

A knowledge of accounting is most valuable in the following three fields:

- **Bookkeeping and accounting** Those who plan to enter the field as a vocation naturally need training in accounting.
- **Business management** Those aspiring to managerial positions must be able to understand financial reports, evaluate operations, and make logical decisions.
- **Personal recordkeeping** Every person—even one who does not plan to be an accountant or a business manager—benefits from a study of accounting, because such a study enables one to keep better records, understand financial reports, engage in financial planning and budgeting, invest savings, and prepare necessary tax returns.

Bookkeeping and Accounting

Considerable confusion exists over the distinction between bookkeeping and accounting. Actually the two are closely related, and there is no universally accepted line of separation. Generally, bookkeeping involves the systematic recording of business transactions in financial terms. Accounting is carried on at a higher level or degree than bookkeeping is. An accountant sets up the system by which business transactions are to be recorded by a bookkeeper. An accountant may supervise the work of the bookkeeper and prepare financial statements and tax reports. Although the work of the bookkeeper is more routine, it is hard to draw a line where the bookkeeper's work ends and the accountant's begins. The bookkeeper must understand the entire accounting system, exercise judgment in recording financial details, and organize and report the appropriate information.

Career Opportunities in Accounting

When it comes to career opportunities, accounting is commonly divided into three main fields, listed here in the order of number of positions available.

- **Private accounting** Most people who are accountants work for private business firms. The growing importance of accounting often provides opportunities for advancement into managerial positions, such as office managers, data processing supervisors, systems analysts, internal auditors, and controllers.
- **Governmental and institutional accounting** Local, state, and federal government bodies employ vast numbers of people in accounting jobs, not only for recordkeeping but also for auditing private businesses and individuals whose dealings are subject to government regulation. Many accountants in the federal government work as internal revenue agents, investigators, bank examiners, and the like. At all levels of government, there are traditional accounting positions.
- **Public accounting** Certified public accountants (or CPAs) are independent professionals, comparable to doctors and lawyers, who offer accounting services to clients for a fee. There are approximately 275,000 CPAs and more than 700,000 noncertified public accountants in the United States today. Accounting is easily the fastest growing of all the professions; it is expanding, in fact, at twice the rate the economy is expanding. Factors responsible for the growth of professional accounting include the increasing size and complexity of business corporations, the broadening of income taxes and other forms of taxation, and the increase in government regulation of business activities.

The Lay Person's Need for Accounting

Anyone who aspires to a position of leadership in business or government needs a knowledge of accounting. Managers and supervisors often have to keep financial records, understand accounting data contained in reports and budgets, and express future plans in financial terms. A study of accounting gives a person the necessary background, as well as an understanding of an organization's scope, functions, and policies. People who have managerial jobs must be aware of how accounting information can be developed for use as a tool in the decision-making process, and they should also be acquainted with the recordkeeping and management functions of accounting.

ASSETS AND OWNER'S EQUITY

Assets are properties or things of value owned by an economic unit or business entity, such as cash, equipment, buildings, and land. Always remember that a **business entity** is considered to be separate and distinct from the persons who supply the assets it uses. Property acquired by the business is an asset of the business. The owner is separate from the business and, in fact, has claims upon it. If no money is owed against the assets, then the owner's right would be equal to the value of the assets. The owner's right or claim is expressed by the word **equity,** or *investment.* You often see these terms in the classified-advertising section of a newspaper, where a person wants to sell the ownership right to a property, such as a house. Other terms that may be used include **capital,** *net worth,* or *proprietorship.*

Assets	= Owner's Equity
Items or property of value owned by the business	Owner's right or investment in the business

Suppose that the total value of the assets is $10,000, and the business entity does not owe any amount against the assets. Then,

Assets	= Owner's Equity
$10,000 =	$10,000

Or suppose that the assets consist of a truck that costs $8,000; the owner has invested $2,000 for the truck, and the business entity has borrowed the remainder from the bank, which is the **creditor** (one to whom money is owed). This can be shown as follows:

Assets	=	Liabilities	+	Owner's Equity
Items owned		Amount owed to creditors		Owner's investment
$8,000	=	$6,000	+	$2,000

We have now introduced a new classification, **liabilities,** which represents debts and includes the amounts that the business entity owes its creditors, or the amount by which it is liable to its creditors. The debts may originate because the business bought goods or services on a credit basis, borrowed money, or otherwise created an obligation to pay. The creditors' claims to the assets have priority over the claims of the owner.

An equation expressing the relationship of these elements is called the **fundamental accounting equation.** We'll be dealing with this equation constantly from now on. If we know two parts of this equation, we can determine the third. Let us look at some examples.

Ms. Smith has $9,000 invested in her advertising agency, and the agency owes creditors $3,000; that is, the agency has liabilities of $3,000. Then,

Assets	=	Liabilities	+	Owner's Equity
?	=	$3,000	+	$9,000

We can find the amount of the business's assets by adding the liabilities and the owner's equity:

$ 3,000 Liabilities
+9,000 Owner's Equity
$12,000 Assets

The completed equation now reads

Assets = Liabilities + Owner's Equity
$12,000 = $3,000   + $9,000

Or take Mr. Jones, who raises mushrooms to sell to canners. His business has assets of $20,000, and it owes creditors $4,000; that is, it has liabilities of $4,000. Then,

Assets = Liabilities + Owner's Equity
$20,000 = $4,000   +   ?

We find the owner's equity by subtracting the liabilities from the assets:

$20,000 Assets
−4,000 Liabilities
$16,000 Owner's Equity

The equation now reads

Assets = Liabilities + Owner's Equity
$20,000 = $4,000   + $16,000

Mr. Anderson, who has an insurance agency, has assets of $18,000; and his investment (his equity) amounts to $12,000. Then,

Assets = Liabilities + Owner's Equity
$18,000 =   ?   + $12,000

In order to find the firm's total liabilities, we subtract the equity from the assets:

$18,000 Assets
−12,000 Owner's Equity
$ 6,000 Liabilities

The completed equation reads

Assets	=	Liabilities	+	Owner's Equity
$18,000	=	$6,000	+	$12,000

Recording Business Transactions

Objective 2

Record a group of business transactions, in columnar form, involving changes in assets, liabilities, and owner's equity.

To repeat: Business transactions are events that have a direct effect on the operations of an economic unit or enterprise and are expressed in terms of money. Each business transaction must be recorded in the accounting records. As one records business transactions, one has to change the amounts listed under the headings Assets, Liabilities, and Owner's Equity. However, **the total of one side of the fundamental accounting equation should always equal the total of the other side.** The subdivisions under these three main headings, as we shall see, are called **accounts.**

Let us now look at a group of business transactions. Although these transactions illustrate a service type of business, they would pertain to a professional enterprise as well. In these transactions, let's assume that Alan Stevenson establishes his own business and calls it NuWay Cleaners.

Transaction (a) Stevenson invests $32,000 cash in his new business. This means that he deposits $32,000 in the bank in a new separate account entitled NuWay Cleaners. This separate bank account will help Stevenson keep his business investment separate from his personal funds. The Cash account consists of bank deposits and money on hand. The business now has $32,000 more in cash than before, and Stevenson's investment has also increased. The account, denoted by the owner's name followed by the word *Capital*, records the amount of the owner's investment, or equity, in the business. The effect of this transaction on the fundamental accounting equation is as follows:

	Assets	=	Liabilities	+	Owner's Equity
	Items owned		Amounts owed to creditors		Owner's investment
	Cash	=			Alan Stevenson, Capital
(a)	+32,000	=			+32,000

Transaction (b) Alan Stevenson's first task is to get his cleaning shop ready for business, and to do that he will need the proper equipment. Accordingly, NuWay Cleaners buys $18,000 worth of equipment for cash. It is important to note that at this point Stevenson has not invested any new money; he simply exchanged part of the business's cash for equipment. Because equipment is a new type of property for the firm, a new account, called Equipment, is created. Equipment is included under assets. As a result of this transaction, the accounting equation is changed as follows.

	Assets		=	Liabilities	+	Owner's Equity
	Items owned			Amounts owed to creditors		Owner's investment
	Cash	+ Equipment	=			Alan Stevenson, Capital
Initial investment	32,000		=			32,000
(b)	−18,000 +	18,000				
New balances	14,000 +	18,000	=			32,000
		32,000				32,000

Transaction (c) NuWay Cleaners buys $4,000 worth of equipment on credit from Sanchez Equipment Company.

The Equipment account shows an increase because the business owns $4,000 worth of additional equipment. There is also an increase in liabilities, because the business now owes $4,000. The liabilities account called Accounts Payable is used for short-term liabilities or charge accounts, usually due within thirty days. There is now a total of $36,000 on each side of the equals sign. Because NuWay Cleaners owes money to Sanchez Equipment Company, Sanchez Equipment is called NuWay's creditor.

	Assets		=	Liabilities	+	Owner's Equity
	Items owned			Amounts owed to creditors		Owner's investment
	Cash	+ Equipment	=	Accounts Payable	+	Alan Stevenson, Capital
Previous balances	14,000 +	18,000	=			32,000
(c)		+4,000		+4,000		
New balances	14,000 +	22,000	=	4,000	+	32,000
		36,000			36,000	

Observe that the recording of each transaction must yield an equation that is in balance. For example, transaction **(c)** resulted in a $4,000 increase to both sides of the equation, and transaction **(b)** resulted in a minus $18,000 and a plus $18,000 *on the same side,* with nothing recorded on the other side. It does not matter whether you change one side or both sides. The important point is that whenever a transaction is properly recorded, the accounting equation remains in balance.

Transaction (d) NuWay Cleaners pays $1,000 to Sanchez Equipment Company, to be applied against the firm's liability of $4,000.

In analyzing this payment, we recognize that cash is being reduced. At the same time, the firm *owes* less than before, so it should be recorded as a reduction in liabilities.

	Assets		=	Liabilities	+	Owner's Equity
	Items owned			Amounts owed to creditors		Owner's investment
	Cash +	Equipment	=	Accounts Payable	+	Alan Stevenson, Capital
Previous balances	14,000 +	22,000	=	4,000	+	32,000
(d)	−1,000			−1,000		
New balances	13,000 +	22,000	=	3,000	+	32,000
		35,000			35,000	

Transaction (e) NuWay Cleaners buys cleaning fluids on credit from Troy Supply Company for $400. Cleaning fluids are listed under Supplies instead of Equipment because a cleaning business uses up cleaning fluids in a relatively short period of time—as a matter of fact, in one or a few cleaning jobs. Equipment, on the other hand, normally lasts a number of years.

	Assets			=	Liabilities	+	Owner's Equity
	Items owned				Amounts owed to creditors		Owner's investment
	Cash +	Equip. +	Supp.	=	Accounts Payable	+	Alan Stevenson, Capital
Previous balances	13,000 +	22,000		=	3,000	+	32,000
(e)		+	400		+400		
New balances	13,000 +	22,000 +	400	=	3,400	+	32,000
		35,400				35,400	

Accounting, as we said before, is the process of analyzing, classifying, recording, summarizing, and interpreting business transactions in financial or monetary terms. In relating these elements to the transactions of NuWay Cleaners, we made an analysis to decide which accounts were involved and then determined whether a transaction resulted in an increase or a decrease in those accounts. Then we recorded the transaction. After each transaction, the equation should still be in balance; the totals of both sides should always be equal. This example serves as an introduction to **double-entry accounting**. We have demonstrated that each transaction must be recorded in at least two accounts and that the equation must always remain in balance.

Summary of Transactions

Let us now summarize the business transactions of NuWay Cleaners in columnar form, identifying each transaction by a letter of the alphabet. To test your understanding of the recording procedure, describe the nature of the transactions that have taken place.

	Assets			=	Liabilities	+	Owner's Equity
	Cash	+ Equip.	+ Supp.		Accounts Payable		Alan Stevenson, Capital
Transaction (a)	+32,000			=			+32,000
Transaction (b)	−18,000	+ 18,000					
Balance	14,000	+ 18,000		=			32,000
Transaction (c)		+	4,000		+4,000		
Balance	14,000	+ 22,000		=	4,000	+	32,000
Transaction (d)	−1,000				−1,000		
Balance	13,000	+ 22,000		=	3,000	+	32,000
Transaction (e)			+ 400		+400		
Balance	13,000	+ 22,000 +	400	=	3,400	+	32,000
		35,400				35,400	

The following observations apply to all types of business transactions:

1. Every transaction is recorded in terms of increases and/or decreases in two or more accounts.
2. One side of the equation is always equal to the other side of the equation.

THE BALANCE SHEET

Objective 3

Prepare a balance sheet.

Earlier we listed *summarizing* as one of the five basic tasks of the accounting process. To accomplish this task, accountants use financial statements. One of these financial statements, the **balance sheet,** summarizes the balances of the assets, liabilities, and owner's equity accounts on a given date (usually at the end of a month or year). The balance sheet shows the financial position of the company and is sometimes referred to as a *statement of financial position*. Financial position is shown by a list of the values of the assets or property, offset by the liabilities or amounts owed to creditors, and the owner's equity or financial interest. **Financial position,** as used in this accounting concept, means the same thing we would mean if we were to speak of the financial position of a person. A statement of financial position is a listing of what a business owns, as well as a listing of the claims of its creditors. The difference between the total amount owned and total amount owed is the owner's equity or net worth.

Perhaps you might have noticed, in the back pages of a newspaper, the balance sheets of commercial banks and savings and loan associations. The law requires them to publish their balance sheets in daily newspapers at certain times of the year. The purpose of these financial statements is to show the financial positions of these institutions; the total of the assets listed must equal the total claims of the depositors plus the owners' equity.

In the next chapter the fundamental accounting equation will be expanded to include revenue and expense elements. For the moment, however, we may refer to the equation as the *balance sheet equation* because only the three elements that appear on the balance sheet—assets, liabilities, and owner's equity—appear in the equation. And instead of presenting the equation in horizontal form as

Assets = Liabilities + Owner's Equity,

we can now present the same balances in the vertical form in which they appear in the balance sheet below:

Assets
=
Liabilities
+
Owner's Equity

After NuWay Cleaners records its initial transactions, the balance sheet as of June 15 would look like Figure 1-1.

Figure 1-1

NuWay Cleaners
Balance Sheet
June 15, 19–

Assets		
Cash		$13 0 0 0 00
Supplies		4 0 0 00
Equipment		22 0 0 0 00
Total Assets		$35 4 0 0 00
Liabilities		
Accounts Payable		$ 3 4 0 0 00
Owner's Equity		
Alan Stevenson, Capital		32 0 0 0 00
Total Liabilities and Owner's Equity		$35 4 0 0 00

Let's note some details about balance sheets:

1. The three-line heading consists of the name of the firm, the title of the financial statement, and the date of the financial statement. The heading is centered at the top of the page.
2. The headings for the major classifications of accounts (Assets, Liabilities, Owner's Equity) are all centered. The classifications are separated by the space of one line.
3. Dollar signs are placed only at the head of each column and with each total.
4. Single lines (drawn with a ruler) are used to show that figures above are being added or subtracted. Lines should be drawn across the entire column.
5. Double lines are used under the totals in a column.

You should know that balance sheets are presented in one of two forms, the report form or the account form. In the **report form,** assets are placed on top (upper part of the page), and liabilities and owner's equity are placed below (lower part of the page). In the account form, assets are placed on the left side of the page, and liabilities and owner's equity are placed on the right side of the page. The report form will be used throughout this text.

GLOSSARY

Accounting   The process of analyzing, classifying, recording, summarizing, and interpreting business transactions in financial or monetary terms.

Accounts   Subdivisions under the main headings of Assets, Liabilities, and Owner's Equity.

Assets   Cash, properties, and other things of value owned.

Balance sheet   A financial statement showing the financial position of a firm or other economic unit at a given point in time, such as June 30 or December 31.

Business entity   A business enterprise, separate and distinct from the persons who supply the assets it uses. Property acquired by a business is an asset of the business. The owner is separate from the business and occupies the status of a claimant of the business.

Capital   The owner's investment, or equity, in an enterprise.

Creditor   One to whom money is owed.

Double-entry accounting   The system by which each business transaction is recorded in at least two accounts and the accounting equation is kept in balance.

Economic units   Business enterprises; also nonprofit entities such as government bodies, churches, clubs, and fraternal organizations.

Equity   The value of a right to or financial interest in an asset or group of assets.

Financial position The resources or assets owned by an economic unit at a point in time, offset by the claims against those resources; shown by a balance sheet.

Fundamental accounting equation An equation expressing the relationship of assets, liabilities, and owner's equity.

Liabilities Debts, or amounts, owed to creditors.

Report form The form of the balance sheet in which assets are placed at the top and the liabilities and owner's equity are placed below.

Transaction An event affecting an economic entity that can be expressed in terms of money and that must be recorded in the accounting records.

QUESTIONS, EXERCISES, AND PROBLEMS

Discussion Questions

1. What do we mean by owner's equity?
2. What is the fundamental accounting equation? Why should the total amount on one side of the equation always equal the total amount on the other side of the equation?
3. Give five examples of assets.
4. What effect will the purchase of supplies on account have on the fundamental accounting equation?
5. What is a business transaction? Give three examples of business transactions.
6. What does a double ruling across an amount column indicate?
7. What are the three sections of the body of a balance sheet?

Exercises

Exercise 1-1 Complete the following equations.

a. Assets of $24,000 = Liabilities of $4,200 + Owner's Equity of $_____
b. Assets of $_____ = Liabilities of $16,000 + Owner's Equity of $31,000 Balance Sheet
c. Assets of $32,000 − Owner's Equity of $15,000 = Liabilities of $_____

Exercise 1-2 Determine the following values:

a. The amount of the liabilities of a business having $49,463 of assets and in which the owner has a $33,900 equity.
b. The equity of the owner of an automobile that cost $8,700 who owes $3,900 on an installment loan payable to the bank.
c. The amount of the assets of a business having $6,170 in liabilities, in which the owner has a $21,000 equity.

Exercise 1-3 Lois Parker, a real estate broker, owns office equipment amounting to $9,600; a car, which is used for business purposes only, valued at $8,150; and other property that is used in her business amounting to $4,600. She owes business creditors a total of $1,720. What is the value of Parker's equity?

Exercise 1-4 Describe the transactions recorded in the following equation.

	Assets		=	Liabilities	+	Owner's Equity
	Cash	+ Equipment		Accounts Payable		L. Parker, Capital
(a)	+9,450		=			+9,450 — *Invested in business*
(b)		+2,400		+2,400		
Bal.	9,450 +	2,400	=	2,400	+	9,450
(c)	−1,700	+1,700				
Bal.	*paid* 7,750 +	4,100	=	2,400	+	9,450
(d)	−800	+3,300		+2,500 *charged*		
Bal.	6,950 +	7,400	=	4,900	+	9,450

Exercise 1-5 Dr. L. C. Jason is a chiropractor. As of April 30, he owned the following property that related to his professional practice: Cash, $960; Supplies, $350; Professional Equipment, $19,500; Office Equipment, $4,260. On the same date, he owed the following business creditors: Weston Supply Company, $1,740; Barton Equipment Sales, $950. Compute the following amounts in the accounting equation.

Assets_____ = Liabilities_____ + Owner's Equity_____

Exercise 1-6 Describe a business transaction that will do the following:

a. Increase an asset and increase a liability. *$4,000 worth of equip. on credit.*
b. Increase an asset and decrease an asset. *bought $4,000 " " " for cash*
c. Decrease an asset and decrease a liability. *Pay 1,100 to — to be applied against a firms liab.*
d. Increase an asset and increase owner's equity. *Invest in business*

Exercise 1-7 Dr. B. A. Stacy is a dentist. Describe the transactions that have been completed involving the asset, liability, and owner's equity accounts.

	Assets				=	Liabilities +	Owner's Equity
	Cash +	Prepaid Insurance	+ Dental Equipment	+ Office Furniture and Equipment	=	Accounts Payable	B. A. Stacy, Capital
Bal.	1,964 +	280	+ 19,628	+ 4,620	=	8,016 +	18,476
(a)	+1,200						+1,200
Bal.	3,164 +	280	+ 19,628	+ 4,620	=	8,016 +	19,676
(b)	−742					−742	
Bal.	2,422 +	280	+ 19,628	+ 4,620	=	7,274 +	19,676
(c)			+326			*charge* +326	
Bal.	2,422 +	280	+ 19,954	+ 4,620	=	7,600 +	19,676
(d)	−750		+1,850			*charge* +1,100	
Bal.	1,672 +	280	+ 21,804	+ 4,620	=	8,700 +	19,676

Paid on Acct (b)
Charged dental equip (c)

Exercise 1-8   Using the ending balances from Exercise 1-7, prepare a balance sheet, dated as of December 31 of this year. Use notebook paper.

Problem Set A

Problem 1-1A   Townhouse Cleaners has just been established by the owner, Jean Moreland. It engages in the following transactions:

a. Moreland deposited $12,800 in the First State Bank in the name of the business.
b. Bought cleaning supplies for cash, $560.
c. Bought equipment for the business on account from Lundborg Company, $7,200.
d. Moreland invested an additional $3,200 in cash.
e. Paid Lundborg Company $1,600 as part payment on account.
f. Bought additional equipment for the business for cash, $1,420.

Instructions

1. Record the transactions in columnar form, using plus and minus signs, and show the balances after each transaction.
2. Prove that the total of one side of the equation equals the total of the other side of the equation.

Problem 1-2A   R. C. Baker owns the Baker Real Estate Agency. On September 30 Baker's books show the following balances in assets, liabilities, and owner's equity accounts.

Cash	$1,200	Building	$36,000
Supplies	435	Land	9,000
Office Equipment	4,680	Accounts Payable	8,670
Office Furniture	5,400	R. C. Baker, Capital	48,045

Instructions

Prepare a balance sheet as of September 30 of this year.

Problem 1-3A   The Clean-Rite Car Wash has just been established by the owner, J. C. Lloyd. The following transactions affect the asset, liability, and owner's equity accounts.

a. Lloyd deposited $18,200 in cash in the Illinois State Bank in the name of the business.
b. Bought equipment for use in the business for cash, $12,620.
c. Bought supplies consisting of brushes and soap on account from Camus Company, $685.
d. Paid cash for additional cleaning supplies for use in the business, $96.
e. Lloyd invested in the business his personal equipment having a value of $720.
f. Paid Camus Company as part payment on account, $120.
g. Bought additional equipment for use in the business on account from Jacobs Company, $1,400.

Instructions

1. Record the transactions in columnar form, using plus and minus signs, and show the balances after each transaction.
2. Prove that the total on one side of the equation equals the total on the other side of the equation.

Problem 1-4A The Dallas Chiropractic Clinic is owned by F. L. Leedy. On August 31 the following accounts are listed in random order.

Professional Equipment	$18,760	Supplies	$ 721
Cash	2,356	Office Equipment	2,424
F. L. Leedy, Capital	23,336	Accounts Payable	925

Instructions

Prepare a balance sheet as of August 31 of this year.

Problem Set B

Problem 1-1B Frome Appliance Repair has just been established by the owner, C. R. Frome, and engages in the following transactions:

a. Frome deposited $14,500 in the Nashua State Bank in the name of the business.
b. Bought equipment for use in the business for cash, $2,600.
c. Paid cash for supplies for use in the business, $720.
d. Bought additional equipment for the business on account from Downey Company, $7,280.
e. Invested an additional $1,860 in cash.
f. Paid Downey Company as part payment on account, $1,650.

Instructions

1. Record the transactions in columnar form, using plus and minus signs, and show the balance after each transaction.
2. Prove that the total on one side of the equation equals the total on the other side of the equation.

Problem 1-2B A. R. Bergman owns the Bergman Advertising Agency. Bergman's books show the following balances in assets, liabilities, and owner's equity accounts as of August 31.

Cash	$1,440	Building	$42,000
Supplies	465	Land	12,000
Office Equipment	7,020	Accounts Payable	3,255
Office Furniture	6,300	A. R. Bergman, Capital	65,970

Instructions

Prepare a balance sheet as of August 31 of this year.

Problem 1-3B   The Safety Insurance Agency has just been established by the owner, R. A. Baxter. The following transactions affect the asset, liability, and owner's equity accounts.

a. Baxter deposited $12,560 in cash in the California State Bank in the name of the business.
b. Bought equipment for use in the business for cash, $5,845.
c. Bought office supplies consisting of stationery and business forms on account from Excell Printers, $486.
d. Baxter invested in the business her own personal office equipment, having a value of $1,420.
e. Paid cash for additional office supplies for use in the business, $126.
f. Paid Excell Printers (creditors) $145 as part payment on account.
g. Bought additional equipment for use in the business on account from Brooks Company, $1,528.

Instructions

1. Record the transactions in columnar form, using plus and minus signs, and show the balances after each transaction.
2. Prove that the total on one side of the equation equals the total on the other side of the equation.

Problem 1-4B   Down-Town Barber Shop is owned by R. P. Gower. On October 31, the following accounts are listed in random order.

Supplies	$783	Professional Equipment	$ 6,849
Cash	461	R. P. Gower, Capital	10,131
Accounts Payable	·127	Furniture and Fixtures	2,165

Instructions

Prepare a balance sheet as of October 31 of this year.

2 Analyzing Business Transactions: Revenue and Expense Accounts

Learning Objectives

After you have completed this chapter, you will be able to do the following:

1. Record a group of business transactions in columnar form, involving all five elements of the fundamental accounting equation.

2. Present an income statement.

3. Present a statement of owner's equity.

In Chapter 1, we analyzed and recorded a number of transactions in asset, liability, and owner's equity accounts and did so in a way that was consistent with the definition of accounting. In this chapter we shall introduce the remaining two classifications of accounts: revenues and expenses. We shall record business transactions involving revenue and expense accounts in the same type of columnar arrangement we used in Chapter 1. Again let us stress that, after each transaction has been recorded, the total of the balances of the accounts on one side of the equals sign should equal the total of the balances of the accounts on the other side of the equals sign. We shall continue to use transactions of NuWay Cleaners as examples.

REVENUE AND EXPENSE ACCOUNTS

Earnings of Company

Revenues are the amounts of assets that a business or other economic unit gains as a result of its operations. For example, revenues represent earnings (inflows) of <u>cash</u>, or other assets, derived from fees earned for the performing of services, sales involving the exchange of goods, rent income for providing the use of property, and interest income for the lending of money. Revenues are *not* only in the form of cash; they may also consist of credit-card receipts or charge accounts maintained for customers.

Expenses are the amounts of assets that a business or other economic unit uses up as a result of its operations. For example, expenses represent payouts (outflows) of cash, or other assets, for services received, such as wages expense for labor performed, rent expense for the use of property, interest expense for the use of money, and supplies expense for supplies used. When payment is to be made at a later time, an increase in an expense will result in an increase in a liability.

Revenues and expenses directly affect owner's equity. If a business earns revenue, there is an increase in owner's equity. If a business incurs or pays expenses, there is a decrease in owner's equity. So, we place revenue and expenses under the "umbrella" of owner's equity.

Recording Business Transactions

Soon after the opening of NuWay Cleaners, the first customers arrive, beginning a flow of revenue for the business. Let us now itemize further transactions of NuWay Cleaners for the first month of operations.

Transaction (f) NuWay Cleaners receives cash revenue for the first week, $600. As we said, revenue has the effect of increasing the owner's

Objective 1

Record a group of business transactions in columnar form, involving all five elements of the fundamental accounting equation.

equity; however, it is better to keep the revenue separate from the capital account until you have prepared the financial statements. As a result of this transaction, the accounting equation is affected as follows (PB stands for previous balance, and NB stands for new balance):

monthly
quarterly
semiannualy
Annually

	Assets			= Liabilities +		Owner's Equity	
	Cash +	Equipment +	Supplies	Accounts Payable		Alan Stevenson, Capital	+ Revenue
PB	13,000 +	22,000 +	400	= 3,400	+	32,000	
(f)	+600						+600
NB	13,600 +	22,000 +	400	= 3,400	+	32,000 +	600
		36,000				36,000	

Transaction (g) Shortly after opening the business, NuWay Cleaners pays the month's rent of $400. Rent is payment for a service—the privilege of occupying a building. Because this service will be used up in one month or less, we record the amount as an expense. If the payment covered a period longer than one month, we would record the amount under Prepaid Rent, which is an asset account.

Expenses have the effect of decreasing the owner's equity. Later, we will consider revenues and expenses as separate elements in the fundamental accounting equation. At that time, through the medium of the financial statements, they will be connected with owner's equity. For now, however, we will list them under the heading Owner's Equity.

	Assets			= Liabilities +		Owner's Equity		
	Cash +	Equipment +	Supplies	Accounts Payable		Alan Stevenson, Capital	+ Revenue −	Expenses
PB	13,600 +	22,000 +	400	= 3,400	+	32,000 +	600	
(g)	−400							+400 (Rent)
NB	13,200 +	22,000 +	400	= 3,400	+	32,000 +	600 −	400
		35,600				35,600		

Transaction (h) NuWay Cleaners pays $240 in wages to employees for June 1 through June 10. This additional expense of $240 is added to the previous balance of $400, resulting in a total deduction of $640, since the incurring of expense has the result of reducing the owner's equity. Now the equation looks like this:

	Assets			= Liabilities +	Owner's Equity		
	Cash +	Equipment +	Supplies	Accounts Payable	Alan Stevenson, Capital	+ Revenue	− Expenses
PB (h)	13,200 + −240	22,000 +	400	= 3,400	+ 32,000	+ 600	− 400 +240 (Wages)
NB	12,960 +	22,000 +	400	= 3,400	+ 32,000	+ 600	− 640
	35,360				35,360		

Transaction (i) NuWay Cleaners pays $320 for a two-year liability insurance policy. As it expires, the insurance will become an expense. However, because it is paid in advance for a period longer than one month, it has value and is therefore recorded as an asset. At the end of the year or financial period, an adjustment will have to be made, taking out the expired portion (that is, the coverage that has been used up) and recording it as an expense. In most cases accountants initially record expenses that are paid for more than one month in advance as assets.

	Assets				= Liabilities +	Owner's Equity		
	Cash +	Equip. +	Supp. +	Ppd. Ins.	Accounts Payable	Alan Stevenson, Capital	+ Revenue	− Expenses
PB (i)	12,960 + −320	22,000 +	400	+320	= 3,400	+ 32,000	+ 600	− 640
NB	12,640 +	22,000 +	400	+ 320	= 3,400	+ 32,000	+ 600	− 640
	35,360					35,360		

Transaction (j) NuWay Cleaners receives cash revenue for the second week, $760.

	Assets				= Liabilities +	Owner's Equity		
	Cash +	Equip. +	Supp. +	Ppd. Ins.	Accounts Payable	Alan Stevenson, Capital	+ Revenue	− Expenses
PB (j)	12,640 + +760	22,000 +	400	+ 320	= 3,400	+ 32,000	+ 600 +760	− 640
NB	13,400 +	22,000 +	400	+ 320	= 3,400	+ 32,000	+ 1,360	− 640
	36,120					36,120		

Observe that each time a transaction is recorded, the total amount on one side of the equation *remains equal* to the total amount on the other side. As proof of this equality, look at the following computation.

	Total
Cash	$13,400
Equipment	22,000
Supplies	400
Prepaid Insurance	320
	$36,120

	Total
Accounts Payable	$ 3,400
Alan Stevenson, Capital	32,000
Revenue	1,360
	$36,760
Expenses	−640
	$36,120

Revenue
Cash & Credit

Let us now continue with the transactions.

Transaction (k) NuWay Cleaners receives a bill from the Daily News for newspaper advertising, $180. NuWay has simply received the bill for advertising; it has not paid any cash. However, an expense has been incurred, and the firm owes $180 more than it did before, so this transaction must be recorded.

	Assets				=	Liabilities	+		Owner's Equity		
	Cash	+ Equip.	+ Supp.	+ Ppd. Ins.	=	Accounts Payable	+	Alan Stevenson, Capital	+ Revenue	−	Expenses
PB (k)	13,400	+ 22,000	+ 400	+ 320	=	3,400 +180	+	32,000	+ 1,360	−	640 +180 (Advertising)
NB	13,400	+ 22,000	+ 400	+ 320	=	3,580	+	32,000	+ 1,360	−	820
			36,120						36,120		

Transaction (l) NuWay Cleaners pays $1,800 to Sanchez Equipment Company, its creditor (the party to whom it owes money), as part payment on account.

	Assets				=	Liabilities	+		Owner's Equity		
	Cash	+ Equip.	+ Supp.	+ Ppd. Ins.	=	Accounts Payable	+	Alan Stevenson, Capital	+ Revenue	−	Expenses
PB (l)	13,400 −1,800	+ 22,000	+ 400	+ 320	=	3,580 −1,800	+	32,000	+ 1,360	−	820
NB	11,600	+ 22,000	+ 400	+ 320	=	1,780	+	32,000	+ 1,360	−	820
			34,320						34,320		

Transaction (m) NuWay Cleaners receives and pays bill for utilities, $220. Because the bill had not been previously recorded as a liability, the accounting equation is affected as follows:

	Assets				= Liabilities +		Owner's Equity		
	Cash	+ Equip.	+ Supp.	+ Ppd. Ins.	Accounts Payable	Alan Stevenson, Capital	+ Revenue	− Expenses
PB	11,600	+ 22,000	+ 400	+ 320 =	1,780	+ 32,000	+ 1,360	−	820
(m)	−220								+220
									(Utilities)
NB	11,380	+ 22,000	+ 400	+ 320 =	1,780	+ 32,000	+ 1,360	−	1,040

34,100   34,100

Transaction (n)   Now NuWay Cleaners pays $180 to the Daily News for advertising. Recall that it had previously recorded this bill as a liability. The equation is shown below.

	Assets				= Liabilities +		Owner's Equity		
	Cash	+ Equip.	+ Supp.	+ Ppd. Ins.	Accounts Payable	Alan Stevenson, Capital	+ Revenue	− Expenses
PB	11,380	+ 22,000	+ 400	+ 320 =	1,780	+ 32,000	+ 1,360	−	1,040
(n)	−180				−180				
NB	11,200	+ 22,000	+ 400	+ 320 =	1,600	+ 32,000	+ 1,360	−	1,040

33,920   33,920

Transaction (o)   NuWay Cleaners receives cash revenue for the third week, $830.

	Assets				= Liabilities +		Owner's Equity		
	Cash	+ Equip.	+ Supp.	+ Ppd. Ins.	Accounts Payable	Alan Stevenson, Capital	+ Revenue	− Expenses
PB	11,200	+ 22,000	+ 400	+ 320 =	1,600	+ 32,000	+ 1,360	−	1,040
(o)	+830						+830		
NB	12,030	+ 22,000	+ 400	+ 320 =	1,600	+ 32,000	+ 2,190	−	1,040

34,750   34,750

Transaction (p)   NuWay Cleaners signs a contract with A-1 Rental to clean their for-hire formal clothes on a credit basis and cleans ten dress suits. NuWay bills A-1 Rental for services performed, $80.

A firm uses the **Accounts Receivable** account to record the amounts owed by charge customers. These receivable accounts represent credit, usually extended for thirty days. Since A-1 Rental owes NuWay Cleaners $80 more than before the transaction took place, it seems logical to add $80 to Accounts Receivable. Revenue is earned when the service is performed, and hence the corresponding increase in revenue. When A-1 pays the $80 bill in cash, NuWay records this as an increase in Cash and a decrease in Accounts Receivable. It does not have to make an entry for the revenue account, as that has already been done.

	Assets					=	Liabilities +		Owner's Equity			
	Cash	+ Equip.	+ Supp.	+ Ppd. Ins.	+ Accts. Rec.	=	Accounts Payable	+	Alan Stevenson, Capital	+ Revenue	− Expenses
PB	12,030	+ 22,000	+ 400	+ 320		=	1,600	+	32,000	+ 2,190	− 1,040
(p)					+80					+80	
NB	12,030	+ 22,000	+ 400	+ 320	+ 80	=	1,600	+	32,000	+ 2,270	− 1,040
			34,830							34,830	

Transaction (q)   NuWay Cleaners pays wages of employees, $390, for June 11 through June 24.

	Assets					=	Liabilities +		Owner's Equity			
	Cash	+ Equip.	+ Supp.	+ Ppd. Ins.	+ Accts. Rec.	=	Accounts Payable	+	Alan Stevenson, Capital	+ Revenue	− Expenses
PB	12,030	+ 22,000	+ 400	+ 320	+ 80	=	1,600	+	32,000	+ 2,270	− 1,040
(q)	−390										+390 (Wages)
NB	11,640	+ 22,000	+ 400	+ 320	+ 80	=	1,600	+	32,000	+ 2,270	− 1,430
			34,440							34,440	

Transaction (r)   NuWay Cleaners buys additional equipment for $940 from Sanchez Equipment Company, paying $140 down, with the remaining $800 on account. Because buying an item on account is the same as buying it on credit, both expressions, *on account* and *on credit*, are used to describe such transactions.

	Assets					=	Liabilities +		Owner's Equity			
	Cash	+ Equip.	+ Supp.	+ Ppd. Ins.	+ Accts. Rec.	=	Accounts Payable	+	Alan Stevenson, Capital	+ Revenue	− Expenses
PB	11,640	+ 22,000	+ 400	+ 320	+ 80	=	1,600	+	32,000	+ 2,270	− 1,430
(r)	−140	+940					+800				
NB	11,500	+ 22,940	+ 400	+ 320	+ 80	=	2,400	+	32,000	+ 2,270	− 1,430
			35,240							35,240	

Again, because the equipment will last a long time, NuWay lists this $940 as an increase in the assets.

Transaction (s) NuWay Cleaners receives revenue from cash customers for the rest of the month, $960.

	Assets					=	Liabilities +		Owner's Equity		
	Cash	+ Equip.	+ Supp.	+ Ppd. Ins.	+ Accts. Rec.	=	Accounts Payable	+	Alan Stevenson, Capital	+ Revenue	− Expenses
PB	11,500	+ 22,940	+ 400	+ 320	+ 80	=	2,400	+	32,000	+ 2,270	− 1,430
(s)	+960									+960	
NB	12,460	+ 22,940	+ 400	+ 320	+ 80	=	2,400	+	32,000	+ 3,230	− 1,430
			36,200						36,200		

Transaction (t) NuWay Cleaners receives $60 from A-1 Rental to apply on the amount previously billed. A-1 Rental now owes NuWay Cleaners less than before, so NuWay deducts the $60 from Accounts Receivable. It previously recorded this amount as revenue, so the equation looks like the one shown below.

	Assets					=	Liabilities +		Owner's Equity		
	Cash	+ Equip.	+ Supp.	+ Ppd. Ins.	+ Accts. Rec.	=	Accounts Payable	+	Alan Stevenson, Capital	+ Revenue	− Expenses
PB	12,460	+ 22,940	+ 400	+ 320	+ 80	=	2,400	+	32,000	+ 3,230	− 1,430
(t)	+60				−60						
NB	12,520	+ 22,940	+ 400	+ 320	+ 20	=	2,400	+	32,000	+ 3,230	− 1,430
			36,200						36,200		

Transaction (u) At the end of the month, Stevenson withdraws $1,000 in cash from the business for his personal living costs. One may consider a **withdrawal** to be the opposite of an investment in cash by the owner.

	Assets					=	Liabilities +		Owner's Equity		
	Cash	+ Equip.	+ Supp.	+ Ppd. Ins.	+ Accts. Rec.	=	Accounts Payable	+	Alan Stevenson, Capital	+ Revenue	− Expenses
PB	12,520	+ 22,940	+ 400	+ 320	+ 20	=	2,400	+	32,000	+ 3,230	− 1,430
(u)	−1,000								−1,000 (Drawing)		
NB	11,520	+ 22,940	+ 400	+ 320	+ 20	=	2,400	+	31,000	+ 3,230	− 1,430
			35,200						35,200		

Because the owner is taking cash out of the business, there is a decrease in Cash. The withdrawal also decreases Capital, because Stevenson has now reduced his equity. One does not consider a withdrawal as a business expense, since money is not paid to anyone outside the business for services performed or for materials received that would benefit the business.

Summary of Transactions

We have summarized the business transactions of NuWay Cleaners in Figure 2-1, identifying the transactions by letter. To test your understanding of the recording procedure, describe the nature of the transactions that have taken place.

Figure 2-1

	Assets					= Liabilities +	Owner's Equity		
	Cash	+ Equip.	+ Supp.	+ Ppd. Ins.	+ Accts. Rec.	Accounts Payable	Alan Stevenson, Capital	+ Revenue	− Expenses
Bal.	13,000	+ 22,000	+ 400			= 3,400 +	32,000		
(f)	+ 600							+ 600	
Bal.	13,600	+ 22,000	+ 400			= 3,400 +	32,000 +	600	
(g)	−400								+ 400 (Rent)
Bal.	13,200	+ 22,000	+ 400			= 3,400 +	32,000 +	600 −	400
(h)	−240								+ 240 (Wages)
Bal.	12,960	+ 22,000	+ 400			= 3,400 +	32,000 +	600 −	640
(i)	−320			+ 320					
Bal.	12,640	+ 22,000	+ 400	+ 320		= 3,400 +	32,000 +	600 −	640
(j)	+ 760							+ 760	
Bal.	13,400	+ 22,000	+ 400	+ 320		= 3,400 +	32,000 +	1,360 −	640
(k)						+ 180			+ 180 (Advertising)
Bal.	13,400	+ 22,000	+ 400	+ 320		= 3,580 +	32,000 +	1,360 −	820
(l)	−1,800					−1,800			
Bal.	11,600	+ 22,000	+ 400	+ 320		= 1,780 +	32,000 +	1,360 −	820
(m)	−220								+ 220 (Utilities)
Bal.	11,380	+ 22,000	+ 400	+ 320		= 1,780 +	32,000 +	1,360 −	1,040
(n)	−180					−180			

(continued)

	Assets					= Liabilities +	Owner's Equity		
	Cash +	Equip. +	Supp. +	Ppd. Ins. +	Accts. Rec.	Accounts Payable	Alan Stevenson, Capital +	Revenue −	Expenses
Bal.	11,200 +	22,000 +	400 +	320		= 1,600 +	32,000 +	1,360 −	1,040
(o)	+ 830							+ 830	
Bal.	12,030 +	22,000 +	400 +	320		= 1,600 +	32,000 +	2,190 −	1,040
(p)				+	80			+80	
Bal.	12,030 +	22,000 +	400 +	320 +	80 =	1,600 +	32,000 +	2,270 −	1,040
(q)	−390								+390 (Wages)
Bal.	11,640 +	22,000 +	400 +	320 +	80 =	1,600 +	32,000 +	2,270 −	1,430
(r)	−140	+940				+800			
Bal.	11,500 +	22,940 +	400 +	320 +	80 =	2,400 +	32,000 +	2,270 −	1,430
(s)	+960							+960	
Bal.	12,460 +	22,940 +	400 +	320 +	80 =	2,400 +	32,000 +	3,230 −	1,430
(t)	+60				−60				
Bal.	12,520 +	22,940 +	400 +	320 +	20 =	2,400 +	32,000 +	3,230 −	1,430
(u)	−1,000						−1,000 (Drawing)		
Bal.	11,520 +	22,940 +	400 +	320 +	20 =	2,400 +	31,000 +	3,230 −	1,430

	Total			Total
Cash	$11,520	Accounts Payable	$ 2,400
Equipment	22,940	Alan Stevenson, Capital	31,000
Supplies	400	Revenue	3,230
Prepaid Insurance	320		$36,630
Accounts Receivable	20	Expenses	−1,430
	$35,200		$35,200

MAJOR FINANCIAL STATEMENTS

A financial statement is a report prepared by accountants for managers and others both inside and outside the economic unit. In Chapter 1, we discussed the balance sheet. We will now consider the income statement and the statement of owner's equity.

The Income Statement

The **income statement** shows total revenue minus total expenses, which yields the net income, or profit. This income statement pictures the results of the business transactions involving revenue and expense accounts over a period of time. In other words, it shows how the business has

Objective 2

Present an income statement.

performed or fared over a period of time, usually a month or year. Other terms that are identical with the name *income statement* are *statement of income and expenses* or *profit and loss statement*. If the total revenue is less than the expenses, the result is a net loss.

The income statement in Figure 2-2 shows the results of the first month of operations of NuWay Cleaners. (It should be noted that the net income figure presented here represents net income before adjustments. We shall discuss adjustments in Chapter 5.)

Note that as in all financial statements, the heading requires three lines:

1. Name of company (or owner, if there is no company name).
2. Title of the financial statement (in this case, income statement).
3. Period of time covered by the financial statement or its date.

Figure 2-2

NuWay Cleaners
Income Statement
For month ended June 30, 19–

Revenue:			
Income from Services			$ 3 2 3 0 00
Expenses:			
Wages Expense	$ 6 3 0 00		
Rent Expense	4 0 0 00		
Utilities Expense	2 2 0 00		
Advertising Expense	1 8 0 00		
Total Expenses		1 4 3 0 00	
Net Income		$ 1 8 0 0 00	

For convenience, the individual expense amounts are recorded in the first amount column. In this way, the total expenses ($1,430) may be subtracted directly from the total revenue ($3,230).

The income statement covers a period of time, whereas the balance sheet has only one date: the end of the financial period. The revenue for June, less the expenses for June, shows the results of operations—a net income of $1,800. To the accountant, the term **net income** means "clear" income, or profit after all expenses have been deducted. Expenses are usually listed in the same order as in the chart of accounts, which is the official list of all the accounts in which transactions are recorded. Some accountants, however, prefer to list expenses in declining order (the largest amount first, followed by the next largest, etc.). In this arrangement, if Miscellaneous Expense is present, it is placed last regardless of the amount. For the present, we'll list the expenses in the order in which they appear in the Expenses column. Miscellaneous Expense, however, is usually placed last.

The Statement of Owner's Equity

We said that revenue and expenses are connected with owner's equity through the medium of the financial statements. Let us now demonstrate this by a **statement of owner's equity,** shown in Figure 2-3, which the accountant prepares after he or she has determined the net income in the income statement. The statement of owner's equity shows how—and why—the owner's equity, or capital, account has changed over the financial period.

Objective 3

Present a statement of owner's equity.

Figure 2-3

NuWay Cleaners
Statement of Owner's Equity
For month ended June 30, 19–

Alan Stevenson, Capital, June 1, 19–		$32 0 0 0 00
Net Income for June	$1 8 0 0 00	
Less Withdrawals for June	1 0 0 0 00	
Increase in Capital		8 0 0 00
Alan Stevenson, Capital, June 30, 19–		$32 8 0 0 00

The Balance Sheet

After preparing the statement of owner's equity, we prepare a balance sheet (shown in Figure 2-4). In it we record the ending capital that we determined when we prepared the statement of owner's equity.

Figure 2-4

NuWay Cleaners
Balance Sheet
June 30, 19–

Assets	
Cash	$11 5 2 0 00
Accounts Receivable	2 0 00
Supplies	4 0 0 00
Prepaid Insurance	3 2 0 00
Equipment	22 9 4 0 00
Total Assets	$35 2 0 0 00
Liabilities	
Accounts Payable	$ 2 4 0 0 00
Owner's Equity	
Alan Stevenson, Capital	32 8 0 0 00
Total Liabilities and Owner's Equity	$35 2 0 0 00

These financial statements are only tentative because adjustments have not been recorded (see Chapter 5).

Income Statement Involving More Than One Revenue Account

When a business firm or other economic unit has more than one distinct source of revenue, separate revenue accounts are set up for each source. See, for example, the income statement of The Ninth Avenue Theater presented in Figure 2-5.

Figure 2-5

The Ninth Avenue Theater
Income Statement
For month ended September 30, 19–

Revenue:												
Admissions Income	$6	9	6	8	00							
Concessions Income	1	7	4	3	00							
Total Revenue						$8	7	1	1	00		
Expenses:												
Film Rental Expense	$3	3	2	5	00							
Wages Expense	1	3	5	3	00							
Advertising Expense		9	2	5	00							
Utilities Expense		3	1	6	00							
Taxes Expense		2	2	1	00							
Miscellaneous Expense		1	4	5	00							
Total Expenses						6	2	8	5	00		
Net Income						$2	4	2	6	00		

Statement of Owner's Equity Involving an Additional Investment and a Net Loss

Any additional investment by the owner during the period covered by the financial statements should be shown in the statement of owner's equity, since such a statement should show what has affected the Capital account from the *beginning* until the *end* of the period covered by the financial statements. For example, assume the following for the C. E. Davis Company, which has a net income:

Balance of C. E. Davis, Capital, on April 1 $86,000
Additional investment by C. E. Davis on April 12   9,000
Net income for the month (from income statement)   1,500
Total withdrawals for the month   1,200

The statement of owner's equity in Figure 2-6 shows this information.

Figure 2-6

C. E. Davis Company
Statement of Owner's Equity
For month ended April 30, 19–

C. E. Davis, Capital, April 1, 19–			$86 0 0 0	00
Additional Investment, April 12, 19–			9 0 0 0	00
Total Investment			$95 0 0 0	00
Net Income for April	$1 5 0 0	00		
Less Withdrawals for April	1 2 0 0	00		
Increase in Capital			3 0 0	00
C. E. Davis, Capital, April 30, 19–			$95 3 0 0	00

As another example, assume the following for the H. L. Spangler Company, which has a net loss:

H. L. Spangler, Capital, on Oct. 1 $70,000
Additional investment by H. L. Spangler on Oct. 25   6,000
Net loss for the month (from income statement)   250
Total withdrawals for the month   420

Again, the statement of owner's equity in Figure 2-7 shows this information.

Figure 2-7

H. L. Spangler Company
Statement of Owner's Equity
For month ended October 31, 19–

H. L. Spangler, Capital, October 1, 19–			$70 0 0 0	00
Additional Investment, October 25, 19–			6 0 0 0	00
Total Investment			$76 0 0 0	00
Less: Net Loss for October	$ 2 5 0	00		
Withdrawals for October	4 2 0	00		
Decrease in Capital			6 7 0	00
H. L. Spangler, Capital, October 31, 19–			$75 3 3 0	00

         CHAPTER 2

IMPORTANCE OF FINANCIAL STATEMENTS

The owners or managers of a business look on their financial statements as a coach looks on the scoreboard and team statistics, as showing the results of the present game as well as the team's standing. The income statement shows the results of operations for the current month or year. It condenses the results of operations into one figure, either net income or net loss. The income statement is prepared first so that the net income can be recorded in the statement of owner's equity, which comes next. It shows why—and how—the owner's investment has changed. The ending capital in the statement of owner's equity is used in the balance sheet, which shows the present standing or financial position of the business. All these relationships are shown in Figure 2-8.

The owner or manager can use the figures on the financial statements to plan future operations. Owners and managers are not the only ones interested in financial statements. Creditors, prospective investors, and government agencies are also interested in the profitability and financial standing of the business. Financial statements are the way in which one takes the pulse of the business. They are extremely important.

Figure 2-8

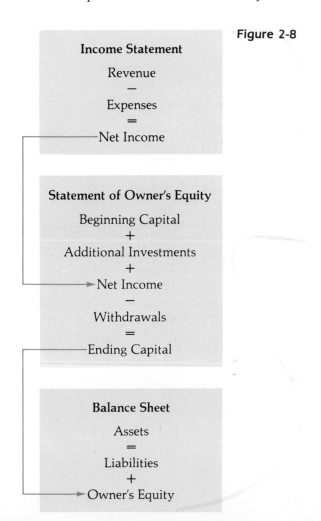

Income Statement

Revenue
−
Expenses
=
Net Income

Statement of Owner's Equity

Beginning Capital
+
Additional Investments
+
Net Income
−
Withdrawals
=
Ending Capital

Balance Sheet

Assets
=
Liabilities
+
Owner's Equity

GLOSSARY

Accounts Receivable   Charge accounts or receivable accounts maintained for customers, representing credit usually extended for thirty-day periods.

Expenses   The amounts of assets that a business or other economic unit uses up as a result of its operations; the cost of services or goods acquired or consumed in the operation of the business or economic unit.

Income statement   A financial statement showing the results of business transactions over a period of time: total revenue minus total expenses.

Net income   Total revenue minus total expenses over a period of time.

Revenues   The amounts of assets that a business or other economic unit gains as a result of its operations; the total price charged for services rendered or goods sold during a period of time; may be in the form of cash or receivables.

Statement of owner's equity   A financial statement showing how—and why—the owner's equity, or capital, account has changed over the financial period.

Withdrawal   The taking of cash or goods out of a business by the owner for his or her own personal use. (This is also referred to as a *drawing*.) One treats a withdrawal as a temporary decrease in the owner's equity, since one anticipates that it will be offset by net income.

QUESTIONS, EXERCISES, AND PROBLEMS

Discussion Questions

1. Define the term *expense*. Does every payment of cash by a business indicate that an expense has been incurred?
2. What titles might you select to describe the kinds of expenses a TV repair shop would incur in its operations?
3. What happens to the elements in the fundamental accounting equation when a sale of services is made on a charge-account basis?
4. What does an income statement show?
5. What is the difference between the headings required for statements of owner's equity and the headings required for balance sheets?
6. Name two ways to increase owner's equity and two ways to decrease owner's equity.
7. Suggest some groups other than the owner or owners of a business who would be interested in data contained in the firm's financial statements. What is the specific interest of each group?

Exercises

Exercise 2-1   Describe a business transaction that will do the following:

a. Decrease a liability and decrease an asset.
b. Increase an asset and increase a revenue.

c. Decrease an asset and increase an expense. *pay an expense*

d. Increase a liability and increase an expense.

Exercise 2-2 Using the following data, determine the total owner's equity.

Equipment	$ 8,000	Accounts Payable	$1,200
Cash	2,000	Accounts Receivable	1,600 — *Asset*
Building	60,000	Supplies	400
Land	10,000		

Exercise 2-3 Describe the transactions recorded in the following equation.

	Assets			= Liabilities +	Owner's Equity		
	Cash	+ Accounts Receivable	+ Equipment	Accounts Payable	C. P. Lee, Capital	+ Revenue	− Expenses
(a)	+12,000		+ 4,000 =		+ 16,000		
(b)	−900						+900
Bal.	11,100		4,000 =		+ 16,000		− 900
(c)		+ 2,100				+ 2,100	
Bal.	11,100 +	2,100	+ 4,000 =		+ 16,000 +	2,100	− 900
(d)	−3,000		+12,000	+9,000			
Bal.	8,100 +	2,100	+ 16,000 =	9,000 +	16,000 + −1,600 (Drawing)	2,100	900
(e)	−1,600						
Bal.	6,500 +	2,100	+ 16,000 =	9,000 +	14,400 +	2,100	− 900

[handwritten left margin: + Investment / Paid expense / Performed service on acct for $2100 / owner took out cash]

Exercise 2-4 From the following balances, in the elements of the fundamental accounting equation, determine the amount of the ending owner's equity.

Assets	$64,000
Liabilities	20,000
Owner's Equity (beginning)	32,000
Revenue	48,000
Expenses	36,000

Exercise 2-5 A. M. Woods is an attorney. Describe the transactions that have been completed.

	Assets				= Liabilities +	Owner's Equity		
	Cash	+ Accts. Rec.	+ Supp.	+ Equip.	Accounts Payable	A. M. Woods, Capital	+ Revenue	− Expenses
Bal.	1,620 +	810	+ 819	+ 7,493 =	2,416 +	8,326		
(a)	+360	−360						
Bal.	1,980 +	450	+ 819	+ 7,493 =	2,416 +	8,326		
(b)	−418							+418 (Rent)

	Assets				= Liabilities +	Owner's Equity		
	Cash +	Accts. Rec. +	Supp. +	Equip.	Accounts Payable	A. M. Woods, + Capital	Revenue	− Expenses
Bal. (c)	1,562 + +2,730	450 +	819 +	7,493 =	2,416 +	8,326	+2,730	− 418
Bal. (d)	4,292 + −300	450 +	819 +	7,493 =	2,416 + −300	8,326 +	2,730 −	418
Bal. (e)	3,992 + −410	450 +	819 +	7,493 =	2,116 +	8,326 +	2,730 −	418 +410 (Wages)
Bal. (f)	3,582 + −1,200	450 +	819 +	7,493 =	2,116 +	8,326 + −1,200 (Drawing)	2,730 −	828
Bal. (g)	2,382 + −875	450 +	819 +	7,493 =	2,116 + −875	7,126 +	2,730 −	828
Bal.	1,507 +	450 +	819 +	7,493 =	1,241 +	7,126 +	2,730 −	828

Exercise 2-6 From Exercise 2-5, present an income statement for the month ending September 30.

Exercise 2-7 From Exercises 2-5 and 2-6, present a statement of owner's equity and a balance sheet.

Exercise 2-8 On January 1, L. P. Romano's equity in his business, Romano's Excavating, was $56,000. On May 22, Romano made an additional investment of $4,000. The firm's net income for the year was $23,500. Romano's total withdrawals amounted to $18,000. Prepare a statement of owner's equity for the year ended December 31.

Problem Set A

Problem 2-1A In June of this year, Lewis Scott established a business under the name Scott Realty. The account headings are presented below. Transactions completed during the month follow.

Assets		= Liabilities +	Owner's Equity		
Cash + Supplies + Equipment		Accounts Payable	Lewis Scott, + Capital	Revenue	− Expenses

a. Deposited $9,000 in a bank account entitled Scott Realty.
b. Paid office rent for the month, $500.
c. Bought supplies consisting of stationery, folders, and stamps for cash, $252.
d. Bought office equipment consisting of desks, chairs, filing cabinets, and other furniture on account from Simcoe Company, $5,400.
e. Received bill for advertising, $360.

f. Paid $800 to Simcoe Company on amount owed on purchase of office equipment recorded previously.
g. Earned sales commissions, receiving cash, $2,820.
h. Received and paid bill for utilities, $136.
i. Paid bill for advertising recorded previously, $360.
j. Paid automobile expenses, $230.
k. Scott withdrew cash for personal use, $970.

Instructions

1. Record the transactions and the balance after each transaction.
2. Prepare an income statement and a statement of owner's equity for June and a balance sheet as of June 30.

Problem 2-2A   A. L. Stone, CPA, opened her public accounting practice on September 1. The account headings are presented below. Transactions completed during the month follow.

Assets	= Liabilities +	Owner's Equity
Cash + Supp. + Ppd. + Library + Equip. Ins.	Accounts Payable	A. L. + Revenue − Expenses Stone, Capital

a. Deposited $14,000 in a bank account in the name of the business, A. L. Stone, CPA.
b. Bought office equipment on account from Jacobs Company, $9,800.
c. Invested a professional library costing $3,800. (Increase the account for Library and the account of A. L. Stone, Capital, and include in the statement of owner's equity as Additional Investment, as shown on page 32.)
d. Paid office rent for the month, $640.
e. Bought office supplies for cash, $590.
f. Paid the premium for a two-year insurance policy on the equipment and the library, $124.
g. Received professional fees for services rendered, $1,640.
h. Received and paid bill for telephone service, $152.
i. Paid salary of part-time receptionist, $640.
j. Paid automobile expense, $192.
k. Received professional fees for services rendered, $1,480.
l. Paid Jacobs Company on amount owed on the purchase of office equipment, $1,000.
m. Stone withdrew cash for personal use, $1,450.

Instructions

1. Record the transactions and the balances after each transaction.
2. Prepare an income statement and a statement of owner's equity for September and a balance sheet as of September 30.

Problem 2-3A   Evans Engineering Consultants hires an accountant, who determines the following account balances, listed in random order, as of November 30.

Cash	$3,528	D. L. Evans, Drawing	$2,400
Wages Expense	2,800	Accounts Receivable	1,442
Professional Fees	7,834	Accounts Payable	2,848
Equipment	7,948	Supplies	232
Rent Expense	1,500	Miscellaneous Expense	220
D. L. Evans, Capital,		Advertising Expense	252
Nov. 1	9,640		

Instructions

Prepare an income statement and a statement of owner's equity for November and a balance sheet as of November 30.

Problem 2-4A   C. P. Moore started the Moore Delivery Service on October 1 of this year. The account headings are presented below. During October, Moore completed the following transactions.

Assets						= Liabilities +	Owner's Equity		
Cash +	Accts. + Rec.	Supp. +	Ppd. Ins.	+ Delivery + Equip.	Office Equip.	Accounts Payable	C. P. Moore, Capital	+ Revenue	− Expenses

a. Invested cash in the business, $4,000.
b. Bought delivery equipment from Acme Motors for $7,500, paying $800 in cash with the remainder due in thirty days.
c. Bought office equipment on account from Dietz and Company, $1,200.
d. Paid rent for the month, $300.
e. Paid cash for insurance on delivery equipment for the year, $384.
f. Cash receipts for the first half of the month from cash customers, $1,850.
g. Bought supplies for cash, $182.
h. Billed customers for services on account, $296.
i. Paid cash for utilities, $64.
j. Received bill for gas and oil used during the current month, $276.
k. Receipts for the remainder of the month from cash customers, $1,720.
l. Moore withdrew cash for personal use, $760.
m. Paid drivers' commissions, $966. (This is an expense.)

Instructions

1. Record the transactions and the balance after each transaction.
2. Prepare an income statement and a statement of owner's equity for October and a balance sheet as of October 31.

Problem Set B

Problem 2-1B   On April 1 of this year, Edward Savage, D.D.S., established an office for the practice of dentistry. The account headings are presented below. Transactions completed during the month follow.

Assets				= Liabilities +	Owner's Equity		
Cash +	Supp. +	Dental +	Office	Accounts	Edward Savage, +	Revenue −	Expenses
		Equip.	Equip.	Payable	Capital		

a. Deposited $9,000 in a bank account entitled Edward Savage, D.D.S.
b. Paid office rent for the month, $570.
c. Bought dental supplies for cash, $1,110.
d. Bought dental equipment consisting of a chair, drills, x-ray equipment, and instruments on account from Peerless Dental Supply, $14,700.
e. Bought a desk and chairs for the reception room from Wagner Office Equipment, for $3,600, paying $600 in cash and the remainder on account.
f. Received cash for professional fees earned, $1,365.
g. Received and paid bill for utilities, $147.
h. Paid Peerless Dental Supply on amount owed on dental equipment recorded previously, $900.
i. Paid salary of assistant, $800.
j. Earned professional fees, receiving $2,142 cash.
k. Savage withdrew cash for personal use, $1,140.

Instructions

1. Record the transactions and the balance after each transaction.
2. Prepare an income statement and a statement of owner's equity for April and a balance sheet as of April 30.

Problem 2-2B   G. N. Little, a photographer, opened a studio for her professional practice on July 1. The account headings are presented below. Transactions completed during the month follow.

Assets				= Liabilities +	Owner's Equity		
Cash +	Supp. +	Ppd. +	Photographic	Accounts	G. N. Little, +	Revenue −	Expenses
		Ins.	Equip.	Payable	Capital		

a. Deposited $13,125 in a bank account in the name of the business, Little Photographic Studio.
b. Bought photographic equipment on account from Precision Equipment, $6,930.
c. Invested personal photographic equipment, $5,040. (Increase the account for Photographic Equipment, and include in the statement of owner's equity as Additional Investment as shown on page 32.)
d. Paid office rent for the month, $525.
e. Bought photographic supplies for cash, $789.
f. Paid premium for a two-year insurance policy on photographic equipment, $108.
g. Received $878 as professional fees for services rendered.
h. Paid salary of part-time assistant, $500.
i. Received and paid bill for telephone service, $58.
j. Paid Precision Equipment on amount owed on the purchase of photographic equipment, $410.
k. Received $1,479 as professional fees for services rendered.
l. Paid for minor repairs to photographic equipment (Repair Expense), $54.
m. Little withdrew cash for personal use, $900.

Instructions

1. Record the transactions and the balances after each transaction.
2. Prepare an income statement and a statement of owner's equity for July and a balance sheet as of July 31.

Problem 2-3B An accountant determines the following balances, listed in random order, for Lambert Auto Repair as of September 30 of this year.

A Cash	$ 3,436	Rent Expense	$ 780
Advertising Expense	630	A Accounts Receivable	5,746
Income from Services	10,032	O E D. C. Lambert, Capital,	
Wages Expense	6,414	Sept. 1	37,638
A Equipment	30,328	D. C. Lambert, Drawing	1,500
L Accounts Payable	2,700	Miscellaneous Expense	308
		A Supplies	1,228

Instructions

Prepare an income statement and a statement of owner's equity for September and a balance sheet as of September 30.

Problem 2-4B On May 1 of this year, C. W. Ennis started the Ennis Advertising Agency. The account headings are presented below. During May, Ennis completed these transactions.

Assets						= Liabilities +	Owner's Equity		
Cash +	Accts. Rec. +	Supp. +	Ppd. Ins. +	Car +	Office Equip.	Accounts Payable	C. W. Ennis, Capital	+ Revenue	− Expenses

a. Invested cash in the business, $11,280.
b. Bought a car for use in the business from Merino Motors for $8,160, paying $1,200 in cash with the balance due in thirty days.
c. Bought office equipment on account from Wallingford Company, $2,210.
d. Paid rent for the month, $430.
e. Cash receipts for the first half of the month from cash customers, $1,840.
f. Paid cash for property and liability insurance on car for the year, $352.
g. Bought office supplies for cash, $148.
h. Received and paid heating bill, $46.
i. Received bill for gas and oil used during the current month from Finch Oil Company for the company car, $91.
j. Billed customers for services performed on account, $374.
k. Receipts for the remainder of the month from cash customers, $2,126.
l. Paid salary of commercial artist, $1,180.
m. Ennis withdrew cash for personal use, $1,850.

Instructions

1. Record the transactions and the balance after each transaction.
2. Prepare an income statement and a statement of owner's equity for May and a balance sheet as of May 31.

3 Recording Business Transactions in Ledger Account Form; The Trial Balance

Learning Objectives

After you have completed this chapter, you will be able to do the following:

1. Record a group of business transactions for a service business directly in T accounts involving changes in assets, liabilities, owner's equity, revenue, and expense accounts.

2. Determine balances of T accounts having entries recorded on both sides of the accounts.

3. Present the fundamental accounting equation with the T account forms, the plus and minus signs, and the debit and credit sides labeled.

4. Prepare a trial balance.

Up to now we have discussed the fundamental accounting equation in two places. In Chapter 1 we described it as *Assets = Liabilities + Owner's Equity*. In Chapter 2 we introduced two more accounts (Revenues and Expenses) and then described the equation as *Assets = Liabilities + Owner's Equity + Revenue − Expenses*. With the last two accounts, the fundamental accounting equation was brought up to its full complement of five account classifications. There are only five; so, as far as you go in accounting—whether you are dealing with a small one-owner business or a large corporation—there will be only these five major classifications of accounts. These classifications relate to the principal financial statements as follows:

Assets = Liabilities +	Owner's Equity	+ Revenue − Expenses
Balance Sheet	**Statement of Owner's Equity**	**Income Statement**
Assets	Beginning Capital	Revenue
=	+	−
Liabilities	Net Income	Expenses
+	−	=
Owner's Equity	Withdrawals	Net Income
	=	
	Ending Capital	

drawing

In this chapter we shall record in T account form the same transactions we used in Chapters 1 and 2, and we shall prove the equality of both sides of the fundamental accounting equation. We'll do this by means of a trial balance, which we'll talk about soon.

THE T ACCOUNT FORM

In Chapters 1 and 2, we recorded business transactions in a columnar arrangement. For example, the Cash account column in the books of NuWay Cleaners is shown at the top of the next page. As an introduction to the recording of transactions, this arrangement has two advantages.

1. In the process of analyzing the transaction, you recognize the need to determine *which* accounts are involved. Next, you must decide whether the transaction results in an increase or a decrease in each of these accounts.
2. You further realize that after each transaction has been recorded, the balance of each account, when combined with the balances of other accounts, proves the equality of the two sides of the fundamental accounting equation.

Cash Account Column

Transaction	(a)	32,000	Balance		12,640	Balance		11,640
Transaction	(b)	−18,000	Transaction	(j)	+760	Transaction	(r)	−140
Balance		14,000	Balance		13,400	Balance		11,500
Transaction	(d)	−1,000	Transaction	(l)	−1,800	Transaction	(s)	+960
Balance		13,000	Balance		11,600	Balance		12,460
Transaction	(f)	+600	Transaction	(m)	−220	Transaction	(t)	+60
Balance		13,600	Balance		11,380	Balance		12,520
Transaction	(g)	−400	Transaction	(n)	−180	Transaction	(u)	−1,000
Balance		13,200	Balance		11,200	Balance		11,520
Transaction	(h)	−240	Transaction	(o)	+830			
Balance		12,960	Balance		12,030			
Transaction	(i)	−320	Transaction	(q)	−390			
Balance		12,640	Balance		11,640			

The **T account form** (that is, an account shaped like the letter T) is the traditional form. It is also known as a ledger account, because the records of *all* the accounts are kept in the **ledger.** The ledger may be as simple as a loose-leaf binder or as complex as a whole filing system.

The T form, developed for convenience as a space-saving device, is divided into two sides: one side to record increases in the account and the other to record decreases. Let us now record in T account form those transactions just listed for NuWay Cleaners that affect the Cash account.

always done to an account
1) Increase
2) Decrease

Cash

+		−	
(a)	32,000	(b)	18,000
(f)	600	(d)	1,000
(j)	760	(g)	400
(o)	830	(h)	240
(s)	960	(i)	320
(t)	60	(l)	1,800
	35,210	(m)	220
		(n)	180
		(q)	390
		(r)	140
		(u)	1,000

Footings → 23,690
Balance → **11,520**

After we record a group of transactions in an account, we add both sides and record the totals in small pencil-written figures called **footings.** Next, we subtract one footing from the other to determine the balance of the account. For the account shown above, the balance would be $11,520 ($35,210 − $23,690).

We now record the balance on the side of the account having the larger footing, which, with a few minor exceptions, is the plus (+) side. The plus side of an account is the side that represents the **normal balance** of the account. The normal balance may, however, fall on either the left or the right side of an account.

Each classification of accounts uses a consistent placement of the plus and minus signs. For example, the T accounts for *all* assets are

+	−
Left	Right

In Chapter 2 we placed revenue and expenses under the "umbrella" of owner's equity. Revenue increases owner's equity, and expenses decrease owner's equity. In T account form, it looks like this:

Owner's Equity

−	+
Left	Right

Expenses		**Revenue**	
+	−	−	+
Left	Right	Left	Right

Also, in Chapter 2, using the five classifications of accounts, we stated the fundamental accounting equation like this:

Assets = Liabilities + <u>Owner's Equity</u>
Capital + Revenue − Expenses

Because revenue and expenses appear separately in the income statement, we'll stretch out the equation to include them as separate headings, like this:

Assets = Liabilities + Owner's Equity + Revenue − Expenses

We can now restate the equation with the T forms and plus and minus signs for each account classification.

Assets		=	**Liabilities**		+	**Owner's Equity**		+	**Revenue**		−	**Expenses**	
+	−		−	+		−	+		−	+		+	−
Left	Right		Left	Right		Left	Right		Left	Right		Left	Right

Revenue has been treated as an addition to owner's equity, so the placement of the plus and minus signs is the same as in owner's equity. On the other hand, expenses have been treated as deductions from owner's equity, so the placement of the plus and minus signs is reversed. We shall use this form of the fundamental accounting equation throughout the remainder of the text.

Your accounting background up to this point has taught you to analyze business transactions in order to determine which accounts are involved and to recognize that the amounts should be recorded as either an increase or a decrease in the accounts. Now, the recording process becomes a simple matter of knowing which side of the T accounts should be used to record increases and which side to record decreases. **Generally speaking, you will not be using the minus side of the revenue and expense accounts, since transactions involving revenue and expense accounts usually result in increases in these accounts.**

RECORDING TRANSACTIONS IN T ACCOUNT FORM

Objective 1

Record a group of business transactions for a service business directly in T accounts.

Our task now is to learn how to record business transactions in the T account form. To facilitate this transition, let's use the transactions of NuWay Cleaners again; we are familiar with them and can readily recognize the increases or decreases in the accounts involved.

There are only five classifications of accounts. These classifications are embodied in the fundamental accounting equation.

Capital

Assets	=	Liabilities	+	Owner's Equity	+	Revenue	−	Expenses
+ | −		− | +		− | +		− | +		+ | −
Left | Right		Left | Right		Left | Right		Left | Right		Left | Right

The fundamental accounting equation with T accounts for NuWay Cleaners is presented below. We have given specific account titles for revenue and expense accounts, as it is necessary to list each account separately in the income statement. The order of Supplies, Prepaid Insurance, and Equipment has been changed, so that the presentation will be consistent with the account number sequence shown in Chapter 4.

Expenses
Decrease
Capital

Drawing
_+ | −_

Capital is B-cause
Opposite of assets
Rev. increases
Capital

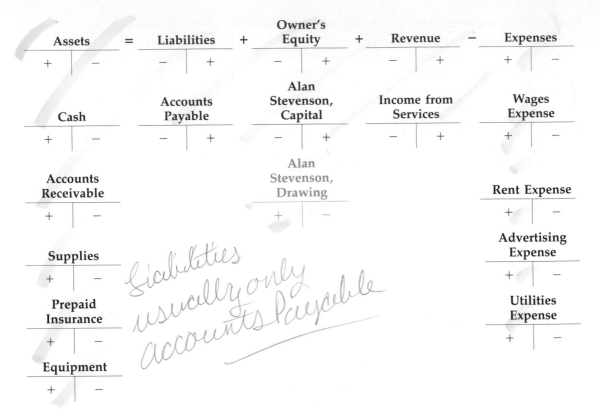

Assets	=	Liabilities	+	Owner's Equity	+	Revenue	−	Expenses
+ | −		− | +		− | +		− | +		+ | −

Cash		Accounts Payable		Alan Stevenson, Capital		Income from Services		Wages Expense
+ | −		− | +		− | +		− | +		+ | −

Accounts Receivable				Alan Stevenson, Drawing				Rent Expense
+ | −				+ | −				+ | −

Supplies
+ | −

Prepaid Insurance
+ | −

Equipment
+ | −

Liabilities usually only accounts Payable

Advertising Expense
+ | −

Utilities Expense
+ | −

To stress the Drawing account, which can cause some confusion, we have printed it in color. One might think of the relationship between Drawing and Capital like this: Amounts put into the business are recorded as increases, and amounts taken out of the business are recorded as decreases.

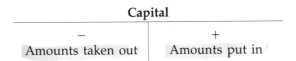

Capital	
−	+
Amounts taken out	Amounts put in

We would, however, like to reserve the minus side of Capital for permanent withdrawals, were the owner to reduce the size of the business permanently. As we said in Chapter 2, amounts taken out for the owner's personal use may be considered to be temporary. Because the owner plans to replenish these amounts from the net income earned by the firm, it is much more convenient to use a separate account to record these withdrawals. Any temporary withdrawals will be listed on the plus side of Drawing. This concept can be illustrated by showing the Drawing T account under the umbrella of the Capital account.

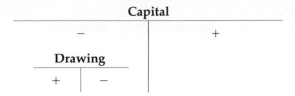

Capital

−	+

Drawing

+	−

Drawing is placed under the heading of owner's equity, because it appears in the statement of owner's equity. As you will recall, in the statement of owner's equity, we list beginning capital, plus net income, minus withdrawals. When we want to treat one account as a deduction from another, we reverse the plus and minus signs.

Transaction (a)   Alan Stevenson invests $32,000 cash in his new business. This transaction results in an increase in Cash and an increase in the Capital account, affecting the T accounts shown below.

Assets		=	Liabilities		+	Owner's Equity		+	Revenue		−	Expenses	
+	−		−	+		−	+		−	+		+	−

Cash			Alan Stevenson, Capital	
+	−		−	+
(a) 32,000				(a) 32,000

Transaction (b)   NuWay Cleaners buys $18,000 worth of equipment, paying cash. This transaction results in an increase in Equipment and a decrease in Cash.

Assets		=	Liabilities		+	Owner's Equity		+	Revenue		−	Expenses	
+	−		−	+		−	+		−	+		+	−

Cash	
+	−
	(b) 18,000

Equipment	
+	−
(b) 18,000	

Transaction (c)   NuWay Cleaners buys equipment on credit from Sanchez Equipment Company, $4,000. This transaction results in an increase in both Equipment and Accounts Payable and is shown in T accounts as follows:

Assets	=	Liabilities	+	Owner's Equity	+	Revenue	−	Expenses
+ | −		− | +		− | +		− | +		+ | −

Equipment		Accounts Payable
+ | −		− | +
(c) 4,000 |		| (c) 4,000

Transaction (d) NuWay Cleaners pays $1,000 to be applied against the firm's liability of $4,000. This transaction results in a decrease in Cash and a decrease in Accounts Payable.

Assets	=	Liabilities	+	Owner's Equity	+	Revenue	−	Expenses
+ | −		− | +		− | +		− | +		+ | −

Cash		Accounts Payable
+ | −		− | +
| (d) 1,000		(d) 1,000 |

Transaction (e) NuWay Cleaners buys cleaning fluids for $400 on credit from Troy Supply Company. This transaction results in an increase in Supplies and an increase in Accounts Payable.

Assets	=	Liabilities	+	Owner's Equity	+	Revenue	−	Expenses
+ | −		− | +		− | +		− | +		+ | −

Supplies		Accounts Payable
+ | −		− | +
(e) 400 |		| (e) 400

Here is a restatement of the accounts after recording **a** through **e**. To test your understanding of the process, trace through the recording of each transaction and describe the nature of the transaction. Footings, or totals—remember always to write them in pencil—are included as a means of determining the balances of the accounts. The balances are inserted in the accounts on the side having the largest total.

Objective 2

Determine balances of T accounts having entries recorded on both sides of the accounts.

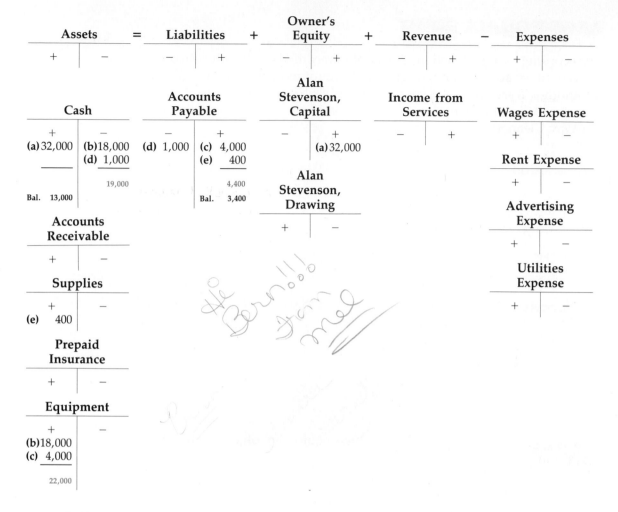

At this point let us pause to determine the equality of the two sides of the equation by listing the balances of the accounts.

Account Name	Accounts with Normal Balances on the Left Side Assets Expenses	Accounts with Normal Balances on the Right Side Liabilities Owner's Equity Revenue
Cash	$13,000	
Supplies	400	
Equipment	22,000	
Accounts Payable		$ 3,400
Alan Stevenson, Capital		32,000
	$35,400	$35,400

LEFT EQUALS RIGHT

In recording each transaction, the amount recorded on the left side of one T account, or accounts, must equal the amount recorded on the right side of another T account, or accounts. This is *double-entry accounting.* To emphasize this point, let us review the recording of the transactions for NuWay Cleaners.

Transaction (a)   Stevenson invests $32,000 cash in his new business.

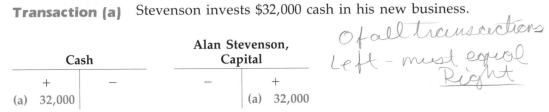

Cash		
+	–	
(a) 32,000		

Alan Stevenson, Capital		
–	+	
	(a) 32,000	

Of all transactions Left – must equal Right

Transaction (b)   NuWay Cleaners buys $18,000 worth of equipment, paying cash.

Cash		
+	–	
	(b) 18,000	

Equipment		
+	–	
(b) 18,000		

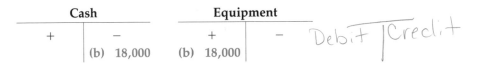

Debit | Credit

Transaction (c)   NuWay Cleaners buys equipment on credit from Sanchez Equipment Company, $4,000.

Equipment		
+	–	
(c) 4,000		

Accounts Payable		
–	+	
	(c) 4,000	

We observe from the foregoing that transactions are recorded in various combinations of pluses and minuses in the accounts. However, the important point to remember is that **the amount recorded on the left side of one T account, or accounts, must equal the amount recorded on the right side of another T account, or accounts.**

Transaction (d)   NuWay Cleaners pays $1,000 to be applied against the firm's liability of $4,000. (Left side of Accounts Payable and right side of Cash.)

Cash		
+	–	
	(d) 1,000	

Accounts Payable		
–	+	
(d) 1,000		

Transaction (e) NuWay Cleaners buys cleaning fluids on credit from Troy Supply Company, $400. (Left side of Supplies and right side of Accounts Payable.)

Supplies		Accounts Payable	
+	−	−	+
(e) 400			(e) 400

Transaction (f) NuWay Cleaners receives $600 cash revenue for the first week. We write $600 on the plus, or left, side of Cash and $600 on the plus, or right, side of Income from Services. In other words, the firm has more cash than before, so we record $600 in the Cash account on the plus side (which happens to be the left side). Also, we recognize that there is an increase in income from services, so we record $600 in Income from Services on the plus side (which happens to be the right side).

Assets		=	Liabilities		+	Owner's Equity		+	Revenue		−	Expenses	
+	−		−	+		−	+		−	+		+	−

Cash				Income from Services	
+	−			−	+
(f) 600					(f) 600

Transaction (g) NuWay Cleaners pays $400 for one month's rent on its shop. We write $400 on the plus, or left, side of Rent Expense. From the point of view of a running record of the Rent Expense account, there is an increase in this account. We also write $400 on the minus, or right, side of Cash.

Assets		=	Liabilities		+	Owner's Equity		+	Revenue		−	Expenses	
+	−		−	+		−	+		−	+		+	−

Cash						Rent Expense	
+	−					+	−
	(g) 400					(g) 400	

Transaction (h) NuWay Cleaners pays wages to employees, $240. We write $240 on the plus, or left, side of Wages Expense and $240 on the minus, or right, side of Cash.

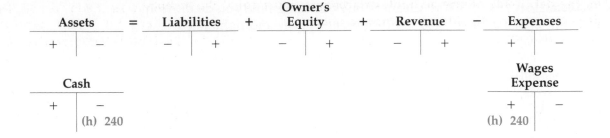

DEBIT AND CREDIT SIDES

In accounting, the *left side* of a T account is called the **debit** side; the *right side* is called the **credit** side. To repeat the fundamental accounting equation with the T's as shown here:

Assets		=	Liabilities		+	Owner's Equity		+	Revenue		−	Expenses	
+	−		−	+		−	+		−	+		+	−
Left	Right		Left	Right		Left	Right		Left	Right		Left	Right
Debit	Credit		Debit	Credit		Debit	Credit		Debit	Credit		Debit	Credit

Note that the left side is always the debit side, regardless of whether it represents the plus or minus side of an account. One may use the word *debit* as a verb. If we debit Wages Expense for $240, for example, this means that we write $240 on the left side of Wages Expense. If the other half of the entry results in a credit to Cash for $240, this means that we write $240 on the right side of Cash.

Objective 3

Present the fundamental accounting equation with the T account forms, the plus and minus signs, and the debit and credit sides labeled.

Rules of Debit and Credit

When we use T accounts to study the fundamental accounting equation, we can make the following observation.

Debits Signify		Credits Signify	
Increases in	{ Assets, Expenses	Decreases in	{ Assets, Expenses
Decreases in	{ Liabilities, Owner's Equity, Revenue	Increases in	{ Liabilities, Owner's Equity, Revenue

Previously we said that when one records each business transaction, the amount placed on the left side of one account (or accounts) must equal the amount placed on the right side of another account (or accounts). Let us now state this rule in terms of debits and credits. **The amount placed**

on the debit side of one account, or accounts, must equal the amount placed on the credit side of another account, or accounts.

In your own personal experience, you may have heard the terms *debit* and *credit* used. So, as an aside, let's talk about these terms. First, keep in mind that the debit side is always the left side of any account and the credit side is always the right side of any account. Here's an example: You deposit $50 in a bank savings account. Every firm keeps its books from its own point of view. From the bank's point of view, the bank now has $50 more in cash, but it also owes you $50 more than before. As you know, you have the right to withdraw $50 at any time. In other words, the bank is liable to you (Deposits Payable account). The bank records the transaction like this:

Assets	=	Liabilities	+	Owner's Equity	+	Revenue	–	Expenses
+ –		– +		– +		– +		+ –
Debit Credit		Debit Credit		Debit Credit		Debit Credit		Debit Credit

Cash	Deposits Payable
+ –	– +
50	50

Note that the bank increased its liability by recording $50 on the plus, or credit, side of Deposits Payable. So, when you deposit $50 in the bank, the bank *credits* your account. Conversely, if you withdraw $50 from the bank, the bank *debits* your account.

Now let's return to the transactions of NuWay Cleaners.

Transaction (i) NuWay Cleaners pays $320 for a two-year insurance policy. We write $320 on the plus, or debit, side of Prepaid Insurance and $320 on the minus, or credit, side of Cash.

Assets	=	Liabilities	+	Owner's Equity	+	Revenue	–	Expenses
+ –		– +		– +		– +		+ –
Debit Credit		Debit Credit		Debit Credit		Debit Credit		Debit Credit

Cash	
+	–
	(i) 320

Prepaid Insurance	
+	–
(i) 320	

Transaction (j) NuWay Cleaners receives cash revenue for the second week, $760. We write $760 on the plus, or debit, side of Cash and $760 on the plus, or credit, side of Income from Services.

Assets		=	Liabilities		+	Owner's Equity		+	Revenue		−	Expenses	
+	−		−	+		−	+		−	+		+	−
Debit	Credit		Debit	Credit		Debit	Credit		Debit	Credit		Debit	Credit

Cash									Income from Services				
+	−								−	+			
(j) 760										(j) 760			

Transaction (k) NuWay Cleaners receives a bill for newspaper advertising, $180. We write $180 on the plus, or debit, side of Advertising Expense and $180 on the plus, or credit, side of Accounts Payable.

Assets		=	Liabilities		+	Owner's Equity		+	Revenue		−	Expenses	
+	−		−	+		−	+		−	+		+	−
Debit	Credit		Debit	Credit		Debit	Credit		Debit	Credit		Debit	Credit

			Accounts Payable									Advertising Expense	
			−	+								+	−
				(k) 180								(k) 180	

Transaction (l) NuWay Cleaners pays $1,800 to creditors as part payment on account. We write $1,800 on the minus, or debit, side of Accounts Payable and $1,800 on the minus, or credit, side of Cash.

Assets		=	Liabilities		+	Owner's Equity		+	Revenue		−	Expenses	
+	−		−	+		−	+		−	+		+	−
Debit	Credit		Debit	Credit		Debit	Credit		Debit	Credit		Debit	Credit

Cash		Accounts Payable											
+	−	−	+										
	(l) 1,800	(l) 1,800											

In order to help you determine how to record debits and credits in the foregoing transactions, we have continually repeated the fundamental accounting equation:

Assets		=	Liabilities		+	Owner's Equity		+	Revenue		–	Expenses	
+	–		–	+		–	+		–	+		+	–
Debit	Credit		Debit	Credit		Debit	Credit		Debit	Credit		Debit	Credit

Let us again stress the steps in the analytical phase of accounting:

1. Decide which accounts are involved.
2. Determine whether there is an increase or a decrease in the accounts.
3. Formulate the entry as a debit to one account (or accounts) and a credit to another account (or accounts).

For the last step, you must be able to visualize this last equation. It is so useful that you ought to engrave it in your mind. For example, in the analysis of transaction **l,** you decide that Accounts Payable is involved; then you mentally classify Accounts Payable as a liability account. You should be able to picture in your mind the T account for Liabilities, with the minus sign on the debit side and the plus sign on the credit side. There is a decrease in Accounts Payable, so the entry should be recorded on the debit side. Without a doubt, this is the most important concept that you will ever learn in accounting. Memorize the fundamental accounting equation and placement of the plus and minus signs in the T accounts. Memorize as well the accounts that are exceptions, such as the Drawing account. It will make everything that follows much, much easier.

Now let's get back to the transactions of NuWay Cleaners.

Transaction (m) NuWay Cleaners receives and pays bill for utilities, $220. We write $220 on the plus, or debit, side of Utilities Expense and $220 on the minus, or credit, side of Cash.

Assets		=	Liabilities		+	Owner's Equity		+	Revenue		–	Expenses	
+	–		–	+		–	+		–	+		+	–
Debit	Credit		Debit	Credit		Debit	Credit		Debit	Credit		Debit	Credit

Cash												Utilities Expense	
+	–											+	–
	(m) 220											(m) 220	

Transaction (n) NuWay Cleaners pays $180 to a newspaper for advertising. (This bill has previously been recorded.) We write $180 on the minus, or debit, side of Accounts Payable and $180 on the minus, or credit, side of Cash.

Credit cash

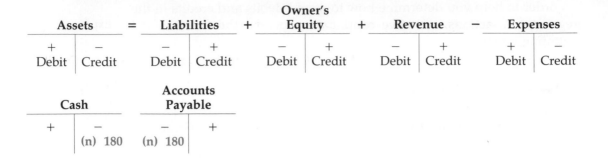

Assets		=	Liabilities		+	Owner's Equity		+	Revenue		−	Expenses	
+	−		−	+		−	+		−	+		+	−
Debit	Credit		Debit	Credit		Debit	Credit		Debit	Credit		Debit	Credit

Cash		Accounts Payable	
+	−	−	+
	(n) 180	(n) 180	

Transaction (o) NuWay Cleaners receives cash revenue for the third week, $830. We write $830 on the plus, or debit, side of Cash and $830 on the plus, or credit, side of Income from Services.

Assets		=	Liabilities		+	Owner's Equity		+	Revenue		−	Expenses	
+	−		−	+		−	+		−	+		+	−
Debit	Credit		Debit	Credit		Debit	Credit		Debit	Credit		Debit	Credit

Cash		Income from Services	
+	−	−	+
(o) 830			(o) 830

Transaction (p) NuWay Cleaners signs a contract with A-1 Rental to clean their for-hire rental clothes on a credit basis. When NuWay bills A-1 Rental $80 for services performed, we write $80 on the plus, or debit, side of Accounts Receivable and $80 on the plus, or credit, side of Income from Services.

Assets		=	Liabilities		+	Owner's Equity		+	Revenue		−	Expenses	
+	−		−	+		−	+		−	+		+	−
Debit	Credit		Debit	Credit		Debit	Credit		Debit	Credit		Debit	Credit

Accounts Receivable		Income from Services	
+	−	−	+
(p) 80			(p) 80

Transaction (q) NuWay Cleaners pays wages of employees, $390. We write $390 on the plus, or debit, side of Wages Expense and $390 on the minus, or credit, side of Cash.

Assets		=	Liabilities		+	Owner's Equity		+	Revenue		−	Expenses	
+	−		−	+		−	+		−	+		+	−
Debit	Credit		Debit	Credit		Debit	Credit		Debit	Credit		Debit	Credit

Cash												Wages Expense	
+	−											+	−
	(q) 390											(q) 390	

Transaction (r) NuWay Cleaners buys additional equipment from Sanchez Equipment Company, $940, paying $140 down with the remaining $800 on account. We write $940 on the plus, or debit, side of Equipment. We write $140 on the minus, or credit, side of Cash and $800 on the plus, or credit, side of Accounts Payable. When a transaction is recorded using two or more debits and/or two or more credits, it is called a **compound entry.**

Assets		=	Liabilities		+	Owner's Equity		+	Revenue		−	Expenses	
+	−		−	+		−	+		−	+		+	−
Debit	Credit		Debit	Credit		Debit	Credit		Debit	Credit		Debit	Credit

Cash		Accounts Payable	
+	−	−	+
	(r) 140		(r) 800

Equipment	
+	−
(r) 940	

Transaction (s) NuWay Cleaners receives revenue from cash customers for the remainder of the month, $960. We write $960 on the plus, or debit, side of Cash and $960 on the plus, or credit, side of Income from Services.

Assets		=	Liabilities		+	Owner's Equity		+	Revenue		−	Expenses	
+	−		−	+		−	+		−	+		+	−
Debit	Credit		Debit	Credit		Debit	Credit		Debit	Credit		Debit	Credit

Cash										Income from Services	
+	−									−	+
(s) 960											(s) 960

Transaction (t) NuWay Cleaners receives $60 from A-1 Rental to apply on the amount previously billed. We write $60 on the plus, or debit, side of Cash and $60 on the minus, or credit, side of Accounts Receivable.

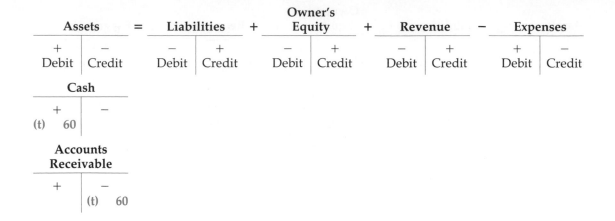

Assets		=	Liabilities		+	Owner's Equity		+	Revenue		−	Expenses	
+	−		−	+		−	+		−	+		+	−
Debit	Credit		Debit	Credit		Debit	Credit		Debit	Credit		Debit	Credit

Cash

+	−
(t) 60	

Accounts Receivable

+	−
	(t) 60

Transaction (u) At the end of the month Stevenson withdraws from the business $1,000 in cash for his personal use. We write $1,000 on the minus, or credit, side of Cash and $1,000 on the plus, or debit, side of Alan Stevenson, Drawing. Because the account, Alan Stevenson, Drawing, is used to record personal withdrawals by the owner, it should be recorded on the plus, or debit, side of this account.

Assets		=	Liabilities		+	Owner's Equity		+	Revenue		−	Expenses	
+	−		−	+		−	+		−	+		+	−
Debit	Credit		Debit	Credit		Debit	Credit		Debit	Credit		Debit	Credit

Cash

+	−
	(u) 1,000

Alan Stevenson, Drawing

+	−
(u) 1,000	

Summary of Transactions

The T accounts that follow show the transactions as they are ordinarily recorded. Footings are shown in color. Note that, in recording expenses, one places the entries only on the plus, or debit, side. Also, in recording revenues, one places the entries on the plus, or credit, side.

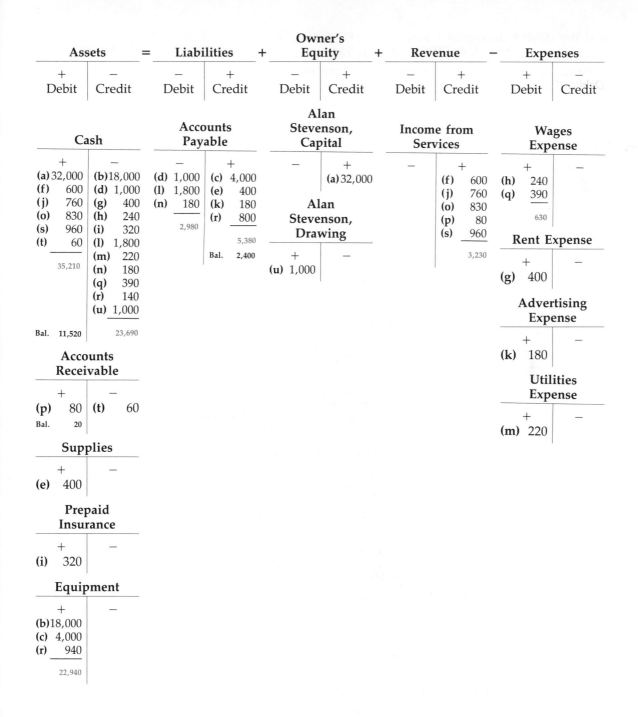

Assets		=	Liabilities		+	Owner's Equity		+	Revenue		−	Expenses	
+	−		−	+		−	+		−	+		+	−
Debit	Credit		Debit	Credit		Debit	Credit		Debit	Credit		Debit	Credit

Cash

+	−
(a) 32,000	(b) 18,000
(f) 600	(d) 1,000
(j) 760	(g) 400
(o) 830	(h) 240
(s) 960	(i) 320
(t) 60	(l) 1,800
35,210	(m) 220
	(n) 180
	(q) 390
	(r) 140
	(u) 1,000
Bal. 11,520	23,690

Accounts Receivable

+	−
(p) 80	(t) 60
Bal. 20	

Supplies

+	−
(e) 400	

Prepaid Insurance

+	−
(i) 320	

Equipment

+	−
(b) 18,000	
(c) 4,000	
(r) 940	
22,940	

Accounts Payable

−	+
(d) 1,000	(c) 4,000
(l) 1,800	(e) 400
(n) 180	(k) 180
2,980	(r) 800
	5,380
Bal. 2,400	

Alan Stevenson, Capital

−	+
	(a) 32,000

Alan Stevenson, Drawing

+	−
(u) 1,000	

Income from Services

−	+
	(f) 600
	(j) 760
	(o) 830
	(p) 80
	(s) 960
	3,230

Wages Expense

+	−
(h) 240	
(q) 390	
630	

Rent Expense

+	−
(g) 400	

Advertising Expense

+	−
(k) 180	

Utilities Expense

+	−
(m) 220	

THE TRIAL BALANCE

You can now prepare a **trial balance** by simply recording the balances of the T accounts. This is not considered to be a financial statement, but, as the name implies, it is in essence a trial run by the accountant to prove that the debit balances of T accounts equal the credit balances of other T accounts. This is evidence of the equality of both sides of the fundamental accounting equation. The trial balance is a prerequisite to the preparation of financial statements.

In preparing a trial balance, record the balances of the accounts in the order in which they appear in the ledger. This order follows the chart of accounts, where first balance sheet accounts and then income statement accounts are listed:

Objective 4

Prepare a trial balance.

- Assets
- Liabilities
- Owner's Equity
- Revenue
- Expenses

NuWay Cleaners
Trial Balance
June 30, 19–

ACCOUNT NAME	DEBIT	CREDIT
Cash	11 5 2 0 00	
Accounts Receivable	2 0 00	
Supplies	4 0 0 00	
Prepaid Insurance	3 2 0 00	
Equipment	22 9 4 0 00	
Accounts Payable		2 4 0 0 00
Alan Stevenson, Capital		32 0 0 0 00
Alan Stevenson, Drawing	1 0 0 0 00	
Income from Services		3 2 3 0 00
Wages Expense	6 3 0 00	
Rent Expense	4 0 0 00	
Advertising Expense	1 8 0 00	
Utilities Expense	2 2 0 00	
	37 6 3 0 00	37 6 3 0 00

The normal balance of each account is on its plus side. Remember that when there is more than one entry in an account, we record the totals in footings and subtract one footing from the other to determine the balance. Record this balance on the side of the account having the larger footing. (Here we record the Drawing account balance in the debit column, because it has a debit balance. We don't deduct Drawing from the Capital account at the time that we prepare the trial balance.) The following table indicates where each of the account balances would normally be shown in a trial balance.

Account Titles	Trial Balance	
	Left or Debit Balances	Right or Credit Balances
	Assets	
		Liabilities
		Owner's Equity
	Drawing	
		Revenue
	Expenses	
Totals	XXXX XX	XXXX XX

Errors Exposed by the Trial Balance

If the debit and credit columns are not equal, then it is evident that we have made an error. Possible causes of errors include the following:

- Recording only half an entry, such as a debit without a corresponding credit, or vice versa.
- Recording both halves of the entry on the same side, such as two debits, rather than a debit and a credit.
- Recording one or more amounts incorrectly.
- Making errors in arithmetic, such as errors in adding the trial balance columns or in finding the balances of the ledger accounts.

Procedure for Locating Errors

Suppose that you are in a business situation in which you have recorded transactions for a month in the account books, and the accounts do not balance. To save yourself time, you need to have a definite procedure for tracking down the errors. The best method is to do everything in reverse, as follows:

- Re-add the trial balance columns.
- Check the transferring of the figures from the ledger accounts to the trial balance.
- Verify the footings and balances of the ledger accounts.

As an added precaution, form the habit of verifying all addition and subtraction as you go along. You can thus correct many mistakes *before* making a trial balance.

When the trial balance totals do not balance, the difference might indicate you forgot to record half of an entry in the accounts. For example, if the difference in the trial balance totals is $20, you may have recorded $20 on the debit side of one account without recording $20 on the credit side of another account. Another possibility is to divide the difference by two; this may provide a clue that you accidentally posted half an entry twice. For example, if the difference in the trial balance is $600, you may have recorded $300 on the debit side of one account and an additional $300 on the debit side of another account. Look for a transaction that involved $300 and then see if you have recorded a debit and a credit. By knowing which transactions to check, you can save a lot of time.

Transpositions and Slides

If the difference is evenly divisible by 9, the discrepancy may be either a **transposition** or a **slide.** A transposition means that the digits have been transposed, or switched around. For example, one transposition of digits in 916 can be written as 619:

$$
\begin{array}{r}
916 \\
-\ 619 \\
\hline
297
\end{array}
\qquad
\begin{array}{r}
33 \\
\hline
9\overline{)297}
\end{array}
$$

A slide refers to an error in placing the decimal point, in other words, a slide in the decimal point. For example, $163 could be inadvertently written as $1.63:

$$
\begin{array}{r}
\$163.00 \\
-\ 1.63 \\
\hline
\$161.37
\end{array}
\qquad
\begin{array}{r}
17.93 \\
\hline
9\overline{)161.37}
\end{array}
$$

Or the error may be a combination of transposition and slide, such as when $216 is written as $6.21:

$$
\begin{array}{r}
\$216.00 \\
-\ 6.21 \\
\hline
\$209.79
\end{array}
\qquad
\begin{array}{r}
23.31 \\
\hline
9\overline{)209.79}
\end{array}
$$

Again, the difference is evenly divisible by 9.

GLOSSARY

Compound entry A transaction that is recorded using two or more debits and/or two or more credits.

Credit The right side of a ledger T account; to credit is to record an amount on the right side of a ledger T account. Credits represent increases in liability, capital, and revenue accounts, and decreases in asset and expense accounts.

Debit The left side of a ledger T account; to debit is to record an amount on the left side of a ledger T account. Debits represent increases in asset and expense accounts, and decreases in liability, capital, and revenue accounts.

Footings The totals of each side of a T account, recorded in pencil.

Ledger A book, a binder, or a file containing all the accounts of an enterprise.

Normal balance The plus side of any T account.

Slide An error in the placement of the decimal point of a number.

T account form A form of ledger account having one side for entries on the debit, or left, side, and one side for entries on the credit, or right, side.

Transposition An error that involves interchanging, or switching around, the digits during the recording of a number.

Trial balance A list of all ledger account balances to prove that the total of all the debit balances equals the total of all the credit balances.

QUESTIONS, EXERCISES, AND PROBLEMS

Discussion Questions

1. Name the five classifications of accounts. Which classifications are identified with the balance sheet? Which classifications are identified with the income statement?
2. Regarding the five classifications of accounts, indicate the normal balance (whether debit or credit) of each account classification.
3. Does the term *debit* always mean increase? Does the term *credit* always mean decrease? Explain.
4. What is the reason for using a separate owner's drawing account?
5. What is a compound entry?
6. Give an example of (a) a transposition and (b) a slide.
7. N. Blacow runs his own grounds maintenance business and keeps his own books. Upon taking a trial balance, Blacow finds the total debits amount to $107,400, and total credits amount to $107,600. What are some possible reasons for the $200 difference between debit and credit totals?

Exercises

Exercise 3-1 Name the account in which each of the following items would be recorded.

a. Premiums paid in advance for two years on a liability insurance policy.
b. Amounts owed to the business by customers.

c. Money on deposit in the business checking account.

d. The value of blank forms used to send out bills to charge customers.

e. Amounts owed to suppliers.

f. D. Aikens's claim against the assets of Aikens's business.

Exercise 3-2   On a sheet of paper set up the fundamental accounting equation with T accounts under each of the five account classifications, noting plus and minus signs on the appropriate sides of each account. Under each of the five classifications, set up T accounts—again with the correct plus and minus signs—for each of the following accounts of the Towncraft Shoe Repair: Cash; Accounts Receivable; Supplies; Equipment; Accounts Payable; Sara Dugan, Capital; Sara Dugan, Drawing; Income from Services; Rent Expense; Telephone Expense; Utilities Expense; Miscellaneous Expense.

Exercise 3-3   James Fulton operates Fulton Carpet Cleaners. The company has the following chart of accounts:

Assets
Cash
Accounts Receivable
Supplies
Prepaid Insurance
Cleaning Equipment
Truck
Office Equipment

Liabilities
Accounts Payable

Owner's Equity
James Fulton, Capital
James Fulton, Drawing

Revenue
Income from Services

Expenses
Wages Expense
Truck Expense
Utilities Expense
Miscellaneous Expense

On a sheet of ordinary notebook paper, record the following transactions directly in pairs of T accounts. (*Example:* Paid telephone bill, $18.)

Utilities Expense		Cash	
+	−	+	−
18			18

a. Paid $440 for liability insurance.

b. Paid $72 for advertising.

c. Fulton withdrew $192 in cash for personal use.

d. Paid creditors on account, $570.

e. Received $882 from charge customers to apply on account.

f. Paid electric bill, $38.

g. Paid gasoline bill for truck, $216.

Exercise 3-4   During the first month of operation, Anderson's Framing Shop recorded the following transactions. Describe transactions **a** through **k**.

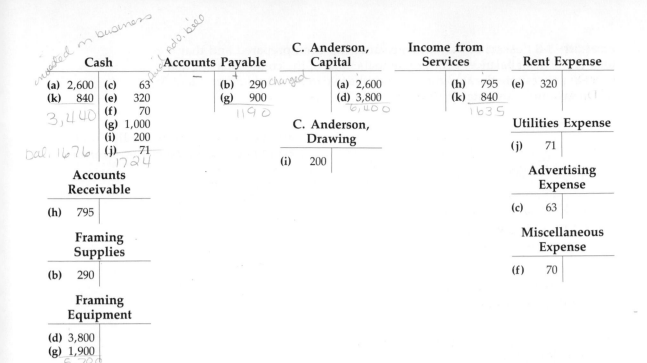

Exercise 3-5 From the accounts in Exercise 4, prepare a trial balance for Anderson's Framing Shop, dated September 30 of this year.

Exercise 3-6 The accounts (all normal balances) of Donna's Beauty Salon as of September 30 of this year are listed in alphabetical order. On a sheet of notebook paper, prepare a trial balance listing the accounts in proper order.

Accounts Payable	$11,400	Insurance Expense	$ 600
Accounts Receivable	16,200	Miscellaneous	
Cash	2,200	Expense	200
Donna Milnor,		Prepaid Insurance	600
Capital	42,200	Rent Expense	4,200
Donna Milnor,		Supplies	6,400
Drawing	1,200	Utilities Expense	2,200
Equipment	40,000	Wages Expense	23,800
Income from Services	44,000		

Exercise 3-7 Answer the following questions by adding the word *debit* or the word *credit*.

a. The Equipment account is increased by entering a _____.
b. The Capital account is increased by entering a _____.
c. The Accounts Receivable account is decreased by entering a _____.
d. The Rent Expense account is increased by entering a _____.
e. The Drawing account is increased by entering a _____.
f. The Accounts Payable account is decreased by entering a debit.

Exercise 3-8 Assume that a trial balance has been prepared and that the total of the debit balances is not equal to the total of the credit balances. On a sheet of paper, note the amount by which the two totals would differ. Identify which column is overstated or understated.

Error	Amount of Difference	Debit or Credit Column Understated or Overstated
Example: A $142 debit to Prepaid Insurance was not posted.	$142	Debit column understated
a. A $47 credit to Cash was not posted.		
b. A $420 debit to Supplies was posted twice.		
c. A $34 debit to Equipment was posted as $340.		
d. A $36 debit to Supplies was posted as a $36 debit to Miscellaneous Expense.		
e. A $91 debit to Accounts Payable was posted twice.		
f. A $48 debit to Accounts Receivable was posted as $84.		

Problem Set A

Problem 3-1A During January of this year, R. L. Ricardo established the Ricardo Autotronics Company. The following asset, liability, and owner's equity accounts are included in the ledger: Cash; Parts and Supplies; Shop Equipment; Store Equipment; Truck; Accounts Payable; R. L. Ricardo, Capital. The following transactions occurred during the month of January.

a. Ricardo invested $16,000 cash in the business.
b. Bought testing equipment for cash, $1,562 (Shop Equipment).
c. Bought repair parts on account from Consolidated Supply, $418; payment is due in 30 days.
d. Bought store fixtures for $924 from Fischer Hardware; payment is due in 30 days.
e. Bought a used service truck for $6,400 from Ludwick Motors, paying $1,500 down; the balance is due in 30 days.
f. Paid $300 on account for the store fixtures in **d**.
g. Ricardo invested his personal tools and testing devices in the business, $1,250.

Instructions

1. Label the account titles under the appropriate headings in the fundamental accounting equation.
2. Correctly place the plus and minus signs under each T account, and label the debit and credit sides of the T account.
3. Record the amounts in the proper positions in the T accounts. Key each entry to the alphabetical symbol identifying each transaction.

Problem 3-2A Dora Shafer established Dora's Fun and Games during October of this year. The accountant prepared the following chart of accounts.

Assets
Cash
Prepaid Insurance
Gaming Equipment
Office Equipment
Neon Sign

Liabilities
Accounts Payable

Owner's Equity
Dora Shafer, Capital
Dora Shafer, Drawing

Revenue
Income from Services

Expenses
Rent Expense
Utilities Expense
Wages Expense
Repair Expense
Miscellaneous Expense

The transactions listed below occurred during the month.

a. Shafer invested $12,200 cash to establish her business.
b. Paid rent for the month, $640.
c. Bought an office desk and filing cabinet for cash, $155.
d. Bought electronic games for use in the business, $10,300; paid $2,300 down, with the balance due in 30 days.
e. Bought a neon sign for $650; paid $200 down, with the balance due in 30 days.
f. Shafer invested her personal electronic games in the business, $740.
g. Received bill for repairs, $52.
h. Received cash for services rendered, $583.
i. Received and paid electric bill, $121.
j. Paid $240 for a two-year liability insurance policy.
k. Paid bill for repairs, billed previously in **g**.
l. Received cash for services rendered, $967.
m. Paid wages to employees, $525.
n. Paid city business license, $27.
o. Shafer withdrew cash for personal use, $325.

Instructions

1. Place the account titles under the appropriate headings in the fundamental accounting equation.
2. Record the plus and minus signs under each T account, and label the debit and credit sides of the T accounts.
3. Record the transactions in the T accounts. Key each entry to the alphabetical symbol identifying each transaction.
4. Foot the T accounts and show balances.
5. Prepare a trial balance with a three-line heading, dated October 31.

Problem 3-3A Doris L. Langdon, an attorney, opens a law office. Her accountant recommends the following chart of accounts:

Assets
Cash
Accounts Receivable
Office Equipment
Office Furniture
Law Library

Liabilities
Accounts Payable

Owner's Equity
Doris L. Langdon, Capital
Doris L. Langdon, Drawing

Revenue
Professional Fees

Expenses
Salary Expense
Rent Expense
Utilities Expense
Travel Expense

The following transactions occurred during June of this year.

a. Langdon invested $12,600 cash in her law practice.
b. Bought a set of filing cabinets on account from Cohn Office Supply (Office Equipment), $270.
c. Paid cash for desks, chairs, and carpets, $110.
d. Bought an electric typewriter for $520 from Macon Office Machines, paying $240 down; the balance is due in 30 days.
e. Received and paid telephone bill, $96.
f. Billed clients for legal services performed, $1,580.
g. Langdon invested her personal law books in the firm, $6,700 (additional investment).
h. Paid $156 in expenses for business trip.
i. Received and paid electric bill, $82.
j. Received $660 from clients previously billed (transaction **f**).
k. Paid $140 on the filing cabinets purchased on credit from Cohn Office Supply.
l. Paid office rent for the month, $400.
m. Paid salary of receptionist, $685.
n. Langdon withdrew cash for personal use, $950.

Instructions

1. Correctly place plus and minus signs under each T account. Label the debit and credit sides of the T accounts.
2. Record the transactions in the T accounts. Key each entry to the alphabetical symbol identifying each transaction.
3. Foot the T accounts and show balances.
4. Prepare a trial balance as of June 30, 19–.
5. Prepare an income statement for June.
6. Prepare a statement of owner's equity for June.
7. Prepare a balance sheet as of June 30, 19–.

Problem 3-4A On August 1, L. C. Kane opened a coin-operated laundry called Modern Self-Service Laundry. Kane's accountant listed the following accounts for the ledger: Cash; Supplies; Prepaid Insurance; Equipment; Furniture and Fixtures; Accounts Payable; L. C. Kane, Capital; L. C. Kane, Drawing; Laundry Revenue; Wages Expense; Rent Expense; Power Expense; Miscellaneous Expense. During August the following transactions were completed.

a. Kane deposited $18,750 in a bank account in the name of the business.
b. Bought tables and chairs for cash, $246.
c. Paid rent for the month, $475.
d. Bought washers and dryers for $15,600, giving $2,700 cash as a down payment with the remainder due in 30 days.
e. Bought washing supplies on account, $423.
f. Received $1,386 from cash customers for the first half of the month.
g. Paid $153 cash for liability insurance for twelve months.
h. Paid $330 as a partial payment on the equipment purchased in **d**.
i. Received and paid electric bill, $172.
j. Paid $115 on account for the washing supplies acquired in **e**.
k. Received $1,160 from cash customers for the second half of the month.
l. Paid $54 for license and other miscellaneous expenses.
m. Paid wages to employee, $815.
n. Kane withdrew cash for personal use, $720.

Instructions

1. Correctly place the plus and minus signs under each T account. Label the debit and credit sides of the T accounts.
2. Record the transactions in the T accounts. Key each entry to the alphabetical symbol identifying each transaction.
3. Foot the T accounts and show balances.
4. Prepare a trial balance as of August 31, 19–.
5. Prepare an income statement for August.
6. Prepare a statement of owner's equity for August.
7. Prepare a balance sheet as of August 31, 19–.

Problem Set B

Problem 3-1B During August of this year, B. L. Chamberlin established the Chamberlin Linen Supply Company. The following asset, liability, and owner's equity accounts are included in the ledger: Cash; Linen Supplies; Laundry Equipment; Office Equipment; Truck; Accounts Payable; B. L. Chamberlin, Capital. During August, the following transactions occurred.

a. Chamberlin invested $15,400 in the business.
b. Bought used washers and dryers for $4,720, paying cash.
c. Bought sheets and pillow cases from Andover Textile Company for cash, $648.
d. Bought towels on account from Restaurant and Hotel Supply Company, $828.

e. Bought a typewriter, desk, and filing cabinet for cash, $516.
f. Bought a used delivery truck for $6,400 from Reliable Used Cars, paying $800 down; the balance is due in 30 days.
g. Paid $200 on account to Restaurant and Hotel Supply Company.

Instructions

1. Label the accounts and put each under the appropriate heading in the fundamental accounting equation.
2. Correctly place plus and minus signs under each T account and label the debit and credit sides of the T accounts.
3. Record the amounts in the proper positions in the T accounts. Key each entry to the alphabetical symbol identifying each transaction.

Problem 3-2B   L. P. Rodriguez established the Supra Game Room during November of this year. The accountant prepared the following chart of accounts.

Assets
Cash
Prepaid Insurance
Gaming Equipment
Office Equipment
Neon Sign
Liabilities
Accounts Payable

Owner's Equity
L. P. Rodriguez, Capital
L. P. Rodriguez, Drawing
Revenue
Income from Services

Expenses
Rent Expense
Utilities Expense
Wages Expense
Repair Expense
Miscellaneous Expense

The transactions listed below occurred during the month.

a. Rodriguez invested $12,400 cash to establish his business.
b. Bought an office desk and filing cabinet for cash, $195.
c. Bought electronic games for use in the business, $8,400, paying $1,400 down; the balance is due in 30 days.
d. Paid rent for the month, $525.
e. Received cash for services rendered, $496.
f. Bought a neon sign for $868, with $200 as a down payment; the balance is due in 30 days.
g. Received bill for repairs, $321.
h. Paid $316 for a two-year liability insurance policy.
i. Received and paid electric bill, $116.
j. Paid bill for repairs, billed previously in **g**.
k. Received cash for services rendered, $915.
l. Paid wages to employee, $520.
m. Rodriguez invested his personal electronic games in the business, $1,425.
n. Rodriguez withdrew cash for personal use, $325.
o. Paid city business license, $32.

Instructions

1. Place the account titles under the appropriate headings in the fundamental accounting equation.
2. Correctly place the plus and minus signs under each T account and label the debit and credit sides of the accounts.
3. Record the transactions in the T accounts. Key each entry to the alphabetical symbol identifying each transaction.
4. Foot the T accounts and show balances.
5. Prepare a trial balance, with a three-line heading, dated November 30.

Problem 3-3B Sylvia A. Koski, an attorney, opens an office for the practice of law. Her accountant recommends the following chart of accounts.

Assets
Cash
Accounts Receivable
Office Equipment
Office Furniture
Law Library

Liabilities
Accounts Payable

Owner's Equity
Sylvia A. Koski, Capital
Sylvia A. Koski, Drawing

Revenue
Professional Fees

Expenses
Salary Expense
Rent Expense
Utilities Expense
Travel Expense

The following transactions occurred during May of this year.

a. Koski invested $9,800 cash in her law practice.
b. Bought a typewriter for $415 from Smithwick Office Machines, paying $250 down; the balance is due in 30 days.
c. Koski invested her personal law books in the firm, $8,430 (additional investment).
d. Bought desks, chairs, and carpets, paying cash, $1,426.
e. Bought a set of filing cabinets on account from Lewis Office Supply (Office Equipment), $312.
f. Received and paid telephone bill, $86.
g. Billed clients for legal services performed, $1,242.
h. Received and paid electric bill for heat and lights, $82.
i. Paid expenses for business trip, $126.
j. Bought bookcases on account from Lewis Office Supply (Office Furniture), $416.
k. Billed clients for additional legal fees, $1,575.
l. Paid office rent for the month, $425.
m. Paid salary of receptionist, $680.
n. Koski withdrew cash for her personal use, $840.

Instructions

1. Correctly place plus and minus signs under each T account, and label the debit and credit sides of the T accounts.
2. Record the transactions in the T accounts. Key each entry to the alphabetical symbol identifying each transaction.

3. Foot the T accounts and show balances.
4. Prepare a trial balance as of May 31, 19–.
5. Prepare an income statement for May.
6. Prepare a statement of owner's equity for May.
7. Prepare a balance sheet as of May 31, 19–.

Problem 3-4B On June 1, A. F. Dukes opened a coin-operated laundry under the name Speedy Self-Service Laundry. Dukes's accountant listed the following accounts for the ledger: Cash; Supplies; Prepaid Insurance; Equipment; Furniture and Fixtures; Accounts Payable; A. F. Dukes, Capital; A. F. Dukes, Drawing; Laundry Revenue; Wages Expense; Rent Expense; Power Expense; Miscellaneous Expense. During June the following transactions were completed.

a. Dukes deposited $15,550 in a bank account in the name of the business.
b. Bought chairs and tables for cash, $232.
c. Bought laundry detergent on account from Oakland Supply Company, $294.
d. Paid rent for the month, $540.
e. Bought washing machines and dryers from Starr Equipment Company, $14,400; paid $2,400 down, with the remainder due in 30 days.
f. Received $1,230 from cash customers for the first half of the month.
g. Paid $210 cash for liability insurance for 12 months.
h. Paid $240 as a partial payment on the equipment purchased from Starr Equipment Company.
i. Received and paid electric bill, $159.
j. Received $1,473 from cash customers for the second half of the month.
k. Paid $36 for license and other miscellaneous expenses.
l. Paid wages to employee, $600.
m. Dukes withdrew cash for his personal use, $575.
n. Paid $225 on account for the washing supplies acquired in **c**.

Instructions

1. Correctly place the plus and minus signs under each T account and label the debit and credit sides of the T accounts.
2. Record the transactions in the T accounts. Key each entry to the alphabetical symbol identifying each transaction.
3. Foot the T accounts and show balances.
4. Prepare a trial balance as of June 30, 19–.
5. Prepare an income statement for June.
6. Prepare a statement of owner's equity for June.
7. Prepare a balance sheet as of June 30, 19–.

4 The General Journal and Posting

Learning Objectives

After you have completed this chapter, you will be able to do the following:

1. Record a group of transactions pertaining to a service-type enterprise in a two-column general journal.

2. Post entries from a two-column general journal to general ledger accounts.

In Chapter 3 we recorded business transactions as debits and credits to T accounts. This enabled you to visualize the accounts and tell which should be debited and which should be credited.

The initial steps in the accounting process are:

1. Record business transactions in a journal.
2. Post to T accounts in the ledger.
3. Foot the T accounts and determine the balances.
4. Prepare a trial balance.

Up to this time we have covered steps 2, 3, and 4. In our previous presentation, we introduced T accounts because, in the process of formulating debits and credits for business transactions, one has to think in terms of T accounts. Now we need to backtrack slightly in order to take up step 1, recording business transactions in a journal. In this chapter we shall present the general journal and the posting procedure.

THE GENERAL JOURNAL

We have seen that an accountant must keep a written record of each transaction. One could record the transactions directly in T accounts; however, one would list only part of the transaction in each T account. A **journal** is a book in which a person makes the original record of a business transaction. The journal serves the function of recording both the debits and credits of the entire transaction. This journal is like a diary for the business, in which one records in day-by-day order all the events involving financial affairs. A journal is called a *book of original entry.* In other words, a transaction is always recorded in the journal first and then recorded in the T accounts. The process of recording in the journal is called **journalizing.** One obtains information about transactions from business papers, such as checks, invoices, receipts, letters, and memos. These **source documents** furnish proof that a transaction has taken place, so we should identify them in the journal entry whenever possible. Later on we shall introduce a variety of special journals. However, the basic form of journal is the two-column general journal. The term *two-column* refers to the two money columns used for debit and credit amounts.

As an example of journalizing business transactions, let's use the transactions for NuWay Cleaners listed in Chapter 3. Each page of the journal is numbered in consecutive order. This is the first page, so we write a 1 in the space for the page number. Also, we must write the date of transaction. Now let's get on with the first entry.

Transaction (a)   June 1: Alan Stevenson deposited $32,000 in a bank account in the name of NuWay Cleaners.

Objective 1

Record a group of transactions pertaining to a service-type enterprise in a two-column general journal.

We write the year and month in the left part of the date column. We don't have to repeat the year and month until we start a new page, or until the year or month changes. (Our illustrations, however, may repeat the month simply to eliminate confusion.) We write the day in the right part of the date column, and repeat it for each journal entry.

	GENERAL JOURNAL			PAGE _1_	
DATE	DESCRIPTION	POST. REF.	DEBIT	CREDIT	
19– Jun. 1					1
					2

Since we are familiar with the accounts, the next step is to decide which accounts should be debited and which credited. We do this by first figuring out which accounts are involved and whether they are increased or decreased. We then visualize the accounts mentally with their respective plus and minus sides.

Cash is involved in our example. Cash is considered to be an asset because it falls within the definition of "things owned." Cash is increased, so we debit Cash.

Cash	
+	–
Debit	Credit
32,000	

Alan Stevenson, Capital is involved; this is an owner's equity account because it represents the owner's investment. Alan Stevenson, Capital is increased, so we credit Alan Stevenson, Capital.

Alan Stevenson, Capital	
–	+
Debit	Credit
	32,000

As we said earlier, you perform this process mentally. If the transaction is more complicated, then use scratch paper, drawing the T accounts. Using T accounts is the accountant's way of drawing a picture of the transaction. This is why we stressed the fundamental accounting equation, with the T accounts and plus and minus signs, so heavily in Chapter 3. You are most definitely urged to get in the T-account habit.

Always record the debit part of the entry first. Enter the account title—in this case, Cash—in the description column. Record the amount—$32,000—in the debit amount column.

GENERAL JOURNAL

PAGE __1__

	DATE		DESCRIPTION	POST. REF.	DEBIT	CREDIT	
1	19– Jun.	1	Cash		32 0 0 0 00		1
2							2

Next, record the credit part of the entry. Enter the account title—in this case, Alan Stevenson, Capital—on the line below the debit, in the Description column, indented about one-half inch. Do not abbreviate account titles, and do not extend them into the Posting Reference column. On the same line, write the amount in the credit column.

GENERAL JOURNAL

PAGE __1__

	DATE		DESCRIPTION	POST. REF.	DEBIT	CREDIT	
1	19– Jun.	1	Cash		32 0 0 0 00		1
2			Alan Stevenson, Capital			32 0 0 0 00	2
3							3

You should now give a brief explanation, in which you may refer to business papers, such as check numbers or invoice numbers; you may also list names of charge customers or creditors, or terms of payment. Enter the explanation below the credit entry, indented an additional one-half inch.

GENERAL JOURNAL

PAGE __1__

	DATE		DESCRIPTION	POST. REF.	DEBIT	CREDIT	
1	19– Jun.	1	Cash		32 0 0 0 00		1
2			Alan Stevenson, Capital			32 0 0 0 00	2
3			Original investment by Stevenson				3
4			in NuWay Cleaners.				4
5							5

In order for an entry in the general journal to be complete, it must contain (1) a debit entry, (2) a credit entry, and (3) an explanation. To anyone thoroughly familiar with the accounts, the explanation may seem to be quite obvious or redundant. This will take care of itself later; but in the meantime, let us record the explanation as a required, integral part of the entry.

Transaction (b) June 2: NuWay Cleaners buys $18,000 worth of equipment, for cash.

Decide which accounts are involved. Next classify them under the five possible classifications. Visualize the plus and minus signs under the classifications. Now decide whether the accounts are increased or decreased. When you use T accounts to analyze the transaction, the results are as follows:

Equipment		Cash	
+	−	+	−
Debit	Credit	Debit	Credit
18,000			18,000

Now journalize this analysis below the first transaction. For the sake of appearance, leave one blank line between transactions. Record the day of the month in the date column. Remember, you don't have to record the month and year again until the month or year changes or you use a new journal page.

		GENERAL JOURNAL			PAGE 1	
	DATE	DESCRIPTION	POST. REF.	DEBIT	CREDIT	
1	19– Jun. 1	Cash		32 0 0 0 00		1
2		Alan Stevenson, Capital			32 0 0 0 00	2
3		Original investment by Stevenson				3
4		in NuWay Cleaners.				4
5						5
6	2	Equipment		18 0 0 0 00		6
7		Cash			18 0 0 0 00	7
8		Bought equipment for cash.				8
9						9

Transaction (c) On June 2 NuWay Cleaners buys $4,000 worth of equipment on account from Sanchez Equipment Company. In order to get organized, think of the T accounts first.

Equipment		Accounts Payable	
+	−	−	+
Debit	Credit	Debit	Credit
4,000			4,000

Skip a line in the journal and record the day of the month and then the entry. In journalizing a transaction involving Accounts Payable, always state the name of the creditor. Similarly, in journalizing a transaction involving Accounts Receivable, always state the name of the charge customer as is done in the example on page 80.

GENERAL JOURNAL PAGE 1

DATE	DESCRIPTION	POST. REF.	DEBIT	CREDIT	
10	2 Equipment		4 0 0 0 00		10
11	Accounts Payable			4 0 0 0 00	11
12	Bought equipment on account				12
13	from Sanchez Equipment				13
14	Company.				14
15					15

Transaction (d)   On June 4, NuWay Cleaners pays $1,000 to be applied against the firm's liability of $4,000. Mentally picture the T accounts like this.

Cash		Accounts Payable	
+	−	−	+
Debit	Credit	Debit	Credit
	1,000	1,000	

Cash is an easy account to recognize. So, in every transaction, ask yourself, "Is Cash involved?" If Cash is involved, determine whether it is coming in or going out. In this case we see that cash is going out, so we record it on the minus side. We now have a credit to Cash and half of the entry. Next, we recognize that Accounts Payable is involved. We ask ourselves, "Do we owe more or less as a result of this transaction?" The answer is "less," so we record it on the minus, or debit, side of the account.

GENERAL JOURNAL PAGE 1

DATE	DESCRIPTION	POST. REF.	DEBIT	CREDIT	
16	4 Accounts Payable		1 0 0 0 00		16
17	Cash			1 0 0 0 00	17
18	Paid Sanchez Equipment				18
19	Company on account.				19
20					20

Now let's list the transactions for June for NuWay Cleaners with the date of each transaction. The journal entries are illustrated on the following pages in Figures 4-1, 4-2, and 4-3.

Jun. 1 Stevenson invests $32,000 cash in his new business.
      2 Buys $18,000 worth of equipment for cash.
      2 Buys $4,000 worth of equipment on credit from Sanchez Equipment Company.

Figure 4-1

	DATE		DESCRIPTION	POST. REF.	DEBIT	CREDIT	
1	19– Jun.	1	Cash		32 0 0 0 00		1
2			Alan Stevenson, Capital			32 0 0 0 00	2
3			Original investment by Stevenson				3
4			in NuWay Cleaners.				4
5							5
6		2	Equipment		18 0 0 0 00		6
7			Cash			18 0 0 0 00	7
8			Bought equipment for cash.				8
9							9
10		2	Equipment		4 0 0 0 00		10
11			Accounts Payable			4 0 0 0 00	11
12			Bought equipment on account				12
13			from Sanchez Equipment				13
14			Company.				14
15							15
16		4	Accounts Payable		1 0 0 0 00		16
17			Cash			1 0 0 0 00	17
18			Paid Sanchez Equipment				18
19			Company on account.				19
20							20
21		4	Supplies		4 0 0 00		21
22			Accounts Payable			4 0 0 00	22
23			Bought cleaning fluids on account				23
24			from Troy Supply Company.				24
25							25
26		7	Cash		6 0 0 00		26
27			Income from Services			6 0 0 00	27
28			For week ended June 7.				28
29							29
30		8	Rent Expense		4 0 0 00		30
31			Cash			4 0 0 00	31
32			For month ended June 30.				32
33							33
34		10	Wages Expense		2 4 0 00		34
35			Cash			2 4 0 00	35
36			Paid wages, June 1 to June 10.				36
37							37

GENERAL JOURNAL — PAGE 1

Jun. 4 Pays $1,000 to Sanchez Equipment Company, to be applied against the firm's liability of $4,000.
      4 Buys cleaning fluids on credit from Troy Supply Company, $400.
      7 Cash revenue received for first week, $600.
      8 Pays rent for the month, $400.
     10 Pays wages to employees, $240, June 1 through June 10.

Figure 4-2

GENERAL JOURNAL   PAGE __2__

	DATE		DESCRIPTION	POST. REF.	DEBIT	CREDIT	
1	19– Jun.	10	Prepaid Insurance		3 2 0 00		1
2			Cash			3 2 0 00	2
3			Premium for two-year liability				3
4			insurance.				4
5							5
6		14	Cash		7 6 0 00		6
7			Income from Services			7 6 0 00	7
8			For week ended June 14.				8
9							9
10		14	Advertising Expense		1 8 0 00		10
11			Accounts Payable			1 8 0 00	11
12			Received bill for advertising				12
13			from Daily News.				13
14							14
15		15	Accounts Payable		1 8 0 0 00		15
16			Cash			1 8 0 0 00	16
17			Paid Sanchez Equipment				17
18			Company on account.				18
19							19
20		15	Utilities Expense		2 2 0 00		20
21			Cash			2 2 0 00	21
22			Paid bill for utilities.				22
23							23
24		15	Accounts Payable		1 8 0 00		24
25			Cash			1 8 0 00	25
26			Paid Daily News for advertising.				26
27							27
28		21	Cash		8 3 0 00		28
29			Income from Services			8 3 0 00	29
30			For week ended June 21.				30
31							31
32		23	Accounts Receivable		8 0 00		32
33			Income from Services			8 0 00	33
34			A-1 Rental, for services rendered.				34
35							35

CHAPTER 4

Jun. 10 Pays for a two-year liability insurance policy, $320.
14 Cash revenue received for second week, $760.
14 Receives bill for newspaper advertising, from the *Daily News*, $180.
15 Pays $1,800 to Sanchez Equipment Company as part payment on account.
15 Receives and pays bill for utilities, $220.
15 Pays the *Daily News* for advertising, $180. (This bill has previously been recorded.)
21 Cash revenue received for third week, $830.
23 NuWay Cleaners enters into a contract with A-1 Rental to clean their for-hire formal garments on a credit basis. Bills A-1 Rental for services performed, $80.
24 Pays wages of employees, $390, June 11 through June 24.

Figure 4-3

GENERAL JOURNAL

PAGE ___3___

	DATE		DESCRIPTION	POST. REF.	DEBIT	CREDIT	
1	19– Jun.	24	Wages Expense		3 9 0 00		1
2			Cash			3 9 0 00	2
3			Paid wages, June 11 to June 24.				3
4							4
5		26	Equipment		9 4 0 00		5
6			Cash			1 4 0 00	6
7			Accounts Payable			8 0 0 00	7
8			Bought equipment on account				8
9			from Sanchez Equipment				9
10			Company.				10
11							11
12		30	Cash		9 6 0 00		12
13			Income from Services			9 6 0 00	13
14			For remainder of June, ended				14
15			June 30.				15
16							16
17		30	Cash		6 0 00		17
18			Accounts Receivable			6 0 00	18
19			A-1 Rental, to apply on account.				19
20							20
21		30	Alan Stevenson, Drawing		1 0 0 0 00		21
22			Cash			1 0 0 0 00	22
23			Withdrawal for personal use.				23
24							24

Jun. 26 Buys additional equipment on account, $940 from Sanchez Equipment Company, paying $140 down with the remaining $800 on account.

30 Cash revenue received for the remainder of the month, $960.

30 Receives $60 from A-1 Rental to apply on amount previously billed.

30 Stevenson withdraws cash for personal use, $1,000.

POSTING TO THE GENERAL LEDGER

From this example, you can see that the journal is indeed the *book of original entry.* Each transaction must first be recorded in the journal in its entirety. Ledger accounts give us a cumulative record of the transactions recorded in each individual account. The general ledger is simply a book that contains all the accounts. The book used for the ledger is usually a loose-leaf binder, so that one can add or remove leaves. The process of transferring figures from the journal to the ledger accounts is called **posting.**

Objective 2

Post entries from a two-column general journal to general ledger accounts.

The Chart of Accounts

One arranges the accounts in the ledger according to the chart of accounts. The **chart of accounts** is the official list of accounts in which transactions may be recorded. Assets are listed first, liabilities second, owner's equity third, revenue fourth, and expenses fifth. The chart of accounts for NuWay Cleaners is as follows.

Chart of Accounts

Assets (100–199)
111 Cash
112 Accounts Receivable
113 Supplies
114 Prepaid Insurance
121 Equipment

Liabilities (200–299)
211 Accounts Payable

Owner's Equity (300–399)
311 Alan Stevenson, Capital
312 Alan Stevenson, Drawing

Revenue (400–499)
411 Income from Services

Expenses (500–599)
511 Wages Expense
512 Rent Expense
513 Advertising Expense
514 Utilities Expense

Notice that the arrangement consists of the balance sheet accounts followed by the income statement accounts. The numbers preceding the account titles are the **account numbers.** Accounts in the ledger are kept by numbers rather than by pages because it's hard to tell in advance how many pages to reserve for a particular account. When you use the number system, you can add sheets quite readily. The digits in the account numbers also indicate *classifications* of accounts: For most companies, assets start with 1, liabilities with 2, owner's equity with 3, revenue with 4, and expenses with 5. The second and third digits indicate the positions of the individual accounts within their respective classifications.

The Ledger Account Form

We have been looking at accounts in the simple T form primarily because T accounts illustrate situations so well. The debit and credit sides are readily apparent. As we have said, accountants usually use the T form to solve problems because it's such a good way to visualize accounts. However, the T form is awkward when you are trying to determine the balance of an account. One must add both columns and subtract the smaller total from the larger. To overcome this disadvantage, accountants generally use the four-column account form with balance columns. Let's look at the Cash account of NuWay Cleaners in four-column form (Figure 4-4) and in T form. Temporarily, the Posting Reference column is left blank. The meaning and use of this column is described in the discussion of the posting process that follows.

Figure 4-4

GENERAL LEDGER

ACCOUNT Cash   ACCOUNT NO. 111

DATE		ITEM	POST. REF.	DEBIT	CREDIT	BALANCE DEBIT	BALANCE CREDIT
19– Jun.	1			32 000 00		32 000 00	
	2				18 000 00	14 000 00	
	4				1 000 00	13 000 00	
	7			6 00 00		13 600 00	
	8				4 00 00	13 200 00	
	10				2 40 00	12 960 00	
	10				3 20 00	12 640 00	
	14			7 60 00		13 400 00	
	15				1 800 00	11 600 00	
	15				2 20 00	11 380 00	
	15				1 80 00	11 200 00	
	21			8 30 00		12 030 00	
	24				3 90 00	11 640 00	
	26				1 40 00	11 500 00	
	30			9 60 00		12 460 00	
	30			6 00 00		12 520 00	
	30				1 000 00	11 520 00	

Cash

+		−	
(a)	32,000	(b)	18,000
(f)	600	(d)	1,000
(j)	760	(g)	400
(o)	830	(h)	240
(s)	960	(i)	320
(t)	60	(l)	1,800
	35,210	(m)	220
		(n)	180
		(q)	390
		(r)	140
		(u)	1,000
			23,690

Bal. 11,520

The Posting Process

In the posting process, you must transfer the following information from the journal to the ledger accounts: the *date of the transaction,* the *debit and credit amounts,* and the *page number* of the journal. Post each account separately, using the following steps. Post the debit part of the entry first.

1. Write the date of transaction.
2. Write the amount of transaction and the new balance.
3. Write the page number of the journal in the Posting Reference column of the ledger account. (This is a **cross-reference**.)
4. Record the ledger account number in the Posting Reference column of the journal. (This is also a cross-reference.)

The transactions for NuWay Cleaners are illustrated in Figure 4-5. Let's look first at the debit part of the entry.

Next we post the credit part of the entry, as shown in Figure 4-6.

Entering the account number in the Posting Reference column of the journal should be the last step. It acts as a verification of the three preceding steps.

The accountant usually uses the Item column only at the end of a financial period. The words that may appear in this column are *balance, closing, adjusting,* and *reversing.* We'll introduce these terms later.

Follow the four steps in the recording of the second transaction, shown in Figure 4-7.

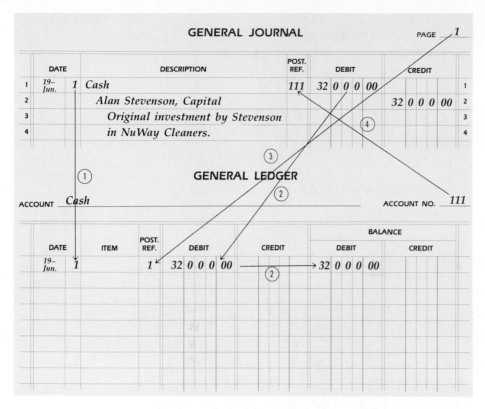

Figure 4-5

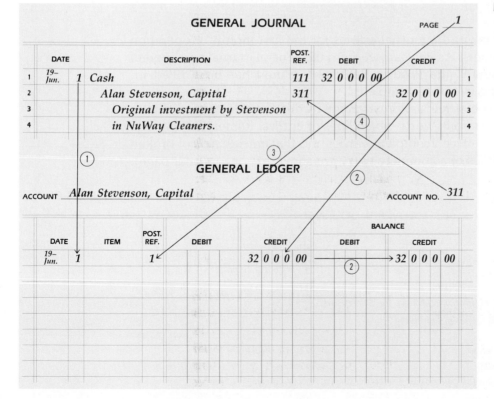

Figure 4-6

Figure 4-7

GENERAL JOURNAL

PAGE ___1___

	DATE		DESCRIPTION	POST. REF.	DEBIT	CREDIT	
6	19– Jun.	2	Equipment	121	18 0 0 0 00		6
7			Cash	111		18 0 0 0 00	7
8			Bought equipment for cash.				8

GENERAL LEDGER

ACCOUNT   Equipment   ACCOUNT NO.   121

							BALANCE	
DATE		ITEM	POST. REF.	DEBIT	CREDIT	DEBIT	CREDIT	
19– Jun.	2		1	18 0 0 0 00		18 0 0 0 00		

ACCOUNT   Cash   ACCOUNT NO.   111

							BALANCE	
DATE		ITEM	POST. REF.	DEBIT	CREDIT	DEBIT	CREDIT	
19– Jun.	1		1	32 0 0 0 00		32 0 0 0 00		
	2		1		18 0 0 0 00	14 0 0 0 00		

Let us now look at the journal entries for the first month of operation for NuWay Cleaners. As you can see from the general journal and general ledger in Figure 4-8, the Posting Reference column has been filled in, since the posting has been completed.

For the purpose of journal illustrations in this chapter, assume that a full journal page permits thirty-seven lines of entries. Remember that one blank line is left between complete entries and that entries are not broken up (that is, all lines of a complete entry are shown on one journal page).

Figure 4-8

GENERAL JOURNAL

PAGE ___1___

	DATE		DESCRIPTION	POST. REF.	DEBIT	CREDIT	
1	19– Jun.	1	Cash	111	32 0 0 0 00		1
2			Alan Stevenson, Capital	311		32 0 0 0 00	2
3			Original investment by Stevenson				3
4			in NuWay Cleaners.				4
5							5
6		2	Equipment	121	18 0 0 0 00		6
7			Cash	111		18 0 0 0 00	7
8			Bought equipment for cash.				8

Figure 4-8 (continued)

		DATE	DESCRIPTION	POST. REF.	DEBIT	CREDIT	
9							9
10		2	Equipment	121	4 0 0 0 00		10
11			Accounts Payable	211		4 0 0 0 00	11
12			Bought equipment on account				12
13			from Sanchez Equipment				13
14			Company.				14
15							15
16		4	Accounts Payable	211	1 0 0 0 00		16
17			Cash	111		1 0 0 0 00	17
18			Paid Sanchez Equipment Company				18
19			on account.				19
20							20
21		4	Supplies	113	4 0 0 00		21
22			Accounts Payable	211		4 0 0 00	22
23			Bought cleaning fluids on account				23
24			from Troy Supply Company.				24
25							25
26		7	Cash	111	6 0 0 00		26
27			Income from Services	411		6 0 0 00	27
28			For week ended June 7.				28
29							29
30		8	Rent Expense	512	4 0 0 00		30
31			Cash	111		4 0 0 00	31
32			For month ended June 30.				32
33							33
34		10	Wages Expense	511	2 4 0 00		34
35			Cash	111		2 4 0 00	35
36			Paid wages, June 1 to June 10.				36
37							37

GENERAL JOURNAL

PAGE ___2___

	DATE	DESCRIPTION	POST. REF.	DEBIT	CREDIT	
1	19– Jun. 10	Prepaid Insurance	114	3 2 0 00		1
2		Cash	111		3 2 0 00	2
3		Premium for two-year liability				3
4		insurance.				4
5						5
6	14	Cash	111	7 6 0 00		6
7		Income from Services	411		7 6 0 00	7
8		For week ended June 14.				8
9						9
10	14	Advertising Expense	513	1 8 0 00		10
11		Accounts Payable	211		1 8 0 00	11
12		Received bill for advertising				12
13		from Daily News.				13
14						14
15	15	Accounts Payable	211	1 8 0 0 00		15
16		Cash	111		1 8 0 0 00	16
17		Paid Sanchez Equipment				17
18		Company on account.				18

Figure 4-8 (continued)

	DATE	DESCRIPTION	POST. REF.	DEBIT	CREDIT	
19						19
20	15	Utilities Expense	514	2 2 0 00		20
21		Cash	111		2 2 0 00	21
22		Paid bill for utilities.				22
23						23
24	15	Accounts Payable	211	1 8 0 00		24
25		Cash	111		1 8 0 00	25
26		Paid Daily News for advertising.				26
27						27
28	21	Cash	111	8 3 0 00		28
29		Income from Services	411		8 3 0 00	29
30		For week ended June 21.				30
31						31
32	23	Accounts Receivable	112	8 0 00		32
33		Income from Services	411		8 0 00	33
34		A-1 Rental, for services rendered.				34
35						35
36						36
37						37

GENERAL JOURNAL   PAGE 3

	DATE	DESCRIPTION	POST. REF.	DEBIT	CREDIT	
1	19— Jun. 24	Wages Expense	511	3 9 0 00		1
2		Cash	111		3 9 0 00	2
3		Paid wages, June 11 to June 24.				3
4						4
5	26	Equipment	121	9 4 0 00		5
6		Cash	111		1 4 0 00	6
7		Accounts Payable	211		8 0 0 00	7
8		Bought equipment on account				8
9		from Sanchez Equipment				9
10		Company.				10
11						11
12	30	Cash	111	9 6 0 00		12
13		Income from Services	411		9 6 0 00	13
14		For remainder of June, ended				14
15		June 30.				15
16						16
17	30	Cash	111	6 0 00		17
18		Accounts Receivable	112		6 0 00	18
19		A-1 Rental, to apply on account.				19
20						20
21	30	Alan Stevenson, Drawing	312	1 0 0 0 00		21
22		Cash	111		1 0 0 0 00	22
23		Withdrawal for personal use.				23
24						24

Figure 4-8
(continued)

GENERAL LEDGER

ACCOUNT _Cash_   ACCOUNT NO. _111_

DATE		ITEM	POST. REF.	DEBIT	CREDIT	BALANCE DEBIT	BALANCE CREDIT
19– Jun.	1		1	32 0 0 0 00		32 0 0 0 00	
	2		1		18 0 0 0 00	14 0 0 0 00	
	4		1		1 0 0 0 00	13 0 0 0 00	
	7		1	6 0 0 00		13 6 0 0 00	
	8		1		4 0 0 00	13 2 0 0 00	
	10		1		2 4 0 00	12 9 6 0 00	
	10		2		3 2 0 00	12 6 4 0 00	
	14		2	7 6 0 00		13 4 0 0 00	
	15		2		1 8 0 0 00	11 6 0 0 00	
	15		2		2 2 0 00	11 3 8 0 00	
	15		2		1 8 0 00	11 2 0 0 00	
	21		2	8 3 0 00		12 0 3 0 00	
	24		3		3 9 0 00	11 6 4 0 00	
	26		3		1 4 0 00	11 5 0 0 00	
	30		3	9 6 0 00		12 4 6 0 00	
	30		3	6 0 00		12 5 2 0 00	
	30		3		1 0 0 0 00	11 5 2 0 00	

ACCOUNT _Accounts Receivable_   ACCOUNT NO. _112_

DATE		ITEM	POST. REF.	DEBIT	CREDIT	BALANCE DEBIT	BALANCE CREDIT
19– Jun.	23		2	8 0 00		8 0 00	
	30		3		6 0 00	2 0 00	

ACCOUNT _Supplies_   ACCOUNT NO. _113_

DATE		ITEM	POST. REF.	DEBIT	CREDIT	BALANCE DEBIT	BALANCE CREDIT
19– Jun.	4		1	4 0 0 00		4 0 0 00	

Figure 4-8
(continued)

ACCOUNT _Prepaid Insurance_   ACCOUNT NO. _114_

DATE	ITEM	POST. REF.	DEBIT	CREDIT	BALANCE DEBIT	BALANCE CREDIT
19– Jun. 10		2	3 2 0 00		3 2 0 00	

ACCOUNT _Equipment_   ACCOUNT NO. _121_

DATE	ITEM	POST. REF.	DEBIT	CREDIT	BALANCE DEBIT	BALANCE CREDIT
19– Jun. 2		1	18 0 0 0 00		18 0 0 0 00	
2		1	4 0 0 0 00		22 0 0 0 00	
26		3	9 4 0 00		22 9 4 0 00	

Liabilities

ACCOUNT _Accounts Payable_   ACCOUNT NO. _211_

DATE	ITEM	POST. REF.	DEBIT	CREDIT	BALANCE DEBIT	BALANCE CREDIT
19– Jun. 2		1		4 0 0 0 00		4 0 0 0 00
4		1	1 0 0 0 00			3 0 0 0 00
4		1		4 0 0 00		3 4 0 0 00
14		2		1 8 0 00		3 5 8 0 00
15		2	1 8 0 0 00			1 7 8 0 00
15		2	1 8 0 00			1 6 0 0 00
26		3		8 0 0 00		2 4 0 0 00

ACCOUNT _Alan Stevenson, Capital_   ACCOUNT NO. _311_

DATE	ITEM	POST. REF.	DEBIT	CREDIT	BALANCE DEBIT	BALANCE CREDIT
19– Jun. 1		1		32 0 0 0 00		32 0 0 0 00

ACCOUNT _Alan Stevenson, Drawing_   ACCOUNT NO. _312_

DATE	ITEM	POST. REF.	DEBIT	CREDIT	BALANCE DEBIT	BALANCE CREDIT
19– Jun. 30		3	1 0 0 0 00		1 0 0 0 00	

**Figure 4-8
(continued)**

Revenue (margin annotation)

ACCOUNT __Income from Services__   ACCOUNT NO. __411__

DATE		ITEM	POST. REF.	DEBIT	CREDIT	BALANCE DEBIT	BALANCE CREDIT
19– Jun.	7		1		6 0 0 00		6 0 0 00
	14		2		7 6 0 00		1 3 6 0 00
	21		2		8 3 0 00		2 1 9 0 00
	23		2		8 0 00		2 2 7 0 00
	30		3		9 6 0 00		3 2 3 0 00

Expenses (margin annotation)

ACCOUNT __Wages Expense__   ACCOUNT NO. __511__

DATE		ITEM	POST. REF.	DEBIT	CREDIT	BALANCE DEBIT	BALANCE CREDIT
19– Jun.	10		1	2 4 0 00		2 4 0 00	
	24		3	3 9 0 00		6 3 0 00	

ACCOUNT __Rent Expense__   ACCOUNT NO. __512__

DATE		ITEM	POST. REF.	DEBIT	CREDIT	BALANCE DEBIT	BALANCE CREDIT
19– Jun.	8		1	4 0 0 00		4 0 0 00	

ACCOUNT __Advertising Expense__   ACCOUNT NO. __513__

DATE		ITEM	POST. REF.	DEBIT	CREDIT	BALANCE DEBIT	BALANCE CREDIT
19– Jun.	14		2	1 8 0 00		1 8 0 00	

ACCOUNT __Utilities Expense__   ACCOUNT NO. __514__

DATE		ITEM	POST. REF.	DEBIT	CREDIT	BALANCE DEBIT	BALANCE CREDIT
19– Jun.	15		2	2 2 0 00		2 2 0 00	

A trial balance is presented in Figure 4-9.

Figure 4-9

NuWay Cleaners
Trial Balance
June 30, 19–

ACCOUNT NAME	DEBIT	CREDIT
Cash	11 5 2 0 00	
Accounts Receivable	2 0 00	
Supplies	4 0 0 00	
Prepaid Insurance	3 2 0 00	
Equipment	22 9 4 0 00	
Accounts Payable		2 4 0 0 00
Alan Stevenson, Capital		32 0 0 0 00
Alan Stevenson, Drawing	1 0 0 0 00	
Income from Services		3 2 3 0 00
Wages Expense	6 3 0 00	
Rent Expense	4 0 0 00	
Advertising Expense	1 8 0 00	
Utilities Expense	2 2 0 00	
	37 6 3 0 00	37 6 3 0 00

If the temporary balance of an account happens to be zero, insert long dashes through both the Debit Balance and Credit Balance columns. We'll use the Donegal Company in this example. Their Accounts Receivable ledger account appears below.

ACCOUNT Accounts Receivable   ACCOUNT NO. 113

						BALANCE	
DATE	ITEM	POST. REF.	DEBIT	CREDIT		DEBIT	CREDIT
19– Oct. 7		96	1 4 0 00			1 4 0 00	
19		97	2 3 8 00			3 7 8 00	
21		97		1 4 0 00		2 3 8 00	
29		98		2 3 8 00		———	———
31		98	1 6 2 00			1 6 2 00	

FLOW OF ACCOUNTING INFORMATION

The journal is a chronological record of the business transactions of a firm. The first step in the accounting process is recording the transactions in the journal. Each journal entry should be based on some material evidence that a transaction has occurred, such as a sales invoice, a receipt, or a check. The second step in the accounting process is posting to the T accounts in the ledger. This step consists of transferring the amounts to the debit or credit columns of the specified accounts in the ledger, using a cross-reference system. The ledger is the book in which all accounts are kept. Accounts are placed in the ledger according to the account numbers in the chart of accounts. After one has journalized and posted a group of transactions for a period of time, one prepares a trial balance to prove that the totals of the debit balances and of the credit balances of the ledger accounts are equal. Figure 4-10 shows the flow of information in the recording process.

Figure 4-10

TROY SUPPLY COMPANY   No. 4-962
2430 East Second Street
Bartell, LA 70990

Sold By: ___203___ Date: ___6/4/___

Name: _NuWay Cleaners_

Address: _1628 East Fifth Avenue_

Bartell, LA 70990

Terms: _Net 30 days_

Quantity	Description	Amount	
20 gal.	Cleaning fluid CR 411 @ $20 per gallon	400	00
	Total	400	00

(continued)

Record in the journal

Figure 4-10
(continued)

21		4	Supplies	113	4 0 0 00		21
22			Accounts Payable	211		4 0 0 00	22
23			Bought cleaning fluids on account				23
24			from Troy Supply Company.				24
25							25

Post to the ledger

ACCOUNT Supplies   ACCOUNT NO. 113

| | | | POST. | | | BALANCE | |
DATE		ITEM	REF.	DEBIT	CREDIT	DEBIT	CREDIT
19– Jun.	4		1	4 0 0 00		4 0 0 00	

ACCOUNT Accounts Payable   ACCOUNT NO. 211

| | | | POST. | | | BALANCE | |
DATE		ITEM	REF.	DEBIT	CREDIT	DEBIT	CREDIT
19– Jun.	2		1		4 0 0 0 00		4 0 0 0 00
	4		1	1 0 0 0 00			3 0 0 0 00
	4		1		4 0 0 00		3 4 0 0 00

} previous
postings

GLOSSARY

Account numbers The numbers assigned to accounts according to the chart of accounts.

Chart of accounts The official list of the ledger accounts in which the transactions of a business are to be recorded.

Cross-reference The ledger account number in the Posting Reference column of the journal or the journal page number in the Posting Reference column of the ledger account.

Journal The book in which a person originally records business transactions; commonly referred to as a *book of original entry.*

Journalizing The process of recording a business transaction in a journal.

Posting The process of recording accounting entries in ledger accounts, the source of information being a journal.

Source documents Business papers such as checks, invoices, receipts, letters, and memos that furnish proof that a transaction has taken place.

QUESTIONS, EXERCISES, AND PROBLEMS

Discussion Questions

1. What is the sequence of the accounts in the general ledger?
2. Is it necessary to add the columns of a two-column general journal?
3. What is a chart of accounts?
4. In the process of recording transactions in a journal, which is recorded first, the title of the account debited or the title of the account credited?
5. Arrange the following steps in the posting process in proper order: (a) Write the page number of the journal in the Posting Reference column of the ledger account. (b) Write the amount of the transaction. (c) Record the ledger account number in the Posting Reference column of the journal. (d) Write the date of the transaction.
6. What is the difference between a journal and a ledger?
7. What is meant by *cross-reference?*

Exercises

Exercise 4-1 In the two-column general journal below, the capital letters represent parts of a journal entry. On notebook paper, write the numbers 1 through 8. Alongside each number, write the letter that indicates where in the journal the items are recorded.

	GENERAL JOURNAL				PAGE 1
DATE	DESCRIPTION	POST. REF.	DEBIT	CREDIT	
G H	I J	O	M		
	K	P.		N	
	L				

1. Ledger account number of account credited P
2. Month H
3. Explanation L
4. Title of account debited J
5. Year G
6. Day of the month I
7. Title of account credited K
8. Amount of debit M

Exercise 4-2 How would the following entry be posted?

| | | GENERAL JOURNAL | | | | | | | | PAGE | _1_ | |

DATE		DESCRIPTION	POST. REF.	DEBIT		CREDIT	
19– Sep.	1	Cash	4) 111	3 6 6 2	00		
		Shop Equipment	121	2 1 8 4	00		
		R. E. Stanfield, Capital	311			5 8 4 6	00
		Original investment in					
		Stanfield Auto Repair					

GENERAL LEDGER

ACCOUNT _Cash_   ACCOUNT NO. _111_

DATE	ITEM	POST. REF.	DEBIT	CREDIT	BALANCE DEBIT	BALANCE CREDIT
19– Sept 1		1	3662 00		3662 00	

ACCOUNT _Shop Equipment_   ACCOUNT NO. _121_

DATE	ITEM	POST. REF.	DEBIT	CREDIT	BALANCE DEBIT	BALANCE CREDIT
19– Sept 1		1	2184 00		2184 00	

ACCOUNT _R. E. Stanfield, Capital_   ACCOUNT NO. _311_

DATE	ITEM	POST. REF.	DEBIT	CREDIT	BALANCE DEBIT	BALANCE CREDIT
19– Sept 1		1		5846 00		5846 00

Cross Referencing

Exercise 4-3   The accounts of Groening Realty on December 31 of this year are listed below in alphabetical order. Prepare a trial balance, with a three-line heading, and list the accounts in the proper sequence by account classification.

Accounts Payable	$ 2,400	G. C. Groening,	
Accounts Receivable	16,200	Drawing	$14,000
Automobile	4,000	Land	8,000
Building	30,000	Office Equipment	5,200
Cash	7,600	Realty Commissions	38,000
G. C. Groening,		Rent Expense	7,200
Capital	61,400	Salary Expense	9,600

Exercise 4-4   The following transactions of Donner Company occurred during this year. Journalize the transactions in general journal form, including brief explanations.

May   8 Bought equipment for $6,000 from Benton Equipment Company, paying $1,500 down; balance due in 30 days.
   10 Paid wages for the period May 1 through 9, $960.
   14 Billed Specker Company for services performed, $156.

Exercise 4-5   Landon Soft-Water Service completed the following selected transactions. Journalize the transactions in general journal form, including brief explanations.

Jun.   3 Collected $646 from C. Buckley, a charge customer.
   9 Issued a check in full payment of an Account Payable to Lafferty Company, $116.
   15 L. E. Landon (the owner) withdrew cash for personal use, $950.

Exercise 4-6   Which of the following errors would cause unequal totals in a trial balance? Explain why or why not.

a. An accountant recorded a $45 payment for advertising as a debit to Advertising Expense of $54 and a credit to Cash of $45.
b. An accountant recorded a withdrawal of $42 in cash by the owner as a debit to Miscellaneous Expense of $42 and a credit to Cash of $42.
c. An accountant recorded an $83 payment to a creditor by a debit to Accounts Payable of $38 and a credit to Cash of $38.

Exercise 4-7   In reviewing the work of the bookkeeper, the office manager discovered the following errors:

a. A typewriter was purchased for $540, and cash was paid and credited. The debit was posted twice in the asset account; the credit was posted correctly.
b. A debit to the Cash account of $1,420 was posted as $1,240; the credit was posted correctly.
c. Cash collections of $1,250 from customers in payment of their accounts were not posted to the Accounts Receivable account but were posted correctly to the Cash account.

For each error, indicate the effect of the error using the following form:

Error	Is the trial balance out of balance?	If yes, by how much?	Which would be incorrect? Debit total	Credit total
a.				
b.				
c.				

Exercise 4-8 The bookkeeper of Newell Company has prepared the following trial balance.

Newell Company
Trial Balance
June 30, 19–

ACCOUNT NAME	DEBIT	CREDIT
Cash		1 6 0 0 00
Accounts Receivable	2 3 0 0 00	
Supplies	2 0 0 00	
Prepaid Insurance	3 0 0 00	
Equipment	10 0 0 0 00	
Accounts Payable		2 2 0 0 00
D. Brogan, Capital		8 0 0 0 00
D. Brogan, Drawing	2 0 0 0 00	
Income from Services		12 3 0 0 00
Rent Expense	4 0 0 0 00	
Miscellaneous Expense	1 0 0 0 00	
	19 8 0 0 00	24 1 0 0 00
	22 3 0 0	22 3 0 0

The bookkeeper is quite upset and has asked you to help prepare a corrected trial balance. In examining the firm's journal and ledger, you discover the following:

a. The debits to the Cash account total $4,000, and the credits total $2,400.
b. A $200 payment to a creditor was entered in the journal but was not posted to the Accounts Payable account.
c. The first two digits in the balance of the Accounts Receivable account were transposed in copying the balance from the ledger to the trial balance.

Problem Set A

Problem 4-1A The chart of accounts of the Roberts Carpet Cleaning Company is given below, followed by the transactions that took place during October.

Assets
111 Cash
112 Accounts Receivable
117 Supplies
121 Equipment
123 Service Truck

Liabilities
211 Accounts Payable

Owner's Equity
311 J. P. Roberts, Capital
312 J. P. Roberts, Drawing

Revenue
411 Cleaning Service Sales

Expenses
511 Wages Expense
512 Service Truck Expense
513 Rent Expense
514 Repair Expense
515 Utilities Expense
516 Miscellaneous Expense

Oct. 1 Bought cleaning supplies on account from Ajax Chemical Company, $94.
      1 Billed First National Bank for services rendered, $316.
      3 Received and paid telephone bill, $62.
      5 Paid rent for the month, $350.
      7 Bought vacuum cleaner on account from Lund Hardware, $229.
     14 Sold cleaning services for cash, $241.
     16 Paid two weeks' wages to employees, $425.
     16 Received and paid gasoline and oil bill relating to the service truck, $64.
     18 Received and paid bill from Fanning Company for repairs to equipment, $75.
     19 J. P. Roberts invested additional cleaning equipment in the business, $327.
     24 Billed Anders Property Management for services performed, $498.
     25 Paid Lund Hardware $100 to apply on account.
     30 Sold services for cash, $942.
     31 Paid two weeks' wages to employees, $540.
     31 J. P. Roberts withdrew cash for personal use, $850.

Instructions

Record the transactions in a general journal, including a brief explanation for each entry. Number the journal pages 17, 18, and 19.

Problem 4-2A The journal entries in the *Working Papers* relate to NuWay Cleaners for its second month of operation. The balances of the accounts as of July 1 have been recorded in the accounts in the ledger.

Instructions

1. Post the journal entries to ledger accounts.
2. Prepare a trial balance as of July 31.
3. Prepare an income statement for the two months ended July 31.
4. Prepare a statement of owner's equity for the two months ended July 31.
5. Prepare a balance sheet as of July 31.

Problem 4-3A Jansen Building Security uses the following chart of accounts.

Assets
111 Cash
112 Accounts Receivable
113 Supplies
114 Prepaid Insurance
115 Weapons and Communication Equipment
121 Patrol Cars

Liabilities
211 Accounts Payable

Owner's Equity
311 C. Jansen, Capital
312 C. Jansen, Drawing

Revenue
411 Security Service Revenue

Expenses
511 Salary Expense
512 Rent Expense
513 Gas and Oil Expense
514 Utilities Expense

The following transactions were completed during October.

Oct. 1 Jansen transferred cash from a personal bank account to an account to be used for the business, $16,200.
1 Jansen invested personal weapons in the business having a fair market value of $742.
4 Bought communication equipment on account from Seegel Audio, $916.
4 Paid rent for the month, $245.
6 Bought a used patrol car for $6,200 from the City of Bristol, paying $3,000 down, with the balance due in 30 days.
9 Received and paid insurance premium to Norwalk Fidelity Group for bonding employees, $514.
11 Performed security services for Limpuri Galleries. Billed Limpuri for services rendered, $550.
15 Received bill from Arrend Printing Company for office stationery, $117.
18 Billed Sinclair Development Company for services rendered, $986.
22 Received and paid bill from City Service for gas and oil for patrol car, $48.
24 Performed security services at a jewelers' convention. Billed Central Gem Association for services rendered, $474.
27 Paid Seegel Audio $300 to apply on account.
29 Received $550 from Limpuri Galleries in full payment of account.
30 Billed Downtown Merchants Association for services rendered, $1,440.
31 Received and paid telephone bill, $69.
31 Paid salaries to employees, $2,100.
31 Jansen withdrew cash for personal use, $1,200.

Instructions

1. Record the transactions in the general journal, giving a brief explanation for each entry.
2. In the general ledger, record the account titles and account numbers. Post the entries to the ledger accounts.
3. Prepare a trial balance dated October 31.

Problem 4-4A The chart of accounts of C. E. Reece, M.D., is as follows.

Assets
111 Cash
112 Accounts Receivable
113 Supplies
114 Prepaid Insurance
121 Equipment

Liabilities
211 Accounts Payable

Owner's Equity
311 C. E. Reece, Capital
312 C. E. Reece, Drawing

Revenue
411 Professional Fees

Expenses
511 Salary Expense
512 Laboratory Expense
513 Rent Expense
514 Utilities Expense

Dr. Reece completed the following transactions during September.

Sep. 2 Bought laboratory equipment on account from Aston Surgical Supply Company, $717.

2 Paid office rent for the month, $465.

3 Received cash on account from patients, $2,720.

6 Bought bandages and other supplies on account, $59.

10 Received and paid bill for laboratory analyses, $183.

12 Paid cash for property insurance policy, $46.

13 Billed patients on account for professional services rendered, $1,518.

16 Received cash for professional services, $281. (Patients were not billed previously.)

17 Part of the laboratory equipment purchased on September 2 was defective; returned equipment and received a reduction in bill, $49.

23 Received cash for professional services, $285. (Patients were not billed previously.)

30 Paid salary of nurse, $640.

30 Received and paid telephone bill for the month, $32.

30 Billed patients on account for professional services rendered, $1,015.

30 Dr. Reece withdrew cash for personal use, $1,010.

Instructions

1. Journalize the transactions for September, beginning with page 21.
2. Post the entries to the ledger accounts. (Because the professional enterprise was in operation previously, the balances have been recorded in the

ledger accounts. A check mark has been placed in the Posting Reference column to represent the various pages of the journal from which the entries were posted.)

3. Prepare a trial balance as of September 30.

Problem Set B

Problem 4-1B   The chart of accounts of Murdoch Carpet Cleaners is given below.

Assets
111 Cash
112 Accounts Receivable
117 Supplies
121 Equipment
123 Service Truck

Liabilities
211 Accounts Payable

Owner's Equity
311 R. L. Murdoch, Capital
312 R. L. Murdoch, Drawing

Revenue
411 Cleaning Service Sales

Expenses
511 Wages Expense
512 Service Truck Expense
513 Rent Expense
514 Repair Expense
515 Utilities Expense
516 Miscellaneous Expense

The following transactions took place during September.

Sep.   1 Received and paid telephone bill, $49.
       1 Received bill from Jenkins Company for repairs to equipment, $91.
       4 Received and paid bill for gasoline and oil used by the service truck, $76.
       6 Paid rent for the month, $315.
       8 R. L. Murdoch invested additional cleaning equipment in the business, $240.
      11 Billed Hotel Randolph for services performed, $298.
      15 Paid two weeks' wages to employees, $375.
      18 Sold services for cash, $879.
      23 Billed Modern Condominiums for services performed, $416.
      26 Paid Acme Electrical Supply on account, $224.
      28 Bought cleaning supplies from Gerhardt Supply Company on account, $72.
      30 Sold services for cash, $785.
      30 Paid two weeks' wages to employees, $392.
      30 R. L. Murdoch withdrew cash for personal use, $800.

Instructions

Record the transactions in a general journal, including a brief explanation for each entry. Number the journal pages 21 and 22.

Problem 4-2B   The journal entries in the *Working Papers* relate to NuWay Cleaners for its second month of operation. The balances of the accounts as of July 1 have been recorded in the accounts in the ledger.

Instructions

1. Post the journal entries to ledger accounts.
2. Prepare a trial balance as of July 31.
3. Prepare an income statement for the two months ended July 31.
4. Prepare a statement of owner's equity for the two months ended July 31.
5. Prepare a balance sheet as of July 31.

Problem 4-3B Modern Building Security had the following transactions during June of this year. The chart of accounts is as follows:

Assets
111 Cash
112 Accounts Receivable
113 Supplies
114 Prepaid Insurance
115 Weapons and Communication Equipment
121 Patrol Cars

Liabilities
211 Accounts Payable

Owner's Equity
311 J. Walsh, Capital
312 J. Walsh, Drawing

Revenue
411 Security Service Revenue

Expenses
511 Salary Expense
512 Rent Expense
513 Gas and Oil Expense
514 Utilities Expense

Jun. 2 Walsh transferred cash from a personal bank account to an account to be used for the business, $12,400.
3 Paid rent for the month, $225.
5 Bought a used patrol car for $5,600 from the City of Anders, paying $4,000 down, with the balance due in 30 days.
6 Walsh invested personal weapons in the business having a present value of $628.
8 Bought communication equipment on account from Noble Electronics, $724.
12 Performed security services at a special rock concert. Billed Music Enterprises for services rendered, $662.
16 Received bill from Perfection Printing for office stationery, $121.
16 Purchased additional weapons for cash from Kimball Hardware, $295.
18 Billed Proctor Property Management for services rendered, $1,620.
19 Paid Noble Electronics $200 to apply on account.
19 Performed security services at a jewelers' convention. Billed Eastern Jewelers' Association for services rendered, $516.
22 Received and paid insurance premiums to Regal Fidelity for bonding employees, $317.
25 Received bill for gas and oil for patrol car from Central Petroleum, $67.
26 Billed City Merchants Association for services rendered, $1,762.
28 Received $662 from Music Enterprises in full payment of account.
30 Paid one month's salary to employees, $2,520.
30 Walsh withdrew cash for personal use, $1,100.
30 Received and paid telephone bill, $71.

Instructions

1. Record the transactions in the general journal, giving a brief explanation for each entry.
2. In the general ledger, record the account names and account numbers. Post the entries to the ledger accounts.
3. Prepare a trial balance dated June 30.

Problem 4-4B The chart of accounts of C. E. Reece, M.D., is as follows.

Assets
111 Cash
112 Accounts Receivable
113 Supplies
114 Prepaid Insurance
121 Equipment

Liabilities
211 Accounts Payable

Owner's Equity
311 C. E. Reece, Capital
312 C. E. Reece, Drawing

Revenue
411 Professional Fees

Expenses
511 Salary Expense
512 Laboratory Expense
513 Rent Expense
514 Utilities Expense

Dr. Reece completed the following transactions during September.

Sep. 2 Bought laboratory equipment from Cox Company on account, $620.
2 Paid office rent for the month, $400.
3 Bought bandages and other supplies on account, $55.
5 Received cash on account from patients, $2,600.
7 Paid cash to creditors on account, $840.
9 Received and paid bill for laboratory analyses, $175.
11 Billed patients on account for professional services rendered, $1,420.
13 Paid cash for property insurance policy for the year, $40.
15 Part of the laboratory equipment purchased on September 2 was defective. Returned the equipment and received a reduction in bill, $40.
16 Received cash for professional services, $260.
29 Paid salary of nurse, $620.
30 Received and paid telephone bill for the month, $26.
30 Received and paid electric bill, $85.
30 Billed patients on account for professional services rendered, $940.
30 Dr. Reece withdrew $975 in cash for personal use.

Instructions

1. Journalize the transactions for September, beginning with page 21.
2. Post the entries to the ledger accounts. (Because the professional enterprise was in operation previously, the balances have been recorded in the ledger accounts. A check mark has been placed in the Posting Reference column to represent the various pages of the journal from which the entries were posted.)
3. Prepare a trial balance as of September 30.

5 Adjustments and the Work Sheet

Learning Objectives

After you have completed this chapter, you will be able to do the following:

1. Complete a work sheet for a service-type enterprise, involving adjustments for supplies consumed, expired insurance, depreciation, and accrued wages.

2. Prepare an income statement and a balance sheet for a service-type business directly from the work sheet.

3. Journalize and post the adjusting entries.

Now that you have become familiar with the classifying and recording phase of accounting for a service-type enterprise, let's look at the remaining steps in the accounting procedure.

FISCAL PERIOD

A **fiscal period** is any period of time covering a complete accounting cycle. A **fiscal year** is a fiscal period consisting of twelve consecutive months. It does not have to coincide with the calendar year. If a business has seasonal peaks, it's a good idea to complete the accounting operations at the end of the most active season. At that time the management wants to know the results of the year and where the business stands financially. As an example, the fiscal period of a resort that is operated during the summer months may be from October 1 of one year to September 30 of the next year. Governments, at some levels, have a fiscal period from July 1 of one year to June 30 of the following year. Department stores often use a fiscal period extending from February 1 of one year to January 31 of the next year. For income tax purposes, any period of twelve consecutive months may be selected. However, you have to be consistent and use the same fiscal period from year to year.

THE ACCOUNTING CYCLE

The **accounting cycle** represents the steps that are involved in the accounting process. In Chapter 4 we summarized the first three steps in the accounting cycle. Figure 5-1 shows all of the steps and their placement in this text.

Figure 5-1

Step	Description	Text Placement
1	Record business transactions in a journal.	
2	Post to the accounts in the ledger.	Chapter 4
3	Prepare a trial balance.	
4	Compile adjustment data and record the adjusting entries in the work sheet.	Chapter 5
5	Complete the work sheet.	
6	Complete the financial statements.	Chapters 1, 2
7	Journalize and post adjusting entries.	Chapter 5
8	Journalize and post closing entries.	Chapter 6
9	Prepare a post-closing trial balance.	Chapter 6

First we shall complete the entire accounting cycle for NuWay Cleaners, which is a service type of business. To show you the accounts for a professional enterprise, Chapter 7 will present the transactions of Dr. Rory T. Barker. We'll go through the entire accounting cycle for each of these examples.

This summary has brought you up to date on what we have accomplished thus far and what we hope to do in the future. The chapters that are not listed cover additional topics about the steps in the accounting cycle.

THE WORK SHEET

At the moment we are concerned with the **work sheet.** As we said in listing the steps of the accounting cycle, the work sheet is a prelude to the preparation of financial statements. The work sheet serves as a medium for recording necessary adjustments and for furnishing the account balances for making up the income statement and balance sheet. We described the income statement and balance sheet that we looked at in Chapter 2 as being tentative, in that adjustments had not been recorded at that time. Often accountants refer to the work sheet as *working papers* because the work sheet is the tool accountants use to bring all the accounts up to date. Accountants use pencil to make entries in the work sheet, since it is a working document.

For our purposes, we will use a ten-column work sheet—so called because two amount columns are provided for each of the work sheet's five major sections. We will discuss the function of each of these sections, again basing our discussion on the accounting activities of NuWay Cleaners. But first, we will fill in the heading, which consists of three lines: the name of the company, the title of the working paper, and the inclusive period of the time covered.

Objective 1

Complete a work sheet for a service-type enterprise, involving adjustments for supplies consumed, expired insurance, depreciation, and accrued wages.

NuWay Cleaners
Work Sheet
For month ended June 30, 19–

ACCOUNT NAME	TRIAL BALANCE		ADJUSTMENTS		ADJUSTED TRIAL BALANCE		INCOME STATEMENT		BALANCE SHEET	
	DEBIT	CREDIT	DEBIT	CREDIT	DEBIT	CREDIT	DEBIT	CREDIT	DEBIT	CREDIT

The Columns of the Work Sheet

When you use a work sheet, you do not have to prepare a trial balance on a separate piece of paper because you enter it in the first two columns of the work sheet. As usual, list the accounts as they appear in the chart of accounts. Thus, in abbreviated form, the accounts are listed in the Trial Balance section of the work sheet as follows:

Trial Balance	
Debit	**Credit**
Assets	
	Liabilities
	Owner's Equity
	Revenue
Expenses	

Entries in the Income Statement section, in abbreviated form, look like the following:

Income Statement	
Debit	**Credit**
	Revenue
Expenses	

Revenue accounts have credit balances, so they are recorded in the Income Statement Credit column. Expense accounts have debit balances, so they are recorded in the Income Statement Debit column.

And in abbreviated form, the accounts in the Balance Sheet section are recorded as follows:

Balance Sheet	
Debit	**Credit**
Assets	Liabilities
	Capital (Owner's Equity)
Drawing	

Asset accounts have debit balances, so they are recorded in the Balance Sheet Debit column. Liability accounts have credit balances, so they are recorded in the Balance Sheet Credit column. The Capital account has a credit balance, so it is recorded in the Balance Sheet Credit column. Because the Drawing account (debit balance) is a deduction from Capital, Drawing is recorded in the Balance Sheet Debit column (the opposite column in which Capital is recorded).

The Classifications of Accounts

It is important that you know where the different classifications of accounts go in the various columns. Observe that all five classifications are placed in the Trial Balance and Adjusted Trial Balance columns. Up-to-date balances are taken directly from the Adjusted Trial Balance columns. The revenue and expense accounts go in the Income Statement columns; the assets, liabilities, and owner's equity accounts go in the Balance Sheet columns.

Account Classification	Trial Balance		Adjustments		Adjusted Trial Balance		Income Statement		Balance Sheet	
	Debit	Credit	Debit	Credit	Debit	Credit	Debit	Credit	Debit	Credit
Assets	X			X	X				X	
Liabilities		X				X				X
Capital		X				X				X
Drawing	X				X				X	
Revenue		X				X		X		
Expenses	X				X		X			

ADJUSTMENTS

Adjustments may be considered *internal transactions*. They have not been recorded in the accounts up to this time because no outside party has been involved. Adjustments are determined after the trial balance has been prepared.

The accounts that require adjusting are few in number and, after one has a limited exposure to accounting, are easy to recognize. They are used by service, merchandising, and all other kinds of businesses. To describe the reasons for—and techniques of handling—adjustments, let's return to NuWay Cleaners. First, let's select the accounts that require adjustments. For the moment, we'll show the adjusting entries by T accounts; later on we'll record them in the work sheet and journalize them.

Supplies   In the trial balance, the Supplies account has a balance of $400. Each time NuWay Cleaners bought supplies, Stevenson wrote the entry as a debit to Supplies and a credit to either Cash or Accounts Payable; so he recorded each purchase of supplies as an increase in the Supplies account.

But we haven't taken into consideration the fact that any business is continually using up supplies in the process of carrying on business operations. For NuWay Cleaners, the items recorded under Supplies consist of cleaning fluids. At the end of the month, obviously some of these supplies have been used. It would be very time consuming to keep a continual record of the exact amount of supplies on hand; so at the end of the month someone takes a physical count of the amount on hand.

When Stevenson takes an inventory on June 30, he finds that there are $320 worth of supplies left. The situation looks like this:

Had	$400	(Recorded under Supplies)
− Have left	− 320	(Determined by taking an inventory)
Used	$ 80	(The amount used is an expense of doing business. This is Supplies Expense.)

To bring the books up to date, Stevenson has to make an **adjusting entry** in NuWay's journal. Let's look at this in the form of T accounts.

(a)

Supplies				Supplies Expense		
+		−		+		−
Balance	400	Adjusting	80	Adjusting	80	

Drawing T accounts on scratch paper is an excellent way of organizing the adjusting entry. By making this entry, Stevenson has merely taken the amount used out of Supplies and put it into Supplies Expense. The new balance of Supplies, $320, represents the cost of supplies that are on hand and should therefore appear in the balance sheet. The $80 figure in Supplies Expense represents the cost of supplies that have been used and should therefore appear in the income statement.

When supplies are bought and originally recorded as an asset (as we have been doing it):

Amount of adjusting entry = Balance of Supplies account
− Amount of supplies remaining

Prepaid Insurance   The $320 balance in Prepaid Insurance stands for the premium paid in advance for a two-year liability insurance policy. One month of the premium has now expired, which amounts to $13.33 (see next page).

$$\frac{\$\ 13.33 \text{ per month}}{24 \text{ months)}\$320.00}$$

In the adjustment, Stevenson deducts the expired or used portion from Prepaid Insurance and transfers it to Insurance Expense.

(b)

Prepaid Insurance		Insurance Expense	
+	−	+	−
Balance 320	Adjusting 13.33	Adjusting 13.33	

The new balance of Prepaid Insurance, $306.67 ($320 − $13.33), represents the cost of insurance that is now paid in advance and should therefore appear in the balance sheet. The $13.33 figure in Insurance Expense represents the cost of insurance that has expired and should therefore appear in the income statement.

Depreciation of Equipment We have followed the policy of recording durable items such as appliances and fixtures under Equipment, because they will last longer than one year. However, since the benefits derived from these assets will eventually be used up, we should systematically apportion their costs over the period of their useful lives. In other words, we write off the cost of the assets as an expense over the estimated useful life of the equipment and call it **depreciation,** because such equipment loses its usefulness. In the case of NuWay Cleaners, the Equipment account has a balance of $22,940. Suppose we estimate that the dry cleaning equipment will have a useful life of six years, with a trade-in value of $2,294 at the end of that time. Then the total depreciation over the estimated useful life of the equipment is $20,646 ($22,940 − $2,294). The calculation of the depreciation for one month is given below.

$$\frac{\$\ 3,441 \text{ per year}}{6 \text{ years)}\$20,646 \text{ full depreciation}}$$

$$\frac{\$\ 286.75 \text{ per month}}{12 \text{ months)}\$3,441}$$

One always records this as a debit to Depreciation Expense and a credit to Accumulated Depreciation. The adjustment in T account form would appear as follows. Note that both accounts are increased.

(c)

Depreciation Expense		Accumulated Depreciation	
+	−	−	+
Adjusting 286.75			Adjusting 286.75

On the balance sheet, the balance of Accumulated Depreciation is a deduction from the balance of the related asset account as illustrated below on the partial balance sheet for NuWay Cleaners.

NuWay Cleaners Balance Sheet June 30, 19–															
Assets															
Equipment			$22	9	4	0	00								
Less Accumulated Depreciation				2	8	6	75	$22	6	5	3	25			

Accumulated Depreciation is contrary to Equipment, so we call it a **contra account.** To show the accounts under their proper headings, let's look at the fundamental accounting equation. (Brackets indicate that Accumulated Depreciation is a deduction from the Equipment account.)

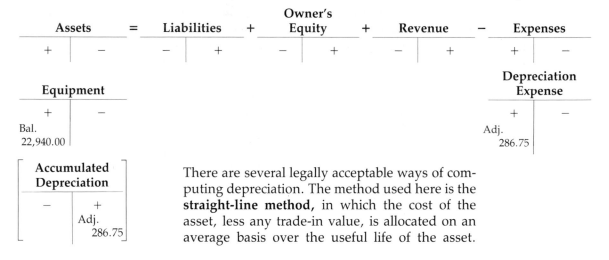

Assets	=	Liabilities	+	Owner's Equity	+	Revenue	−	Expenses
+ | −		− | +		− | +		− | +		+ | −

Equipment

+ | −

Bal.
22,940.00

Depreciation
Expense

+ | −

Adj.
286.75

Accumulated
Depreciation

− | +

Adj.
286.75

There are several legally acceptable ways of computing depreciation. The method used here is the **straight-line method,** in which the cost of the asset, less any trade-in value, is allocated on an average basis over the useful life of the asset.

Accumulated Depreciation, as the title implies, is the total depreciation that the company has taken since the original purchase of the asset. Rather than crediting the Equipment account, NuWay Cleaners keeps track of the total depreciation taken since it first acquired the asset in a separate account. The maximum depreciation it could take would be the cost of the equipment, $22,940, less trade-in value of $2,294. So, for the first year, Accumulated Depreciation will increase at the rate of $286.75 per month, assuming that no additional equipment has been purchased.

For example, at the end of the second month, Accumulated Depreciation will amount to $573.50 ($286.75 + $286.75). The **book value** of an asset is the cost of the asset minus the accumulated depreciation.

Wages Expense The end of the fiscal period and the end of the employees' payroll period rarely fall on the same day. A diagram of the situation looks like this.

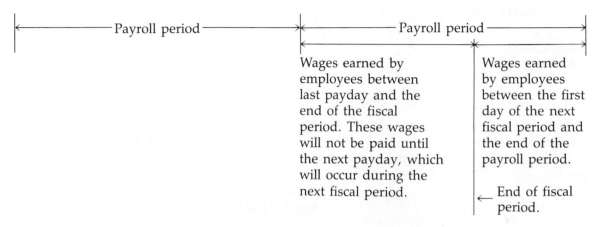

As an example, assume that a firm pays its employees a total of $400 per day and that payday falls on Friday throughout the year. When the employees pick up their paychecks on Friday, at the end of the work day, the amount of the checks includes their wages for that day as well as for the preceding four days. The employees work a five-day week. And suppose that the last day of the fiscal period falls on Wednesday, December 31. We can diagram this as shown in the following illustration.

							End of Fiscal Year		
				Dec. 26	Dec. 29	Dec. 30	Dec. 31	Jan. 1	Jan. 2
Mon	Tue	Wed	Thur	Fri	Mon	Tue	Wed	Thur	Fri
400	400	400	400	400	400	400	400	400	400

—————— Payroll period —————— * —————— Payroll period ——————→

Payday $2,000   Payday $2,000

December						
S	M	T	W	T	F	S
	1	2	3	4	⑤	6
7	8	9	10	11	⑫	13
14	15	16	17	18	⑲	20
21	22	23	24	25	㉖	27
28	29	30	31			

—Paydays

In order to have the Wages Expense account reflect an accurate balance for the fiscal period, you should add $1,200 for the cost of labor between the last payday, December 26, and the end of the year, December 31 (for December 29, $400; for December 30, $400; for December 31, $400). Because the $1,200 is owed to the employees at December 31, you should also add $1,200 to Wages Payable, a liabilities account.

Wages Expense		Wages Payable	
+	−	−	+
Balance 104,000			Adjusting 1,200
Adjusting 1,200			

Returning to our illustration of NuWay Cleaners: The last payday was June 24. NuWay Cleaners owes an additional $100 in wages at the end of the month. Accountants refer to this extra amount that has not been recorded at the end of the month as **accrued wages.** Note that both accounts are increased.

Wages Expense		Wages Payable	
+	−	−	+
Balance 630			Adjusting 100
Adjusting 100			

Placement of Accounts in the Work Sheet   First we have to enter the adjustments in the work sheet. But before doing so, let's digress briefly to discuss the Drawing and Accumulated Depreciation accounts, as well as net income, and their effect on the work sheet.

The Drawing account looks like this:

Alan Stevenson, Drawing

+	−
Balance	

Drawing is a deduction from capital and is shown in the column opposite the normal balance of the Capital account.

The Accumulated Depreciation account looks like this:

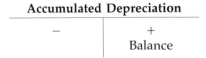

Accumulated Depreciation

−	+
	Balance

Accumulated depreciation is a deduction from the respective asset account; and, as we have said, it is shown in the column opposite the normal balance of the asset account.

Net income (or net loss) is the difference between revenue and expenses. It is used to balance off the Income Statement columns; and, since revenue is normally larger than expenses, the balancing-off amount must be added to the expense side. Net income (or net loss) is also used to balance off the Balance Sheet columns. As in the statement of owner's equity, one adds net income to the owner's equity. The following illustration shows these relationships in diagram form:

Account Name	Trial Balance		Adjustments		Adjusted Trial Balance		Income Statement		Balance Sheet	
	Debit	Credit	Debit	Credit	Debit	Credit	Debit	Credit	Debit	Credit
	A + E + Draw.	L + Cap. + R + Accum. Depr.			A + E + Draw.	L + Cap. + R + Accum. Depr.	E	R	A + Draw.	L + Cap. + Accum. Depr.
Net Income							NI			NI

On the other hand, if expenses are larger than revenue, the result is a net loss. One must add net loss to the revenue side to balance off the Income Statement columns. Also, because one deducts a net loss from the owner's equity, one includes net loss in the debit side of the Balance Sheet columns, thereby balancing off these columns. To show this, let's look at the Income Statement and Balance Sheet columns diagrammed here.

	Income Statement		Balance Sheet	
	Debit	Credit	Debit	Credit
	E	R	A + Draw.	L + Cap. + Accum. Depr.
Net Loss		NL	NL	

Summary of Adjustments by T Accounts

To test your understanding, describe why the following adjustments are necessary. The answers are shown below the accounts.

(a)

	Supplies				Supplies Expense		
	+		−		+		−
Balance	400.00	Adjusting	80.00	Adjusting	80.00		

(b)

	Prepaid Insurance				Insurance Expense		
	+		−		+		−
Balance	320.00	Adjusting	13.33	Adjusting	13.33		

(c)

	Depreciation Expense				Accumulated Depreciation		
	+		−		−		+
Adjusting	286.75					Adjusting	286.75

(d)

	Wages Expense				Wages Payable		
	+		−		−		+
Balance	630					Adjusting	100
Adjusting	100						

a. To record the cost of supplies used during June
b. To record the insurance expired during June
c. To record the depreciation for the month of June
d. To record accrued wages owed at the end of June

Recording the Adjustments in the Work Sheet

In the examples above, we used T accounts to explain how to handle adjustments. T accounts, as you are aware, represent a reliable method of organizing any type of accounting entry. Now it is time to record adjustments in the work sheet. To help you remember which classifications of accounts appear in each column of the work sheet, we will label the columns by letter, for example, *A* for assets and *L* for liabilities.

After completing the trial balance in the first two columns of the work sheet, enter the adjustments directly in the Adjustments columns.

Adjustments Columns of the Work Sheet

When we enter the adjustments, we identify them as **(a)**, **(b)**, **(c)**, and **(d)** to indicate the relationships between the debit and credit sides of the individual adjusting entries, as shown in Figure 5-2.

Note that Supplies Expense, Insurance Expense, Depreciation Expense, and Wages Payable did not appear in the trial balance because there were no balances in the accounts to record. So we wrote them below

NuWay Cleaners
Work Sheet
For month ended June 30, 19–

	ACCOUNT NAME	TRIAL BALANCE DEBIT (A + E + Draw.)	TRIAL BALANCE CREDIT (L + C + R + Accum. Deprec.)	ADJUSTMENTS DEBIT	ADJUSTMENTS CREDIT	
1	Cash	11 5 2 0 00				1
2	Accounts Receivable	2 0 00				2
3	Supplies	4 0 0 00			(a) 8 0 00	3
4	Prepaid Insurance	3 2 0 00			(b) 1 3 33	4
5	Equipment	22 9 4 0 00				5
6	Accounts Payable		2 4 0 0 00			6
7	Alan Stevenson, Capital		32 0 0 0 00			7
8	Alan Stevenson, Drawing	1 0 0 0 00				8
9	Income from Services		3 2 3 0 00			9
10	Wages Expense	6 3 0 00		(d) 1 0 0 00		10
11	Rent Expense	4 0 0 00				11
12	Advertising Expense	1 8 0 00				12
13	Utilities Expense	2 2 0 00				13
14		37 6 3 0 00	37 6 3 0 00			14
15	Supplies Expense			(a) 8 0 00		15
16	Insurance Expense			(b) 1 3 33		16
17	Depreciation Expense			(c) 2 8 6 75		17
18	Accumulated Depreciation				(c) 2 8 6 75	18
19	Wages Payable				(d) 1 0 0 00	19
20				4 8 0 08	4 8 0 08	20

Figure 5-2

the Trial Balance totals. Some people consider them to be new accounts, because they were never used during the fiscal period. But observe that they all have one thing in common: *They are all increased.* In other words, you bring a new account into existence in order to increase it; definitely not to decrease it. This hint can help you formulate any adjusting entry correctly.

Steps in the Completion of the Work Sheet

Before proceeding to the completion of the work sheet, let us list the recommended steps to follow.

1. Complete the Trial Balance columns—making sure both columns are equal. In the Account Name column above the trial balance totals, we list only the accounts having balances, as in the trial balances in Chap-

ters 3 and 4. However, as an alternative, many accountants list all the accounts in the ledger.

2. Complete the Adjustments columns—labeling each adjustment as (a), (b), (c), and so on, and making sure both columns are equal.
3. Complete the Adjusted Trial Balance columns—carrying across any balance from the Trial Balance columns plus or minus any amounts appearing in the Adjustments columns. Make sure both columns are equal.
4. Complete the Income Statement and Balance Sheet columns—distributing each amount from the Adjusted Trial Balance columns, according to the account classification, to either the Income Statement or the Balance Sheet columns, but never to more than one column. For example, Accounts Payable is a liability, and liabilities are recorded in the Balance Sheet Credit column only.

NuWay Cleaners
Work Sheet
For month ended June 30, 19–

	ACCOUNT NAME	TRIAL BALANCE		ADJUSTMENTS	
		DEBIT A + E + Draw.	CREDIT L + C + R + Accum. Deprec.	DEBIT	CREDIT
1	Cash	11 5 2 0 00			
2	Accounts Receivable	2 0 00			
3	Supplies	4 0 0 00			(a) 8 0 00
4	Prepaid Insurance	3 2 0 00			(b) 1 3 33
5	Equipment	22 9 4 0 00			
6	Accounts Payable		2 4 0 0 00		
7	Alan Stevenson, Capital		32 0 0 0 00		
8	Alan Stevenson, Drawing	1 0 0 0 00			
9	Income from Services		3 2 3 0 00		
10	Wages Expense	6 3 0 00		(d) 1 0 0 00	
11	Rent Expense	4 0 0 00			
12	Advertising Expense	1 8 0 00			
13	Utilities Expense	2 2 0 00			
14		37 6 3 0 00	37 6 3 0 00		
15	Supplies Expense		*Step 1*	(a) 8 0 00	
16	Insurance Expense			(b) 1 3 33	
17	Depreciation Expense			(c) 2 8 6 75	
18	Accumulated Depreciation				(c) 2 8 6 75
19	Wages Payable				(d) 1 0 0 00
20				4 8 0 08	4 8 0 08
21					
22					*Step 2*
23					

5. Add the Income Statement Debit and Credit columns and find the difference between the two columns. (The difference represents the net income or net loss.) Use the amount of the net income or net loss to balance off the two columns.
6. Add the Balance Sheet Debit and Credit columns and insert the amount of the net income or net loss to balance off the two columns.

Now we include the Adjusted Trial Balance columns, as shown in Figure 5-3, bringing the balances of the accounts that were adjusted up to date.

After the Adjusted Trial Balance columns are completed, we go through the mental process of classifying the accounts so that we know where to place the classifications in the various columns; and we enter each account balance in the appropriate column. We now carry forward

Figure 5-3

ADJUSTED TRIAL BALANCE		INCOME STATEMENT		BALANCE SHEET		
DEBIT	CREDIT	DEBIT	CREDIT	DEBIT	CREDIT	
A + E + Draw.	L + C + R + Accum. Deprec.	E	R	A + Draw.	L + C + Accum. Deprec.	
11 5 2 0 00						1
2 0 00						2
3 2 0 00						3
3 0 6 67						4
22 9 4 0 00						5
	2 4 0 0 00					6
	32 0 0 0 00					7
1 0 0 0 00						8
	3 2 3 0 00					9
7 3 0 00						10
1 0 0 00						11
1 8 0 00						12
2 2 0 00						13
						14
8 0 00						15
1 3 33						16
2 8 6 75						17
	2 8 6 75					18
	1 0 0 00					19
38 0 1 6 75	38 0 1 6 75					20
						21
Step 3						22
						23

	ACCOUNT NAME	TRIAL BALANCE		ADJUSTMENTS	
		DEBIT A + E + Draw.	CREDIT L + C + R + Accum. Deprec.	DEBIT	CREDIT
1	*Cash*	11 5 2 0 00			
2	*Accounts Receivable*	2 0 00			
3	*Supplies*	4 0 0 00			(a) 8 0 00
4	*Prepaid Insurance*	3 2 0 00			(b) 1 3 33
5	*Equipment*	22 9 4 0 00			
6	*Accounts Payable*		2 4 0 0 00		
7	*Alan Stevenson, Capital*		32 0 0 0 00		
8	*Alan Stevenson, Drawing*	1 0 0 0 00			
9	*Income from Services*		3 2 3 0 00		
10	*Wages Expense*	6 3 0 00		(d) 1 0 0 00	
11	*Rent Expense*	4 0 0 00			
12	*Advertising Expense*	1 8 0 00			
13	*Utilities Expense*	2 2 0 00			
14		37 6 3 0 00	37 6 3 0 00		
15	*Supplies Expense*			(a) 8 0 00	
16	*Insurance Expense*	Step 1		(b) 1 3 33	
17	*Depreciation Expense*			(c) 2 8 6 75	
18	*Accumulated Depreciation*				(c) 2 8 6 75
19	*Wages Payable*				(d) 1 0 0 00
20				4 8 0 08	4 8 0 08
21	*Net Income*				
22				Step 2	
23					
24					
25					
26					
27					
28					
29					
30					

the amounts in the Adjusted Trial Balance columns to the remaining four columns, recording each amount in only one column. Net income or net loss is recorded in both the Income Statement column and the Balance Sheet column to balance off the columns. The completed work sheet is shown in Figure 5-4.

Accountants refer to accounts such as Supplies and Prepaid Insurance, as they appear in the trial balance, as **mixed accounts**—accounts with

Figure 5-4

	ADJUSTED TRIAL BALANCE		INCOME STATEMENT		BALANCE SHEET		
	DEBIT	CREDIT	DEBIT	CREDIT	DEBIT	CREDIT	
	A + E + Draw.	L + C + R + Accum. Deprec.	E	R	A + Draw.	L + C + Accum. Deprec.	
1	11 5 2 0 00				11 5 2 0 00		
2	2 0 00				2 0 00		
3	3 2 0 00				3 2 0 00		
4	3 0 6 67				3 0 6 67		
5	22 9 4 0 00				22 9 4 0 00		
6		2 4 0 0 00				2 4 0 0 00	
7		32 0 0 0 00				32 0 0 0 00	
8	1 0 0 0 00				1 0 0 0 00		
9		3 2 3 0 00		3 2 3 0 00			
10	7 3 0 00		7 3 0 00				
11	4 0 0 00		4 0 0 00				
12	1 8 0 00		1 8 0 00				
13	2 2 0 00		2 2 0 00				
14							
15	8 0 00		8 0 00				
16	1 3 33		1 3 33				
17	2 8 6 75		2 8 6 75				
18		2 8 6 75				2 8 6 75	
19		1 0 0 00				1 0 0 00	
20	38 0 1 6 75	38 0 1 6 75	1 9 1 0 08	3 2 3 0 00	36 1 0 6 67	34 7 8 6 75	
21			1 3 1 9 92			1 3 1 9 92	
22			3 2 3 0 00	3 2 3 0 00	36 1 0 6 67	36 1 0 6 67	
23							
24							

Step 3

Steps 4, 5, 6

(handwritten annotations at right:)
3239.80
1910.08
1319.92

36106.67
34786.75
1319.92

balances that are partly income statement amounts and partly balance sheet amounts. For example, Supplies is recorded as $400 in the Trial Balance, but after adjustment this is apportioned as $80 in Supplies Expense in the Income Statement columns and $320 in Supplies in the Balance Sheet columns. Similarly, Prepaid Insurance is recorded as $320 in the trial balance, but is apportioned as $13.33 in Insurance Expense in the Income Statement columns and as $306.67 in Prepaid Insurance in the

Balance Sheet columns. In other words, portions of these accounts are recorded in each section.

After the first fiscal period, Accumulated Depreciation will always have a balance until the related asset is sold or disposed of. Consequently, it will be listed in the Trial Balance columns immediately below the appropriate asset (Equipment, in this case).

Sometimes it may be necessary to continue the work sheet on another page. Using a different company as an example, follow this procedure:

(First Page)

Account Name	Trial Balance	Adjustments	
Depreciation Expense		(c)220 50	
Totals carried forward		962 50	126 50

(Second Page)

| | Trial Balance | | Adjustments | |
Account Name	Debit	Credit	Debit	Credit
Totals brought forward			962 50	126 50
Accumulated Depreciation				(c)220 50

COMPLETION OF THE FINANCIAL STATEMENTS

Objective 2

Prepare an income statement and a balance sheet for a service-type business directly from the work sheet.

We now prepare the income statement, the statement of owner's equity, and the balance sheet, taking the figures directly from the work sheet. These statements are shown in Figure 5-5.

Note that one records Accumulated Depreciation in the asset section of the balance sheet as a direct deduction from Equipment. As we have said, accountants refer to it as a *contra account*, because it is contrary to its companion account. The difference, $22,653.25, is called the *book value*, because it represents the cost of the assets after Accumulated Depreciation has been deducted.

ADJUSTING ENTRIES

Objective 3

Journalize and post the adjusting entries.

In order to change the balance of an account, you need a journal entry as evidence of the change. Up to this time, we have been listing adjustments in the Adjustments columns of the work sheet only. Since the work sheet

Figure 5-5

NuWay Cleaners
Income Statement
For month ended June 30, 19–

Revenue:							
Income from Services					$3 2 3 0 00
Expenses:						
Wages Expense	$ 7 3 0 00				
Rent Expense	4 0 0 00				
Advertising Expense	1 8 0 00				
Utilities Expense	2 2 0 00				
Supplies Expense	8 0 00				
Insurance Expense	1 3 33				
Depreciation Expense	2 8 6 75				
Total Expenses					1 9 1 0 08
Net Income					$1 3 1 9 92

NuWay Cleaners
Statement of Owner's Equity
For month ended June 30, 19–

Alan Stevenson, Capital, June 1, 19–					$32 0 0 0 00
Net Income for month of June	$1 3 1 9 92				
Less Withdrawals for month of June	1 0 0 0 00				
Increase in Capital					3 1 9 92
Alan Stevenson, Capital, June 30, 19–					$32 3 1 9 92

Figure 5-5
(continued)

NuWay Cleaners
Balance Sheet
June 30, 19–

Assets									
Cash						$11	5 2 0	00	
Accounts Receivable							2 0	00	
Supplies							3 2 0	00	
Prepaid Insurance							3 0 6	67	
Equipment	$22	9 4 0	00						
Less Accumulated Depreciation		2 8 6	75			22	6 5 3	25	
Total Assets						$34	8 1 9	92	
Liabilities									
Accounts Payable	$ 2	4 0 0	00						
Wages Payable		1 0 0	00						
Total Liabilities						$ 2	5 0 0	00	
Owner's Equity									
Alan Stevenson, Capital						32	3 1 9	92	
Total Liabilities and Owner's Equity						$34	8 1 9	92	

Figure 5-6

GENERAL JOURNAL

PAGE _4_

DATE		DESCRIPTION	POST. REF.	DEBIT	CREDIT
		Adjusting Entries			
19– Jun.	30	Supplies Expense	515	8 0 00	
		Supplies	113		8 0 00
	30	Insurance Expense	516	1 3 33	
		Prepaid Insurance	114		1 3 33
	30	Depreciation Expense	517	2 8 6 75	
		Accumulated Depreciation	122		2 8 6 75
	30	Wages Expense	511	1 0 0 00	
		Wages Payable	212		1 0 0 00

does not constitute a journal, we must journalize the entries. You can take the information for these entries directly from the Adjustments columns of the work sheet, debiting and crediting exactly the same accounts.

In the Description column of the general journal, write "Adjusting Entries" before you begin making these entries. This does away with the need to write explanations for each entry. The adjusting entries for NuWay Cleaners are shown in Figure 5-6.

When you post the adjusting entries to the ledger accounts, write the word "Adjusting" in the Item column of the ledger account. For example, the adjusting entry for Supplies is posted as shown below.

GENERAL LEDGER

ACCOUNT _Supplies_   ACCOUNT NO. _113_

DATE		ITEM	POST. REF.	DEBIT	CREDIT	BALANCE DEBIT	BALANCE CREDIT
19– Jun.	4		1	4 0 0 00		4 0 0 00	
	30	Adjusting	4		8 0 00	3 2 0 00	

ACCOUNT _Supplies Expense_   ACCOUNT NO. _515_

DATE		ITEM	POST. REF.	DEBIT	CREDIT	BALANCE DEBIT	BALANCE CREDIT
19– Jun.	30	Adjusting	4	8 0 00		8 0 00	

Businesses with More Than One Revenue Account and More Than One Accumulated Depreciation Account

NuWay Cleaners's only revenue account is Income from Services. However, a business may have several distinct sources of revenue. For example, City Veterinary Clinic has two revenue accounts, Professional Fees and Boarding Fees. Figure 5-7 illustrates the placement of these accounts in the income statement.

Figure 5-7

City Veterinary Clinic
Income Statement
For year ended December 31, 19–

Revenue:		
Professional Fees	$ 111 7 2 0 00	
Boarding Fees	22 0 8 0 00	
Total Revenue		$ 133 8 0 0 00
Expenses:		
Salaries Expense	$ 84 0 0 0 00	
Depreciation Expense, Building	6 4 8 0 00	
Depreciation Expense, Furniture		
and Equipment	3 8 4 0 00	
Supplies Expense	3 7 2 0 00	
Prepaid Insurance	7 2 0 00	
Miscellaneous Expense	2 1 6 0 00	
Total Expenses		100 9 2 0 00
Net Income		$ 32 8 8 0 00

In the example of NuWay Cleaners, Equipment is the only type of asset that is subject to depreciation, so the related accounts are simply titled Depreciation Expense and Accumulated Depreciation. On the other hand, if NuWay Cleaners buys a building that is also subject to depreciation, NuWay would have to separate the depreciation taken on the equipment from the depreciation taken on the building. As a result, separate related accounts would be set up for each type of asset: Depreciation Expense, Equipment and Accumulated Depreciation, Equipment; Depreciation Expense, Building and Accumulated Depreciation, Building.

To illustrate the placement of these accounts in a balance sheet, let's use another example. Standard Travel Agency has the balance sheet shown in Figure 5-8.

Land supposedly will last forever; consequently, land is not depreciated. Separate adjustments would already have been recorded in the work sheet for depreciation of office equipment and building.

GLOSSARY

Accounting cycle The steps in the accounting process that are completed during the fiscal period.

Accrued wages The amount of unpaid wages owed to employees for the time between the last payday and the end of the fiscal period.

Adjusting entry An entry to help bring the books up to date at the end of the fiscal period.

Figure 5-8

Standard Travel Agency
Balance Sheet
September 30, 19–

Assets									
Cash							$ 6	2 4 0	00
Supplies								2 0 0	00
Office Equipment	$ 4	6 0 0	00						
Less Accumulated Depreciation	2	2 0 0	00		2	4 0 0	00		
Building	$26	7 0 0	00						
Less Accumulated Depreciation	1	4 0 0	00		25	3 0 0	00		
Land					4	4 0 0	00		
Total Assets					$38	5 4 0	00		
Liabilities									
Accounts Payable					$ 2	8 0 0	00		
Owner's Equity									
Stanley C. Clay, Capital					35	7 4 0	00		
Total Liabilities and Owner's Equity					$38	5 4 0	00		

Adjustments Internal transactions that bring ledger accounts up to date, as a planned part of the accounting procedure. They are first recorded in the Adjustments columns of the work sheet.

Book value The cost of an asset minus the accumulated depreciation.

Contra account An account that is contrary to, or a deduction from, another account; for example, Accumulated Depreciation entered as a deduction from Equipment.

Depreciation An expense, based on the expectation that an asset will gradually decline in usefulness due to time, wear and tear, or obsolescence; the cost of the asset is therefore spread out over its estimated useful life. A part of depreciation expense is apportioned to each fiscal period.

Fiscal period or year The period of time covered by the entire accounting cycle, generally consisting of twelve consecutive months.

Mixed accounts The balances of certain accounts that appear in the trial balance that are partly income statement amounts and partly balance sheet amounts—for example, Prepaid Insurance and Supplies.

Straight-line method A means of calculating depreciation by taking the cost of an asset, less any trade-in value, and allocating this amount, on an average basis, over the useful life of the asset.

Work sheet A chart for recording necessary adjustments and for furnishing the account balances for making up the income statement and balance sheet.

QUESTIONS, EXERCISES, AND PROBLEMS

Discussion Questions

1. If it is agreed that there is a need to make adjusting entries at the end of a fiscal period, does this mean that errors were made in the accounts during the period? Explain.
2. Why is it necessary to journalize adjusting entries?
3. What is meant by a mixed account? Give an example.
4. What is a contra account? Give an example.
5. What is the nature of the balance in the prepaid insurance account at the end of the fiscal period (a) before the adjusting entry? (b) after the adjusting entry?
6. In which column of a work sheet (Income Statement columns or Balance Sheet columns) would the adjusted balances of the following accounts appear?
   a. Depreciation Expense
   b. Prepaid Insurance
   c. Wages Payable
   d. Income from Services
   e. Insurance Expense
   f. Supplies
   g. Accumulated Depreciation
   h. C. D. Jones, Drawing
7. At the end of the fiscal period, the usual adjusting entry to record supplies used was unintentionally omitted. What is the effect of the omission on (a) the amount of net income for the period? (b) the balance sheet as of the end of the fiscal period?

Exercises

Exercise 5-1   Using a form similar to the one shown, list the following classifications of accounts in all the columns in which they appear in the work sheet, with the exception of the Adjustments columns: Liabilities, Capital, Expenses, Accumulated Depreciation, Revenue, Net Income, Drawing. (*Example:* Assets)

Trial Balance		Adjustments		Adjusted Trial Balance		Income Statement		Balance Sheet	
Debit	Credit	Debit	Credit	Debit	Credit	Debit	Credit	Debit	Credit
Assets				Assets				Assets	

Exercise 5-2   From the following ledger accounts, journalize adjusting entries (a) through (e).

Supplies		Depreciation Expense		Accumulated Depreciation		Prepaid Insurance	
916	(a) 510	(b) 728			1,960	640	(c) 418
					(b) 728		

Wages Payable	Taxes Expense	Prepaid Taxes		Wages Expense
(d) 420	(e) 406	523	(e) 406	4,296
				(d) 420

Insurance Expense	Supplies Expense
(c) 418	(a) 510

Exercise 5-3 Journalize the necessary adjusting entries at June 30, the close of the current fiscal year, based on the following data.

a. The Prepaid Insurance account before adjustments on June 30 has a balance of $1,260. You now figure out that $820 worth of the insurance has expired during the year.

b. The Supplies account before adjustments on June 30 has a balance of $872. By taking a physical inventory, you now determine that the amount of supplies on hand is worth $260.

c. The last payday was June 27. From June 28 to 30, $590 of wages accrue.

Exercise 5-4   From the ledger accounts for Supplies, determine the missing figures.

a.

Supplies			
Balance	310	Used	728
Bought	916		
End. Inv.	___		

b.

Supplies			
Balance	___	Used	114
Bought	260		
End. Inv.	210		

c.

Supplies			
Balance	148	Used	___
Bought	480		
End. Inv.	160		

d.

Supplies			
Balance	670	Used	820
Bought	___		
End. Inv.	711		

Exercise 5-5 Journalize the year-end adjusting entry for each of the following.

a. Depreciation on equipment was estimated at $3,460 for the year.

b. The payment of the $360 insurance premium for three years in advance was originally recorded as Prepaid Insurance. One year of the policy has now expired.

c. The Supplies account had a balance of $116 on January 1, the beginning of the year; $340 worth of supplies were bought during the year; a year-end inventory shows that $180 worth are still on hand.

d. Two employees earn a total of $200 per day for a five-day week beginning on Monday and ending on Friday. They were paid for the workweek ending December 28. They worked on Monday, December 31.

Exercise 5-6   If the required adjusting entries for Exercise 5 were not made at the end of the year, what would be the cumulative effect of the omissions on net income?

Exercise 5-7 Presented below is a partial work sheet in which the Trial Balance and Income Statement columns have been completed. All amounts are in dollars. Check the adjustments and then journalize the adjusting entries. Why is the Wages Payable line left blank here?

Account Name	Trial Balance		Income Statement	
	Debit	Credit	Debit	Credit
Cash	500			
Accounts Receivable	2,000			
Supplies	800			
Prepaid Insurance	600			
Building	50,000			
Accumulated Depreciation		16,000		
Accounts Payable		700		
L. Bryan, Capital		35,200		
L. Bryan, Drawing	1,000			
Income from Services		4,000		4,000
Wages Expense	900		1,100	
Miscellaneous Expense	100		100	
	55,900	55,900		
Insurance Expense			100	
Supplies Expense			300	
Depreciation Expense			1,200	
Wages Payable				
			2,800	4,000
Net Income			1,200	
			4,000	4,000

Exercise 5-8 Record the adjusting entry in each of the following situations.

a.

Supplies			Supplies Expense	
+	–		+	–
Bal. 260				
Purchases 490				

Ending inventory, $135.

b.

Supplies			Supplies Expense	
+	–		+	–
Bal. 400				
Purchases 920				

Supplies used, $840.

Problem Set A

Problem 5-1A   Here is the trial balance for the A. C. Jones Insurance Agency as of March 31, after it has completed its first month of operations.

A. C. Jones Insurance Agency
Trial Balance
March 31, 19–

ACCOUNT NAME	DEBIT	CREDIT
Cash	2 7 3 2 00	
Accounts Receivable	1 0 8 7 00	
Prepaid Insurance	2 8 6 00	
Office Equipment	2 9 6 4 00	
Automobile	3 2 0 0 00	
A. C. Jones, Capital		9 9 2 2 00
A. C. Jones, Drawing	4 2 0 00	
Commissions Earned		1 3 3 5 00
Rent Expense	2 6 0 00	
Advertising Expense	1 4 4 00	
Travel Expense	9 8 00	
Utility Expense	1 6 00	
Telephone Expense	3 2 00	
Miscellaneous Expense	1 8 00	
	11 2 5 7 00	11 2 5 7 00

Instructions

1. Record the trial balance in the Trial Balance columns of the work sheet.
2. Record the letters standing for the account classifications at the top of each column of the work sheet (as shown in Figure 5-2).
3. Complete the work sheet. (Data for the adjustments: depreciation expense of office equipment, $26; depreciation expense of automobile, $63; expired insurance, $21.)

Problem 5-2A   The *Working Papers* present the completed work sheet for N. L. Smith, Attorney at Law, for Smith's law practice for August.

Instructions

1. Prepare an income statement.
2. Prepare a statement of owner's equity.
3. Prepare a balance sheet.
4. Journalize the adjusting entries.

Problem 5-3A   The trial balance of Supreme Hair Salon as of December 31, the end of the current fiscal year, and data needed for year-end adjustments are shown on the next page.

Supreme Hair Salon
Trial Balance
December 31, 19–

ACCOUNT NAME	DEBIT	CREDIT
Cash	1 4 7 1 00	
Beauty Supplies	1 9 8 0 00	
Prepaid Insurance	4 8 4 00	
Shop Equipment	28 1 8 0 00	
Accumulated Depreciation, Shop Equipment		18 1 3 5 00
Accounts Payable		4 9 2 00
C. Everett, Capital		17 5 4 8 00
C. Everett, Drawing	7 3 0 0 00	
Income from Services		17 6 2 0 00
Wages Expense	11 6 5 8 00	
Rent Expense	1 8 0 0 00	
Utilities Expense	4 8 6 00	
Telephone Expense	1 2 0 00	
Miscellaneous Expense	3 1 6 00	
	53 7 9 5 00	53 7 9 5 00

Data for the adjustments are as follows:

a. Inventory of beauty supplies at December 31, $826.
b. Wages accrued at December 31, $126.
c. The amount in Prepaid Insurance represents twenty-four months' premium paid on July 1 of the current year. Six months' insurance has now expired.
d. Depreciation of shop equipment for the year is $4,030.

Instructions

1. Complete the work sheet.
2. Journalize the adjusting entries.

Problem 5-4A The trial balance for Donovan Miniature Golf at September 30, the end of the current fiscal year, is on the next page. Data for year-end adjustments are as follows:

a. Inventory of supplies at September 30, $146.
b. Insurance expired during the year, $184.
c. Depreciation of field equipment during the year, $3,860.
d. Depreciation of lighting fixtures during the year, $416.
e. Wages accrued at September 30, $288.

Donovan Miniature Golf
Trial Balance
September 30, 19–

ACCOUNT NAME	DEBIT	CREDIT
Cash	1 9 6 2 00	
Supplies	5 1 9 00	
Prepaid Insurance	4 7 6 00	
Golf Clubs	5 1 5 00	
Field Equipment	19 7 6 0 00	
Accumulated Depreciation, Field Equipment		6 4 6 6 00
Lighting Fixtures	1 8 7 8 00	
Accumulated Depreciation, Lighting Fixtures		4 2 0 00
Accounts Payable		3 2 1 00
Contracts Payable		9 6 0 00
J. C. Donovan, Capital		10 1 8 1 00
J. C. Donovan, Drawing	4 8 7 8 00	
Golf Fees Income		20 6 6 7 00
Concession Income		9 2 3 00
Wages Expense	6 8 2 0 00	
Repair Expense	1 9 8 6 00	
Advertising Expense	4 8 9 00	
Utilities Expense	3 6 4 00	
Miscellaneous Expense	2 9 1 00	
	39 9 3 8 00	39 9 3 8 00

Instructions

1. Complete the work sheet.
2. Journalize the adjusting entries.
3. Prepare an income statement and a statement of owner's equity for the year and a balance sheet as of September 30.

Problem Set B

Problem 5-1B   The trial balance of the C. R. Lind Company, as of November 30, after the company has completed the first month of operations, is on the next page.

Instructions

1. Record the trial balance in the Trial Balance columns of the work sheet.
2. Record the letters standing for the account classifications at the top of each column of the work sheet (as shown in Figure 5-2).
3. Complete the work sheet. (Data for the adjustments: depreciation expense of office equipment, $96; accrued salaries, $108.)

C. R. Lind Company
Trial Balance
November 30, 19—

ACCOUNT NAME	DEBIT	CREDIT
Cash	4 1 1 6 00	
Accounts Receivable	5 6 2 1 00	
Office Equipment	3 1 1 0 00	
Accounts Payable		6 5 4 00
C. R. Lind, Capital		11 3 0 8 00
C. R. Lind, Drawing	1 2 0 0 00	
Commissions Earned		3 0 7 2 00
Salary Expense	6 5 0 00	
Rent Expense	2 1 0 00	
Advertising Expense	8 5 00	
Utilities Expense	2 5 00	
Miscellaneous Expense	1 7 00	
	15 0 3 4 00	15 0 3 4 00

Problem 5-2B The *Working Papers* present the completed work sheet for N. L. Smith, Attorney at Law, for Smith's law practice for August.

Instructions

1. Prepare an income statement.
2. Prepare a statement of owner's equity.
3. Prepare a balance sheet.
4. Journalize the adjusting entries.

Problem 5-3B The trial balance of Collier Launderette as of December 31, the end of the current fiscal year, is shown on the next page. The data needed for year-end adjustments are shown below.

Data for the adjustments are as follows:

a. Inventory of supplies at December 31, $382.
b. The amount in Prepaid Insurance represents twenty-four months' premium paid January 2 of the current year. Twelve months' insurance has now expired.
c. Depreciation of furniture and equipment for the year is $6,000.
d. Wages accrued at December 31, $220.

Instructions

1. Complete the work sheet.
2. Journalize the adjusting entries.

Collier Launderette
Trial Balance
December 31, 19–

ACCOUNT NAME	DEBIT	CREDIT
Cash	2 3 9 2 00	
Laundry Supplies	2 8 4 1 00	
Prepaid Insurance	6 2 6 00	
Furniture and Equipment	25 6 0 0 00	
Accumulated Depreciation, Furniture and Equipment		14 1 6 0 00
Accounts Payable		4 1 9 00
J. L. Collier, Capital		18 2 7 6 00
J. L. Collier, Drawing	8 6 4 0 00	
Income from Services		23 5 4 8 00
Wages Expense	10 6 4 0 00	
Rent Expense	3 6 0 0 00	
Utilities Expense	1 2 7 1 00	
Advertising Expense	4 1 8 00	
Miscellaneous Expense	3 7 5 00	
	56 4 0 3 00	56 4 0 3 00

Problem 5-4B Shown on page 136 is the trial balance of Recreation Lanes, a bowling alley, as of June 30, the end of the current fiscal year. Data for the year-end adjustments are given below.

a. Inventory of supplies at June 30, $272.
b. Insurance expired during the year, $418.
c. Depreciation of bowling equipment during the year, $14,000.
d. Depreciation of furniture and fixtures during the year, $1,610.
e. Depreciation of building during the year, $2,700.
f. Wages accrued at June 30, $384.

Instructions

1. Complete the work sheet.
2. Journalize the adjusting entries.
3. Prepare an income statement and a statement of owner's equity for the year and a balance sheet as of June 30.

ACCOUNT NAME	DEBIT	CREDIT
Cash	2 9 8 4 00	
Supplies	8 6 2 00	
Prepaid Insurance	6 2 0 00	
Bowling Equipment	90 4 6 0 00	
Accumulated Depreciation, Bowling Equipment		47 2 0 0 00
Furniture and Fixtures	8 4 0 0 00	
Accumulated Depreciation, Furniture and Fixtures		4 1 6 0 00
Building	70 5 0 0 00	
Accumulated Depreciation, Building		20 0 0 0 00
Land	8 0 0 0 00	
Accounts Payable		3 8 2 0 00
Mortgage Payable		42 0 0 0 00
E. L. Boulding, Capital		42 3 3 8 00
E. L. Boulding, Drawing	12 5 0 0 00	
Bowling Fees Income		47 6 6 4 00
Concession Income		5 8 2 0 00
Wages Expense	10 6 0 0 00	
Advertising Expense	3 8 2 0 00	
Repair Expense	2 1 7 0 00	
Utilities Expense	1 5 7 0 00	
Miscellaneous Expense	5 1 6 00	
	213 0 0 2 00	213 0 0 2 00

APPENDIX A

Methods of Depreciation

Depreciation methods will all be calculated using the same example. At the beginning of a year, a delivery truck was bought at a cost of $10,000. The truck is estimated to have a useful life of five years and a trade-in value of $2,500 at the end of the five-year period.

Assets Acquired Before January 1, 1981

For assets bought before January 1, 1981, a business has a choice of depreciation methods, both for general financial reporting and for tax purposes. Three of these methods will be presented here: straight line, sum of the years' digits, and double declining balance.

For assets acquired after 1980, the business may still select any of these methods for general financial reporting so long as it uses just one method consistently for each asset. But it must use a different method for tax purposes; we will discuss that method later in the appendix. Now, let's turn to the three standard methods of depreciation.

Straight-Line Method

$$\text{Yearly depreciation} = \frac{\text{Cost of asset} - \text{Trade-in value}}{\text{Years of life}} = \frac{\$10,000 - \$2,500}{5 \text{ years}} = \$1,500 \text{ per year}$$

Year	Depreciation for the Year	Accumulated Depreciation	Book Value (Cost Less Accumulated Depreciation)
1	$7,500 ÷ 5 years = $1,500	$1,500	$10,000 − $1,500 = $8,500
2	$7,500 ÷ 5 years = $1,500	$1,500 + $1,500 = $3,000	$10,000 − $3,000 = $7,000
3	$7,500 ÷ 5 years = $1,500	$3,000 + $1,500 = $4,500	$10,000 − $4,500 = $5,500
4	$7,500 ÷ 5 years = $1,500	$4,500 + $1,500 = $6,000	$10,000 − $6,000 = $4,000
5	$7,500 ÷ 5 years = $1,500	$6,000 + $1,500 = $7,500	$10,000 − $7,500 = $2,500
	$7,500		

Sum-of-the-Years'-Digits Method   Add the number of years and use the sum as the denominator of the fractions. As numerators in the fractions, use the years in reverse order.

$$1 + 2 + 3 + 4 + 5 = 15$$

$$\frac{5}{15} + \frac{4}{15} + \frac{3}{15} + \frac{2}{15} + \frac{1}{15} = \frac{15}{15}$$

Year	Depreciation for the Year	Accumulated Depreciation	Book Value (Cost Less Accumulated Depreciation)
1	$7,500 × $\frac{5}{15}$ = $2,500	$2,500	$10,000 − $2,500 = $7,500
2	$7,500 × $\frac{4}{15}$ = $2,000	$2,500 + $2,000 = $4,500	$10,000 − $4,500 = $5,500
3	$7,500 × $\frac{3}{15}$ = $1,500	$4,500 + $1,500 = $6,000	$10,000 − $6,000 = $4,000
4	$7,500 × $\frac{2}{15}$ = $1,000	$6,000 + $1,000 = $7,000	$10,000 − $7,000 = $3,000
5	$7,500 × $\frac{1}{15}$ = $500	$7,000 + $500 = $7,500	$10,000 − $7,500 = $2,500
15	$\frac{15}{15}$ $7,500		

Double-Declining-Balance Method   With a life of five years, the straight-line rate is $\frac{1}{5}$. Twice, or double, the straight-line rate is $\frac{2}{5}$ ($\frac{1}{5} \times 2$). The trade-in value is not counted until the end of the schedule. Multiply *book value* at beginning of year by twice the straight-line rate.

Year	Depreciation for the Year	Accumulated Depreciation	Book Value (Cost Less Accumulated Depreciation)
1	$10,000 × $\frac{2}{5}$ = $4,000	$4,000	$10,000 − $4,000 = $6,000
2	$6,000 × $\frac{2}{5}$ = $2,400	$4,000 + $2,400 = $6,400	$10,000 − $6,400 = $3,600
3	$3,600 − $2,500 = $1,100	$6,400 + $1,100 = $7,500	$10,000 − $7,500 = $2,500
4	0	$7,500	$10,000 − $7,500 = $2,500
5	0	$7,500	$10,000 − $7,500 = $2,500
	$7,500		

In the third year, if we calculate depreciation as $3,600 × ⅖, the amount equals $1,440. In this case, the book value would amount to $2,160 ($3,600 − $1,440), which is less than the $2,500 set as the trade-in value. Because the book value cannot be less than the established trade-in value of $2,500, the maximum depreciation that can be taken in Year 3 is $1,100 ($3,600 − $1,100 = $2,500).

In this case, after the end of the third year, no more depreciation may be taken. In other words, the truck has been fully depreciated for income-tax purposes before the end of its estimated useful life.

Assets Acquired After December 31, 1980

For assets bought after 1980, a business must use the Accelerated Cost Recovery System (ACRS) for tax purposes. Property is divided into four categories: three-year, such as automobiles and light trucks; five-year, such as other machinery and equipment; fifteen-year, for certain buildings; and eighteen-year, for other buildings. Under the ACRS method, trade-in value is ignored. Percentage tables have been established; however, Congress may change the percentages from time to time.

Our light truck qualifies as three-year property. The established rates are: first year, 25 percent; second year, 38 percent; third year, 37 percent.

Year	Depreciation for the Year	Accumulated Depreciation	Book Value (Cost Less Accumulated Depreciation)
1	$10,000 × .25 = $2,500	$2,500	$10,000 − $ 2,500 = $7,500
2	$10,000 × .38 = $3,800	$2,500 + $3,800 = $ 6,300	$10,000 − $ 6,300 = $3,700
3	$10,000 × .37 = $3,700	$6,300 + $3,700 = $10,000	$10,000 − $10,000 = 0

In preparing financial reports for its own use, a company may calculate depreciation using any of the methods described in this appendix. However, for tax purposes, a company must use ACRS for assets acquired after December 31, 1980.

Problems

Problem A-1 A delivery van was bought for $7,200 before January 1, 1981. The estimated life of the van is four years. The trade-in value at the end of four years is estimated to be $800. Prepare a schedule of depreciation for the four-year period using the straight-line method.

Problem A-2 Using the information in Problem A-1, prepare a schedule of depreciation using the sum-of-the-years'-digits method.

Problem A-3 Assume the van was purchased after January 1, 1981. Using the information in Problem A-1, prepare a schedule of depreciation under ACRS.

6 Closing Entries and the Post-Closing Trial Balance

Learning Objectives

After you have completed this chapter, you will be able to do the following:

1. Journalize and post closing entries for a service-type enterprise.

2. Prepare a post-closing trial balance for any type of enterprise.

After you have prepared the financial statements from the work sheet and journalized and posted the adjusting entries, the remaining steps of the accounting cycle consist of (1) journalizing and posting the closing entries, and (2) preparing a post-closing trial balance.

This chapter explains the functions of and procedures for accomplishing these final steps in the accounting cycle.

INTERIM STATEMENTS

Interim statements consist of the financial statements that are prepared during the fiscal year for periods of *less* than twelve months. For example, a business may prepare the income statement, the statement of owner's equity, and the balance sheet *monthly*. These statements provide up-to-date information about the results and status of operations. Suppose a company has a fiscal period extending from January 1 of one year through December 31 of the same year; it might have the following interim statements.

Jan. 1	Jan. 31	Feb. 28	Mar. 31	Apr. 30
	Income statement for month ended Jan. 31	Income statement for month ended Feb. 28	Income statement for month ended Mar. 31	Income statement for month ended Apr. 30

Beginning of fiscal period

	Jan. 31	Feb. 28	Mar. 31	Apr. 30
	Balance sheet dated Jan. 31	Balance sheet dated Feb. 28	Balance sheet dated Mar. 31	Balance sheet dated Apr. 30

Income statement for 2 months ended Feb. 28

Income statement for 3 months ended Mar. 31

Income statement for 4 months ended Apr. 30

In this case, the company would prepare statements of owner's equity for the same periods as the income statements.

The work sheet and the financial statements would be completed at each of the interim dates. However, the accountant would perform the remaining steps—journalizing the adjusting and closing entries and preparing the post-closing trial balance—only at the end of the fiscal year. As an example and to gain practice, however, let's assume that a fiscal year, with the closing entries and post-closing trial balance, consists of only one month. We need to make this assumption so that we can thoroughly cover the material. The entire accounting cycle is presented graphically in Figure 6-1.

CLOSING ENTRIES

So that you will understand the reason for the closing entries, let us first repeat the fundamental accounting equation:

Assets = Liabilities + Owner's Equity + Revenue − Expenses

We know that the income statement, as stated in the third line of its heading, covers a definite period of time. It consists of revenue minus expenses for this period of time only. So, when this period is over, we should start from zero for the next period. In other words, we wipe the slate clean, so that we can start all over again next period.

Purposes of Closing Entries

This brings us to the *purpose* of the closing entries, which is to close off the revenue and expense accounts. We do this because their balances apply to only one fiscal period. As stated before, with the coming of the next fiscal period, we want to start from scratch, recording brand-new revenue and expenses. Accountants also refer to this as *clearing the accounts.* For income tax purposes, this is certainly understandable. No one wants to pay income tax more than once on the same income, and the Internal Revenue Service frowns on counting an expense more than once. So now we have this:

(closed)   (closed)
Assets = Liabilities + Owner's Equity + ~~Revenue~~ − ~~Expenses~~

The assets, liabilities, and owner's equity accounts remain open. The balance sheet, with its one date in the heading, merely gives the present balances of these accounts. The accountant carries them over to the next fiscal period.

During the accounting period

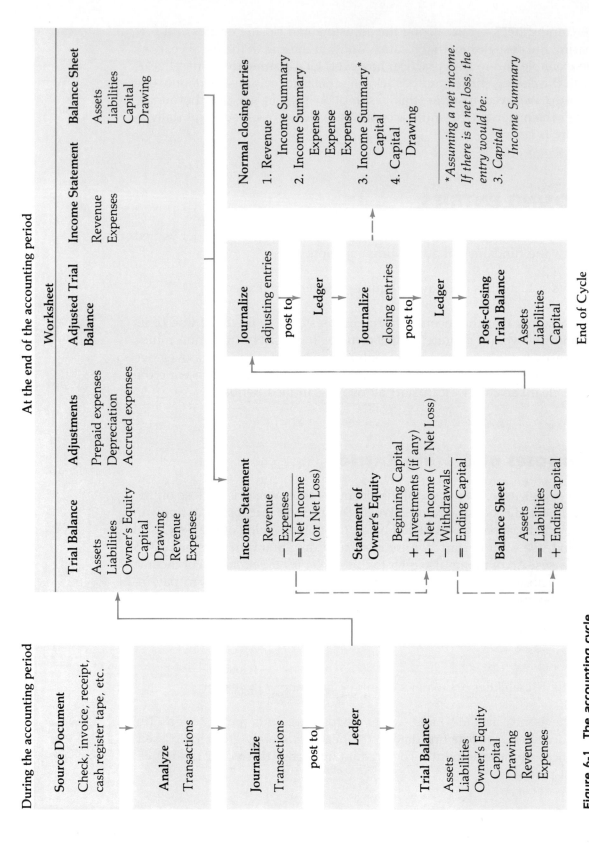

Figure 6-1 The accounting cycle

Procedure for Closing

Objective 1

Journalize and post closing entries for a service-type enterprise.

The procedure for closing is simply to balance off the account, in other words, to make the balance *equal to zero*. This meets our objective, which is to start from zero in the next fiscal period. Let's illustrate this first with T accounts. Suppose an account happens to have a debit balance; then, to make the balance equal zero, we *credit* the account. We write *closing* in the Item column of the ledger account.

Debit		Credit	
Balance	960	Closing	960

To take another example, suppose an account happens to have a credit balance; then, to make the balance equal to zero, we *debit* the account.

Debit		Credit	
Closing	1,200	Balance	1,200

Every entry must have both a debit and a credit. So, in order to record the other half of the closing entry, we bring into existence **Income Summary.** Thus, there are four steps in the closing procedure:

1. Close the revenue accounts into Income Summary.
2. Close the expense accounts into Income Summary.
3. Close the Income Summary account into the Capital account.
4. Close the Drawing account into the Capital account.

To illustrate by making the entries directly in T accounts, we again fall back on the accounts of our friendly neighborhood business, NuWay Cleaners. For the purpose of the illustration, assume that NuWay Cleaners's fiscal period consists of one month. We now have the following revenue and expense accounts.

Income from Services			Utilities Expense		
−	+		+	−	
	Balance	3,230	Balance 220.00		

Wages Expense			Supplies Expense		
+	−		+	−	
Balance 730.00			Balance 80.00		

Rent Expense			Insurance Expense		
+	−		+	−	
Balance 400.00			Balance 13.33		

Advertising Expense		Depreciation Expense	
+	−	+	−
Balance 180.00		Balance 286.75	

Step 1 Close the revenue account, or accounts, into Income Summary. In order to make the balance of Income from Services equal to zero, we *balance it off*, or debit it, in the amount of $3,230. Because we need an offsetting credit, we credit Income Summary for the same amount.

Income from Services		Income Summary	
−	+		
Closing 3,230.00	Balance 3,230.00		3,230.00

In essence, the balance of Income from Services is transferred to Income Summary. Now let's look at the journal entry for this step.

	GENERAL JOURNAL			PAGE __4__	
DATE	DESCRIPTION	POST. REF.	DEBIT	CREDIT	
	Closing Entries				
30	Income from Services		3 2 3 0 00		
	Income Summary			3 2 3 0 00	

Writing *Closing Entries* in the Description column eliminates the need to write explanations for all the closing entries.

Step 2 Close the expense accounts into Income Summary. In order to make the balances of the expense accounts equal to zero, we need to balance them off, or credit them. Again the T accounts are a basis for formulating the journal entry. In essence, the balances of the expense accounts are transferred to Income Summary, as shown in Figure 6-2.

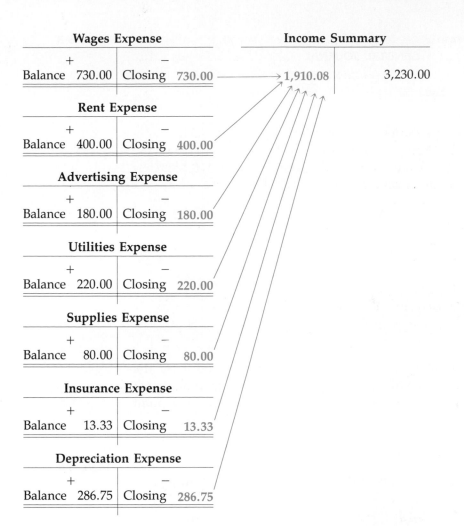

Figure 6-2

The journal entries for step 2 are shown in Figure 6-3 (next page).

Step 3 Recall that we created Income Summary so that we could have a debit and credit with each closing entry. Now that it has done its job, we close it out. We use the same procedure as before, in that we make the balance equal to zero, or balance off the account. In essence, we transfer, or close, the balance of the Income Summary account into the Capital account, as shown in the T accounts and in Figure 6-4 (next page).

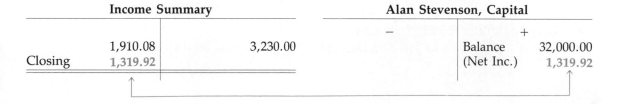

Figure 6-3

			GENERAL JOURNAL					PAGE 4						
DATE			DESCRIPTION	POST. REF.		DEBIT					CREDIT			
			Closing Entries											
	30		Income from Services		3	2	3	0	00					
			Income Summary							3	2	3	0	00
	30		Income Summary		1	9	1	0	08					
			Wages Expense								7	3	0	00
			Rent Expense								4	0	0	00
			Advertising Expense								1	8	0	00
			Utilities Expense								2	2	0	00
			Supplies Expense									8	0	00
			Insurance Expense									1	3	33
			Depreciation Expense								2	8	6	75

Income Summary is always closed into the Capital account by the amount of the net income or the net loss. Comparing net income or net loss with the closing entry for Income Summary can serve as a check point or verification for you.

Figure 6-4

			GENERAL JOURNAL					PAGE 4						
DATE			DESCRIPTION	POST. REF.		DEBIT					CREDIT			
			Closing Entries											
	30		Income from Services		3	2	3	0	00					
			Income Summary							3	2	3	0	00
	30		Income Summary		1	9	1	0	08					
			Wages Expense								7	3	0	00
			Rent Expense								4	0	0	00
			Advertising Expense								1	8	0	00
			Utilities Expense								2	2	0	00
			Supplies Expense									8	0	00
			Insurance Expense									1	3	33
			Depreciation Expense								2	8	6	75
	30		Income Summary		1	3	1	9	92					
			Alan Stevenson, Capital							1	3	1	9	92

Net income is added or credited to the Capital account because in the statement of owner's equity, as we have seen, net income is treated as an addition. Net loss, on the other hand, should be subtracted from or debited to the Capital account because net loss is treated as a deduction in the statement of owner's equity. Here's how one would close Income Summary for J. Doe Company, which had a net loss.

Income Summary			J. Doe, Capital	
(Expenses) 900	(Revenue) 700		(Net Loss) 200	Balance 30,000
	Closing 200			

For a situation involving a net loss of $200, the entry to close Income Summary into the Capital account would look like this.

GENERAL JOURNAL   PAGE __3__

DATE	DESCRIPTION	POST. REF.	DEBIT	CREDIT
	Closing Entries			
31	*J. Doe, Capital*		2 0 0 00	
	Income Summary			2 0 0 00

Step 4   Let us return to the example of NuWay Cleaners. The Drawing account applies to only one fiscal period, so it too must be closed. You may recall from Chapter 2 that Drawing is not an expense because no money is paid to anyone outside the business. And because Drawing is not an expense, it cannot affect net income or net loss. It appears in the statement of owner's equity as a deduction from the Capital account, and so it is closed directly into the Capital account. So we balance off the Drawing account, or make the balance of it equal to zero. The balance of Drawing is transferred to the Capital account.

Alan Stevenson, Drawing			Alan Stevenson, Capital	
+	–		–	+
Balance 1,000.00	Closing 1,000.00		1,000	Balance 32,000.00
				(Net Inc.) 1,319.92

The four journal entries in the closing procedure are illustrated in Figure 6-5.

Figure 6-5

GENERAL JOURNAL				PAGE __4__	

DATE	DESCRIPTION	POST. REF.	DEBIT	CREDIT
	Closing Entries			
30	*Income from Services*		3 2 3 0 00	
	Income Summary			3 2 3 0 00
30	*Income Summary*		1 9 1 0 08	
	Wages Expense			7 3 0 00
	Rent Expense			4 0 0 00
	Advertising Expense			1 8 0 00
	Utilities Expense			2 2 0 00
	Supplies Expense			8 0 00
	Insurance Expense			1 3 33
	Depreciation Expense			2 8 6 75
30	*Income Summary*		1 3 1 9 92	
	Alan Stevenson, Capital			1 3 1 9 92
30	*Alan Stevenson, Capital*		1 0 0 0 00	
	Alan Stevenson, Drawing			1 0 0 0 00

These closing entries show that NuWay Cleaners has net income of $1,319.92, the owner has withdrawn $1,000 for personal expenses, and $319.92 has been retained or plowed back into the business, thereby increasing capital.

Closing Entries Taken Directly from the Work Sheet

One can gather the information for the closing entries either directly from the ledger accounts or from the work sheet. Since the Income Statement columns of the work sheet consist entirely of revenues and expenses, one can pick up the figures for the closing entries from these columns. Figure 6-6 shows a partial work sheet for NuWay Cleaners.

You may formulate the closing entries by simply balancing off all the figures that appear in the Income Statement columns. For example, in the Income Statement column, there is a credit for $3,230; so we debit that account for $3,230 and credit Income Summary for $3,230.

There are debits for $730, $400, $180, $220, $80, $13.33, and $286.75. So now we *credit* these accounts for the same amounts, and we debit Income Summary for their total.

#	ACCOUNT NAME	TRIAL BALANCE DEBIT	TRIAL BALANCE CREDIT	ADJUSTMENTS DEBIT	ADJUSTMENTS CREDIT	INCOME STATEMENT DEBIT	INCOME STATEMENT CREDIT	#
1	Cash	11 5 2 0 00						1
2	Accounts							2
3	Receivable	2 0 00						3
4	Supplies	4 0 0 00			(a) 8 0 00			4
5	Prepaid Insurance	3 2 0 00			(b) 1 3 33			5
6	Equipment	22 9 4 0 00						6
7	Accounts Payable		2 4 0 0 00					7
8	Alan Stevenson,							8
9	Capital		32 0 0 0 00					9
10	Alan Stevenson,							10
11	Drawing	1 0 0 0 00						11
12	Income from							12
13	Services		3 2 3 0 00				3 2 3 0 00	13
14	Wages Expense	6 3 0 00		(d) 1 0 0 00		7 3 0 00		14
15	Rent Expense	4 0 0 00				4 0 0 00		15
16	Advertising							16
17	Expense	1 8 0 00				1 8 0 00		17
18	Utilities Expense	2 2 0 00				2 2 0 00		18
19		37 6 3 0 00	37 6 3 0 00					19
20	Supplies Expense			(a) 8 0 00		8 0 00		20
21	Insurance Expense			(b) 1 3 33		1 3 33		21
22	Depreciation							22
23	Expense			(c) 2 8 6 75		2 8 6 75		23
24	Accumulated							24
25	Depreciation				(c) 2 8 6 75			25
26	Wages Payable				(d) 1 0 0 00			26
27				4 8 0 08	4 8 0 08	1 9 1 0 08	3 2 3 0 00	27
28	Net Income					1 3 1 9 92		28
29						3 2 3 0 00	3 2 3 0 00	29
30								30

Figure 6-6

Next, as usual, we close Income Summary into Capital, by using the net income figure already shown on the work sheet.

We would of course have to pick up the last entry from the Balance Sheet columns to close Drawing.

Collectively, we call the accounts that are closed **temporary-equity accounts,** or nominal accounts. In this context they are temporary in that the balances apply to one fiscal period only. A **closing entry** is simply an entry made at the end of a fiscal period in order to make the balance of a temporary-equity account equal to zero. In the last analysis, temporary-equity accounts are closed into the Capital account.

We indicate that the accounts are closed by writing the word *Closing* in the Item column of the ledger, and by extending a line through both the debit and credit balance columns.

Posting the Closing Entries

After we have posted the closing entries, the Capital, Drawing, Income Summary, revenue, and expense accounts of NuWay Cleaners appear as follows.

GENERAL LEDGER

ACCOUNT _Alan Stevenson, Capital_   ACCOUNT NO. _311_

DATE		ITEM	POST. REF.	DEBIT	CREDIT	BALANCE DEBIT	BALANCE CREDIT
19– Jun.	1		1		32 0 0 0 00		32 0 0 0 00
	30		4		1 3 1 9 92		33 3 1 9 92
	30		4	1 0 0 0 00			32 3 1 9 92

ACCOUNT _Alan Stevenson, Drawing_   ACCOUNT NO. _312_

DATE		ITEM	POST. REF.	DEBIT	CREDIT	BALANCE DEBIT	BALANCE CREDIT
19– Jun.	30		4	1 0 0 0 00		1 0 0 0 00	
	30	Closing	4		1 0 0 0 00	—	—

ACCOUNT _Income Summary_   ACCOUNT NO. _313_

DATE		ITEM	POST. REF.	DEBIT	CREDIT	BALANCE DEBIT	BALANCE CREDIT
19– Jun.	30		4		3 2 3 0 00		3 2 3 0 00
	30		4	1 9 1 0 08			1 3 1 9 92
	30	Closing	4	1 3 1 9 92		—	—

GENERAL LEDGER

ACCOUNT **Income from Services**   ACCOUNT NO. **411**

DATE		ITEM	POST. REF.	DEBIT	CREDIT	BALANCE	
						DEBIT	CREDIT
19– Jun.	7		1		6 0 0 00		6 0 0 00
	14		2		7 6 0 00	1 3 6 0 00	
	21		2		8 3 0 00	2 1 9 0 00	
	23		3		8 0 00	2 2 7 0 00	
	30		3		9 6 0 00	3 2 3 0 00	
	30	Closing	4	3 2 3 0 00			

ACCOUNT **Wages Expense**   ACCOUNT NO. **511**

DATE		ITEM	POST. REF.	DEBIT	CREDIT	BALANCE	
						DEBIT	CREDIT
19– Jun.	10		2	2 4 0 00		2 4 0 00	
	24		3	3 9 0 00		6 3 0 00	
	30	Adjusting	4	1 0 0 00		7 3 0 00	
	30	Closing	4		7 3 0 00		

ACCOUNT **Rent Expense**   ACCOUNT NO. **512**

DATE		ITEM	POST. REF.	DEBIT	CREDIT	BALANCE	
						DEBIT	CREDIT
19– Jun.	8		1	4 0 0 00		4 0 0 00	
	30	Closing	4		4 0 0 00		

ACCOUNT **Advertising Expense**   ACCOUNT NO. **513**

DATE		ITEM	POST. REF.	DEBIT	CREDIT	BALANCE	
						DEBIT	CREDIT
19– Jun.	14		2	1 8 0 00		1 8 0 00	
	30	Closing	4		1 8 0 00		

GENERAL LEDGER

ACCOUNT _Utilities Expense_   ACCOUNT NO. _514_

DATE		ITEM	POST. REF.	DEBIT	CREDIT	BALANCE DEBIT	BALANCE CREDIT
19– Jun.	15		2	2 2 0 00		2 2 0 00	
	30	Closing	4		2 2 0 00		

ACCOUNT _Supplies Expense_   ACCOUNT NO. _515_

DATE		ITEM	POST. REF.	DEBIT	CREDIT	BALANCE DEBIT	BALANCE CREDIT
19– Jun.	30	Adjusting	4	8 0 00		8 0 00	
	30	Closing	4		8 0 00		

ACCOUNT _Insurance Expense_   ACCOUNT NO. _516_

DATE		ITEM	POST. REF.	DEBIT	CREDIT	BALANCE DEBIT	BALANCE CREDIT
19– Jun.	30	Adjusting	4	1 3 33		1 3 33	
	30	Closing	4		1 3 33		

ACCOUNT _Depreciation Expense_   ACCOUNT NO. _517_

DATE		ITEM	POST. REF.	DEBIT	CREDIT	BALANCE DEBIT	BALANCE CREDIT
19– Jun.	30	Adjusting	4	2 8 6 75		2 8 6 75	
	30	Closing	4		2 8 6 75		

Figure 6-7

NuWay Cleaners
Post-Closing Trial Balance
June 30, 19–

ACCOUNT NAME	DEBIT	CREDIT
Cash	11 5 2 0 00	
Accounts Receivable	2 0 00	
Supplies	3 2 0 00	
Prepaid Insurance	3 0 6 67	
Equipment	22 9 4 0 00	
Accumulated Depreciation		2 8 6 75
Accounts Payable		2 4 0 0 00
Wages Payable		1 0 0 00
Alan Stevenson, Capital		32 3 1 9 92
	35 1 0 6 67	35 1 0 6 67

THE POST-CLOSING TRIAL BALANCE

After posting the closing entries and before going on to the next fiscal period, one should verify the balances of the accounts that remain open. To do so, make up a **post-closing trial balance,** using the final-balance figures from the ledger accounts. This represents a last-ditch effort to make absolutely sure that the debit balances equal the credit balances.

The accounts listed in the post-closing trial balance (assets, liabilities, owner's equity, balance sheet accounts) are called **real accounts** or **permanent accounts.** (See Figure 6-7.) The accountant carries forward the balances of real accounts from one fiscal period to another.

Contrast this to the handling of temporary-equity accounts, which, as you have seen, are closed at the end of each fiscal period.

Objective 2

Prepare a post-closing trial balance for any type of enterprise.

GLOSSARY

Closing entry   An entry made at the end of a fiscal period to make the balance of a temporary-equity account equal to zero. This is also referred to as *clearing the accounts.*

Income Summary   An account brought into existence in order to have a debit and credit with each closing entry.

Interim statements   Financial statements prepared during the fiscal year, covering a period of time less than the entire twelve months.

Post-closing trial balance   The listing of the final balances of the real accounts at the end of the fiscal period.

Real accounts   Assets, liabilities, and the Capital account in owner's equity, having balances that are carried forward from one fiscal period to another. Also known as *permanent accounts.*

Temporary-equity accounts Accounts that apply to only one fiscal period and that are closed at the end of that fiscal period, such as revenue, expense, Income Summary, and Drawing accounts. This category may also be described as all accounts except assets, liabilities, and the Capital account. Also known as *nominal accounts*.

QUESTIONS, EXERCISES, AND PROBLEMS

Discussion Questions

1. For the first two months of the year, what interim statements would you suggest for a restaurant that operates on a fiscal year of January 1 through December 31?
2. Explain the functions served by the Income Summary account?
3. What is the difference between a real account and a temporary-equity account?
4. What is the closing entry required for a firm that made a profit for the fiscal period? What entry is required for a firm that had a loss for the fiscal period?
5. Name the four steps in the closing procedure.
6. What is the purpose of the post-closing trial balance?
7. What accounts appear in the post-closing trial balance?

Exercises

Exercise 6-1 As of December 31, the end of the current year, the ledger of the Harmon Company contained the following account balances: Cash, $4,000; Equipment, $24,000; Accounts Payable, $3,000; L. H. Harmon, Capital, $28,000; L. H. Harmon, Drawing, $20,000; Income from Services, $62,000; Concession Income, $2,000; Salary Expense, $36,000; Taxes Expense, $4,000; Depreciation Expense, Equipment, $6,000; Miscellaneous Expense, $1,000. All the accounts have normal balances. Journalize the closing entries.

Exercise 6-2 Complete the posting of the closing entry for this account.

GENERAL LEDGER

ACCOUNT *Commissions Earned*　　　　　　　　　　　　　　　　ACCOUNT NO. __411__

DATE		ITEM	POST. REF.	DEBIT	CREDIT	BALANCE DEBIT	BALANCE CREDIT
19– Mar.	31		56		16 4 0 0 00		16 4 0 0 00
Jun.	30		71		18 4 6 0 00		34 8 6 0 00
Sep.	30		84		19 7 2 0 00		54 5 8 0 00
Dec.	31		96		13 1 7 0 00		67 7 5 0 00
	31		97	67 7 5 0 00			

Exercise 6-3 The Income Statement columns of the work sheet of M. R. Zeller Company for the fiscal year ended April 30 contain the following.

ACCOUNT NAME	INCOME STATEMENT		BALANCE SHEET		
	DEBIT	CREDIT	DEBIT	CREDIT	
1					1
2 Income from Services		52 0 0 0 00			2
3 Salary Expense	26 0 0 0 00				3
4 Rent Expense	4 8 0 0 00				4
5 Supplies Expense	1 2 0 0 00				5
6 Miscellaneous Expense	1 0 0 0 00				6
7					7

The Balance Sheet columns of the work sheet contain the following.

ACCOUNT NAME	INCOME STATEMENT		BALANCE SHEET		
	DEBIT	CREDIT	DEBIT	CREDIT	
1					1
2 M. R. Zeller, Capital				80 0 0 0 00	2
3 M. R. Zeller, Drawing			17 0 0 0 00		3
4					4

Record the four closing entries.

Exercise 6-4 The Income Summary ledger account is as follows.

Income Summary

8,700	10,200

1. Total revenue is _____ .
2. Total expenses are _____ .
3. Net income is _____ .

Exercise 6-5 After all revenues and expenses have been closed at the end of the fiscal period, Income Summary has a debit of $29,000 and a credit of $27,000. On the same date, A. C. Marker, Drawing, has a debit balance of $6,000, and A. C. Marker, Capital, has a credit balance of $46,000. On a sheet of paper, record the journal entries necessary to complete the closing of the accounts. What is the new balance of A. C. Marker, Capital?

Exercise 6-6 From the following ledger accounts, journalize the adjusting entries and closing entries that have been posted to the accounts.

Accumulated Depreciation			Prepaid Insurance			Depreciation Expense		
		1,900	360	(b)	120	(a)	500	(2)	500
	(a)	500	90					

Insurance Expense			Income from Services			Wages Expense		
(b)	120	(2)	120	(1)	3,500		300		800	(2)	1,670
						2,900		800	
						300	(c)	70	

Wages Payable			Miscellaneous Expense			Income Summary		
	(c)	70		160	(2)	160	(2)	2,450	(1)	3,500

Exercise 6-7   The ledger accounts of D. L. Minor Company are as follows. Prepare a statement of owner's equity.

Income Summary				D. L. Minor, Capital			
Dec. 31	60,000	Dec. 31	90,000	Dec. 31	24,000	Jan. 1 Bal.	67,000
Dec. 31 Closing	30,000					Dec. 31	30,000

D. L. Minor, Drawing			
Mar. 31	6,000	Dec. 31	24,000
Oct. 30	9,000		
Nov. 30	9,000		

Exercise 6-8   Financial information for three different one-owner businesses is shown below. Fill in the missing figures. (Assume no additional investments were made during the year.)

	a	b	c
Net income (loss) for the year	$ 75,000	$?	$(12,000)
Owner's equity at beginning of year	?	105,000	45,000
Owner's equity at end of year	142,000	102,000	30,000
Withdrawals by owner during year	12,000	9,000	?

Problem Set A

Problem 6-1A   The partial work sheet for Precision Termite Control for the fiscal year ending December 31 of this year is presented on the next page.

Instructions

Journalize the closing entries with the four steps in order.

	ACCOUNT NAME	TRIAL BALANCE DEBIT	TRIAL BALANCE CREDIT	INCOME STATEMENT DEBIT	INCOME STATEMENT CREDIT	
1	Cash	2 9 6 3 00				1
2	Accounts					2
3	Receivable	1 7 8 1 00				3
4	Supplies	8 8 7 00				4
5	Equipment	4 9 1 4 00				5
6	Accumulated					6
7	Depreciation,					7
8	Equipment		3 2 9 8 00			8
9	Truck	3 5 8 4 00				9
10	Accumulated					10
11	Depreciation,					11
12	Truck		2 7 8 0 00			12
13	Accounts Payable		8 2 6 00			13
14	N. B. Petrie, Capital		3 8 9 9 00			14
15	N. B. Petrie,					15
16	Drawing	10 4 0 0 00				16
17	Service Income		25 7 1 6 00		25 7 1 6 00	17
18	Wages Expense	7 4 2 0 00		7 4 2 0 00		18
19	Rent Expense	2 4 0 0 00		2 4 0 0 00		19
20	Truck Operating					20
21	Expense	1 9 3 0 00		1 9 3 0 00		21
22	Telephone Expense	2 4 0 00		2 4 0 00		22
23		36 5 1 9 00	36 5 1 9 00			23
24	Supplies Expense			2 3 2 00		24
25	Depreciation					25
26	Expense,					26
27	Equipment			3 1 2 00		27
28	Depreciation					28
29	Expense, Truck			4 4 0 00		29
30				12 9 7 4 00	25 7 1 6 00	30
31	Net Income			12 7 4 2 00		31
32				25 7 1 6 00	25 7 1 6 00	32

Problem 6-2A After the adjusting entries have been posted, the ledger of S. T. Dixon, consulting engineer, contains the following account balances as of March 31.

Cash	$14,166	Income Summary	$ 0
Office Supplies	1,413	Professional Fees	15,189
Furniture and Fixtures	8,637	Salary Expense	6,780
Accumulated Depreciation,		Rent Expense	1,050
Furniture and Fixtures	5,523	Telephone Expense	156
Accounts Payable	2,823	Office Supplies Expense	360
Salaries Payable	120	Depreciation Expense,	
S. T. Dixon, Capital	13,200	Furniture and Fixtures	228
S. T. Dixon, Drawing	3,240	Miscellaneous Expense	825

Instructions

Journalize the closing entries with the four steps in order.

Problem 6-3A The trial balance section of the work sheet for Clean-Sweep Chimney Service as of December 31, the end of the current fiscal year, is as follows.

ACCOUNT NAME	TRIAL BALANCE DEBIT	TRIAL BALANCE CREDIT
Cash	1 2 9 8 00	
Accounts Receivable	2 1 1 0 00	
Cleaning Supplies	4 2 6 00	
Cleaning Equipment	3 8 6 4 00	
Accumulated Depreciation, Cleaning Equipment		1 9 3 2 00
Truck	2 9 8 0 00	
Accumulated Depreciation, Truck		2 1 2 0 00
Accounts Payable		8 7 2 00
R. A. Fallon, Capital		1 8 3 9 00
R. A. Fallon, Drawing	10 8 0 0 00	
Service Income		24 8 4 0 00
Wages Expense	8 6 4 0 00	
Advertising Expense	2 6 2 00	
Truck Operating Expense	4 2 4 00	
Utilities Expense	3 1 9 00	
Miscellaneous Expense	4 8 0 00	
	31 6 0 3 00	31 6 0 3 00

Data for the adjustments are as follows.

a. Accrued wages, $116.
b. Inventory of cleaning supplies, $304.
c. Depreciation of cleaning equipment, $120.
d. Depreciation of truck, $296.

Instructions

1. Complete the work sheet.
2. Prepare an income statement.
3. Prepare a statement of owner's equity.
4. Prepare a balance sheet.
5. Journalize the closing entries, with the four steps in order.

Problem 6-4A The completed work sheet for Twinning Employment Agency is presented in the *Working Papers*.

Instructions

1. Journalize and post the adjusting entries.
2. Journalize and post the closing entries.
3. Prepare a post-closing trial balance.

Problem Set B

Problem 6-1B The partial work sheet for Jarris Tree-Spraying Service for the fiscal year ending December 31 of this year is presented below.

	ACCOUNT NAME	TRIAL BALANCE DEBIT	TRIAL BALANCE CREDIT	INCOME STATEMENT DEBIT	INCOME STATEMENT CREDIT	
1	Cash	3 4 0 0 00				1
2	Accounts					2
3	Receivable	1 8 0 0 00				3
4	Supplies	9 1 0 00				4
5	Equipment	4 2 2 0 00				5
6	Accumulated					6
7	Depreciation,					7
8	Equipment		2 6 0 0 00			8
9	Truck	3 1 9 0 00				9
10	Accumulated					10
11	Depreciation,					11
12	Truck		1 4 7 2 00			12
13	Accounts Payable		6 4 0 00			13
14	T. Jarris, Capital		7 5 9 8 00			14
15	T. Jarris, Drawing	9 6 0 0 00				15
16	Service Income		23 6 7 0 00		23 6 7 0 00	16
17	Wages Expense	8 4 2 0 00		8 4 2 0 00		17
18	Rent Expense	2 4 0 0 00		2 4 0 0 00		18
19	Truck Operating					19
20	Expense	1 8 6 0 00		1 8 6 0 00		20
21	Telephone Expense	1 8 0 00		1 8 0 00		21
22		35 9 8 0 00	35 9 8 0 00			22
23	Supplies Expense			2 2 7 00		23
24	Depreciation					24
25	Expense,					25
26	Equipment			3 2 6 00		26
27	Depreciation					27
28	Expense, Truck			4 8 2 00		28
29				13 8 9 5 00	23 6 7 0 00	29
30	Net Income			9 7 7 5 00		30
31				23 6 7 0 00	23 6 7 0 00	31
32						32

Instructions

Journalize the closing entries with the four steps in order.

Problem 6-2B After the adjusting entries have been posted, the ledger of N. L. Francis, marriage counselor, contains the following account balances as of May 31.

Cash	$10,911	Income Summary	$ 0
Office Supplies	570	Income from Professional	
Furniture and Fixtures	4,758	Fees	11,460
Accumulated Depreciation,		Salary Expense	5,064
Furniture and Fixtures	3,252	Rent Expense	624
Accounts Payable	2,559	Telephone Expense	72
Salaries Payable	492	Office Supplies Expense	1,263
N. L. Francis, Capital	9,747	Depreciation Expense,	
N. L. Francis, Drawing	3,600	Furniture and Fixtures	648

Instructions

Journalize the closing entries with the four steps in order.

Problem 6-3B The trial balance section of the work sheet for the Super Janitorial Service as of December 31, the end of the current fiscal year, is as follows.

ACCOUNT NAME	TRIAL BALANCE	
	DEBIT	CREDIT
Cash	1 6 8 3 00	
Accounts Receivable	1 7 9 0 00	
Cleaning Supplies	2 4 3 00	
Cleaning Equipment	2 9 7 0 00	
Accumulated Depreciation, Cleaning Equipment		1 8 6 0 00
Truck	3 1 7 5 00	
Accumulated Depreciation, Truck		1 4 2 5 00
Accounts Payable		6 2 7 00
S. A. Maki, Capital		3 3 3 2 00
S. A. Maki, Drawing	9 6 0 0 00	
Service Income		19 6 4 1 00
Wages Expense	6 4 2 0 00	
Advertising Expense	2 6 4 00	
Truck Operating Expense	4 1 5 00	
Utilities Expense	3 2 5 00	
	26 8 8 5 00	26 8 8 5 00

Data for the adjustments are as follows.

a. Accrued wages, $128.
b. Inventory of cleaning supplies, $120.
c. Depreciation of cleaning equipment, $225.
d. Depreciation of truck, $340.

Instructions

1. Complete the work sheet.
2. Prepare an income statement.
3. Prepare a statement of owner's equity.
4. Prepare a balance sheet.
5. Journalize the closing entries with the four steps in order.

Problem 6-4B The completed work sheet for Twinning Employment Agency is presented in the *Working Papers*.

Instructions

1. Journalize and post the adjusting entries.
2. Journalize and post the closing entries.
3. Prepare a post-closing trial balance.

APPENDIX B

Computers and Accounting

Businesses, governments, and nonprofit organizations use computers to improve their efficiency and reduce the cost of doing business. Computers can provide more timely and accurate management information, which enhances efficiency, as well as improving customer relations.

Large business organizations began to use computers in the 1950s. Since that time, the size and cost of computers have been gradually reduced. Today medium-sized and small business firms enjoy the benefits of computer use. Only a brief overview is presented in this appendix, but it is vitally important that people going into business become acquainted with computers.

Types of Computers

Mainframe Computers Computers may be divided into three categories by size: mainframe computers (large), minicomputers (medium), and microcomputers (small). Large economic units, such as petroleum and airline companies, research laboratories, banks, universities, and government agencies, invest several million dollars in mainframe computers. These computers are able to process 100 million operations per second.

Many other organizations also use mainframe computers. Typical examples include a stock exchange that executes customer buy and sell orders from locations throughout the country; travel agents, who verify space availability as well as departure and arrival times; the Internal Revenue Service, which matches taxable income with tax returns; and police organizations that check criminal records and traffic violations.

Minicomputers   Minicomputers are compact, powerful machines used in business, education, and government. The cost begins at about $25,000. By using remote terminals or keyboards, these computers can link branch offices to an organization's main office. Or they may be used entirely in one location. Minicomputers are used to monitor patients in health-care facilities, handle the record keeping of car rental agencies, and make hotel reservations. Libraries and insurance companies are likely to use minicomputers.

Microcomputers   Microcomputers have changed both business and personal information management. As their cost has fallen to under $5,000, they have become increasingly popular. Small businesses use these computers for accounting applications such as accounts receivable and payable, payroll records, and inventory records. Many businesses use microcomputers for data management, text editing, creation and updating of membership or mailing lists, and maintenance of personnel files. Today many tax preparers rely on microcomputers. New applications are unveiled regularly as schools, businesses, public institutions, and individuals acquire these machines.

Definitions

Data are facts, concepts, or instructions that can be communicated, interpreted, or processed. *Data processing* consists of recording, coding, sorting, calculating, summarizing, communicating, storing, retrieving, and arranging information in a usable form—with or without the aid of a computer. Data processing converts raw data into usable information. A *system* is a series of procedures designed to do a specific task. A *computer* is an electronic machine that processes data quickly.

Parts of a Computer

Computers consist of three major segments—input, central processing, and output. *Input devices* give instructions and data to the computer system. *Input mediums* may include disks, magnetic or punched card readers, magnetic tapes, paper tape readers, optical scanners, magnetic ink readers, audio units, numeric pads, and alphabetic keyboards.

The second part of a computer is the *Central Processing Unit* (CPU). It has a *control unit* that interprets instructions from a program, an *arithmetic-logic unit* that performs calculations and executes the actual instructions, and a *memory section*. The Read Only Memory (ROM) unit stores programs built into the computer by the manufacturer. The Random Access Memory (RAM) allows the computer to receive information and store it efficiently. Memory is measured in kilobytes. One kilobyte stores 1,024 characters. The word *kilobyte*, for example, has eight characters.

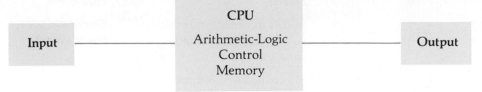

The third part of a computer is an *output device,* which may provide permanent or temporary storage of the results of the data processed. It may be a disk, printer, card punch, magnetic tape unit, paper tape unit, or a visual display unit (screen). A disk system is very flexible. The disk looks like a phonograph record with a cover, and the computer can select data quickly from different sections of the disk's surface. A tape system, on the other hand, must run in sequence, like a tape recorder. Only a fraction of a second is needed for the computer to search a disk, but it could take several minutes to locate a specific section on a tape. Today both "floppy disk" and hard disk systems are available. Hard disks provide more storage and faster processing times, but their high cost makes them inappropriate for many small users.

Hardware and Software

Hardware includes the physical machines or display screens and printer. *Software* consists of specific *programs* that provide a set of instructions for the CPU to follow to perform a particular job. Software also contains instructions for the computer operator on how to use the program. Separate programs are needed for different applications, such as the general ledger, accounts payable, accounts receivable, inventory, and payroll. *User friendly software* helps a person follow the program by indicating what choices can be made at a specific point. Well-designed software helps eliminate operator mistakes by anticipating possible errors and by building in controls that prevent those errors. It can also include internal controls to prevent fraud.

Some companies purchase accounting programs, which can cost as much as 25 percent of the price of the hardware. A good list of available accounting software programs can be found in the most recent updates of DataPro Research Corporation's reports on software (available at many college and university libraries). Other companies hire programmers to custom design programs for their special needs. Still other companies buy data-processing services, such as the handling of accounts receivable or payroll, from banks or specialized data-processing companies.

Computer Personnel

A systems analyst precisely describes every logical step needed in a new computer program by creating a flow chart or graphic presentation of the process to be performed. Analysts consider such matters as source documents, the personnel needed to enter data into the computer, the type of calculations to be performed and their sequence, the ways in which one pro-

Screen

Shows information keyed in, such as debits and credits for a transaction.

Shows updated information, such as account balances after new amounts have been entered.

Figure B-2

Electronic computer system

Keyboard

Requests processing, such as posting amounts to accounts.

CPU sends processed information to screen, such as debits and credits for a transaction and account balances updated.

Central Processing Unit (CPU)

Arithmetic-Logic
Control
Memory

CPU saves processed information for permanent storage, such as account balances.

CPU retrieves processed information from storage for further processing, such as making account balances ready for another entry.

Permanent Storage for Programs and Data

Magnetic tape
Punch card
Big disk
Diskette

Printer

Presents processed data in final form, such as a printout of a trial balance.

gram should relate to others, the kinds of reports that will be needed, and other potential applications of the program.

A programmer may either adapt an existing program or create a new program that will tell the computer how to read, record, and store information. Programs are written in languages that the computers understand. Two languages frequently used for business applications are COBOL and BASIC. Common Business Oriented Language (COBOL) is a high-level language developed for business data processing applications. The Beginner's All-Purpose Symbolic Instruction Code (BASIC) is used for programming in personal as well as business computing. Each brand of computer has its own adaptation of BASIC.

An accounting computer operator enters data from source documents and may also be responsible for selecting the correct data file, entering correct raw information for calculations, creating various records, and printing the necessary forms and reports. Business transactions are recorded in the computer in terms of debits and credits to specific accounts, much as hand-written entries are.

Implementation

As mentioned earlier, some firms send their work to a *service bureau*. This arrangement provides many of the benefits of computer use without the problems or expense of computer ownership. Sometimes a firm sends its source documents to the service bureau, where the data are entered for the customer. This is called *batch processing*. In other cases, terminals may be hooked up in the firm's own office, thereby allowing the firm's employees to enter transactions. This is known as *on-line processing*.

Other companies purchase their own *in-house* computers. Smaller companies often buy microcomputers or minicomputers.

Introducing Computers to a Company A firm may elect to begin with only one phase of the accounting cycle. In many cases the phase selected is accounts receivable; it is often followed by accounts payable, payroll, inventory control, and general ledger. As the complete accounting cycle becomes involved, special reports may be generated to enhance management decision-making.

Whether a firm starts with one portion of the accounting cycle or implements the complete cycle, it should use a dual system, manual and computer, until all the "bugs" have been worked out.

Back-up System If a firm has its own computer system, it is imperative that a back-up system be maintained. Many microprocessor systems rely on disks, and disks are easily damaged or erased. To prevent fraud, as well as to have a record available, a duplicate disk should be made daily and stored in a safe place. This procedure allows information to be stored in two different places at the same time, limiting the potential damage of natural disasters, fire, theft, malicious destruction of company property, or simple human error.

Advantages

There are many advantages to using computerized accounting procedures. For instance, computerizing Accounts Receivable may help to ensure that prompt, accurate, and legible statements are sent to customers. This procedure results in faster collections.

Computerizing Accounts Payable helps the business take advantage of cash discounts. Computerized inventories allow firms to upgrade purchasing and delivery systems. In addition, a computer can make up-to-date financial reports available at any time.

Other advantages include faster, more accurate computations and the automatic updating of balances, which eliminate possible transposition and footing errors. Sales analysis of the activity of individual salespeople is a valuable tool for evaluating the efforts of the sales force. *Spreadsheets,* or "what if" programs, are also commonly used in businesses. The spreadsheet considers what would happen if certain amounts or figures were changed. For example, a firm can see what is likely to happen if it changes its mark-up on merchandise, adjusts the size of the inventory, adds or deletes a product line, or leases facilities instead of buying them. Spreadsheets are particularly valuable for analyzing changes in interest rates and various repayment schedules.

The microcomputer has given all sizes and types of business organizations access to computerized accounting systems. As computers become used more widely, accounting records are likely to become more standardized. Software programs will evolve that allow each type of business to have its own accounting system. Organizations will no longer need to adapt programs designed for another type of business.

Disadvantages

The computer only does what it is told to do. Accurate data will not be available unless information from the source documents is entered into the computer correctly. It is important to select software that will encourage accuracy. The software should have controls built in that will ensure the input of correct data and that will protect against fraud and theft. In general, compatible software and hardware must be teamed with accounting personnel who are comfortable working with computers. The machine is no better than the people who use it.

Summary

The computer operator inputs data from source documents. Someone who understands the accounting cycle must formulate the debits and credits of the transactions and adjustments to be keyed into the computer. The computer will post, prepare a trial balance, provide a work sheet, and prepare financial statements and certain schedules such as those for accounts receivable and accounts payable.

Management uses data-based systems for making decisions. It recognizes that effective decisions must be based on reliable data. Accurate financial data that can be quickly obtained are essential to business success. Basic accounting concepts, with or without the aid of computers, will always be the foundation for accurate financial records and reports.

REVIEW OF T ACCOUNT PLACEMENT AND REPRESENTATIVE TRANSACTIONS CHAPTERS 1 THROUGH 6

Review of T Account Placement

The following display sums up the placement of T accounts covered in Chapters 3 through 6 in relation to the fundamental accounting equation.

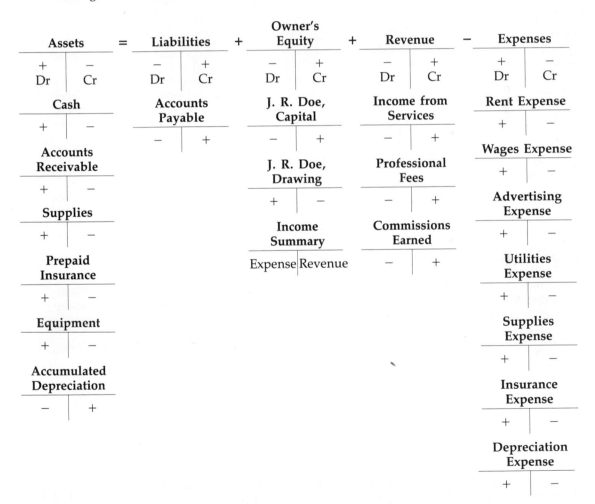

Review of Representative Transactions

The following table summarizes the recording of the various transactions described in Chapters 1 through 6. It also summarizes the classification of the accounts involved.

Transaction	Accounts Involved	Class.	Increase or Decrease	Therefore Debit or Credit	Financial Statement
Owner invested cash in business	Cash J. R. Doe, Capital	A OE	I I	Debit Credit	Bal. Sheet Bal. Sheet
Bought equipment for cash	Equipment Cash	A A	I D	Debit Credit	Bal. Sheet Bal. Sheet
Bought supplies on account	Supplies Accounts Payable	A L	I I	Debit Credit	Bal. Sheet Bal. Sheet
Bought equipment paying a down payment with the remainder on account	Equipment Cash Accounts Payable	A A L	I D I	Debit Credit Credit	Bal. Sheet Bal. Sheet Bal. Sheet
Paid premium for insurance policy	Prepaid Insurance Cash	A A	I D	Debit Credit	Bal. Sheet Bal. Sheet
Paid creditor on account	Accounts Payable Cash	L A	D D	Debit Credit	Bal. Sheet Bal. Sheet
Sold services for cash	Cash Income from Services	A R	I I	Debit Credit	Bal. Sheet Inc. State.
Paid rent for month	Rent Expense Cash	E A	I D	Debit Credit	Inc. State. Bal. Sheet
Billed customers for services performed	Accounts Receivable Income from Services	A R	I I	Debit Credit	Bal. Sheet Inc. State.
Owner withdrew cash for personal use	J. R. Doe, Drawing Cash	OE A	I D	Debit Credit	State. of O. E. Bal. Sheet

Transaction	Accounts Involved	Class.	Increase or Decrease	Therefore Debit or Credit	Financial Statement
Received cash from charge customers to apply on account	Cash Accounts Receivable	A A	I D	Debit Credit	Bal. Sheet Bal. Sheet
Paid wages to employees	Wages Expense Cash	E A	I D	Debit Credit	Inc. State. Bal. Sheet
Adjusting entry for supplies used	Supplies Expense Supplies	E A	I D	Debit Credit	Inc. State. Bal. Sheet
Adjusting entry for insurance expired	Insurance Expense Prepaid Insurance	E A	I D	Debit Credit	Inc. State. Bal. Sheet

Adjusting entry for depreciation of assets	Depreciation Expense
	   Accumulated
	     Depreciation
		E
		A
			I
			I
				Debit
				Credit
					Inc. State.
					Bal. Sheet

Adjusting entry for accrued wages	Wages Expense Wages Payable	E L	I I	Debit Credit	Inc. State. Bal. Sheet
Closing entry for revenue accounts	Revenue accounts Income Summary	R OE	D —	Debit Credit	Inc. State. —
Closing entry for expense accounts	Income Summary Expense accounts	OE E	— D	Debit Credit	— Inc. State.
Closing entry for Income Summary account (Net Income)	Income Summary J. R. Doe, Capital	OE OE	— I	Debit Credit	— Bal. Sheet
Closing entry for Drawing account	J. R. Doe, Capital J. R. Doe, Drawing	OE OE	D D	Debit Credit	Bal. Sheet State. of O. E.

Accounting Cycle Review Problem

This problem is designed to get you to review and apply the knowledge that you have acquired in the preceding chapters. In accounting, the ultimate test is being able to handle data in real-life situations. This problem will give you valuable experience.

Chart of Accounts

Assets
111 Cash
112 Accounts Receivable
114 Prepaid Insurance
121 Electronic Games
122 Accumulated Depreciation, Electronic Games
123 Furniture and Fixtures
124 Accumulated Depreciation, Furniture and Fixtures
127 Building
128 Accumulated Depreciation, Building
129 Land

Liabilities
211 Accounts Payable
212 Wages Payable
221 Mortgage Payable

Owner's Equity
311 R. C. Belko, Capital
312 R. C. Belko, Drawing
313 Income Summary

Revenue
411 Income from Services
412 Concession Income

Expenses
511 Equipment Rental Expense
512 Wages Expense
513 Advertising Expense
514 Utilities Expense
515 Interest Expense
516 Insurance Expense
517 Depreciation Expense, Electronic Games
518 Depreciation Expense, Furniture and Fixtures
519 Depreciation Expense, Building
522 Miscellaneous Expense

You are to record transactions in a two-column general journal. To get in a little more practice, assume that the fiscal period is one month. You will then be able to complete all the steps in the accounting cycle.

When you are analyzing the transactions, think them through by mentally visualizing the T accounts or by writing them down on scratch paper. In the case of unfamiliar types of transactions, specific instructions for recording them are included. However, go ahead and reason them out for yourself as well. Check off each transaction as it is recorded.

The following transactions were completed during June of this year.

Jun. 1 Belko deposited $41,600 in a bank account for the purpose of buying The Gamerama, a business offering the use of electronic games to the public.

2 Bought The Gamerama in its entirety for a total price of $106,650. The assets include games, $10,400; furniture and fixtures, $4,250; building, $72,000; land, $20,000. Paid $32,200 down, and signed a mortgage note for the remainder. (Debit the assets and credit Cash and the liability.)

3 Received and paid bill for newspaper advertising, $74.

3 Received and paid bill for property and liability insurance for the coming year, $518.

3 Bought additional games from Royer Electronics for $3,260, paying $1,600 down, with the remainder due in 30 days.

3 Signed a contract for leasing out space for vending machines. The rental income is to be 10 percent of sales, with the estimated total payable in advance. Received cash payment for June, $90. (Debit Cash and credit Concession Income.)

3 Received bill from Pronto Printing for promotional handouts, $184.

3 Signed a contract for leasing games from Vue Fine Amusement Company and paid rental fee for June, $316.

3 Paid cash for miscellaneous expenses, $46.22.

8 Received $1,316.25 in cash as income for the use of games.

9 Bought stools on account from Smithwick Furniture Company, $418.

15 Paid wages to employees for the period ending June 14, $2,100.

16 Paid the bill for promotional handouts already recorded on June 3.

16 Belko withdrew cash for personal use, $526.

16 Bought additional games on account from Peterson Electronic, $427; payment due in 30 days.

16 Received $1,521.50 in cash as income for the use of games.

19 Paid cash for miscellaneous expenses, $21.32.

20 Paid cash to Royer Electronics as part payment on account, $240.

22 Received $2,541 in cash as income for the use of games.

23 Returned one game to Royer Electronics purchased on June 3 and received full credit (a reduction in the outstanding bill), $226.

24 Received and paid telephone bill, $42.

29 Paid wages for period June 15 through 28, $2,326.

30 Paid cash to Smithwick Furniture Company to apply on account, $209.

30 Received and paid electric bill, $216.

30 Paid cash as an installment payment on the mortgage, $940. Of this amount, $340 represents a reduction in the principal, and the remainder is interest. (Debit Mortgage Payable, debit Interest Expense, and credit Cash.)

30 Received and paid water bill, $21.

Jun. 30 Bought additional games from Moyer Company for $2,426, paying
     $226 down, with the remainder due in 30 days.
   30 Received $2,316 in cash as income for the use of games.
   30 Belko withdrew cash for personal use, $578.
   30 Sales for vending machines for the month amounted to $1,160. (Ten
     percent of $1,160 equals $116. Since you have already recorded $90
     as concession income, list the additional $26 revenue from the
     vending machine operator.)

Instructions

1. Journalize the transactions, starting on page 1 of the general journal.
2. Post the transactions to the ledger accounts.
3. Prepare a trial balance in the first two columns of the work sheet.
4. Complete the work sheet. Data for the adjustments are as follows:
   a. Insurance expired during the month, $43.
   b. Depreciation of electronic games for the month, $402.
   c. Depreciation of furniture and fixtures for the month, $81.50.
   d. Depreciation of building for the month, $300.
   e. Wages accrued at June 30, $348.
5. Prepare the income statement.
6. Prepare the statement of owner's equity.
7. Prepare the balance sheet.
8. Journalize adjusting entries.
9. Post adjusting entries to the ledger accounts.
10. Journalize closing entries.
11. Post closing entries to the ledger accounts.
12. Prepare a post-closing trial balance.

7 Accounting for Professional Enterprises: The Combined Journal (optional)

Learning Objectives

After you have completed this chapter, you will be able to do the following:

1. Define the following methods of accounting: accrual basis, cash-receipts-and-disbursements basis, modified cash basis.

2. Record transactions for both a professional and a service-type enterprise in a combined journal.

3. Complete the entire accounting cycle for a professional enterprise.

Professional Enterprises include the practice of medicine, dentistry, law, architecture, engineering, optometry, and so forth. Your knowledge of accounting procedures can be readily applied to professional enterprises. Generally, the accounting records for professional enterprises are kept on a modified cash basis. Let us digress briefly to define the three bases of accounting currently in use and officially recognized.

ACCRUAL BASIS VERSUS CASH BASIS OF ACCOUNTING

Up to this time we have been dealing with the **accrual basis** of accounting, and therefore we shall look at it first in this section. **When we use the accrual basis, we record revenue when it is earned and expenses when they are incurred.** In this way, revenue and expenses are matched up with the appropriate fiscal period. For example, the books of NuWay Cleaners were recorded on the accrual basis; as proof, let us recall two transactions that we first looked at in Chapter 3.

Objective 1

Define the following methods of accounting: accrual basis, cash-receipts- and- disbursements basis, modified cash basis.

Transaction (k)   Received the bill for newspaper advertising, $180. The expense was recorded before it was paid in cash. The expense is matched up with the fiscal period in which it was incurred.

Advertising Expense	Accounts Payable
(k) 180	(k) 180

Transaction (p)   Entered into a contract with A-1 Rental to clean their for-hire garments on a credit basis. Billed A-1 Rental for services performed, $80.

Accounts Receivable	Income from Services
(p) 80	(p) 80

The revenue was recorded before it was received in cash. The revenue is matched up with the fiscal period in which it was earned. Incidentally, accountants feel strongly that the accrual basis gives the most realistic picture of the revenue and expense accounts and hence the net income. (Net income equals total revenue minus total expenses.) We shall depart from the accrual basis temporarily because we are now concerned with professional enterprises and their accounting records. As we said, the books of professional firms are often kept on a modified cash basis.

The *cash basis* is used primarily for convenience and simplicity. As a practical matter, the cash basis is divided into two types: the cash-receipts-and-disbursements basis and the modified cash basis.

Cash-Receipts-and-Disbursements Basis

The term *disbursements* refers to cash payments. A firm that uses the **cash-receipts-and-disbursements basis** records revenue only when it is received in cash and expenses when they are paid in cash. The only type of business that could use this basis is a firm having practically no equipment. Consequently, no adjusting entries need be made. Actually, the cash-receipts-and-disbursements basis is used by most individuals in filing their personal income tax returns. Revenue in the form of salaries, wages, dividends, and so on is recorded in the year in which it is received. Likewise, expenditures—to be counted as employee business expenses or personal deductions—are recorded in the year they are paid.

Modified Cash Basis

Professional enterprises are not alone in using a modified cash basis; many small business firms use it as well. It is also suitable for accounting for income from rental units. In Internal Revenue Service publications, the **modified cash basis** is referred to as the *hybrid method*. It is similar to the cash-receipts-and-disbursements basis in that revenue is recorded only when received in cash, and expenses are ordinarily recorded only when paid in cash. However, exceptions are made for expenditures on items with an economic life of more than one year and on some prepaid items. Examples would be supplies, insurance, and equipment. Costs of these items must be spread out over their useful lives, and so adjusting entries are made for supplies used, insurance expired, and depreciation of equipment. There is no need to make further adjusting entries, such as an adjustment for accrued salaries or other adjustments that we shall introduce later.

EXAMPLE: RECORDS OF A DENTIST

To understand the accounting system used for a professional enterprise, let us look at the records of Dr. Rory T. Barker, a dentist. The basic records used in his office are the appointment record and the patient's ledger record. The chart of accounts for the office is shown on the top of the following page.

Chart of Accounts

Assets
111 Cash
112 X-ray Supplies
113 Dental Supplies
114 Office Supplies
115 Prepaid Insurance
121 Dental Equipment
122 Accumulated Depreciation, Dental
     Equipment
123 Office Furniture and Equipment
124 Accumulated Depreciation, Office
     Furniture and Equipment

Liabilities
211 Notes Payable

Owner's Equity
311 R. T. Barker, Capital
312 R. T. Barker, Drawing
313 Income Summary

Revenue
411 Professional Fees

Expenses
511 Dental Instruments Expense
512 Laundry and Cleaning Expense
513 Office Salary Expense
514 Laboratory Expense
515 Dental Supplies Expense
516 Rent Expense
517 Depreciation Expense, Dental
     Equipment
518 Depreciation Expense, Office
     Furniture and Equipment
519 X-ray Supplies Expense
520 Office Supplies Expense
521 Insurance Expense
522 Telephone Expense
523 Utilities Expense
524 Repairs and Maintenance Expense
525 Miscellaneous Expense

Appointment Record

The dentist's receptionist keeps a daily appointment record, showing the time of appointment and the name of each patient and gives a copy of the appointment record to the dentist the day before the scheduled appointments. Dr. Barker's appointment record is shown in Figure 7-1.

Patient's Ledger Record

The receptionist also maintains a patient's ledger record card for each patient. One side of this card shows a daily record of the services performed, amount of any cost estimate given, plan of payment, information regarding collections, and the like. A card is shown in Figure 7-2.

The other side of the card contains a diagram of the patient's teeth and a space for personal information about the patient.

After Dr. Barker has completed the work, he (or an assistant) describes the services performed and writes the amount of the fees in the debit column. The card is returned to the receptionist, who records the services rendered and the fees charged on the appointment record.

Figure 7-1

APPOINTMENT RECORD

DATE ____12/1____

HOUR	PATIENT	SERVICE RENDERED	FEES	RECEIPTS
8 00	Donald Rankin			
15	Patricia Fischer			
30				
45	Cecil Hansen			
9 00				
15				
30				
45	Donna Heller			
10 00	C. F. Elliott			
15				
30				
45	Ralph Simons			
11 00	Peter Smithson			
15				
30				
45				
1 00	Donald C. Kraft			
15				
30	N. C. Byers			
45				
2 00	Mrs. N. D. Silversmith			
15				
30	John F. Piper			
45	Nolan F. Sanderson			
3 00				
15	Nancy Stacy			
30				
45	C. D. Harper			
4 00	Ardis Newell			
15				
30				
45				
5 00				
15				

When a patient sends in a payment, the receptionist records the amount on the appointment record on the day the payment was received and on the patient's ledger record in the credit column. Remember that the fees charged are not recorded in the Professional Fees account until they are received in cash. The record showing the amounts patients owe is much like Accounts Receivable, except that these amounts are not offi-

Figure 7-2

Elliott, C. F. 365-2619
1629 S. W. Arbor St.
Denver

DATE		SERVICE RENDERED	TIME	DEBIT	CREDIT	BALANCE
Jun.	15	#31—M.O.D. (4)	10:00	4 0 00		4 0 00
Jul.	4	Ck.			4 0 00	
	16	#27—D.O. (Amal.)	9:15	3 3 00		3 3 00
Aug.	5	Ck.			3 3 00	
Sep.	24	#25—P.J.C.	10:00	1 8 8 00		1 8 8 00
Oct.	6	Ck.			7 5 00	1 1 3 00
	18	#24—D. (Porc.)	9:00	3 0 00		1 4 3 00
Nov.	3	Ck.			7 5 00	6 8 00
	9	#18—full gold crown	10:00	1 5 0 00		2 1 8 00
Dec.	1	B.W. X-rays (6)		4 2 00		2 6 0 00
		Impression upper 7/1		3 6 8 00		6 2 8 00
	1	C.S.			9 0 00	5 3 8 00

PLAN OF SERVICE	PLAN OF PAYMENT	COLLECTION EFFORTS
1–2 surf. ⎫ amalgam	30-day basis	
2–3 surf. ⎬ 1 full gold crown	or $75 per	
1–1 surf. ⎭ 1 ceramic crown	month	
2 anterior porcelain		

ESTIMATE IF ANY	
$410 upper denture (6 appt.)	$90 per month

cially recorded in the books. As with Accounts Receivable, debits mean increases in the amounts owed by patients and credits mean decreases in the amounts owed by patients. The balance columns show the final amounts owed by patients at the time of the latest entry.

The services to be performed may require a number of appointments. Some patients may make partial payments each time they have appointments. Others may pay the entire amount at—or after—the last appointment. Patients' bills are compiled directly from the ledger cards. The dentist or receptionist keeps a constant watch on the patients' ledger records to determine which accounts are past due and to take the necessary steps to speed up collections. The statement shown in Figure 7-3 was mailed to a patient at the end of the month.

Figure 7-3

Rory T. Barker, D.D.S.
1620 South Canton Place
Denver, Colorado 80226

STATEMENT

C. F. ELLIOTT
1629 S.W. ARBOR STREET
DENVER, CO 80232

Date	Professional Service	Charges	Payments	Balance
6/15	#31-MOD (4)	40.00		40.00
7/4	Ck		40.00	—
7/16	#27-DO (Amal.)	33.00		33.00
8/5	Ck		33.00	—
9/24	#25-PJC	188.00		188.00
10/6	Ck		75.00	113.00
10/18	#24-D (Porc.)	30.00		143.00
11/3	Ck		75.00	68.00
11/9	#18-full gold crown	150.00		218.00
12/1	B. W. X-rays (6)	42.00		260.00
	Impression upper	368.00		628.00
12/1	CS		90.00	538.00

Pay last amount in Balance column. ▲

Receipt of Payments from Patients

Depending on the size of the office, the person who receives payments may be the receptionist or the cashier in the accounting office. Whoever receives them issues a written receipt for all incoming cash, filled out in duplicate, sending the first copy to the patient and filing the second copy as evidence of the transaction. Receipts should be prenumbered, so that they can all be accounted for. The payment is recorded in the Receipts column of the appointment record.

The form in Figure 7-4 is a typical appointment record for a day, showing services rendered, fees (recorded by the dentist on the patients' ledger records), and payments received (recorded by the receptionist). The receptionist deposits $608 in the bank.

Figure 7-4

APPOINTMENT RECORD

DATE ___12/1___

HOUR	PATIENT	SERVICE RENDERED	FEES		RECEIPTS	
8 00	Donald Rankin	Extraction	22	00		
15	Patricia Fischer	Three amalgam fillings				
30		D.O. (3)	68	00	16	00
45	Cecil Hansen	Gold inlay filling	97	00		
9 00						
15						
30						
45	Donna Heller	Amalgam filling D.O.	18	00		
10 00	C. F. Elliott	Denture—full upper	410	00	90	00
15		(6 appointments)				
30						
45	Ralph Simons	Prophylaxis	24	00	24	00
11 00	Peter Smithson	Endodontia treatment	120	00	15	00
15						
30						
45						
1 00	Donald C. Kraft	Amalgam filling M.O.D.	27	00	22	00
15						
30	N. C. Byers	Porcelain jacket crown	173	00		
45						
2 00	Mrs. N. D. Silversmith	Extraction	26	00		
15						
30	John F. Piper	Amalgam filling 1 surf.	12	00		
45	Nolan F. Sanderson	Prophylaxis and full-				
3 00		mouth X-ray (14)	27	00		
15	Nancy Stacy	Fixed bridge 3 units	540	00	60	00
30		(Gold) (5 appointments)				
45	C. D. Harper	Prophylaxis & bitewing				
4 00		X-rays	30	00		
15	Ardis Newell	Periodontal treatment	62	00		
30						
45						
5 00						
15						
	Ronald T. McCaw				60	00
	Helen Bower				55	00
	Eugene Sampson				72	00
	Sidney Weeks				27	00
	C. D. Sanderson				100	00
	Roger Lindsay				27	00
	Gilbert Rae				40	00
			1,656	00	608	00

Summary of Procedures

1. Patients request appointments.
2. Receptionist records appointments on appointment record: date, time, and name of patient.
3. Receptionist furnishes dentist with appointment record for the day, plus the patients' ledger records.
4. Dentist performs services and records on each patient's ledger card descriptions of the services performed and lists the fees to be charged in the Debit column.
5. Receptionist accepts payments from patients both in the office and through the mail and records receipt of payments in the Receipts column of the appointment record.
6. At the end of the day, receptionist deposits in the bank any cash received.
7. Receptionist lists the description of services and the amount charged on the appointment record.
8. Receptionist records the payments received from patients on the patients' ledger cards in the Credit column. The source is the appointment record.
9. The receptionist compiles monthly statements directly from the patients' ledger records.

This procedure may vary, depending on the size of the office staff. It could be further shortened by describing the services rendered only once. For the sake of security or internal control, if the size of the office staff is sufficiently large, the function of accepting and depositing money should be separated from the function of recording payments.

Here is a list of Dr. Barker's transactions for December, the last month of the fiscal period. To save time and space, cash receipts are recorded on a weekly basis.

Dec.
  1 Paid rent for the month, $1,000.
  1 Paid telephone bill, $32.
  1 Paid electric bill, $66.
  3 Issued check to First-Rate Printing for patient statement forms, $132.
  5 Bought short-term supply of drills for cash from Murdoch Dental Supply, $254.
  5 Total cash received from patients during the week, $5,524.
  8 Paid bill for repair of typewriter to Greeley Office Supply, $58.
  9 Barker withdrew cash for personal use, $400.
  11 Paid Reliable Building Maintenance Company for janitorial service, $120.

Figure 7-5

19–Dec.	1	Rent Expense	1 0 0 0	00		
		Cash			1 0 0 0	00
		Rent for December.				
	1	Telephone Expense	3 2	00		
		Cash			3 2	00
		Telephone bill for November.				
	1	Utilities Expense	6 6	00		
		Cash			6 6	00
		Electric bill for November.				
	3	Office Supplies	1 3 2	00		
		Cash			1 3 2	00
		First-Rate Printing for				
		statement forms.				
	5	Dental Instruments Expense	2 5 4	00		
		Cash			2 5 4	00
		Murdoch Dental Supply for				
		drills.				
	5	Cash	5 5 2 4	00		
		Professional Fees			5 5 2 4	00
		For period December 1 through 5.				
	8	Repairs and Maintenance Expense	5 8	00		
		Cash			5 8	00
		Greeley Office Supply,				
		typewriter.				
	9	R. T. Barker, Drawing	4 0 0	00		
		Cash			4 0 0	00
		For personal use.				
	11	Laundry and Cleaning Expense	1 2 0	00		
		Cash			1 2 0	00
		Reliable Building Maintenance				
		Company.				

Because you are now used to a general journal, we'll record these transactions first in this form (Figure 7-5). However, our objective is to introduce the combined journal; so we will record the same transactions, as well as the rest of the month's transactions, in a combined journal.

Dec. 12 Total cash received from patients during the week, $1,842.

16 Paid Pender Dental Supply for miscellaneous dental supplies, $432.

16 Paid salaries of dental assistant and receptionist, $980.

19 Bought new dental chair from Murdoch Dental Supply, $1,234; $434 down, the balance to be paid in eight monthly payments of $100 each.

19 Total cash received from patients during the week, $620.

22 Barker withdrew $520 for personal use.

23 Paid bill for laboratory expense to Nollen Dental Laboratory, $296.

23 Paid Pender Dental Supply $320 as a contract payment on dental equipment purchased in October.

27 Total cash received from patients during the week, $392.

29 Barker wrote check to garage for repairing his car, $128 (to be recorded as Drawing).

31 Paid Murdoch Dental Supply for miscellaneous dental supplies, $192.

31 Paid salaries of dental assistant and receptionist, $980.

31 Barker withdrew $780 for personal use.

31 Paid $54 to Jersey Publishers Service for magazines for the office.

31 Paid Clement Linen Supply for laundry service, $84.

31 Total cash received from patients up until last day of year, $266.

THE COMBINED JOURNAL

The **combined journal** is designed to make the recording and posting of transactions more efficient. It is used widely by professional and service-type enterprises, where it replaces the general journal. Notice that no explanations are given in the combined journal. Special columns are set up to record accounts that are used frequently by a particular business.

Compare the recording of the first nine transactions in the combined journal in Figure 7-6 with the same transactions portrayed in the general journal in Figure 7-5. For example, in the first transaction (paid rent for the month, $1,000), you determine that the entry is a debit to Rent Expense and a credit to Cash. There is a Cash Credit column, so you list $1,000 in this column; that $1,000 will be posted as a part of the column total. The Sundry columns are used to record any accounts for which there are no special columns. Since there is no Rent Expense Debit column, the $1,000 debit to Rent Expense must be recorded in the Sundry Debit column. Notice, however, that the Sundry column does not tell you where to post $1,000. Therefore, you need to write the title of the account to be posted in the Account Name column. This amount will be posted separately.

Objective 2

Record transactions for both a professional and a service-type enterprise in a combined journal.

COMBINED JOURNAL

	DATE	ACCOUNT NAME	POST. REF.	SUNDRY DEBIT	SUNDRY CREDIT	DENTAL SUPPLIES DEBIT	R. T. BARKER, DRAWING DEBIT
1	19– Dec. 1	Rent Expense	516	1 0 0 0 00			
2	1	Telephone Expense	522	3 2 00			
3	1	Utilities Expense	523	6 6 00			
4	3	Office Supplies	114	1 3 2 00			
5	5	Dental Instruments Expense	511	2 5 4 00			
6	5	Professional Fees	–				
7	8	Repairs and Maintenance					
8		Expense	524	5 8 00			
9	9	R. T. Barker, Drawing	–				4 0 0 00
10	11	Laundry and Cleaning					
11		Expense	–				
12	12	Professional Fees	–				
13	16	Dental Supplies	–			4 3 2 00	
14	16	Office Salary Expense	–				
15	19	Dental Equipment	121	1 2 3 4 00			
16		Notes Payable	211		8 0 0 00		
17	19	Professional Fees	–				
18	22	R. T. Barker, Drawing	–				5 2 0 00
19	23	Laboratory Expense	–				
20	23	Notes Payable	211	3 2 0 00			
21	27	Professional Fees	–				
22	29	R. T. Barker, Drawing	–				1 2 8 00
23	31	Dental Supplies	–			1 9 2 00	
24	31	Office Salary Expense	–				
25	31	R. T. Barker, Drawing	–				7 8 0 00
26	31	Miscellaneous Expense	–				
27	31	Laundry and Cleaning					
28		Expense	–				
29	31	Professional Fees	–				
30	31			3 0 9 6 00	8 0 0 00	6 2 4 00	1 8 2 8 00
31				(✓)	(✓)	(1 1 3)	(3 1 2)
32							

Figure 7-6

In the entry of December 5 to record professional fees received in cash, special columns are available to handle both the debit to Cash and the credit to Professional Fees. In this case, Professional Fees is entered in the Account Name column purely as a means of filling up the space; some accountants prefer to leave the space blank.

After you have added all columns at the end of the month, prove on scratch paper that the sum of the debit totals equals the sum of the credit totals, as shown in the following example.

PROFESSIONAL FEES CREDIT	LAUNDRY AND CLEANING EXPENSE DEBIT	OFFICE SALARY EXPENSE DEBIT	LABORATORY EXPENSE DEBIT	MISC. EXPENSE DEBIT	CASH DEBIT	CASH CREDIT	
						1 000 00	1
						32 00	2
						66 00	3
						1 32 00	4
						2 54 00	5
5 5 2 4 00					5 5 2 4 00		6
							7
						58 00	8
						4 00 00	9
							10
	1 20 00					1 20 00	11
1 8 4 2 00					1 8 4 2 00		12
						4 32 00	13
		9 80 00				9 80 00	14
						4 34 00	15
							16
6 20 00					6 20 00		17
						5 20 00	18
			2 96 00			2 96 00	19
						3 20 00	20
3 92 00					3 92 00		21
						1 28 00	22
						1 92 00	23
		9 80 00				9 80 00	24
						7 80 00	25
				5 4 00		5 4 00	26
							27
	8 4 00					8 4 00	28
2 66 00					2 66 00		29
8 6 4 4 00	2 04 00	1 9 6 0 00	2 96 00	5 4 00	8 6 4 4 00	7 2 6 2 00	30
(4 1 1)	(5 1 2)	(5 1 3)	(5 1 4)	(5 2 5)	(1 1 1)	(1 1 1)	31
							32

Column	Debit totals	Credit totals
Sundry	$ 3,096.00	$ 800.00
Dental Supplies	624.00	
R. T. Barker, Drawing	1,828.00	
Professional Fees		8,644.00
Laundry and Cleaning Expense	204.00	
Office Salary Expense	1,960.00	
Laboratory Expense	296.00	
Miscellaneous Expense	54.00	
Cash	8,644.00	7,262.00
	$16,706.00	$16,706.00

Posting from the Combined Journal

The person who is keeping records posts items in the Sundry columns individually, usually daily. After posting the ledger account, the person records the ledger account number in the Posting Reference column of the combined journal. This procedure is similar to posting from a general journal.

Special columns, used only for the debit or credit to specific accounts, are posted as totals. After posting the ledger account, the accountant records the ledger account number in the special column immediately below the total. The account number is placed in parentheses. The total of the Cash debit column in Figure 7-6 may be used as an example. After the Cash account in the general ledger has been debited for $8,644.00, the account number of Cash (111) is placed in parentheses below the total of the Cash debit column in the combined journal. Notice that the accountant puts a check mark in parentheses below the totals of the Sundry columns. The check mark indicates that the amounts have been posted individually and should not be posted again.

A dash in the Posting Reference column indicates that individual amounts in the special columns are being posted as totals. Selected accounts from Dr. Barker's completed general ledger are shown in Figure 7-7. Cash, Dental Supplies, and Rent Expense are used to illustrate the posting process.

Figure 7-7

GENERAL LEDGER

ACCOUNT Cash   ACCOUNT NO. 111

	DATE		ITEM	POST. REF.	DEBIT	CREDIT	BALANCE DEBIT	BALANCE CREDIT	
1	19– Dec.	1	Balance	✓			6 4 0 4 00		1
2		31		12	8 6 4 4 00		15 0 4 8 00		2
3		31		12		7 2 6 2 00	7 7 8 6 00		3

ACCOUNT Dental Supplies   ACCOUNT NO. 113

	DATE		ITEM	POST. REF.	DEBIT	CREDIT	BALANCE DEBIT	BALANCE CREDIT	
1	19– Dec.	1	Balance	✓			4 8 5 6 00		1
2		31		12	6 2 4 00		5 4 8 0 00		2

ACCOUNT Rent Expense   ACCOUNT NO. 516

	DATE		ITEM	POST. REF.	DEBIT	CREDIT	BALANCE DEBIT	BALANCE CREDIT	
1	19– Dec.	1	Balance	✓			11 0 0 0 00		1
2		1		12	1 0 0 0 00		12 0 0 0 00		2

Determining Cash Balance

The cash balance may be determined at any time during the month by taking the beginning balance of cash, adding the total cash debits so far during the month, and subtracting the total cash credits so far during the month. For example, to determine the balance of cash on December 5:

Cash

Dec. 1 Balance 6,404

	COMBINED JOURNAL			PAGE __12__

			CASH	
DATE	MISC. EXPENSE	DEBIT	DEBIT	CREDIT
19– Dec. 1				1 0 0 0 00
1				3 2 00
1				6 6 00
3				1 3 2 00
5				2 5 4 00
5		5 5 2 4 00		
		5 5 2 4 00		1 4 8 4 00

Beginning balance (Dec. 1)	$ 6,404
Add cash debits	5,524
Total	$11,928
Less cash credits	1,484
Ending balance (Dec. 5)	$10,444

Work Sheet for a Professional Enterprise

Assume that Dr. Barker's receptionist has posted the journal entries to the ledger accounts and has recorded the trial balance in the first two columns of the work sheet. Dr. Barker uses the modified cash basis of accounting, recording revenue only when he has received it in cash, and recording expenses only when he has paid for them in cash. In addition, when Dr. Barker buys an item that is going to last a number of years, he records this item as an asset and writes it off or depreciates it by making an adjusting

	ACCOUNT NAME	TRIAL BALANCE DEBIT	TRIAL BALANCE CREDIT	ADJUSTMENTS DEBIT	ADJUSTMENTS CREDIT
1	Cash	7 7 8 6 00			
2	X-ray Supplies	2 7 6 2 00			(c)2 1 4 4 00
3	Dental Supplies	5 4 8 0 00			(d)3 8 6 4 00
4	Office Supplies	1 3 0 8 00			(e)1 1 1 2 00
5	Prepaid Insurance	8 4 8 00			(f) 7 2 0 00
6	Dental Equipment	85 2 3 4 00			
7	Accum. Depr., Dental Equipment		17 2 0 0 00		(a)8 4 0 0 00
8	Office Furniture and Equipment	7 8 0 0 00			
9	Accum. Depr., Office Furniture & Equipment		4 2 0 0 00		(b)1 5 2 0 00
10	Notes Payable		7 6 0 0 00		
11	R. T. Barker, Capital		52 5 5 8 00		
12	R. T. Barker, Drawing	33 2 8 0 00			
13	Professional Fees		112 0 2 4 00		
14	Dental Instruments Expense	1 9 8 2 00			
15	Laundry and Cleaning Expense	3 0 2 4 00			
16	Office Salary Expense	23 5 2 0 00			
17	Laboratory Expense	5 8 5 6 00			
18	Rent Expense	12 0 0 0 00			
19	Telephone Expense	4 1 2 00			
20	Utilities Expense	7 7 8 00			
21	Repairs and Maintenance Expense	8 8 8 00			
22	Miscellaneous Expense	6 2 4 00			
23		193 5 8 2 00	193 5 8 2 00		
24	Depreciation Expense, Dental Equipment			(a)8 4 0 0 00	
25	Depreciation Expense, Off. Furn. & Equip.			(b)1 5 2 0 00	
26	X-ray Supplies Expense			(c)2 1 4 4 00	
27	Dental Supplies Expense			(d)3 8 6 4 00	
28	Office Supplies Expense			(e)1 1 1 2 00	
29	Insurance Expense			(f) 7 2 0 00	
30				17 7 6 0 00	17 7 6 0 00
31	Net Income				
32					
33					

entry each year of its useful life. He also makes adjusting entries for expired insurance, as well as for supplies used.

Data for the adjustments are as follows:

a. Additional depreciation on dental equipment, $8,400.
b. Additional depreciation on office furniture and equipment, $1,520.
c. Inventory of x-ray supplies, $618.
d. Inventory of dental supplies, $1,616.

ADJUSTED TRIAL BALANCE		INCOME STATEMENT		BALANCE SHEET		
DEBIT	CREDIT	DEBIT	CREDIT	DEBIT	CREDIT	
7 7 8 6 00				7 7 8 6 00		1
6 1 8 00				6 1 8 00		2
1 6 1 6 00				1 6 1 6 00		3
1 9 6 00				1 9 6 00		4
1 2 8 00				1 2 8 00		5
85 2 3 4 00				85 2 3 4 00		6
	25 6 0 0 00				25 6 0 0 00	7
7 8 0 0 00				7 8 0 0 00		8
	5 7 2 0 00				5 7 2 0 00	9
	7 6 0 0 00				7 6 0 0 00	10
	52 5 5 8 00				52 5 5 8 00	11
33 2 8 0 00				33 2 8 0 00		12
	112 0 2 4 00		112 0 2 4 00			13
1 9 8 2 00		1 9 8 2 00				14
3 0 2 4 00		3 0 2 4 00				15
23 5 2 0 00		23 5 2 0 00				16
5 8 5 6 00		5 8 5 6 00				17
12 0 0 0 00		12 0 0 0 00				18
4 1 2 00		4 1 2 00				19
7 7 8 00		7 7 8 00				20
8 8 8 00		8 8 8 00				21
6 2 4 00		6 2 4 00				22
						23
8 4 0 0 00		8 4 0 0 00				24
1 5 2 0 00		1 5 2 0 00				25
2 1 4 4 00		2 1 4 4 00				26
3 8 6 4 00		3 8 6 4 00				27
1 1 1 2 00		1 1 1 2 00				28
7 2 0 00		7 2 0 00				29
203 5 0 2 00	203 5 0 2 00	66 8 4 4 00	112 0 2 4 00	136 6 5 8 00	91 4 7 8 00	30
		45 1 8 0 00			45 1 8 0 00	31
		112 0 2 4 00	112 0 2 4 00	136 6 5 8 00	136 6 5 8 00	32
						33

Figure 7-8

e. Inventory of office supplies, $196.

f. Insurance expired, $720.

With these adjusting entries, the rest of the work sheet can now be completed as shown in Figure 7-8. First the balances of the accounts that were adjusted are brought up to date in the Adjusted Trial Balance columns. Then these amounts are carried forward to the remaining columns.

Financial Statements

From the work sheet, Dr. Barker's accountant prepares the financial statements shown in Figure 7-9. In this case, there was no additional investment made to R. T. Barker, Capital, during the year. However, whenever you are preparing a statement of owner's equity, always look into the capital account to see if any additional investment was recorded.

Figure 7-9

R. T. Barker, D.D.S.
Income Statement
For year ended December 31, 19–

Revenue:		
Professional Fees		$ 112 0 2 4 00
Expenses:		
Dental Instruments Expense	$ 1 9 8 2 00	
Laundry and Cleaning Expense	3 0 2 4 00	
Office Salary Expense	23 5 2 0 00	
Laboratory Expense	5 8 5 6 00	
Dental Supplies Expense	3 8 6 4 00	
Rent Expense	12 0 0 0 00	
Depreciation Expense,		
Dental Equipment	8 4 0 0 00	
Depreciation Expense,		
Office Furniture and Equipment	1 5 2 0 00	
X-ray Supplies Expense	2 1 4 4 00	
Office Supplies Expense	1 1 1 2 00	
Insurance Expense	7 2 0 00	
Telephone Expense	4 1 2 00	
Utilities Expense	7 7 8 00	
Repairs and Maintenance Expense	8 8 8 00	
Miscellaneous Expense	6 2 4 00	
Total Expenses		66 8 4 4 00
Net Income		$ 45 1 8 0 00

R. T. Barker, D.D.S.
Statement of Owner's Equity
For year ended December 31, 19–

R. T. Barker, Capital, Jan. 1, 19–		$52 5 5 8 00
Net Income for year	$45 1 8 0 00	
Less Withdrawals for year	33 2 8 0 00	
Increase in Capital		11 9 0 0 00
R. T. Barker, Capital, Dec. 31, 19–		$64 4 5 8 00

Figure 7-9
(continued)

R. T. Barker, D.D.S.
Balance Sheet
December 31, 19–

Assets													
Cash								$ 7	7	8	6	00
X-ray Supplies									6	1	8	00
Dental Supplies								1	6	1	6	00
Office Supplies									1	9	6	00
Prepaid Insurance									1	2	8	00
Dental Equipment	$85	2	3	4	00							
Less Accumulated Depreciation,												
Dental Equipment	25	6	0	0	00	59	6	3	4	00	
Office Furniture and Equipment	$ 7	8	0	0	00							
Less Accumulated Depreciation,												
Office Furniture and Equipment	5	7	2	0	00	2	0	8	0	00	
Total Assets						$72	0	5	8	00	
Liabilities												
Notes Payable								$ 7	6	0	0	00
Owner's Equity												
R. T. Barker, Capital								64	4	5	8	00
Total Liabilities and Owner's Equity								$72	0	5	8	00

Adjusting and Closing Entries

Dr. Barker (or his receptionist) records the adjusting and closing entries in the Sundry columns of the combined journal. These entries must be posted individually. For example, the adjusting and closing entries are shown in Figure 7-10, two pages of a shortened combined journal (see pages 194 and 195).

There are a number of aspects of the accounting for a professional enterprise which we have not yet considered:

1. Special funds, such as the change fund and the petty cash fund. (We shall discuss these in Chapter 8.)
2. Payroll deductions, such as withholdings for employees' income taxes, Social Security taxes, and other salary deductions. (We shall discuss these in Chapter 9.)
3. Payroll taxes levied on the employer, such as the matching for Social Security, and unemployment taxes. (We shall discuss these in Chapter 10.)

Objective 3

Complete the entire accounting cycle for a professional enterprise.

Figure 7-10

										SUNDRY								
DATE		ACCOUNT NAME	POST. REF.	DEBIT							CREDIT							

COMBINED JOURNAL   PAGE 13

DATE		ACCOUNT NAME	POST. REF.	DEBIT						CREDIT					
		Adjusting Entries													
19–Dec.	31	Depreciation Expense,													
		Dental Equipment	517	8	4	0	0	00							
		Accumulated Deprecia-													
		tion, Dental Equipment	122							8	4	0	0	00	
	31	Depreciation Expense,													
		Office Furniture and													
		Equipment	518	1	5	2	0	00							
		Accumulated Deprecia-													
		tion, Office Furniture													
		and Equipment	124							1	5	2	0	00	
	31	X-ray Supplies Expense	519	2	1	4	4	00							
		X-ray Supplies	112							2	1	4	4	00	
	31	Dental Supplies													
		Expense	515	3	8	6	4	00							
		Dental Supplies	113							3	8	6	4	00	
	31	Office Supplies Expense	520	1	1	1	2	00							
		Office Supplies	114							1	1	1	2	00	
	31	Insurance Expense	521		7	2	0	00							
		Prepaid Insurance	115								7	2	0	00	
	31			17	7	6	0	00		17	7	6	0	00	

ACCOUNTING FOR OTHER PROFESSIONAL ENTERPRISES

Accounting records for other professional enterprises are similar to our dentist's records. Professional people often use the modified cash basis, recording revenue when received in cash and recording expenses when paid in cash. Adjusting entries may be made for supplies used, expired insurance, and depreciation on specialized equipment. Ledger cards for patients or clients are used, although they may be given special titles. Lawyers, for example, call their clients' ledger cards Collection Dockets.

Lawyers have an additional asset account, Advances for Clients, representing amounts they have paid on behalf of their clients. Advances for Clients is a receivable, similar to Accounts Receivable. Lawyers also have an additional liability account, Collections for Clients, representing amounts they receive on behalf of their clients. Collections for Clients is a payable, similar to Accounts Payable. All in all, the same general accounting principles and procedures prevail in all professional enterprises.

COMBINED JOURNAL   PAGE   14

DATE		ACCOUNT NAME	POST. REF.	SUNDRY			
				DEBIT		CREDIT	
		Closing Entries					
19– Dec.	31	Professional Fees	411	112 0 2 4	00		
		Income Summary	313			112 0 2 4	00
	31	Income Summary	313	66 8 4 4	00		
		Dental Instruments Expense	511			1 9 8 2	00
		Laundry and Clean- ing Expense	512			3 0 2 4	00
		Office Salary Expense	513			23 5 2 0	00
		Laboratory Expense	514			5 8 5 6	00
		Dental Supplies Expense	515			3 8 6 4	00
		Rent Expense	516			12 0 0 0	00
		Depreciation Expense, Dental Equipment	517			8 4 0 0	00
		Depreciation Expense, Office Furniture and Equipment	518			1 5 2 0	00
		X-ray Supplies Expense	519			2 1 4 4	00
		Office Supplies Expense	520			1 1 1 2	00
		Insurance Expense	521			7 2 0	00
		Telephone Expense	522			4 1 2	00
		Utilities Expense	523			7 7 8	00
		Repairs and Main- tenance Expense	524			8 8 8	00
		Miscellaneous Expense	525			6 2 4	00
	31	Income Summary	313	45 1 8 0	00		
		R. T. Barker, Capital	311			45 1 8 0	00
	31	R. T. Barker, Capital	311	33 2 8 0	00		
		R. T. Barker, Drawing	312			33 2 8 0	00
	31			257 3 2 8	00	257 3 2 8	00

DESIGNING A COMBINED JOURNAL

As we have said, the combined journal is widely used in professional offices and service-type business firms. It is interesting to look over the varieties of combined journals that are available at stores that sell office supplies. Some are bound journals, and others are loose-leaf type books. The number of columns may vary from six to twenty, and they are available with or without column headings. Those that have printed column headings represent a "canned" type of combined journal. In other words, these combined journals are set up for a particular kind of business enterprise and describe how to channel routine transactions into the journal. These journals are available for service stations, dry cleaners, doctors' offices, and many other types of businesses.

A person with even a limited knowledge of accounting can keep books as long as the transactions are routine and fall into the established channels. In every business, however, unusual or nonroutine transactions pop up from time to time. You need to have enough knowledge and background to be able to handle them, and you will have to understand the entire accounting system if you are ever going to see *why* transactions are recorded as they are.

Combined journals with blank columns can be customized to meet the specific requirements of a given business. Prior to labeling the columns, one first studies the operations of the business and makes up a chart of accounts. Next one identifies those accounts that are likely to be used frequently in recording typical transactions of the business. Naturally, if these accounts are used over and over again, one needs to set up special columns for them. The combined journal is appropriate for businesses using either the accrual basis or the modified cash basis of accounting.

GLOSSARY

Accrual basis An accounting method by which revenue is recorded when it is earned, regardless of when it is received. Expenses are recorded when they are incurred, regardless of when they are paid.

Cash-receipts-and-disbursements basis An accounting method by which revenue is recorded only when it is received in cash, and expenses, consisting of all expenditures, are recorded only when they are paid in cash.

Combined journal A journal format widely used by professional and service-type businesses in place of a general journal. Designed to make the recording and posting of transactions more efficient.

Modified cash basis An accounting method by which revenue is recorded only when it is received in cash. Expenditures classified as expenses are recorded only when they are paid in cash. Exceptions can be made in cases of expenditures for items having a useful life of more than one year and for certain prepaid items. For example, expenditures for supplies and insurance premiums can be *prorated,* or apportioned over the fiscal periods covered. Expenditures for long-lived items are recorded as assets and later depreciated or written off as an expense during their useful lives.

QUESTIONS, EXERCISES, AND PROBLEMS

Discussion Questions

1. What is meant by the modified cash basis of accounting?
2. In regard to a combined journal, describe the procedure followed in posting amounts in the following columns: Cash Debit, Professional Fees Credit, Sundry Debit, Miscellaneous Expense Debit, Sundry Credit.
3. Where is a check mark ($\checkmark$) used in a combined journal, and what does it indicate?
4. What is the meaning of the numbers that appear in the Posting Reference column of the combined journal?
5. What is the purpose of the dashes that appear in the Posting Reference column of the combined journal?
6. Describe the process of proving the combined journal at the end of the month.
7. You have been asked to set up a combined journal for Jack's Appliance Repair. The business maintains charge accounts for customers and buys parts on account from creditors. The space occupied by the shop is rented on a monthly basis. J. Rowe, the owner, makes withdrawals on a weekly basis. The firm subscribes to a telephone answering service on a monthly basis. There are no employees. What money columns would you suggest?

Exercises

Exercise 7-1   The Champion Insurance Agency, operating on the accrual basis, uses a combined journal that has the following columns.

Date	Accounts Payable Debit
Account Name	Accounts Payable Credit
Post. Ref.	Commissions Income Credit
Cash Debit	Salary Expense Debit
Cash Credit	Miscellaneous Expense Debit
Accounts Receivable Debit	Sundry Debit
Accounts Receivable Credit	Sundry Credit

Answer the following.

a. Which money column totals are not posted?
b. How do you record an investment of additional cash in the business by C. T. Champion?
c. How do you determine the balance of Cash at any time during the month?
d. Which columns are used to record the payment of rent for the month?

Exercise 7-2 Journalize the closing entries in the proper sequence for the following ledger accounts.

Professional Fees		Utilities Expense	
	37,640	560	

Salary Expense		Miscellaneous Expense	
16,400		420	

Rent Expense		J. D. Cameron, Drawing	
4,800		14,600	

Supplies Expense		Depreciation Expense	
365		2,980	

Exercise 7-3 On the appointment record for the dentist, the total of the fees column is $624, and the total of the receipts column is $386. The dentist deposits $386 in the bank at the end of the day. Record the journal entry for the deposit. Assume the dentist uses the modified cash basis.

Exercise 7-4 Record the proper account or classification of accounts in the blank spaces of the partial work sheet shown in this exercise. Number 1 is given as an example. (Omit the Adjustments column.)

1. Assets
2. Expenses
3. Revenue
4. Liabilities
5. Drawing
6. Accumulated Depreciation
7. Capital

Account Name	Trial Balance		Adjustments		Adjusted Trial Balance		Income Statement		Balance Sheet	
	Debit	Credit	Debit	Credit	Debit	Credit	Debit	Credit	Debit	Credit
	1	___			1	___	___	___	1	___
	___	___			___	___	___	___	___	___
	___	___			___	___			___	___

Exercise 7-5 Determine the cash balance after September 6.

Cash

Sep. 1 Balance 941.60

Combined Journal

Date				Cash Dr.		Cash Cr.	
19–							
Sept.	1			600	00		
	3					425	00
	4			172	60		
	4			21	52		
	5					341	58
	6			83	22		

Exercise 7-6 In the following T accounts, record the plus and minus signs and $418 depreciation for the fiscal period.

Depreciation Expense, Equipment	Accumulated Depreciation, Equipment

Exercise 7-7 Record the depreciation in Exercise 7-6 in the following partial work sheet.

Account Name	Trial Balance		Adjustments		Adjusted Trial Balance	
	Debit	Credit	Debit	Credit	Debit	Credit
Equipment	12,000.00					
Accumulated Depreciation, Equipment		4,650.00				
	56,720.00	56,720.00				
Depreciation Expense, Equipment						

Exercise 7-8 Number the steps in the accounting cycle in the proper sequence.

___ Financial statements
___ Trial balance
___ Journalizing and posting adjusting entries
___ Journalizing transactions
___ Journalizing and posting closing entries

___ Completing the work sheet
___ Formulating the data for the adjustments
___ Posting to the ledger accounts
___ Post-closing trial balance

Problem Set A

Problem 7-1A The following chart of accounts is used by L. E. Benson, M.D.

Assets
111 Cash
112 Medical Supplies
113 X-ray Supplies
114 Office Supplies
115 Medical Equipment
116 Accumulated Depreciation, Medical Equipment
117 Office Furniture and Equipment
118 Accumulated Depreciation, Office Furniture and Equipment
119 Automobile
120 Accumulated Depreciation, Automobile

Liabilities
211 Notes Payable

Owner's Equity
311 L. E. Benson, Capital
312 L. E. Benson, Drawing
313 Income Summary

Revenue
411 Professional Fees

Expenses
511 Salaries Expense
512 Rent Expense
513 Equipment Rental Expense
514 Medical Supplies Expense
515 X-ray Supplies Expense
516 Laboratory Expense
517 Laundry and Cleaning Expense
518 Office Supplies Expense
519 Depreciation Expense, Medical Equipment
520 Depreciation Expense, Office Furniture and Equipment
521 Depreciation Expense, Automobile
522 Automobile Expense
523 Insurance Expense
524 Telephone Expense
525 Utilities Expense
526 Miscellaneous Expense

Dr. Benson's records consist of an appointment record book, examination and charge reports, patients' ledger records, a general journal, and a general ledger. The doctor fills out an examination and charge report each time a patient visits. The reports contain a description or listing of the treatments and tests administered and the amount of the charges. The charges are then recorded in the patient's ledger record. Monthly statements based on the patients' ledger records are mailed to patients. Dr. Benson's books are kept on the modified cash basis.

The following transactions took place during September.

Sep. 1 Bought medical supplies for cash from Porter Surgical Supply, $285.
  1 Paid rent for the month to Dolan Realty, $850.
  5 Paid office salaries for the month, $590.

Sep.   6 Received cash from patients during the week, $4,916.
        7 Bought an examination table from Malcom Surgical Supply, costing
          $420, paying $120 in cash and agreeing by contract to pay the bal-
          ance in three monthly installments of $100 each. (Credit Notes Pay-
          able.)
        8 Paid telephone bill, $62.
        9 Paid Superior Laboratories for laboratory expense, $216 (not previ-
          ously recorded).
       13 Total cash received from patients during the week, $3,114.
       16 Paid for x-ray supplies to Modern Supply Company, $129.
       16 Dr. Benson withdrew $615 for personal use.
       20 Total cash received from patients during the week, $1,222.
       23 Bought postage stamps, $60 (Miscellaneous Expense); paid cash.
       25 Paid Mike's Service Station for gas and oil, $65.50.
       29 Paid United Building Maintenance for janitorial service, $40.
       30 Paid nurses' salaries, $1,342.
       30 Dr. Benson withdrew $920 for personal use.
       30 Paid Peerless Laundry for laundry service through September 30,
          $61.40 (not previously recorded).

Instructions

1. Journalize these transactions in the combined journal. Record them on
   page 41 of the journal.
2. Prove the equality of the debit and credit totals on a sheet of scratch paper.

Problem 7-2A   The completed work sheet for D. D. Paige, Architect, is
presented on the next two pages.

Instructions

Journalize the adjusting and closing entries and record column totals.

Problem 7-3A   Donna C. Perkins, M.D., completed the transactions described below during November of this year. Her chart of accounts is as follows.

Assets
111 Cash
112 Accounts Receivable
113 Supplies
114 Prepaid Insurance
121 Equipment
122 Accumulated Depreciation,
    Equipment

Liabilities
211 Accounts Payable

Owner's Equity
311 Donna C. Perkins, Capital
312 Donna C. Perkins, Drawing
313 Income Summary

Revenue
411 Professional Fees

Expenses
511 Salary Expense
512 Rent Expense
513 Laboratory Expense
514 Utilities Expense
515 Depreciation Expense
516 Miscellaneous Expense

	ACCOUNT NAME	TRIAL BALANCE DEBIT	TRIAL BALANCE CREDIT	ADJUSTMENTS DEBIT	ADJUSTMENTS CREDIT
1	Cash	3 1 7 9 00			
2	Supplies	2 1 7 2 00			(b)1 1 9 3 00
3	Office Equipment	31 7 1 8 00			
4	Accumulated Depreciation, Office Equipment		9 7 6 0 00		(a)2 9 8 2 00
5	D. D. Paige, Capital		22 4 9 6 56		
6	D. D. Paige, Drawing	15 7 8 0 00			
7	Professional Fees		46 7 5 8 00		
8	Salary Expense	17 1 6 4 00			
9	Blueprint Expense	2 0 0 8 64			
10	Rent Expense	4 2 0 0 00			
11	Automobile Expense	8 8 6 19			
12	Travel Expense	1 2 9 2 00			
13	Entertainment Expense	4 1 6 53			
14	Miscellaneous Expense	1 9 8 20			
15		79 0 1 4 56	79 0 1 4 56		
16	Depreciation Expense, Office Equipment			(a)2 9 8 2 00	
17	Supplies Expense			(b)1 1 9 3 00	
18				4 1 7 5 00	4 1 7 5 00
19	Net Income				
20					
21					

Problem 7-3A   (continued)

Nov. 2 Bought laboratory equipment on account, $1,872.
 2 Paid office rent for month, $920.
 2 Received cash on account from patients, $940: A. C. Cummings, $170; Agnes Denton, $296; Frank Curtis, $384; Simon Russell, $90. (Dr. Perkins is on the accrual basis. Use four lines, recording individual amounts in both the Cash Debit column and the Accounts Receivable Credit column. List each patient's name in the Account Name column.)
 4 Received cash for professional services rendered, $284.
 6 Received and paid telephone bill for the month, $52.
 6 Received and paid electric bill, $164.76.
 9 Recorded fees charged to patients on account for professional services rendered, $938: Derek Stevens, $498; Mildred Wendt, $440.
 16 Paid salary of nurse, $670.
 19 Received cash for professional services, $632.
 23 Returned part of equipment purchased on November 2 and received a reduction on the bill, $84.
 27 Billed patients on account, $1,280: Emerson Schultz, $720; Mary MacIntyre, $290; David Allen, $270. (Use three lines.)

ADJUSTED TRIAL BALANCE		INCOME STATEMENT		BALANCE SHEET		
DEBIT	CREDIT	DEBIT	CREDIT	DEBIT	CREDIT	
3 1 7 9 00				3 1 7 9 00		1
9 7 9 00				9 7 9 00		2
31 7 1 8 00				31 7 1 8 00		3
	12 7 4 2 00				12 7 4 2 00	4
	22 4 9 6 56				22 4 9 6 56	5
15 7 8 0 00				15 7 8 0 00		6
	46 7 5 8 00		46 7 5 8 00			7
17 1 6 4 00		17 1 6 4 00				8
2 0 0 8 64		2 0 0 8 64				9
4 2 0 0 00		4 2 0 0 00				10
8 8 6 19		8 8 6 19				11
1 2 9 2 00		1 2 9 2 00				12
4 1 6 53		4 1 6 53				13
1 9 8 20		1 9 8 20				14
						15
2 9 8 2 00		2 9 8 2 00				16
1 1 9 3 00		1 1 9 3 00				17
81 9 9 6 56	81 9 9 6 56	30 3 4 0 56	46 7 5 8 00	51 6 5 6 00	35 2 3 8 56	18
		16 4 1 7 44			16 4 1 7 44	19
		46 7 5 8 00	46 7 5 8 00	51 6 5 6 00	51 6 5 6 00	20
						21

Nov.   30 Paid salary of nurse, $670.
    30 Paid salary of receptionist, $840.
    30 Dr. Perkins withdrew cash for personal use, $1,970.

Instructions

1. Record these transactions in the combined journal.
2. On scratch paper, prove the equality of the debit and credit totals.
3. Post to the accounts in the general ledger.
4. Prepare a trial balance.

Problem 7-4A   On September 1 of this year, C. T. Pitts decided to open a moving business serving the local area. Pitts completed the following transactions related to "Pitts the Mover."

Sep.   1 Pitts invested $16,000 cash in the new business.
    2 Bought a used moving van from Chelsea Van and Storage for $12,450, paying $4,000 down with the balance on account.
    2 Placed an advertisement in *The Guardian* and received a bill for $94.
    3 Bought three hand trucks from Sanderson Rent-All for $227, paying cash.

Sep. 4 Paid Steve's Fast Service for gas and oil for moving van, $84.
      6 Paid rent for subletting office space, $85.
      7 Received revenue for the week, $476.
      7 Paid wages to part-time employee, $184.
      9 Paid for city business license, $32.
     12 Paid for telephone answering service for the month, $58.
     14 Bought two piano dollies on account from Sanderson Rent-All for $118.
     14 Received revenue for the week, $588.
     14 Paid wages to part-time employee, $192.
     14 Pitts withdrew $318 for personal use.
     17 Paid Chelsea Van and Storage $800 as part payment on account.
     18 Paid Steve's Fast Service for gas and oil for moving van, $116.
     18 Paid $62 for advertisement in the telephone directory.
     21 Paid utilities for the month, $47.
     21 Received revenue for the week, $646.
     23 Paid wages to part-time employee, $212.
     26 Paid Sanderson Rent-All in full payment of account, $118.
     30 Received revenue for the week, $784.
     30 Received bill from Steve's Fast Service for performing a tune-up on the moving van, $91.
     30 Paid wages of part-time employee, $220.
     30 Pitts withdrew $425 for personal use.

Instructions

1. By reviewing the transactions, formulate a chart of accounts for "Pitts the Mover."
2. Label the appropriate columns in the combined journal. Next to the date column, list a check number and record checks beginning with check number one.
3. Record the transactions in the combined journal.
4. Prove the equality of debits and credits on scratch paper.

Problem Set B

Problem 7-1B   N. B. Carter, M.D., uses the following chart of accounts.

Assets
111 Cash
112 Medical Supplies
113 X-ray Supplies
114 Office Supplies
115 Medical Equipment
116 Accumulated Depreciation, Medical Equipment
117 Office Furniture and Equipment
118 Accumulated Depreciation, Office Furniture and Equipment
119 Automobile
120 Accumulated Depreciation, Automobile

Liabilities
211 Notes Payable

Owner's Equity
311 N. B. Carter, Capital
312 N. B. Carter, Drawing
313 Income Summary

Revenue
411 Professional Fees

Expenses

511 Nurses' Salaries Expense
512 Office Salaries Expense
513 Rent Expense
514 Equipment Rental Expense
515 Medical Supplies Expense
516 X-ray Supplies Expense
517 Laboratory Expense
518 Laundry and Cleaning Expense
519 Office Supplies Expense
520 Depreciation Expense, Medical
    Equipment

521 Depreciation Expense, Office Furniture
    and Equipment
522 Depreciation Expense, Automobile
523 Automobile Expense
524 Insurance Expense
525 Telephone Expense
526 Utilities Expense
527 Miscellaneous Expense

Dr. Carter's records consist of an appointment record book, examination and charge reports, patients' ledger records, a general journal, and a general ledger. The doctor fills out an examination and charge report each time a patient visits. The reports contain a description or listing of the treatments and tests administered and the amount of the charges. The charges are then recorded in the patient's ledger record. Monthly statements based on the patient's ledger record are mailed to the patient. Dr. Carter's books are kept on the modified cash basis.

These transactions took place during April.

Apr. 1 Paid rent for the month to M. B. Faris, $900.
      3 Bought medical supplies for cash from Shinn Surgical Supply, $260.
      4 Paid office salaries for the month, $520.
      6 Received cash from patients during week, $4,160.
     10 Paid telephone bill, $54.
     12 Paid for laboratory expense to Shelton Laboratories, $210.
     13 Total cash received from patients during week, $2,932.
     16 Paid for x-ray supplies to Meier Supply Company, $122.
     17 Dr. Carter withdrew $520 for personal use.
     19 Bought postage stamps, $26 (Miscellaneous Expense); paid cash.
     20 Received cash from patients during week, $1,184.
     23 Paid Roy's Service Station for gas and oil, $62.
     24 Paid Speedy News Service for magazines, $41.
     27 Paid Modern Laundry for laundry service, $56.
     30 Paid nurses' salaries for the month, $1,260.
     30 Dr. Carter withdrew $680 for personal use.
     30 Paid Johnson Janitorial Service, $82.
     30 Received cash from patients (April 21 through 30), $917.

Instructions

1. Journalize these transactions in the combined journal. Record them on page 39 of the journal.
2. Prove the equality of the debit and credit totals on a sheet of scratch paper.

A. L. Brown, Architect
Work Sheet
For year ended December 31, 19–

	ACCOUNT NAME	TRIAL BALANCE		ADJUSTMENTS	
		DEBIT	CREDIT	DEBIT	CREDIT
1	Cash	4 2 8 0 00			
2	Supplies	1 4 2 6 00			(b)1 2 1 4 00
3	Office Equipment	23 7 0 0 00			
4	Accumulated Depreciation, Office Equipment		10 8 7 0 00		(a)3 4 1 0 00
5	A. L. Brown, Capital		12 5 4 1 00		
6	A. L. Brown, Drawing	16 2 0 0 00			
7	Professional Fees		50 6 8 0 00		
8	Salary Expense	18 7 2 0 00			
9	Blueprint Expense	2 1 7 2 00			
10	Rent Expense	4 2 0 0 00			
11	Automobile Expense	9 2 0 00			
12	Travel Expense	1 4 8 0 00			
13	Entertainment Expense	5 6 4 00			
14	Miscellaneous Expense	4 2 9 00			
15		74 0 9 1 00	74 0 9 1 00		
16	Depreciation Expense, Office Equipment			(a)3 4 1 0 00	
17	Supplies Expense			(b)1 2 1 4 00	
18				4 6 2 4 00	4 6 2 4 00
19	Net Income				
20					
21					

Problem 7-2B   The work sheet for A. L. Brown, Architect, is above.

Instructions

Journalize the adjusting and closing entries and record column totals.

Problem 7-3B   Donna C. Perkins, M.D., uses the following chart of accounts.

Assets
111 Cash
112 Accounts Receivable
113 Supplies
114 Prepaid Insurance
121 Equipment

Liabilities
211 Accounts Payable

Owner's Equity
311 Donna C. Perkins, Capital
312 Donna C. Perkins, Drawing
313 Income Summary

Revenue
411 Professional Fees

Expenses
511 Salary Expense
512 Rent Expense
513 Laboratory Expense
514 Utilities Expense
515 Depreciation Expense
516 Miscellaneous Expense

ADJUSTED TRIAL BALANCE		INCOME STATEMENT		BALANCE SHEET		
DEBIT	CREDIT	DEBIT	CREDIT	DEBIT	CREDIT	
4 2 8 0 00				4 2 8 0 00		1
2 1 2 00				2 1 2 00		2
23 7 0 0 00				23 7 0 0 00		3
	14 2 8 0 00				14 2 8 0 00	4
	12 5 4 1 00				12 5 4 1 00	5
16 2 0 0 00				16 2 0 0 00		6
	50 6 8 0 00		50 6 8 0 00			7
18 7 2 0 00		18 7 2 0 00				8
2 1 7 2 00		2 1 7 2 00				9
4 2 0 0 00		4 2 0 0 00				10
9 2 0 00		9 2 0 00				11
1 4 8 0 00		1 4 8 0 00				12
5 6 4 00		5 6 4 00				13
4 2 9 00		4 2 9 00				14
						15
3 4 1 0 00		3 4 1 0 00				16
1 2 1 4 00		1 2 1 4 00				17
77 5 0 1 00	77 5 0 1 00	33 1 0 9 00	50 6 8 0 00	44 3 9 2 00	26 8 2 1 00	18
		17 5 7 1 00			17 5 7 1 00	19
		50 6 8 0 00	50 6 8 0 00	44 3 9 2 00	44 3 9 2 00	20
						21

These transactions were completed during November of this year.

Nov. 2 Paid office rent for the month, $920.

2 Bought laboratory equipment on account, $1,880.

3 Received cash on account from patients, $940: R. C. Striker, $320; Dennis Horton, $380; Angela Higgins, $240. (Dr. Perkins is on the accrual basis. Use three lines, recording individual amounts in both the Cash Debit column and the Accounts Receivable Credit column. List each patient's name in the Account Name column.)

4 Received cash for professional services rendered, $250.

6 Received and paid telephone bill for the month, $48.

9 Recorded fees charged to patients on account for professional services rendered, $1,090: J. C. Prescott, $520; Arthur Lewis, $570. (Use two lines.)

9 Received and paid electric bill for the month, $170.

16 Paid salary of nurse, $630.

23 Received cash for professional services, $620.

23 Returned part of equipment purchased on November 2 and received a reduction on the bill, $120.

Nov.   27 Billed patients on account for professional services rendered, $740:
            R. L. Graves, $180; C. C. Simon, $320; Charles Marshall, $240.
        30 Paid receptionist's salary for the month, $780.
        30 Paid salary of nurse, $630.
        30 Dr. Perkins withdrew cash for personal use, $1,680.

Instructions

1. Record these transactions in the combined journal.
2. On scratch paper, prove the equality of the debit and credit totals.
3. Post to the accounts in the general ledger.
4. Prepare a trial balance.

Problem 7-4B   On October 1 of this year, R. D. Spargo decided to open a tree trimming service. Spargo completed the following transactions related to Spargo's Tree Service.

Oct.   1 Spargo invested cash in the business by depositing $6,000 in the
            bank under the name Spargo's Tree Service.
        1 Paid office rent for the month, $125.
        2 Bought a used truck from Midland Truck and Tractor for $8,200,
            paying $1,500 down, with the balance on account.
        2 Bought a used chipper from Jones Equipment for $2,400, paying
            $1,000 as a down payment and the balance on account.
        3 Received a bill for advertising from the City Chronicle, $72.
        4 Bought two chain saws on account from Scott's Hardware, $578.
        4 Paid City Service for gas and oil for the truck, $76.
        6 Received revenue for the week, $564.
        7 Paid wages of part-time employee, $121.
        7 Paid for telephone answering service for the month, $61.
        10 Paid City Service for gas and oil for the truck, $59.
        13 Received $628 revenue for the week.
        15 Paid City Chronicle $72 for advertising previously recorded.
        18 Spargo withdrew $420 for personal use.
        20 Received revenue for the week, $642.
        21 Paid wages to part-time employee, $132.
        26 Paid utilities for the month, $58.
        26 Paid $24 for city business license.
        30 Paid Midland Truck and Tractor $900 to apply on account.
        30 Paid City Service $47 for gas and oil for the truck plus $18 for a
            wheel alignment for the truck.
        31 Received revenue for the week, $786.
        31 Paid wages of part-time employee, $143.
        31 Spargo withdrew $325 for personal use.

Instructions

1. By reviewing the transactions, formulate a chart of accounts.
2. Label appropriate columns in the combined journal. Next to the Date column, list a Check Number column, and record checks beginning with number one.
3. Record the transactions in the combined journal.
4. Prove the equality of debits and credits on scratch paper.

8 Bank Accounts and Cash Funds

Learning Objectives

After you have completed this chapter, you will be able to do the following:

1. Reconcile a bank statement.

2. Journalize the requisite entries directly from the bank reconciliation.

3. Journalize entries to establish and reimburse Petty Cash Fund.

4. Complete petty cash vouchers and petty cash payments records.

5. Journalize the entries to establish a Change Fund.

6. Journalize transactions involving Cash Short and Over.

A very important aspect of any system of financial accounting, either for an individual or for a business enterprise, is the efficient management of cash. For a business of any size, all cash received during a working day should be deposited at the end of the day, and all disbursements—with the exception of payments from Petty Cash—should be made by check. When we talk about cash, we mean currency, coins, checks, money orders, and bank drafts or bank cashier's checks. Personal checks are accepted on a conditional-payment status, that is, based on the condition that they're valid. In other words, we consider checks to be good until they are proved to be no good.

In this chapter, we're also going to talk about **cash funds**—petty cash funds and change funds—which, in this sense, are separately held stores of cash.

USING A CHECKING ACCOUNT

Although you may be familiar with the process of opening a checking account, making deposits, and writing checks, let's review these and other procedures associated with opening and maintaining a business checking account. We'll discuss signature cards, deposit slips, night deposits, and ways of endorsing checks.

Signature card

When Eugene L. Madison founded East Phoenix Rental Equipment, he opened a checking account in the name of the business. When he made his first deposit, he filled out a **signature card** for the bank's files. Madison gave his accountant the right to sign checks too, so the accountant also signed the card. This card gives the bank a copy of the official signatures of any persons authorized to sign checks. The bank can use it to verify any signatures on checks of East Phoenix Rental Equipment presented for payment. This, of course, helps the bank detect forgeries. Figure 8-1 shows a typical signature card.

Deposit slips

The bank provides **deposit slips** on which customers record the amount of coins and currency they are depositing and list each individual check being deposited. A typical deposit slip is shown in Figure 8-2. For identification purposes, each check should be listed according to its American Bankers Association (ABA) transit number. The **ABA number** is the small

Figure 8-1

Title	East Phoenix Rental Equipment	Account Number

In consideration of the acceptance by lmlmmllmllmmllm lmmmlmllm lmllmlmmlln of my/our account of the type indicated below, I/we agree to be bound by such rules and regulations and/or such schedules of interest, fees and charges applicable to such account as may now or hereafter be adopted by and in effect at said Bank, and also by the provisions printed hereon. It is understood that the acceptance by said Bank of my/our account is subject to the receipt by said Bank of satisfactory credit information.

(1) Sign Here *Eugene L. Madison*

(2) Sign Here *Gloria B. Masters*

Address 3011 N.W. Ventura Street

City Phoenix **State** Arizona **Zip** 85280

☑ CHECKING ☐ MULTIPLE MATURITY ☐ CASH MANAGER
☐ SAVINGS ☐ GUARANTEED INTEREST (Multiple Maturity) ☐ SAFE DEPOSIT ☐ OTHER_____

IF THIS IS A JOINT ACCOUNT, BOTH OWNERS MUST SIGN ABOVE

Each of the signers guarantees the genuineness of the signature of the other. Each signer also agrees with the other and the Bank that deposits now or hereafter made to this account may be withdrawn in whole or part by either or survivor, and that each may endorse for deposit to this account any instrument payable to the order of either or both. Provisions respecting this agreement shall be modified only upon receipt by the Bank of written notice, signed by both.

fraction located in the upper right corner of a check. The numerator (top of the fraction) indicates the city or state in which the bank is located and the specific bank on which the check is drawn. The denominator (bottom of the fraction) indicates the Federal Reserve District in which the check is cleared and the routing number used by the Federal Reserve Bank. For example,

$$\frac{68\text{-}420}{1210}$$

The 68 identifies the city or state, and the 420 indicates the specific bank within that area. That is all you need to list on the deposit slip. However, for your information, the 12 in the denominator represents the Twelfth

Figure 8-2

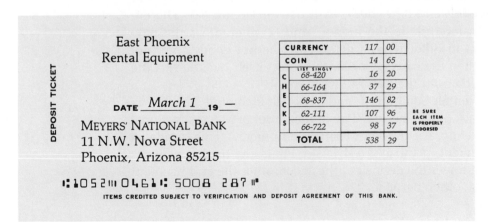

	CURRENCY	117	00
	COIN	14	65
C	LIST SINGLY 68-420	16	20
H	66-164	37	29
E	68-837	146	82
C	62-111	107	96
K S	66-722	98	37
	TOTAL	538	29

East Phoenix Rental Equipment

DEPOSIT TICKET

DATE *March 1* 19 —

MEYERS' NATIONAL BANK
11 N.W. Nova Street
Phoenix, Arizona 85215

⑆1052⑈0461⑆ 5008 287⑈

BE SURE EACH ITEM IS PROPERLY ENDORSED

ITEMS CREDITED SUBJECT TO VERIFICATION AND DEPOSIT AGREEMENT OF THIS BANK.

Federal Reserve District, and the 10 represents the routing number used by the Federal Reserve Bank.

The depositor fills out the deposit slip in duplicate, giving one copy to the bank teller and keeping the other copy. (This procedure may vary from bank to bank.)

When the bank receives the deposited checks, it prints the amount of each check on the lower right side of the check in a very distinctive script called **MICR,** which stands for *magnetic ink character recognition.* The routing number used by the Federal Reserve Bank was previously printed on the lower left side of the blank check. The reason banks use this MICR script is that the electronic equipment used to process the checks is able to read the script identifying the bank on which the check is drawn as well as the amount of the check. Clearing checks electronically speeds up the process considerably.

Night Deposits

Most banks provide night depositories so that firms can make deposits after regular banking hours. Depositories are steel-lined chutes into which a firm's representative can drop a bag of cash and checks, knowing that their day's receipts will be safe until the bank opens in the morning.

Endorsements

The bank refuses to accept for deposit a check made out to a firm until someone from the firm has endorsed the check. The **endorsement** may be made by signature or by using a stamp. The endorsement should appear on the back of the left end of a check, as it does in Figure 8-3. The endorsement (1) transfers title to the money, and (2) guarantees the payment of the check. In other words, if the check is not good, NSF (not sufficient funds), then the bank, in order to protect itself, will deduct the amount of the check from the depositor's account.

East Phoenix Rental Equipment endorses all incoming checks by stamping on the back of the checks: "Pay to the Order of Meyers National Bank, For Deposit Only, East Phoenix Rental Equipment." This is called a **restrictive endorsement,** because it restricts or limits any further negotiation of the check; it forces the deposit of the check, since the endorsement is not valid for any other purpose.

Figure 8-3

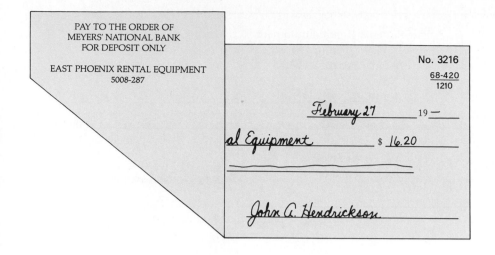

PAY TO THE ORDER OF
MEYERS' NATIONAL BANK
FOR DEPOSIT ONLY

EAST PHOENIX RENTAL EQUIPMENT
5008-287

No. 3216

$\dfrac{68\text{-}420}{1210}$

February 27   19 —

al Equipment $ _16.20_

John C. Hendrickson

WRITING CHECKS

As you know, you have to use a check to withdraw money from a checking account. A check represents an order by the depositor, directing the bank to pay money to a designated person or firm: the **payee.**

The checks may be attached to check stubs. Each stub has spaces to record the check number and amount, the date and payee, the purpose of the check, and the beginning and ending balances. _Note well:_ The information recorded on the check stub is the basis for the journal entry, so check stubs are vitally important. A person in a hurry, or working under pressure, can sometimes neglect to fill in the check stubs. Therefore, it is best to record all the information on the check stub _before making out the check._

It goes without saying that all checks should be written carefully, so that no dishonest person can successfully alter them. Write the payee's name on the first long line. Write the amount of the check in figures close to the dollar sign, then write the amount in words at the extreme left of the line provided for this information. Write cents as a fraction of 100. For example, write $727.50 as "seven hundred twenty-seven and 50/100," or $69.00 as "sixty-nine and 00/100." From a legal standpoint, if there is a discrepancy between the amount in figures and the written amount, the written amount prevails. However, as a general practice, the bank gets in touch with the depositor and asks what the correct amount should be.

Many firms use a **check writer,** which is a machine used to imprint the amount in figures and in words on the check itself. Using this machine neatly prevents anyone from altering the amount of the check.

Finally, the depositor's signature on the face of the check should match that of the signature card on file at the depositor's bank.

In Figure 8-4 we see a check, with the accompanying stub, drawn on the account of East Phoenix Rental Equipment.

Figure 8-4

BANK STATEMENTS

Once a month the bank sends all of its customers a **bank statement.** This statement provides the following information about their accounts.

- The balance at the beginning of the month
- Additions in the form of deposits and credit memos
- Deductions in the form of checks and debit memos
- The final balance at the end of the month

A bank statement for East Phoenix Rental Equipment is shown in Figure 8-5. The following code symbols are listed on the statement:

- **CM Credit memo**   Increases or credits to the account, such as notes or accounts left with the bank for collection.
- **DM Debit memo**   Decreases or debits to the account, items returned such as NSF checks and special charges levied by the bank against the account.
- **EC Error correction**   Corrections of errors made by the bank, such as mistakes in transferring figures.
- **OD Overdraft**   An overwithdrawal, resulting in a negative balance in the account.
- **SC Service charge**   The amount charged by the bank for servicing the account, based on the number of items processed and the average balance of the account.

The bank statement is a valuable aid to efficiency because it gives a double record of the Cash account. If a business entity deposits all cash receipts in the bank and makes all payments by check, then the bank is keeping an independent record of the firm's cash. Offhand, you might think that the two balances—the firm's and the bank's—should be equal,

MEYERS NATIONAL BANK
11 N.W. Nova Street
Phoenix, Arizona 85215

STATEMENT OF ACCOUNT		ACCOUNT NO.
East Phoenix Rental Equipment 3011 N.W. Ventura Street Phoenix, Arizona 85280		5008-287 STATEMENT DATE October 31, 19–

CHECKS AND OTHER DEBITS			DEPOSITS	DATE	BALANCE
		BALANCE BROUGHT FORWARD FROM LAST STATEMENT		Oct. 1, 19–	7,495.13
50.00	200.00	400.00	921.00	Oct. 1	7,766.13
46.00	174.23	671.74	1,476.22	Oct. 2	8,350.38
846.20	664.56		463.62	Oct. 3	7,303.24
719.00	61.68	591.84	789.43	Oct. 4	6,720.15
36.92	817.22	DM125.00	1,063.14	Oct. 7	6,804.15
523.00	786.40	374.00	1,211.96	Oct. 8	6,332.71
	943.64		CM606.00	Oct. 30	7,812.62
			873.19	Oct. 30	8,685.81
843.17	21.92	SC5.50	946.78	Oct. 31	8,762.00

CHECKING SUMMARY

BEGINNING BALANCE	TOTAL AMOUNT OF CHECKS & DEBITS		TOTAL AMOUNT OF DEPOSITS & CREDITS		SERVICE CHARGE AMOUNT	ENDING BALANCE
	NO.	AMOUNT	NO.	AMOUNT		
7,495.13	66	25,153.41	23	26,425.78	5.50	8,762.00

PLEASE EXAMINE THIS STATEMENT CAREFULLY. REPORT ANY POSSIBLE ERRORS IN 10 DAYS.

CODE SYMBOLS

CM	Credit Memo		OD	Overdraft
DM	Debit Memo		SC	Service Charge
EC	Error Correction			

Figure 8-5

but this is most unlikely. Some transactions may have been recorded in the firm's account before being recorded in the bank's. In addition, there are unavoidable delays (by either the firm or the bank) in recording transactions. Ordinarily, there is a time lag of one day or more between the date a check is written and the date it is presented to the bank for payment. Also, banks usually do not record deposits until the following business day. During this time, deposits made or checks written are recorded in the firm's checkbook, but they are not yet recorded on the bank statement.

The bank usually mails statements to its depositors shortly after the end of the month. In the same envelope with the statement are the **canceled checks** (checks that have been cashed or cleared by the bank) and debit or credit memos. As we mentioned before, debit memos represent deductions and credit memos represent additions to a bank account. Each business entity keeps its accounts from its *own* point of view. As far as the bank is concerned, each customer's deposits are liabilities, in that the bank owes the customer the amount of the deposits. Using T accounts, it looks like this.

Liabilities		Deposits Payable	
−	+	−	+
Debits	Credits	Debits	Credits
		Checks written	Deposits
	Debit	{ Service charges	Notes } Credit
	memos	{ NSF checks	collected } memos

On the customer's books, of course, this comes under the account titled Cash, or Cash in Bank, or simply the name of the bank. Regardless of what title is used for the account, the balance of the account is referred to as the *book balance of Cash*.

Need for Reconciling Bank Balance and Book Balance

The **book balance** is the balance of the Cash account in the general ledger. Since the bank statement balance and the book balance are not equal, a firm makes a **bank reconciliation** to uncover the reasons for the difference between the two balances and to correct any errors that may have been made by either the bank or the firm. This makes it possible to wind up with the same balance in each account, which is called the *adjusted balance*, or *true balance*, of the Cash account.

There are a variety of reasons for differences between the bank statement balance and the customer's cash balance. Here are some of the more usual ones:

• **Outstanding checks**   Checks that have been written but that have not yet been received for payment by the time the bank sends out its statement. The depositor, when writing out his or her checks, deducted the amounts from the Cash account in the company's books, which explains the difference.

Objective 1

Reconcile a bank statement.

- **Deposits in transit**   A deposit made after the bank statement was issued. Many accountants call this a *late deposit*. The depositor has naturally already added the amount to the Cash account in his or her books.
- **Service charge**   A bank charge for services rendered: for issuing checks, for collecting money, for receiving payment of notes turned over to it by the customer for collection, and for other such services. The bank notifies the depositor with a debit memorandum, and immediately deducts the fee from the balance of the bank account.
- **Collections**   When the bank acts as a collection agent for its customers by accepting payments on promissory notes, installment accounts, and charge accounts, it adds the proceeds to the customer's bank account and sends a credit memorandum to notify the customer of the transaction.
- **NSF (Not Sufficient Funds) checks**   When a bank customer deposits a check, she or he counts it as cash. Occasionally, however, a check is not paid (bounces), and then the bank notifies the customer. The customer must then make a deduction from the Cash account.
- **Errors**   In spite of internal control and systems designed to double-check against errors, sometimes either the customer or the bank makes a mistake. Often these errors do not become evident until the bank reconciliation is performed.

Steps in Reconciling the Bank Statement

Follow these steps in reconciling a bank statement:

1. **Canceled checks**   Compare the amount of each canceled check with the bank statement, and note any discrepancies. Also, on the stub that matches each canceled check, list the date of the bank statement. In some cases, a bank may not pay a check until one or two months after it was written. If a question arises as to whether or not you have paid a particular bill, you can look at the check stub. Next, you can refer directly to the bank statement to pick up the canceled check as proof of payment.
2. **Deposits**   Look over the deposits in transit, or unrecorded deposits listed on the bank reconciliation of the previous month. Compare these with the deposits listed on this month's bank statement. These deposits should all be accounted for; note any discrepancy. Now compare the remaining deposits listed on the current bank statement with deposits written in the firm's accounting records. Consider any deposits not shown on the bank statement as deposits in transit.
3. **Outstanding checks**   Next, arrange the canceled checks in the order of the check numbers. Look over the list of outstanding checks left over from the bank reconciliation of the previous month, and note the

checks that have now been returned. Compare each canceled check with the entry in the journal. If the journal is not available, then compare the canceled checks with the check stubs. In either case, use a check mark (√) to indicate that the check has been paid and that the amount is correct. To further verify that money has been sent to the right payee, review the endorsements on the backs of the checks. Any payments that have *not* been checked off, including the outstanding checks from the previous bank reconciliation, are the present outstanding checks. In other words, they were not presented for payment by the time of the cutoff date of the bank statement.

4. **Bank memorandums** Trace the credit memos and the debit memos to the journal. If the memos have not been recorded, make separate journal entries for them.

As you can see, a bank can be an accountant's best friend. A large firm should require that the reconciliation be prepared by an employee who is not involved in recording business transactions or in handling cash receipts and disbursements.

Examples of Bank Reconciliations

Let's go through the reconciliation process for two firms. First we'll take the case of A. R. Conolly and Company, then we'll look at East Phoenix Rental Equipment.

A. R. Conolly and Company The bank statement of A. R. Conolly and Company indicates a balance of $2,119 as of March 31. The balance of the Cash account in their ledger as of that date is $1,552. Conolly's accountant has taken the steps we've listed.

1. Verified that canceled checks were recorded correctly on the bank statement.
2. Noted the deposit made on March 31 that was not recorded on the bank statement, $762.
3. Noted outstanding checks: no. 921, $626; no. 985, $69; no. 986, $438.
4. Noted credit memo: note collected by the bank from S. Alden, $200, not recorded in the journal. Noted debit memo: collection charge and service charge not recorded in the journal, $4.

The bank reconciliation may be made on a separate sheet of paper or on the back of the bank statement, since some banks print the main headings on the form. Here are Conolly's bank reconciliation and journal entries. The items in the reconciliation that require journal entries are shown in color in Figure 8-6.

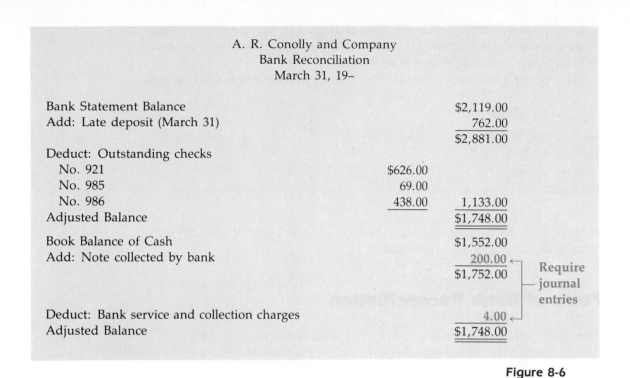

A. R. Conolly and Company
Bank Reconciliation
March 31, 19–

Bank Statement Balance		$2,119.00
Add: Late deposit (March 31)		762.00
		$2,881.00
Deduct: Outstanding checks		
No. 921	$626.00	
No. 985	69.00	
No. 986	438.00	1,133.00
Adjusted Balance		$1,748.00
Book Balance of Cash		$1,552.00
Add: Note collected by bank		200.00
		$1,752.00
Deduct: Bank service and collection charges		4.00
Adjusted Balance		$1,748.00

Require journal entries

Figure 8-6

Objective 2

Journalize the requisite entries directly from the bank reconciliation.

Note that journal entries should be based on the bank reconciliation, since the true balance of Cash is $1,748, whereas the current balance on the firm's books is $1,552. You can't change the balance of an account unless you first make a journal entry and then post the entry to the accounts involved. *Consequently, you have to make journal entries only from the book-balance-of-cash section of the bank reconciliation.* Debit additions to Cash and credit deductions from Cash. A. R. Conolly and Company records the entries in their general journal.

GENERAL JOURNAL PAGE _____

DATE		DESCRIPTION	POST. REF.	DEBIT	CREDIT
19– Mar.	31	Cash		2 0 0 00	
		Notes Receivable			2 0 0 00
		Non-interest-bearing note signed			
		by S. Alden was collected by			
		the bank.			
	31	Miscellaneous Expense		4 00	
		Cash			4 00
		Service charge and collection			
		charge levied by the bank.			

Here service charges and collection charges are recorded in the same account because the amounts are relatively small. However, some accountants use separate expense accounts.

After posting the above entries, the T account for Cash looks like this:

Cash

Balance	1,552	Mar. 31	4
Mar. 31	200		
	1,752		
Bal. 1,748			

Note that the balance in the T account is now equal to the adjusted balance on the bank reconciliation.

Form of Bank Reconciliation

Now that you have seen an example of a bank reconciliation, let's look at the standard form of a bank reconciliation for a hypothetical company.

Bank Statement Balance (last figure on the statement)		$4,000
Add		
Deposits in transit (late deposits already added to the Cash account)	$300	
Bank errors	20	320
		$4,320
Deduct		
Outstanding checks (they have already been deducted from the Cash account)	$960	
Bank errors	40	1,000
Adjusted balance (the true balance of Cash)		$3,320
Book Balance of Cash (the latest balance of the Cash account if it has been posted up to date; otherwise take the beginning balance of Cash, plus cash receipts and minus cash payments)		$2,850
Add		
Credit memos (additions by the bank not recorded in the Cash account, such as collections of notes)	$500	
Book errors (that understate balance)	40	540
		$3,390

Deduct

Debit memos (deductions by the bank not recorded in the Cash account, such as service charges or collection charges)	$ 20	
Book errors (that overstate balance)	50	70
Adjusted balance (the true balance of Cash)		$3,320

East Phoenix Rental Equipment The bank statement of East Phoenix Rental Equipment shows a final balance of $8,762 as of October 31 (see Figure 8-7). The present balance of the Cash account in the ledger, after East Phoenix's accountant has posted from the journal, is $7,806.50. The accountant took the following steps:

1. Verified that canceled checks were recorded correctly on the bank statement.
2. Discovered that a deposit of $1,003 made on October 31 was not recorded on the bank statement.

Figure 8-7

East Phoenix Rental Equipment
Bank Reconciliation
October 31, 19–

Bank Statement Balance		$8,762.00
Add: Late deposit (October 31)		1,003.00
		$9,765.00
Deduct: Outstanding checks		
No. 1916	$461.00	
No. 2022	119.00	
No. 2023	827.00	
No. 2024	67.00	1,474.00
Adjusted Balance		$8,291.00
Book Balance of Cash		$7,806.50
Add: Note collected (principal $600.00, interest $6.00, Ryan Plumbing and Heating)	$606.00 ←	
Error in recording Check No. 2001 payable to Mahon, Inc.	9.00 ←	615.00
		$8,421.50
Deduct: Bank service and collection charges	$ 5.50 ←	
NSF check from C. M. Lang Company	125.00 ←	130.50
Adjusted Balance		$8,291.00

Require journal entries

3. Noted outstanding checks: no. 1916, $461; no. 2022, $119; no. 2023, $827; no. 2024, $67.
4. Noted that a credit memo for a note collected by the bank from Ryan Plumbing and Heating, $600 principal plus $6 interest, was not recorded in the journal.
5. Found that check no. 2001 for $523, payable to Mahon, Inc., on account was recorded in the journal as $532. (The correct amount is $523.)
6. Noted that a debit memo for a collection charge and service charge of $5.50 was not recorded in the journal.
7. Noted that debit memo for an NSF check for $125 from C. M. Lang Company was not recorded.

Look at Figure 8-7 to see how each step relates to the bank reconciliation.

The accountant has to make the journal entries shown in Figure 8-8 in order to change the Cash account from the present balance of $7,806.50 to the true balance of $8,291. Again, those items that require journal entries are highlighted in Figures 8-7 and 8-8.

A bank reconciliation form is ordinarily printed on the back of the bank statement. In a typical form, it is assumed that the adjusted balance of the book-balance-of-cash section has already been determined. Conse-

Figure 8-8

GENERAL JOURNAL PAGE _____

DATE		DESCRIPTION	POST. REF.	DEBIT	CREDIT
19– Oct.	31	Cash		6 0 6 00	
		Notes Receivable			6 0 0 00
		Interest Income			6 00
		Bank collected note signed by			
		Ryan Plumbing and Heating.			
	31	Cash		9 00	
		Accounts Payable			9 00
		Error in recording check no.			
		2001 payable to Mahon, Inc.			
	31	Miscellaneous Expense		5 50	
		Cash			5 50
		Bank service charge and			
		collection charge.			
	31	Accounts Receivable		1 2 5 00	
		Cash			1 2 5 00
		NSF check received from			
		C. M. Lang.			

THIS FORM IS PROVIDED TO HELP YOU BALANCE YOUR BANK STATEMENT

CHECKS OUTSTANDING—NOT CHARGED TO ACCOUNT			
No. 1916	$	461	00
2022		119	00
2023		827	00
2024		67	00
TOTAL	$	1,474	00

BEFORE YOU START—

PLEASE BE SURE YOU HAVE ENTERED IN YOUR CHECKBOOK ALL AUTOMATIC TRANSACTIONS SHOWN ON THE FRONT OF YOUR STATEMENT.

YOU SHOULD HAVE ADDED IF ANY OCCURRED:
1. Loan advances.
2. Credit memos.
3. Other automatic deposits.

YOU SHOULD HAVE SUBTRACTED IF ANY OCCURRED:
1. Automatic loan payments.
2. Automatic savings transfers.
3. Service charges.
4. Debit memos.
5. Other automatic deductions and payments.

BANK BALANCE SHOWN ON THIS STATEMENT $ 8,762.00

ADD
DEPOSITS NOT SHOWN ON THIS STATEMENT (IF ANY) $ 1,003.00

TOTAL $ 9,765.00

SUBTRACT—
► CHECKS OUTSTANDING $ 1,474.00

BALANCE $ 8,291.00

SHOULD AGREE WITH YOUR CHECKBOOK BALANCE AFTER DEDUCTING SERVICE CHARGE (IF ANY) SHOWN ON THIS STATEMENT.

Please examine immediately and report if incorrect. If no reply is received within 15 days the account will be considered correct.

Figure 8-9

Bank reconciliation form

quently, the bank form only provides for calculating the adjusted bank statement balance of the bank-statement section of the bank reconciliation. The bank form for East Phoenix Rental Equipment is shown in Figure 8-9.

THE PETTY CASH FUND

Day after day, business firms are confronted with transactions involving small immediate payments, such as the cost of a telegram, delivery charges, postage due for mail, or a new typewriter ribbon. If the firm had to go through the usual procedure of making all payments by check, the time consumed would be frustrating and the whole process unduly expensive. For many firms, the cost of writing each check is more than $.50; this includes the cost of an employee's time in writing and reconciling the check. Suppose the mail carrier is at the door with a letter on which there is $.20 postage due. To write a check would be ridiculous. It only makes sense to pay in cash, out of the **Petty Cash Fund.** *Petty* means small; so the firm sets a maximum amount that can be paid out of petty cash. Payments that exceed this maximum must be processed by regular check through the journal.

Establishing the Petty Cash Fund

After the firm has decided on the maximum amount of a payment from petty cash, the next step is to estimate how much cash will be needed during a given period of time, such as a month. Small payments are made during the month from the petty cash fund.

It is also important to consider the element of security when keeping cash in the office. If risk is great, the amount kept in the fund should be small, and the fund should be reimbursed at intervals of perhaps one or two weeks.

East Phoenix Rental Equipment decided to establish a petty cash fund of $50 and put it under the control of the secretary. Accordingly, their accountant writes a check, cashes it at the bank, and records this transaction in the journal as follows.

Objective 3

Journalize entries to establish and reimburse Petty Cash Fund.

		GENERAL JOURNAL				PAGE _____	
DATE		DESCRIPTION	POST. REF.	DEBIT		CREDIT	
19— Sep.	1	*Petty Cash Fund*		5 0 00			
		Cash				5 0 00	
		Established a petty cash fund.					

T accounts for the entry look like this:

Petty Cash Fund			Cash	
+	−		+	−
50				50

Because the Petty Cash Fund is an asset account, it is listed in the balance sheet immediately below Cash. Remember: **The Petty Cash Fund account is debited only once, and this happens when the fund is established initially.**

There is only one exception: When the original amount is not large enough to handle the necessary transactions, the accountant has to make the Petty Cash Fund bigger—maybe change the $50 to $75. But, barring such a change in the size of the fund, Petty Cash is debited only once.

After the accountant cashes that original $50 check, he or she converts it into convenient **denominations,** such as quarters and dimes, and one and five dollar bills. Then the accountant puts the money in a locked drawer in the secretary's desk, telling the secretary not to pay anything larger than $5 out of petty cash.

Payments from the Petty Cash Fund

The secretary now takes the responsibility for the petty cash fund; he or she is designated as the only person who can make payments from it. In case of his or her illness, some other employee should be named as stand-in. A **petty cash voucher** must be used to account for every payment from the fund. The voucher constitutes a receipt signed by the person who authorized the payment and by the person receiving payment. Thus, even for small payments of $5 or less, there would have to be collusion between the payee and the secretary for any theft to occur. Figure 8-10 shows what a petty cash voucher looks like.

Objective 4

Complete petty cash vouchers and petty cash payments records.

Reimbursement of the Petty Cash Fund

When the fund is nearly exhausted, for example at month end, the accountant reimburses the fund for expenditures made to bring the fund back up to the original amount. Consequently, it may be considered to be

Figure 8-10

PETTY CASH VOUCHER

No. *1*   Date *September 2, 19–*

Paid to *Excell Delivery Service* $ *2.00*

For *Delivery*

Account *Delivery Expense*

Approved by   Payment received by

R. Jason   *C J Comstock*

a revolving fund. If the amount initially put in the Petty Cash Fund is $50 and at the end of the month only $4 is left, the accountant puts $46 in the fund as a reimbursement, thereby bringing it back up to $50 to start the new month.

For example, take voucher no. 1 (shown in Figure 8-10), in which $2 is charged to Delivery Expense. Let's say that, as the month goes by, $12 more is charged to Delivery Expense on other petty cash vouchers. Assume that the total amount spent from the fund during the month for all purposes is $43. At the end of the month, the accountant makes a summarizing entry, debiting the accounts recorded on the petty cash vouchers and crediting Cash. For this month, she or he debits Delivery Expense for $14, debits other accounts for $29, and credits Cash for $43. By doing this, she or he officially journalizes the transactions so that they can be posted to the proper ledger accounts. The accountant then writes a check for $43 payable to Cash, cashes it, and has the secretary put the money in the drawer, bringing the fund back up to the original $50.

Some firms prefer to have a written record on one sheet of paper, so they keep a **petty cash payments record,** with columns in the Distribution of Payments section labeled with the types of expenditures they make most often.

East Phoenix Rental Equipment made the following payments from its petty cash fund during September.

Sep.   2 Paid $2 to Excell Delivery Service, voucher no. 1.
       3 Bought pencils and pens, $3.20, voucher no. 2.
       5 Paid local newspaper for advertising, $5, voucher no. 3.
       7 Paid for mailing packages, $2.90, voucher no. 4.
      10 Eugene L. Madison, the owner, withdrew $5 for personal use, voucher no. 5.
      14 Postage due on incoming mail, $.16, voucher no. 6.
      21 Bought typewriter ribbons, $4.10, voucher no. 7.
      22 Paid $3 to Excell Delivery Service, voucher no. 8.
      26 Paid for mailing packages, $3.80, voucher no. 9.
      27 Paid $3.50 to Fast Way Delivery, voucher no. 10.
      29 Bought memo pads, $4.40, voucher no. 11.
      29 Paid for collect telegram, $2.60, voucher no. 12.
      30 Paid $3.20 to Excell Delivery Service, voucher no. 13.
      30 Paid for having windows cleaned, $5, voucher no. 14.

East Phoenix Rental Equipment uses a petty cash payments record to keep track of the payments according to purpose. This is only a supplementary record, *not* a journal. It is merely used as a basis for compiling the journal entry to reimburse the fund. At the end of the month the accountant makes the summarizing entry in order to officially journalize the transactions that have taken place. He or she takes the information directly from the petty cash payments record (shown in Figure 8-11 on the next two pages). The T accounts and the journal entry are shown below on this page.

   Note that in the summarizing entry the accountant debits the accounts on whose behalf the payments were made and credits the Cash account. He or she leaves the Petty Cash Fund strictly alone. Then the accountant cashes a check for $47.86 and puts the cash in the secretary's desk drawer, thereby restoring the amount in the Petty Cash Fund to the original $50.

	DATE	DESCRIPTION	POST. REF.	DEBIT	CREDIT	
			GENERAL JOURNAL		PAGE _____	
1	19– Sep. 30	Office Supplies		1 1 70		1
2		Delivery Expense		1 8 40		2
3		Miscellaneous Expense		7 76		3
4		Advertising Expense		5 00		4
5		Eugene L. Madison, Drawing		5 00		5
6		Cash			4 7 86	6
7		Reimbursed the petty cash fund.				7
8						8

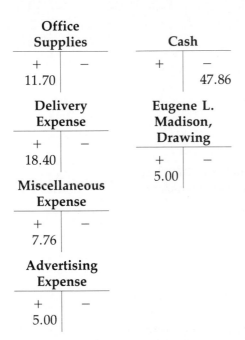

PETTY CASH PAYMENTS RECORD
Month of September 19–

	DATE	VOU. NO.	EXPLANATION	PAYMENTS	
1	Sep. 1		Established fund, check no. 88, $50		
2	2	1	Excell Delivery Service	2	00
3	3	2	Pencils and pens	3	20
4	5	3	Local newspaper	5	00
5	7	4	Postage for mailings	2	90
6	10	5	Eugene L. Madison	5	00
7	14	6	Postage on incoming mail		16
8	21	7	Typewriter ribbons	4	10
9	22	8	Excell Delivery Service	3	00
10	26	9	Postage for mailings	3	80
11	27	10	Fast Way Delivery	3	50
12	29	11	Memo pads	4	40
13	29	12	Collect telegram	2	60
14	30	13	Excell Delivery Service	3	20
15	30	14	Cleaning windows	5	00
16	30		Totals	4 7	86
17			Balance in Fund $ 2.14		
18			Reimbursed check no. 136 47.86		
19			Total $50.00		
20					

THE CHANGE FUND

Anyone who has ever tried to pay for a small item by handing the clerk a $20 bill knows that a firm that carries out numerous cash transactions needs a **Change Fund.**

Establishing the Change Fund

Before setting up a change fund, one has to decide on two things: (1) how much money needs to be in the fund, and (2) what denominations of bills and coins are needed. Like the Petty Cash Fund, **the Change Fund is debited only once: when it is established.** It is left at the initial figure unless the person in charge decides to make it larger. The Change Fund account, like the Petty Cash account, is an asset. It is recorded in the balance sheet immediately below Cash. If the Petty Cash account is larger than the Change Fund account, it precedes the Change Fund.

Figure 8-11

PAGE _1_

OFFICE SUPPLIES	DELIVERY EXPENSE	MISCELLANEOUS EXPENSE	SUNDRY ACCOUNT	AMOUNT	
					1
	2 00				2
3 20					3
			Advertising Expense	5 00	4
	2 90				5
			E. L. Madison, Drawing	5 00	6
		16			7
4 10					8
	3 00				9
	3 80				10
	3 50				11
4 40					12
		2 60			13
	3 20				14
		5 00			15
11 70	18 40	7 76		10 00	16
					17
					18
					19
					20

The owner of East Phoenix Rental Equipment, Mr. Madison, decides to establish a change fund; he decides this at the same time he sets up his petty cash fund. The entries for both transactions look like this.

Objective 5

Journalize the entries to establish a Change Fund.

GENERAL JOURNAL

PAGE _____

	DATE		DESCRIPTION	POST. REF.	DEBIT	CREDIT	
1	19– Sep.	1	Petty Cash Fund		5 0 00		1
2			Cash			5 0 00	2
3			Established a petty cash fund.				3
4							4
5		1	Change Fund		1 0 0 00		5
6			Cash			1 0 0 00	6
7			Established a change fund.				7
8							8

The T accounts for establishing the fund are as follows.

Change Fund			Cash	
+	−		+	−
100				100

So Madison cashes a check for $100 and gets the money in several denominations. He is now prepared to make change in any normal business transactions.

Depositing Cash

At the end of each business day, Madison deposits the cash taken in during the day, but he holds back the amount of the Change Fund, being sure that it's in convenient denominations.

When he makes up the Change Fund depends on what time his shop closes for the day and what time the bank closes. Let's say that on September 1, East Phoenix Rental Equipment has $325 on hand at the end of the day.

$325 Total cash count
− 100 Change fund
$225 New cash

The T accounts look like this.

Cash			Rental Income	
+	−		−	+
225				225

Madison records this in the journal as follows.

	DATE		DESCRIPTION	POST. REF.	DEBIT	CREDIT	
1	19– Sep.	1	Cash		2 2 5 00		1
2			Rental Income			2 2 5 00	2
3			To record revenue earned during				3
4			the day.				4
5							5

GENERAL JOURNAL   PAGE _____

Now recall that the amount of the cash deposit is the total cash count less the amount of the Change Fund, so that's how the deposit happens to be $225. On another day the cash count is $327. So Madison deposits $227; the deposit is shown below.

	DATE		DESCRIPTION	POST. REF.	DEBIT	CREDIT	
			GENERAL JOURNAL			PAGE _____	
1	19– Sep.	9	Cash		2 2 7 00		1
2			Rental Income			2 2 7 00	2
3			To record revenue earned during				3
4			the day.				4
5							5

Some business firms label the Cash account *Cash in Bank* and label the Change Fund *Cash on Hand*.

CASH SHORT AND OVER

There is an inherent danger in making change: Human beings make mistakes, especially when there are many customers to be waited on or when the business is temporarily short-handed. Ideally, mistakes should be eliminated. However, because mistakes do happen, accounting records must be set up to cope with the situation. One reason that a business uses a cash register is to detect mistakes in the handling of cash. If, after removing the change fund, the day's receipts are less than the machine reading, then a cash shortage exists. Conversely, when the day's receipts are greater than the machine reading, a cash overage exists. Both shortages and overages are recorded in the same account, which is called Cash Short and Over. (The Cash Short and Over account may also be used to handle shortages and overages in the Petty Cash Fund.) Shortages are considered to be an expense of operating a business and, therefore, are recorded on the debit side of the account. Overages are treated as another form of revenue and so are recorded on the credit side of the account.

Objective 6

Journalize transactions involving Cash Short and Over.

For example, let's say that on September 14 East Phoenix Rental Equipment is faced with the following situation.

Cash Register Tape	Cash Count	Amount of the Change Fund
$281	$378	$100

After deducting the $100 in the Change Fund, Madison will deposit $278. Note that this amount is less than the amount indicated by the cash register; therefore, a cash shortage exists. The following T accounts show how Madison entered this transaction into the books.

Cash		Rental Income		Cash Short and Over	
+	−	−	+		
278			281	3	

The next day, September 15, the pendulum happens to swing in the other direction.

Cash Register Tape	Cash Count	Amount of the Change Fund
$356	$457	$100

The amount to be deposited is $357 ($457 − $100). This figure is $1 greater than the $356 in rental income indicated by the cash register tape. Thus, there is a $1 cash overage on this occasion. The analysis of this transaction is shown below in T accounts.

Cash		Rental Income		Cash Short and Over	
+	−	−	+		
357			356		1

Now let's summarize our discussion of the Cash Short and Over account by drawing these conclusions from the illustration.

1. At the close of the business day, the firm deposits the total day's receipts, holding back the Change Fund.
2. The firm records its rental income as being the amount shown on the cash register tape.
3. If the amount of cash actually received disagrees with the record of receipts, Cash Short and Over takes up the difference. In the first situation just described, there was a shortage of $3, so there was a debit to Cash Short and Over. In the second situation, there was an overage of $1, so there was a credit to Cash Short and Over. It is apparent that as a result of these transactions the account looks like this.

Cash Short and Over	
Shortage 3	Overage 1

East Phoenix Rental Equipment's revenue for September 14 and 15 is recorded in the general journal (Figure 8-12) as follows:

Figure 8-12

	DATE		DESCRIPTION	POST. REF.	DEBIT		CREDIT		
1	19– Sep.	14	Cash		2 7 8 00				1
2			Cash Short and Over		3 00				2
3			Rental Income				2 8 1 00		3
4			To record revenue earned during						4
5			the day involving a cash						5
6			shortage of $3.00.						6
7									7
8		15	Cash		3 5 7 00				8
9			Rental Income				3 5 6 00		9
10			Cash Short and Over				1 00		10
11			To record revenue earned during						11
12			the day involving a cash						12
13			overage of $1.00.						13
14									14

GENERAL JOURNAL — PAGE ____

As far as errors are concerned, one would think that shortages would be offset by overages. However, customers receiving change are more likely to report shortages than overages. Consequently, to the firm shortages predominate. A firm may set a tolerance level for the cashiers. If the shortages consistently exceed the level of tolerance, either fraud is considered or somebody is making entirely too many careless mistakes.

Throughout any fiscal period, the accountant must continually record shortages and overages in the Cash Short and Over account. Let's say that East Phoenix's final balance is $21 on the debit side. East Phoenix winds up with a net shortage of $21.

At the end of the fiscal period, if the account has a debit balance or net shortage, the accountant classifies it as an expense and puts it in the income statement under Miscellaneous Expense. The T account would look like this.

Cash Short and Over

Short		Over	
	3		1
	4		1
	3		2
	7		2
	5		1
	2		2
	3		1
	4		10
	31		
Bal. 21			

Conversely, if the account has a credit balance or net overage, the accountant classifies it as a revenue account and puts it in the income statement under Miscellaneous Income. This is an exception to the policy of recording accounts under their exact account title in financial statements. Rather than attaching plus and minus signs to the Cash Short and Over account immediately, we wait until we find out its final balance.

GLOSSARY

ABA number The number assigned by the American Bankers Association to a given bank. The first part of the numerator denotes the city or state in which the bank is located; the second part denotes the bank on which the check is drawn. The denominator indicates the Federal Reserve District and the routing number used by the Federal Reserve Bank.

Bank reconciliation A process by which an accountant determines whether there is a difference between the balance shown on the bank statement and the balance of the Cash account in the firm's general ledger. The object is to determine the adjusted (or true) balance of the Cash account.

Bank statement Periodic statement that a bank sends to the holder of a checking account listing deposits received and checks paid by the bank, as well as debit and credit memorandums.

Book balance The balance of the Cash account in the general ledger before it is reconciled with the bank statement.

Canceled checks Checks issued by the depositor that have been paid by the bank and listed on the bank statement. They are called canceled checks because they are canceled by a stamp or perforation, indicating that they have been paid.

Cash fund Sums of money set aside for specific purposes.

Change fund A cash fund used by a firm to make change for customers who pay cash for goods or services.

Check writer A machine used to imprint the amount in figures and words on the check itself.

Denominations Varieties of currency and coins, such as $5 bills, $1 bills, quarters, dimes, and nickels.

Deposit in transit A deposit not recorded on the bank statement because the deposit was made between the time of the bank's closing date for compiling items for its statement and the time the statement is received by the depositor; also known as a *late deposit*.

Deposit slips Printed forms provided by a bank so that a customer can list all items being deposited; also known as a *deposit ticket*.

Endorsement The process by which the payee transfers ownership of the check to a bank or another party. A check must be endorsed when deposited in a bank because the bank must have legal title to it in order to collect payment from the drawer of the check (the person or firm who wrote the check). In case the check cannot be collected, the endorser guarantees all subsequent holders (*Exception:* an endorsement "without recourse").

MICR Magnetic ink character recognition; the script the bank uses to print the number of the depositor's account and the bank's number at the bottom of checks and deposit slips. The bank also prints the amount of the check in MICR when the check is deposited. A number written in this script can be read by electronic equipment used by banks in clearing checks.

NSF check A check drawn against an account in which there are *Not Sufficient Funds:* this check is returned by the depositor's bank to the drawer's bank because of nonpayment; also known as a *dishonored check.*

Outstanding checks Checks that have been issued by the depositor and deducted on his or her records but have not reached the bank for payment and deduction by the time the bank issues its statement.

Payee The person to whom a check is payable.

Petty Cash Fund A cash fund used to make small immediate cash payments.

Petty cash payments record A record indicating the amount of each petty cash voucher and the accounts to which they should be charged.

Petty cash voucher A form stating who got what from the Petty Cash Fund, signed by (1) the person in charge of the fund, and (2) the person who received the cash.

Restrictive endorsement An endorsement, such as "Pay to the order of (name of bank), for deposit only," that limits further negotiation of a check. It forces the check's deposit, since the endorsement is not valid for any other purpose.

Service charge The fee the bank charges for handling checks, collections, and other items. It is in the form of a debit memorandum.

Signature card The form a depositor signs to give the bank a sample of his or her signature. The bank uses it to verify the depositor's signature on checks, on cash items that he or she may endorse for deposit, and on other business papers that he or she may present to the bank.

QUESTIONS, EXERCISES, AND PROBLEMS

Discussion Questions

1. What is the purpose of a signature card?
2. What is the purpose of a bank reconciliation?
3. Indicate whether the following items in a bank reconciliation should be (a) added to the cash account balance, (b) deducted from the cash account balance, (c) added to the bank statement balance, (d) deducted from the bank statement balance.

- Deposit in transit
- NSF check
- Outstanding check
- Bank error charging the firm's account with another company's check

4. Describe in order the steps in reconciling a bank statement.
5. Explain the purpose of a petty cash fund. Describe the entries to establish and reimburse the fund.

6. What is the purpose of a petty cash payments record?
7. What does a debit balance in Cash Short and Over represent? Where does it appear in the financial statements? What does a credit balance in Cash Short and Over represent? Where does it appear in the financial statements?

Exercises

Exercise 8-1 Tiny's Restaurant deposits all receipts in the bank on the day received and makes all payments by check. On September 30, the Cash account showed a balance of $443 after all posting was completed. The bank statement received on September 30 had an ending balance of $301. Prepare a bank reconciliation, using the following information, and record the necessary entries in general journal form.

a. The bank included with the September canceled checks a $2 debit memorandum for service charges.
b. Outstanding checks, $194.
c. The September 30 cash receipts, $316, were placed in the bank's night depository after banking hours on that date and were not listed on the bank statement.
d. Check no. 928, returned with the canceled checks, was correctly drawn for $31 in payment of the electric bill and was paid by the bank on September 16, but it had been erroneously recorded in the checkbook and debited to the Utilities Expense account as though it were $13.

Exercise 8-2 The Hinman Company made the following bank reconciliation on April 30 of this year. Record the necessary entries in general journal form.

Bank Reconciliation

Bank Statement Balance		$1,856.00
Add deposit of April 30		145.00
		$2,001.00
Deduct outstanding checks		
No. 191	$200.00	
No. 192	150.00	350.00
Adjusted Balance		$1,651.00
Book Balance of Cash		$1,380.00
Add proceeds of note collected		300.00
		$1,680.00
Deduct: NSF check of Thomas Baxter	$ 27.00	
Collection charge for note	2.00	29.00
Adjusted Balance		$1,651.00

Exercise 8-3 Identify each of the following reconciling items as: (1) an addition to the bank statement balance, (2) a deduction from the bank statement balance, (3) an addition to the book balance of cash, (4) a deduction from the book balance of cash. (None of the transactions reported by bank debit and credit memorandums have been recorded by the depositor.)

a. Check for $100 charged by bank as $1,000.
b. Deposit in transit, $673.15.
c. Outstanding checks, $617.23.
d. Note collected by bank, $525.
e. Check of a customer returned by bank to depositor because of insufficient funds, $31.
f. Bank service charge, $9.20.
g. Check drawn by depositor for $23 but recorded in the checkbook and Cash account as $32.

Exercise 8-4 Make entries in general journal form to record the following.

a. Established a Petty Cash Fund, $80.
b. Reimbursed the Petty Cash Fund for expenditures of $69: store supplies, $21; office supplies, $18; miscellaneous expense, $30.

Exercise 8-5 Make entries in general journal form to record the following.

a. Established a Change Fund, $250.
b. Record the cash sales for the day; the cash in the cash register is $862.

Exercise 8-6 The cash register tape for today indicates $961.16 as sales for the day. The cash count, including a $200 Change Fund, is $1,160.22. Make entries to record how much cash you will deposit in the bank today.

Exercise 8-7 Describe the nature of the entries that have been posted to the following accounts after the Change Fund was established.

Change Fund		Sales		Cash		Cash Short and Over	
Bal. 200			946	944		2	1
			998	999		3	
			1,069	1,066			

Exercise 8-8 The Vaughn Company's Cash account shows a balance of $6,978 as of October 31 of this year. The balance on the bank statement on that date is $10,127.04. Checks for $123, $1,062, and $221.20 are outstanding. The bank statement shows a charge for a check made out by another depositor for $250. The statement also shows a credit of $2,000 for a customer's note that had been left with the bank for collection. Service charges for the month were $7.16. What is the true balance of cash as of October 31?

Problem Set A

Problem 8-1A Marge's Clothes and Things deposits all receipts in the bank and makes all payments by check. On September 30 its Cash in Bank account has a balance of $3,073.60. The bank statement on September 30 shows a balance of $3,321.29. You are given the following information with which to reconcile the bank statement.

a. The reconciliation for August, the previous month, showed three checks outstanding on August 31: no. 786 for $71.50, no. 789 for $117.60, and no. 790 for $49.43. Checks no. 786 and 789 were returned with the September bank statement; however, check no. 790 was not returned.
b. A deposit of $398.36 was placed in the night depository on September 30 and did not appear on the bank statement.
c. Checks no. 801 for $31, no. 803 for $18.40, no. 804 for $103, and no. 805 for $15.62 were written during September but were not returned by the bank.
d. A bank debit memo for service charges, $2.40.
e. A bank credit memo for collection of a note signed by Franklin C. Hough, $404, including $400 principal and $4 interest.
f. You compare the canceled checks with the entries in the check register and find that check no. 797 for $69 was written correctly, payable to M. E. Francis, the owner, for her personal use. However, the check was recorded in the checkbook as $96.

Instructions

1. Prepare a bank reconciliation.
2. Journalize the necessary entries in general journal form, assuming that the debit and credit memos have not been recorded.

Problem 8-2A On April 1 of this year, the Nordic Ski Shop established a Petty Cash Fund, and the following petty cash transactions took place during the month.

Apr. 1 Cashed check no. 1116 for $60 to establish a Petty Cash Fund and put the $60 in a locked drawer in the office.
    4 Issued voucher no. 1 for telegram, $3 (Miscellaneous Expense).
    7 Issued voucher no. 2 for typewriter ribbons, $4.90.
    9 Paid $4.50 for an advertisement in college basketball program, voucher no. 3.
   16 Bought postage stamps, $4, voucher no. 4 (Office Supplies).
   20 Paid $4.90 to have snow removed from sidewalk in front of store, voucher no. 5 (Miscellaneous Expense).
   25 Issued voucher no. 6 for delivery charge on outgoing merchandise, $2.40.
   28 L. R. Francis, the owner, withdrew $5 for personal use, voucher no. 7.
   29 Paid $1.60 for telegram, voucher no. 8.

Apr. 30 Paid Reliable Delivery Service $4.20 for delivery charges on outgoing merchandise, voucher no. 9.

30 Issued and cashed check no. 1304 for $34.50 to reimburse Petty Cash Fund.

Instructions

1. Journalize the entry establishing the Petty Cash Fund in the general journal.
2. Record the disbursements of petty cash in the petty cash payments record.
3. Journalize the summarizing entry to reimburse the Petty Cash Fund.

Problem 8-3A   During May of this year, the Eastside Cycle Shop has the following transactions involving its Change Fund, its Cash Short and Over account, and its cash sales.

May   1 Established a Change Fund, $200, check no. 714.

6 Recorded cash sales for the week: cash register tape, $1,291; cash count, $1,490.25.

13 Recorded cash sales for the week: cash register tape, $1,424.30; cash count, $1,622.10.

20 Recorded cash sales for the week: cash register tape, $1,378.25; cash count, $1,579.15.

31 Recorded cash sales for the week: cash register tape, $1,813.28; cash count, $2,009.74.

Instructions

1. Record the entry establishing the Change Fund in the general journal.
2. Record the cash sales in the general journal. (In making deposits, the firm holds back the amount of the Change Fund.)
3. Post the appropriate entries to the Cash Short and Over ledger account. Where will the balance of this account appear in the income statement?

Problem 8-4A   On July 31, Riverside Inn receives its bank statement (next page). The company deposits its receipts in the bank and makes all payments by check. The debit memo is for a $37 NSF check written by Thomas R. Beeler. The other debit memo is for a service charge.

The balance of the Cash account as of July 31 is $1,446.82. Outstanding checks as of July 31 are: no. 1631, $110; no. 1632, $71.19; no. 1633, $163.20. The accountant notes a deposit of $165.69 that did not appear on the bank statement.

Instructions

1. Prepare a bank reconciliation as of July 31.
2. Journalize the necessary entries, assuming that the debit memos have not been recorded.
3. Complete the bank form to determine the adjusted balance of cash.

Riverside Inn
8619 East Castle Blvd.
Chicago, Illinois 60611

ACCOUNT NO.: 761-142-786
STATEMENT DATE: July 31, 19–

Checks and Other Debits		Deposits	Date		Balance	
	Balance Brought Forward		July	1	1,163	16
72 50	167 00	491 50		3	1,415	16
137 20				5	1,277	96
236 25	159 89	415 72		6	1,297	54
120 00				8	1,177	54
429 60		439 16		9	1,187	10
		378 20		11	1,565	30
37 40	38 49			12	1,489	41
		291 76		15	1,781	17
182 71	368 70			17	1,229	76
96 87		142 90		18	1,275	79
DM 37 00				22	1,238	79
19 20				25	1,219	59
DM 3 10		368 93		28	1,585	42

PLEASE EXAMINE THIS STATEMENT CAREFULLY. REPORT ANY POSSIBLE ERRORS IN 10 DAYS.

CODE SYMBOLS

CM   Credit Memo
DM   Debit Memo
EC   Error Correction

OD   Overdraft
SC   Service Charge

Problem Set B

Problem 8-1B   Hagen's Western Store deposits all receipts in the bank each evening and makes all payments by check. On November 30 its Cash in Bank account has a balance of $1,967.65. The bank statement of November 30 shows a balance of $1,920.25. The following information pertains to reconciling the bank statement.

a. The reconciliation for October, the previous month, showed three checks outstanding on October 31: no. 1416 for $85, no. 1419 for $76.50, and no. 1420 for $126. Checks no. 1416 and 1420 were returned with the November bank statement; however, check no. 1419 was not returned.

b. Checks no. 1499 for $39, no. 1516 for $21.60, no. 1517 for $101.50, and no. 1518 for $17 were written during November and have not been returned by the bank.

c. A deposit of $410 was placed in the night depository on November 30 and did not appear on the bank statement.

d. The canceled checks were compared with the entries in the check register, and it was observed that check no. 1487, for $78, was written correctly, payable to C. T. Melton, the owner, for personal use, but was recorded in the checkbook as $87.

e. A bank debit memo for service charges, $3.

f. A bank credit memo for collection of a note signed by T. R. Salmon, $101, including $100 principal and $1 interest.

Instructions

1. Prepare a bank reconciliation.
2. Journalize the necessary entries in general journal form, assuming that the debit and credit memos have not been recorded.

Problem 8-2B On March 1 of this year, Bolen Janitorial Supply Company established a Petty Cash Fund. The following petty cash transactions took place during the month.

Mar.   1 Cashed check no. 956 for $50 to establish a Petty Cash Fund and put the $50 in a locked drawer in the office.

3 Bought postage stamps, $4, voucher no. 1 (Office Supplies).

4 Issued voucher no. 2 for telegram, $2 (Miscellaneous Expense).

6 Issued voucher no. 3 for delivery charges on outgoing merchandise, $5.

9 B. W. Bolen withdrew $4.50 for personal use, voucher no. 4.

13 Bought postage stamps, $5, voucher no. 5.

19 Bought pens for office, $4.90, voucher no. 6.

23 Paid $3 for trash removal, voucher no. 7 (Miscellaneous Expense).

28 Paid $5 for window cleaning service, voucher no. 8.

29 Paid $1.50 for telegram, voucher no. 9.

31 Issued and cashed check no. 1098 for $34.90 to reimburse Petty Cash Fund.

Instructions

1. Journalize the entry establishing the Petty Cash Fund in the general journal.
2. Record the disbursements of petty cash in the petty cash payments record.
3. Journalize the summarizing entry to reimburse the Petty Cash Fund.

Problem 8-3B Henry's Drive-In made the following transactions during July involving its Change Fund, its Cash Short and Over account, and its cash sales.

Jul.   1 Established a Change Fund, $300, check no. 986.

7 Recorded cash sales for the week: cash register tape, $1,546; cash count, $1,842.35.

14 Recorded cash sales for the week: cash register tape, $1,214.10; cash count, $1,511.

21 Recorded cash sales for the week: cash register tape, $1,482; cash count, $1,783.25.

31 Recorded cash sales for the remainder of the month: cash register tape, $1,892; cash count, $2,188.50.

Instructions

1. Record the entry establishing the Change Fund in the general journal.
2. Record the cash sales in the general journal. (In making bank deposits, the firm holds back the amount of the Change Fund.)
3. Post the appropriate entries to the Cash Short and Over ledger account. Where will the balance of this account appear in the income statement?

Problem 8-4B   On August 31, Frank's Auto Repair receives its bank statement (next page). The company deposits its receipts in the bank and makes all payments by check. The debit memo for $49 is for an NSF check written by D. Carter. The debit memo for $2 is for a service charge.

The balance of the Cash account as of August 31 is $1,247. Outstanding checks as of August 31 are: no. 928, $119; no. 929, $243. The accountant notes a deposit of $224 that did not appear on the bank statement.

Instructions

1. Prepare a bank reconciliation as of August 31.
2. Journalize the necessary entries, assuming that the debit memos have not been recorded.
3. Complete the bank form to determine the adjusted balance of cash.

PARAMOUNT NATIONAL BANK

Frank's Auto Repair
3152 East Senegal Ave.
Toledo, Ohio 44366

ACCOUNT NO.: 168-652-219

STATEMENT DATE: August 31, 19–

CHECKS AND OTHER DEBITS				DEPOSITS	DATE		BALANCE	
			BALANCE BROUGHT FORWARD		Aug.	1	972	00
				326 00		2	1298	00
172	00	76	00			4	1050	00
146	00			412 00		5	1316	00
206	00	139	00			7	971	00
200	00					8	771	00
621	00			437 00		9	587	00
				368 00		14	955	00
37	00	14	00			17	904	00
				419 00		18	1323	00
533	00					23	790	00
				398 00		24	1188	00
94	00			291 00		28	1385	00
DM 49	00	DM 2	00			31	1334	00

PLEASE EXAMINE THIS STATEMENT CAREFULLY. REPORT ANY POSSIBLE ERRORS IN 10 DAYS.

CODE SYMBOLS

CM Credit Memo
DM Debit Memo
EC Error Correction

OD Overdraft
SC Service Charge

9 Payroll Accounting: Employee Earnings and Deductions

Learning Objectives

After you have completed this chapter, you will be able to do the following:

1. Calculate total earnings based on an hourly, piece-rate, or commission basis.

2. Determine deductions from tables of employees' income tax withholding.

3. Complete a payroll register.

4. Journalize the payroll entry from a payroll register.

5. Maintain employees' individual earnings records.

Up to now, we've been recording employees' wages as a debit to Salaries or Wages Expense and a credit to Cash, but we've really been talking only about **gross pay.** We haven't said a word about the various deductions that we all know are taken out of our gross pay before we get to the **net pay** or take-home pay. In this chapter we'll be talking about types and amounts of deductions and how to enter them in payroll records, as well as journal entries for recording the payroll and paying the employees.

OBJECTIVES OF PAYROLL RECORDS AND ACCOUNTING

There are two primary reasons for maintaining accurate payroll records. First, we must collect the necessary data to compute the compensation for each employee for each payroll period.

Second, we must provide information needed to complete the various government reports—federal and state—that are required of all employers. All business enterprises, both large and small, are required by law to withhold certain amounts from employees' pay for taxes, to make payments to government agencies by specified deadlines, and to submit reports on official forms. Because governments impose penalties if the requirements are not met, employers are vitally concerned with payroll accounting. Anyone going into accounting, or involved with the management of any business, should be thoroughly acquainted with payroll accounting.

EMPLOYER/EMPLOYEE RELATIONSHIPS

Payroll accounting is concerned only with employees and their compensations, withholdings, records, reports, and taxes. *Note:* There is a distinction between an employee and an independent contractor. An **employee** is one who is under the direction and control of the employer, such as a secretary, bookkeeper, sales clerk, vice president, controller, and so on. An **independent contractor,** on the other hand, is someone who is engaged for a definite job or service who may choose her or his own means of doing the work (*examples:* an appliance repair person, a plumber, a CPA firm). Payments made to independent contractors are in the form of fees or charges. Independent contractors submit bills or invoices for the work they do. The invoice is paid in a lump sum and is not subject to any withholding or payroll taxes.

LAWS AFFECTING COMPENSATION OF EMPLOYEES

Both federal and state laws require the employer to act as a collecting agent and deduct specified amounts from employees' gross earnings. The employer sends the withholdings to the appropriate government agencies, along with reports substantiating the figures. In addition, certain payroll taxes, based on the total wages paid to employees, are levied on the employer. Let's look at some of the more important laws that pertain to compensation of employees.

Federal Income Tax Withholding

The **Current Tax Payment Act** requires employers not only to withhold the tax and then pay it to the Internal Revenue Service, but also to keep records of the names and addresses of persons employed, their earnings and withholdings, and the amounts and dates of payment. The employer has to submit reports to the Internal Revenue Service on a quarterly basis (Form 941) and to the employee on an annual basis (W-2 form). With few exceptions, this requirement applies to employers of one or more persons. We'll discuss these reports and the related deposits in Chapter 10.

Federal Insurance Contributions Act (FICA)

This act, passed in 1935, provides for retirement pensions after a worker reaches age 62, disability benefits for any worker who becomes disabled (and for her or his dependents), and a health insurance program or Medicare after age 65. Both the employee and the employer have to pay **FICA taxes,** which are commonly referred to as Social Security taxes. The employer withholds FICA taxes from employees' wages and pays them to the Internal Revenue Service. The employer has to match the amount of FICA tax withheld from the employees' wages, and the employer's share is recorded under Payroll Tax Expense. We'll cover this in Chapter 10, as our concern here is with employees' deductions.

FICA tax rates apply to the gross earnings of an employee during the calendar year. After an employee has paid FICA tax on the maximum taxable earnings, the employer stops deducting FICA tax until the next calendar year begins. Congress has frequently changed the schedule of rates and taxable incomes. A rate of 7.1 percent applied to earnings up to $36,000, or a maximum of $2,556, will be assumed and used in this text for the examples and the problems. (Future changes in FICA tax rates are already on the books: 1985, 7.05 percent; 1986, 7.15 percent; 1988, 7.51

percent; 1990, 7.65 percent. The earnings base will increase automatically with growth in average earnings.)

The employer is required to keep records of the following information.

1. **Personal data on employee** Name, address, Social Security number, date of birth
2. **Data on wage payments** Dates and amounts of payments, and payroll periods
3. **Amount of taxable wages paid** Total amount earned so far during the year
4. **Amount of tax withheld from each employee's earnings**

Every three months the employer has to submit reports to the Internal Revenue Service, recording the information on Form 941, the same form that is used to report the income tax withheld. The employer's payment to the Internal Revenue Service consists of (1) the employee's share of the FICA tax, (2) the employer's matching portion of the FICA tax, and (3) the employee's income tax withheld. We'll talk about this in detail in Chapter 10.

Fair Labor Standards Act

The **Fair Labor Standards Act (Wages and Hours Law)** specifies that employers engaged in interstate commerce must pay their employees overtime at the rate of 1½ times the regular rate (time-and-a-half) for hours worked in excess of 40 per week. Frequently, union contracts stipulate additional overtime pay for work performed on Sundays and holidays. The act provides that certain management and supervisory employees are exempt from its regulations—these exempt employees are usually referred to as salaried personnel.

Federal Unemployment Tax Act (FUTA)

The purpose of the Federal Unemployment Tax Act is to provide financial support for the maintenance of government-run employment offices throughout the country. **FUTA taxes** are paid by employers only.

The federal unemployment tax is based on the total earnings of each employee during the calendar year. Congress has frequently changed the rates and the taxable income base.

For the examples and problems in this text, we will assume that employers pay an effective federal unemployment tax rate of .8 percent (.008) of the first $7,000 of earnings of each employee during the calendar year (January 1 through December 31).

Reports to the federal government (Form 940) must be submitted annually. We'll discuss these reports in Chapter 10.

State Unemployment Taxes

Each state is responsible for paying its own unemployment compensation benefits. The revenue provided by **state unemployment taxes** is used exclusively for this purpose. However, there is considerable variation among the states concerning the tax rates and the amount of taxable income. The minimum tax rate levied by any state is 2.7 percent based on the taxable income stipulated in the Federal Unemployment Tax Act. States require employers to file reports on a quarterly, or three-month, basis, listing employees' names, amount of wages paid to each employee, and a computation of the unemployment tax. We'll discuss these reports in Chapter 10.

Our example of payroll accounting deals with the firm of Harding and Associates. This business is located in the state of Washington, which has an assumed unemployment tax rate of 3 percent on the first $12,000 of wages paid to each employee during the calendar year (January 1 through December 31). This tax is paid by employers only.

Workers' Compensation Laws

Workers' compensation laws protect employees and their dependents against losses due to death or injury incurred on the job. Most states require employers either to contribute to a state compensation insurance fund or to buy similar insurance from a private insurance company. The employer ordinarily pays the cost of the insurance premiums. The premium rates vary according to the degree of danger inherent in each job category and the employer's number of accidents. The employer has to keep records of job descriptions and classifications, as well as claims of insured persons.

State and City Income Taxes

Besides requiring employers to deduct money from employees' earnings for federal income taxes, two-thirds of the states require employers to deduct money to pay state income taxes. A number of cities also require withholding for *city* income taxes. When these laws are in effect, the employer handles the reporting and payments in much the same way as for federal income taxes. Separate liability accounts may be set up for employees' state and city income taxes withheld.

HOW EMPLOYEES GET PAID

Employees may be paid a salary or wages, depending on the type of work and the period of time covered. Money paid to a person for managerial or administrative services is usually called a salary, and the time period covered is generally a month or a year. Money paid for either skilled or unskilled labor is usually called wages, and the time period covered is hours or weeks. Wages may also be paid on a piecework basis. In practice, the words *salaries* and *wages* are somewhat interchangeable. A company may supplement an employee's salary or wage by commissions, bonuses, cost-of-living adjustments, and profit-sharing plans. As a rule, employees are paid by check or in cash. However, their compensation may take the form of merchandise, lodging, meals, or other property as well. When the compensation is in these forms, one has to determine the fair value of property or service given in payment for an employee's labor.

Calculating Total Earnings

When compensation is based on the amount of time worked, the accountant of course has to have a record of the number of hours worked by each employee. When there are only a few employees, this can be accomplished by means of a book record. When there are many employees, time clocks are the traditional method. Nowadays, for computer-operated time-keeping systems, employers use punched cards.

Objective 1

Calculate total earnings based on an hourly, piece-rate, or commission basis.

Wages

Let's take the case of Graham C. Laboe, who works for Harding and Associates. His regular rate of pay is $12 per hour. The company pays time-and-a-half for hours worked in excess of 40. In addition, it pays him double time for any work he does on Sundays and holidays. Laboe has a ½-hour lunch break during an 8½-hour day. He is not paid for the lunch break. His time card for the week is shown in Figure 9-1.

Laboe's gross wages can be computed by one of two methods. The first method works like this:

40 hours at straight time	$40 \times \$12$ per hour = $480
2 hours overtime on Thursday	$2 \times \$18$ per hour = 36
1 hour overtime on Friday	$1 \times \$18$ per hour = 18
5 hours overtime on Saturday	$5 \times \$18$ per hour = 90
4 hours overtime on Sunday	$4 \times \$24$ per hour = 96
Total gross wages	$720

Figure 9-1

TIME CARD

Name   _Laboe, Graham C._

Week ending   _Nov. 7, 19–_

Day	In	Out	In	Out	Hours Worked Regular	Overtime
M	7⁵⁷	12⁰⁰	12³⁰	4³²	8	
T	7⁵⁶	12⁰⁶	12³⁶	4³⁷	8	
W	7⁵⁷	12⁰²	12³¹	4³¹	8	
T	8⁰⁰	12¹¹	12⁴⁰	6³²	8	2
F	8⁰⁰	12⁰³	12³³	5³³	8	1
S	7⁵⁹	1⁰²				5
S	7⁵⁵	12⁰⁴				4

The second method of calculating gross wages is often used when machine accounting is involved.

52 hours at straight time: 52 × $12 per hour = $624
Overtime premium:
   8 hours × $ 6 per hour premium = $48
   4 hours × $12 per hour premium = <u> 48</u>

   Total overtime premium   <u>96</u>

   Total gross wages $720

Salaries

Employees who are paid a regular salary may also be entitled to premium pay for overtime. It is necessary to figure out their regular hourly rate of pay before you can determine their overtime rate. Let's consider the case of Donna Garcia, who gets a salary of $1,872 per month. She is entitled to overtime pay for all hours worked in excess of 40 during a week at the rate of 1½ times her regular hourly rate. This past week she worked 44 hours, so we calculate her overtime pay as follows.

$1,872 per month × 12 months = $22,464 per year
 $22,464 per year ÷ 52 weeks = $432 per week
  $432 per week ÷ 40 hours = $10.80 per regular hour

Earnings for 44 hours:
40 hours at straight time   40 × $10.80 = $432.00
 4 hours overtime   4 × $16.20 =   64.80

Total gross earnings $496.80

Piece Rate

Workers under the piece-rate system are paid at the rate of so much per unit of production. For example, Peter Ryan, an apple picker, gets paid $8 for picking a bin of apples. If he picks 6 bins during the day, his total earnings are 6 × $8 = $48.

Commissions and Bonuses

Some salespersons are paid on a purely commission basis. However, a more common arrangement is a salary plus a commission or bonus. Assume that Rosie Perkins receives an annual salary of $9,600. Her employer agrees to pay her a 6 percent commission on all sales during the year in excess of $120,000. Her sales for the year total $210,000. Her bonus amounts to $90,000 × .06 = $5,400. Therefore her total earnings are $9,600 + $5,400 = $15,000.

DEDUCTIONS FROM TOTAL EARNINGS

Anyone who has ever earned a paycheck has encountered some of the many types of deductions that account for the shrinkage. The most usual deductions are due to the following.

1. Federal income tax withholding
2. State income tax withholding
3. FICA tax (Social Security), employee's share
4. Purchase of U.S. savings bonds
5. Union dues
6. Medical and life insurance premiums
7. Contributions to a charitable organization
8. Repayment of personal loans from the company credit union
9. Savings through the company credit union

Employees' Federal Income Tax Withholding

The amount of federal income tax withheld from an employee's wages depends on the amount of her or his total earnings and the number of exemptions claimed. An **exemption** is the amount of an individual's earnings that is exempt from income taxes (nontaxable). An employee is entitled to one personal exemption, plus an additional exemption if he or she is over 65 or blind, and an exemption for each dependent. Each employee has to fill out an **Employee's Withholding Allowance Certificate (Form W-4),** shown in Figure 9-2.

The employer retains this form, as authorization to withhold money for the employee's federal income tax.

For convenience, most employers use the wage-bracket withholding tables in *Circular E, Employer's Tax Guide,* an Internal Revenue Service publication, to determine the amount of federal tax to be withheld for each employee. These tables cover monthly, semimonthly, biweekly, weekly, and daily payroll periods; they are also subdivided on the basis of married and unmarried persons.

In order to determine the tax to be withheld from an employee's gross wages, first locate the wage bracket in the first two columns of the table. Next, find the column for the number of exemptions claimed and read down this column until you get to the wage-bracket line. A portion of the weekly federal income tax withholding table for married persons is reproduced in Figure 9-3.

Assume that Graham C. Laboe, who claims three exemptions, has $720 gross wages for the week. At first sight, it appears that $720 could fall in

Objective 2

Determine deductions from tables of employees' income tax withholding.

Figure 9-2

Form **W-4**	Department of the Treasury—Internal Revenue Service **Employee's Withholding Allowance Certificate**	OMB No. 1545-0010

1 Type or print your full name
Graham C. Laboe

2 Your social security number
543-24-1680

Home address (number and street or rural route)
1582 North Pierce Street

City or town, State, and ZIP code
Spokane, WA 99204

3 Marital Status
☐ Single ☒ Married
☐ Married, but withhold at higher Single rate
Note: If married, but legally separated, or spouse is a nonresident alien, check the Single box.

4 Total number of allowances you are claiming (from line F of the worksheet on page 2)   3

5 Additional amount, if any, you want deducted from each pay . . . . $

6 I claim exemption from withholding because (see instructions and check boxes below that apply):

a ☐ Last year I did not owe any Federal income tax and had a right to a full refund of **ALL** income tax withheld, **AND**

b ☐ This year I do not expect to owe any Federal income tax and expect to have a right to a full refund of **ALL** income tax withheld. If both a and b apply, enter the year effective and "EXEMPT" here . . . ▶   Year

c If you entered "EXEMPT" on line 6b, are you a full-time student? . . . .   ☐Yes ☐No

Under penalties of perjury, I certify that I am entitled to the number of withholding allowances claimed on this certificate, or if claiming exemption from withholding, that I am entitled to claim the exempt status
Employee's signature ▶ *Graham C. Laboe.*   Date ▶ February 1   , 19 --

7 Employer's name and address **(Employer: Complete 7, 8, and 9 only if sending to IRS)**

8 Office code

9 Employer identification number

MARRIED Persons—WEEKLY Payroll Period

And the wages are—		And the number of withholding allowances claimed is—										
At least	But less than	0	1	2	3	4	5	6	7	8	9	10 or more
		The amount of income tax to be withheld shall be—										
$310	$320	$42.70	$39.10	$35.40	$31.80	$28.10	$24.80	$21.70	$18.70	$15.60	$12.50	$9.40
320	330	44.60	41.00	37.30	33.70	30.00	26.40	23.30	20.30	17.20	14.10	11.00
330	340	46.50	42.90	39.20	35.60	31.90	28.30	24.90	21.90	18.80	15.70	12.60
340	350	48.40	44.80	41.10	37.50	33.80	30.20	26.50	23.50	20.40	17.30	14.20
350	360	50.30	46.70	43.00	39.40	35.70	32.10	28.40	25.10	22.00	18.90	15.80
360	370	52.70	48.60	44.90	41.30	37.60	34.00	30.30	26.70	23.60	20.50	17.40
370	380	55.10	50.50	46.80	43.20	39.50	35.90	32.20	28.60	25.20	22.10	19.00
380	390	57.50	52.80	48.70	45.10	41.40	37.80	34.10	30.50	26.80	23.70	20.60
390	400	59.90	55.20	50.60	47.00	43.30	39.70	36.00	32.40	28.70	25.30	22.20
400	410	62.30	57.60	53.00	48.90	45.20	41.60	37.90	34.30	30.60	26.90	23.80
410	420	64.70	60.00	55.40	50.80	47.10	43.50	39.80	36.20	32.50	28.80	25.40
420	430	67.10	62.40	57.80	53.20	49.00	45.40	41.70	38.10	34.40	30.70	27.10
430	440	69.50	64.80	60.20	55.60	51.00	47.30	43.60	40.00	36.30	32.60	29.00
440	450	71.90	67.20	62.60	58.00	53.40	49.20	45.50	41.90	38.20	34.50	30.90
450	460	74.30	69.60	65.00	60.40	55.80	51.20	47.40	43.80	40.10	36.40	32.80
710	720	155.30	148.20	141.10	134.00	127.80	121.70	115.50	109.40	103.20	97.80	92.60
720	730	159.00	151.90	144.80	(137.70)	131.00	124.90	118.70	112.60	106.40	100.50	95.30
730	740	162.70	155.60	148.50	141.40	134.30	128.10	121.90	115.80	109.60	103.50	98.00
740	750	166.40	159.30	152.20	145.10	138.00	131.30	125.10	119.00	112.80	106.70	100.70
750	760	170.10	163.00	155.90	148.80	141.70	134.50	128.30	122.20	116.00	109.90	103.70
760	770	173.80	166.70	159.60	152.50	145.40	138.20	131.50	125.40	119.20	113.10	106.90
770	780	177.50	170.40	163.30	156.20	149.10	141.90	134.80	128.60	122.40	116.30	110.10
780	790	181.20	174.10	167.00	159.90	152.80	145.60	138.50	131.80	125.60	119.50	113.30
790	800	184.90	177.80	170.70	163.60	156.50	149.30	142.20	135.10	128.80	122.70	116.50
800	810	188.60	181.50	174.40	167.30	160.20	153.00	145.90	138.80	132.00	125.90	119.70
810	820	192.30	185.20	178.10	171.00	163.90	156.70	149.60	142.50	135.40	129.10	122.90
820	830	196.00	188.90	181.80	174.70	167.60	160.40	153.30	146.20	139.10	132.30	126.10
830	840	199.70	192.60	185.50	178.40	171.30	164.10	157.00	149.90	142.80	135.70	129.30
840	850	203.40	196.30	189.20	182.10	175.00	167.80	160.70	153.60	146.50	139.40	132.50
850	860	207.10	200.00	192.90	185.80	178.70	171.50	164.40	157.30	150.20	143.10	136.00
		37 percent of the excess over $860 plus—										
$860 and over		209.00	201.90	194.70	187.60	180.50	173.40	166.30	159.20	152.00	144.90	137.80

Figure 9-3

either the $710–$720 bracket or the $720–$730 bracket. However, note the headings of the bracket columns: "At least" and "But less than." A strict interpretation of the $710–$720 bracket really means $710–$719.99. Therefore $720 must be included in the $720–$730 bracket. As can be seen from the table, $137.70 should be withheld.

Many states that levy state income taxes also furnish employers with withholding tables. Other states use a fixed percentage of the federal income tax withholding as the amount to be withheld for state taxes.

Employees' FICA Tax Withholding (Social Security)

To determine the FICA tax for each employee, simply multiply the FICA taxable wages by the FICA tax rate.

Let's get back to Graham C. Laboe, who had gross wages of $720 for the week ending November 7. Suppose that the total accumulated gross wages Laboe earned this year prior to this payroll period were $25,316. His total gross wages including this payroll period were $26,036 ($25,316 + $720), which is well below the $36,000 assumed maximum taxable income. Therefore, multiply the FICA taxable wages ($720) by the FICA tax rate (7.1 percent).

$$\$720 \times .071 = \$51.12$$

Of course, if Laboe's gross earnings prior to this payroll period had been greater than $36,000, then there would be *no* FICA tax deduction. (Tables for FICA tax withholding are published in the Internal Revenue Service's *Circular E, Employer's Tax Guide*.)

PAYROLL REGISTER

The payroll register is a form that summarizes the information about employees' wages and salaries for a given payroll period. In Figure 9-4 we see a payroll register that shows the data for each employee on a separate line. This would be suitable for a firm, such as Harding and Associates, that has a small number of employees.

Objective 3

Complete a payroll register.

State Unemployment Taxable Earnings Column

The columns marked Taxable Earnings refer to the amount of pay that is subject to taxation. The employer uses the information in these columns to calculate the amount of unemployment taxes as well as the employer's portion of FICA. (We'll discuss these calculations in Chapter 10.)

For the present, however, we are concerned only with recording the amount of taxable income (the amount on which the actual tax is figured). First, let's take the State Unemployment Taxable Earnings column. Remember, however, that taxable earnings may differ from one state to another. Harding and Associates operates in the state of Washington, which has an assumed unemployment tax based on the first $12,000 paid to each employee during the calendar year (January 1 through December 31). After an employee's earnings top $12,000 in one year, the employer no longer pays state unemployment tax on that employee. For example, Graham C. Laboe's total earnings before the payroll period ended November 7 were $25,316 (as shown in his earnings record in Figure 9-7). Since he has already earned more than $12,000, no amount is recorded in the State

NAME	TOTAL HOURS	EARNINGS			TAXABLE EARNINGS			FEDERAL INCOME TAX
		REGULAR	OVERTIME	TOTAL	STATE UNEMPL.	FEDERAL UNEMPL.	FICA	
1 Anderson, Dennis L.	45	4 0 0 00	7 5 00	4 7 5 00	2 4 0 00		4 7 5 00	7 4 50
2 Bowlen, Ralph P.	46	3 2 0 00	7 2 00	3 9 2 00	3 9 2 00		3 9 2 00	5 0 60
3 Daniels, John N.	49	4 0 0 00	1 3 5 00	5 3 5 00			5 3 5 00	8 0 30
4 Drew, Nancy R.	40	3 6 0 00		3 6 0 00	3 6 0 00	3 6 0 00	3 6 0 00	4 4 90
5 Farrell, Steven L.	40	3 8 4 00		3 8 4 00	3 8 4 00	3 8 4 00	3 8 4 00	4 8 70
6 Harwood, Lance C.	40	9 5 0 00		9 5 0 00				2 2 8 00
7 Laboe, Graham C.	52	4 8 0 00	2 4 0 00	7 2 0 00			7 2 0 00	1 3 7 70
8 Lyman, Mary C.	40	6 0 0 00		6 0 0 00			6 0 0 00	1 0 4 90
9 Miller, Robert M.	44	4 4 0 00	6 6 00	5 0 6 00			5 0 6 00	8 2 60
10 Olsen, Marvin C.	45	4 0 0 00	7 5 00	4 7 5 00	2 4 0 00		4 7 5 00	7 4 50
11 Stanfield, John D.	40	8 5 0 00		8 5 0 00				1 8 5 80
12 Tucker, Norma P.	52	4 8 0 00	2 1 6 00	6 9 6 00			6 9 6 00	1 2 7 60
13		6 0 6 4 00	8 7 9 00	6 9 4 3 00	1 6 1 6 00	7 4 4 00	5 1 4 3 00	1 2 4 0 10
14								

Unemployment Taxable Earnings column. A blank space indicates that the employee has already earned more than $12,000 (prior to this payroll period) so far this year. On the other hand, Ralph P. Bowlen's total earnings so far this year, including the $392 during this pay period, amount to $8,460. Because his earnings are still less than $12,000, the entire $392 is recorded in the State Unemployment Taxable Earnings column. Dennis L. Anderson's cumulative earnings prior to this week were $11,760. As a result, only $240 of this week's earnings are taxable for state unemployment, to bring him up to the $12,000 maximum. After this week, none of Anderson's earnings will be taxable for state unemployment.

Federal Unemployment Taxable Earnings Column

Regarding the Federal Unemployment Taxable Earnings column, we assume a tax rate of .8 percent on the first $7,000 paid to each employee during the calendar year. After a given employee's earnings top $7,000 in one year, the employer doesn't have to pay any more federal unemployment tax on that employee. For example, Laboe has already earned more than $7,000 during the year, so no amount is recorded in the Federal Unemployment Taxable Earnings column. On the other hand, Steven L. Farrell's cumulative earnings so far this year, including the $384 during this pay period, amount to $6,242. Consequently, the entire $384 is placed in the Federal Unemployment Taxable Earnings column as well as in the State Unemployment Taxable Earnings column.

	DEDUCTIONS							PAYMENTS		EXPENSE ACCOUNT DEBITED		
					OTHER							
FICA	U.S. BONDS	UNION DUES	MEDICAL INSURANCE		CODE	AMOUNT	TOTAL	NET AMOUNT	CK. NO.	SALES SALARY EXPENSE	OFFICE SALARY EXPENSE	
33 73	20 00	10 00	16 00		CC	4 00	158 23	316 77	931	475 00		1
27 83		10 00	16 00				104 43	287 57	932	392 00		2
37 99	32 00	10 00	20 00		CC	6 00	186 29	348 71	933		535 00	3
25 56		10 00	16 00				96 46	263 54	934		360 00	4
27 26		10 00	16 00				101 96	282 04	935	384 00		5
	40 00		20 00		CC	6 00	294 00	656 00	936	950 00		6
51 12	10 00	10 00	20 00		CC	6 00	234 82	485 18	937	720 00		7
42 60	10 00		20 00		CC	5 00	182 50	417 50	938	600 00		8
35 93			16 00				144 53	361 47	939	506 00		9
33 73			20 00		AR	40 00	178 23	296 77	940	475 00		10
			20 00		CC	6 00	211 80	638 20	941	850 00		11
49 42			16 00		CC	4 00	207 02	488 98	942		696 00	12
365 17	112 00	90 00	216 00			77 00	2100 27	4842 73		5352 00	1591 00	13
												14

Figure 9-4

FICA Taxable Earnings Column

We have assumed a FICA tax rate of 7.1 percent on the first $36,000. In the case of Graham C. Laboe, his total earnings so far this year, including the $720 during this pay period, amount to $26,036 (see Laboe's individual earnings record, Figure 9-7). Consequently, the entire $720 is listed as FICA taxable. On the line of Lance C. Harwood, there is a blank, indicating that he has already earned more than $36,000 before this pay period.

As we said, the three taxable earnings columns are used to calculate the employer's payroll tax expense, which is discussed in Chapter 10. However, the FICA Taxable Earnings column is also used to determine the amount of the *employees'* FICA tax deductions. For example, to find Laboe's FICA deduction multiply $720 (FICA taxable) by 7.1 percent (FICA tax rate): $720 \times .071 = 51.12.

Deductions Columns

The federal income tax withholding and the FICA (Social Security) deductions are employee deductions required by law; the others are usually voluntary. One could set up special columns for any frequently used deductions. Here, Community Chest and Accounts Receivable are included as other deductions.

The Net Amount column represents the employee's take-home pay. The last two columns show the distribution of the salary accounts to be debited. Harding and Associates uses Sales Salary Expense and Office Salary Expense. The sum of these two columns equals the total earnings.

Figure 9-5

	DATE		DESCRIPTION	POST. REF.	DEBIT				CREDIT				
1	19– Nov.	7	Sales Salary Expense		5	3	5	2	00				1
2			Office Salary Expense		1	5	9	1	00				2
3			Employees' Income Tax Payable						1	2	4	0	10	3
4			FICA Tax Payable ($5,143 × .071)							3	6	5	17	4
5			Employees' Bond Deductions										5
6			Payable							1	1	2	00	6
7			Employees' Union Dues Payable								9	0	00	7
8			Employees' Medical Insurance										8
9			Payable							2	1	6	00	9
10			Employees' Community Chest										10
11			Payable								3	7	00	11
12			Accounts Receivable								4	0	00	12
13			Salaries Payable						4	8	4	2	73	13
14			Payroll register, page 68, for week										14
15			ended November 7.										15
16													16
17													17
18													18

GENERAL JOURNAL — PAGE 31

The Payroll Entry

Because the payroll register summarizes the payroll data for the period, it seems logical that it should be used as the basis for recording the payroll in the ledger accounts. Since the payroll register does not have the status of a journal, a journal entry is necessary. Figure 9-5 shows the entry in general journal form. (The calculation is given purely as further explanation; it is not ordinarily a part of the journal entry.)

Note that a firm records the total cost to the company for services of employees as debits to the salary expense accounts. To pay the employees, the firm now makes the following journal entry.

Objective 4

Journalize the payroll entry from a payroll register.

			DEBIT		CREDIT	
	7	Salaries Payable	4 8 4 2	73		
		Cash			4 8 4 2	73
		Paid salaries for week ended				
		November 7. Issued check no.				
		667 payable to special payroll				
		bank account.				

In the two journal entries, the debit and credit to the Salaries Payable account cancel out each other. It would be possible to combine the two entries by making one credit to Cash. If a combined journal were in use, both of the above entries would be recorded in it, instead of in the general journal.

A firm having a large number of employees would probably open a special payroll account with its bank. One check drawn on the regular bank account is made payable to the special payroll account for the amount of the total net pay for a payroll period. All payroll checks for the period are then written on the special payroll account. With the use of the special payroll account, if employees delay cashing their paychecks, then the checks do not have to be listed on the bank reconciliation of the firm's regular bank account. Balances of Employees' Bond Deductions Payable, Employees' Union Dues Payable, and other employee deductions are paid out of the firm's regular bank account.

Small businesses that have just a few workers will not find it worthwhile to use a special payroll bank account. Instead, these firms will use their regular bank account to write the employees' payroll checks, crediting Cash directly rather than crediting Salaries Payable.

PAYCHECK

All the data needed to make out a payroll check are available in the payroll register. Graham C. Laboe's paycheck is shown in Figure 9-6.

Figure 9-6

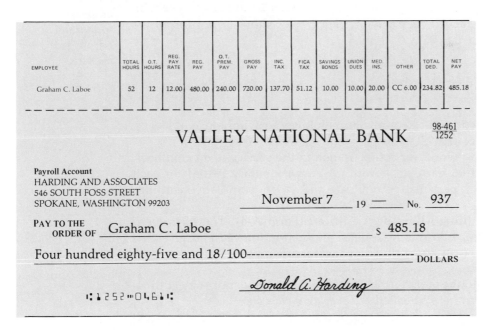

EMPLOYEE	TOTAL HOURS	O.T. HOURS	REG. PAY RATE	REG. PAY	O.T. PREM. PAY	GROSS PAY	INC. TAX	FICA TAX	SAVINGS BONDS	UNION DUES	MED. INS.	OTHER	TOTAL DED.	NET PAY
Graham C. Laboe	52	12	12.00	480.00	240.00	720.00	137.70	51.12	10.00	10.00	20.00	CC 6.00	234.82	485.18

VALLEY NATIONAL BANK 98-461/1252

Payroll Account
HARDING AND ASSOCIATES
546 SOUTH FOSS STREET
SPOKANE, WASHINGTON 99203   November 7   19 ——   No. 937

PAY TO THE ORDER OF   Graham C. Laboe $ 485.18

Four hundred eighty-five and 18/100----------------------------------- DOLLARS

Donald A. Harding

⑆1252⑈0461⑆

EMPLOYEE'S INDIVIDUAL

NAME _Laboe, Graham Charles_

ADDRESS _1582 North Pierce Street_

Spokane, Washington   99204

MALE _X_   FEMALE _____

MARRIED _X_   SINGLE _____

PHONE NO. _663-2556_   DATE OF BIRTH _9/19/39_

| LINE NO. | PERIOD ENDED | DATE PAID | HOURS WORKED | | EARNINGS | | | ACCUMULATED EARNINGS | INCOME TAX |
			REG.	O.T.	REGULAR	OVERTIME	TOTAL		
40	10/3	10/4	40	8	4 8 0 00	1 4 4 00	6 2 4 00	23 1 6 2 00	1 0 5 20
41	10/10	10/11	40	2	4 8 0 00	3 6 00	5 1 6 00	23 6 7 8 00	7 4 90
42	10/17	10/18	40	2	4 8 0 00	3 6 00	5 1 6 00	24 1 9 4 00	7 4 90
43	10/24	10/24	40	5	4 8 0 00	9 0 00	5 7 0 00	24 7 6 4 00	9 1 10
44	10/30	11/1	40	4	4 8 0 00	7 2 00	5 5 2 00	25 3 1 6 00	8 5 70
45	11/7	11/8	40	$13\frac{1}{3}$	4 8 0 00	2 4 0 00	7 2 0 00	26 0 3 6 00	1 3 7 70

Employees' Individual Earnings Records

To comply with government regulations, a firm has to keep current data on each employee's accumulated earnings, deductions, and net pay. The information is transferred from the payroll register to the **employee's individual earnings record** each payday. Figure 9-7 shows a portion of the earnings record for Graham C. Laboe.

Objective 5

Maintain employees' individual earnings records.

GLOSSARY

Current Tax Payment Act   Requires an employer to withhold employees' federal income tax as well as to pay and report the tax.

Employee   One who works for compensation in the service of an employer.

Employee's individual earnings record   A supplementary record for each employee showing personal payroll data and yearly cumulative earnings and deductions.

Employee's Withholding Allowance Certificate (Form W-4)   This form specifies the number of exemptions claimed by each employee and gives the employer the authority to withhold money for an employee's income taxes and FICA taxes.

Exemption   An amount of an employee's annual earnings not subject to income tax. The term is also called a _withholding allowance_.

EARNINGS RECORD

EMPLOYEE NO. _5_   DATE EMPLOYED _2/1/—_

SOC. SEC. NO. _543-24-1680_   NO. OF EXEMPTIONS _3_

PAY RATE _$12.00_   PER HOUR _X_   PER DAY _____

EQUIVALENT HOURLY RATE _$12.00_   PER WEEK _____   PER MONTH _____

DATE TERMINATED _____

CLASSIFICATION FOR WORKMEN'S COMPENSATION INSURANCE _Warehouse_

			DEDUCTIONS					PAID	
FICA	BONDS	UNION DUES	HOSPITAL INSURANCE	CODE	OTHER AMOUNT	TOTAL	NET AMOUNT	CK. NO.
4 4 30	1 0 00	1 0 00	2 0 00	cc	6 00	1 9 5 50	4 2 8 50	887
3 6 64	1 0 00	1 0 00	2 0 00	cc	6 00	1 5 7 54	3 5 8 46	889
3 6 64	1 0 00	1 0 00	2 0 00	cc	6 00	1 5 7 54	3 5 8 46	901
4 0 47	1 0 00	1 0 00	2 0 00	cc	6 00	1 7 7 57	3 9 2 43	913
3 9 19	1 0 00	1 0 00	2 0 00	cc	6 00	1 7 0 89	3 8 1 11	925
5 1 12	1 0 00	1 0 00	2 0 00	cc	6 00	2 3 4 82	4 8 5 18	937

Figure 9-7

Fair Labor Standards Act (Wages and Hours Law) An act requiring employers whose products are involved in interstate commerce to pay their employees time-and-a-half for all hours worked in excess of 40 per week.

FICA taxes Social Security taxes paid by both employers and employees under the provisions of the Federal Insurance Contributions Act. The proceeds are used to pay old-age and disability pensions.

FUTA taxes Taxes paid only by employers under the provisions of the Federal Unemployment Tax Act. The proceeds are used to pay part of the costs of the federal-state unemployment programs.

Gross pay The total amount of an employee's pay before any deductions.

Independent contractor Someone who is engaged for a definite service who may choose her or his own means of doing the work; not an employee of the firm for which the service is provided. (*Examples:* appliance repair person, plumber, freelance artist, CPA firm.)

Net pay Gross pay minus deductions.

State unemployment taxes Taxes paid by employers only. The proceeds are used to pay unemployment benefits.

Workers' compensation laws State laws guaranteeing benefits for employees who are injured or killed on the job.

QUESTIONS, EXERCISES, AND PROBLEMS

Discussion Questions

1. Distinguish between an employee and an independent contractor.
2. Suggest seven possible deductions from total earnings of an employee.

3. Explain the requirements of the Fair Labor Standards Act.
4. What are the main provisions of the Federal Insurance Contributions Act?
5. What is a wage-bracket withholding table?
6. Describe how a special payroll bank account is useful in paying the wages of employees.
7. What information is included in an employee's individual earnings record, and what is its function?

Exercises

Exercise 9-1   Using the table in Figure 9-3 (page 254), determine the amount of federal income tax an employer should withhold weekly for married employees with the following wages and exemptions.

	Total Weekly Wages	Number of Exemptions	Amount of Withholding
a	$315.52	1	_____
b	$712.16	5	_____
c	$710.00	6	_____

Exercise 9-2   Henry R. Gallo works for the Central Roofing Corporation, which must abide by the Fair Labor Standards Act. It must pay its employees time-and-a-half for all hours worked per week in excess of 40. Gallo's pay rate is $9.20 per hour. His wages are subject to federal income tax and FICA deductions at the rate of 7.1 percent. He claims four income tax exemptions. Gallo has a ½-hour lunch during an 8½-hour day. His time card is shown below.

TIME CARD

Name   *Henry R. Gallo*

Week ending   *March 11, 19–*

Day	In	Out	In	Out	Hours Worked Regular	Overtime
M	7^{56}	12^{09}	12^{39}	4^{32}	8	
T	7^{52}	12^{05}	12^{35}	5^{04}	8	½
W	7^{59}	12^{20}	12^{40}	5^{03}	8	½
T	8^{00}	12^{08}	12^{38}	4^{34}	8	
F	7^{56}	12^{09}	12^{39}	6^{33}	8	2
S	8^{00}	11^{01}				3
S						

Complete the following.

a. _____ hours at straight time × $9.20 per hour $_____
b. _____ hours overtime × $13.80 per hour $_____
c. Total gross wages $_____
d. Federal income tax withholding
   (from tax tables in Figure 9-3, page 254) $_____
e. FICA withholding at 7.1 percent $_____
f. Total withholding $_____
g. Net pay $_____

Exercise 9-3   On January 31, Sato and Company's column totals of its payroll register showed that its sales employees had earned $4,560 and its office employees had earned $960. FICA taxes were withheld at an assumed rate of 7.1 percent. Other deductions consisted of federal income tax, $501.60; U.S. savings bonds, $240; and hospital insurance, $320. Determine the amount of FICA taxes to be withheld and record the general journal entry for the payroll, crediting Salaries Payable for the net pay.

Exercise 9-4   Sandra Lund works for Fine Fabrics, a company engaged in interstate commerce, which is subject to the provisions of the Fair Labor Standards Act. Fine Fabrics has just adopted a four-day, 40-hour workweek.

Lund's pay rate is $7.40 per hour. During the four-day week, her working hours were as follows: Monday, 12 hours; Tuesday, 10 hours; Wednesday, 11½ hours; Thursday, 10½ hours. Compute the amount of her gross earnings for the week.

Exercise 9-5   The following information was taken from the records of Rasmussen Tea Company, which is subject to the Fair Labor Standards Act, for the first week of January.

NAME	HOURLY RATE	HOURS WORKED REG.	HOURS WORKED O.T.	TOTAL EARNINGS	FEDERAL INCOME TAX	FICA	SAVINGS BONDS	HOSPITAL INSURANCE	TOTAL	NET PAY
Murray, A.	7.50	40	6				4 00	16 00		
Smith, B.	7.90	40	8				10 00	18 00		

Using the table in Figure 9-3 (page 254), determine the income tax withheld. The FICA tax rate is 7.1 percent. Murray and Smith claim two exemptions each. In general journal form, record the payroll entry, debiting Wages Expense for the amount of the total earnings and crediting Cash for the net pay.

Exercise 9-6   June Ames is employed by the Solar Company. During the week ended July 7, she worked 9 hours on Monday and 7 hours each day during the remaining four days of the five-day week. The existing union contract defines overtime as time worked over 8 hours each day. She earns $10 per hour and time-and-a-half for overtime. Ames's deductions include the following.

Federal income tax withheld	$50.50
Union dues withheld	12.00
Medical insurance withheld	20.00

Her total earnings through July 1 were $9,800. Assume that the FICA tax is 7.1 percent of the first $36,000 earned during the calendar year. Compute Ames's total earnings and the net amount of her check for the week.

Exercise 9-7 The Booker Camera Company has two employees. The information shown below was taken from their individual earnings record cards for the month of October. Determine the missing amounts, assuming that the FICA tax is 7.1 percent.

	Davis	Finch
Regular earnings	$?	$670.00
Overtime earnings	30.00	?
Total earnings	?	684.00
FICA taxes withheld	?	48.56
Federal income taxes withheld	140.00	132.00
State income taxes withheld	10.00	?
Medical insurance withheld	15.00	15.00
Total deductions	216.83	204.56
Net amount paid	513.17	479.44

Exercise 9-8 Assume the employees in Exercise 9-7 are paid from the firm's regular bank account. Journalize the payroll entry in general journal form.

Problem Set A

Problem 9-1A Jan R. Franco, an employee of Carpets, Inc., worked 47 hours during the week of February 15 to 21. Her rate of pay is $8.40 per hour, and she gets time-and-a-half for work in excess of 40 hours per week. She is married and claims one exemption on her W-4 form. Her wages are subject to the following deductions.

a. Federal income tax (use the table in Figure 9-3, page 254)
b. FICA tax at 7.1 percent
c. Union dues, $6.20
d. Medical insurance, $17.20

Instructions

Compute her regular pay, overtime pay, gross pay, and net pay.

Problem 9-2A The Falcon Motor Inn has the following payroll information for the week ended April 26.

Name	Daily Time							Pay Rate	Federal Income Tax	Union Dues	Earnings at End of Previous Week
	M	T	W	T	F	S	S				
Baker, Loren	8	0	0	8	10	8	8	5 40	28 60	4 00	3,960 00
Collier, Douglas	0	0	8	8	8	8	8	3 50	14 00	4 00	2,172 60
Edwards, Roberta	8	8	8	8	4	0	8	4 00	19 20	4 00	2,548 22
Stanski, Louise	0	4	8	8	8	8	8	4 00	22 50	4 00	3,980 10
Tolliver, Elwood	8	8	4	8	8	0	8	4 50	22 60	4 00	861 30

The firm is subject to the Fair Labor Standards Act regarding minimum wages. However, being a motel, it is exempt from paying time-and-a-half for 44 hours or less. In this case, all hours are compensated at the regular rate. For each employee, taxable earnings for FICA are based on the first $36,000, and taxable earnings for unemployment insurance (state and federal) are based on the first $7,000.

Instructions

1. Complete the payroll register, using 7.1 percent for calculating FICA tax withholding.
2. Prepare a general journal entry to record the payroll. The firm's general ledger contains a Wages Expense account and a Wages Payable account.
3. Assuming that the firm uses a special payroll bank account, make the entry in the general journal to record check no. 53.

Problem 9-3A The Illinois Products Company is subject to the Fair Labor Standards Act and, accordingly, pays its employees time-and-a-half for all hours worked in excess of 40 per week. The following information is available from time cards and employee's individual earnings records for the pay period ended February 28.

Name	Clock Card No.	Daily Time							Regular Rate	Income Tax Exemp.	Union Dues	Medical Insurance	Earnings at End of Previous Week
		M	T	W	T	F	S	S					
Bush, Paula C.	69	8	8	8	10	9	0	0	7 20	1	6 00	13 60	2,298 00
Carlson, John D.	70	8	8	8	8	8	5	0	7 20	3	6 00	15 00	2,388 00
Dodge, R. C.	71	8	10	8	9	8	0	0	7 70	5	6 00	15 40	2,446 00
Klein, Louis A.	72	8	8	9	8	8	2	0	7 70	4	6 00	15 20	2,424 00
Lewis, David	73	8	8	8	8	8	0	0	9 00	4	6 00	15 20	2,736 00

For each employee, taxable earnings for FICA are based on the first $36,000, and taxable earnings for unemployment insurance (state and federal) are based on the first $7,000.

Instructions

1. Complete the payroll register, using the wage-bracket income tax withholding tables in Figure 9-3 (page 254). The FICA tax is 7.1 percent. Assume that all employees are married.
2. Prepare a general journal entry to record the payroll. The firm's general ledger contains a Wages Expense account and a Wages Payable account.
3. Assume that the firm uses a special payroll bank account and issues check no. 113.

Problem 9-4A The Brewster Trailer Company is subject to the Fair Labor Standards Act and, accordingly, pays its employees time-and-a-half for all hours worked in excess of 40 per week. The following information is available from the time books and employee's individual earnings records for the pay period ended December 10.

Name	Pay Rate	Hours Worked	Federal Income Tax	Union Dues	Medical Insurance	Earnings at End of Previous Week
Cooper, C. R.	$7.20 per hour	41	37 40	8 00	13 00	14,600 00
Crane, J. P.	$400 per week	40	53 00		13 00	19,600 00
Kimball, A. L.	$350 per week	40	43 00		14 00	17,150 00
Woods, C. N.	$6.50 per hour	42	31 70	8 00	11 00	6,920 00

For each employee, taxable earnings for FICA are based on the first $36,000, and taxable earnings for unemployment insurance are based on the first $7,000 (state and federal).

Instructions

1. Complete the payroll register, using a FICA tax of 7.1 percent.
2. Prepare a general journal entry to record the payroll and the payment of the employees. Assume that the company issues individual checks out of its regular bank account beginning with check no. 864.

Problem Set B

Problem 9-1B James Noble, an employee of Andrews Motors, worked 46 hours during the week of March 16 to 22. His rate of pay is $9.20 per hour, and he receives time-and-a-half for all work in excess of 40 hours per week. Noble is married and claims two exemptions on his W-4 form. His wages are subject to the following deductions.

a. Federal income tax (use the table in Figure 9-3, page 254)
b. FICA tax at 7.1 percent
c. Union dues, $7.40
d. Medical insurance, $25.50

Instructions

Compute his regular pay, overtime pay, gross pay, and net pay.

Problem 9-2B The Lakeside Motel has the following payroll information for the week ended April 18.

Name	Daily Time M	T	W	T	F	S	S	Pay Rate	Federal Income Tax	Union Dues	Earnings at End of Previous Week
Albers, John	0	8	8	8	8	8	0	5 60	26 60	4 00	3,510 00
Conrad, Jean	8	8	8	8	8	0	0	7 10	41 60	4 00	2,392 00
Johnson, Donna	0	0	8	8	8	8	8	4 00	20 70		1,280 00
Mennen, Roy	0	4	8	8	8	8	8	4 00	19 20		1,686 00
Palmer, Ronald	8	8	8	8	8	4	0	6 20	39 20	4 00	3,430 00

The firm is subject to the Fair Labor Standards Act regarding minimum wages. However, being a motel, it is exempt from paying time-and-a-half for 44 hours of work or less. In this case, all hours are compensated at the regular rate. For each employee, taxable earnings for FICA are based on the first $36,000, and taxable earnings for unemployment insurance (state and federal) are based on the first $7,000. The amounts of employees' income tax withheld are given.

Instructions

1. Complete the payroll register, using 7.1 percent of earnings for calculating FICA tax withholding.
2. Prepare a general journal entry to record the payroll. The firm's general ledger contains a Wages Expense account and a Wages Payable account.
3. Assuming that the firm uses a special payroll bank account, make the entry in the general journal to record check no. 53.

Problem 9-3B The Rhode Island Products Company is subject to the Fair Labor Standards Act and, accordingly, pays time-and-a-half for all hours worked in excess of 40 per week. The following information is available from the time cards and employees' individual earnings records for the pay period ended March 16.

Name	Clock Card No.	Daily Time M	T	W	T	F	S	S	Regular Rate	Income Tax Exemption	Union Dues	Medical Insurance	Earnings at End of Previous Week
Clark, C. R.	76	8	8	8	10	8	0	0	7 80	2	5 00	9 60	2,580 00
Dillon, L. C.	77	8	8	8	8	8	0	0	8 55	2	5 00	9 60	1,815 00
Evans, M. E.	78	8	8	8	8	8	4	4	7 50	4	5 00	10 50	3,255 00
Keller, D. N.	79	8	8	9	9	8	6	0	7 80	3	5 00	10 00	3,345 00
Norton, T. C.	80	8	8	8	8	8	0	0	9 00	4	5 00	10 50	3,480 00

For each employee, taxable earnings for FICA are based on the first $36,000, and taxable earnings for unemployment insurance (state and federal) are based on the first $7,000.

Instructions

1. Complete the payroll register, using the wage-bracket income tax withholding table in Figure 9-3 (page 254). The FICA tax is 7.1 percent. Assume that all employees are married.
2. Prepare a general journal entry to record the payroll. The firm's general ledger contains a Wages Expense account and a Wages Payable account.
3. Assume that the firm uses a special payroll bank account and issues check no. 113.

Problem 9-4B The Quincy Insurance Company is subject to the Fair Labor Standards Act and, accordingly, pays its employees time-and-a-half for all hours worked in excess of 40 per week. The following information is available from Quincy's time book and the employee's individual earnings records for the payroll period ended December 8.

Name	Pay Rate	Hours Worked	Federal Income Tax		Union Dues		Medical Insurance		Earnings at End of Previous Week	
Glenn, D. N.	$7.10 per hour	46	41	10	6	00	14	00	16,950	00
Sharp, D. L.	$460.00 per week	40	72	00			16	00	22,540	00
Vaughn, J. A.	$325.00 per week	40	41	00			12	00	15,925	00
Wise, T. C.	$5.90 per hour	48	42	70	6	00	12	00	6,946	00

For each employee, taxable earnings for FICA are based on the first $36,000, and taxable earnings for unemployment are based on the first $7,000 (state and federal).

Instructions

1. Complete the payroll register, using a FICA tax of 7.1 percent.
2. Prepare a general journal entry to record the payroll and the payment of the employees. Assume that the company issues individual checks out of its regular bank account beginning with check no. 716.

10 Payroll Accounting: Employer's Taxes, Payments, and Reports

Learning Objectives

After you have completed this chapter, you will be able to do the following:

1. Journalize the entry to record payroll tax expense.

2. Journalize the entry for the deposit of employees' income taxes withheld and FICA taxes (both employees' withheld and employer's matching share).

3. Journalize the entries for the payment of employer's state and federal unemployment taxes.

4. Complete Employer's Quarterly Federal Tax Return, Form 941.

5. Prepare W-2 forms and W-3 forms.

6. Prepare state and federal unemployment insurance reports and the related journal entries.

7. Calculate the premium for workers' compensation insurance, and prepare the entry for payment in advance.

8. Determine the amount of adjustment for workers' compensation insurance at end of year, and record adjustment.

In Chapter 9, we talked about the computing and recording of such payroll data as gross pay, employees' income tax withheld, employees' FICA tax withheld, and various deductions requested by employees. Now we're going to get around to the payment of these withholdings and the taxes levied on the employer based on total payroll.

EMPLOYER'S IDENTIFICATION NUMBER

As you know quite well, everyone who works has a Social Security number, a number that is a vital part of his or her federal income tax returns. For an employer, a counterpart to the Social Security number is the **employer identification number.** Each employer of one or more persons is required to have such a number, and it must be listed on all reports and payments of employees' federal income tax withholding and FICA taxes.

EMPLOYER'S PAYROLL TAXES

An employer's payroll taxes are levied on the employer on the basis of the gross wages paid to the employees. Payroll taxes—like property taxes—are an expense of doing business. Harding and Associates records these taxes in the Payroll Tax Expense account and debits the account for the company's FICA taxes as well as for state and federal unemployment taxes. In T account form Payroll Tax Expense for Harding and Associates would look like the following example.

Payroll Tax Expense

+	−
FICA (employer's matching portion)	Closed at the end of the year along with all other expense accounts
Federal Unemployment Tax	
State Unemployment Tax	

As you can see, FICA tax (employer's share), **federal unemployment tax,** and **state unemployment tax** are included under the "umbrella" of Payroll Tax Expense. The unemployment taxes are levied on the employer only.

Employer's Matching Portion of FICA Tax

The FICA tax is imposed on both employer and employee. The firm's accountant deducts the employee's share from gross wages and records it in the payroll entry under FICA Tax Payable (the same liability account as shown in Chapter 9). Next, he or she determines the employer's share by multiplying the employer's FICA tax rate (assumed to be 7.1 percent) times the total FICA-taxable earnings (gross annual earnings for the calendar year for each employee up to an assumed $36,000). In this text, we shall assume that the same tax rate applies to both the employer and the employee. The accountant gets the FICA-taxable earnings figure from the payroll register. In Figure 10-1 we take another look at the Taxable Earnings columns from the payroll register for the week ended November 7, 19–, shown in Figure 9-4.

By T accounts, the entry to record the employer's portion of the FICA tax looks like this.

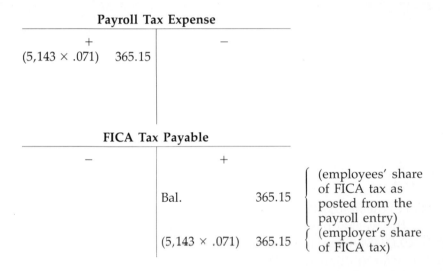

Note particularly that the FICA Tax Payable account is often used for the tax liability of both the employer and the employee. This is logical because both FICA taxes are paid at the same time and the same place. There might be a slight difference between the employer's and the employee's share of FICA taxes, due to the rounding-off process (or to slightly different rates, as in 1984). In our example, the accountant calculates the employee's share by taking 7.1 percent (assumed rate) of the taxable earnings of each worker, then adding these figures to find the total amount due for all employees. At the same time, she or he determines the employer's share by taking 7.1 percent of the total taxable earnings of all the employees. The two figures may vary, but only by a few cents.

Figure 10-1

Amount of employees' earnings that are less than $7,000 per employee for the year

Amount of employees' earnings that are less than $12,000 per employee for the year (Many states use $7,000 for each employee.)

Amount of employees' earnings that are less than $36,000 per employee for the year

TAXABLE EARNINGS		
STATE UNEMPLOYMENT	FEDERAL UNEMPLOYMENT	FICA
2 4 0 00		4 7 5 00
3 9 2 00		3 9 2 00
		5 3 5 00
3 6 0 00	3 6 0 00	3 6 0 00
3 8 4 00	3 8 4 00	3 8 4 00
		7 2 0 00
		6 0 0 00
		5 0 6 00
2 4 0 00		4 7 5 00
		6 9 6 00
1 6 1 6 00	7 4 4 00	5 1 4 3 00

Employer's state unemployment tax $1,616 × .03 = $48.48

Employer's federal unemployment tax $1,136 × .008 = $9.09

Employer's FICA tax 5,143 × .071 = $365.15

Employer's Federal Unemployment Tax (FUTA)

The employer's federal unemployment tax is levied on the employer only. Congress may from time to time change the rate. But for now, let's assume a rate of .8 percent (.008) of the first $7,000 earned by each employee during the calendar year. For the weekly payroll period for Harding and Associates, the tax liability is $9.09 ($1,136 of unemployment taxable earnings taken from the payroll register multiplied by .008, the tax rate). By T accounts, the entry is as follows.

Payroll Tax Expense		Federal Unemployment Tax Payable	
+	−	−	+
(1,136 × .008) 9.09			(1,136 × .008) 9.09

Employer's State Unemployment Tax

This tax, like the federal unemployment tax, is paid by the employer only. The rate of the state unemployment tax varies considerably among the states. During recent years, with the trend toward higher unemployment benefits, many states have adopted a base of at least $7,000 and rates of 2.7 percent or higher. However, let us assume here that Harding and Associates is subject to a rate of 3 percent of the first $12,000 of each employee's earnings. As shown in the portion of the payroll register illustrated in Figure 10-1, $1,616 of earnings are subject to the state unemployment tax. Accordingly, by T accounts, the state unemployment tax based on taxable earnings is as follows.

Payroll Tax Expense		State Unemployment Tax Payable	
+	−	−	+
(1,616 × .03) 48.48			(1,616 × .03) 48.48

To make things clearer in the foregoing discussion, figures for the three employer's payroll taxes have been presented separately. Now let's combine this information into one entry, which follows the regular payroll entry. Harding and Associates pays its employees weekly, so it also makes its Payroll Tax Expense entry weekly.

Objective 1

Journalize the entry to record payroll tax expense.

	DATE	DESCRIPTION	POST. REF.	DEBIT	CREDIT	
		GENERAL JOURNAL			PAGE _31_	
17	19– Nov. 7	Payroll Tax Expense		4 2 2 72		17
18		FICA Tax Payable			3 6 5 15	18
19		Federal Unemployment Tax Payable			9 09	19
20		State Unemployment Tax Payable			4 8 48	20
21		To record employer's share of				21
22		FICA tax and employer's federal				22
23		and state unemployment taxes.				23
24						24
25						25
26						26
27						27

JOURNAL ENTRIES FOR RECORDING PAYROLL

At this point let us restate in general journal form the entries that have been recorded, using the payroll register illustrated in Chapter 9 (Figure 9-4) as the source of information. First, we record the payroll entry.

1	19– Nov.	7	Sales Salary Expense		5	3	5	2	00										1
2			Office Salary Expense		1	5	9	1	00										2
3			Employees' Income Tax Payable								1	2	4	0	10			3
4			FICA Tax Payable									3	6	5	17			4
5			Employees' Bond Deductions															5
6			Payable									1	1	2	00			6
7			Employees' Union Dues Payable										9	0	00			7
8			Employees' Medical Insurance															8
9			Payable									2	1	6	00			9
10			Employees' Community Chest															10
11			Payable										3	7	00			11
12			Accounts Receivable										4	0	00			12
13			Salaries Payable								4	8	4	2	73			13
14			Payroll register page 68, for week															14
15			ended November 7.															15
16																		16

Next, the entry to record the employer's payroll taxes is journalized.

17		7	Payroll Tax Expense		4	2	2	72							17
18			FICA Tax Payable							3	6	5	15		18
19			Federal Unemployment Tax Payable									9	09		19
20			State Unemployment Tax Payable								4	8	48		20
21			To record employer's share of												21
22			FICA tax and employer's federal												22
23			and state unemployment taxes.												23
24															24

Finally, Harding and Associates, on the basis of the previous entry, issues one check payable to a payroll bank account. To pay its employees, it will draw separate payroll checks on this payroll bank account.

25		7	Salaries Payable		4	8	4	2	73						25
26			Cash							4	8	4	2	73	26
27			To record payment of employees												27
28			(by issuing one check payable												28
29			to payroll bank account).												29
30															30

As stated previously, in the first payroll entry, small employers will credit Cash directly instead of Salaries Payable.

PAYMENTS OF FICA TAXES AND EMPLOYEES' INCOME TAX WITHHOLDING

After an employer has paid the employees, he or she has to make payments in the form of federal tax deposits for (1) employees' federal income taxes withheld, (2) employees' FICA taxes withheld, and (3) the employer's share of FICA taxes. These deposits, which put the employers on a pay-as-you-go basis, are made during the three-month quarter.

For *large-sized employers*, if the combined total of undeposited employees' income taxes and FICA taxes levied on both employees and employer is greater than $3,000 for an **eighth-of-a-month period** (approximately three or four days), the employer has to make deposits within three banking days after the end of the period and must include at least 95 percent of the tax liability. Note that these amounts are cumulative. These eighth-of-a-month periods end on the 3rd, 7th, 11th, 15th, 19th, 22nd, 25th, and last day of any month. For example, assume that an employer has $4,950 of undeposited taxes for an eighth-of-a-month period ending on Friday, September 7. Since the banks are traditionally closed on Saturday and Sunday, the employer would have to make the deposit by Wednesday, September 12.

For *medium-sized employers*, if the total undeposited income taxes and FICA taxes for any *month* is between $500 and $3,000, the employer has to make the deposit within fifteen days after the end of the month.

But now suppose you're just a *small-sized employer*, and the total amount of your undeposited income taxes and FICA taxes at the end of the calendar **quarter** (three months) is less than $500; you don't have to make a deposit until you submit your quarterly return, Form 941. Now, remember that we're talking about a quarter (three months). You keep records on the basis of a calendar year, with the first quarter ending March 31, the second quarter ending June 30, the third quarter ending September 30, and the fourth quarter ending December 31. (If taxes are less than $500 at the end of a single month, they can be carried over to the following month within the quarter.)

Harding and Associates, for the week ended November 7, had the following taxes due:

Employees' income tax withheld	$1,240.10
Employees' FICA taxes withheld	365.17
Employer's FICA tax	365.15
Total	$1,970.42

Because Harding's tax liability is less than $3,000, it is not necessary to make a federal tax deposit at this time.

Assume that for the week ended November 14 Harding and Associates had the following taxes due:

Employees' income tax withheld	$1,364.11
Employees' FICA taxes withheld	401.68
Employer's FICA tax	401.68
Total	$2,167.47

The total cumulative liability for the two-week period is now $4,137.89 ($1,970.42 + $2,167.47). Because the total cumulative liability is greater than $3,000, it is necessary for the firm to make a federal tax deposit at the end of the second week, or within three banking days thereafter.

Harding receives a federal tax deposit card (preprinted with the company's name and tax number) from the Internal Revenue Service. The accountant records the amount of the deposit and the name of the bank where the deposit is to be submitted (any authorized commercial bank or Federal Reserve bank). The deposits are forwarded to the U.S. Treasury. The entry in general journal form to record the deposit of two weeks' taxes looks like this.

Objective 2

Journalize the entry for the deposit of employees' income taxes withheld and FICA taxes.

1	19— Nov.	15	Employees' Income Tax Payable	2 6 0 4 21		1
2			FICA Tax Payable	1 5 3 3 68		2
3			Cash		4 1 3 7 89	3
4			Issued check to record payment			4
5			of federal tax deposit.			5
6						6
7						7
8						8
9						9

The T accounts are as follows.

Employees' Income Tax Payable

Nov. 15	2,604.21	Nov. 7	1,240.10
		Nov. 14	1,364.11

FICA Tax Payable

Nov. 15	1,533.68	Nov. 7	365.17
		Nov. 7	365.15
		Nov. 14	401.68
		Nov. 14	401.68

Cash

		Nov. 15	4,137.89

PAYMENTS OF STATE UNEMPLOYMENT INSURANCE

States differ with regard to both the rate and the taxable base for unemployment insurance. The state tax is usually due by the end of the month following the end of the calendar quarter. Here's the general journal entry made by Harding and Associates for the first quarter (January, February, and March).

Objective 3

Journalize the entries for the payment of employer's state and federal unemployment taxes.

1	19– Apr.	27	State Unemployment Tax Payable	2 0 3 0 69		1
2			Cash		2 0 3 0 69	2
3			To record payment of state			3
4			unemployment tax.			4
5						5
6						6
7						7
8						8
9						9
10						10

The T accounts are as follows.

State Unemployment Tax Payable			Cash	
−	+		+	−
Apr. 27 2,030.69	Apr. 27 Bal. 2,030.69		Apr. 27	2,030.69

The balance in State Unemployment Tax Payable is the result of weekly entries recording payroll tax expense.

PAYMENTS OF FEDERAL UNEMPLOYMENT INSURANCE

The FUTA tax is calculated quarterly, during the month following the end of each calendar quarter. **If the accumulated tax liability is greater than $100, the tax is deposited in a commercial bank or Federal Reserve bank, accompanied by a preprinted federal tax deposit card,** like the form used to deposit employees' federal income tax withholding and FICA taxes. The due date for this deposit is the last day of the month following the end of the quarter, the same as the due dates for the Employer's Quarterly Federal Tax Return and for state unemployment taxes.

19– Apr.	27	Federal Unemployment Tax Payable		4 7 6 30*		
		Cash			4 7 6 30	
		To record payment of federal				
		unemployment tax.				

*The calculation of $476.30 is shown on page 283.

The T accounts are as follows.

Federal Unemployment Tax Payable			Cash	
−	+		+	−
Apr. 27 476.30	Apr. 27 Bal. 476.30		Apr. 27	476.30

The balance in Federal Unemployment Tax Payable is taken from the weekly entries recording payroll tax expense.

Employer's Quarterly Federal Tax Return (Form 941)

This return, which applies to federal income taxes withheld and FICA taxes, must be filed by the end of the month following the end of the quarter. Consequently, the due dates for a calendar-year taxpayer are: first quarter, April 30; second quarter, July 31; third quarter, October 31; fourth quarter, January 31. Once an employer has secured an identification number and has filed his or her first return, the Internal Revenue Service sends forms directly to the employer. These forms will have the employer's name, address, and identification number filled in.

Harding's sources of information for its Employer's Quarterly Federal Tax Return are the payroll registers and the general ledger accounts. Its Form 941 for the fourth quarter is shown in Figure 10-2. Note that in the illustration the taxable FICA wages are multiplied by 14.2 percent (the 7.1 percent portion contributed by the employees plus the 7.1 percent matching portion contributed by the employer). Also note the tax deposit section indicating the amount and date of each deposit. In this case, the deposits are up to date and no payment is due. However, if an amount is shown on line 15 for undeposited taxes due, the entry for payment is a debit to Employees' Income Tax Payable, a debit to FICA Tax Payable (employees' and employer's share), and a credit to Cash.

Objective 4

Complete Employer's Quarterly Federal Tax Return, Form 941.

Form **941** (Rev. January 19) Department of the Treasury Internal Revenue Service	**Employer's Quarterly Federal Tax Return** ► For Paperwork Reduction Act Notice, see page 2.	OMB No. 1545-0029

		T
		FF

Your name, address, employer identification number, and calendar quarter of return. (If not correct, please change.)

Name (as distinguished from trade name)
Donald A. Harding

Date quarter ended
December 31, 19--

Employer identification number
64-7218463

Trade name, if any
Harding and Associates

Address and ZIP code
546 South Foss Street
Spokane, WA 99203

T
FF
FD
FP
I
T

If address is different from prior return, check here ►

Record of Federal Tax Liability
(Complete if line 13 is $500 or more)

See the instructions under rule 4 on page 4 for details before checking these boxes.

Check only if you made eighth-monthly deposits using the 95% rule. . . . . . ► ☐
Check only if you are a first-time 3-banking-day depositor. . . . . ► ☐

Date wages paid	Tax liability
Day	
1st-3rd A	
4th-7th B	2,153.68
8th-11th C	
12th-15th D	2,028.56
16th-19th E	
20th-22nd F	2,244.60
23rd-25th G	
26th-last H	2,212.82
I Total . ►	8,639.66
1st-3rd I	
4th-7th J	1,970.42
8th-11th K	
12th-15th L	2,167.47
16th-19th M	
20th-22nd N	2,005.36
23rd-25th O	
26th-last P	2,151.19
II Total . ►	8,294.44
1st-3rd Q	
4th-7th R	2,225.52
8th-11th S	
12th-15th T	2,228.36
16th-19th U	
20th-22nd V	2,177.80
23rd-25th W	
26th-last X	1,870.70
III Total . ►	8,502.38
IV Total for quarter (add lines I, II, and III)	25,436.48

(First month of quarter / Second month of quarter / Third month of quarter as row-group labels on left margin)

If you are not liable for returns in the future, write "FINAL" . . . . ►
Date final wages paid . . . . ►

Complete for First Quarter Only

1 a Number of employees (except household) employed in the pay period that includes March 12th . ► **12**

b If you are a subsidiary corporation AND your parent corporation files a consolidated Form 1120, enter parent corporation's employer identification number (EIN) ►

2 Total wages and tips subject to withholding, plus other compensation . . . . ►	91,376	40
3 a Income tax withheld from wages, tips, pensions, annuities, sick pay, gambling, etc. . . . . ►	13,305	93
b Backup withholding . . . . ►	0	
c Total income tax withheld (add lines 3a and 3b) . ►	13,305	93
4 Adjustment of withheld income tax for preceding quarters of calendar year:		
a From wages, tips, pensions, annuities, sick pay, gambling, etc. . . . . ►	0	
b From backup withholding . . . . ►	0	
c Total adjustments (add lines 4a and 4b) . . . ►	0	
5 Adjusted total of income tax withheld (line 3c as adjusted by line 4c)	13,305	93
6 Taxable social security wages paid: $ 85,426 40 x 14.2% (.142) . .	12,130	55
7 a Taxable tips reported: $ 0 x 7.1% (.071) . .	0	
h Tips deemed to be wages (see instructions): $ 0 x 7.1% (.071) . .	0	
8 Total social security taxes (add lines 6, 7a, and 7b) . .	12,130	55
9 Adjustment of social security taxes (see instructions) ►	0	
10 Adjusted total of social security taxes . . . . . ►	12,130	55
11 Total taxes (add lines 5 and 10) . . . . ►	25,436	48
12 Advance earned income credit (EIC) payments, if any ►	0	
13 Net taxes (subtract line 12 from line 11). This must equal line IV (plus line IV of Schedule A (Form 941) if you have treated backup withholding as a separate liability.) . . . . ►	25,436	48

14 Total deposits for quarter, including any overpayment applied from a prior quarter, from your records . . . . ►	25,436	48
15 Undeposited taxes due (subtract line 14 from line 13). Enter here and pay to Internal Revenue Service . . . . . . ►	0	
16 If line 14 is more than line 13, enter overpayment here ► $		

and check if to be: ☐ Applied to next return, or ☐ Refunded.

Under penalties of perjury, I declare that I have examined this return, including accompanying schedules and statements, and to the best of my knowledge and belief it is true, correct, and complete.

Signature ► *Donald A. Harding*   Title ► Owner   Date ► 1/29/19--

Please file this form with your Internal Revenue Service Center (see instructions on "Where to File").   Form **941** (Rev.   )

Figure 10-2

Withholding Statements for Employees
(W-2 forms)

The employer has to furnish W-2 forms to employees on or before the January 31 following the close of the preceding year or within 30 days after an employee leaves service. The source of the information on the W-2 form is the employee's individual earnings record. Graham C. Laboe's earnings record, presented in Chapter 9, will be our source for this example (see Figure 9-7). The accountant fills out Form W-2 (Figure 10-3) in quadruplicate and gives copies B and C to the employee.

Notice the squares in block 5. Statutory employees are life insurance and traveling salespersons; legal representatives include attorneys and parents; 942 employees include household workers; subtotal is used if the employer is submitting more than forty-one W-2 forms. Block 7 shows the total paid to employees as advance earned income credit payments. For qualifying low-income taxpayers, earned income credit is a deduction from income tax owed.

Objective 5

Prepare W-2 forms and W-3 forms.

Figure 10-3

1 Control number 22222	For Paperwork Reduction Act Notice, see back of Copy D. OMB No. 1545-0008	For Official Use Only	
2 Employer's name, address, and ZIP code Harding and Associates 546 South Foss Street Spokane, WA 99203	3 Employer's identification number 64-7218463		4 Employer's State number 462-718
	5 Stat. employee ☐ Deceased ☐ Legal rep. ☐ 942 emp. ☐ Subtotal ☐ Void ☐		
	6 Allocated tips		7 Advance EIC payment
8 Employee's social security number 543-24-1680	9 Federal income tax withheld $5,768.29	10 Wages, tips, other compensation $30,161.00	11 Social security tax withheld $2,141.43
12 Employee's name (first, middle, last) Graham Charles Laboe		13 Social security wages $30,161.00	14 Social security tips None
	16 *		
1582 North Pierce Street Spokane, WA 99204	17 State income tax	18 State wages, tips, etc.	19 Name of State
	20 Local income tax	21 Local wages, tips, etc.	22 Name of locality
15 Employee's address and ZIP code			

Form **W-2 Wage and Tax Statement** 19   **Copy A For Social Security Administration** • See Instructions for Forms W-2 and W-2P   Department of the Treasury Internal Revenue Service

Employer's Annual Federal Income
Tax Reports

Harding sends copy A of each employee's W-2 form to the District Director of Internal Revenue on or before February 28. The accountant attaches these to Form W-3, the Transmittal of Income and Tax Statements, shown in Figure 10-4.

To sum up thus far: The employer must submit the following at the end of the calendar year: (1) Employer's Quarterly Federal Tax Return for the fourth quarter, (2) copy A of all employees' W-2 forms, and (3) Form W-3. The employer keeps copy D of the W-2 forms.

Form W-3

1 Control number	**33333**	OMB No. 1545-0008			

Kind of Payer and Tax Statements Transmitted ☐	2 941/941E ☐ Military ☐ 943 ☐ CT-1 ☐ 942 ☐ Medicare Fed. emp. ☐	3 W-2 ☒ W-2P ☐	4.	5 Number of statements attached **12**

6 Allocated tips	7 Advance EIC payments 0	8

9 Federal income tax withheld **61,093.22**	10 Wages, tips, and other compensation **343,220.32**	11 Social security (FICA) tax withheld **23,048.04**

12 Employer's State number **462–718**	13 Social security (FICA) wages **324,620.32**	14 Social security (FICA) tips 0

15 Employer's identification number **64— 7218463**	16 Establishment number 0

17 Employer's name Harding and Associates	18 Gross annuity, pension, etc. (Form W-2P) 0

546 South Foss Street Spokane, WA 99203	20 Taxable amount (Form W-2P) 0 21 Income tax withheld by third-party payer 0

| 19 Employer's address and ZIP code (If available, place label over boxes 15, 17, and 19.) | |

Under penalties of perjury, I declare that I have examined this return and accompanying documents, and to the best of my knowledge and belief, they are true, correct, and complete. In the case of documents without recipients' identifying numbers, I have complied with the requirements of the law in attempting to secure such numbers from the recipients.

Signature ► *Donald A. Harding*   Title ► Owner   Date ►1/31/--

Form **W-3** Transmittal of Income and Tax Statements

Department of the Treasury
Internal Revenue Service

Figure 10-4

Reports and Payments of State Unemployment Insurance

Figure 10-5 shows the state unemployment insurance return for Harding and Associates for the first quarter with an assumed state rate of 3 percent on the first $12,000 paid to each employee during the calendar year. The source for the wage report section is the employees' individual earnings records.

Various states differ with regard to both the rate and the taxable base for unemployment insurance. The state tax is usually due by the end of the month following the end of the calendar quarter; the due dates consequently coincide with the due dates for Form 941.

Here is the general journal entry made by Harding and Associates for the first quarter (January, February, and March).

Objective 6

Prepare state and federal unemployment insurance reports and the related journal entries.

1	19– Apr.	27	State Unemployment Tax Payable	2 0 3 0 69		1
2			Cash		2 0 3 0 69	2
3			To record payment of state			3
4			unemployment tax.			4

ATTACH ADDITIONAL WAGE LISTING HERE

2. FEDERAL I.D. NO.	TAX OFFICE	EMP. CLASS	3. CALENDAR QUARTER ENDING DATE MO. DAY YR.	TAX RATE %	4. EMPLOYMENT SEC. NO. ACCOUNT	BR
64-7218463	15	7	3 31 -	3.0	462-718	810

STATE OF WASHINGTON
EMPLOYMENT SECURITY DEPARTMENT
OLYMPIA, WASHINGTON 98504

EMPLOYER'S QUARTERLY REPORT OF EMPLOYEE'S WAGES

LINE	5. EMPLOYEE'S SOCIAL SECURITY NUMBER	6. EMPLOYEE'S NAME LAST FIRST INITIAL	7. HOURS WORKED THIS QTR.	8. TOTAL WASHINGTON WAGES PAID THIS QUARTER
L1	533 16 7285	Anderson, Dennis L.	582	2,840 00
L2	541 27 6982	Bowlen, Ralph P.	598	2,620 00
L3	539 87 1643	Daniels, John N.	572	5,980 00
L4	533 98 5379	Drew, Nancy R.	520	2,756 00
L5	526 71 8478	Farrell, Steven L.	520	2,150 00
L6	541 19 6143	Harwood, Lance C.	520	11,400 00
L7	543 24 1680	Laboe, Graham C.	520	7,176 00
L8	533 62 1745	Lyman, Mary C.	520	7,200 00
L9	541 38 9394	Miller, Robert M.	598	5,769 50
L10	540 29 7162	Olsen, Marvin C.	582	2,422 00
L11	538 12 2796	Stanfield, John D.	520	10,200 00
L12	529 92 8131	Tucker, Norma P.	572	7,176 00

▶ READ INSTRUCTIONS ON BACK OF PAGE 3 BEFORE COMPLETING THIS FORM.

▶ IF ANY BUSINESS CHANGES HAVE OCCURRED, COMPLETE PAGE 3.

1. EMPLOYER'S NAME AND ADDRESS

Donald A. Harding
Harding and Associates
546 South Foss Street
Spokane, WA 99203

TOTALS FOR THIS PAGE	NO. OF PAGES	9. NO. OF EMPLOYEES 12	10.	WAGES 67,689 50
GRAND TOTALS ALL PAGES	11. 1	12. 12	13.	67,689 50

PAGE 1 - ORIGINAL
EMPLOYMENT SECURITY DEPARTMENT COPY

— **DO NOT DETACH**   **DO NOT DETACH**

EMS 5208

▶ ATTACH CHECK HERE

25. EMPLOYER'S NAME AND ADDRESS

Donald A. Harding
Harding and Associates
546 South Foss Street
Spokane, WA 99203

STATE OF WASHINGTON
EMPLOYMENT SECURITY DEPARTMENT
OLYMPIA, WASHINGTON 98504

EMPLOYER'S QUARTERLY TAX REPORT

▶ DO NOT MAKE ENTRIES IN THE SHADED AREAS.

COMPUTATION OF PAYMENT

		FOR DEPARTMENT USE	
14.	TOTAL WAGES (SAME AS ITEM 13)		67,689 50
15.	EXCESS WAGES		0
16.	TAXABLE WAGES (ITEM 14 LESS ITEM 15)		67,689 50
17.	TAX DUE YOUR TAX RATE 3% TIMES ITEM 16		2,030 69
18.	PENALTY - LATE PAYMENT (MINIMUM PENALTY - $2.00)		0
19.	INTEREST		0
20.	ADJUSTMENT (ATTACH STATEMENT OF ACCOUNT - FORM EMS 5229)		0
21.	PENALTY - LATE REPORT ($10.00)		0
22.	REMITTANCE (MAKE CHECKS PAYABLE TO: EMPLOYMENT SECURITY DEPARTMENT)		2,030 69

23. NUMBER OF COVERED EMPLOYEES	1ST MONTH 12	2ND MONTH 12	3RD MONTH 12

24. I CERTIFY THAT THE INFORMATION CONTAINED IN THIS REPORT IS TRUE AND CORRECT AND THAT NO PART OF THE TAX REPORTED WAS OR IS TO BE DEDUCTED FROM WORKERS WAGES.

SIGNATURE *Donald A. Harding*   TITLE Owner

DATE April 27, 19--   TELEPHONE NO. (509) 272-4414

26. ANNUAL TAXABLE WAGE BASE EACH EMPLOYEE	27. FEDERAL I.D. NO.	TAX OFFICE	EMP. CLASS	28. CALENDAR QUARTER ENDING DATE MO. DAY YR.	29. TAX RATE %	30. EMPLOYMENT SEC. NO. ACCOUNT	BR
$12,000	64-7218463	15	7	3 31 -	3.0	462-718	810

PAGE 1 - ORIGINAL
EMPLOYMENT SECURITY DEPARTMENT COPY

FOR DEPARTMENTAL USE			
DATE RECEIVED	TAX	PENALTY	INTEREST
RECEIVED BY	AUDITED BY		

Figure 10-5

REPORTS AND PAYMENTS OF FEDERAL UNEMPLOYMENT INSURANCE

Each employer who is subject to the Federal Unemployment Tax Act, as outlined in Chapter 9, must submit an Employer's Annual Federal Unemployment Tax Return, Form 940, not later than the January 31 following the close of the calendar year. This deadline may be extended until February 10 if the employer has made deposits paying the FUTA tax liability in full. The FUTA tax is calculated quarterly, during the month following the end of each calendar quarter. **If the accumulated tax liability is greater than $100, the tax is deposited in a commercial bank or Federal Reserve bank, accompanied by a preprinted federal tax deposit card.** The due date for this deposit is the last day of the month following the end of the quarter, the same as the dates for the Employer's Quarterly Federal Tax Return and state unemployment taxes.

The accountant computes the tax liability for the first quarter as follows: Suppose that unemployment-taxable earnings are $59,537.50 and that the FUTA tax rate is .8 percent. Then $59,537.50 × .008 = $476.30. As stated on page 278, the entry for the deposit of the tax, in general journal form, is as follows.

19–							
Apr.	27	Federal Unemployment Tax Payable		4 7 6 30			
		Cash				4 7 6 30	
		To record payment of federal					
		unemployment tax.					

Unemployment taxable earnings for the second quarter are $15,240, which means a tax liability of $121.92. As the year goes on, many employees' total earnings will pass the $7,000 mark and the firm's tax liability will be reduced accordingly.

Harding does not have to make a deposit following the third quarter because the total accumulated liability is less than $100. Harding can pay the unpaid tax liability of $73.78 ($51.62 for the third quarter, and $22.16 for the fourth quarter) when the Employer's Annual Federal Unemployment Tax Return (Form 940) is filed.

Figure 10-6 presents the annual return (Form 940) for Harding and Associates. The employer should complete the quarterly state unemployment tax return for the last quarter of the year before he or she tries to prepare the Employer's Annual Federal Unemployment Tax Return. Data from the state returns are the source of information for the federal Form 940.

Form 940

Department of the Treasury
Internal Revenue Service

Employer's Annual Federal Unemployment (FUTA) Tax Return

▶ For Paperwork Reduction Act Notice, see page 2.

OMB No. 1545-0028

19—

T	
FF	
FD	
FP	
I	
T	

If incorrect, make any necessary change. ▶

Name (as distinguished from trade name)
Donald A. Harding

Trade name, if any
Harding and Associates

Address and ZIP code
546 South Foss Street
Spokane, WA 99203

Calendar Year
19—

Employer identification number
64-7218463

A Did you pay all required contributions to your State unemployment fund by the due date of Form 940? . . . . ☒ Yes ☐ No

If you check the "Yes" box, enter amount of contributions paid to your State unemployment fund . . . . . ▶ $ ___9,856__56_

B Are you required to pay contributions to only one State? . . . . ☒ Yes ☐ No

If you checked the "Yes" box, (1) Enter the name of the State where you are required to pay contributions . . . . ▶ Washington
(2) Enter your State reporting number(s) as shown on State unemployment tax return . . . . . ▶ 462-718

PART I.—Computation of Taxable Wages and Credit Reduction (To Be Completed by All Taxpayers)

1	Total payments (including exempt payments) during the calendar year for services of employees	**1**	343,220	32
2	Exempt payments. (Explain each exemption shown, attaching additional sheets if necessary) ▶	Amount paid			
		2			
3	Payments for services in excess of $7,000. Enter only the excess over the first $7,000 paid to individual employees exclusive of exempt amounts entered on line 2. Do not use State wage limitation	**3**	259,220	32	
4	Total exempt payments (add lines 2 and 3)	**4**	259,220	32
5	**Total taxable wages** (subtract line 4 from line 1). (If any portion is exempt from State contributions, see instructions)▶	**5**	84,000	00

6 Credit reduction for unpaid advances to the States listed. Enter the wages included on line 5 above for each State and multiply by the rate shown.

(a) AR _____x.006 _____	(g) MI _____ x.006 _____	(m) VT _____ x .006 _____
(b) CT _____x.007 _____	(h) MN _____ x .006 _____	(n) WV _____ x .006 _____
(c) DE _____x.006 _____	(i) NJ _____ x .006 _____	**Outside the U.S.**
(d) DC _____x.011 _____	(j) OH _____ x .006 _____	(o) PR _____ x .006 _____
(e) IL _____x.007 _____	(k) PA _____ x.007 _____	(p) VI _____ x .006 _____
(f) KY _____x.003 _____	(l) RI _____ x .006 _____	

7 Total credit reduction (add lines 6(a) through 6(p) and enter on line 2, Part II or line 4, Part III) . . . . ▶ | **7** | 0 |

PART II.—Tax Due or Refund (Complete If You Checked the "Yes" Boxes in Both Items A and B Above)

1	FUTA tax. Multiply the wages on line 5, Part I, by .008 and enter here	**1**	672	00
2	Enter amount from line 7, Part I	**2**	0	
3	**Total FUTA tax** (add lines 1 and 2)	**3**	672	00
4	Less: Total FUTA tax deposited for the year from your records	**4**	598	22
5	**Balance due** (subtract line 4 from line 3—if over $100, see Part IV instructions). Pay to IRS . . ▶	**5**	73	78
6	**Overpayment** (subtract line 3 from line 4). Check if to be: ☐ Applied to next return, or ☐ Refunded . . ▶	**6**		

PART III.—Tax Due or Refund (Complete If You Checked the "No" Box in Either Item A or Item B Above. Also complete Part V)

1	Gross FUTA tax. Multiply the wages on line 5, Part I, by .035			**1**	
2	Maximum credit. Multiply the wages on line 5, Part I, by .027	**2**			
3	Enter the smaller of the amount on line 11, Part V, or line 2, Part III . .	**3**			
4	Enter amount from line 7, Part I			**4**	
5	**Credit allowable** (subtract line 4 from line 3)			**5**	
6	Total FUTA tax (subtract line 5 from line 1)			**6**	
7	Less: Total FUTA tax deposited for the year from your records			**7**	
8	**Balance due** (subtract line 7 from line 6—if over $100, see Part IV instructions). Pay to IRS . . ▶			**8**	
9	**Overpayment** (subtract line 6 from line 7). Check if to be: ☐ Applied to next return, or ☐ Refunded . . ▶			**9**	

PART IV.—Record of Quarterly Federal Tax Liability for Unemployment Tax (Do not include State liability)

Quarter	First	Second	Third	Fourth	Total for Year
Liability for quarter .	$476.30	$121.92	$51.62	$22.16	$672.00

If you will not have to file returns in the future, write "Final" here (see general instruction "Who Must File") . . ▶

Under penalties of perjury, I declare that I have examined this return, including accompanying schedules and statements, and to the best of my knowledge and belief, it is true, correct, and complete, and that no part of any payment made to a State unemployment fund claimed as a credit was or is to be deducted from the payments to employees.

Date ▶ 1/26/--   Signature ▶ *Donald A. Harding*   Title (Owner, etc.) ▶ Owner

Form **940**

Figure 10-6

WORKERS' COMPENSATION INSURANCE

Objective 7

Calculate the premium for workers' compensation insurance, and prepare the entry for payment in advance.

As we said in Chapter 9 when we were describing the laws affecting employment, most states require employers to provide **workers' compensation insurance** or industrial accident insurance, either through plans administered by the state or through private insurance companies authorized by the state. The employer usually has to pay all the premiums. The premium rate varies with the amount of risk the job entails and the company's number of accidents. Handling molten steel ingots is a lot more dangerous than typing reports. So it is very important that employees be identified properly according to the insurance premium classifications. For example, the rate for office work may be .15 percent of the payroll for office work; the rate for industrial labor in heavy manufacturing may be 3.5 percent of the payroll for that category. These same figures may be expressed as $.15 per $100 of payroll and $3.50 per $100 of payroll.

Generally, the employer pays a premium in advance, based on the estimated payrolls for the year. After the year ends, the employer knows the exact amounts of the payrolls and can calculate the exact premium. At this time, depending on the difference between the estimated and the exact premium, the employer either pays an additional premium or gets a credit for overpayment.

At Harding and Associates, there are two types of work classifications: office work and sales work. At the beginning of the year, the firm's accountant computed the estimated annual premium, based on the predicted payrolls for the year, as follows.

Classification	Predicted Payroll	Rate (Percent)	Estimated Premium
Office work	$ 76,000	.15	$ 76,000 × .0015 = $ 114
Sales work	280,000	.5	280,000 × .005 = 1,400
			Total estimated premium $1,514

As shown by T accounts, the accountant made the following entry.

Prepaid Insurance, Workers' Compensation		Cash	
+	−	+	−
Jan. 10 1,514			Jan. 10 1,514

Then, at the end of the calendar year, the accountant calculated the exact premium.

Classification	Exact Payroll	Rate (Percent)	Exact Premium
Office work	$ 78,000	.15	$ 78,000 × .0015 = $ 117.00
Sales work	286,512	.5	286,512 × .005 = 1,432.56
			Total exact premium $1,549.56

Therefore, the amount of the unpaid premium is

$1,549.56   Total exact premium
 1,514.00   Less total estimated premium paid

$ 35.56   Additional premium owed

Now the accountant makes an adjusting entry, similar to the adjusting entry for expired insurance; this entry appears on the work sheet. The accountant then makes an additional adjusting entry for the extra premium owed. By T accounts, the entries are as follows.

Objective 8

Determine the amount of adjustment for workers' compensation insurance at end of year, and record adjustment.

Workers' Compensation Insurance Expense

+	−
Dec. 31 Adj. 1,514.00	
Dec. 31 Adj. 35.56	

Prepaid Insurance, Workers' Compensation

+	−
Jan. 10 Bal. 1,514	Dec. 31 Adj. 1,514

Workers' Compensation Insurance Payable

−	+
	Dec. 31 Adj. 35.56

Harding and Associates will pay this amount of unpaid premium in January, together with the estimated premium for the next year.

ADJUSTING FOR ACCRUED SALARIES AND WAGES

Assume that $800 of salaries accrue for the time between the last payday and the end of the year. The adjusting entry is the same as that introduced in Chapter 5.

	DATE		DESCRIPTION	POST. REF.	DEBIT	CREDIT	
1			*Adjusting Entry*				1
2			*Salary Expense*		8 0 0 00		2
3			*Salaries Payable*			8 0 0 00	3

Salaries Payable is considered a liability account, as are employees' withholding taxes and deductions payable. Actually, federal income taxes and FICA taxes levied on employees do not legally become effective until the employees are paid. Therefore, for the purpose of recording the adjusting entry, one includes the entire liability of the gross salaries and wages under Salaries Payable or Wages Payable. In other words, in the adjusting entry, such accounts as Employees' Income Tax Payable, FICA Tax Payable (employees' share), and Employees' Union Dues Payable, are not used.

Adjusting Entry for Accrual of Payroll Taxes

As we have seen, the following taxes come under the Payroll Tax Expense account: the employer's share of the FICA tax, the state unemployment tax, and the federal unemployment tax. The employer becomes liable for these taxes only when the employees are actually paid, rather than at the time the liability to the employees is incurred. From the standpoint of legal liability, there should be no adjusting entry for Payroll Tax Expense. From the standpoint of the income statement, however, failure to make this entry means that this accrued expense for payroll taxes is not included; thus the expenses are understated and the net income is overstated, although by a rather inconsequential amount. Although the legal element is not consistent with good accounting practice, we have to abide by the law.

TAX CALENDAR

Now let's put it all together: Assume that the employer's combined monthly totals of employees' FICA taxes, employer's FICA tax, and employees' income tax withheld are usually greater than $500 and less than $3,000. So the accountant, in order to keep up with the task of paying and reporting the various taxes, compiles a chronological list of the due dates. We are including only the payroll taxes here; however, sales taxes and property taxes should also be listed. When you think about the penalties for nonpayment of taxes by the due dates, this chronological list seems to be well worth the trouble.

Jan. 10 Pay estimated annual premium for workers' compensation insurance. (This is an approximate date, as it varies among the states.)

31 Complete Employer's Quarterly Federal Tax Return, Form 941, for the fourth quarter and pay employees' income tax withholding, employees' FICA tax withholding, and employer's FICA tax for wages paid during the month of December.

31 Issue copies B and C of Wage and Tax statement, Form W-2, to employees.

31 Pay state unemployment tax liability for the previous quarter and submit state return, employer's tax report.

31 Pay federal unemployment tax liability for previous year and submit Form 940, Employer's Annual Federal Unemployment Tax Return.

Feb. 15 Make federal tax deposit for employees' income tax withholding, employees' FICA tax withholding, and employer's FICA tax for wages paid during the month of January.

28 Complete Transmittal of Income and Tax Statements, Form W-3, and attach copy A of W-2 forms for employees.

Mar. 15 Make federal tax deposit for employees' income tax withholding, employees' FICA tax withholding, and employer's FICA tax for wages paid during the month of February.

Apr. 30 Pay state unemployment tax liability for the previous quarter and submit state return, employer's tax report.

30 Complete Employer's Quarterly Federal Tax Return, Form 941, for the first quarter, and pay employees' income tax withholding, employees' FICA tax withholding, and employer's FICA tax for wages paid during the month of March.

30 Make federal tax deposit for federal unemployment tax liability if it exceeds $100.

PAYROLL SUMMARY

An employer's taxes (with assumed rates) based on the payroll are as follows. Remember that rates are always subject to change.

1. FICA tax, 7.1 percent of taxable income (the first $36,000 for each employee)
2. Federal unemployment tax, .8 percent of taxable income (the first $7,000 for each employee)
3. State unemployment tax, which varies from state to state, approximately 3 percent of taxable income (approximately the first $12,000 for each employee)

After recording each payroll entry from the payroll register, the accountant makes the following type of entry to record the employer's payroll taxes.

				Debit				Credit				
17		Payroll Tax Expense		4 2 2 72								17
18		FICA Tax Payable					3 6 5 15					18
19		Federal Unemployment Tax										19
20		Payable					9 09					20
21		State Unemployment Tax Payable					4 8 48					21
22		To record employer's share of										22
23		FICA tax and employer's federal										23
24		and state unemployment taxes.										24
25												25

Payment of the tax liabilities and sample journal entries are as follows.

1. Payment of the combined amounts of employees' income tax withheld, employees' FICA tax withheld, and employer's FICA tax falls into three brackets:

   a. **Large** If at the end of any eighth of a month (approximately three or four days) the cumulative amount of undeposited taxes so far for the calendar quarter (three months) is $3,000 or more, deposit the taxes within three banking days after the end of the period. The Internal Revenue Service divides any month into eight periods ending on the 3rd, 7th, 11th, 15th, 19th, 22nd, 25th, and last day of the month.

   b. **Medium** If at the end of any month (except the last month of a quarter) the cumulative amount of undeposited taxes for the quarter is at least $500 but less than $3,000, deposit the taxes within fifteen days after the end of the month. For the last month of the quarter, make the payment by the end of the next month.

   c. **Small** If at the end of a calendar month or calendar quarter (three months) the total amount of undeposited taxes is less than $500, make the payment when submitting the Employer's Quarterly Federal Tax Return.

					Debit				Credit				
1	19– Nov.	15	Employees' Income Tax Payable		2 6 0 4 21								1
2			FICA Tax Payable		1 5 3 3 68								2
3			Cash						4 1 3 7 89				3
4			Issued check to record payment										4
5			of federal tax deposit.										5
6													6
7													7
8													8

2. State unemployment tax is paid on a quarterly basis. Payment is due by the end of the next month following the end of the calendar quarter.

	19– Apr.	27	State Unemployment Tax Payable		2 0 3 0 69		
1					2 0 3 0 69		1
2			Cash			2 0 3 0 69	2
3			To record payment of state				3
4			unemployment tax.				4
5							5
6							6
7							7
8							8

3. If the amount of the accumulated federal unemployment tax liability exceeds $100, pay the tax by the end of the next month following the end of the quarter. If the federal unemployment tax payable is less than $100 at the end of the year, pay it by January 31 of the next year.

	19– Apr.	27	Federal Unemployment Tax Payable		4 7 6 30		
1					4 7 6 30		1
2			Cash			4 7 6 30	2
3			To record payment of federal				3
4			unemployment tax.				4
5							5
6							6

4. Workers' compensation insurance is based on a state plan or private insurance. At the beginning of the year, pay the premium in advance based on the estimated annual payroll. At the end of the year, when you know the actual payroll, adjust for the exact amount of the premium.

GLOSSARY

Eighth-of-a-month period A period used to determine the due date of tax deposits, designated by the Internal Revenue Service as follows: from the 1st to the 3rd of the month, from the 4th to the 7th of the month, from the 8th to the 11th of the month, from the 12th to the 15th of the month, from the 16th to the 19th of the month, from the 20th to the 22nd of the month, from the 23rd to the 25th of the month, and from the 26th to the last day of the month. (All dates are inclusive.)

Employer identification number The number assigned each employer by the Internal Revenue Service for use in the submission of reports and payments for FICA taxes and federal income tax withheld.

Federal unemployment tax A tax levied on the employer only, amounting to .8 percent of the first $7,000 of total earnings paid to each employee during the calendar year. This tax is used to supplement state unemployment benefits.

Payroll Tax Expense A general expense account used for recording the employer's matching portion of the FICA tax, the federal unemployment tax, and the state unemployment tax.

Quarter A three-month interval of the year, also referred to as a *calendar quarter*, as follows: first quarter, January, February, and March; second quarter, April, May, and June; third quarter, July, August, and September; fourth quarter, October, November, and December.

State unemployment tax A tax levied on the employer only. Rates differ among the various states; however, they are generally 2.7 percent or higher of the first $7,000 of total earnings paid to each employee during the calendar year. The proceeds are used to pay subsistence benefits to unemployed workers.

Workers' compensation insurance This insurance, usually paid for by the employer, provides benefits for employees injured or killed on the job. The rates vary according to the degree of risk inherent in the job. The plans may be sponsored by states or by private firms. The employer pays the premium in advance at the beginning of the year, based on the estimated payroll, and rates are adjusted after the exact payroll is known.

QUESTIONS, EXERCISES AND PROBLEMS

Discussion Questions

1. What payroll taxes are included under Payroll Tax Expense?
2. What information concerning the employee is included on a W-2 form?
3. How many copies of a W-2 form are prepared? To whom are the copies given?
4. What are Forms 940 and 941? How often are they prepared, and what are the due dates?
5. Explain the deposit requirement for federal unemployment insurance.
6. Generally, what is the time schedule for payment of premiums of workers' compensation insurance?
7. Explain the advantage of establishing a tax calendar.

Exercises

Exercise 10-1 The earnings for the calendar year for the employees of Computer Services are as follows.

Employee	Cumulative Earnings
Bach, Ralph P.	$ 12,400.00
Lindahl, Doreen C.	37,500.00
Luhr, Alan D.	36,200.00
Weist, Terry D.	18,400.00
	$104,500.00

The employees had to pay FICA tax during the year at the rate of 7.1 percent on the first $36,000 of their earnings; the employer had to pay a matching FICA tax. Unemployment insurance rates were 2.7 percent for the state and .8 percent for the federal government on the first $7,000 of an employee's earnings.

a. Determine the taxable earnings for FICA, state unemployment, and federal unemployment.
b. Determine the amount of taxes paid by the employees.
c. Determine the total amount of payroll taxes paid by the employer.
d. What percentage of the employer's total payroll of $104,500 was represented by payroll taxes?

Exercise 10-2   The salary expense of the Erskine Company this year was $150,000, of which $30,000 was not subject to FICA tax and $60,000 was not subject to state and federal unemployment taxes. Calculate Erskine's payroll tax expense for the year, using the following rates: FICA, 7.1 percent; state unemployment, 3 percent; federal unemployment, .8 percent.

Exercise 10-3   On January 13, at the end of the second weekly pay period during the year, the totals of Cooper Transfer's payroll register showed that its driver employees had earned $2,200 and its office employees had earned $600. The employees were to have FICA taxes withheld at the rate of 7.1 percent of the first $36,000, plus $275 of federal income taxes, and $90 of union dues.

a. Calculate the amount of FICA taxes to be withheld, and write the general journal entry to record the payroll.
b. Write the general journal entry to record the employer's payroll taxes, assuming that the state unemployment tax rate is 2.7 percent of the first $7,000 paid each employee, and that the federal unemployment tax is .8 percent of the same base.

Exercise 10-4   The payroll for the Quinn Company is as follows.

Gross earnings of employees	$100,000
Earnings subject to FICA tax	88,000
Earnings subject to federal unemployment tax	26,000
Earnings subject to state unemployment tax	26,000

Assuming that the payroll is subject to a FICA tax of 7.1 percent (.071), a state unemployment tax of 2.7 percent (.027), and a federal unemployment tax of .8 percent (.008), give the entry in general journal form to record the payroll tax expense.

Exercise 10-5   The following information on earnings and deductions for the pay period ended December 14 is from J. C. Willms and Company's payroll records.

Name	Gross Pay	Earnings to End of Previous Week
Fowler, Earl C.	$190.00	$ 2,500.00
Minski, Carl A.	720.00	36,000.00
Woods, Norma M.	200.00	10,000.00
Zimmer, Axel L.	210.00	10,500.00

Prepare a general journal entry to record the employer's payroll taxes. The FICA tax is 7.1 percent of the first $36,000 of earnings for each employee. The state unemployment tax rate is 3 percent of the first $7,000 of earnings of each employee, and the federal unemployment tax is .8 (.008) percent of the same base.

Exercise 10-6   On March 31 Dover Company's selected payroll accounts are as follows.

FICA Tax Payable		State Unemployment Tax Payable	
	Mar. 31 980.04		Mar. 31 414.11
	Mar. 31 980.02		

Federal Unemployment Tax Payable		Employees' Federal Income Tax Payable	
	Mar. 31 112.14		Mar. 31 1,819.82

Prepare general journal entries to record payment of the taxes.

Apr.   14 Record payment of federal tax deposit of FICA and income tax.
       30 Record payment of state unemployment tax.
       30 Record deposit of federal unemployment tax.

Exercise 10-7   Suppose that you are an accountant for a small business, and you get a premium notice for workers' compensation insurance, stipulating the rates for the coming year. You have estimated that the year's premium will be as follows.

Classification	Estimated Wages and Salaries	Rate	Estimated Premium
Office work	$ 9,000	.10%	$ 9.00
Sales work	36,000	.78%	280.80
Warehouse work	9,000	1.80%	162.00
		Total estimated premium	$451.80

On January 27 the owner issued a check for $451.80. Record the entry in general journal form.

Exercise 10-8   Still with reference to Exercise 10-7, at the end of the year the exact figures for the payroll are as follows.

Classification	Estimated Wages and Salaries	Rate	Estimated Premium	
Office work	$ 9,000	.10%		$ 9.00
Sales work	37,800	.78%		294.84
Warehouse work	9,600	1.80%		172.80
			Total actual premium	$476.64
			Less estimated premium paid	451.80
			Balance of premium due	$ 24.84

Record the adjusting entries for the insurance expired as well as for the additional premium due.

Problem Set A

Problem 10-1A   Robert Johnson and Company had the following payroll for the week ended June 24.

Salaries		Deductions	
Sales salaries	$1,640.00	Income tax withheld	$230.00
Office salaries	280.00	FICA tax withheld	136.32
	$1,920.00	U.S. Savings Bonds	150.00
		Medical insurance	160.00

Assumed tax rates are as follows.

a. FICA tax, 7.1 percent (.071) on the first $36,000 for each employee
b. State unemployment tax, 2.7 percent (.027) on the first $7,000 for each employee
c. Federal unemployment tax, .8 percent (.008) on the first $7,000 for each employee

Instructions

Record the following entries in general journal form.

1. The payroll entry as of June 24
2. The entry to record the employer's payroll taxes as of June 24, assuming that the total payroll is subject to the FICA tax and that $1,410 is subject to unemployment taxes
3. The payment of the employees as of June 27, assuming that Johnson and Company issues one check payable to a payroll bank account

Problem 10-2A   The column totals of the payroll register of Rivera and Son, for the week ended January 14 of this year, show that the sales employees have earned $1,700 and the office employees $300. Rivera has deducted from the salaries of employees $336 for income taxes, $85 for medical insurance, $68 for union dues, and FICA tax at the rate of 7.1 percent (.071) on the first $36,000 of their earnings.

Instructions

Record the following entries in general journal form:

1. The payroll entry as of January 14
2. The entry to record the employer's payroll taxes as of January 14, assuming 2.7 percent (.027) of $7,000 for state unemployment insurance and .8 percent (.008) of $7,000 for federal unemployment insurance
3. The payment of the employees as of January 16, assuming that Rivera issues one check payable to a payroll bank account

Problem 10-3A   For the third quarter of the year, Sprague Company, 2116 Highland Street, Boston, MA 02102, received Form 941 from the Director of Internal Revenue. The identification number of Sprague Company is 66-7125961. Its payroll for the quarter ended September 30 is as follows.

| NAME | TOTAL EARNINGS | TAXABLE EARNINGS | | FICA WITHHELD | INCOME TAX WITHHELD |
		UNEMPLOYMENT INSURANCE	FICA		
Lange, M. C.	3 6 4 8 00		3 6 4 8 00	2 5 9 01	4 8 9 60
Larken, A. L.	3 4 5 6 00		3 4 5 6 00	2 4 5 38	4 7 6 80
McBride, F. C.	2 9 9 2 00	4 1 6 00	2 9 9 2 00	2 1 2 43	3 5 0 40
Randich, P. G.	3 1 3 6 00	1 2 8 00	3 1 3 6 00	2 2 2 65	3 6 9 60
Webb, A. L.	1 9 2 0 00	1 9 2 0 00	1 9 2 0 00	1 3 6 32	2 3 3 60
	15 1 5 2 00	2 4 6 4 00	15 1 5 2 00	10 7 5 79	19 2 0 00

The company has had five employees throughout the year. Assume that the FICA tax payable by the employees is 7.1 percent of the first $36,000 of their earnings and that the FICA tax payable by the employer is also 7.1 percent of the first $36,000 paid to the employees. Sprague Company has submitted the following federal tax deposits and written the accompanying checks.

On August 14, for the July Payroll	On September 12, for the August Payroll	On October 14, for the September Payroll
Employees' income tax withheld $ 608.00	Employees' income tax withheld $ 672.00	Employees' income tax withheld $ 640.00
Employees' FICA tax withheld 340.66	Employees' FICA tax withheld 376.03	Employees' FICA tax withheld 359.10
Employer's FICA tax 340.66	Employer's FICA tax 376.03	Employer's FICA tax 359.10
$1,289.32	$1,424.06	$1,358.20

Instructions

Complete Form 941 dated October 28. Record the tax liability and deposits (the same amounts) in the spaces marked "Total."

Problem 10-4A   The Martin Company has the following balances in its general ledger as of March 1 of this year.

a. FICA tax payable (liability for February), $948.56
b. Employees' income tax payable (liability for February), $1,004.91
c. Federal unemployment tax payable (liability for January and February), $106.88
d. State unemployment tax payable (liability for January and February), $360.72
e. Medical insurance payable (liability for January and February), $1,244

The company completed the following transactions involving the payroll during March and April.

Mar. 12 Issued check for $1,953.47, payable to the Security Bank and Trust, for the monthly deposit of February FICA taxes and employees' federal income tax withheld.

12 Issued check for $106.88, payable to the Security Bank and Trust, for the deposit of February federal unemployment tax.

31 Recorded the payroll entry in the general journal from the payroll register for March. The payroll register has the following column totals.

Sales salaries	$5,600.00	
Office salaries	1,080.00	
Total earnings		$6,680.00
Employees' income tax deductions	$1,004.91	
Employees' FICA tax deductions	474.28	
Medical insurance deductions	622.00	
Total deductions		2,101.19
Net pay		$4,578.81

31 Recorded payroll taxes in the general journal. Employees' FICA tax is 7.1 percent, employer's is 7.1 percent, state unemployment insurance is 2.7 percent, and federal unemployment insurance is .8 percent.

31 Issued check for $4,578.81 payable to a payroll bank account.

Apr. 14 Issued check for $1,866, payable to Noble Insurance Company, in payment of employees' medical insurance for January, February, and March.

14 Issued check for $541.08, payable to the State Tax Commission, for state unemployment taxes for January, February, and March. The check was accompanied by the quarterly tax return.

14 Issued check for $1,953.47, payable to the Security Bank and Trust, for the monthly deposit of March FICA taxes and employees' federal income tax withheld.

Instructions

Record the transactions listed above in the general journal.

Problem Set B

Problem 10-1B   The Draper Clinical Laboratory had the following payroll for the week ended June 15.

Salaries		Deductions	
Technicians' salaries	$1,860.00	Income tax withheld	$287.00
Office salaries	390.00	FICA tax withheld	159.75
	$2,250.00	U.S. Savings Bonds	160.00
		Medical insurance	180.00

Assumed tax rates are as follows.

a. FICA tax, 7.1 percent (.071) on the first $36,000 for each employee
b. State unemployment tax, 2.7 percent (.027) on the first $9,000 for each employee
c. Federal unemployment tax, .8 percent (.008) on the first $7,000 for each employee

Instructions

Record the following entries in general journal form.

1. The payroll entry as of June 15
2. The entry to record the employer's payroll taxes as of June 15, assuming that the total payroll is subject to the FICA tax and that $1,400 is subject to unemployment taxes
3. The payment of the employees as of June 18, assuming that Draper Clinical Laboratory issued one check payable to a payroll bank account

Problem 10-2B   The column totals of the payroll register of the Sheridan Chair Company for the week ended January 28 of this year show that the sales employees have earned $1,920 and the office employees $360. Sheridan has deducted from the salaries of employees $296 for income taxes, $90 for medical insurance, $72 for union dues, and FICA tax at the rate of 7.1 percent (.071) on the first $36,000 of their earnings.

Instructions

Record the following entries in general journal form:

1. The payroll entry as of January 28
2. The entry to record the payroll taxes as of January 28, assuming 2.7 percent (.027) for state unemployment insurance and .8 percent (.008) for federal unemployment insurance on the first $7,000
3. The payment of the employees as of January 31, assuming that Sheridan issues one check payable to a payroll bank account

Problem 10-3B Nowell Machine Shop, of 3216 Stanich Boulevard, Los Angeles, California 90028, received Form 941 from the Director of Internal Revenue. The identification number for Nowell Machine Shop is 75-3959166. Its payroll for the quarter ended September 30 is as follows.

NAME	TOTAL EARNINGS	TAXABLE EARNINGS UNEMPLOYMENT INSURANCE	FICA	FICA WITHHELD	INCOME TAX WITHHELD
Ballard, F. N.	5 0 5 9 20		5 0 5 9 20	3 5 9 20	6 8 4 80
Carrier, M. A.	3 8 1 4 40		3 8 1 4 40	2 7 0 83	5 0 5 60
Couch, H. E.	3 0 6 5 60		3 0 6 5 60	2 1 7 66	4 0 4 80
Edwards, J. A.	3 4 7 2 00		3 4 7 2 00	2 4 6 51	4 7 0 40
Goode, D. L.	2 3 6 1 60	1 6 7 6 80	2 3 6 1 60	1 6 7 67	3 1 8 40
	17 7 7 2 80	1 6 7 6 80	17 7 7 2 80	1 2 6 1 87	2 3 8 4 00

The company has had five employees during the year. Assume that the employees have paid a FICA tax of 7.1 percent on the first $36,000 of their earnings and that the employer has paid the same percentage on their earnings. F. R. Nowell, the owner, has submitted the following federal tax deposits and written the accompanying checks.

On August 12, for the July Payroll	On September 13, for the August Payroll	On October 12, for the September Payroll
Employees' income tax withheld $ 754.02	Employees' income tax withheld $ 789.98	Employees' income tax withheld $ 840.00
Employees' FICA tax withheld 384.38	Employees' FICA tax withheld 411.48	Employees' FICA tax withheld 466.01
Employer's FICA tax 384.38	Employer's FICA tax 411.48	Employer's FICA tax 466.01
$1,522.78	$1,612.94	$1,772.02

Instructions

Complete Form 941 dated October 28. Record the tax liability and deposits (the same amounts) in the spaces marked "Total."

Problem 10-4B The Lafke Company has the following balances in its general ledger as of March 1 of this year.

a. FICA tax payable (liability for February), $1,931.20
b. Employees' federal income tax payable (liability for February), $2,040
c. Federal unemployment tax payable (liability for the months of January and February), $217.60
d. State unemployment tax payable (liability for the months of January and February), $734.40
e. Medical insurance payable (liability for January and February), $1,608

The company completed the following transactions involving the payroll during March and April.

Mar. 3 Issued check for $3,971.20 to Common Bank and Trust, for monthly deposit of February FICA taxes and employees' federal income tax withheld.

31 Recorded the payroll entry in the general journal from the payroll register for March. The payroll register had the following column totals.

Sales salaries	$10,400.00	
Office salaries	3,200.00	
Total earnings		$13,600.00
Employees' federal income tax deductions	$ 2,016.00	
Employees' FICA tax deductions	965.60	
Medical insurance deductions	804.00	
Total deductions		3,785.60
Net pay		$ 9,814.40

31 Recorded payroll taxes in the general journal. Employees' FICA tax is 7.1 percent, employer's is 7.1 percent, state unemployment insurance is 2.7 percent, and federal unemployment insurance is .8 percent.

31 Issued check for $9,814.40, payable to a payroll bank account.

31 Issued check for $108.80, payable to Common Bank and Trust for deposit of federal unemployment tax for January and February.

Apr. 3 Issued check for $3,947.20, payable to Common Bank and Trust, for monthly deposit of March FICA taxes and employees' federal income tax withheld.

6 Issued check for $2,412, payable to Fidelity Insurance Company, in payment of employees' medical insurance for January, February, and March.

14 Issued check for $1,101.60, payable to the State Tax Commission, for state unemployment taxes for January, February, and March. The check was accompanied by the quarterly tax return.

Instructions

Record the transactions listed above in the general journal.

REVIEW OF T ACCOUNT PLACEMENT AND REPRESENTATIVE TRANSACTIONS CHAPTERS 7 THROUGH 10

Review of T-account Placement

The following sums up the placement of T accounts covered in Chapters 7 through 10 in relation to the fundamental accounting equation.

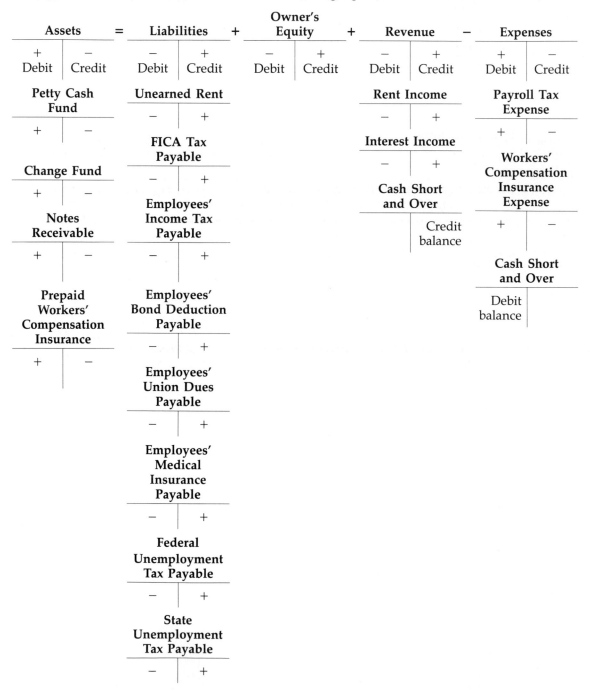

Review of Representative Transactions

The following summarizes the recording of transactions covered in Chapters 7 through 10, along with a classification of the accounts involved.

Transaction	Accounts Involved	Class.	Increase or Decrease	Therefore Debit or Credit	Financial Statement
Established a Petty Cash Fund	Petty Cash Fund Cash	A A	I D	Debit Credit	Bal. Sheet Bal. Sheet

Reimbursed Petty Cash Fund	Expenses or
	  Assets or
	  Drawing
	Cash
		E,
		A,
		OE
		A
			I
			
			D
				Debit
				
				Credit
					Balance Sheet, State. of O.E., or Inc. Stat.

Established a Change Fund	Change Fund Cash	A A	I D	Debit Credit	Bal. Sheet Bal. Sheet
Recorded cash sales (amount on cash register tape was larger than cash count)	Cash Cash Short and Over Sales	A E R	I — I	Debit Debit Credit	Bal. Sheet Inc. State. Inc. State.

Recorded cash sales (amount on cash register tape was less than cash count)	Cash
	  Sales
	  Cash Short and Over
		A
		R
		R
			I
			I
			—
				Debit
				Credit
				Credit
					Bal. Sheet
					Inc. State.
					Inc. State.

Recorded service charges on bank account	Miscellaneous Expense Cash	E A	I D	Debit Credit	Inc. State. Bal. Sheet
Recorded NSF check received from customer	Accounts Receivable Cash	A A	I D	Debit Credit	Bal. Sheet Bal. Sheet

Transaction	Accounts Involved	Class.	Increase or Decrease	Therefore Debit or Credit	Financial Statement
Recorded interest-bearing note receivable collected by our bank	Cash	A	I	Debit	Bal. Sheet
	Notes Receivable	A	D	Credit	Bal. Sheet
	Interest Income	R	I	Credit	Inc. State.
Recorded the payroll entry from the payroll register	Sales Salary Expense	E	I	Debit	Inc. State.
	Office Salary Expense	E	I	Debit	Inc. State.
	FICA Tax Payable	L	I	Credit	Bal. Sheet
	Employees' Income Tax Payable	L	I	Credit	Bal. Sheet
	Employees' Bond Deduction Payable	L	I	Credit	Bal. Sheet
	Employees' Union Dues Payable	L	I	Credit	Bal. Sheet
	Salaries Payable	L	I	Credit	Bal. Sheet
Issued check payable to payroll bank account	Salaries Payable	L	D	Debit	Bal. Sheet
	Cash	A	D	Credit	Bal. Sheet
Recorded employer's payroll taxes	Payroll Tax Expense	E	I	Debit	Inc. State.
	FICA Tax Payable	L	I	Credit	Bal. Sheet
	State Unemployment Tax Payable	L	I	Credit	Bal. Sheet
	Federal Unemployment Tax Payable	L	I	Credit	Bal. Sheet
Recorded deposit of FICA taxes and employees' income tax withheld	Employees' Income Tax Payable	L	D	Debit	Bal. Sheet
	FICA Tax Payable	L	D	Debit	Bal. Sheet
	Cash	A	D	Credit	Bal. Sheet
Recorded deposit of federal unemployment tax	Federal Unemployment Tax Payable	L	D	Debit	Bal. Sheet
	Cash	A	D	Credit	Bal. Sheet

Transaction	Accounts Involved	Class.	Increase or Decrease	Therefore Debit or Credit	Financial Statement
Paid state unemploy-ment tax	State Unemployment Tax Payable Cash	L A	D D	Debit Credit	Bal. Sheet Bal. Sheet
Paid for workers' compensation insurance in advance	Prepaid Workers' Compensation Insurance Cash	A A	I D	Debit Credit	Bal. Sheet Bal. Sheet
Adjusting entry for workers' compensation insurance, assuming an additional amount is owed	Workers' Compensation Insurance Expense Prepaid Workers' Compensation Insurance Workers' Compensation Insurance Payable	E A L	I D I	Debit Credit Credit	Inc. State. Bal. Sheet Bal. Sheet

11 Accounting for Merchandise: Sales

Learning Objectives

After you have completed this chapter, you will be able to do the following:

1. Record transactions in sales journals.

2. Post from sales journals to an accounts receivable ledger and a general ledger.

3. Prepare a schedule of accounts receivable.

4. Post directly from sales invoices to an accounts receivable ledger and a general ledger.

By now you've had enough experience to complete the full accounting cycle for service-type and professional enterprises. To enlarge your accounting knowledge, let us now introduce accounting systems for merchandising enterprises. The same general principles of double-entry accounting prevail. This chapter describes specific accounts of merchandising firms; such a merchandising firm could be anything from a dress shop to a supermarket. The sales journal and the accounts receivable ledger are also presented. Just as we used NuWay Cleaners as a continuous example of a service-type business, we shall use C. L. Frederickson Plumbing Supply as an example of a merchandising business.

SPECIAL JOURNALS

In our previous descriptions of the accounting process, we have intentionally shown the entire procedure. In other words, we have taken the long way home, but there are certain shortcuts available. Moreover, as far as understanding accounting is concerned, if you fully understand the long way, it's relatively easy to learn the shortcuts. The reverse is not true; you cannot readily understand the entire system if you are exposed to shortcuts only.

Any accounting system must be as efficient as possible. As a matter of fact, accounting is a means, or tool, by which to measure efficiency in a business. Consequently, one should take shortcuts wherever one can do so without sacrificing internal control (discussed in detail in Chapter 12).

As we shall see, **special journals** provide one shortcut. Using a two-column general journal for recording transactions that take place day after day is extremely time-consuming, because each individual debit and credit entry must be posted separately. Special journals make it easier to handle specialized transactions and delegate work. The following table lists the special journals that we shall introduce separately in the next few chapters.

When any of these four journals are used, the general journal must also be used to record any *non*specialized transactions—in other words, any transactions that the special journals cannot handle. In this case the letter designation for the general journal is J.

Chapter	Special Journal	Letter Designation	Specialized Transaction
11	Sales journal	S	Sales of merchandise on account only
12	Purchases journal	P	Purchase of merchandise on account only
13	Cash receipts journal	CR	All cash received from any source
13	Cash payments journal	CP	All cash paid out for any purpose

SPECIFIC ACCOUNTS FOR MERCHANDISING FIRMS

A service or professional enterprise, such as the ones we have encountered, depends for its revenue on the rendering of services; a service or professional enterprise uses such accounts as Income from Services or Professional Fees. A merchandising business, on the other hand, depends for its revenue on the sale of goods or merchandise, recording the amount of the sale under the account titled Sales.

Merchandise inventory consists of a stock of goods that a firm buys and intends to resell, in the same physical condition, at a profit. Merchandise should be differentiated from other assets, such as equipment and supplies, which are acquired for use in the business and are not for resale.

Because the merchandising firm has to record transactions involving the purchase, handling, and sale of its merchandise, it uses accounts and procedures that we have not yet discussed. Let's look at the fundamental accounting equation with the new T accounts that are introduced in this chapter, as well as the T accounts introduced in Chapters 12 and 13 (which are shown in color).

Assets		=	Liabilities		+	Owner's Equity		+	Revenue		−	Expenses	
+	−		−	+		−	+		−	+		+	−
Debit	Credit		Debit	Credit		Debit	Credit		Debit	Credit		Debit	Credit

Merchandise Inventory		Sales Tax Payable				Sales		Purchases	
+	−	−	+			−	+	+	−

						Sales Returns and Allowances		Purchases Returns and Allowances	
						+	−	−	+

						Sales Discount		Purchases Discount	
						+	−	−	+

The **Sales** account, as we have said, is a revenue account; it records the sale of merchandise.

The **Purchases** account records the cost of merchandise acquired for resale. Remember that the Purchases account is used strictly for the buying of merchandise. The plus and minus signs are the same as the signs for Merchandise Inventory. Purchases is placed under the heading of Expenses only because the accountant closes it, along with the expense accounts, at the end of the fiscal period.

The **Sales Returns and Allowances** account records the physical return of merchandise by customers or a reduction in a bill because merchandise was damaged. It is treated as a deduction from Sales.

The **Purchases Returns and Allowances** account records the firm's return of merchandise it has purchased or a reduction in the bill due to damaged merchandise. It is treated as a deduction from Purchases.

The **Sales Discount** and **Purchases Discount** accounts record cash discounts granted for prompt payments, in accordance with the credit terms. We'll discuss these accounts along with cash journals in Chapter 13.

The T accounts for returns and allowances and for discounts are shown in color to emphasize that we are treating them as deductions from the related accounts placed above them. We list these accounts as deductions because they appear as deductions in the financial statements. Their relationship is similar to that between the Drawing account and the Capital account; remember that we deduct Drawing from Capital in the statement of owner's equity.

The firm's accountant makes entries involving Merchandise Inventory only when the firm takes an actual physical count of the goods in stock; otherwise the accountant leaves this account strictly alone.

The type of transaction most frequently encountered in a merchandising business is the sale of merchandise. Some businesses sell on a cash-and-carry basis only; others sell only on credit. Many firms offer both arrangements. The same general types of entries pertain to retail and wholesale enterprises. Here are some examples.

Sale of merchandise for cash, $100.

	Cash				Sales	
+		−		−		+
100						100

Debit Cash and credit Sales; record this in the cash receipts journal.

Sale of merchandise on account, $200.

Accounts Receivable			Sales	
+	−		−	+
200				200

Debit Accounts Receivable and credit Sales; record this in the sales journal.

HANDLING SALES ON ACCOUNT

Sales are only recorded in response to a customer order. The routines for processing orders and recording sales vary with the type and size of the business.

In a retail business, a salesperson usually prepares a sales ticket—either in duplicate or triplicate—for a sale on account. One copy is given to the customer, and another to the accounting department, where it will serve as the basis for an entry in the sales journal. A third copy may be used as a record of sales—when one is computing sales commissions or is involved in inventory control, for example.

In a wholesale business, the company usually receives a written order from a customer or from a salesperson who obtained the order from the customer. The order must then be approved by the credit department, after which it is sent to the billing department, where the sales invoice is prepared. Like a sales ticket, the sales invoice may be made out in duplicate or triplicate.

For our model business, we shall use C. L. Frederickson Plumbing Supply, a wholesaler. One of its invoices is shown in Figure 11-1.

We shall introduce the sales journal by looking at three transactions on the books of C. L. Frederickson Plumbing Supply.

Figure 11-1

C. L. FREDERICKSON PLUMBING SUPPLY
1968 N.E. Allen Street
Portland, OR 97201

INVOICE

Sold To: T. L. Long Co.
620 S.W. Kennedy Street
Portland, OR 97110

Date: *August 1, 19–*
Invoice No.: *320*
Order No.: *5384*
Shipped By: *Their truck*
Terms: *2/10, n/30*

Quantity	Description	Unit Price	Total
1,000	¾" galv. pipe, 10'	.32	320.00
50	1½" cast-iron 90° reg. elbow	.96	48.00
40	1½" cast-iron 90° street elbow	1.40	56.00
			424.00

Aug.   1 Sold merchandise on account to T. L. Long Company, invoice no. 320, $424.

      3 Sold merchandise on account to Maley, Inc., invoice no. 321, $116.

      6 Sold merchandise on account to Abel Plumbing and Heating, invoice no. 322, $94.

We can use T accounts to visualize these transactions.

Accounts Receivable		Sales	
+	−	−	+
424			424
116			116
94			94

If the transactions were recorded in a general journal, they would appear as they do in Figure 11-2.

Next the journal entries would be posted to the accounts in the general ledger, as shown here. (In each of the following ledger accounts, assume that there were no beginning balances.)

GENERAL LEDGER

ACCOUNT   *Accounts Receivable*   ACCOUNT NO. *113*

	DATE	ITEM	POST. REF.	DEBIT	CREDIT	BALANCE DEBIT	BALANCE CREDIT	
1	19– Aug. 1		23	4 2 4 00		4 2 4 00		1
2	3		23	1 1 6 00		5 4 0 00		2
3	6		23	9 4 00		6 3 4 00		3
4								4

ACCOUNT   *Sales*   ACCOUNT NO. *411*

	DATE	ITEM	POST. REF.	DEBIT	CREDIT	BALANCE DEBIT	BALANCE CREDIT	
1	19– Aug. 1		23		4 2 4 00		4 2 4 00	1
2	3		23		1 1 6 00		5 4 0 00	2
3	6		23		9 4 00		6 3 4 00	3
4								4

Figure 11-2

		DATE	DESCRIPTION	POST. REF.	DEBIT				CREDIT				
			GENERAL JOURNAL					PAGE	23				
1		19– Aug.	1 Accounts Receivable	113	4	2	4	00					1
2			Sales	411					4	2	4	00	2
3			Invoice no. 320, T. L. Long										3
4			Company.										4
5													5
6			3 Accounts Receivable	113	1	1	6	00					6
7			Sales	411					1	1	6	00	7
8			Invoice no. 321, Maley, Inc.										8
9													9
10			6 Accounts Receivable	113		9	4	00					10
11			Sales	411						9	4	00	11
12			Invoice no. 322, Abel Plumbing										12
13			and Heating.										13
14													14

Obviously, there is a great deal of repetition in both journalizing and posting. The credit sales require three separate journal entries, three debit postings to Accounts Receivable, and three credit postings to Sales. We have presented all of this to show the advantages of the sales journal. Using a *sales journal* eliminates all this repetition.

THE SALES JOURNAL

The **sales journal** records sales of merchandise *on account only*. This specialized type of transaction calls for debits to Accounts Receivable and credits to Sales. Let's see how to record the three transactions for C. L. Frederickson Plumbing Supply in the sales journal *instead of* in the general journal.

Objective 1

Record transactions in sales journals.

		DATE	INV. NO.	CUSTOMER'S NAME	POST. REF.	ACCOUNTS RECEIVABLE DR., SALES CR.				
				SALES JOURNAL		PAGE	38			
1		19– Aug.	1 320	T. L. Long Company		4	2	4	00	1
2			3 321	Maley, Inc.		1	1	6	00	2
3			6 322	Abel Plumbing and Heating			9	4	00	3
4										4

Because *one* money column is headed *Accounts Receivable Debit and Sales Credit*, each transaction requires only a single line. Repetition is avoided, and all entries for sales of merchandise on account are found in one place.

Listing the invoice number makes it easier to check the details of a particular sale at a later date.

Posting from the Sales Journal

Using the sales journal also saves time and space in posting to the ledger accounts. The transactions involving the sales of merchandise on account for the entire month of August are shown in Figure 11-3.

Objective 2

Post from sales journals to an accounts receivable ledger and a general ledger.

	DATE	INV. NO.	CUSTOMER'S NAME	POST. REF.	ACCOUNTS RECEIVABLE DR., SALES CR.	
1	19– Aug. 1	320	T. L. Long Company		4 2 4 00	1
2	3	321	Maley, Inc.		1 1 6 00	2
3	6	322	Abel Plumbing and Heating		9 4 00	3
4	9	323	Manning Service Company		9 6 1 00	4
5	11	324	Craig and Fraser Hardware		8 6 00	5
6	16	325	Home Hardware Company		2 1 5 00	6
7	20	326	Henning's Plumbing		2 9 3 00	7
8	23	327	Baker Building Supplies		5 6 0 00	8
9	24	328	Craig and Fraser Hardware		2 8 6 00	9
10	28	329	Home Hardware Company		7 5 00	10
11	30	330	Baker Building Supplies		3 8 7 00	11
12	31	331	T. L. Long Company		5 6 00	12
13	31	332	Robert D. Bishop, Inc.		8 7 1 00	13
14	31				4 4 2 4 00	14
15					(113)(411)	15
16						16
17						17

SALES JOURNAL   PAGE 38

Figure 11-3

Because all the entries are a debit to Accounts Receivable and a credit to Sales, one can now make a single posting to these accounts for the amount of the total as of the last day of the month. In the Posting Reference columns of the ledger accounts, the letter S designates the sales journal.

GENERAL LEDGER

ACCOUNT Accounts Receivable   ACCOUNT NO. 113

	DATE	ITEM	POST. REF.	DEBIT	CREDIT	BALANCE DEBIT	BALANCE CREDIT	
1	19– Aug. 31		S38	4 4 2 4 00		4 4 2 4 00		1
2								2

	DATE	ITEM	POST. REF.	DEBIT	CREDIT	BALANCE DEBIT	BALANCE CREDIT	
1	19– Aug. 31		S38		4 4 2 4 00		4 4 2 4 00	1
2								2

ACCOUNT Sales ACCOUNT NO. 411

After posting to the Accounts Receivable account, go back to the sales journal and record the account number in parentheses directly below the total. The account number for the account being debited (Accounts Receivable) goes on the left. The account number for the account being credited (Sales) goes on the right. Again, as a precaution, don't record these account numbers until you have completed the postings.

If you should find an error, do not erase it. If the error is caught in a journal entry before it is posted to the ledger, simply draw a single line through the error (with a ruler), write in the correct information, and add your initials. If an amount is entered incorrectly in the ledger (although the journal entry is correct), follow the same procedure. However, if an entry has been posted to the wrong accounts in the ledger, then you must prepare a new journal entry correcting the first one.

Sales Journal Provision for Sales Tax

Most states and some cities levy a **sales tax** on retail sales of goods and services. The retailer collects the sales tax from customers and later pays it to the tax authorities.

When goods or services are sold on credit, the sales tax is charged to the customer and recorded at the time of the sale. The sales journal must be designed to handle this type of transaction. For example, if a retail store sells an item for $100 and the sales tax is 4 percent, the transaction would be recorded in T accounts like this.

Accounts Receivable		Sales		Sales Tax Payable	
+	−	−	+	−	+
104			100		4

The accountant debits Sales Tax Payable and credits Cash when the sales tax is paid to the government.

Because we want to illustrate a sales journal for a retail merchandising firm operating in a state having a sales tax, we shall talk about the transactions of Milner and Salter Fabrics. Its sales journal is presented on the next page.

SALES JOURNAL

	DATE	INV. NO.	CUSTOMER'S NAME	POST. REF.	ACCOUNTS RECEIVABLE DEBIT	SALES TAX PAYABLE CREDIT	SALES CREDIT	
1	19– Apr.	1 9382	B. T. Lawson		1 6 64	64	1 6 00	1
2		1 9383	Culver Apartments		2 2 88	88	2 2 00	2
3		1 9384	Richard Gladdon		5 2 00	2 00	5 0 00	3
4		2 9385	T. R. Sears		1 2 48	48	1 2 00	4
10		30 10121	Paul Murphy		1 2 4 80	4 80	1 2 0 00	10
11		30			2 5 1 6 80	9 6 80	2 4 2 0 00	11
12					(1 1 3)	(2 1 4)	(4 1 1)	12
13								13

Each column is posted to the ledger accounts as a total at the end of the month. After posting the figures, the accountant records the account numbers in parentheses immediately below the totals.

GENERAL LEDGER

ACCOUNT **Accounts Receivable**   ACCOUNT NO. 113

	DATE	ITEM	POST. REF.	DEBIT	CREDIT	BALANCE DEBIT	BALANCE CREDIT	
1	19– Apr. 30		S96	2 5 1 6 80		2 5 1 6 80		1
2								2

ACCOUNT **Sales Tax Payable**   ACCOUNT NO. 214

	DATE	ITEM	POST. REF.	DEBIT	CREDIT	BALANCE DEBIT	BALANCE CREDIT	
1	19– Apr. 30		S96		9 6 80		9 6 80	1
2								2

ACCOUNT **Sales**   ACCOUNT NO. 411

	DATE	ITEM	POST. REF.	DEBIT	CREDIT	BALANCE DEBIT	BALANCE CREDIT	
1	19– Apr. 30		S96		2 4 2 0 00		2 4 2 0 00	1
2								2
3								3

THE ACCOUNTS RECEIVABLE LEDGER

Accounts Receivable, as we have seen, represents the total amount owed to a business by its charge customers.

There is a major deficiency with the account, however. The business can't tell at a glance *how much each* individual charge customer owes, which handicaps the credit department. To correct this shortcoming, businesses keep a separate account for each charge customer.

When a business has very few charge customers, it is possible to have a separate Accounts Receivable account in the general ledger for each charge customer. However, if there are many charge customers (which is the usual case), such an arrangement is too cumbersome. When each charge customer's account is included, the trial balance is very long, and of course, the possibility for errors increases accordingly.

It is more practical to have a separate book containing a list of all the charge customers and each one's respective balance. This is called the **accounts receivable ledger.** In the accounts receivable ledger, the individual charge customer accounts are listed in alphabetical order. Most accountants prefer a loose-leaf binder so that they can insert accounts for new customers and remove other accounts; they don't use account numbers.

The Accounts Receivable account should still be maintained in the general ledger; when all the postings are up to date, the balance of this account should equal the total of all the individual balances of the charge customers. The Accounts Receivable account in the general ledger is called a **controlling account.** The accounts receivable *ledger*, containing the accounts or listing of all the charge customers, is really a special ledger, called a **subsidiary ledger**. Figure 11-4 diagrams the interrelationship of these books.

The accountant posts the individual amounts to the accounts receivable ledger every day, so that this ledger will have up-to-date information. At the end of the month, the accountant posts the total of the sales journal (in Figure 11-4 it happens to be $2,900) to the general ledger accounts as a debit to the Accounts Receivable (controlling) account and a credit to the Sales account. As indicated in Figure 11-4, the balance of the Accounts Receivable (controlling) account at the end of the month must equal the total of the balances of the charge customer accounts in the accounts receivable ledger. The schedule of accounts receivable is merely a listing of charge customers' individual balances.

After you post the amount from the sales journal to the charge customer's account in the accounts receivable ledger, put a check mark ($\checkmark$) in the Posting Reference column of the sales journal.

Let us now look at the sales journal of C. L. Frederickson Plumbing Supply for August with the daily postings that its accountant has made to the accounts receivable ledger, as well as the schedule of accounts

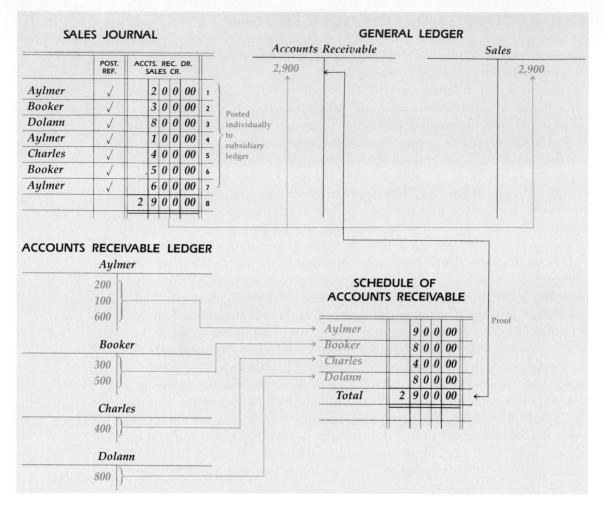

Figure 11-4

SALES JOURNAL

PAGE 38

	DATE	INV. NO.	CUSTOMER'S NAME	POST. REF.	ACCOUNTS RECEIVABLE DR., SALES CR.	
1	19– Aug. 1	320	T. L. Long Company	√	4 2 4 00	1
2	3	321	Maley, Inc.	√	1 1 6 00	2
3	6	322	Abel Plumbing and Heating	√	9 4 00	3
4	9	323	Manning Service Company	√	9 6 1 00	4
5	11	324	Craig and Fraser Hardware	√	8 6 00	5
6	16	325	Home Hardware Company	√	2 1 5 00	6
7	20	326	Henning's Plumbing	√	2 9 3 00	7
8	23	327	Baker Building Supplies	√	5 6 0 00	8
9	24	328	Craig and Fraser Hardware	√	2 8 6 00	9
10	28	329	Home Hardware Company	√	7 5 00	10
11	30	330	Baker Building Supplies	√	3 8 7 00	11
12	31	331	T. L. Long Company	√	5 6 00	12
13	31	332	Robert D. Bishop, Inc.	√	8 7 1 00	13
14	31				4 4 2 4 00	14
15					(113)(411)	15

Figure 11-5

receivable. These entries are shown in Figure 11-5 and the ledger accounts that follow.

ACCOUNTS RECEIVABLE LEDGER

NAME _Abel Plumbing and Heating_

ADDRESS _1015 Broadway, S.W._

Seattle, WA 98102

DATE		ITEM	POST. REF.	DEBIT	CREDIT	BALANCE
19– Aug.	6		S38	9 4 00		9 4 00

NAME _Baker Building Supplies_

ADDRESS _17 No. Second St._

Renton, WA 98055

DATE		ITEM	POST. REF.	DEBIT	CREDIT	BALANCE
19– Aug.	23		S38	5 6 0 00		5 6 0 00
	30		S38	3 8 7 00		9 4 7 00

NAME _Robert D. Bishop, Inc._

ADDRESS _2168 Main St._

Kent, WA 98031

DATE		ITEM	POST. REF.	DEBIT	CREDIT	BALANCE
19– Aug.	31		S38	8 7 1 00		8 7 1 00

NAME   *Craig and Fraser Hardware*
ADDRESS *2005 N. Powder St.*
         Everett, WA 98201

DATE		ITEM	POST. REF.	DEBIT				CREDIT				BALANCE			
19– Aug.	11		S38		8	6	00						8	6	00
	24		S38	2	8	6	00					3	7	2	00

NAME   *Henning's Plumbing*
ADDRESS *21680 S.E. Twelfth Ave.*
         Portland, OR 97208

DATE		ITEM	POST. REF.	DEBIT				CREDIT				BALANCE			
19– Aug.	20		S38	2	9	3	00					2	9	3	00

NAME   *Home Hardware Company*
ADDRESS *7810 N.W. Cherburg St.*
         Portland, OR 97206

DATE		ITEM	POST. REF.	DEBIT				CREDIT				BALANCE			
19– Aug.	16		S38	2	1	5	00					2	1	5	00
	28		S38		7	5	00					2	9	0	00

NAME   *T. L. Long Company*
ADDRESS *620 S.W. Kennedy St.*
         Portland, OR 97110

DATE		ITEM	POST. REF.	DEBIT				CREDIT				BALANCE			
19– Aug.	1		S38	4	2	4	00					4	2	4	00
	31		S38		5	6	00					4	8	0	00

NAME __Maley, Inc.__

ADDRESS __1720 Ninth St., N.W.__

__Seattle, WA 98107__

DATE	ITEM	POST. REF.	DEBIT	CREDIT	BALANCE
19– Aug. 3		S38	1 1 6 00		1 1 6 00

NAME __Manning Service Company__

ADDRESS __2720 N.W. 43rd Ave.__

__Portland, OR 97210__

DATE	ITEM	POST. REF.	DEBIT	CREDIT	BALANCE
19– Aug. 9		S38	9 6 1 00		9 6 1 00

Assuming that these were the only transactions involving charge customers, the accountant prepares a schedule of accounts receivable, listing the balance of each charge customer.

Objective 3

Prepare a schedule of accounts receivable.

C. L. Frederickson Plumbing Supply
Schedule of Accounts Receivable
August 31, 19–

Abel Plumbing and Heating	$	9 4 00
Baker Building Supplies		9 4 7 00
Robert D. Bishop, Inc.		8 7 1 00
Craig and Fraser Hardware		3 7 2 00
Henning's Plumbing		2 9 3 00
Home Hardware Company		2 9 0 00
T. L. Long Company		4 8 0 00
Maley, Inc.		1 1 6 00
Manning Service Company		9 6 1 00
Total Accounts Receivable	$	4 4 2 4 00

Again we assume that there were no previous balances in the customers' accounts. Under this circumstance, the Accounts Receivable (controlling) account in the general ledger will have the same balance, $4,424, as the schedule of accounts receivable.

GENERAL LEDGER

ACCOUNT *Accounts Receivable*   ACCOUNT NO. 113

	DATE	ITEM	POST. REF.	DEBIT	CREDIT	BALANCE DEBIT	BALANCE CREDIT	
1	19– Aug. 31		S38	4 4 2 4 00		4 4 2 4 00		1
2								2

SALES RETURNS AND ALLOWANCES

The Sales Returns and Allowances account handles two types of transactions having to do with merchandise that has previously been sold. A *return* is a physical return of the goods. An *allowance* is a reduction from the original price because the goods were defective or damaged. It may not be economically worthwhile to have customers return the goods; each situation is a special case. In order to avoid writing a separate letter each time to inform customers of their account adjustments, businesses use a special form called a **credit memorandum,** such as the one in Figure 11-6.

The Sales Returns and Allowances account is considered to be a deduction from Sales. Using an account separate from Sales provides a better record of the total returns and allowances. Accountants deduct Sales Returns and Allowances from Sales in the income statement, as we shall see later. Let's consider this situation by using T accounts.

Transaction (a)   On August 24, C. L. Frederickson sold merchandise on account to Craig and Fraser Hardware, $286, and recorded this in the sales journal.

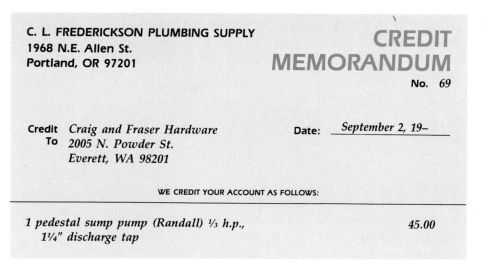

Figure 11-6

C. L. FREDERICKSON PLUMBING SUPPLY
1968 N.E. Allen St.
Portland, OR 97201

CREDIT MEMORANDUM

No. 69

Credit   *Craig and Fraser Hardware*   Date: *September 2, 19–*
To   *2005 N. Powder St.*
        Everett, WA 98201

WE CREDIT YOUR ACCOUNT AS FOLLOWS:

1 pedestal sump pump (Randall) ⅓ h.p.,   45.00
  1¼" discharge tap

Transaction (b) On September 2, Craig and Fraser Hardware returned $45 worth of the merchandise. C. L. Frederickson issued credit memorandum no. 69 (see Figure 11-6).

Assets		=	Liabilities		+	Owner's Equity		+	Revenue		−	Expenses	
+	−		−	+		−	+		−	+		+	−
Debit	Credit		Debit	Credit		Debit	Credit		Debit	Credit		Debit	Credit

Accounts Receivable

+	−
(a) 286	(b) 45

Sales

−	+
	(a) 286

Sales Returns and Allowances

+	−
(b) 45	

C. L. Frederickson's accountant debits Sales Returns and Allowances because C. L. Frederickson has greater returns and allowances than it did before. The accountant credits Accounts Receivable because the charge customer (Craig and Fraser) owes less than before.

One uses the word *credit* in "credit memorandum" because one credits Accounts Receivable. Suppose that during September, C. L. Frederickson Plumbing Supply issues two credit memorandums and makes the following entries in the general journal.

GENERAL JOURNAL   PAGE __27__

	DATE		DESCRIPTION	POST. REF.	DEBIT	CREDIT	
1	19– Sep.	2	Sales Returns and Allowances		4 5 00		1
2			Accounts Receivable, Craig and				2
3			Fraser Hardware			4 5 00	3
4			Credit memorandum no. 69.				4
5							5
6		2	Sales Returns and Allowances		1 1 6 00		6
7			Accounts Receivable, Home				7
8			Hardware Company			1 1 6 00	8
9			Credit memorandum no. 70.				9
10							10

The general journal entry serves as the posting source for crediting the Accounts Receivable controlling account in the general ledger. It also serves as the posting source for updating the accounts receivable ledger and therefore includes the name of the charge customer. If the balance of the Accounts Receivable (controlling) account is to equal the total of the individual balances in the accounts receivable ledger, one must post to *both* the Accounts Receivable account in the general ledger *and* the account of Craig and Fraser Hardware in the accounts receivable ledger. To take care of this double posting, one puts a slant line in the Posting Reference column. When the amount has been posted as a credit to the general ledger account, the accountant puts the account number of Accounts Receivable in the left part of the Posting Reference column. After the account of Craig and Fraser Hardware has been posted as a credit, the accountant puts a check mark in the right portion of the Posting Reference column, then posts Sales Returns and Allowances in the usual manner. Here are the entries with posting completed.

GENERAL JOURNAL PAGE 27

	DATE		DESCRIPTION	POST. REF.	DEBIT	CREDIT	
1	19– Sep.	2	Sales Returns and Allowances	412	4 5 00		1
2			Accounts Receivable, Craig and				2
3			Fraser Hardware	113/√		4 5 00	3
4			Credit memorandum no. 69.				4
5							5
6		2	Sales Returns and Allowances	412	1 1 6 00		6
7			Accounts Receivable, Home				7
8			Hardware Company	113/√		1 1 6 00	8
9			Credit memorandum no. 70.				9
10							10

GENERAL LEDGER

ACCOUNT Accounts Receivable   ACCOUNT NO. 113

	DATE		ITEM	POST. REF.	DEBIT	CREDIT	BALANCE DEBIT	BALANCE CREDIT	
1	19– Aug.	31		S38	4 4 2 4 00		4 4 2 4 00		1
2	Sep.	2		J27		4 5 00	4 3 7 9 00		2
3		2		J27		1 1 6 00	4 2 6 3 00		3
4									4

ACCOUNT *Sales Returns and Allowances* ACCOUNT NO. 412

	DATE	ITEM	POST. REF.	DEBIT	CREDIT	BALANCE DEBIT	BALANCE CREDIT	
1	19– Sep. 2		J27	4 5 00		4 5 00		1
2	2		J27	1 1 6 00		1 6 1 00		2
3								3
4								4

ACCOUNTS RECEIVABLE LEDGER

NAME *Craig and Fraser Hardware*

ADDRESS *2005 N. Powder St.*

Everett, WA 98201

DATE	ITEM	POST. REF.	DEBIT	CREDIT	BALANCE
19– Aug. 11		S38	8 6 00		8 6 00
24		S38	2 8 6 00		3 7 2 00
Sep. 2		J27		4 5 00	3 2 7 00

NAME *Home Hardware Company*

ADDRESS *7810 N.W. Cherburg St.*

Portland, OR 97206

DATE	ITEM	POST. REF.	DEBIT	CREDIT	BALANCE
19– Aug. 16		S38	2 1 5 00		2 1 5 00
28		S38	7 5 00		2 9 0 00
Sep. 2		J27		1 1 6 00	1 7 4 00

If a customer who returns merchandise to a retail store was originally charged a sales tax, the sales tax must be returned to the customer. To illustrate, first, refer to the sales journal of Milner and Salter Fabrics on page 314 involving sales taxes. On April 3, assume that B. T. Lawson returns the merchandise bought on April 1 for $16 plus $.64 sales tax. The general journal entry for the return is on the next page.

GENERAL JOURNAL

PAGE 12

	DATE		DESCRIPTION	POST. REF.	DEBIT	CREDIT	
1	19– Apr.	3	Sales Returns and Allowances		1 6 00		1
2			Sales Tax Payable		64		2
3			Accounts Receivable, B. T. Lawson			1 6 64	3
4			Credit memorandum no. 371.				4
5							5

POSTING DIRECTLY FROM SALES INVOICES

An accountant can take a further shortcut by posting directly from sales invoices or sales slips. The accountant posts to the charge customer accounts in the accounts receivable ledger daily, directly from carbon copies of the sales invoices or sales slips. He or she writes the *invoice number* rather than the journal page number in the Posting Reference column. Then, at the end of the month, the accountant brings the Accounts Receivable (controlling) account in the general ledger up to date by totaling all the sales invoices for the month, then making a general journal entry debiting Accounts Receivable and crediting Sales.

Let's use a different firm to show how this procedure works. The Marsden Sports Equipment Company posts directly from its sales invoices; the total of its sales invoices for December is $17,296. Its accountant journalizes and posts the entry as follows.

Objective 4

Post directly from sales invoices to an accounts receivable ledger and a general ledger.

GENERAL JOURNAL

PAGE 36

	DATE		DESCRIPTION	POST. REF.	DEBIT	CREDIT	
1	19– Dec.	31	Accounts Receivable	113	17 2 9 6 00		1
2			Sales	411		17 2 9 6 00	2
3			Summarizing entry for the total				3
4			of the sales invoices for the				4
5			month.				5
6							6

GENERAL LEDGER

ACCOUNT Accounts Receivable   ACCOUNT NO. 113

	DATE	ITEM	POST. REF.	DEBIT	CREDIT	BALANCE DEBIT	BALANCE CREDIT	
1	19– Dec. 31		J36	17 2 9 6 00		17 2 9 6 00		1
2								2

ACCOUNT Sales   ACCOUNT NO. 411

	DATE	ITEM	POST. REF.	DEBIT	CREDIT	BALANCE DEBIT	BALANCE CREDIT	
1	19– Dec. 31		J36		17 2 9 6 00		17 2 9 6 00	1
2								2

This is called a *summarizing entry* because it summarizes the credit sales for one month. Because the company's accountant posts the entry to the accounts in the general ledger, there is no need for a sales journal; the one summarizing entry in the general journal records the total sales for the month.

One invoice and the corresponding entry in the accounts receivable ledger might look like Figure 11-7.

Figure 11-7

MARSDEN SPORTS EQUIPMENT COMPANY
1610 Alhambra Blvd.
San Diego, CA 92002

INVOICE

Sold To Garcia and Cranston, Sporting Goods
1600 Santa Clara Ave.
San Francisco, CA 94133

Date: Dec. 4, 19–
Invoice No.: 6075
Order No.: 359
Shipped By: Express Collect
Terms: 2/10, n/30

Quantity	Description	Unit Price	Total
10	Molded unicellular foam ski/life vest (Davis) lg.	16.80	168.00

ACCOUNTS RECEIVABLE LEDGER

NAME *Garcia and Cranston, Sporting Goods*

ADDRESS *1600 Santa Clara Ave.*

San Francisco, CA 94133

DATE	ITEM	POST. REF.	DEBIT	CREDIT	BALANCE
19– Dec. 4		6075	1 6 8 00		1 6 8 00

The $168 would, of course, be posted to the general ledger as a part of the total comprising the monthly summarizing entry.

GLOSSARY

Accounts receivable ledger A subsidiary ledger that lists the individual accounts of charge customers in alphabetical order.

Controlling account An account in the general ledger that summarizes the balances of a subsidiary ledger.

Credit memorandum A written statement indicating a seller's willingness to reduce the amount of a buyer's debt. The seller records the amount of the credit memorandum under the Sales Returns and Allowances account.

Merchandise inventory A stock of goods that a firm buys with the intent of reselling the goods in the same physical condition.

Purchases An account for recording the cost of merchandise acquired for resale.

Purchases Discount An account that records cash discounts granted by suppliers in return for prompt payment; it is treated as a deduction from Purchases.

Purchases Returns and Allowances An account that records allowances and cash refunds granted by a supplier for returned or defective merchandise; it is treated as a deduction from Purchases.

Sales A revenue account for recording the sale of merchandise.

Sales Discount An account that records a deduction from the original price, granted by the seller to the buyer for the prompt payment of an invoice.

Sales journal A special journal for recording the sale of merchandise on account only.

Sales Returns and Allowances The account a seller uses to record the amount of a reduction granted to a customer either for the physical return of merchandise previously sold to the customer or as compensation for merchandise that is defective or damaged. This account is usually evidenced by a credit memorandum issued by the seller.

Sales tax A tax levied by a state or local government on the sale of goods. The tax is paid by the consumer but collected by the merchant.

Special journals Books of original entry in which one records specialized types of transactions.

Subsidiary ledger A group of accounts representing individual subdivisions of a controlling account.

QUESTIONS, EXERCISES, AND PROBLEMS

Discussion Questions

1. What information typically appears on a sales invoice?
2. What kind of ledger is an accounts receivable ledger? Are account numbers used? Why or why not?
3. Why does a business with a large number of charge customers need an accounts receivable ledger?
4. What is a schedule of accounts receivable?
5. What is the difference between a sales return and a sales allowance?
6. Why is it worthwhile to set up an account for sales returns and allowances instead of debiting Sales for any transaction involving a return or allowance?
7. Describe the method of posting directly from sales invoices.

Debit Sales
Ret. & Allowances

Exercises

Exercise 11-1   Label the blanks as debit or credit.

					ACCOUNTS RECEIVABLE	SALES TAX PAYABLE	SALES
					SALES JOURNAL		PAGE _____
	DATE	SALES SLIP	CUSTOMER's NAME	POST. REF.	*Debit*	*Credit*	*Credit*
1							

Exercise 11-2   Describe how the following sales journal of Bancroft Company would be posted to the ledgers.

1. Post to his individual Account
2.   PAGE __26__

	DATE	INV. NO.	CUSTOMER'S NAME	POST. REF.	ACCOUNTS RECEIVABLE DR., SALES CR.
1	19– Nov. 2	723	Sanderson Company		2 2 1 62
2	6	724	J. C. Farnsworth		1 6 4 2 00
3	12	725	A. R. Dombroski		1 2 6 8 71
4	20	726	Bannion and Worthy		3 6 8 4 00
5	30	727	Craig and Luckman		1 8 7 4 68
6	30				8 6 9 1 01
7					

debit A/R
credit Sales

Don't forget Account #'s

Exercise 11-3   Record the following transactions in general journal form.

a. Sold merchandise on account to L. B. Simpson, invoice no. 318, $120.
b. Issued credit memo no. 18 to L. B. Simpson for merchandise returned, $20.
c. Received full payment from L. B. Simpson.

Exercise 11-4   Describe the transactions recorded in the following T accounts.

Cash			Accounts Receivable		
(b)	210		**(a)**	210	**(b)**	210

Sales			Sales Tax Payable		
	(a)	200		**(a)**	10

Exercise 11-5   Post the following entry to the general ledger and subsidiary ledger accounts.

GENERAL JOURNAL   PAGE _43_

	DATE		DESCRIPTION	POST. REF.	DEBIT	CREDIT	
1	19– May	1	Sales Returns and Allowances	412	1 2 1 16		1
2			Accounts Receivable, J. B. Stokes	113/✓		1 2 1 16	2
3			Issued credit memo no. 129.				3
4							4

GENERAL LEDGER

ACCOUNT _Accounts Receivable_   ACCOUNT NO. _113_

	DATE		ITEM	POST. REF.	DEBIT	CREDIT	BALANCE DEBIT	BALANCE CREDIT	
1	19– May	1	Balance	✓			6 3 2 1 70		1
2				J43		1 2 1 16	6 2 0 0 54		2

ACCOUNT _Sales Returns and Allowances_   ACCOUNT NO. _412_

	DATE		ITEM	POST. REF.	DEBIT	CREDIT	BALANCE DEBIT	BALANCE CREDIT	
1	19– May	1	Balance	✓	3 2 9 80		3 2 9 80		1
2				J43	1 2 1 16		4 5 0 96		2

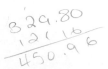

ACCOUNTS RECEIVABLE LEDGER

ACCOUNT _J. B. Stokes_

492.60
121.16
371.44

	DATE	INVOICE NO.	ITEM	POST. REF.	DEBIT	CREDIT	BALANCE	
1	19– Apr. 30	761		S26	4 9 2 60		4 9 2 60	1
2			cm 129	J43		1 2 1 16	3 7 1 44	2

Exercise 11-6 A business firm uses carbon copies of its sales invoices to record sales of merchandise on account and carbon copies of its credit memorandums to record its sales returns and allowances. During September, the firm issued 214 invoices for $82,729.82 and 12 credit memorandums for $1,768.20. Present the summarizing entries, dated September 30, in general journal form to record the sales and sales returns and allowances for the month.

Exercise 11-7 An accountant made the following errors in journalizing sales of merchandise on account in a single-column sales journal and posting to the general ledger and accounts receivable ledger. The errors were discovered at the end of the month before the closing entries were journalized and posted. Describe how to correct the errors.

a. The sales journal was footed correctly as $34,760, but it was posted as a debit and credit of $34,670.
b. A sale of $56 to T. R. Prentice was posted to his account as $5.60.
c. A sale of $72 to A. C. Freese was entered in the sales journal correctly, but it was posted to Freese's account as $27.

Exercise 11-8 Record the following transactions in general journal form.

a. Sold merchandise for cash to Paul Bremmer, $100 plus 5 percent sales tax.
b. Bremmer returned $20 of the merchandise; issued credit memo no. 323, and paid Bremmer $21 in cash, $20 for the amount of the returned merchandise plus $1 for the amount of the sales tax.

Problem Set A

Problem 11-1A Martin Brothers sells scaffolding equipment on a wholesale basis. The following transactions took place during March of this year.

Mar. 1 Sold merchandise on account to Duncan Construction Company, invoice no. 623, $482.
  7 Sold merchandise on account to T. R. Gibson Company, invoice no. 624, $386.
  8 Issued credit memorandum no. 41 to Richards Company for merchandise returned, $46.
  13 Sold merchandise on account to Spencer and Lucas, invoice no. 625, $106.

Mar. 15 Sold merchandise on account to Snyder and Pierce, invoice no. 626, $933.

20 Sold merchandise on account to Sprague Painting, invoice no. 627, $481.

24 Issued credit memorandum no. 42 to Snyder and Pierce for merchandise returned, $97.

26 Sold merchandise on account to Richards Company, invoice no. 628, $398.

29 Sold merchandise on account to Spencer and Lucas, invoice no. 629, $861.

30 Issued credit memorandum no. 43 to Spencer and Lucas for damage to merchandise, $43.

Instructions

1. Record these sales of merchandise on account in the sales journal. Record the sales returns and allowances in the general journal.
2. Immediately after recording each transaction, post to the accounts receivable ledger.
3. Post the amounts from the general journal daily. Post the sales journal amount as a total at the end of the month.
4. Prepare a schedule of accounts receivable.

Problem 11-2A   Margold Electronics, which opened for business during May of this year, had the following sales of merchandise on account and sales returns and allowances during the month.

May   3 Sold merchandise on account to Dempsey Automotive Electric, invoice no. 1, $272.65.

9 Sold merchandise on account to William T. Brocklin, invoice no. 2, $318.

11 Sold merchandise on account to L. T. Barber, Inc., invoice no. 3, $864.20.

16 Sold merchandise on account to N. C. Farmer, invoice no. 4, $788.16.

17 Issued credit memorandum no. 1, $26, to William T. Brocklin for merchandise returned.

22 Sold merchandise on account to Dempsey Automotive Electric, invoice no. 5, $976.70.

24 Issued credit memorandum no. 2, $118.10, to L. T. Barber, Inc., for merchandise returned.

27 Sold merchandise on account to N. C. Farmer, invoice no. 6, $227.18.

29 Sold merchandise on account to William T. Brocklin, invoice no. 7, $698.

30 Sold merchandise on account to Dempsey Automotive Electric, invoice no. 8, $163.72.

31 Issued credit memorandum no. 3, $44, to L. T. Barber, Inc., for merchandise damaged in transit.

Instructions

1. Record these sales of merchandise on account in the sales journal. Record the sales returns and allowances in the general journal.
2. Immediately after recording each transaction, post to the accounts receivable ledger.
3. Post the amounts from the general journal daily. Post the sales journal amount as a total at the end of the month.
4. Prepare a schedule of accounts receivable. Compare the balance of the Accounts Receivable controlling account with the total of the schedule of accounts receivable.

Problem 11-3A Hall's Camera sells merchandise on a retail basis. Most sales are for cash; however, a few steady customers have charge accounts. The salesclerks fill out sales slips for each sale. The state government levies a 5 percent retail sales tax, which is collected by the retailer. Hall's Camera's charge sales for November are as follows:

Nov.   3 Sold a Tendex Four-speed Projector with f/1.5 zoom lens to A. T. Albers, sales slip no. 238, $180, plus sales tax of $9, total $189.

5 Sold a Nasha K-3 Autowinder to Sheila Nelson, sales slip no. 263, $70, plus sales tax of $3.50, total $73.50.

10 Sold a Simpson Automatic-opening Screen to Roger Scott, sales slip no. 271, $48, plus sales tax of $2.40.

15 Sold a Tendex 35mm Auto Camera with Auto Focus (N16) to C. T. Abernathy, $260, plus sales tax, sales slip no. 282.

16 Giffin Photos bought a Miko SL Portrait Camera with Semco tripod and two Semco light stands on account, sales slip no. 296, $800, plus sales tax.

19 Giffin Photos returned the Semco tripod and two Semco light stands. Hall's Camera allowed full credit on the sale, $140, plus $7 sales tax, sales slip no. 296.

20 The Daily Chronicle bought ten Kadette 35mm Autofocus Viewfinder Cameras (K6), $1,100, plus sales tax, sales slip no. 303.

22 Allowed the Daily Chronicle credit, $110 plus tax, because of a defective camera, sales slip no. 303.

Instructions

1. Record these sales of merchandise on account in either the sales journal or the general journal.
2. Immediately after recording each transaction, post to the accounts receivable ledger.
3. Post the amounts from the general journal daily. Post the sales journal amount as a total at the end of the month.
4. Prepare a schedule of accounts receivable.

Problem 11-4A Worthington Company uses carbon copies of its charge sales invoices as a sales journal and posts to the accounts receivable ledger directly from the sales invoices. The invoices are totaled at the end of the month; an entry is made in the general journal summarizing the charge sales for the month. The charge sales invoices for March are as follows.

Mar. 2 T. R. Timmins Company, invoice no. 3912, $348.
      7 Northern Novelty Company, invoice no. 3925, $104.
      9 Harold J. Townsend, invoice no. 3936, $542.
    11 Vance and Harris, invoice no. 3944, $744.
    16 Coolidge and Roe, Inc., invoice no. 3962, $148.
    21 Prentice and Thomas, Inc., invoice no. 3978, $432.
    25 Perez Specialty Company, invoice no. 3989, $539.
    27 Singleton Amusement, invoice no. 3999, $268.
    31 Northern Novelty Company, invoice no. 4011, $189.

Instructions

1. Post to the accounts receivable ledger directly from the sales invoices, listing the invoice number in the Posting Reference column.
2. Record the summarizing entry in the general journal for the total amount of the sales invoices.
3. Post the general journal entry to the appropriate accounts in the general ledger.
4. Prepare a schedule of accounts receivable.

Problem Set B

Problem 11-1B Martin Brothers sells scaffolding equipment on a wholesale basis. The following transactions took place during April of this year.

Apr. 1 Sold merchandise on account to Duncan Construction Company, invoice no. 621, $457.
    6 Sold merchandise on account to T. R. Gibson Company, invoice no. 622, $353.
    7 Issued credit memorandum no. 30 to Richards Company for merchandise returned, $34.
    12 Sold merchandise on account to Spencer and Lucas, invoice no. 623, $98.
    14 Sold merchandise on account to Snyder and Pierce, invoice no. 624, $921.
    19 Sold merchandise on account to Sprague Painting, invoice no. 625, $469.
    23 Issued credit memorandum no. 31 to Snyder and Pierce for merchandise returned, $96.
    25 Sold merchandise on account to Richards Company, invoice no. 626, $392.
    29 Sold merchandise on account to Spencer and Lucas, invoice no. 627, $872.
    30 Issued credit memorandum no. 32 to Spencer and Lucas for damage to merchandise, $29.

Instructions

1. Record these sales of merchandise on account in the sales journal. Record the sales returns and allowances in the general journal.
2. Immediately after recording each transaction, post to the accounts receivable ledger.
3. Post the amounts from the general journal daily. Post the sales journal amount as a total at the end of the month.
4. Prepare a schedule of accounts receivable.

Problem 11-2B Margold Electronics, which opened for business during October of this year, had the following sales of merchandise on account and sales returns and allowances during the month.

Oct. 6 Sold merchandise on account to Dempsey Automotive Electric, invoice no. 1, $260.
      9 Sold merchandise on account to William T. Brocklin, invoice no. 2, $315.
     11 Sold merchandise on account to L. T. Barber, Inc., invoice no. 3, $870.
     16 Sold merchandise on account to N. C. Farmer, invoice no. 4, $776.
     17 Issued credit memorandum no. 1, $48, to William T. Brocklin for merchandise returned.
     21 Sold merchandise on account to Dempsey Automotive Electric, invoice no. 5, $964.
     23 Issued credit memorandum no. 2 to L. T. Barber, Inc., for merchandise returned, $120.
     27 Sold merchandise on account to N. C. Farmer, invoice no. 6, $229.
     29 Sold merchandise on account to William T. Brocklin, invoice no. 7, $694.
     30 Sold merchandise on account to Dempsey Automotive Electric, invoice no. 8, $161.
     31 Issued credit memorandum no. 3 to L. T. Barber, Inc., for damage done to merchandise during shipping, $40.

Instructions

1. Record the above sales of merchandise on account in the sales journal. Record the sales returns and allowances in the general journal.
2. Immediately after recording each transaction, post to the accounts receivable ledger.
3. Post the amounts from the general journal daily. Post the sales journal amount as a total at the end of the month.
4. Prepare a schedule of accounts receivable. Compare the balance of the Accounts Receivable controlling account with the total of the schedule of accounts receivable.

Problem 11-3B Pasara's Camera sells merchandise on a retail basis. Most sales are for cash; however, a few steady customers have charge accounts.

The salesclerks fill out sales slips for each sale. The state government levies a 5 percent retail sales tax, which is collected by the retailer. Pasara's Camera's charge sales for November are as follows.

Nov. 4 Sold a Pasha Electro 35mm PTN Rangefinder camera with f/1.6 lens to Sheila Nelson, sales slip no. 217, $160, plus sales tax of $8, total $168.

6 Sold a Tendex SV Flash to A. T. Albers, sales slip no. 262, $80, plus sales tax of $4, total $84.

12 Sold Giffin Photos a Laashi TN Portrait Camera with Semte tripod and two Semte light stands, sales slip no. 272, $600, plus sales tax of $30.

14 Sold a Rognor 3 C Tele-Converter to Roger Scott, sales slip no. 284, $60, plus sales tax.

18 Sold the Daily Chronicle two Bannion DE-2 35mm cameras with f/1.7 lens and two Bannion C Strobes, $900, plus sales tax, sales slip no. 294.

21 Giffin Photos returned a Semte tripod and two Semte light stands from sales slip no. 272. Pasara's Camera allowed full credit on the sale of $180 and the related sales tax of $9.

27 C. T. Abernathy bought a Bannion 28mm f/2.8 Wide Angle Lens for $240, plus sales tax, sales slip no. 306.

30 Allowed the Daily Chronicle credit for the return of two Bannion C Strobes, $80, plus tax, purchased on sales slip no. 294.

Instructions

1. Record the transactions in either the sales journal or the general journal.
2. Immediately after recording each transaction, post to the accounts receivable ledger.
3. Post the amounts from the general journal daily. Post the sales journal amount as a total at the end of the month.
4. Prepare a schedule of accounts receivable.

Problem 11-4B Best-Goods Company uses carbon copies of its charge sales invoices as a sales journal and posts to the accounts receivable ledger directly from the sales invoices. At the end of the month, the accountant totals the invoices and makes an entry in the general journal summarizing the charge sales for the month. The charge sales invoices are as follows.

Mar. 3 T. R. Timmins Company, invoice no. 2016, $360.

9 Northern Novelty Company, invoice no. 2019, $789.

12 Harold J. Townsend, invoice no. 2021, $219.

16 Vance and Harris, invoice no. 2024, $1,068.

17 Coolidge and Roe, Inc., invoice no. 2025, $724.

19 Prentice and Thomas, Inc., invoice no. 2027, $191.

25 Perez Specialty Company, invoice no. 2028, $783.

29 Singleton Amusement Company, invoice no. 2039, $860.

30 Northern Novelty Company, invoice no. 2040, $1,216.

Instructions

1. Post to the accounts receivable ledger directly from the sales invoices, listing the invoice number in the Posting Reference column.
2. Record the summarizing entry in the general journal for the total amount of the sales invoices.
3. Post the general journal entry to the appropriate accounts in the general ledger.
4. Prepare a schedule of accounts receivable.

12 Accounting for Merchandise: Purchases

Learning Objectives

After you have completed this chapter, you will be able to do the following:

1. Record transactions in a one-column purchases journal.

2. Post from a one-column purchases journal to an accounts payable ledger and a general ledger.

3. Prepare a schedule of accounts payable.

4. Journalize transactions involving transportation charges on incoming goods.

5. Post directly from purchase invoices to an accounts payable ledger and a general ledger.

We've been talking about the procedures, accounts, and special journals used to record the *selling* of merchandise. Now let's talk about those same elements as they apply to the *buying* of merchandise. We'll be dealing with the Purchases account and with Purchases Returns and Allowances. In this chapter you'll see that Accounts Payable is a controlling account, just as you saw in Chapter 11 that Accounts Receivable is a controlling account.

PURCHASING PROCEDURES

When you think of the great variety in types and sizes of merchandising firms, it comes as no surprise to learn that there is also considerable variety in the procedures used to buy goods for resale. Some purchases may be for cash; however, in most cases, purchases are on a credit basis. In a small retail store, the owner may do the buying. In large retail and wholesale concerns, department heads or division managers do the buying, after which the Purchasing Department goes into action: placing purchase orders, following up the orders, receiving the goods, and seeing that deliveries are made to the right departments. The Purchasing Department also acts as a source of information on current prices, price trends, quality of goods, prospective suppliers, and reliability of suppliers.

The Purchasing Department normally requires that any buying orders be in writing, in the form of a **purchase requisition.** After the purchase requisition is approved, the Purchasing Department sends a **purchase order** to the supplier. A purchase order is the company's written offer to buy certain goods. The accountant does not make any entry at this point, because the supplier has not yet indicated acceptance of the order. A purchase order is made out in triplicate: One copy goes to the supplier, one stays in the Purchasing Department (as proof of what was ordered), and one goes to the department that sent out the requisition (telling them that the goods they wanted have indeed been ordered).

To continue with the accounts of C. L. Frederickson Plumbing Supply: The Pipe Department submits a purchase requisition to the Purchasing Department as shown in Figure 12-1.

The Purchasing Department completes the bottom part of the purchase requisition and then sends out a purchase order, as shown in Figure 12-2.

The seller now sends an **invoice** to the buyer. This invoice should arrive in advance of the goods (or at least *with* the goods). From the seller's point of view, this is a sales invoice. If the sale is on credit, as we saw in Chapter 11, the seller's accountant makes an entry debiting Accounts Receivable and crediting Sales. To the buyer, this is a purchase invoice, so

Figure 12-1

C. L. FREDERICKSON
1968 N.E. Allen St.
Portland, OR 97201

PURCHASE REQUISITION

No. C-726

Department _Pipe_

Advise on delivery _Mr. Holloway_

Date of request _July 2, 19–_

Date required _Aug. 5, 19–_

Quantity	Description
1,000'	Flexible copper tubing ⅝", Type L, (50' roll)

Approved by _Ronald Schmidt_   Requested by _J. H. Holloway_

FOR PURCHASING DEPT. USE ONLY

Purchase Order No. _7918_

Date _July 5, 19–_

Issued to: _Darvik, Inc._
1616 Madera Ave.
Los Angeles, CA 90026

Figure 12-2

C. L. FREDERICKSON PLUMBING SUPPLY
1968 N.E. Allen St.
Portland, OR 97201

PURCHASE ORDER

To: _Darvik, Inc._
1616 Madera Ave.
Los Angeles, CA 90026

Date: _July 5, 19–_
Order No.: _7918_
Shipped By: _Freight Truck_
Terms: _2/10, n/30_

Quantity	Description	Unit Price	Total
1,000'	Flexible copper tubing ⅝", Type L (50' roll)	.42	420.00

Ronald Schmidt

the buyer's accountant makes an entry debiting Purchases and crediting Accounts Payable. C. L. Frederickson Plumbing Supply receives an invoice (Figure 12-3) from Darvik, Inc.

Let us now extract from the fundamental accounting equation (recall Chapter 11) the T accounts involved in buying merchandise. Again, color is used to emphasize the accounts that are deductions from Purchases.

Assets		=	Liabilities		+	Owner's Equity		+	Revenue		−	Expenses	
+	−		−	+		−	+		−	+		+	−
Debit	Credit		Debit	Credit		Debit	Credit		Debit	Credit		Debit	Credit

Purchases	
+	−

Purchases Returns and Allowances	
−	+

Purchases Discount	
−	+

Figure 12-3

DARVIK, INC.
1616 Madera Ave.
Los Angeles, CA 90026

INVOICE

Sold To *C. L. Frederickson Plumbing Supply*
1968 N.E. Allen St.
Portland, OR 97201

Date: *July 31, 19–*
No.: *2706*
Order No.: *7918*
Shipped By: *Western Freight Line*
Terms: *2/10, n/30*

Quantity	Description	Unit Price	Total
1,000'	*Flexible copper tubing ⅝",* *Type L (50' roll)*	*.42*	*420.00*

Bear in mind that the Purchases account is used exclusively for the buying of merchandise intended for resale. *If the firm buys anything else, the accountant records the amount under the appropriate asset or expense account.* At the end of the fiscal period, the balance in the Purchases account represents the total cost of merchandise bought during the period. As we said in Chapter 11, Purchases is classified as an expense only for the sake of convenience. The classification is permissible because Purchases is closed at the end of the fiscal period along with the expense accounts.

Purchases Returns and Allowances is a deduction from Purchases. A separate account is set up to keep track of the amount of the returns and of the reductions in bills due to damaged merchandise. In the income statement, we treat Purchases Returns and Allowances and Purchases Discount as deductions from Purchases; so, for consistency they are presented below Purchases in the fundamental accounting equation just shown.

To get back to C. L. Frederickson Plumbing Supply: as in Chapter 11, we'll record three transactions in the general journal. Then—just to reemphasize the advantage of special journals as opposed to the general journal—we'll record the same three transactions in a special journal.

During the first week in August, the following transactions took place.

Aug. 2 Bought merchandise on account from Darvik, Inc., their invoice no. 2706, dated July 31; terms 2/10, n/30; $420.
   3 Bought merchandise on account from Reiter and Simon Company, their invoice no. 982, dated August 2, terms net 30 days, $760.
   5 Bought merchandise on account from Alman Manufacturing Company, their invoice no. 10611, dated August 3; terms 2/10, n/30; $692.

Let's take a minute to explain the credit terms in the transactions. The notation "net 30 days" means that the bill is due within 30 days after the date of the invoice. The notation "2/10, n/30" refers to the **purchases discount** or cash discount. It means that the seller offers a 2 percent discount if the bill is paid within 10 days after the date of the invoice, and that the whole bill must be paid within 30 days after the invoice date. We will be working with these credit terms in Chapter 13.

For the present, we are concerned with recording the purchases. Let's visualize these transactions in terms of T accounts.

Purchases		Accounts Payable	
+	−	−	+
420			420
760			760
692			692

Figure 12-4

GENERAL JOURNAL

PAGE 22

	DATE		DESCRIPTION	POST. REF.	DEBIT	CREDIT	
1	19– Aug.	2	Purchases	511	4 2 0 00		1
2			Accounts Payable	211		4 2 0 00	2
3			Darvik, Inc., their invoice no.				3
4			2706, terms 2/10, n/30, dated				4
5			July 31.				5
6							6
7		3	Purchases	511	7 6 0 00		7
8			Accounts Payable	211		7 6 0 00	8
9			Reiter and Simon Company, their				9
10			invoice no. 982, terms net 30				10
11			days, dated August 2.				11
12							12
13		5	Purchases	511	6 9 2 00		13
14			Accounts Payable	211		6 9 2 00	14
15			Alman Manufacturing Company,				15
16			their invoice no. 10611, terms				16
17			2/10, n/30, dated August 3.				17
18							18
19							19
20							20
21							21

If these transactions are recorded in the general journal, they look like Figure 12-4, above.

Next the general journal entries would be posted to the general ledger.

GENERAL LEDGER

ACCOUNT Accounts Payable   ACCOUNT NO. 211

	DATE		ITEM	POST. REF.	DEBIT	CREDIT	BALANCE DEBIT	BALANCE CREDIT	
1	19– Aug.	1	Balance	√				3 5 6 00	1
2		2		22		4 2 0 00		7 7 6 00	2
3		3		22		7 6 0 00		1 5 3 6 00	3
4		5		22		6 9 2 00		2 2 2 8 00	4
5									5
6									6
7									7
8									8

GENERAL LEDGER

ACCOUNT *Purchases*   ACCOUNT NO. *511*

	DATE	ITEM	POST. REF.	DEBIT	CREDIT	BALANCE DEBIT	BALANCE CREDIT	
1	19– Aug. 1	Balance	✓			20 6 1 2 00		1
2	2		22	4 2 0 00		21 0 3 2 00		2
3	3		22	7 6 0 00		21 7 9 2 00		3
4	5		22	6 9 2 00		22 4 8 4 00		4
5								5

PURCHASES JOURNAL

Objective 1

Record transactions in a one-column purchases journal.

The above repetition can be avoided if the accountant uses a **purchases journal** instead of the general journal. The purchases journal is used to record the purchase of merchandise *on account only*. In each case, with this special type of transaction, the accountant debits Purchases and credits Accounts Payable.

PURCHASES JOURNAL   PAGE _29_

	DATE	SUPPLIER'S NAME	INVOICE NO.	INVOICE DATE	TERMS	POST. REF.	PURCHASES DR., ACCOUNTS PAYABLE CR.	
1	19– Aug. 2	Darvik, Inc.	2706	7/31	2/10, n/30		4 2 0 00	1
2	3	Reiter and Simon						2
3		Company	982	8/2	n/30		7 6 0 00	3
4	5	Alman Manufacturing						4
5		Company	10611	8/3	2/10, n/30		6 9 2 00	5
6								6

Note that the one money column is headed Purchases Debit, Accounts Payable Credit.

Objective 2

Post from a one-column purchases journal to an accounts payable ledger and a general ledger.

Posting from the Purchases Journal to the General Ledger

Figure 12-5 shows the journal entries for all transactions involving the purchase of merchandise on account for August.

The next step in the accounting cycle is posting. Since all the entries are debits to Purchases and credits to Accounts Payable, one can post the totals to these accounts at the end of the month.

Figure 12-5

PURCHASES JOURNAL

PAGE _29_

	DATE		SUPPLIER'S NAME	INVOICE NO.	INVOICE DATE	TERMS	POST. REF.	PURCHASES DR., ACCOUNTS PAYABLE CR.	
1	19– Aug.	2	Darvik, Inc.	2706	7/31	2/10, n/30		4 2 0 00	1
2		3	Reiter and Simon						2
3			Company	982	8/2	n/30		7 6 0 00	3
4		5	Alman Manufacturing						4
5			Company	10611	8/3	2/10, n/30		6 9 2 00	5
6		9	Sullivan Manufacturing						6
7			Company	B643	8/6	1/10, n/30		1 6 5 00	7
8		18	Tru-Fit Valve, Inc.	46812	8/17	n/60		2 2 8 00	8
9		25	Donaldson and Farr	1024	8/23	2/10, n/30		3 7 6 00	9
10		26	Darvik, Inc.	2801	8/25	n/30		4 0 6 00	10
11		31						3 0 4 7 00	11
12								(511)(211)	12
13									13

In the Posting Reference column of the ledger accounts, P designates the purchases journal. After posting to the ledger accounts, the accountant goes back to the purchases journal and records the account numbers in parentheses directly below the total, placing the account number for the account being debited on the left. **Transactions involving the buying**

GENERAL LEDGER

ACCOUNT _Accounts Payable_   ACCOUNT NO. _211_

	DATE		ITEM	POST. REF.	DEBIT	CREDIT	BALANCE DEBIT	BALANCE CREDIT	
1	19– Aug.	1	Balance	√				3 5 6 00	1
2		31		P29		3 0 4 7 00		3 4 0 3 00	2
3									3

GENERAL LEDGER

ACCOUNT _Purchases_   ACCOUNT NO. _511_

	DATE		ITEM	POST. REF.	DEBIT	CREDIT	BALANCE DEBIT	BALANCE CREDIT	
1	19– Aug.	1	Balance	√			20 6 1 2 00		1
2		31		P29	3 0 4 7 00		23 6 5 9 00		2
3									3

of supplies or other assets should *not* be recorded in the purchases journal, because the purchases journal may be used only for the purchases of merchandise for resale.

THE ACCOUNTS PAYABLE LEDGER

In Chapter 11 we called the Accounts Receivable account in the general ledger a *controlling* account, and we saw that the accounts receivable ledger consists of an individual account for each charge customer. We also saw that the accountant posts to the accounts receivable ledger every day.

Accounts Payable is a parallel case; it, too, is a controlling account in the general ledger. The accounts payable ledger is a subsidiary ledger, and it consists of individual accounts for all the creditors. Again, in the accounts payable ledger, posting is done daily. After posting to the individual creditors' accounts, the accountant puts a check mark ($\sqrt{}$) in the Posting Reference column of the purchases journal. After he or she has finished all the posting to the controlling account at the end of the period, the total of the schedule of accounts payable should equal the balance of the Accounts Payable (controlling) account. Incidentally, one always uses the three-column form for the accounts payable ledger. Because the T account for Accounts Payable is

it follows that the three-column form looks like this.

Accounts Payable Ledger		
Debit	Credit	Balance
−	+	+

Now let's see the purchases journal (Figure 12-6) and the postings to the ledger (Figure 12-7).

Note that in the accounts payable ledger—as in the accounts receivable ledger—the accounts of the individual creditors are listed in alphabetical order. Accountants usually use a loose-leaf binder with no page numbers or account numbers.

Figure 12-6

PURCHASES JOURNAL

PAGE __29__

	DATE		SUPPLIER'S NAME	INVOICE NO.	INVOICE DATE	TERMS	POST. REF.	PURCHASES DR., ACCOUNTS PAYABLE CR.	
1	19– Aug.	2	Darvik, Inc.	2706	7/31	2/10, n/30	√	4 2 0 00	1
2		3	Reiter and Simon						2
3			Company	982	8/2	n/30	√	7 6 0 00	3
4		5	Alman Manufacturing						4
5			Company	10611	8/3	2/10, n/30	√	6 9 2 00	5
6		9	Sullivan Manufacturing						6
7			Company	B643	8/6	1/10, n/30	√	1 6 5 00	7
8		18	Tru-Fit Valve, Inc.	46812	8/17	n/60	√	2 2 8 00	8
9		25	Donaldson and Farr	1024	8/23	2/10, n/30	√	3 7 6 00	9
10		26	Darvik, Inc.	2801	8/25	n/30	√	4 0 6 00	10
11		31						3 0 4 7 00	11
12								(511)(211)	12
13									13

Figure 12-7

ACCOUNTS PAYABLE LEDGER

NAME __Alman Manufacturing Company__

ADDRESS __2510 Madeira Ave.__
__San Francisco, CA 94130__

DATE		ITEM	POST. REF.	DEBIT	CREDIT	BALANCE
19– Aug.	5		P29		6 9 2 00	6 9 2 00

NAME __Darvik, Inc.__

ADDRESS __1616 Madera Ave.__
__Los Angeles, CA 90026__

DATE		ITEM	POST. REF.	DEBIT	CREDIT	BALANCE
19– Aug.	2		P29		4 2 0 00	4 2 0 00
	26		P29		4 0 6 00	8 2 6 00

NAME __Donaldson and Farr__

ADDRESS __1600 S.W. Yelm St.__
__Portland, OR 97216__

DATE		ITEM	POST. REF.	DEBIT	CREDIT	BALANCE
19– Aug.	25		P29		3 7 6 00	3 7 6 00

Figure 12-7
(continued)

NAME _____ *Reiter and Simon Company* _____

ADDRESS _____ *21325 186th Ave. No.* _____

_____ *Seattle, WA 98101* _____

DATE		ITEM	POST. REF.	DEBIT	CREDIT	BALANCE
19– Jul.	27		P28		1 8 0 00	1 8 0 00
Aug.	3		P29		7 6 0 00	9 4 0 00

NAME _____ *Sullivan Manufacturing Company* _____

ADDRESS _____ *1068 Casino Ave.* _____

_____ *Los Angeles, CA 90023* _____

DATE		ITEM	POST. REF.	DEBIT	CREDIT	BALANCE
19– Aug.	9		P29		1 6 5 00	1 6 5 00

NAME _____ *Tru-Fit Valve, Inc.* _____

ADDRESS _____ *1620 Minard St.* _____

_____ *San Francisco, CA 94130* _____

DATE		ITEM	POST. REF.	DEBIT	CREDIT	BALANCE
19– Jul.	29		P28		1 7 6 00	1 7 6 00
Aug.	18		P29		2 2 8 00	4 0 4 00

PURCHASES RETURNS AND ALLOWANCES

This account, as the title implies, handles either a return of merchandise previously purchased or an allowance made for merchandise that arrived in damaged condition. In both cases there is a reduction in the amount owed to the supplier. The buyer sends a letter or printed form to the supplier, who acknowledges the reduction by sending a **credit memorandum.** The buyer should wait for notice of the agreed deduction before making an entry.

The Purchases Returns and Allowances account is considered to be a deduction from Purchases. Using a separate account provides a better record of the total returns and allowances. Purchases Returns and Allowances is deducted from the Purchases account in the income statement. (We'll talk about this point later.) For now, let's look at an example consisting of two entries on the books of C. L. Frederickson Plumbing Supply.

Transaction (a) On August 5, bought merchandise on account from Alman Manufacturing Co., their invoice no. 10611 of August 3; terms 2/10, n/30; $692. Recorded this as a debit to Purchases and a credit to Accounts Payable. On August 6, returned $70 worth of the merchandise. Made no entry.

Transaction (b) On August 8, received credit memorandum no. 629 from Alman Manufacturing Company for $70. Recorded this as a debit to Accounts Payable and a credit to Purchases Returns and Allowances.

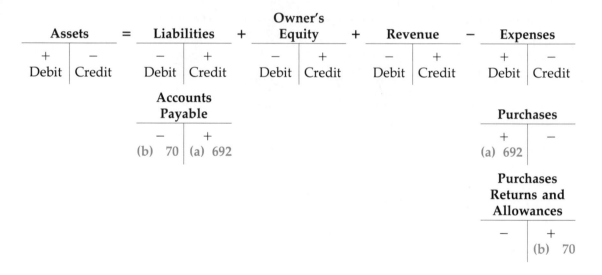

Purchases Returns and Allowances is credited because C. L. Frederickson has more returns and allowances than before. Accounts Payable is debited because C. L. Frederickson owes less than before.

Suppose that C. L. Frederickson Plumbing Supply returned merchandise on two occasions during August and received credit memorandums from the suppliers; the entries are recorded in the general journal.

GENERAL JOURNAL
PAGE __27__

	DATE		DESCRIPTION	POST. REF.	DEBIT	CREDIT	
1	19– Aug.	8	Accounts Payable, Alman				1
2			Manufacturing Company		7 0 00		2
3			Purchases Returns and Allowances			7 0 00	3
4			Credit memo 629, invoice				4
5			no. 10611.				5
6							6
7		12	Accounts Payable, Sullivan				7
8			Manufacturing Company		3 6 00		8
9			Purchases Returns and Allowances			3 6 00	9
10			Credit memo 482, invoice				10
11			no. B643.				11
12							12
13							13

In these entries, Accounts Payable is followed by the name of the individual creditor's account. The accountant must post to both the Accounts Payable controlling account and the individual creditor's account in the accounts payable ledger. The journal entries are shown below as they appear when the posting is completed. The account numbers in the Posting Reference column indicate postings to the accounts in the general ledger, and the check marks indicate postings to the accounts in the accounts payable ledger.

GENERAL JOURNAL
PAGE __27__

	DATE		DESCRIPTION	POST. REF.	DEBIT	CREDIT	
1	19– Aug.	8	Accounts Payable, Alman				1
2			Manufacturing Company	211/✓	7 0 00		2
3			Purchases Returns and Allowances	512		7 0 00	3
4			Credit memo 629, invoice				4
5			no. 10611.				5
6							6
7		12	Accounts Payable, Sullivan				7
8			Manufacturing Company	211/✓	3 6 00		8
9			Purchases Returns and Allowances	512		3 6 00	9
10			Credit memo 482, invoice				10
11			no. B643.				11
12							12
13							13

GENERAL LEDGER

ACCOUNT __Purchases Returns and Allowances__ ACCOUNT NO. __512__

	DATE		ITEM	POST. REF.	DEBIT	CREDIT	BALANCE DEBIT	BALANCE CREDIT	
1	19– Aug.	1	Balance					6 9 0 00	1
2		8		J27		7 0 00		7 6 0 00	2
3		12		J27		3 6 00		7 9 6 00	3
4									4

GENERAL LEDGER

ACCOUNT __Accounts Payable__ ACCOUNT NO. __211__

	DATE		ITEM	POST. REF.	DEBIT	CREDIT	BALANCE DEBIT	BALANCE CREDIT	
1	19– Aug.	1	Balance	√				3 5 6 00	1
2		8		J27	7 0 00			2 8 6 00	2
3		12		J27	3 6 00			2 5 0 00	3
4									4

ACCOUNTS PAYABLE LEDGER

NAME __Alman Manufacturing Company__
ADDRESS __2150 Madeira Ave.__
__San Francisco, CA 94130__

DATE		ITEM	POST. REF.	DEBIT	CREDIT	BALANCE
19– Aug.	5		P29		6 9 2 00	6 9 2 00
	8		J27	7 0 00		6 2 2 00

NAME __Sullivan Manufacturing Company__
ADDRESS __1068 Casino Ave.__
__Los Angeles, CA 90023__

DATE		ITEM	POST. REF.	DEBIT	CREDIT	BALANCE
19– Aug.	9		P29		1 6 5 00	1 6 5 00
	12		J27	3 6 00		1 2 9 00

Schedule of Accounts Payable

Assuming that no other transactions involved Accounts Payable, the schedule of accounts payable would appear as follows. Note that the balances of the creditors' accounts, with the exception of the accounts for Alman Manufacturing Company and Sullivan Manufacturing Company, are taken from the accounts payable ledger shown in Figure 12-7.

Objective 3

Prepare a schedule of accounts payable.

C. L. Frederickson Plumbing Supply
Schedule of Accounts Payable
August 31, 19–

Alman Manufacturing Company	$ 6 2 2 00
Darvik, Inc.	8 2 6 00
Donaldson and Farr	3 7 6 00
Reiter and Simon Company	9 4 0 00
Sullivan Manufacturing Company	1 2 9 00
Tru-Fit Valve, Inc.	4 0 4 00
Total Accounts Payable	$3 2 9 7 00

The Accounts Payable controlling account in the general ledger is now posted up to date.

GENERAL LEDGER

ACCOUNT **Accounts Payable**   ACCOUNT NO. **211**

	DATE	ITEM	POST. REF.	DEBIT	CREDIT	BALANCE DEBIT	BALANCE CREDIT	
1	19– Aug. 1	Balance	√				3 5 6 00	1
2	8		J27	7 0 00			2 8 6 00	2
3	12		J27	3 6 00			2 5 0 00	3
4	31		P29		3 0 4 7 00		3 2 9 7 00	4
5								5
6								6
7								7

TRANSPORTATION CHARGES ON INCOMING MERCHANDISE AND OTHER ASSETS

When a firm buys merchandise, the total of the purchase invoice may include the transportation charges. If it does, this means that the supplier is selling on the basis of **FOB destination.** In other words, the supplier loads the goods *free on board* (FOB) the carrier and ships them to the customer without charge. Since the supplier is paying the freight charges, these charges naturally have to be included in the selling price of the goods.

For example, C. L. Frederickson Plumbing Supply (remember, it's in Portland) buys pipe fittings from a supplier in Chicago. A note on the supplier's invoice indicates that the terms are FOB Portland (destination). The total of the invoice is $1,200, and C. L. Frederickson knows that this figure includes the freight charges but does not account for them separately. We show this situation by T accounts as follows.

Purchases		Accounts Payable	
+	−	−	+
1,200			1,200

Objective 4

Journalize transactions involving transportation charges on incoming goods.

What happens when the transportation charges are separate? In that case, there's a note on the invoice that the terms are **FOB shipping point.** This term means that the supplier will load the goods free on board the carrier at the shipping point, but any freight charges from there on have to be paid by the buyer.

Suppose, for example, that C. L. Frederickson Plumbing Supply buys lavatories from a manufacturer in Detroit with terms FOB Detroit (shipping point). Now the total of the invoice is $1,750, but in this case C. L. Frederickson Plumbing Supply has to pay the freight charges from Detroit to Portland separately. The lavatories are shipped by rail, and C. L. Frederickson pays the railroad $125. In our minds we can picture the T accounts this way.

Purchases		Accounts Payable		Cash	
+	−	−	+	+	−
1,750			1,750		125
125					

Any merchandising concern must base its markups on the *delivered* cost of the merchandise. So, for this reason, **the buyer debits any freight charges on incoming merchandise to Purchases.** Thus the Purchases account represents both the *cost* of the merchandise and the *freight charges* the buyer has to pay for transporting the goods. In the case of FOB destination, the freight charges have already been included in the total price of the merchandise and debited to the Purchases account when recording the invoice. In the case of FOB shipping point, the buyer pays the freight charges separately and debits the Purchases account at the time of payment. So, with both FOB destination and FOB shipping point, the freight charges on incoming merchandise all wind up in the Purchases account.

Any firm that sells on the basis of FOB destination must be able to cover all its costs, which of course include freight costs. Therefore the firm must include freight costs when it sets the price for its goods. There is an interesting legal point here. Ordinarily, unless the title is definitely retained by the seller, whoever pays the freight charges on the goods has title to the goods during shipment.

Some business firms, instead of debiting Purchases for freight charges on incoming merchandise, set up an expense account entitled Freight In or Transportation In. In the income statement, the accountant adds the balance of this account to the balance of the Purchases account to determine the *delivered* cost of the purchases. However, here we shall follow the policy of debiting Purchases for freight charges on incoming merchandise.

Any shipping charges involved in the buying of any other assets, such as supplies or equipment, are debited to their respective asset accounts. For example, C. L. Frederickson Plumbing Supply bought display cases on account, at a cost of $2,700 plus freight charges of $90. As a convenience, the seller of the display cases paid the transportation costs for C. L. Frederickson Plumbing Supply and then added the $90 to the invoice price of the cases. Let's visualize this by means of T accounts.

Store Equipment		Accounts Payable	
+	−	−	+
2,790			2,790

On the other hand, if C. L. Frederickson had paid the freight charges separately, the entry for the payment would be a debit to Store Equipment for $90 and a credit to Cash for $90.

POSTING DIRECTLY FROM PURCHASE INVOICES

Posting from purchase invoices is a shortcut like posting from sales invoices (described in Chapter 11). The accountant posts to the individual creditors' accounts daily, directly from the purchase invoices. The suppliers' invoice numbers are recorded in the Posting Reference column in place of the journal page number. The Accounts Payable controlling account in the general ledger is brought up to date at the end of the month by making a summarizing entry in the general journal. The accountant debits Purchases and any asset accounts that may be involved and credits Accounts Payable.

Since posting directly from purchase invoices is a variation of the accounting system, we shall use a different example: Sam's Towing and Trailer Service. This firm sorts its purchase invoices for the month and finds that the totals are as follows: purchase of merchandise, $8,610; store supplies, $168; office supplies, $126; store equipment, $520. The accountant then makes a summarizing entry in the general journal, as follows.

Objective 5

Post directly from purchase invoices to an accounts payable ledger and a general ledger.

GENERAL JOURNAL — PAGE 37

	DATE		DESCRIPTION	POST. REF.	DEBIT	CREDIT	
1	19– Oct.	31	Purchases	511	8 6 1 0 00		1
2			Store Supplies	114	1 6 8 00		2
3			Office Supplies	115	1 2 6 00		3
4			Store Equipment	121	5 2 0 00		4
5			Accounts Payable	211		9 4 2 4 00	5
6			Summarizing entry for total				6
7			purchase of goods on account.				7
8							8

The accountant posts the above entry to the general ledger accounts.

GENERAL LEDGER

ACCOUNT Store Supplies — ACCOUNT NO. 114

	DATE		ITEM	POST. REF.	DEBIT	CREDIT	BALANCE DEBIT	BALANCE CREDIT	
1	19– Oct.	31		J37	1 6 8 00		1 6 8 00		1
2									2

ACCOUNT Office Supplies — ACCOUNT NO. 115

	DATE		ITEM	POST. REF.	DEBIT	CREDIT	BALANCE DEBIT	BALANCE CREDIT	
1	19– Oct.	31		J37	1 2 6 00		1 2 6 00		1
2									2

CHAPTER 12

Store Equipment

ACCOUNT _Store Equipment_   ACCOUNT NO. _121_

	DATE	ITEM	POST. REF.	DEBIT	CREDIT	BALANCE DEBIT	BALANCE CREDIT	
1	19– Oct. 31		J37	5 2 0 00		5 2 0 00		1
2								2

Accounts Payable

ACCOUNT _Accounts Payable_   ACCOUNT NO. _211_

	DATE	ITEM	POST. REF.	DEBIT	CREDIT	BALANCE DEBIT	BALANCE CREDIT	
1	19– Oct. 31		J37		9 4 2 4 00		9 4 2 4 00	1
2								2

Purchases

ACCOUNT _Purchases_   ACCOUNT NO. _511_

	DATE	ITEM	POST. REF.	DEBIT	CREDIT	BALANCE DEBIT	BALANCE CREDIT	
1	19– Oct. 31		J37	8 6 1 0 00		8 6 1 0 00		1
2								2

This procedure does away with the need for a purchases journal, and it also includes the buying of any assets on account in the same summarizing entry. An example of an invoice is shown in Figure 12-8.

Sam's Towing and Trailer Service posts the amount of the invoice to the account of the supplier in the accounts payable ledger.

ACCOUNTS PAYABLE LEDGER

NAME — _Reinbold Electronics_

ADDRESS — _9600 Alhambra St._
San Francisco, CA 94132

	DATE	ITEM	POST. REF.	DEBIT	CREDIT	BALANCE
	19– Oct. 7		13168		1 7 6 00	1 7 6 00

Sam's Towing and Trailer Service will also include the $176 figure in the summarizing entry recorded in the general journal, debiting Purchases and crediting Accounts Payable. Note that the supplier's invoice number is recorded in the Post. Ref. column in the Reinbold Electronics account.

Figure 12-8

REINBOLD ELECTRONICS
9600 Alhambra St.
San Francisco, CA 94132

INVOICE

Sold To *Sam's Towing and Trailer Service*
2716 Brighton Road
Burlingame, CA 94011

Rec'd Oct. 7, 19—

Date: *Oct. 4, 19—*
No.: *13168*
Order No.: *1635*
Shipped By: *Pacific Express Co.*
Terms: *1/10, n/30*

Quantity	Description	Unit Price	Total
20	*Mobile home antenna—TV*	*8.80*	*176.00*

SUBSIDIARY LEDGERS

The place of subsidiary ledgers in the accounting cycle is shown in Figure 12-9. The figure also shows how the schedules of accounts receivable and accounts payable fit into the accounting cycle.

INTERNAL CONTROL

We have already spoken briefly about the efficient management of cash in Chapter 8. We stated that all payments should be made either by check or from the petty cash fund, and all cash received should be deposited in the bank at the end of the day. The handling of cash in this manner is an example of **internal control.** When there is internal control, plans and procedures for the control of operations are made a part of the accounting system. Doing this is necessary when the owner or management must delegate authority. The owner has to take measures to (1) protect assets against fraud and waste, (2) provide for accurate accounting data, (3) promote an efficient operation, and (4) encourage adherence to management policies. We'll be talking about the concept of internal control quite often in the rest of the text.

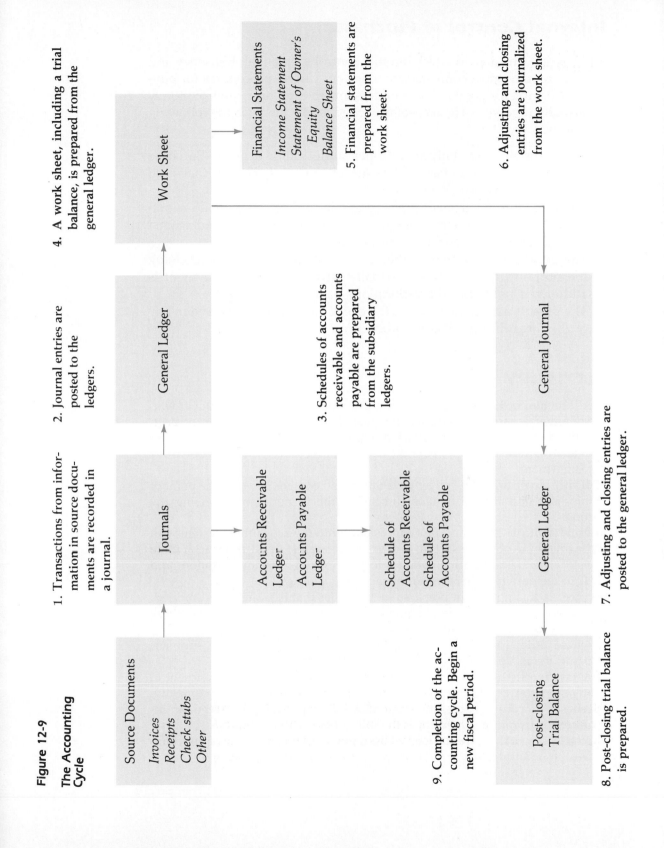

Figure 12-9

The Accounting Cycle

1. Transactions from information in source documents are recorded in a journal.

2. Journal entries are posted to the ledgers.

3. Schedules of accounts receivable and accounts payable are prepared from the subsidiary ledgers.

4. A work sheet, including a trial balance, is prepared from the general ledger.

5. Financial statements are prepared from the work sheet.

6. Adjusting and closing entries are journalized from the work sheet.

7. Adjusting and closing entries are posted to the general ledger.

8. Post-closing trial balance is prepared.

9. Completion of the accounting cycle. Begin a new fiscal period.

Source Documents
Invoices
Receipts
Check stubs
Other

Journals

General Ledger

Work Sheet

Financial Statements
Income Statement
Statement of Owner's Equity
Balance Sheet

Accounts Receivable Ledger
Accounts Payable Ledger

Schedule of Accounts Receivable
Schedule of Accounts Payable

General Journal

General Ledger

Post-closing Trial Balance

Internal Control of Purchases

Purchases is one area in which internal control is essential. Efficiency and security require most companies to work out careful procedures for buying and paying for goods. This is understandable, as large sums of money are usually involved. The control aspect generally involves the following measures.

1. Purchases are made only after proper authorization is given. Purchase requisitions and purchase orders are all prenumbered, so that each form can be accounted for.
2. The receiving department carefully checks and counts all goods upon receipt. Later the report of the receiving department is verified against the purchase order and the purchase invoice.
3. The person who authorizes the payment is neither the person doing the ordering nor the person actually writing the check. Payment is authorized only after the verifications have been made.
4. The person who actually writes the check has not been involved in any of the foregoing purchasing procedures.

GLOSSARY

Credit memorandum A business form provided by the seller to a buyer who has either returned a purchase (or part of a purchase) for credit or been granted an allowance for damaged goods.

FOB destination The seller pays the freight charges and includes them in the selling price.

FOB shipping point The buyer pays the freight charges between the point of shipment and the destination directly to the carrier upon receiving the goods.

Internal control Plans and procedures built into the accounting system with the following objectives: (1) to protect assets against fraud and waste, (2) to yield accurate accounting data, (3) to promote an efficient operation, and (4) to encourage adherence to management policies.

Invoice A business form prepared by the seller that lists the items shipped, their cost, and the mode of shipment. The buyer considers it a purchase invoice; the seller considers it a sales invoice.

Purchase order A written order from the buyer of goods to the supplier, listing items wanted as well as terms of the transaction.

Purchase requisition A form used to request the Purchasing Department to buy something. This form is intended for internal use within a company.

Purchases discount A cash discount allowed for prompt payment of an invoice; for example, 2 percent if the bill is paid within 10 days.

Purchases journal A special journal used to record the purchase of merchandise on account only.

Purchases Returns and Allowances The account used by the buyer to record a reduction granted by the supplier either for the return of merchandise or as compensation for damage to the merchandise. The entry in the buyer's account is based on a credit memorandum received from the supplier.

QUESTIONS, EXERCISES, AND PROBLEMS

Discussion Questions

1. How many copies of a purchase order are usually made, and who receives each copy?
2. What business document authorizes the recording of a purchase transaction?
3. What does a check mark in the Posting Reference column of a purchases journal indicate?
4. How will an error in posting to an individual creditor's account generally be detected?
5. Why is it necessary for a business firm to account for transportation charges on incoming merchandise?
6. When an owner delegates authority, what measures must be taken to maintain control over the operations?
7. Describe the four procedures that most companies follow to maintain internal control of purchases?

Exercises

Exercise 12-1   Label the blanks in the column headings as debit or credit.

						PURCHASES (_____)
DATE	SUPPLIER'S NAME	INVOICE NO.	INVOICE DATE	TERMS	POST. REF.	ACCOUNTS PAYABLE (_____)

PURCHASES JOURNAL   PAGE _____

Exercise 12-2   Record the following transactions in general journal form.

a. Bought merchandise on account from Drexel Company, invoice no. 7197, FOB shipping point, $416.
b. Paid Acme Fast Freight for shipping charges on the above purchase, $36.

Exercise 12-3   On the above purchase, the markup is 20 percent of cost. Determine the selling price of the new merchandise.

Exercise 12-4   Record the following transactions in general journal form.

a. Bought merchandise on account from Bingham and Harvey, invoice no. D716, $640.
b. Received credit memo no. 216 from Bingham and Harvey for merchandise returned on invoice no. D716, $30.
c. Issued a check to Bingham and Harvey in full payment of invoice no. D716.

Exercise 12-5 A business firm that posts directly from its purchase invoices sorts the invoices for the month and finds that the totals are as follows: purchases of merchandise, $7,624; store supplies, $118; office supplies, $97; office equipment, $136. Record the summarizing entry in general journal form.

Exercise 12-6 Describe the transactions in the following T accounts.

Cash	Purchases	Purchases Returns and Allowances	Accounts Payable
(c) 670	(a) 720	(b) 50	(b) 50 | (a) 720
			(c) 670

Exercise 12-7 Record the following transactions in general journal form.

a. Bought a desk for use in the office from Modern Office Supply, invoice no. D419, $240.
b. Paid Mountain States Freight Company for shipping the desk, $9.

Exercise 12-8 Post the following entry to the general ledger and subsidiary ledger accounts.

	DATE	DESCRIPTION	POST. REF.	DEBIT	CREDIT	
1	19– Jun. 15	Accounts Payable, L. B. Dixon				1
2		Company	09	3 7 40		2
3		Purchases Returns and Allowances	512		3 7 40	3
4		Received credit memo no. 1087.				4
5						5
6						6
7						7
8						8
9						9
10						10
11						11

GENERAL JOURNAL   PAGE 44

GENERAL LEDGER

ACCOUNT *Accounts Payable* ACCOUNT NO. __212__

	DATE		ITEM	POST. REF.	DEBIT	CREDIT	BALANCE DEBIT	BALANCE CREDIT	
1	19– Jun.	1	Balance	✓				1 6 5 4 20	1
2		15		J44	37 40			1 6 1 6 80	2

ACCOUNT *Purchases Returns and Allowances* ACCOUNT NO. __512__

	DATE		ITEM	POST. REF.	DEBIT	CREDIT	BALANCE DEBIT	BALANCE CREDIT	
1	19– Jun.	1	Balance	✓				8 4 20	1
2		15		J44		37 40		1 2 1 60	2

ACCOUNTS PAYABLE LEDGER

NAME __L. B. Dixon Company__

ADDRESS _____

DATE		ITEM	POST. REF.	DEBIT	CREDIT	BALANCE
19– May	27		G729		1 2 8 00	1 2 8 00
	15		J44	37 40		9 0 60

Problem Set A

Problem 12-1A Morgan and Stern, Jewelers, uses a single-column purchases journal. On January 1 of this year, the balances in the ledger accounts are Accounts Payable, $400.86; Purchases, zero. In addition to a general ledger, Morgan and Stern uses an accounts payable ledger. Transactions for January related to the buying of merchandise are as follows.

Jan. 5 Bought sixty Soules Mortenson Automatic Day/Date watches in Karecki yellow cases from Spencer Watch Company, invoice no. 2117D, dated January 4, terms net 60 days, $5,920.

7 Bought ten Precision Chronograph ILD watches from Bell and Taylor, invoice no. C3946, dated January 7; terms 2/10, n/30; $482.

8 Bought four Farrell Deep Diver watches from Ferrano Imports, invoice no. 15148, dated January 8, terms net 30 days, $268.

11 Bought ten Unico Boy's Sport watches, model 14K, from Cooper and Larkin, invoice no. 359FE, dated January 9; terms 1/10, n/30; $282.

Jan. 19 Bought ten Mercer Antiqued Gold-tone Vest Chains from Ferrano Imports, invoice no. 15224, dated January 18, terms net 30 days, $73.60.

24 Purchased ten Tenser PCL Pocket watches from Spencer Watch Company, invoice no. 2218D, dated January 23, terms net 60 days, $1,326.

29 Bought two Fidelity Diamond Sharon watches from Campbell Manufacturing Company, invoice no. 764LC, dated January 27; terms 2/10, n/30; $293.16.

31 Bought one Champton Diamond Minuet watch from Simmons, Inc., invoice no. 36049, dated January 28; terms 2/10, n/30; $326.82.

Instructions

1. Open the following accounts in the accounts payable ledger and record the January 1 balances, if any, as given: Bell and Taylor, $128; Campbell Manufacturing Company, $74.16; Cooper and Larkin; Ferrano Imports; Simmons, Inc., $198.70; Spencer Watch Company.
2. Record the balance of $400.86 as of January 1 in the Accounts Payable controlling account.
3. Record the transactions in the purchases journal beginning with page 72.
4. Post to the accounts payable ledger.
5. Post to the Accounts Payable controlling account and the Purchases account.
6. Prepare a schedule of accounts payable, and compare the balance of the Accounts Payable controlling account with the total of the schedule of accounts payable.

Problem 12-2A The Heathwood Gift Shop had the following purchases of merchandise and supplies and related returns and allowances during March.

Mar. 3 Bought merchandise on account from Merrill Pottery Company, invoice no. 8792, dated March 1; terms 2/10, n/30; $682.

4 Bought merchandise on account from Danville Supply Company, invoice no. 21863D, dated March 2; terms net 30 days; $583.20.

7 Bought merchandise on account from Dawes and Son, invoice no. 28860, dated March 7; terms net 30 days; $291.72.

11 Bought office supplies on account from Nielson Office Supply, invoice no. 3849, dated March 11; terms net 30 days; $169.48.

13 Received credit memo no. 316 from Merrill Pottery Company for merchandise returned, $22.

15 Bought merchandise on account from Unique Card Company, invoice no. 77281, dated March 15; terms 1/10, n/30; $789.60.

20 Bought office equipment on account from Carlton Equipment Company, invoice no. 6582, dated March 18; terms net 30 days; $717.

25 Bought merchandise on account from Unique Card Company, invoice no. 77472, dated March 25; terms 1/10, n/30; $989.60.

28 Received credit memo no. 49 from Danville Supply Company for merchandise returned, $73.

Mar. 29 Bought merchandise on account from Merrill Pottery Company, invoice no. 8871, dated March 28; terms 2/10, n/30; $1,273.10.

30 Bought store supplies on account from Lassiter and Foss, invoice no. 87616, dated March 30; terms net 30 days; $41.

30 Bought merchandise on account from Dawes and Son, invoice no. 29143, dated March 29; terms net 30 days; $142.30.

30 Bought merchandise on account from Danville Supply Company, invoice no. 21914D, dated March 28; terms net 30 days; $348.16.

Instructions

1. Open the following accounts in the general ledger and enter the March 1 balances as given.

113	Store Supplies	$ 315.18
114	Office Supplies	136.32
121	Office Equipment	4,775.00
211	Accounts Payable	2,744.01
511	Purchases	6,881.19
512	Purchases Returns and Allowances	262.46

2. Open the following accounts in the accounts payable ledger and enter the balances, if any, in the Balance columns as of March 1: Carlton Equipment Company; Danville Supply Company; Dawes and Son, $924.18; Lassiter and Foss; Merrill Pottery Company, $1,480; Nielson Office Supply; Unique Card Company, $339.83.

3. Record the transactions either in the general journal, page 31, or the purchases journal, page 9, as appropriate.

4. Post the entries to the creditors' accounts in the accounts payable ledger immediately after you record each journal entry.

5. Post the entries to the general ledger after you record each general journal entry.

6. Post the total of the purchases journal at the end of the month.

7. Prepare a schedule of accounts payable, and compare the balance of the Accounts Payable controlling account with the total of the schedule of accounts payable.

Problem 12-3A Frankhurst Products Company records sales of merchandise daily by posting directly from its sales invoices to the accounts receivable ledger. At the end of the month it makes a summarizing entry in the general journal. It records purchases of goods on account the same way, daily, posting directly from the invoices to the accounts payable ledger and making a summarizing entry in the general journal at the end of the month. Sales of merchandise and purchases of goods on account during October of this year were as follows.

Sales of merchandise

Oct. 4 Allentown Specialty Shop, no. 3216, $348.17.

7 I. D. Miller, no. 3217, $548.19.

11 R. D. Blanchard and Company, no. 3218, $918.65.

15 Myron and Nelson, no. 3219, $1,080.72.

Oct. 22 Lane P. Jackson, no. 3220, $877.25.
24 Eldon P. Wenzel, no. 3221, $967.60.
25 Rex P. Ruller, no. 3222, $1,110.
28 Dante and Rubin, no. 3223, $540.35.
30 Myron and Nelson, no. 3224, $318.
31 I. D. Miller, no. 3225, $225.70.

Purchases of goods on account

Oct. 3 Denham and Lancaster, merchandise, no. C1189, $566.
7 Dugan Wood Products, merchandise, no. 23229, $1,400.
9 Precision Manufacturing Company, merchandise, no. 83118, $3,870.
10 Singleton Supply Company, office supplies, no. AD776, $112.
19 C. C. Russo and Company, merchandise, no. C1146, $129.76.
26 Nelson and Nelson, store supplies, no. S9825, $54.60.
28 Dugan Wood Products, merchandise, no. 23313, $2,874.
31 Denton Equipment Company, store equipment, no. 31192, $210.

Instructions

1. Record the summarizing entry for the sales of merchandise on account in the general journal.
2. Record the summarizing entry for the purchase of goods on account in the general journal.

Problem 12-4A The following transactions relate to the Pembrook Company during March of this year. Terms of sale are 2/10, n/30.

Mar. 1 Sold merchandise on account to Arthur Yeager, invoice no. 16116, $800.
3 Bought merchandise on account from Newton Manufacturing Company, invoice no. A1121, March 1; terms 1/10, n/30; $450.
9 Sold merchandise on account to Anderson and Low, invoice no. 16117, $1,250.
11 Bought merchandise on account from N. D. Stonewall Company, invoice no. 7892, dated March 10; terms 2/10, n/30; $4,300.
14 Received credit memo no. 84 for merchandise returned to N. D. Stonewall Company, for $110, related to invoice no. 7892.
17 Sold merchandise on account to Martin Dahl, invoice no. 16118, $840.
17 Issued credit memo no. 26 to Anderson and Low, for merchandise returned, $80, related to invoice no. 16117.
26 Bought merchandise on account from George T. Williams and Son, invoice no. 9986, dated March 25; 2/10, EOM (within 10 days after the end of the month); $1,600.
28 Bought office supplies on account from Freeport Stationery Company, invoice no. R2686, dated March 28, 30 days net, $65.
29 Sold merchandise on account to Sutton and Thomas, invoice no. 16119, $2,960.
30 Issued credit memo no. 27 to Sutton and Thomas for merchandise returned, $190, related to invoice no. 16119.

Instructions

1. Open the following accounts in the accounts receivable ledger, and enter the March 1 balances, if any, in the Balance columns as given: Anderson and Low, $417; Dahl, Martin; Sutton and Thomas, $983; Yeager, Arthur.
2. Open the following accounts in the accounts payable ledger, and enter the March 1 balances, if any, in the Balance columns as given: Freeport Stationery Company; Newton Manufacturing Company; N. D. Stonewall Company, $378; George T. Williams and Son.
3. Record the transactions in the sales, purchases, and general journals as appropriate.
4. Post to the accounts receivable ledger daily.
5. Post to the accounts payable ledger daily.
6. Post to the general ledger provided.
7. Prepare a schedule of accounts receivable.
8. Prepare a schedule of accounts payable.
9. Compare the totals of the schedules with the balances of the controlling accounts.

Problem Set B

Problem 12-1B Stevens Appliance uses a single-column purchases journal. On January 1 of this year, the balances of the ledger accounts are Accounts Payable, $539.06; Purchases, zero. In addition to a general ledger, Stevens Appliance also uses an accounts payable ledger. Transactions for January related to the buying of merchandise are as follows.

Jan.   3 Bought eighty Mulholland Two-Burner Buffet Ranges from Skelton, Inc., invoice no. 2718C, dated January 2, terms net 60 days, $2,376.
        5 Bought ten White Swan Immersible Griddles from Shattuck Company, invoice no. 27418, dated January 2; terms 2/10, n/30; $325.
        8 Bought ten Supra Deluxe Waffle Bakers from Thomas and Finch, invoice no. 321AC, dated January 5; terms 1/10, n/30; $264.
       11 Bought twenty-four Simpo Popcorn Pumpers, Model 2800, from Ulmer Company, invoice no. C8741, dated January 10; terms 2/10, n/30; $480.
       15 Bought four Trendo Automatic Egg Cookers, Model 24-10, from Foster Products Company, invoice no. 2621, dated January 14, terms net 30 days, $98.
       23 Bought forty Sebas Hot Baskets, Model BC1, from Skelton, Inc., invoice no. 2823C, dated January 21; terms net 60 days; $980.
       29 Bought ten Trendo Pizza Baker/Grills, Model 5122, from Foster Products Company, invoice no. 2719, dated January 28, terms net 30 days, $263.
       30 Bought ten Isenware 6½ qt. Electric Woks, Model 210, from Penfield Manufacturing Company, invoice no. 732AL, dated January 27; terms 2/10, n/30; $286.

Instructions

1. Open the following accounts in the accounts payable ledger and record the balances, if any, as of January 1: Foster Products Company; Penfield Manufacturing Company, $143.17; Shattuck Company, $167.19; Skelton, Inc.; Thomas and Finch, $228.70; Ulmer Company.
2. Record the balance of $539.06 in the Accounts Payable controlling account as of January 1.
3. Record the transactions in the purchases journal beginning with page 81.
4. Post to the accounts payable ledger.
5. Post to the Accounts Payable controlling account and the Purchases account.
6. Prepare a schedule of accounts payable, and compare the balance of the Accounts Payable controlling account with the total of the schedule of accounts payable.

Problem 12-2B   The Remco Gift Shop bought the following merchandise and supplies and had the following returns and allowances during May of this year.

May   2 Bought merchandise on account from Trevino Pottery Company, invoice no. 9761, dated May 1; terms 2/10, n/30; $680.

4 Bought merchandise on account from Tenet Card Company, invoice no. 16728, dated May 1; terms 1/10, n/30; $268.

6 Bought merchandise on account from Dow Supply Company, invoice no. 21792D, dated May 5, terms net 30 days, $586.

10 Bought office supplies on account from Drexel and Son, invoice no. 2995C, dated May 10, terms net 30 days, $162.

12 Received credit memorandum no. 746 from Tenet Card Company for merchandise returned, $26.

16 Bought merchandise on account from Axel Printing Company, invoice no. 99821, dated May 15; terms 1/10, n/30; $580.

21 Bought office equipment on account from Dalton Equipment Company, invoice no. 6616, dated May 18; terms net 30 days; $624.

26 Bought merchandise on account from Tenet Card Company, invoice no. 17118, dated May 23; terms 1/10, n/30; $982.

27 Received credit memorandum no. 28C from Dow Supply Company for merchandise returned, $76.

28 Bought merchandise on account from Trevino Pottery Company, invoice no. 10096, dated May 27; terms 2/10, n/30; $1,642.

29 Bought store supplies on account from Towne and Truvall, invoice no. 98621, dated May 29, terms net 30 days, $32.

Instructions

1. Open the following accounts in the general ledger and enter the May 1 balances as given:

113	Store Supplies	$ 210
114	Office Supplies	121
121	Office Equipment	4,680
211	Accounts Payable	2,788

| 511 | Purchases | 6,984 |
| 512 | Purchases Returns and Allowances | 270 |

2. Open the following accounts in the accounts payable ledger and enter the balances in the Balance columns as of May 1: Axel Printing Company; Dalton Equipment Company; Dow Supply Company, $1,800; Drexel and Son; Tenet Card Company, $28; Towne and Truvall; Trevino Pottery Company, $960.
3. Record the transactions in either the general journal, starting on page 27, or the purchases journal, listing them on page 6, as appropriate.
4. Post the entries to the creditors' accounts in the accounts payable ledger immediately after you make each journal entry.
5. Post the entries in the general journal immediately after you make each journal entry.
6. Post the total of the purchases journal at the end of the month.
7. Prepare a schedule of accounts payable, and compare the balance of the Accounts Payable controlling account with the total of the schedule of accounts payable.

Problem 12-3B   The Trotter Products Company records sales of merchandise daily by posting directly from its sales invoices to the accounts receivable ledger. At the end of the month, a summarizing entry is made in the general journal. The purchase of goods on account is recorded in a similar manner. Each day's posting is done directly from the invoices to the accounts payable ledger, and a summarizing entry is made in the general journal at the end of the month. Sales of merchandise and purchases of goods on account during September of this year were as follows.

Sales of merchandise

Sep.   3 Arnold Store Corp., no. 2611, $2,300.
   6 T. D. Mitchell, no. 2612, $3,400.
   10 C. A. Howard and Company, no. 2613, $1,612.
   14 Bartor and Bartell, no. 2614, $2,680.
   21 Franklin P. Ellis, no. 2615, $1,470.
   23 George H. Anderson, no. 2616, $424.
   24 Daniel B. Tyne, no. 2617, $2,900.
   27 Marshall and Miner, no. 2618, $640.
   28 T. D. Mitchell, no. 2619, $1,876.
   30 Bartor and Bartell, no. 2620, $1,920.
   30 Marshall and Miner, no. 2621, $3,268.

Purchases of goods on account

Sep.   2 Lanham Corp., merchandise, no. 6382, $2,170.
   6 Unique Wood Products, merchandise, no. 2198A, $1,800.
   8 Modern Manufacturing Company, merchandise, no. 82116, $4,620.
   16 Slessor and Smith, store supplies, no. D9682, $210.
   25 B. R. Rogers and Company, store supplies, no. 9621, $180.
   28 Lanham Corp., merchandise, no. B726, $3,960.
   30 Unique Wood Products, merchandise, no. 2716A, $4,215.
   30 Johnson Equipment Company, store equipment, no. 72116, $325.

Instructions

1. Record the summarizing entry for sales of merchandise on account in the general journal.
2. Record the summarizing entry for the purchase of goods on account in the general journal.

Problem 12-4B The transactions described below relate to the Snyder Supply Company during March of this year. Terms of sale are 2/10, n/30.

Mar. 1 Sold merchandise on account to Spangler Hardware, invoice no. 36442, $762.

4 Bought merchandise on account from Northern Manufacturing Company, invoice no. C1149, dated March 4; 1/10, n/30; $320.

8 Sold merchandise on account to Meadowland Department Store, invoice no. 36443, $942.

10 Bought merchandise on account from Superior Products Company, invoice no. 9119, dated March 10; 2/10, n/30; $3,776.75.

13 Received credit memo no. 96 for merchandise returned from Roxford and Son for $341, related to invoice no. D1198.

16 Sold merchandise on account to Nancy Girard, invoice no. 36444, $442.70.

17 Issued credit memo no. 31 to Meadowland Department Store for merchandise related to invoice no. 36443, $96.

25 Bought merchandise on account from Danforth Manufacturing Company, invoice no. B4491, dated March 23; 2/10, n/30; $1,562.

27 Bought office supplies on account from Hosford and Randall Company, invoice no. D3179, dated March 26, 30 days net, $56.20.

27 Sold merchandise on account to Hadley Specialty Company, invoice no. 36445, $3,006.

30 Issued credit memo no. 32 to Hadley Specialty Company for merchandise related to invoice no. 36445, $258.

Instructions

1. Open the following accounts in the accounts receivable ledger, and enter the March 1 balances, if any, in the Balance columns as given: Girard, Nancy; Hadley Specialty Company, $1,400; Meadowland Department Store; Spangler Hardware.
2. Open the following accounts in the accounts payable ledger, and enter the March 1 balances, if any, in the Balance columns as given: Danforth Manufacturing Company; Hosford and Randall; Northern Manufacturing Company; Roxford and Son, $378; Superior Products Company.
3. Record the transactions in the sales, purchases, and general journals.
4. Post to the accounts receivable ledger daily.
5. Post to the accounts payable ledger daily.
6. Post to the general ledger provided.
7. Prepare a schedule of accounts receivable.
8. Prepare a schedule of accounts payable.
9. Compare the totals of the schedules with the balances of the controlling accounts.

13 Cash Receipts and Cash Payments

Learning Objectives

After you have completed this chapter, you will be able to do the following:

1. Record transactions for a retail merchandising business in a cash receipts journal.

2. Post from a cash receipts journal to a general ledger and an accounts receivable ledger.

3. Determine cash discounts according to credit terms, and record cash receipts from charge customers who are entitled to deduct the cash discount.

4. Record transactions for a wholesale merchandising business in a cash receipts journal.

5. Record transactions in a cash payments journal for a service enterprise.

6. Record transactions in a cash payments journal for a merchandising enterprise.

7. Record transactions in a check register.

8. Record transactions involving trade discounts.

We have seen that using a sales journal and a purchases journal enables an accountant to carry out the journalizing and posting processes much more efficiently. These special journals make it possible to post column totals rather than individual figures. This procedure also makes possible a more efficient division of labor, because the journalizing functions can be delegated to different persons. The *cash receipts journal* and *cash payments journal* further extend these advantages.

CASH RECEIPTS JOURNAL

The **cash receipts journal** records all transactions in which cash comes in, or increases. When the cash receipts journal is used, all transactions in which cash is debited *must* be recorded in it. It may be used for a service as well as a merchandising business. To get acquainted with the cash receipts journal, let's list some typical transactions of a retail merchandising business that result in an increase in cash. To get a better picture of the transactions, let's record them immediately in T accounts.

Objective 1

Record transactions for a retail merchandising business in a cash receipts journal.

May 3: Sold merchandise for cash, $100, plus $4 sales tax.

Cash		Sales		Sales Tax Payable	
+	−	−	+	−	+
104			100		4

May 4: Sold merchandise, $100 plus $4 sales tax, and the customer used a **bank charge card.** Millions of people use these cards every day and pay the bank directly at the end of the month. The firm, on the other hand, deposits the bank credit card receipts every day. The bank *deducts a discount* and credits the firm's account with cash. This discount is often 2 percent of the total of sales plus sales tax. The firm therefore records the amount of the discount under Credit Card Expense. (From the amount that would ordinarily be debited to Cash, deduct the bank charge, consisting of 2 percent of the total of sales plus sales tax, and debit this amount to Credit Card Expense instead of to Cash: $104 × .02 = $2.08 credit card expense; $100 + $4 − $2.08 = $101.92.)

Cash		Credit Card Expense		Sales Tax Payable		Sales	
+	−	+	−	−	+	−	+
101.92		2.08			4		100

May 5: Collected cash on account from J. C. Rowe, a charge customer, $208.

Cash		Accounts Receivable	
+	−	+	−
208			208

May 7: The owner, A. P. Hall, invested cash in the business, $3,000.

Cash		A. P. Hall, Capital	
+	−	−	+
3,000			3,000

May 8: Sold equipment for cash at cost, $150.

Cash		Equipment	
+	−	+	−
150			150

Now let's appraise these five transactions: The first three would occur frequently; the last two could conceivably take place, but they would be rather infrequent. If one is designing a cash receipts journal, it is logical to include a Cash Debit column because all the transactions involve an increase in cash. If a business regularly collects cash from charge customers, there should be an Accounts Receivable Credit column. If a firm often sells merchandise for cash and collects a sales tax, there should be a Sales Credit column and a Sales Tax Payable Credit column. If the business honors bank charge cards, there should be a Credit Card Expense Debit column to take care of the amount deducted by the bank.

However, the credit to A. P. Hall, Capital, and the credit to Equipment occur very seldom, so it wouldn't be practical to set up special columns for them. They can be handled adequately by a Sundry Credit column, which can be used for credits to all accounts that have no special column.

Now let's record the same transactions in a cash receipts journal (see Figure 13-1 on page 372). First we'll repeat the transactions:

May   3 Sold merchandise for cash, $100, plus $4 sales tax.
      4 Sold merchandise, $100 plus $4 sales tax, and the customer used a bank charge card. Discount charged by the bank is 2 percent of the amount of the total of sales plus sales tax.
      5 Collected cash from J. C. Rowe, a charge customer, on account, $208.

CASH RECEIPTS JOURNAL

	DATE	ACCOUNT CREDITED	POST. REF.	SUNDRY ACCOUNTS CREDIT	ACCOUNTS RECEIVABLE CREDIT	SALES CREDIT	SALES TAX PAYABLE CREDIT	CREDIT CARD EXPENSE DEBIT	CASH DEBIT	
1	19— May 3	Sales				1 0 0 00	4 00		1 0 4 00	1
2	4	Sales				1 0 0 00	4 00	2 08	1 0 1 92	2
3	5	J. C. Rowe			2 0 8 00				2 0 8 00	3
4	7	A. P. Hall, Capital		3 0 0 0 00					3 0 0 0 00	4
5	8	Equipment		1 5 0 00					1 5 0 00	5
6										6

Figure 13-1

CASH RECEIPTS JOURNAL

	DATE	ACCOUNT CREDITED	POST. REF.	SUNDRY ACCOUNTS CREDIT	ACCOUNTS RECEIVABLE CREDIT	SALES CREDIT	SALES TAX PAYABLE CREDIT	CREDIT CARD EXPENSE DEBIT	CASH DEBIT	
1	19— May 3	Sales	–			1 0 0 00	4 00		1 0 4 00	1
2	4	Sales	–			1 0 0 00	4 00	2 08	1 0 1 92	2
3	5	J. C. Rowe	√		2 0 8 00				2 0 8 00	3
4	7	A. R. Hall, Capital	311	3 0 0 0 00					3 0 0 0 00	4
5	8	Equipment	121	1 5 0 00					1 5 0 00	5
6	11	Notes Payable	211	3 0 0 00					3 0 0 00	6
7	16	Sales	–			2 0 0 00	8 00		2 0 8 00	7
8	21	Sales	–			5 0 00	2 00	1 04	5 0 96	8
9	26	Kenneth Ralston	√		6 2 40				6 2 40	9
10	28	Sales	–			4 0 00	1 60		4 1 60	10
11	31	Sales	–			1 5 0 00	6 00	3 12	1 5 2 88	11
12	31	Sylvia Harlow	√		2 6 00				2 6 00	12
13	31			3 4 5 0 00	2 9 6 40	6 4 0 00	2 5 60	6 24	4 4 0 5 76	13
14				(√)	(1 1 3)	(4 1 1)	(2 1 3)	(5 1 3)	(1 1 1)	14
15										15

Figure 13-2

May   7 The owner, A. P. Hall, invested cash in the business, $3,000.
       8 Sold equipment for cash at cost, $150.

Posting from the Cash Receipts Journal

At the end of the month we can post the special columns in the cash receipts journal as totals to the general ledger accounts. These include Accounts Receivable Credit, Sales Credit, Sales Tax Payable Credit, Credit Card Expense Debit, and Cash Debit. We post the items in the Sundry Accounts Credit column individually; we post the figures in the Accounts Receivable Credit column separately to accounts in the accounts receivable ledger. The posting letter designation for the cash receipts journal is CR.

Objective 2

Post from a cash receipts journal to a general ledger and an accounts receivable ledger.

Here are some other transactions made during the month that involve increases in cash. (Remember that these transactions are for a retail business.)

May   11 Borrowed $300 from the bank, receiving cash and giving the bank a promissory note.
       16 Sold merchandise for cash, $200, plus $8 sales tax.
       21 Sold merchandise for cash, $50, plus $2 sales tax; customer used a bank charge card. Credit card expense charge is 2 percent of sales plus tax.
       26 Collected cash from Kenneth Ralston, a charge customer, on account, $62.40.
       28 Sold merchandise for cash, $40, plus $1.60 sales tax.
       31 Sold merchandise for cash, $150, plus $6 sales tax; customer used a bank charge card. Credit card expense charge is 2 percent of sales plus tax.
       31 Collected cash from Sylvia Harlow, a charge customer, on account, $26.

Let us assume that all the month's transactions involving debits to Cash have now been recorded in the cash receipts journal. The cash receipts journal (Figure 13-2) and the T accounts on page 374 illustrate the postings to the general ledger and the accounts receivable ledger.

Individual amounts in the Accounts Receivable credit column of the cash receipts journal are posted daily. Individual amounts in the Sundry credit column are posted daily. Totals are posted at the end of the month.

Accounts Receivable Ledger

Sylvia Harlow

+	−	
	May 31	26

J. C. Rowe

+	−	
	May 5	208

Kenneth Ralston

+	−	
	May 26	62.40

General Ledger

A. P. Hall, Capital

−	+	
	May 7	3,000

Equipment

+	−	
	May 8	150

Notes Payable

−	+	
	May 11	300

Cash

+	−
May 31 4,405.76	

Credit Card Expense

+	−
May 31 6.24	

Sales Tax Payable

−	+	
	May 31	25.60

Sales

−	+	
	May 31	640

Accounts Receivable

+	−	
	May 31	296.40

In the Posting Reference column, the check marks (√) indicate that the amounts in the Accounts Receivable Credit column have been posted to the individual charge customers' accounts as credits. The account numbers show that the amounts in the Sundry Accounts Credit column have been posted separately to the accounts described in the Account Credited column. A check mark (√) also goes under the total of the Sundry column, where it means "do not post—the figures have already been posted separately." A check mark in our example thus has two meanings: (1) *the individual account has been posted in the subsidiary ledger,* as in the Accounts Receivable Credit column; and (2) *the total is not to be posted,* as in the Sundry column.

A dash in the Posting Reference column indicates that an individual amount is being posted as a part of a column total. For example, the $100 credit to Sales on May 3 will be posted as a part of the $640 total.

Let's say it's the end of the month. We total the columns, then check the accuracy of the footings by proving that the sum of the debit totals equals the sum of the credit totals. This process is referred to as **crossfooting** the journal. It must be done before one posts the totals to the general ledger accounts.

	Debit Totals
Cash	$4,405.76
Credit Card Expense	6.24
	$4,412.00

	Credit Totals
Sundry Accounts	$3,450.00
Accounts Receivable	296.40
Sales	640.00
Sales Tax Payable	25.60
	$4,412.00

After posting the total amounts of the special columns, write the general ledger account number in parentheses below the total in the appropriate column.

CREDIT TERMS

Objective 3

Determine cash discounts according to credit terms, and record cash receipts from charge customers who are entitled to deduct the cash discount.

The seller always stipulates credit terms: How much credit can be allowed to a customer? And how much time should the customer be given to pay the full amount? The **credit period** is the time the seller allows the buyer before full payment has to be made. Retailers generally allow 30 days.

Wholesalers and manufacturers often specify a **cash discount** in their credit terms. A cash discount is the amount a customer can deduct if she or he pays the bill within a short time. The discount is based on the total amount of the invoice after deducting any returns and allowances. Naturally this discount acts as an incentive for charge customers to pay their bills promptly.

Let's say that a wholesaler offers customers credit terms of 2/10, n/30. These terms mean that the customer gets a 2 percent discount if the bill is paid within 10 days after the invoice date. If the bill is not paid within the 10 days, then the entire amount is due within 30 days after the invoice date. Other cash discounts that may be used are the following.

- **1/15, n/60** The seller offers a 1 percent discount if the bill is paid within 15 days after the invoice date, or the whole bill must be paid within 60 days after the invoice date.
- **2/10, EOM, n/60** The seller offers a 2 percent discount if the bill is paid within 10 days after the end of the month, and the whole bill must be paid within 60 days after the invoice date.

A wholesaler or manufacturer offering a cash discount adopts a single cash discount as a credit policy and makes this available to all its customers. The seller considers cash discounts as **sales discounts;** the buyer, on the other hand, considers cash discounts as purchases discounts. In this section we are concerned with the sales discount. The Sales Discount account, like Sales Returns and Allowances, is a deduction from Sales.

To illustrate, we return to C. L. Frederickson Plumbing Supply. We'll record the following transactions in T accounts so we can see them at a glance.

Transaction (a) August 1: Sold merchandise on account to T. L. Long Company, invoice no. 320; terms 2/10, n/30; $424.

Transaction (b) August 10: Received check from T. L. Long Company for $415.52 in payment of invoice no. 320, less cash discount ($424.00 − $8.48 = $415.52).

Assets		=	Liabilities		+	Owner's Equity		+	Revenue		−	Expenses	
+	−		−	+		−	+		−	+		+	−
Debit	Credit		Debit	Credit		Debit	Credit		Debit	Credit		Debit	Credit

Accounts Receivable			Sales	
+	−		−	+
(a) 424.00	(b) 424.00			(a) 424.00

Cash			Sales Discount	
+	−		+	−
(b) 415.52			(b) 8.48	

Since C. L. Frederickson Plumbing Supply offers this cash discount to all its customers, and since charge customers often pay their bills within the discount period, C. L. Frederickson sets up a Sales Discount Debit column in the cash receipts journal. Note that C. L. Frederickson Plumbing Supply is a wholesaler. Therefore, a column for Sales Tax Payable is not used, since few states levy a tax on sales at the wholesale level.

Objective 4

Record transactions for a wholesale merchandising business in a cash receipts journal.

DATE	ACCOUNT CREDITED	POST. REF.	SUNDRY ACCOUNTS CREDIT	ACCOUNTS RECEIVABLE CREDIT	SALES CREDIT	SALES DISCOUNT DEBIT	CASH DEBIT	
19– Aug. 10	T. L. Long Co.			4 2 4 00		8 48	4 1 5 52	1
								2

Several other transactions of C. L. Frederickson Plumbing Supply involve increases in cash during August. Remember that the standard credit terms for all charge customers are 2/10, n/30.

Aug. 15 Cash sales for first half of the month, $460.

16 Received check from Abel Plumbing and Heating for $92.12 in payment of invoice no. 322, less cash discount ($94.00 − $1.88 = $92.12).

17 Received payment on a promissory note given by John R. Stokes, $300 principal, plus $3 interest. (The amount of the interest is recorded in Interest Income.)

21 Received check from Craig and Fraser Hardware for $84.28 in payment of invoice no. 324, less cash discount ($86.00 − $1.72 = $84.28).

23 Sold store equipment for cash at cost, $126.

26 C. L. Frederickson, the owner, invested an additional $4,000 cash in the business.

26 Received a check from Home Hardware Company for $97.02 in payment of invoice no. 325, less the amount of credit memorandum no. 70, $99, less cash discount ($215 − $116 = $99; $99.00 × .02 = $1.98; $99.00 − $1.98 = $97.02).

30 Received check from Henning's Plumbing for $287.14 in payment of invoice no. 326, less cash discount ($293.00 − $5.86 = $287.14).

31 Cash sales for second half of the month, $620.

31 Received check from Maley, Inc., in payment of invoice no. 321, for $116. (This is longer than the 10-day period, so they missed the cash discount.)

C. L. Frederickson records these transactions in its cash receipts journal (Figure 13-3, next page).

After that has been done, the company's accountant proves the equality of debits and credits:

Debit Totals		Credit Totals	
Cash	$6,601.08	Sundry Accounts	$4,429.00
Sales Discount	19.92	Accounts Receivable	1,112.00
	$6,621.00	Sales	1,080.00
			$6,621.00

CASH RECEIPTS JOURNAL

	DATE	ACCOUNT CREDITED	POST. REF.	SUNDRY ACCOUNTS CREDIT	ACCOUNTS RECEIVABLE CREDIT	SALES CREDIT	SALES DISCOUNT DEBIT	CASH DEBIT	
1	19– Aug. 10	T. L. Long Company			4 2 4 00		8 48	4 1 5 52	1
2	15	Sales				4 6 0 00		4 6 0 00	2
3	16	Abel Plumbing and Heating			9 4 00		1 88	9 2 12	3
4	17	Notes Receivable		3 0 0 00					4
5		Interest Income		3 00				3 0 3 00	5
6	21	Craig and Fraser Hardware			8 6 00		1 72	8 4 28	6
7	23	Store Equipment		1 2 6 00				1 2 6 00	7
8	26	C. L. Frederickson, Capital		4 0 0 0 00				4 0 0 0 00	8
9	26	Home Hardware Company			9 9 00		1 98	9 7 02	9
10	30	Heming's Plumbing			2 9 3 00		5 86	2 8 7 14	10
11	31	Sales				6 2 0 00		6 2 0 00	11
12	31	Maley, Inc.			1 1 6 00			1 1 6 00	12
13	31			4 4 2 9 00	1 1 1 2 00	1 0 8 0 00	1 9 92	6 6 0 1 08	13
14									14
15									15
16									16
17									17
18									18
19									19
20									20
21									21
22									22
23									23
24									24

Figure 13-3

CASH PAYMENTS JOURNAL: SERVICE ENTERPRISE

The cash payments journal, as the name implies, records all transactions in which cash goes out, or decreases. When the cash payments journal is used, all transactions in which cash is credited *must* be recorded in it. It may be used for a service as well as a merchandising business.

To get acquainted with the cash payments journal, let's list some typical transactions of a service firm (such as a dry cleaner or a bowling alley) or a professional enterprise that result in a decrease in cash. So that you'll see the transactions at a glance, let's record them directly in T accounts.

May 2: Paid C. C. Hardy Company, a creditor, on account, check no. 63, $220.

Accounts Payable		Cash	
−	+	+	−
220			220

May 4: Bought supplies for cash, check no. 64, $90.

Supplies		Cash	
+	−	+	−
90			90

May 5: Paid wages for two weeks, check no. 65, $1,216 (previously recorded in the payroll entry).

Wages Payable		Cash	
−	+	+	−
1,216			1,216

May 6: Paid rent for the month, check no. 66, $350.

Rent Expense		Cash	
+	−	+	−
350			350

Now let's appraise these four transactions. The first one would occur very often, as payments to creditors are made several times a month. Of the last three transactions, the debit to Wages Payable might occur twice a month, the debit to Rent Expense once a month, and the debit to Supplies only occasionally.

It is logical to include a Cash Credit column in a cash payments journal, because all transactions recorded in it involve a decrease in cash. Since payments to creditors are made often, there should also be an Accounts Payable Debit column. One can set up any other column that is used often enough to warrant it. Otherwise, a Sundry Debit column takes care of all the other transactions.

Now let's record these same transactions in a cash payments journal and include a column entitled Check Number. If you think a moment, you'll see that this is consistent with good management of cash. All expenditures but Petty Cash expenditures should be paid for by check. First let's repeat the transactions.

Objective 5

Record transactions in a cash payments journal for a service enterprise.

May 2 Paid C. C. Hardy Company, a creditor, on account, check no. 63, $220.
    4 Bought supplies for cash, check no. 64, $90.
    5 Paid wages for two weeks, check no. 65, $1,216 (previously recorded in the payroll entry).
    6 Paid rent for the month, check no. 66, $350.

CASH PAYMENTS JOURNAL   PAGE 62

	DATE	CK. NO.	ACCOUNT DEBITED	POST. REF.	SUNDRY ACCOUNTS DEBIT	ACCOUNTS PAYABLE DEBIT	CASH CREDIT	
1	19– May 2	63	C. C. Hardy					1
2			Company			2 2 0 00	2 2 0 00	2
3	4	64	Supplies		9 0 00		9 0 00	3
4	5	65	Wages Payable		1 2 1 6 00		1 2 1 6 00	4
5	6	66	Rent Expense		3 5 0 00		3 5 0 00	5
6								6

Note that you list all checks in consecutive order, even those checks that must be voided. In this way, *every* check is accounted for, which is necessary for internal control.

At the end of the month, post the special columns as totals to the general ledger accounts; do not post the total of the Sundry Accounts Debit column. A check mark (√) is written below the total of the Sundry Accounts Debit column to indicate that the total amount is not posted. Post the figures in this column individually, then place the account number in the Posting Reference column. Post the amounts in the Accounts Payable Debit column separately to individual accounts in the accounts payable ledger. After posting, put a check mark (√) in the Posting Reference column. The posting letter designation for the cash payments journal is CP. Other transactions involving decreases in cash during May are as follows.

May 7 Paid a three-year premium for fire insurance, check no. 67, $360.

9 Paid Treadwell, Inc., a creditor, on account, check no. 68, $418.

11 Issued check no. 69 in payment of delivery expense, $62.

14 Paid Johnson and Son, a creditor, on account, check no. 70, $110.

16 Issued check no. 71 to the Melton State Bank, for a Note Payable, $660, $600 on the principal and $60 interest.

19 Voided check no. 72.

19 Bought equipment from Burns Company for $800, paying $200 down. Issued check no. 73. The rest of this entry is recorded in the general journal as explained below.

20 Paid wages for two weeks, check no. 74, $1,340 (previously recorded in the payroll entry).

22 Issued check no. 75 to Peter R. Morton Advertising Agency for advertising, $94.

26 Paid telephone bill, check no. 76, $26.

31 Issued check for freight bill on equipment purchased on May 19, check no. 77, $28.

31 Paid Teller and Noble, a creditor, on account, check no. 78, $160.

These transactions are recorded in the cash payments journal as illustrated in Figure 13-4.

Figure 13-4

CASH PAYMENTS JOURNAL

PAGE 62

	DATE	CK. NO.	ACCOUNT DEBITED	POST. REF.	SUNDRY ACCOUNTS DEBIT	ACCOUNTS PAYABLE DEBIT	CASH CREDIT	
1	19— May	2 63	C. C. Hardy Co.	✓		2 2 0 00	2 2 0 00	1
2		4 64	Supplies	113	9 0 00		9 0 00	2
3		5 65	Wages Payable	411	1 2 1 6 00		1 2 1 6 00	3
4		6 66	Rent Expense	412	3 5 0 00		3 5 0 00	4
5		7 67	Prepaid Insurance	114	3 6 0 00		3 6 0 00	5
6		9 68	Treadwell, Inc.	✓		4 1 8 00	4 1 8 00	6
7		11 69	Delivery Expense	413	6 2 00		6 2 00	7
8		14 70	Johnson and Son	✓		1 1 0 00	1 1 0 00	8
9		16 71	Notes Payable	211	6 0 0 00			9
10			Interest Expense	414	6 0 00		6 6 0 00	10
11		19 72	Void	✓				11
12		19 73	Equipment	✓	2 0 0 00		2 0 0 00	12
13		20 74	Wages Payable	411	1 3 4 0 00		1 3 4 0 00	13
14		22 75	Advertising Expense	415	9 4 00		9 4 00	14
15		26 76	Telephone Expense	416	2 6 00		2 6 00	15
16		31 77	Equipment	121	2 8 00		2 8 00	16
17		31 78	Teller and Noble	✓		1 6 0 00	1 6 0 00	17
18		31			4 4 2 6 00	9 0 8 00	5 3 3 4 00	18
19					(✓)	(2 1 1)	(1 1 1)	19
20								20

When the purchase of an asset involves a cash down payment with the remainder on account, it is necessary to record the transactions in two journals. For example, this transaction: Bought equipment for $800 from Burns Company, paying $200 down with the remainder to be paid in 30 days. In the general journal, debit Equipment for $800, credit Accounts Payable, Burns Company for $600, and credit Cash for $200. In the Posting Reference column of this entry, place a check mark on the line with Cash so that the $200 credit to Cash will not be posted. Record the second entry in the cash payments journal, debiting Equipment for $200 in the Sundry Accounts Debit column and crediting Cash for $200 in the Cash Credit column. In the Posting Reference column of this entry, place a check mark on the line with Equipment so that the $200 debit to Equipment will not be posted. The net result is that Equipment is debited for the full amount of $800, Cash is credited for $200, and Accounts Payable is credited for $600. The general journal entry looks like this.

	GENERAL JOURNAL				PAGE __94__	
	DATE	DESCRIPTION	POST. REF.	DEBIT	CREDIT	
1	19– May 19	Equipment	121	8 0 0 00		1
2		Accounts Payable, Burns Company	211√		6 0 0 00	2
3		Cash	√		2 0 0 00	3
4		Payment is due in 30 days.				4
5						5

Let us return to the cash payments journal. At the end of the month, after totaling the columns, check the accuracy of the footings by proving that the sum of the debit totals equals the sum of the credit totals. Since you have posted the individual amounts in the Sundry Debit column to the general ledger, the only posting that remains is the credit to the Cash account for $5,334 and the debit to the Accounts Payable (controlling) account for $908.

Debit Totals		Credit Totals	
Sundry	$4,426.00	Cash	$5,334.00
Accounts Payable	908.00		
	$5,334.00		

The posting is summarized in the following T accounts. Individual amounts in the Accounts Payable Debit column and the general journal are posted daily to the subsidiary ledger. Individual amounts in the Sundry debit column of the special journal and individual amounts in the general journal are posted daily to the general ledger. Totals of the Cash Credit column and the Accounts Payable Debit column are posted at the end of the month.

Accounts Payable Ledger

C. C. Hardy Company

−	+
May 2 220	

Johnson and Son

−	+
May 14 110	

Teller and Noble

−	+
May 31 160	

Treadwell, Inc.

−	+
May 9 418	

Burns Company

−	+
	May 19 600

General Ledger

Cash

+	−
	May 31 5,334

Supplies

+	−
May 4 90	

Accounts Payable

−	+
May 31 908	May 19 600

Wages Payable

−	+
May 5 1,216	
20 1,340	

Rent Expense

+	−
May 6 350	

Prepaid Insurance

+	−
May 7 360	

Delivery Expense

+	−
May 11 62	

Notes Payable

−	+
May 16 600	

Interest Expense

+	−
May 16 60	

Equipment

+	−
May 19 800	
31 28	

Advertising Expense

+	−
May 22 94	

Telephone Expense

+	−
May 26 26	

CASH PAYMENTS JOURNAL: MERCHANDISING ENTERPRISE

There is one slight difference between the **cash payments journal** for a merchandising enterprise and that for a service enterprise. This difference has to do with the cash discounts available to a merchandising business. Recall that a cash discount is the amount that the buyer may deduct from the bill; this acts as an incentive to make the buyer pay the bill promptly. The buyer considers the cash discount to be a Purchases Discount, because it relates to his or her purchase of merchandise. The Purchases Discount account, like Purchases Returns and Allowances, is treated as a deduction from Purchases in the buyer's income statement.

Objective 6

Record transactions in a cash payments journal for a merchandising enterprise.

Let us return to C. L. Frederickson Plumbing Supply and assume that the following transactions take place. To demonstrate the debits and credits, let's show some typical transactions in the form of T accounts.

Transaction (a)   August 2: Bought merchandise on account from Darvik, Inc., their invoice no. 2706, dated July 31; terms 2/10, n/30; $420.

Transaction (b)   August 8: Issued check no. 76 to Darvik, Inc., in payment of invoice no. 2706 less the cash discount of $8.40, $411.60.

Assets	=	Liabilities	+	Owner's Equity	+	Revenue	−	Expenses
+ / −		− / +		− / +		− / +		+ / −
Debit / Credit		Debit / Credit		Debit / Credit		Debit / Credit		Debit / Credit

Cash
+	−
	(b) 411.60

Accounts Payable
−	+
(b) 420	(a) 420

Purchases
+	−
(a) 420	

Purchases Discount
−	+
	(b) 8.40

Any well-managed business takes advantage of a purchases discount whenever possible. So if a discount is generally available to the business, it is worthwhile to set up a special Purchases Discount credit column in the cash payments journal.

	DATE	CK. NO.	ACCOUNT NAME	POST. REF.	SUNDRY ACCOUNTS DEBIT	ACCOUNTS PAYABLE DEBIT	PURCHASES DISCOUNT CREDIT	CASH CREDIT	
1	19– Aug. 8	76	Darvik, Inc.			4 2 0 00	8 40	4 1 1 60	1
2									2

Here are some other transactions of C. L. Frederickson Plumbing Supply involving decreases in cash during August. Note that credit terms vary among the different creditors.

Aug.   10   Paid wages for two-week period, check no. 77, $1,680 (previously recorded in the payroll entry).

      11   Issued check no. 78 to Alman Manufacturing Company, in payment of invoice no. 10611, less return; less cash discount, 2/10, n/30; $609.56 ($692 − $70 = $622; $622.00 × .02 = $12.44; $622.00 − $12.44 = $609.56).

      12   Bought supplies for cash, issued check no. 79 payable to Davenport Office Supplies, $70.

      15   Issued check no. 80 to Sullivan Manufacturing Company in payment of their invoice no. B643, less return; less cash discount, 1/10, n/30; $127.71 ($165 − $36 = $129; $129.00 × .01 = $1.29; $129.00 − $1.29 = $127.71).

      16   Bought merchandise for cash, check no. 81, payable to Jones Sheet and Tube, $200.

      19   Issued check no. 82 to Reliable Express Company for freight cost on merchandise purchased, $60.

      23   Voided check no. 83.

      23   Issued check no. 84 to American Fire Insurance Company for insurance premium for one year, $120.

      25   Paid wages for two-week period, check no. 85, $1,750 (previously recorded in the payroll entry).

      27   Paid F. R. Waller for merchandise he returned on a cash sale, check no. 86, $46.

      31   Issued check no. 87 to Reiter and Simon Company in payment of invoice no. 982, net 30 days, $760.

Now let's record these transactions in the cash payments journal (Figure 13-5). After that has been done, C. L. Frederickson's accountant proves the equality of debits and credits:

Debit Totals		**Credit Totals**	
Sundry	$3,926.00	Cash	$5,834.87
Accounts Payable	1,931.00	Purchases Discount	22.13
	$5,857.00		$5,857.00

CASH PAYMENTS JOURNAL

	DATE 19—	CK. NO.	ACCOUNT NAME	POST. REF.	SUNDRY ACCOUNTS DEBIT	ACCOUNTS PAYABLE DEBIT	PURCHASES DISCOUNT CREDIT	CASH CREDIT	
1	Aug. 8	76	Darvik, Inc.			420 00	8 40	411 60	1
2	10	77	Wages Payable		1680 00			1680 00	2
3	11	78	Alman Manufacturing Co.			622 00	12 44	609 56	3
4	12	79	Supplies		70 00			70 00	4
5	15	80	Sullivan Manufacturing Co.			129 00	1 29	127 71	5
6	16	81	Purchases		200 00			200 00	6
7	19	82	Purchases		60 00			60 00	7
8	23	83	Void						8
9	23	84	Prepaid Insurance		120 00			120 00	9
10	25	85	Wages Payable		1750 00			1750 00	10
11	27	86	Sales Returns and						11
12			Allowances		46 00			46 00	12
13	31	87	Reiter and Simon						13
14			Company			760 00		760 00	14
15	31				3926 00	1931 00	22 13	5834 87	15
16									16

merchandise

Figure 13-5

CHECK REGISTER

Instead of using a cash payments journal as a book of original entry, one can use a check register. The check register is merely a large checkbook with perforations that make it easy to tear out the checks. The page opposite the checks has columns labeled for special accounts, such as Bank Credit (in place of Cash), Accounts Payable Debit, and so on. The checks are prenumbered, and each check issued is recorded on the columnar sheet. This is common practice for a small business in which the owner writes the checks himself or herself. One posts directly from the check register.

Suppose C. L. Frederickson Plumbing Supply had used a check register instead of the cash payments journal. Its August transactions would appear as they do in Figure 13-6.

You can see for yourself that the difference between the cash payments journal and the check register is minor. Recall that one substitutes the Bank Credit column for the Cash Credit column. The check register lists the payee of the check. The Accounts Payable Debit column and the Purchases Discount Credit column are included to handle payments to creditors.

Two additional columns, Deposits and Bank Balance, can be added, to give a current balance of the Valley National Bank or Cash account. The posting process for each book of original entry is the same.

Objective 7

Record transactions in a check register.

CHECK REGISTER

DATE	CK. NO.	PAYEE	ACCOUNT DEBITED	POST. REF.	SUNDRY ACCOUNTS DEBIT	ACCOUNTS PAYABLE DEBIT	PURCHASES DISCOUNT CREDIT	VALLEY BANK CREDIT	
19— Aug. 8	76	Darvik, Inc.	Darvik, Inc.			4 2 0 00	8 40	4 1 1 60	1
10	77	Payroll	Wages Payable		1 6 8 0 00			1 6 8 0 00	2
11	78	Alman Manufacturing	Alman Manufacturing			6 2 2 00	1 2 44	6 0 9 56	3
12	79	Davenport	Supplies		7 0 00			7 0 00	4
15	80	Sullivan Mfg. Co.	Sullivan Mfg. Co.			1 2 9 00	1 29	1 2 7 71	5
16	81	Jones Sheet and Tube	Purchases		2 0 0 00			2 0 0 00	6
19	82	Reliable Express Co.	Purchases		6 0 00			6 0 00	7
23	83	Void							8
23	84	American Fire Insurance	Prepaid Insurance		1 2 0 00			1 2 0 00	9
25	85	Payroll	Wages Payable		1 7 5 0 00			1 7 5 0 00	10
27	86	F. R. Waller	Sales Ret. and Allow.		4 6 00			4 6 00	11
31	87	Reiter & Simon Co.	Reiter & Simon Co.			7 6 0 00		7 6 0 00	12
31					3 9 2 6 00	1 9 3 1 00	2 2 13	5 8 3 4 87	13
									14
									15
									16
									17
									18
									19
									20
									21
									22
									23

Figure 13-6

In a small business, the owner or manager usually signs all the checks. However, if the owner delegates the authority to sign checks to some other person, that person should *not* have access to the accounting records. Why? Well, this helps to prevent fraud, because a dishonest employee could conceal a cash disbursement in the accounting records. In other words, for a medium- to large-size business, it's worth a manager's while to keep a separate book, which in this case is the cash payments journal. One person writes the checks; another person records the checks in the cash payments journal. In this way, one person acts as a check on the other. There would have to be collusion between the two people for embezzlement to take place. Again, this precaution is consistent with a good system of internal control.

TRADE DISCOUNTS

Manufacturers and wholesalers of many lines of products publish annual catalogs listing their products at retail prices. These concerns offer their customers substantial reductions (often as much as 40 percent) from the list or catalog prices. The reductions from the list prices are called **trade discounts.** Remember, firms grant cash discounts for prompt payment of invoices. Trade discounts are *not related* to cash payments. Manufacturers and wholesalers use trade discounts to avoid reprinting catalogs when selling prices change. They simply issue a new list of trade discounts to be applied to the catalog prices, effectively changing prices.

Objective 9

Record transactions involving trade discounts.

Firms may quote trade discounts as a single percentage. Example: A distributor of furnaces grants a single discount of 40 percent off the listed catalog price of $8,000. In this case, the selling price is calculated as follows.

List or catalog price	$8,000
Less trade discount of 40% ($8,000 × .4)	3,200
Selling price	$4,800

Neither the seller nor the buyer records trade discounts in the accounts; they enter only the selling price. By T accounts, the furnace distributor records the sale like this:

Accounts Receivable			Sales	
+	−		−	+
4,800				4,800

The buyer records the purchase as follows:

Purchases			Accounts Payable	
+	−		−	+
4,800				4,800

Firms may also quote trade discounts as a chain, or series of percentages. For example, a distributor of automobile parts grants discounts of 30 percent, 10 percent, and 10 percent off the listed catalog price of $900. In this case, the selling price is calculated as follows.

List or catalog price	$900.00
Less first trade discount of 30% ($900 × .3)	270.00
Remainder after first discount	$630.00
Less second trade discount of 10% ($630 × .1)	63.00
Remainder after second discount	$567.00
Less third discount of 10% ($567 × .1)	56.70
Selling price	$510.30

By T accounts, the automobile parts distributor records the sale as follows:

Accounts Receivable			Sales	
+	−		−	+
510.30				510.30

The buyer records the purchase as follows:

Purchases			Accounts Payable	
+	−		−	+
510.30				510.30

In the situation involving a chain of discounts, the additional discounts are granted for large-volume transactions, either in dollar amount or in size of shipment, such as carload lots.

Cash discounts could also apply in situations involving trade discounts. Example: Suppose that the credit terms of the above sale include a cash discount of 2/10, n/30, and the buyer pays the invoice within 10 days. The seller applies the cash discount to the selling price. By T accounts, the seller records the transaction as

Cash		Sales Discount		Accounts Receivable	
+	−	+	−	+	−
500.09		10.21			510.30

Types of Transactions

Sale of merchandise on account	Purchase of merchandise on account	Receipt of cash	Payment of cash	All other

Evidenced by Source Documents

Sales invoice	Purchase invoice	Credit card receipts / Cash / Checks	Check stub	Miscellaneous

Types of Journals

Sales journal	Purchases journal	Cash receipts journal	Cash payments journal	General journal

Posting to Ledger Accounts

Sales journal	Purchases journal	Cash receipts journal	Cash payments journal	General journal
Individual amounts posted daily to the accounts receivable ledger and the total posted monthly to the general ledger.	*Individual amounts posted daily to the accounts payable ledger and the total posted monthly to the general ledger.*	*Individual amounts in the Accounts Receivable credit column posted daily to the accounts receivable ledger.* *Individual amounts in the Sundry columns posted daily to the general ledger.* *Totals of special columns posted monthly.*	*Individual amounts in the Accounts Payable debit column posted daily to the accounts payable ledger.* *Individual amounts in the Sundry columns posted daily to the general ledger.* *Totals of special columns posted monthly.*	*Entries posted daily to the subsidiary ledgers and the general ledger.*

Figure 13-7

Choice of the Correct Journal

The buyer records the transaction as

Cash		Purchases Discount		Accounts Payable	
+	−	−	+	−	+
	500.09		10.21	510.30	

We have now looked at four special journals and the general journal. It is very important for a business to select and use the journals that will provide the most efficient accounting system possible. Figure 13-7 summarizes the applications of and correct procedures for using the journals we have discussed.

GLOSSARY

Bank charge card A bank credit card, like the credit cards used by millions of private citizens. The card holder pays what she or he owes directly to the issuing bank. The business firm deposits the credit card receipts; the amount of the deposit equals the total of the receipts, less a discount deducted by the bank.

Cash discount The amount a customer can deduct for paying a bill within a specified period of time; to encourage prompt payment. Not all sellers offer cash discounts.

Cash payments journal A special journal used to record all transactions in which cash goes out, or decreases.

Cash receipts journal A special journal used to record all transactions that increase cash.

Credit period The time the seller allows the buyer before full payment on a charge sale must be made.

Crossfooting The process of totaling columns in a journal or work sheet to make sure that the sum of the debit totals equals the sum of the credit totals.

Sales discount The cash discount from the seller's point of view; in the buyer's books this is a *purchases discount.*

Trade discounts Substantial reductions from the list or catalog prices of goods, granted by the seller.

QUESTIONS, EXERCISES, AND PROBLEMS

Discussion Questions

1. Describe the posting procedure for a cash receipts journal that has a Sundry Accounts credit column and several special columns including an Accounts Receivable credit column.

2. When a cash receipts journal and a cash payments journal are used, how does one determine the exact balance of cash on a specific date during the month?
3. What does "1/10, n/30" mean?
4. Is the normal balance of Sales Discount a debit or a credit?
5. In a cash receipts journal, both the Accounts Receivable credit column and the Cash debit column were erroneously under added by $100. How will this error be discovered?
6. Explain the difference between the handling of delivery costs on merchandise sold and the handling of freight costs on merchandise purchased.
7. What is the difference between a cash discount and a trade discount?

Exercises

Exercise 13-1 Describe the transactions recorded in the following T accounts.

Cash	Sales Tax Payable	Accounts Receivable	Sales
(b) 208	(a) 8	(a) 208 | (b) 208	(a) 200

Exercise 13-2 Record the transactions listed below in general journal form.

Aug.   2 Sold merchandise on account to T. Clancy; 2/10, n/30; $800.
      4 Issued credit memo no. 493 to T. Clancy for damaged merchandise, $35.
     12 Received a check from T. Clancy in full payment of bill.

Exercise 13-3 Describe the transaction recorded in the following T accounts.

Cash	Sales Tax Payable	Sales	Credit Card Expense
102.90	5	100	2.10

Exercise 13-4 Record the transactions listed here in general journal form.

Mar.   9 Bought merchandise on account from Columbia Electrical Supply; 2/10, n/30; $1,500.
      21 Received a credit memo for $100 for defective goods returned.
Apr.   8 Paid Columbia Electrical Supply in full of account.

Exercise 13-5 Label the blanks in the column heads as debit or credit.

CASH PAYMENTS JOURNAL

PAGE _____

	DATE	CK. NO.	ACCOUNT NAME	POST. REF.	SUNDRY ACCOUNTS Debit	ACCOUNTS PAYABLE Debit	PURCHASES DISCOUNT Credit	CASH Credit	
1									1
2									2
3									3
4									4

Exercise 13-6 Describe the transactions recorded in the following T accounts.

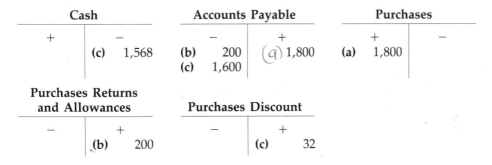

Cash			Accounts Payable			Purchases		
+	−		−	+		+	−	
	(c) 1,568		(b) 200	(a) 1,800		(a) 1,800		
			(c) 1,600					

Purchases Returns and Allowances			Purchases Discount		
−	+		−	+	
	(b) 200			(c) 32	

Exercise 13-7 Shown below is a page from a special journal.

1. What kind of journal is this?
2. Explain each of the transactions.
3. Explain the notations in the Posting Reference column.
4. Explain the notations below the column totals.

	DATE	ACCOUNT CREDITED	POST. REF.	SUNDRY ACCOUNTS CREDIT	ACCOUNTS RECEIVABLE CREDIT	SALES CREDIT	SALES DISCOUNT DEBIT	CASH DEBIT	
1	19–May 2	Della Simpson	✓		5 0 0 00		1 0 00	4 9 0 00	1
2	7	Sales	−			7 1 0 00		7 1 0 00	2
3	11	Notes Payable	211	2 5 0 0 00				2 5 0 0 00	3
4	21	Harry Walls	✓		2 1 0 00			2 1 0 00	4
5	31	L. R. Lee,							5
6		Capital	311	5 0 0 0 00				5 0 0 0 00	6
7				7 5 0 0 00	7 1 0 00	7 1 0 00	1 0 00	8 9 1 0 00	7
8				(✓)	(1 1 3)	(4 1 1)	(4 1 3)	(1 1 1)	8
9									9

Exercise 13-8 Record the transactions listed here in general journal form.

Jun. 1 Sold merchandise on account to the Bayliss Company; 2/10, n/30; $460.

 9 Purchased merchandise on account from the Mueller Company; 1/10, n/30, F.O.B. shipping point; $720.

Jun. 10 Paid freight charges on the merchandise purchased from the Mueller Company, $10.

10 Received payment from the Bayliss Company, less the cash discount.

12 Received a credit memo from the Mueller Company for defective merchandise returned, $70.

18 Paid the Mueller Company in full.

Problem Set A

Problem 13-1A Sommerset and Vaughn, a retail sales concern, sells on the bases of (1) cash, (2) charge accounts, and (3) bank credit cards. The following transactions involved cash receipts for the firm during April of this year. The state imposes a 4 percent sales tax on retail sales.

Apr. 7 Total cash sales for the week, $900, plus $36 sales tax.

7 Total sales for the week paid for by bank credit cards, $800, plus $32 sales tax. The bank charges 2 percent on the total of the sales plus tax ($832 × .02 = $16.64).

8 N. T. Nolan, the owner, invested an additional $2,000.

11 Collected cash from Robert Stone, a charge customer, $47.80.

12 Sold store equipment for cash, at cost, $160.

14 Total cash sales for the week, $1,100, plus $44 sales tax.

14 Total sales for the week paid for by bank credit cards, $600, plus $24 sales tax.

18 Borrowed $1,600 from the bank, receiving cash and giving the bank a promissory note.

20 Collected cash from Ruth Aiken, a charge customer, $52.

21 Total sales for the week paid for by bank credit cards, $700, plus $28 sales tax.

21 Total cash sales for the week, $1,600, plus $64 sales tax.

23 Received cash as refund for return of merchandise bought, $90.

25 Collected cash from J. R. Finch, a charge customer, $104.

30 Total sales for the week paid for by bank credit cards, $160.00, plus $6.40 sales tax.

30 Collected cash from Nathan Turnbull, a charge customer, $72.80.

30 Total cash sales for the week, $1,550, plus $62 sales tax.

Instructions

1. Open the following accounts in the accounts receivable ledger and record the April 1 balances as given: Ruth Aiken, $52.00; J. R. Finch, $124.00; Stella Roe, $76.48; Robert Stone, $47.80; Nathan Turnbull, $72.80; C. R. Zellers, $81.20. Place a check mark in the Posting Reference column.
2. Record a balance of $454.28 in the Accounts Receivable controlling account as of April 1.
3. Record the transactions in the cash receipts journal beginning with page 57.
4. Post daily to the accounts receivable ledger.

5. Total and rule the cash receipts journal.
6. Prove the equality of debit and credit totals.
7. Post to the Accounts Receivable account in the general ledger.

Problem 13-2A The H. G. Seton Company sells snacks wholesale, primarily to vending-machine operators. Terms of sales on account are 2/10, n/30, FOB shipping point. The following selected transactions involving cash receipts and sales of merchandise took place in May of this year.

May 1 Received $490 cash from P. Kline in payment of April 23 invoice of $500, less cash discount.
    4 Received $840 cash in payment of $800 note receivable and interest of $40.
    7 Sold merchandise on account to F. Stevens, invoice no. 871, $360.
    8 Received $686 in cash from Donald Pihl in payment of April 30 invoice of $700, less cash discount.
  14 Received cash from F. Stevens in payment of invoice no. 871, less discount.
  15 Cash sales for the first half of May, $2,772.
  18 Received $152 in cash from Randy Sims in payment of April 14 invoice, no discount.
  21 Sold merchandise on account to S. T. Thompson, invoice no. 898, $416.
  24 Received $218 cash refund for return of defective equipment bought in April for cash.
  27 Sold merchandise on account to C. C. Cummins, invoice no. 921, $432.
  31 Cash sales for the second half of May, $2,027.

Instructions

1. Journalize the transactions for May in the cash receipts journal and the sales journal.
2. Total and rule the journals.

Problem 13-3A The Matthews Bookstore uses a check register to keep track of expenditures. The following transactions occurred during February of this year.

Feb. 2 Issued check no. 3118 to National Book Company for their invoice no. 1113B, $520, less cash discount of $10.40, $509.60.
    3 Paid freight bill to Newton Express Company for merchandise purchased, check no. 3119, $47.
    5 Paid rent for month of February, check no. 3120, to Standard Realty, $215.
  10 Paid for advertising in *Campus News*, check no. 3121, $42.
  11 Paid Piedmont Publishing Company, check no. 3122, for their invoice no. C755 in the amount of $1,000 less 1 percent cash discount of $10, $990.
  16 Paid wages for the first half of month, check no. 3123, $426 (payroll entry previously recorded).

Feb. 20 R. Matthews, the owner, withdrew cash for personal use, check no. 3124, $425.

26 Made payment to Fenway National Bank on bank loan, check no. 3125, consisting of $600 on principal and $20 interest, $620.

28 Issued to Southern Publishing Company, check no. 3126, for their invoice no. 3126 (no discount previously recorded), $358.

28 Voided check no. 3127.

28 Paid wages for the second half of month, check no. 3128, $426 (payroll entry previously recorded).

28 Received and paid telephone bill, check no. 3129, payable to Nationwide Telephone Company, $32.

Instructions

1. Record the transactions in the check register.
2. Total and rule the check register.
3. Prove the equality of the debit and credit totals.

Problem 13-4A   The following transactions were completed by Thompson Electronics Supply during January, the first month of this fiscal year. Terms of sale are 2/10, n/30.

Jan. 2 Paid rent for month, check no. 6981, $825.

2 J. M. Thompson, the owner, invested an additional $3,360 in the business.

4 Bought merchandise on account from Meyer and Company, their invoice no. A691, dated January 2; 2/10, n/30; $4,065.

4 Received check from Worden Appliance for $1,470 in payment of invoice for $1,500, less discount.

4 Sold merchandise on account to C. R. Larsen, invoice no. 6483, $975.

6 Received check from Metcalf and Schafer for $955.50 in payment of $975 invoice, less discount, $19.50.

7 Issued check no. 6982 to Hunter and Jared, in payment of their invoice no. C1271, for $900, less discount, $882.

7 Bought supplies on account from Conley Office Supply, their invoice no. 1906B, $127.20.

7 Sold merchandise on account to Bridges and Spear, invoice no. 6484, $1,275.

9 Issued credit memo no. 43 to C. R. Larsen, for merchandise returned, $45.

11 Cash sales for January 1 to 10, $6,663.90.

11 Issued check no. 6983 to Meyer and Company in payment of their invoice, $4,065, less discount; $3,983.70.

14 Sold merchandise on account to Worden Appliance, invoice no. 6485, $2,850.

14 Received check from C. R. Larsen, $911.40, in payment of $975 invoice, less return of $45, less discount, $18.60.

18 Bought merchandise on account from Chapman Products, their invoice no. 7281D, dated January 16; 2/10, n/60; $5,610.

Jan. 21 Issued check no. 6984, for advertising, $397.50.

21 Cash sales for January 11 to 20, $5,347.50.

23 Received credit memo no. 163 from Chapman Products for merchandise returned, $144.

23 Paid Acme Fast Freight, check no. 6985, for transportation of merchandise purchased, $117.

29 Sold merchandise on account to Allen Supply, invoice no. 6486, $2,796.

31 Cash sales for January 21 to 31, $5,980.50.

31 Issued check no. 6986, for miscellaneous expenses, $67.50.

31 Recorded payroll entry from the payroll register: total salaries, $8,700; employees' income tax withheld, $1,218; FICA tax withheld, $522.

31 Recorded the payroll taxes: FICA, $522; state unemployment tax, $348; federal unemployment tax, $69.60.

31 Issued check no. 6987, for salaries for the month, $6,960.

31 J. M. Thompson, the owner, withdrew cash for personal use, check no. 6988, $1,455.

Instructions

1. Journalize the transactions.
2. Post daily all entries involving customer accounts to the accounts receivable ledger.
3. Post daily all entries involving creditor accounts to the accounts payable ledger.
4. Post daily those entries involving the Sundry columns and the general journal to the general ledger.
5. Add the columns of the special journals, and prove the equality of debit and credit totals on scratch paper.
6. Post the appropriate totals of the special journals to the general ledger.
7. Prepare a trial balance.
8. Prepare a schedule of accounts receivable and a schedule of accounts payable. Do the totals equal the balances of the related controlling accounts?

Problem Set B

Problem 13-1B   Flegel and Rossiter, a retail store, sells on the bases of (1) cash, (2) charge accounts, and (3) bank credit cards. The following transactions involve cash receipts for the firm for March of this year. The state imposes a 4 percent sales tax on retail sales.

Mar. 8 Total cash sales for the week, $850, plus $34 sales tax.

8 Total sales from bank credit cards for the week, $900, plus $36 sales tax. The bank charges 2 percent of the total sales plus tax ($936 × .02 = $18.72).

12 C. T. Kohler, the owner, invested an additional $2,364.

13 Sold office equipment for cash, at cost, $183.

13 Collected cash from Robert Alston, a charge customer, $26.92.

Mar. 15 Total cash sales for the week, $1,296.52, plus $51.86 sales tax.

15 Total sales for the week on the basis of bank credit cards, $720.00, plus $28.80 sales tax.

19 Collected cash from Betsy Wagoner, a charge customer, $39.26.

20 Borrowed $2,780 from the bank, receiving cash and giving the bank a promissory note.

22 Total cash sales for the week, $1,627.00, plus $65.08 sales tax.

22 Total sales from bank credit cards for the week, $740.00, plus $29.60 sales tax.

23 Collected cash from T. E. French, a charge customer, $116.76.

25 Flegel and Rossiter received cash as a refund for the return of merchandise they purchased, $186.

28 Collected cash from Norbert Truman, a charge customer, $71.56.

31 Total sales from bank credit cards for the week, $176.40, plus $7.06 sales tax.

31 Total cash sales for the week, $1,927.84, plus $77.11 sales tax.

Instructions

1. Open the following accounts in the accounts receivable ledger and record the March 1 balances as given: Robert Alston, $46.92; T. E. French, $116.76; Megan Green, $53.23; Douglas Lowe, $89.76; Norbert Truman, $71.56; Betsy Wagoner, $39.26. Place a check mark in the Posting Reference column.
2. Record balance of $417.49 in the Accounts Receivable controlling account as of March 1.
3. Record the transactions in the cash receipts journal beginning with page 14.
4. Post daily to the accounts receivable ledger.
5. Total and rule the cash receipts journal.
6. Prove the equality of debit and credit totals.
7. Post to the Accounts Receivable account in the general ledger.

Problem 13-2B Parkins Company sells snacks wholesale, primarily to vending machine operators. Terms of sales on account are 2/10, n/30, FOB shipping point. The following transactions involving cash receipts and sales of merchandise took place in May of this year.

May 1 Received cash from G. Payne in payment of April 22 invoice of $1,000, less cash discount; $980.

3 Received $660 cash in payment of a $600 note receivable and interest of $60.

6 Received cash from J. R. Potter in payment of April 29 invoice of $600, less cash discount; $588.

7 Sold merchandise on account to N. Olson, invoice no. 286, $400.

15 Cash sales for the first half of May, $2,160.

16 Received cash from N. Olson in payment of invoice no. 286, less discount.

19 Received cash from Ralph Porter in payment of April 16 invoice, no discount, $160.

May   20 Sold merchandise on account to P. R. Thresher, invoice no. 298, $810.
       23 Received cash refund for return of defective equipment bought in April for cash, $216.
       26 Sold merchandise on account to T. E. Bannister, invoice no. 306, $460.
       31 Cash sales for the second half of May, $3,290.

Instructions

1. Journalize the transactions for May in the cash receipts journal and the sales journal.
2. Total and rule the journals.

Problem 13-3B   The Runyan Bookshop uses a check register to keep track of expenditures. The following transactions occurred during February of this year.

Feb.   2 Issued check no. 6210 to Amalgamated Publishers for the amount of their invoice no. 68172 for $640.00, less 2 percent cash discount of $12.80, $627.20.
        3 Paid freight bill to Midway Express Company, books purchased, check no. 6211, $40.
        5 Paid rent for the month, to Beale Land Company, check no. 6212, $190.
       10 Paid for advertising in *Campus News,* check no. 6213, $40.
       11 Issued check no. 6214 to New England Book Company for their invoice no. A3322 for $860 less 1 percent cash discount of $8.60, $851.40.
       16 Paid wages for the first half of February, check no. 6215, $320 (payroll entry previously recorded).
       20 N. D. Runyan, the owner, withdrew $200 for personal use, check no. 6216.
       25 Made payment on bank loan to Coast National Bank, check no. 6217, consisting of $400 on the principal and $40 interest, $440.
       28 Paid Midwest Publishing Company for their invoice no. 7768 (no discount previously recorded), check no. 6218, $940.
       28 Voided check no. 6219.
       28 Paid wages for the second half of February, check no. 6220, $320 (payroll entry previously recorded).

Instructions

1. Record the transactions in the check register.
2. Total and rule the check register.
3. Prove the equality of the debit and credit totals.

Problem 13-4B   The following transactions were completed by Thompson Electronics Supply during January, the first month of this fiscal year. Terms of sale are 2/10, n/30.

Jan. 2 J. M. Thompson, the owner, invested an additional $3,300 in the business.

2 Paid rent for the month, check no. 6981, $900.

4 Bought merchandise on account from Meyer and Company, their invoice no. A691, dated January 2; 2/10, n/30; $4,260.

4 Received check from Worden Appliance, in payment of $1,500 invoice, less discount, $30; $1,470.

4 Sold merchandise on account to C. R. Larsen, invoice no. 6483, $1,125.

6 Received check from Metcalf and Moody for $955.50 in payment of $975.00 invoice, less discount, $19.50.

7 Issued check no. 6982 to Hunter and Jared, in payment of their invoice no. C1272 for $750, less discount of $15, $735.

7 Bought supplies on account from Conley Office Supply, their invoice no. 1906B, $147.

7 Sold merchandise on account to Bridges and Spear, invoice no. 6484, $1,335.

9 Issued credit memo no. 43 to C. R. Larsen, for merchandise returned, $75.

11 Cash sales for January 1 to 10, $6,771.

11 Paid Meyer and Company, check no. 6983, in payment of $4,260.00 invoice, less discount of $85.20, $4,174.80.

14 Sold merchandise on account to Worden Appliance, invoice no. 6485, $2,925.

18 Bought merchandise on account from Chapman Products, their invoice no. 7281D, dated January 16; 2/10, n/60; $7,395.

21 Issued check no. 6984, for advertising, $423.

21 Cash sales for January 11 to 20, $5,985.

23 Paid Acme Fast Freight, check no. 6985, for transportation of merchandise purchased, $129.

23 Received credit memo no. 163 from Chapman Products, for merchandise returned, $637.50.

29 Sold merchandise on account to Allen Supply, invoice no. 6486, $2,910.

31 Cash sales, January 21 to 31, $6,642.

31 Issued check no. 6986, for miscellaneous expenses, $73.50.

31 Recorded payroll entry from the payroll register: total salaries, $9,150; employees' income tax withheld, $1,281; FICA tax withheld, $549.

31 Recorded the payroll taxes: FICA, $549; state unemployment tax, $366; federal unemployment tax, $73.20.

31 Issued check no. 6987, for salaries for the month, $7,320.

31 J. M. Thompson, the owner, withdrew cash for personal use, check no. 6988, $1,425.

Instructions

1. Journalize the transactions.
2. Post daily all entries involving customer accounts to the accounts receivable ledger.

3. Post daily all entries involving creditor accounts to the accounts payable ledger.
4. Post daily those entries involving the Sundry columns and the general journal to the general ledger.
5. Add the columns of the special journals. Prove the equality of debit and credit totals on scratch paper.
6. Post the appropriate totals from the special journals to the general ledger.
7. Prepare a trial balance.
8. Prepare a schedule of accounts receivable and a schedule of accounts payable. Do the totals equal the balances of the related controlling accounts?

14 Work Sheet and Adjusting Entries for a Merchandising Business

Learning Objectives

After you have completed this chapter, you will be able to do the following:

1. Complete a work sheet for a merchandising business involving adjustments for merchandise inventory, unearned revenue, depreciation, expired insurance, supplies used, and accrued wages or salaries.

2. Journalize the adjusting entries for a merchandising business.

For quite some time we've been talking about keeping special journals and accounts for a merchandising enterprise. Now let's take another step forward in the accounting cycle for a merchandising business: let's make *adjustments* and prepare *work sheets*.

The columnar classifications and procedures for completing the work sheet are basically the same as those described in Chapter 5. A merchandising business—like a service business—requires adjustments for supplies used, expired insurance, depreciation, and accrued wages. However, one adjustment applies exclusively to a merchandising enterprise: the adjustment for merchandise inventory. Still another adjustment, which could apply to either a merchandising or a service business, is the adjustment for unearned revenue. Previously, in introducing the work sheet, we included the Adjusted Trial Balance columns as a means of verifying that the accounts were in balance after recording the adjustments. To reduce the size of the work sheet, we will now eliminate the Adjusted Trial Balance columns. The account balances after the adjustments will be carried directly into the Income Statement and Balance Sheet columns of the work sheet.

This chapter will also discuss the work sheet with respect to handling the specialized accounts of a merchandising business.

ADJUSTMENT FOR MERCHANDISE INVENTORY

When we introduced the Merchandise Inventory account in Chapter 11, we put it under the heading of assets and said that in our example the balance of the account is changed only after a **physical inventory** (or actual count) has been taken. This is consistent with a system of periodic inventories in which one records the purchase of merchandise as a debit to Purchases for the amount of the cost, and the sale of merchandise as a credit to Sales for the amount of the selling price.

Consider this example: A firm has a Merchandise Inventory balance of $18,000, which represents the cost of the inventory at the beginning of the fiscal period. At the end of the fiscal period, the firm takes an actual count of the stock on hand and determines the cost of the ending inventory to be $22,000. Naturally, in any business, goods are constantly being bought, sold, and replaced. Evidently the reason that the cost of the ending inventory is larger than the cost of the beginning inventory is that the firm bought more than it sold. When we adjust the Merchandise Inventory account, we want to install the new figure of $22,000 in the account. We do this by a two-step process.

Objective 1

Complete a work sheet for a merchandising business involving adjustments for merchandise inventory, unearned revenue, depreciation, expired insurance, supplies used, and accrued wages or salaries.

Step 1 Eliminate or close the Merchandise Inventory account into Income Summary by the amount of the beginning inventory. (Transfer the balance into Income Summary.)

Let's look at this entry in the form of T accounts.

Merchandise Inventory				Income Summary	
Bal.	18,000	Adj.	18,000	Adj.	18,000

We handle this just as we handle the closing of any other account, by balancing off the account, or making the balance equal to zero. We treat the entry as a credit to Merchandise Inventory and then do the opposite to Income Summary, which means we debit this account.

Step 2 Enter the ending Merchandise Inventory, because one must record on the books the cost of the asset remaining on hand. (Add on the ending inventory.)

Let's repeat the T accounts, showing Step 1 and adding Step 2.

Merchandise Inventory				Income Summary			
Bal.	18,000	Adj.	18,000	Adj.	18,000	Adj.	22,000
Adj.	22,000						

In step 2, we debit Merchandise Inventory (recording the asset on the plus side of the account), and we do the opposite to Income Summary.

The reason for adjusting the Merchandise Inventory account in these two steps is that both the beginning and the ending figures appear separately in the income statement (see page 430), which is prepared directly from the Income Statement columns of the work sheet. This method of adjusting the inventory is considered to be more meaningful than taking a shortcut and adjusting for the difference between the beginning and the ending inventory values, since the amount of the difference does not appear as a distinct figure in the income statement.

ADJUSTMENT FOR UNEARNED REVENUE

Let us now introduce another adjusting entry: **unearned revenue.** As we said, this entry could pertain to a service as well as to a merchandising business. Occasionally, cash is received in advance for services to be performed in the future. For example, a dining hall sells meal tickets in advance, a concert association sells season tickets in advance, a magazine receives subscriptions in advance, and an insurance company receives premiums in advance. If the amounts to be received by each of these organizations will be earned during the present fiscal period, the amounts should be credited to revenue accounts. On the other hand, if the amounts to be received will *not* be earned during the present fiscal period, the amounts should be credited to unearned revenue accounts. An unearned revenue account is classified as a liability because an organization is liable for the amount received in advance until it is earned.

To illustrate, assume that Mark Publishing Company receives $60,000 in cash for subscriptions covering two years and records them originally as debits to Cash and credits to Unearned Subscriptions. At the end of the year, Mark finds that $44,000 of the subscriptions have been earned. Accordingly, Mark's accountant makes an adjusting entry, debiting Unearned Subscriptions and crediting Subscriptions Income. In other words, the accountant takes the earned portion out of Unearned Subscriptions and adds it to Subscriptions Income. T accounts show the situation as follows.

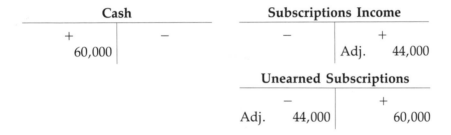

To take another example, suppose that C. L. Frederickson offers a course in plumbing repairs for home owners and apartment managers. On November 1, C. L. Frederickson receives $900 in fees for a three-month course. Because C. L. Frederickson's present fiscal period ends on December 31, the three months' worth of fees received in advance will not be earned during this fiscal period. Therefore, C. L. Frederickson's accountant records the transaction as a debit to Cash of $900 and a credit to Unearned Course Fees of $900. Unearned Course Fees is a liability account because C. L. Frederickson must complete the how-to course or refund a portion of the money it collected. Any account beginning with the word *Unearned* is always a liability.

On December 31, because two months' worth of course fees have now been earned, C. L. Frederickson's accountant makes an adjusting entry to transfer $600 (⅔ of $900) from Unearned Course Fees to Course Fees Income. By T accounts, the situation looks like this:

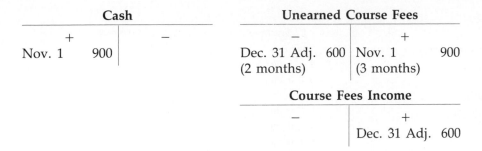

Cash		Unearned Course Fees	
+	−	−	+
Nov. 1 900		Dec. 31 Adj. 600 (2 months)	Nov. 1 900 (3 months)

Course Fees Income	
−	+
	Dec. 31 Adj. 600

C. L. Frederickson Plumbing Supply's chart of accounts is presented below. The account-number arrangement will be discussed in Chapter 15.

Assets (100–199)
111 Cash
112 Notes Receivable
113 Accounts Receivable
114 Merchandise Inventory
115 Supplies
116 Prepaid Insurance
121 Equipment
122 Accumulated Depreciation,
      Equipment
125 Building
126 Accumulated Depreciation,
      Building
127 Land

Liabilities (200–299)
211 Notes Payable
212 Accounts Payable
213 Wages Payable
217 Unearned Course Fees
221 Mortgage Payable

Owner's Equity (300–399)
311 C. L. Frederickson, Capital
312 C. L. Frederickson, Drawing
313 Income Summary

Revenue (400–499)
411 Sales
412 Sales Returns
      and Allowances
413 Sales Discount
421 Course Fees Income
422 Interest Income

Expenses (500–599)
511 Purchases
512 Purchases Returns
      and Allowances
513 Purchases Discount
521 Wages Expense
522 Depreciation Expense,
      Equipment
523 Supplies Expense
531 Depreciation Expense,
      Building
532 Taxes Expense
533 Insurance Expense
534 Interest Expense

Before we demonstrate how to record adjustments, let's first look at the trial balance section of C. L. Frederickson Plumbing Supply's work sheet (Figure 14-1). Notice that the adjustments for supplies used, insurance expired, depreciation, and accrued wages are the same type of adjustment we discussed for a service business in earlier chapters.

	ACCOUNT NAME	TRIAL BALANCE								ADJUSTMENTS								
		DEBIT					CREDIT					DEBIT			CREDIT			
1	Cash	21	9	2	2	00												1
2	Notes Receivable	4	0	0	0	00												2
3	Accounts Receivable	29	3	6	0	00												3
4	Merchandise Inventory	63	0	0	0	00												4
5	Supplies	1	4	4	0	00												5
6	Prepaid Insurance		9	6	0	00												6
7	Equipment	33	6	0	0	00												7
8	Accum. Depreciation, Equipment						16	4	0	0	00							8
9	Building	100	0	0	0	00												9
10	Accum. Depreciation, Building						32	0	0	0	00							10
11	Land	12	0	0	0	00												11
12	Notes Payable						3	0	0	0	00							12
13	Accounts Payable						36	4	0	0	00							13
14	Unearned Course Fees							9	0	0	00							14
15	Mortgage Payable						8	0	0	0	00							15
16	C. L. Frederickson, Capital						146	5	7	4	00							16
17	C. L. Frederickson, Drawing	19	2	0	0	00												17
18	Sales						176	1	8	0	00							18
19	Sales Returns and Allowances		8	4	0	00												19
20	Sales Discount	1	8	8	0	00												20
21	Interest Income							1	2	0	00							21
22	Purchases	85	6	0	0	00												22
23	Purchases Returns and Allowances							8	3	2	00							23
24	Purchases Discount						1	2	4	8	00							24
25	Wages Expense	45	8	0	0	00												25
26	Taxes Expense	1	9	6	0	00												26
27	Interest Expense			9	2	00												27
28		421	6	5	4	00	421	6	5	4	00							28

Figure 14-1

DATA FOR THE ADJUSTMENTS

The data for adjustments are as follows.

a–b. Ending merchandise inventory, $58,800
   c. Course fees earned, $600
   d. Ending supplies inventory, $412
   e. Insurance expired, $320
   f. Additional year's depreciation of equipment, $4,800
   g. Additional year's depreciation of building, $4,000
   h. Wages owed but not paid to employees at end of year, $1,220

Listing the adjustment data appears to be a relatively minor task. In a business situation, however, one must take actual physical counts of the inventories and match them up with costs. One must check insurance policies to determine the amount of insurance that has expired. Finally, one must systematically write off, or depreciate, the cost of equipment and buildings. Incidentally, for income tax and accounting purposes, land cannot be depreciated. Even if the building and lot were bought as one package for one price, the buyer must separate the cost of the building from the cost of the land. For real estate taxes, the county assessor appraises the building and the land separately. If there is no other qualified appraisal available, one can use the assessor's ratio or percentage as a basis for separating building cost and land cost.

Now let's look at these adjustments in the form of T accounts.

Merchandise Inventory			
+		−	
Bal.	63,000	(a) Adj. 63,000	
(b) Adj. 58,800			

Income Summary			
(a) Adj. 63,000	(b) Adj. 58,800		

Unearned Course Fees			
−		+	
(c) Adj.	600	Bal.	900

Course Fees Income		
−	+	
	(c) Adj.	600

Supplies			
+		−	
Bal.	1,440	(d) Adj. 1,028	

Supplies Expense	
+	−
(d) Adj. 1,028	

Prepaid Insurance			
+		−	
Bal.	960	(e) Adj.	320

Insurance Expense	
+	−
(e) Adj. 320	

Accumulated Depreciation, Equipment	
−	+
	Bal. 16,400
	(f) Adj. 4,800

Depreciation Expense, Equipment	
+	−
(f) Adj. 4,800	

Accumulated Depreciation, Building	
−	+
	Bal. 32,000
	(g) 4,000

Depreciation Expense, Building	
+	−
(g) 4,000	

Wages Payable	
−	+
	(h) 1,220

Wages Expense	
+	−
Bal. 45,800	
(h) 1,220	

We now record these in the Adjustments columns of the work sheet, using the same letters to identify the adjustments (see Figure 14-2).

COMPLETION OF THE WORK SHEET

Now we carry the account balances from the Trial Balance and Adjustments columns directly to the Income Statement and Balance Sheet columns. In the interest of efficiency and to save space, we do away with the Adjusted Trial Balance columns. In the earlier presentation they acted as a teaching device and as an intermediate checkpoint to prove that the accounts were in balance before we carried them forward. Obviously, however, the Adjusted Trial Balance columns are not necessary to complete the work sheet. For the sake of efficiency and economy, therefore, we often eliminate the Adjusted Trial Balance columns.

Figure 14-2

	ACCOUNT NAME	TRIAL BALANCE DEBIT	TRIAL BALANCE CREDIT	ADJUSTMENTS DEBIT	ADJUSTMENTS CREDIT	
1	Cash	21 9 2 2 00				1
2	Notes Receivable	4 0 0 0 00				2
3	Accounts Receivable	29 3 6 0 00				3
4	Merchandise Inventory	63 0 0 0 00		(b)58 8 0 0 00	(a)63 0 0 0 00	4
5	Supplies	1 4 4 0 00			(d) 1 0 2 8 00	5
6	Prepaid Insurance	9 6 0 00			(e) 3 2 0 00	6
7	Equipment	33 6 0 0 00				7
8	Accum. Depreciation, Equipment		16 4 0 0 00		(f) 4 8 0 0 00	8
9	Building	100 0 0 0 00				9
10	Accum. Depreciation, Building		32 0 0 0 00		(g) 4 0 0 0 00	10
11	Land	12 0 0 0 00				11
12	Notes Payable		3 0 0 0 00			12
13	Accounts Payable		36 4 0 0 00			13
14	Unearned Course Fees		9 0 0 00	(c) 6 0 0 00		14
15	Mortgage Payable		8 0 0 0 00			15
16	C. L. Frederickson, Capital		146 5 7 4 00			16
17	C. L. Frederickson, Drawing	19 2 0 0 00				17
18	Sales		176 1 8 0 00			18
19	Sales Returns and Allowances	8 4 0 00				19
20	Sales Discount	1 8 8 0 00				20
21	Interest Income		1 2 0 00			21
22	Purchases	85 6 0 0 00				22
23	Purchases Returns and Allowances		8 3 2 00			23
24	Purchases Discount		1 2 4 8 00			24
25	Wages Expense	45 8 0 0 00		(h) 1 2 2 0 00		25
26	Taxes Expense	1 9 6 0 00				26
27	Interest Expense	9 2 00				27
28		421 6 5 4 00	421 6 5 4 00			28
29	Income Summary			(a)63 0 0 0 00	(b)58 8 0 0 00	29
30	Course Fees Income				(c) 6 0 0 00	30
31	Supplies Expense			(d) 1 0 2 8 00		31
32	Insurance Expense			(e) 3 2 0 00		32
33	Depreciation Expense, Equipment			(f) 4 8 0 0 00		33
34	Depreciation Expense, Building			(g) 4 0 0 0 00		34
35	Wages Payable				(h) 1 2 2 0 00	35
36				133 7 6 8 00	133 7 6 8 00	36

Observe in particular the way we carry forward the figures for Merchandise Inventory and Income Summary. **Income Summary is the only account in which we don't combine the debit and credit figures;** instead we carry them into the Income Statement columns in Figure 14-3 as *two distinct figures.* As we said, the reason is that both figures appear in the income statement itself. We'll talk about this topic in greater detail in Chapter 15.

When you are developing the work sheet, complete one stage at a time:

1. Record the trial balance, and make sure that the total of the Debit column equals the total of the Credit column.
2. Record the adjustments in the Adjustments columns, and make sure that the totals are equal.
3. Complete the Income Statement and Balance Sheet columns by recording the adjusted balance of each account, as indicated by the following classification of accounts.

Income Statement		Balance Sheet	
Debit	**Credit**	**Debit**	**Credit**
Expenses	Revenues	Assets	Liabilities
+	+	+	+
Sales Returns	Purchases Returns	Drawing	Capital
and Allowances	and Allowances		+
+	+		Accumulated
Sales Discount	Purchases		Depreciation
+	Discount		
Purchases	+		
+	Income Summary		
Income Summary			

Study the following example, noting especially the way we treat these special accounts for a merchandising business:

	Location in Work Sheet			
	Income Statement		Balance Sheet	
Account Name	**Debit**	**Credit**	**Debit**	**Credit**
Merchandise Inventory			58,800 00	
Sales		176,180 00		
Sales Returns and Allowances	840 00			
Sales Discount	1,880 00			
Purchases	85,600 00			
Purchases Returns and				
Allowances		832 00		
Purchases Discount		1,248 00		
Income Summary	63,000 00	58,800 00		

The completed work sheet looks like Figure 14-3, below.

	ACCOUNT NAME	TRIAL BALANCE DEBIT	TRIAL BALANCE CREDIT
1	Cash	21 9 2 2 00	
2	Notes Receivable	4 0 0 0 00	
3	Accounts Receivable	29 3 6 0 00	
4	Merchandise Inventory	63 0 0 0 00	
5	Supplies	1 4 4 0 00	
6	Prepaid Insurance	9 6 0 00	
7	Equipment	33 6 0 0 00	
8	Accumulated Depreciation, Equipment		16 4 0 0 00
9	Building	100 0 0 0 00	
10	Accumulated Depreciation, Building		32 0 0 0 00
11	Land	12 0 0 0 00	
12	Notes Payable		3 0 0 0 00
13	Accounts Payable		36 4 0 0 00
14	Unearned Course Fees		9 0 0 00
15	Mortgage Payable		8 0 0 0 00
16	C. L. Frederickson, Capital		146 5 7 4 00
17	C. L. Frederickson, Drawing	19 2 0 0 00	
18	Sales		176 1 8 0 00
19	Sales Returns and Allowances	8 4 0 00	
20	Sales Discount	1 8 8 0 00	
21	Interest Income		1 2 0 00
22	Purchases	85 6 0 0 00	
23	Purchases Returns and Allowances		8 3 2 00
24	Purchases Discount		1 2 4 8 00
25	Wages Expense	45 8 0 0 00	
26	Taxes Expense	1 9 6 0 00	
27	Interest Expense	9 2 00	
28		421 6 5 4 00	421 6 5 4 00
29	Income Summary		
30	Course Fees Income		
31	Supplies Expense		
32	Insurance Expense		
33	Depreciation Expense, Equipment		
34	Depreciation Expense, Building		
35	Wages Payable		
36			
37	Net Income		
38			
39			
40			
41			

Figure 14-3

ADJUSTMENTS DEBIT	ADJUSTMENTS CREDIT	INCOME STATEMENT DEBIT	INCOME STATEMENT CREDIT	BALANCE SHEET DEBIT	BALANCE SHEET CREDIT	
				21 9 2 2 00		1
				4 0 0 0 00		2
				29 3 6 0 00		3
(b)58 8 0 0 00	(a)63 0 0 0 00			58 8 0 0 00		4
	(d) 1 0 2 8 00			4 1 2 00		5
	(e) 3 2 0 00			6 4 0 00		6
				33 6 0 0 00		7
	(f) 4 8 0 0 00				21 2 0 0 00	8
				100 0 0 0 00		9
	(g) 4 0 0 0 00				36 0 0 0 00	10
				12 0 0 0 00		11
					3 0 0 0 00	12
					36 4 0 0 00	13
(c) 6 0 0 00					3 0 0 00	14
					8 0 0 0 00	15
					146 5 7 4 00	16
				19 2 0 0 00		17
			176 1 8 0 00			18
		8 4 0 00				19
		1 8 8 0 00				20
			1 2 0 00			21
		85 6 0 0 00				22
			8 3 2 00			23
			1 2 4 8 00			24
(h) 1 2 2 0 00		47 0 2 0 00				25
		1 9 6 0 00				26
		9 2 00				27
						28
(a)63 0 0 0 00	(b)58 8 0 0 00	63 0 0 0 00	58 8 0 0 00			29
	(c) 6 0 0 00		6 0 0 00			30
(d) 1 0 2 8 00		1 0 2 8 00				31
(e) 3 2 0 00		3 2 0 00				32
(f) 4 8 0 0 00		4 8 0 0 00				33
(g) 4 0 0 0 00		4 0 0 0 00				34
	(h) 1 2 2 0 00				1 2 2 0 00	35
133 7 6 8 00	133 7 6 8 00	210 5 4 0 00	237 7 8 0 00	279 9 3 4 00	252 6 9 4 00	36
		27 2 4 0 00			27 2 4 0 00	37
		237 7 8 0 00	237 7 8 0 00	279 9 3 4 00	279 9 3 4 00	38
						39
						40
						41

Figure 14-4

	DATE		DESCRIPTION	POST. REF.	DEBIT		CREDIT		
1			*Adjusting Entries*						1
2	19– Dec.	31	Income Summary		63 0 0 0 00				2
3			Merchandise Inventory				63 0 0 0 00		3
4									4
5		31	Merchandise Inventory		58 8 0 0 00				5
6			Income Summary				58 8 0 0 00		6
7									7
8		31	Unearned Course Fees		6 0 0 00				8
9			Course Fees Income				6 0 0 00		9
10									10
11		31	Supplies Expense		1 0 2 8 00				11
12			Supplies				1 0 2 8 00		12
13									13
14		31	Insurance Expense		3 2 0 00				14
15			Prepaid Insurance				3 2 0 00		15
16									16
17		31	Depreciation Expense, Equipment		4 8 0 0 00				17
18			Accumulated Depreciation,						18
19			Equipment				4 8 0 0 00		19
20									20
21		31	Depreciation Expense, Building		4 0 0 0 00				21
22			Accumulated Depreciation,						22
23			Building				4 0 0 0 00		23
24									24
25		31	Wages Expense		1 2 2 0 00				25
26			Wages Payable				1 2 2 0 00		26
27									27

GENERAL JOURNAL — PAGE 96

ADJUSTING ENTRIES

See above for the way the adjusting entries look when they are taken from the Adjustments columns of the work sheet and recorded in the general journal (Figure 14-4).

Objective 2

Journalize the adjusting entries for a merchandising business.

GLOSSARY

Physical inventory An actual count of the stock of goods on hand; also referred to as a *periodic inventory*.

Unearned revenue Revenue received in advance for goods or services to be delivered later; considered to be a liability until the revenue is earned.

QUESTIONS, EXERCISES, AND PROBLEMS

Discussion Questions

1. Explain the two-step process for adjusting Merchandise Inventory.
2. What is the difference between merchandise inventory and supplies?
3. What is a physical, or periodic, inventory?
4. For a firm using a system of periodic inventories, which inventory (beginning merchandise or ending merchandise) appears in the firm's unadjusted trial balance at the end of the fiscal period?
5. On the income summary line of a work sheet, $31,500 appears in the Income Statement Debit column and $29,400 appears in the Income Statement Credit column. Which figure represents the beginning merchandise inventory?
6. In which columns of the work sheet is Sales Discount recorded?
7. When a dormitory received a semester's rent in advance, an entry was made debiting Cash and crediting Unearned Rent. At the end of the calendar year, a large portion of the rent had been earned. What adjusting entry would you have made?

Exercises

Exercise 14-1 Prepare the complete entry (in the general journal) from which each of the items identified by number below was posted.

							BALANCE	
			POST.					
	DATE	ITEM	REF.	DEBIT	CREDIT	DEBIT	CREDIT	

ACCOUNT _Wages Expense_   ACCOUNT NO. _514_

	DATE	ITEM	POST. REF.	DEBIT	CREDIT	DEBIT	CREDIT	
2	19– Dec. 28	(1)	CP39	2 2 0 0 00		91 7 0 0 00		2
3	31	(2)	J42	6 0 0 00		92 3 0 0 00		3
4	31	(3)	J43		92 3 0 0 00			4

Exercise 14-2 The beginning inventory of a merchandising business was $27,000, and the ending inventory is $31,000. What entries are needed at the end of the fiscal period to adjust Merchandise Inventory?

Exercise 14-3 In the Income Statement columns of the work sheet, we record the Income Summary account as $68,000 in the Debit column and $72,000 in the Credit column. Identify the beginning and ending merchandise inventory.

Exercise 14-4 The Inquisitive Magazine credited Unearned Subscriptions for $48,000 received from subscribers to its new monthly magazine. All subscriptions were for twelve issues. The first issue was mailed during October of the present year. Make the adjusting entry on December 31 of this year.

Exercise 14-5 Determine the amount of expired insurance for the fiscal year, January 1 through December 31, from the following account.

									BALANCE			
	DATE		ITEM	POST. REF.	DEBIT		CREDIT		DEBIT		CREDIT	
1	19– Jan.	1	Balance									1
2			(4 months)	✓					4 2 0 00			2
3	May	1	(12 months)	CP59	1 6 8 0 00				2 1 0 0 00			3

ACCOUNT *Prepaid Insurance*   ACCOUNT NO. **118**

Exercise 14-6 From the ledger account for Supplies, prepare the complete entries (in the general journal) from which each of the items identified by journal reference was posted.

ACCOUNT *Supplies*   ACCOUNT NO. **126**

									BALANCE			
	DATE		ITEM	POST. REF.	DEBIT		CREDIT		DEBIT		CREDIT	
1	19– Jan.	1	Balance	✓					9 6 0 00			1
2	Apr.	16		CP51	3 2 0 00				1 2 8 0 00			2
3	Sept.	22		CP72	2 1 0 00				1 4 9 0 00			3
4		29		CR76			3 0 00		1 4 6 0 00			4
5	Dec.	31	Adjusting	J121			6 0 0 00		8 6 0 00			5
6												6
7												7

Exercise 14-7 Because of a sudden illness, McGregor Company's accountant was unable to return to the job by the close of the company's fiscal year. The accountant did not have a chance to discuss what adjusting entries would be necessary at the end of the year, December 31. Fortunately, however, he did jot down a few notes that provided some leads. Here are his notes.

a. Charge off $1,450 of expired insurance from prepaid account for the year.
b. No bill received yet from car rental agency for salespeople's cars—should be about $8,400 for the year.
c. Depreciation on furniture and equipment for the year is $6,000.
d. Two days' salaries will be unpaid at year-end; total weekly (5 days) salary is $2,400.

Instructions

Record the adjusting entries.

Exercise 14-8 Complete each horizontal line of the selected accounts in the work sheet on pages 418–419. (Equipment and Insurance Expense are given as examples.)

Problem Set A

Problem 14-1A The trial balance of Carter Company as of December 31, the end of its fiscal year, is as follows.

Carter Company
Trial Balance
December 31, 19–

ACCOUNT NAME	DEBIT	CREDIT
Cash	4 5 6 8 27	
Merchandise Inventory	31 4 2 7 41	
Store Supplies	7 3 3 42	
Prepaid Insurance	5 1 0 00	
Store Equipment	18 6 7 0 00	
Accumulated Depreciation, Store Equipment		12 4 1 8 00
Accounts Payable		7 1 4 3 48
Sales Tax Payable		1 2 3 49
L. O. Carter, Capital		27 5 2 9 92
L. O. Carter, Drawing	14 5 0 0 00	
Sales		88 9 8 3 17
Sales Returns and Allowances	7 4 6 92	
Purchases	40 7 1 8 92	
Purchases Returns and Allowances		9 2 8 91
Purchases Discount		7 5 1 82
Salary Expense	18 2 8 4 43	
Rent Expense	7 2 0 0 00	
Miscellaneous Expense	5 1 9 42	
	137 8 7 8 79	137 8 7 8 79

Here are the data for the adjustments.

a–b. Merchandise inventory at December 31, $32,874.90
  c. Store supplies inventory, $202.16
  d. Insurance expired, $368.00
  e. Salaries accrued, $293.40
  f. Depreciation of store equipment, $1,960.00

Instructions

Complete the work sheet.

	ACCOUNT NAME	TRIAL BALANCE	
		DEBIT	CREDIT
1	Accounts Receivable	18 0 0 0 00	
2	Merchandise Inventory	60 0 0 0 00	
3	Prepaid Insurance	1 6 2 0 00	
4	Equipment	26 0 0 0 00	
5	Accumulated Depreciation, Equipment		15 2 0 0 00
6	Unearned Concession Income		1 8 0 0 00
7	Concession Income		
8	Sales		80 0 0 0 00
9	Sales Returns and Allowances	3 0 0 00	
10	Purchases	42 0 0 0 00	
11	Purchases Discount		1 0 5 0 00
12	Wages Expense	29 0 0 0 00	
13	Income Summary		
14	Wages Payable		
15	Depreciation Expense, Equipment		
16	Insurance Expense		
17			

Problem 14-2A   The balances of the ledger accounts of Harris Frame Shop as of June 30, the end of its fiscal year, are as follows.

Cash	$ 9,850
Accounts Receivable	34,200
Merchandise Inventory	48,600
Supplies	980
Prepaid Insurance	720
Store Equipment	17,860
Accumulated Depreciation, Store Equipment	10,800
Office Equipment	6,400
Accumulated Depreciation, Office Equipment	3,210
Notes Payable	2,400
Accounts Payable	28,600
Salaries Payable	—
Unearned Equipment Rental	1,800
Mary C. Harris, Capital	63,560
Mary C. Harris, Drawing	16,000
Income Summary	—
Sales	311,000
Sales Returns and Allowances	2,140
Equipment Rental Income	—
Purchases	261,000
Purchases Returns and Allowances	4,780
Purchases Discount	1,520

	ADJUSTMENTS		INCOME STATEMENT		BALANCE SHEET		
	DEBIT	CREDIT	DEBIT	CREDIT	DEBIT	CREDIT	
					18000		1
	56000				56000		2
		820			800		3
					26 0 0 0 00		4
		2400			17000		5
	1600					200	6
		1 6 0 0 00		1600			7
				80000			8
			300				9
			42000				10
				1050			11
	200		29200				12
	60 0 0 0 00	56 0 0 0 00	60000	56000			13
		2 0 0 00		200			14
	2 4 0 0 00		2400				15
	8 2 0 00		8 2 0 00				16
	121020	61020	134720	138850	117800		17

Salary Expense	$29,500
Depreciation Expense, Store Equipment	—
Depreciation Expense, Office Equipment	—
Insurance Expense	—
Supplies Expense	—
Interest Expense	420

Here are the data for the adjustments.

a–b. Merchandise inventory at June 30, $76,400
   c. Salaries accrued at June 30, $960
   d. Insurance expired during the year, $600
   e. Supplies inventory at June 30, $190
   f. Depreciation of store equipment, $2,500
   g. Depreciation of office equipment, $1,300
   h. Equipment rent earned, $1,500

Instructions

1. Complete the work sheet.
2. Journalize the adjusting entries.

Problem 14-3A   A portion of the work sheet of Morris Dow and Company for the year ended December 31 is at the top of the next page.

ACCOUNT NAME	INCOME STATEMENT DEBIT	INCOME STATEMENT CREDIT	BALANCE SHEET DEBIT	BALANCE SHEET CREDIT
Cash			4 6 7 0 00	
Merchandise Inventory			38 4 7 0 00	
Supplies			1 2 8 00	
Prepaid Insurance			1 2 0 00	
Store Equipment			19 6 4 0 00	
Accumulated Deprecia-tion, Store Equipment				13 1 1 0 00
Accounts Payable				7 3 0 0 00
Morris Dow, Capital				34 4 7 0 00
Morris Dow, Drawing			13 8 0 0 00	
Sales		86 7 1 0 00		
Sales Returns and Allowances	7 6 0 00			
Purchases	42 1 3 0 00			
Purchases Returns and Allowances		4 7 0 00		
Purchases Discount		8 0 0 00		
Salary Expense	18 7 8 0 00			
Rent Expense	7 4 0 0 00			
Income Summary	32 8 4 0 00	38 4 7 0 00		
Depreciation Expense, Store Equipment	2 0 2 0 00			
Insurance Expense	3 8 0 00			
Supplies Expense	4 7 2 00			
Salaries Payable				2 8 0 00
	104 7 8 2 00	126 4 5 0 00	76 8 2 8 00	55 1 6 0 00

Instructions

1. Determine the entries that appeared in the Adjustments columns and present them in general journal form.
2. Determine the net income for the year and the amount of the owner's capital at the end of the year (assuming that no capital contributions were made during the year).

Problem 14-4A Here are the accounts in the ledger of Reiner's Health Foods Store, with the balances as of December 31, the end of its fiscal year.

Cash	$ 3,760	Income Summary	—
Accounts Receivable	518	Sales	$126,418
Merchandise Inventory	38,700	Sales Returns and Allowances	1,296
Store Supplies	428	Purchases	87,656
Prepaid Insurance	762	Purchases Returns and	
Store Equipment	25,830	Allowances	1,087
Accumulated Depreciation,		Purchases Discount	1,470
Store Equipment	5,720	Salary Expense	7,800
Building	26,000	Advertising Expense	642
Accumulated Depreciation,		Depreciation Expense,	
Building	9,780	Store Equipment	—
Land	5,000	Depreciation Expense,	
Accounts Payable	4,690	Building	—
Sales Tax Payable	928	Store Supplies Expense	—
Salaries Payable	—	Insurance Expense	—
Mortgage Payable	14,620	Utilities Expense	386
C. C. Reiner, Capital	50,610	Miscellaneous Expense	325
C. C. Reiner, Drawing	15,500	Interest Expense	720

Here are the data for the adjustments.

a–b. Merchandise inventory at December 31, $37,690
  c. Insurance expired during the year, $418
  d. Depreciation of store equipment (life of eight years with a trade-in value of $2,950 at the end of eight years, straight-line rate)
  e. Depreciation of building (life of seventeen years with a value of $2,200 remaining at the end of seventeen years, straight-line rate)
  f. Salaries accrued at December 31, $140
  g. Store supplies inventory at December 31, $106

Instructions

1. Complete the work sheet.
2. Journalize the adjusting entries.

Problem Set B

Problem 14-1B The trial balance of Parkhurst Company as of December 31, the end of its current fiscal year, is at the top of the next page.

Here are the data for the adjustments.

a–b. Merchandise inventory at December 31, $33,416.28
  c. Store supplies inventory, $198.20
  d. Insurance expired, $360
  e. Salaries accrued, $281.50
  f. Depreciation of store equipment, $1,940

Instructions

Complete the work sheet.

Parkhurst Company
Trial Balance
December 31, 19–

ACCOUNT NAME	DEBIT	CREDIT
Cash	4 7 8 1 96	
Merchandise Inventory	31 7 6 1 42	
Store Supplies	7 2 0 56	
Prepaid Insurance	4 8 0 00	
Store Equipment	18 7 4 0 00	
Accumulated Depreciation, Store Equipment		12 1 6 0 00
Accounts Payable		7 2 8 9 40
Sales Tax Payable		1 2 1 68
C. R. Ross, Capital		27 8 1 5 00
C. R. Ross, Drawing	14 7 2 0 00	
Sales		89 5 1 8 37
Sales Returns and Allowances	7 2 1 52	
Purchases	40 6 2 1 73	
Purchases Returns and Allowances		9 3 9 47
Purchases Discount		7 4 8 95
Salary Expense	18 3 2 9 40	
Rent Expense	7 2 0 0 00	
Miscellaneous Expense	5 1 6 28	
	138 5 9 2 87	138 5 9 2 87

Problem 14-2B The balances of the ledger accounts of Belfair Music as of December 31, the end of its fiscal year, are as follows.

Cash	$ 5,796	Income Summary	—
Accounts Receivable	21,481	Sales	$326,000
Merchandise Inventory	60,919	Sales Returns and Allowances	4,874
Supplies	785	Equipment Rental Income	—
Prepaid Insurance	814	Purchases	271,549
Store Equipment	18,462	Purchases Returns and	
Accumulated Depreciation,		Allowances	6,720
Store Equipment	14,710	Purchases Discount	3,817
Office Equipment	4,718	Wages Expense	27,600
Accumulated Depreciation,		Depreciation Expense,	
Office Equipment	860	Store Equipment	—
Notes Payable	2,000	Depreciation Expense,	
Accounts Payable	15,411	Office Equipment	—
Wages Payable	—	Supplies Expense	—
Unearned Equipment Rental	1,600	Insurance Expense	—
C. K. Hennings, Capital	60,266	Interest Expense	386
C. K. Hennings, Drawing	14,000		

Data for the adjustments are as follows.

a–b. Merchandise inventory at December 31, $50,838
  c. Wages accrued at December 31, $978
  d. Supplies inventory at December 31, $372
  e. Depreciation of store equipment, $2,934
  f. Depreciation of office equipment, $866
  g. Insurance expired during the year, $316
  h. Equipment rent earned, $1,200

Instructions

1. Complete the work sheet.
2. Journalize the adjusting entries.

Problem 14-3B   Here is a portion of the work sheet of Donna Easely & Company for the year ended December 31.

6

ACCOUNT NAME	INCOME STATEMENT DEBIT	INCOME STATEMENT CREDIT	BALANCE SHEET DEBIT	BALANCE SHEET CREDIT
Cash			3 8 6 8 00	
Merchandise Inventory			37 1 4 9 00	
Supplies			1 4 9 00	
Prepaid Insurance			1 2 5 00	
Store Equipment			18 9 8 0 00	
Accumulated Deprecia-				
tion, Store Equipment				14 7 2 0 00
Accounts Payable				6 8 8 0 00
Donna Easely, Capital				37 5 7 1 00
Donna Easely, Drawing			15 4 0 0 00	
Sales		85 9 0 8 00		
Sales Returns and				
Allowances	7 1 7 00			
Purchases	44 2 9 6 00			
Purchases Returns				
and Allowances		4 8 2 00		
Purchases Discount		8 1 8 00		
Salary Expense	18 9 2 6 00			
Rent Expense	7 2 0 0 00			
Income Summary	34 1 1 4 00	37 1 4 9 00		
Depreciation Expense,				
Store Equipment	2 1 8 0 00			
Insurance Expense	2 7 6 00			
Supplies Expense	4 4 2 00			
Salaries Payable				2 9 4 00
	108 1 5 1 00	124 3 5 7 00	75 6 7 1 00	59 4 6 5 00
	16206—			16206—
	124357—	124357 —	75671 —	75671—

Instructions

1. Determine the entries that appeared in the Adjustments columns and present them in general journal form.
2. Determine the net income for the year and the amount of the owner's capital at the end of the year (assuming that no capital contributions were made during the year).

Problem 14-4B   The accounts in the ledger of Roberts Variety, with the balances as of December 31, the end of its fiscal year, are as follows.

Cash	$ 4,200	Income Summary	—
Accounts Receivable	680	Sales	$156,000
Merchandise Inventory	40,200	Sales Returns and Allowances	2,900
Store Supplies	540	Purchases	101,000
Prepaid Insurance	980	Purchases Returns and	
Store Equipment	18,700	Allowances	2,300
Accumulated Depreciation,		Purchases Discount	1,600
Store Equipment	4,200	Salary Expense	17,500
Building	30,000	Advertising Expense	2,050
Accumulated Depreciation,		Depreciation Expense,	
Building	12,200	Store Equipment	—
Land	6,000	Depreciation Expense,	
Notes Payable	3,600	Building	—
Accounts Payable	6,420	Store Supplies Expense	—
Sales Tax Payable	1,980	Insurance Expense	—
Salaries Payable	—	Utilities Expense	1,870
F. T. Roberts, Capital	57,000	Miscellaneous Expense	420
F. T. Roberts, Drawing	18,000	Interest Expense	260

Data for the adjustments are as follows.

a–b. Merchandise inventory at December 31, $41,600
  c. Store supplies inventory at December 31, $180
  d. Depreciation of store equipment (life of ten years with a trade-in value of $6,700 at the end of ten years, straight-line rate)
  e. Depreciation of building (life of twenty years with a value of $2,000 remaining at the end of twenty years, straight-line rate)
  f. Salaries accrued at December 31, $550
  g. Insurance expired during the year, $760

Instructions

1. Complete the work sheet.
2. Journalize the adjusting entries.

15 Financial Statements and Closing Entries for a Merchandising Firm

Learning Objectives

After you have completed this chapter, you will be able to do the following:

1. Prepare a classified income statement for a merchandising firm.

2. Prepare a classified balance sheet for any type of business.

3. Compute working capital and current ratio.

4. Journalize the closing entries for a merchandising firm.

5. Determine which adjusting entries should be reversed.

Chapters 5 and 7 discussed at length the income statements for a service and a professional enterprise, respectively. Then, in Chapters 11 and 14, we discussed the specialized accounts and journals for merchandising enterprises; in Chapter 14 we also explained the work sheet.

This chapter will show you how to formulate financial statements directly from work sheets. We will also explain the functions of closing entries and reversing entries as means of completing the accounting cycle. In Figure 15-1 (pages 428–429) we'll reproduce part of the work sheet for C. L. Frederickson Plumbing Supply that we presented in Chapter 14. First we'll look at the financial statements in their entirety, and then we'll explain their various subdivisions.

THE INCOME STATEMENT

As you know, the work sheet is merely a tool used by accountants to prepare the financial statements. In Figure 15-1, we present the partial work sheet for C. L. Frederickson Plumbing Supply, which includes the Income Statement columns. Of course, each of the amounts that appear in the Income Statement columns of the work sheet will also be used in the income statement. Notice that the amounts for the beginning and ending Merchandise Inventory now appear separately on the Income Summary line. Figure 15-2 (page 430) shows the entire income statement. Pause for a while and look it over; then we'll break it down into its component parts.

The outline of the income statement follows a logical pattern that is much the same for any type of merchandising business. The ability to interpret the income statement and extract parts from it is very useful when one is gathering information for decisions. To realize the full value of an income statement, however, you need to know the skeleton outline of an income statement backward and forward; you must be able to visualize it at a moment's notice. So, let's look at the statement piece by piece.

Objective 1

Prepare a classified income statement for a merchandising firm.

Net Sales	$173,460
− Cost of Merchandise Sold	87,720
Gross Profit	$85,740
− Operating Expenses	59,128
Income from Operations	$26,612

To hammer home the concepts of *gross* and *net*, let's imagine a simple transaction that takes place many thousands of times a day, all over the world: selling a house.

Cynthia Jones, a few years back, bought a house and a lot for $32,000. Last week she sold the house and lot for $60,000. The real estate agent who did the actual selling got a sales commission of 7 percent. How much did Jones make as clear profit?

Sale price of property	$60,000
Less Cost of property sold	32,000
Gross Profit (or Gross Margin)	$28,000
Less Agent's commission expense	4,200
Net Income or Net Profit (gain on the sale)	$23,800

Gross profit is the profit on the sale of the property before any expense has been deducted. **Net income** or *net profit* is the final or clear profit after all the expenses have been deducted. On a single-sale situation such as this, we refer to the final outcome as the net profit. But for a business that has many sales and expenses, most accountants prefer the term *net income*. Regardless of which word one uses, *net* refers to clear profit.

Revenue from Sales

All right, now let's look at the Revenue from Sales section in the income statement of C. L. Frederickson Plumbing Supply.

Revenue from Sales:			
Sales		$ 176 1 8 0 00	
Less: Sales Returns and Allowances	$ 8 4 0 00		
Sales Discount	1 8 8 0 00	2 7 2 0 00	
Net Sales			$ 173 4 6 0 00

When we introduced Sales Returns and Allowances and Sales Discount, we treated them as deductions from Sales. You can see that in the income statement they are deducted from Sales to give us **net sales.** Note that we recorded these items in the same order in which they appear in the ledger.

Cost of Merchandise Sold

The section of the income statement that requires the greatest amount of concentration is the **Cost of Merchandise Sold.** Let us therefore repeat it in its entirety.

C. L. Frederickson Plumbing Supply
Work Sheet
For year ended December 31, 19–

	ACCOUNT NAME	TRIAL BALANCE	
		DEBIT	CREDIT
1	Cash	21 9 2 2 00	
2	Notes Receivable	4 0 0 0 00	
3	Accounts Receivable	29 3 6 0 00	
4	Merchandise Inventory	63 0 0 0 00	
5	Supplies	1 4 4 0 00	
6	Prepaid Insurance	9 6 0 00	
7	Equipment	33 6 0 0 00	
8	Accum. Depreciation, Equipment		16 4 0 0 00
9	Building	100 0 0 0 00	
10	Accum. Depreciation, Building		32 0 0 0 00
11	Land	12 0 0 0 00	
12	Notes Payable		3 0 0 0 00
13	Accounts Payable		36 4 0 0 00
14	Unearned Course Fees		9 0 0 00
15	Mortgage Payable		8 0 0 0 00
16	C. L. Frederickson, Capital		146 5 7 4 00
17	C. L. Frederickson, Drawing	19 2 0 0 00	
18	Sales		176 1 8 0 00
19	Sales Returns and Allowances	8 4 0 00	
20	Sales Discount	1 8 8 0 00	
21	Interest Income		1 2 0 00
22	Purchases	85 6 0 0 00	
23	Purchases Returns and Allowances		8 3 2 00
24	Purchases Discount		1 2 4 8 00
25	Wages Expense	45 8 0 0 00	
26	Taxes Expense	1 9 6 0 00	
27	Interest Expense	9 2 00	
28		421 6 5 4 00	421 6 5 4 00
29	Income Summary		
30	Course Fees Income		
31	Supplies Expense		
32	Insurance Expense		
33	Depreciation Expense, Equipment		
34	Depreciation Expense, Building		
35	Wages Payable		
36			
37	Net Income		
38			
39			

Figure 15-1

	ADJUSTMENTS		INCOME STATEMENT		
	DEBIT	CREDIT	DEBIT	CREDIT	
					1
					2
					3
	(b)58 8 0 0 00	(a)63 0 0 0 00			4
		(d)1 0 2 8 00			5
		(e) 3 2 0 00			6
					7
		(f) 4 8 0 0 00			8
					9
		(g) 4 0 0 0 00			10
					11
					12
					13
	(c) 6 0 0 00				14
					15
					16
					17
				176 1 8 0 00	18
			8 4 0 00		19
			1 8 8 0 00		20
				1 2 0 00	21
			85 6 0 0 00		22
				8 3 2 00	23
				1 2 4 8 00	24
	(h)1 2 2 0 00		47 0 2 0 00		25
			1 9 6 0 00		26
			9 2 00		27
					28
	(a)63 0 0 0 00	(b)58 8 0 0 00	63 0 0 0 00	58 8 0 0 00	29
		(c) 6 0 0 00		6 0 0 00	30
	(d)1 0 2 8 00		1 0 2 8 00		31
	(e) 3 2 0 00		3 2 0 00		32
	(f)4 8 0 0 00		4 8 0 0 00		33
	(g)4 0 0 0 00		4 0 0 0 00		34
		(h)1 2 2 0 00			35
	133 7 6 8 00	133 7 6 8 00	210 5 4 0 00	237 7 8 0 00	36
			27 2 4 0 00		37
			237 7 8 0 00	237 7 8 0 00	38
					39

C. L. Frederickson Plumbing Supply
Income Statement
For year ended December 31, 19–

Revenue from Sales:			
Sales		$176 1 8 0 00	
Less: Sales Returns and Allowances	$ 8 4 0 00		
Sales Discount	1 8 8 0 00	2 7 2 0 00	
Net Sales			$ 173 4 6 0 00
Cost of Merchandise Sold:			
Merchandise Inventory,			
January 1, 19–		$ 63 0 0 0 00	
Purchases	$85 6 0 0 00		
Less: Purchases Returns and			
Allowances $ 832.00			
Purchases Discount 1,248.00	2 0 8 0 00		
Net Purchases		83 5 2 0 00	
Merchandise Available for Sale		$ 146 5 2 0 00	
Less Merchandise Inventory,			
December 31, 19–		58 8 0 0 00	
Cost of Merchandise Sold			87 7 2 0 00
Gross Profit			$ 85 7 4 0 00
Operating Expenses:			
Wages Expense		$ 47 0 2 0 00	
Depreciation Expense, Equipment		4 8 0 0 00	
Supplies Expense		1 0 2 8 00	
Depreciation Expense, Building		4 0 0 0 00	
Taxes Expense		1 9 6 0 00	
Insurance Expense		3 2 0 00	
Total Operating Expenses			59 1 2 8 00
Income from Operations			$ 26 6 1 2 00
Other Income:			
Course Fees Income		$ 6 0 0 00	
Interest Income		1 2 0 00	
Total Other Income		$ 7 2 0 00	
Other Expenses:			
Interest Expense		9 2 00	6 2 8 00
Net Income			$ 27 2 4 0 00

Figure 15-2

Cost of Merchandise Sold:			
Merchandise Inventory,			
January 1, 19–		$ 63 0 0 0 00	
Purchases	$85 6 0 0 00		
Less: Purchases Returns			
and Allowances $ 832.00			
Purchases Discount 1,248.00	2 0 8 0 00		
Net Purchases		83 5 2 0 00	
Merchandise Available for Sale		$146 5 2 0 00	
Less: Merchandise Inventory,			
December 31, 19–		58 8 0 0 00	
Cost of Merchandise Sold			87 7 2 0 00

First let's look closely at the Purchases section.

Purchases	$85 6 0 0 00		
Less: Purchases Returns			
and Allowances $ 832.00			
Purchases Discount 1,248.00	2 0 8 0 00		
Net Purchases		83 5 2 0 00	

Note the parallel to the Sales section; in order to arrive at Net Purchases, we deduct both Purchases Returns and Allowances and Purchases Discount from Purchases. We list the items in account-number order.

Now let's take in the full Cost of Merchandise Sold section. Does this seem like a reasonable summing up of the situation?

Amount we started with (beginning inventory)	$ 63,000
+ Net amount we purchased	83,520
Total amount that could have been sold (available)	$146,520
− Amount left over (ending inventory)	58,800
Cost of the merchandise that was actually sold	$ 87,720

An alternative way of presenting this information follows:

Merchandise Inventory, January 1, 19–	$ 63,000
+ Net Purchases	83,520
Merchandise Available for Sale	$146,520
− Merchandise Inventory, December 31, 19–	58,800
Cost of Merchandise Sold	$ 87,720

Remember that **net purchases** means total Purchases less both Purchases Returns and Allowances and Purchases Discount.

Operating Expenses

Operating expenses, as the name implies, are the regular expenses of doing business. They may be listed in descending order, with the largest amount first, if account numbers are unavailable. A Miscellaneous Expense account goes last regardless of its amount, however. Many accountants prefer to list the accounts and their respective balances in the order that the accounts appear in the ledger. We shall follow this order in this chapter.

Many firms may use subclassifications of operating expenses, such as the following.

1. **Selling expenses**   Any expenses directly connected with the selling activity, such as these:

- Sales Salaries Expense
- Sales Commissions Expense
- Advertising Expense
- Store Supplies Expense
- Delivery Expense
- Depreciation Expense, Store Equipment

2. **General expenses**   Any expenses related to the office or the administration, or any expense that cannot be directly connected with a selling activity:

- Office Salaries Expense
- Taxes Expense
- Depreciation Expense, Office Equipment
- Rent Expense
- Insurance Expense
- Office Supplies Expense

If the Cash Short and Over account has a debit balance (net shortage), the balance is added to and reported as Miscellaneous General Expense. Conversely, if the Cash Short and Over account has a credit balance (net overage), the balance is added to and reported as Miscellaneous Income, which is classified as Other Income.

In preparing the income statement, classifying expense accounts as selling expenses or general expenses is a matter of judgment. The only reason we're not using this breakdown here is that we're trying to keep the number of accounts to a minimum. In other words, getting bogged down in a large number of accounts could make it more difficult for you to understand the main concepts. We don't want you to lose sight of the forest on account of the trees.

Income from Operations

Now let's repeat the skeleton outline.

Net Sales
− Cost of Merchandise Sold

Gross Profit
− Operating Expenses

Income from Operations

If the Operating Expenses are the regular, recurring expenses of doing business, then Income from Operations should be the regular or recurring net income. When you are comparing the results of operations over a number of years, the income from operations is the most significant figure to use each year as a basis for comparison.

Other Income

The Other Income classification, as the name implies, records any revenue account other than revenue from Sales. What we are trying to do is to isolate Sales at the top of the income statement as the major revenue account, so that the gross profit figure represents the profit made on the sale of merchandise *only*. Additional accounts that may appear under the heading of Other Income are Rent Income (the firm is subletting part of its premises), Interest Income (the firm holds an interest-bearing note or contract), Gain on Disposal of Plant and Equipment (the firm makes a profit on the sale of plant and equipment), Miscellaneous Income (the firm has an overage recorded in the Cash Short and Over account).

Other Expenses

The classification of Other Expenses records various nonoperating expenses, such as Interest Expense or Loss on Disposal of Plant and Equipment.

Skeleton Outline of the Income Statement

Net Sales }
{
Gross Sales
− Sales Returns and
   Allowances
− Sales Discount
─────────────
= Net Sales
}

− Cost of Merchandise Sold }
{
Beginning Merchandise Inventory

+ Net Purchases }
{
Gross Purchases
− Purchases Returns and Allowances
− Purchases Discount
─────────────
= Net Purchases
}

= Merchandise Available for Sale
− Ending Merchandise Inventory
─────────────
= Cost of Merchandise Sold
}

= Gross Profit
− Operating Expenses }
{
Selling Expenses
General Expenses
}

= Income from Operations

+ Other Income }
{
Interest Income
Rent Income
Gain on Disposal of Plant and Equipment
}

− Other Expenses }
{
Interest Expense
Loss on Disposal of Plant and Equipment
}

= Net Income

THE BALANCE SHEET

Figure 15-3 (see pages 436–437) is a partial work sheet for C. L. Frederick-son Plumbing Supply (again, based on the one in Chapter 14). Here again we find that every figure in the Balance Sheet columns of the work sheet is used in either the statement of owner's equity or the balance sheet. The first of these statements appears below.

C. L. Frederickson, Capital,												
January 1, 19–							$138	5	7	4	00	
Additional Investment, August 26, 19–							8	0	0	0	00	
Total Investment							$146	5	7	4	00	
Net Income for the Year	$27	2	4	0	00							
Less Withdrawals for the Year	19	2	0	0	00							
Increase in Capital							8	0	4	0	00	
C. L. Frederickson, Capital,												
December 31, 19–							$154	6	1	4	00	

C. L. Frederickson Plumbing Supply
Statement of Owner's Equity
For year ended December 31, 19–

We have already discussed the statement of owner's equity. C. L. Frederickson Plumbing Supply's statement of owner's equity shows why the balance of the Capital account has changed from the beginning of the fiscal period to the end of it. The statement shows that an additional investment was made during the period. Data relating to additional investments are available from an analysis of the Capital account, not from the work sheet. After one has added the additional investment to the beginning capital, the remainder of the statement is the same as our illustrations in Chapter 2. When there has been no additional investment, one simply records the net income, less withdrawals, and the resulting increase or decrease in capital.

Balance sheet classifications are generally uniform for all types of business enterprises. You are strongly urged to take the time to learn the following definitions of the classifications and the order of accounts within them. If you do, you will forever after have a standard routine for compiling a balance sheet, and this routine will save you a lot of grief and time. As you read, refer to Figure 15-4 on page 438.

Objective 2

Prepare a classified balance sheet for any type of business.

Current Assets

Current assets consist of cash and any other assets or resources that are expected to be realized in cash or to be sold or consumed during the normal operating cycle of the business or one year, if the normal operating cycle is less than twelve months.

ACCOUNT NAME	TRIAL BALANCE								
	DEBIT					CREDIT			
Cash	21	9	2	2	00				
Notes Receivable	4	0	0	0	00				
Accounts Receivable	29	3	6	0	00				
Merchandise Inventory	63	0	0	0	00				
Supplies	1	4	4	0	00				
Prepaid Insurance		9	6	0	00				
Equipment	33	6	0	0	00				
Accum. Depreciation, Equipment						16	4	0	0	00
Building	100	0	0	0	00				
Accum. Depreciation, Building						32	0	0	0	00
Land	12	0	0	0	00				
Notes Payable						3	0	0	0	00
Accounts Payable						36	4	0	0	00
Unearned Course Fees							9	0	0	00
Mortgage Payable						8	0	0	0	00
C. L. Frederickson, Capital						146	5	7	4	00
C. L. Frederickson, Drawing	19	2	0	0	00				
Sales						176	1	8	0	00
Sales Returns and Allowances		8	4	0	00				
Sales Discount	1	8	8	0	00				
Interest Income							1	2	0	00
Purchases	85	6	0	0	00				
Purchases Returns and Allowances							8	3	2	00
Purchases Discount						1	2	4	8	00
Wages Expense	45	8	0	0	00				
Taxes Expense	1	9	6	0	00				
Interest Expense		9	2	00					
	421	6	5	4	00	421	6	5	4	00
Income Summary									
Course Fees Income									
Supplies Expense									
Insurance Expense									
Depreciation Expense, Equipment									
Depreciation Expense, Building									
Wages Payable									
Net Income									

Figure 15-3

ADJUSTMENTS		BALANCE SHEET	
DEBIT	CREDIT	DEBIT	CREDIT
		21 9 2 2 00	
		4 0 0 0 00	
		29 3 6 0 00	
(b) 58 8 0 0 00	(a) 63 0 0 0 00	58 8 0 0 00	
	(d) 1 0 2 8 00	4 1 2 00	
	(e) 3 2 0 00	6 4 0 00	
		33 6 0 0 00	
	(f) 4 8 0 0 00		21 2 0 0 00
		100 0 0 0 00	
	(g) 4 0 0 0 00		36 0 0 0 00
		12 0 0 0 00	
			3 0 0 0 00
			36 4 0 0 00
(c) 6 0 0 00			3 0 0 00
			8 0 0 0 00
			146 5 7 4 00
		19 2 0 0 00	
(h) 1 2 2 0 00			
(a) 63 0 0 0 00	(b) 58 8 0 0 00		
	(c) 6 0 0 00		
(d) 1 0 2 8 00			
(e) 3 2 0 00			
(f) 4 8 0 0 00			
(g) 4 0 0 0 00			
	(h) 1 2 2 0 00		1 2 2 0 00
133 7 6 8 00	133 7 6 8 00	279 9 3 4 00	252 6 9 4 00
			27 2 4 0 00
		279 9 3 4 00	279 9 3 4 00

C. L. Frederickson Plumbing Supply
Balance Sheet
December 31, 19–

Assets					
Current Assets:					
Cash			$ 21 9 2 2 00		
Notes Receivable			4 0 0 0 00		
Accounts Receivable			29 3 6 0 00		
Merchandise Inventory			58 8 0 0 00		
Supplies			4 1 2 00		
Prepaid Insurance			6 4 0 00		
Total Current Assets				$ 115 1 3 4 00	
Plant and Equipment:					
Equipment	$ 33 6 0 0 00				
Less Accumulated Depreciation	21 2 0 0 00	$ 12 4 0 0 00			
Building	$ 100 0 0 0 00				
Less Accumulated Depreciation	36 0 0 0 00	64 0 0 0 00			
Land		12 0 0 0 00			
Total Plant and Equipment				88 4 0 0 00	
Total Assets				$ 203 5 3 4 00	
Liabilities					
Current Liabilities:					
Notes Payable			$ 3 0 0 0 00		
Mortgage Payable (current portion)			2 0 0 0 00		
Accounts Payable			36 4 0 0 00		
Wages Payable			1 2 2 0 00		
Unearned Course Fees			3 0 0 00		
Total Current Liabilities				$ 42 9 2 0 00	
Long-term Liabilities:					
Mortgage Payable				6 0 0 0 00	
Total Liabilities				$ 48 9 2 0 00	
Owner's Equity					
C. L. Frederickson, Capital				154 6 1 4 00	
Total Liabilities and Owner's Equity				$ 203 5 3 4 00	

Figure 15-4

Accountants list current assets in the order of their convertibility into cash, or, in other words, their **liquidity.** (If you've got an asset such as a car or a diamond, and you sell it quickly and turn it into cash, you are said to be turning it into a *liquid* state.) If the first four accounts under Current Assets (see Figure 15-4) are present, always record them in the same order: (1) Cash, (2) Notes Receivable, (3) Accounts Receivable, and (4) Merchandise Inventory.

Notes receivable (current) are short-term promissory notes (promise-to-pay notes) held by the firm. (*Example:* Suppose you own a lumber yard and sell lumber to a builder who does not have enough cash to pay for the lumber but does have a ready buyer for the finished house. The builder therefore gives you a *promissory note,* stating that you will be paid within 90 days.) Notes Receivable is generally placed ahead of Accounts Receivable, because promissory notes are considered to be more liquid than Accounts Receivable. (*Reason:* The holder of the note can raise more cash by borrowing from a bank, pledging the notes as security for the loan.) Supplies and Prepaid Insurance are considered to be prepaid items that will be used up or expire within the following operating cycle or year. That's why they appear at the bottom of the Current Assets section. (There is no particular reason to list Supplies before Prepaid Insurance. Prepaid Insurance could just as easily have preceded Supplies.)

Plant and Equipment

Plant and equipment are relatively long-lived assets that are held for use in the production or sale of other assets or services; some accountants refer to them as *fixed assets*. The three types of accounts that usually appear in this category are equipment, buildings, and land (refer to Figure 15-4 once again). Note that the Equipment and Building accounts are followed by their respective Accumulated Depreciation accounts. (Remember how we spoke of Accumulated Depreciations as being deductions from assets?) Plant and equipment are sometimes listed in the order of their length of life, with the shortest-lived asset (equipment) recorded first. A firm that owns delivery equipment, for example, lists it first, because of its relatively short life. In other words, plant and equipment go in order from the least fixed to the most fixed; land is placed last in this category.

Current Liabilities

Current liabilities are debts that will become due within the normal operating cycle of the business, usually within one year; they will normally be paid, when due, from current assets. List current liabilities in the order of their expected payment. Notes Payable (current) generally precedes Accounts Payable, just as Notes Receivable precedes Accounts Receivable. The Mortgage Payable (current portion), which may precede Accounts Payable, is the payment one makes to reduce the principal of the mortgage in a given year. Wages Payable and any other accrued liabilities, such as Commissions Payable and the current portion of unearned revenue accounts, usually fall at the bottom of the list of current liabilities.

Long-term Liabilities

Long-term liabilities are debts that are payable over a comparatively long period, usually more than one year. Ordinarily Mortgage Payable is the only account in this category for a sole-proprietorship (or one-owner) type of business. One single amount in a category can be recorded in the column on the extreme right.

Working Capital and Current Ratio

Both the management and the short-term creditors of a firm are vitally interested in two questions.

1. Does the firm have a sufficient amount of capital to operate?
2. Does the firm have the ability to pay its debts?

Two measures used to answer these questions are a firm's working capital and its current ratio, and the necessary data is taken from a classified balance sheet.

Working capital is determined by subtracting current liabilities from current assets, thus

Working capital = Current assets − Current liabilities

The normal operating cycle for most firms is one year. Because current assets equal cash—or items that can be converted into cash or used up within one year—and current liabilities equal the total amount that the company must pay out within one year, "working capital" is appropriately named. It is the amount of capital the company has available to use or work with. The working capital for C. L. Frederickson Plumbing Supply is as follows.

Working capital = $115,134 − $42,920 = $72,214

A firm's ability to pay its debts is revealed by the firm's **current ratio.** The current ratio is determined by dividing current assets by current liabilities.

$$\text{Current ratio} = \frac{\text{Current assets (amount coming in within one year)}}{\text{Current liabilities (amount going out within one year)}}$$

The current ratio for C. L. Frederickson Plumbing Supply is calculated like this:

Current ratio $= \dfrac{\$115{,}134}{\$42{,}920} = 2.68:1$

$$\begin{array}{r} 2.68 \\ \hline 42{,}920{\overline{)}}115{,}134.00 \end{array}$$

In the case of C. L. Frederickson Plumbing Supply, $2.68 is available to pay every dollar currently due on December 31.

When banks are considering granting loans to merchandising firms, a minimum current ratio of 2:1 is generally required.

Chart of Accounts

In Chapter 4, when we introduced the chart of accounts and the account-number arrangement, we said that the first digit represents the classification of the accounts. A common organization is:

Assets	1__
Liabilities	2__
Owner's Equity	3__
Revenue	4__
Expenses	5__

The second digit stands for the subclassification.

Assets	1__
Current Assets	11_
Plant and Equipment	12_
Liabilities	2__
Current Liabilities	21_
Long-term Liabilities	22_
Owner's Equity	3__
Capital	31_
Revenue	4__
Revenue from Sales	41_
Other income	42_
Expenses	5__
Cost of Merchandise Sold	51_
Selling Expenses	52_
General Expenses	53_
Other Expenses	54_

| | TRIAL BALANCE | | INCOME STATEMENT | | |
ACCOUNT NAME	DEBIT	CREDIT	DEBIT	CREDIT	
1 Cash	21 9 2 2 00				1
2 Notes Receivable	4 0 0 0 00				2
3 Accounts Receivable	29 3 6 0 00				3
4 Merchandise Inventory	63 0 0 0 00				4
5 Supplies	1 4 4 0 00				5
6 Prepaid Insurance	9 6 0 00				6
7 Equipment	33 6 0 0 00				7
8 Accum. Depreciation, Equipment		16 4 0 0 00			8
9 Building	100 0 0 0 00				9
10 Accum. Depreciation, Building		32 0 0 0 00			10
11 Land	12 0 0 0 00				11
12 Notes Payable		3 0 0 0 00			12
13 Accounts Payable		36 4 0 0 00			13
14 Unearned Course Fees		9 0 0 00			14
15 Mortgage Payable		8 0 0 0 00			15
16 C. L. Frederickson, Capital		146 5 7 4 00			16
17 C. L. Frederickson, Drawing	19 2 0 0 00				17
18 Sales		176 1 8 0 00		176 1 8 0 00	18
19 Sales Returns and Allowances	8 4 0 00		8 4 0 00		19
20 Sales Discount	1 8 8 0 00		1 8 8 0 00		20
21 Interest Income		1 2 0 00		1 2 0 00	21
22 Purchases	85 6 0 0 00		85 6 0 0 00		22
23 Purchases Returns and Allowances		8 3 2 00		8 3 2 00	23
24 Purchases Discount		1 2 4 8 00		1 2 4 8 00	24
25 Wages Expense	45 8 0 0 00		47 0 2 0 00		25
26 Taxes Expense	1 9 6 0 00		1 9 6 0 00		26
27 Interest Expense	9 2 00		9 2 00		27
28	421 6 5 4 00	421 6 5 4 00			28
29 Income Summary			63 0 0 0 00	58 8 0 0 00	29
30 Course Fees Income				6 0 0 00	30
31 Supplies Expense			1 0 2 8 00		31
32 Insurance Expense			3 2 0 00		32
33 Depreciation Expense, Equipment			4 8 0 0 00		33
34 Depreciation Expense, Building			4 0 0 0 00		34
35 Wages Payable					35
36			210 5 4 0 00	237 7 8 0 00	36
37 Net Income			27 2 4 0 00		37
38			237 7 8 0 00	237 7 8 0 00	38
39					39

Figure 15-5

The third digit indicates the placement of the account within the sub-classification. As an example, account number 411 represents Sales, which is the first account listed under revenue. Account number 312 represents Drawing, which is the second account listed under owner's equity.

CLOSING ENTRIES

In Chapter 6 we discussed closing entries for a service business; now let's look at closing entries for a merchandising business. The same methods apply to both. You follow the same four steps to balance off the revenue, expense, and Drawing accounts.

At the end of a fiscal period, you close the revenue and expense accounts so that you can start the next fiscal period with a clean slate. You also close the Drawing account, because it, too, applies to one fiscal period. As you recall from our discussion in Chapter 6, these accounts are called temporary-equity accounts.

You can speed up the preparation of closing entries by balancing off each figure in the Income Statement columns of the work sheet. Figure 15-5 shows the Income Statement columns. After you have looked them over, let's take up those four steps and see how we come out.

Four Steps in the Closing Procedure

To repeat, these four steps should be followed when closing:

1. Close the revenue accounts as well as the other accounts appearing in the income statement and having credit balances. (**Debit the figures that are credited in the Income Statement column of the work sheet, except the figure on the Income Summary line.**) This entry is illustrated in Figure 15-6.

Objective 4

Journalize the closing entries for a merchandising firm.

Figure 15-6

	DATE		DESCRIPTION	POST. REF.	DEBIT	CREDIT	
			GENERAL JOURNAL			PAGE _97_	
1			*Closing Entries*				1
2	19– Dec.	31	Sales		176 1 8 0 00		2
3			Purchases Returns and Allowances		8 3 2 00		3
4			Purchases Discount		1 2 4 8 00		4
5			Course Fees Income		6 0 0 00		5
6			Interest Income		1 2 0 00		6
7			*Income Summary*			178 9 8 0 00	7
8							8

Figure 15-7

	DATE		DESCRIPTION	POST. REF.	DEBIT		CREDIT		
1	Dec.	31	Income Summary		147 5 4 0 00				1
2			Sales Returns and Allowances				8 4 0 00		2
3			Sales Discount				1 8 8 0 00		3
4			Purchases				85 6 0 0 00		4
5			Wages Expense				47 0 2 0 00		5
6			Taxes Expense				1 9 6 0 00		6
7			Interest Expense				9 2 00		7
8			Supplies Expense				1 0 2 8 00		8
9			Insurance Expense				3 2 0 00		9
10			Depreciation Expense, Equipment				4 8 0 0 00		10
11			Depreciation Expense, Building				4 0 0 0 00		11
12									12

2. Close the expense accounts as well as the other accounts appearing in the income statement that have debit balances. (**Credit the figures that are debited in the Income Statement column of the work sheet, except the figure on the Income Summary line.** The entry appears in Figure 15-7.)

3. Close the Income Summary account into C. L. Frederickson, Capital. (**Debit Income Summary by the amount of the net income; credit it by the amount of a net loss.**)

	DATE		DESCRIPTION	POST. REF.	DEBIT		CREDIT		
1	Dec.	31	Income Summary		27 2 4 0 00				1
2			C. L. Frederickson, Capital				27 2 4 0 00		2
3									3

Income Summary

Adjusting 63,000 (Beginning Merchandise Inventory)	Adjusting 58,800 (Ending Merchandise Inventory)
(Expenses) 147,540	(Revenue) 178,980
Clos. (Net Inc.) 27,240	

C. L. Frederickson, Capital

−	+
	Balance 146,574
	(Net Inc.) 27,240

4. Close the Drawing account into the Capital account.

GENERAL JOURNAL

	DATE	DESCRIPTION	POST. REF.	DEBIT	CREDIT	
1	Dec. 31	C. L. Frederickson, Capital		19 2 0 0 00		1
2		C. L. Frederickson, Drawing			19 2 0 0 00	2
3						3

C. L. Frederickson, Drawing

	+			−	
Balance		19,200	Closing		19,200

C. L. Frederickson, Capital

	−			+	
(Drawing)		19,200	Balance		146,574
			(Net Inc.)		27,240

Note that you close Purchases Discount and Purchases Returns and Allowances in step 1 along with the revenue accounts. Note also that in step 2 you close Sales Discount and Sales Returns and Allowances along with the expense accounts. Finally, bear in mind that the Income Summary account already contains adjusting entries for merchandise inventory.

REVERSING ENTRIES

Reversing entries are general journal entries that are the exact reverse of certain adjusting entries. A reversing entry enables the accountant to record routine transactions in the usual manner, *even though* an adjusting entry affecting one of the accounts involved in the transaction has intervened. We can see this concept best by looking at an example.

Suppose there's an adjusting entry for accrued wages owed to employees at the end of the fiscal year. (We talked about this in Chapter 5.) Assume that the employees of a certain firm are paid altogether $200 per day for a five-day week, and that payday occurs every Friday throughout the year. When the employees get their checks at 5:00 P.M. on Friday, the checks include their wages for that day as well as the preceding four days. And say that one year the last day of the fiscal period happens to fall on Wednesday, December 31. A diagram of this situation would look like this.

Mon	Tue	Wed	Thur	Dec. 26 Fri	Dec. 29 Mon	Dec. 30 Tue	Dec. 31 Wed	Jan. 1 Thur	Jan. 2 Fri
200	200	200	200	200	200	200	200	200	200

←————————Payroll period————————→ ←————————Payroll period————————→

Payday $1,000   Accrued $600   Payday $1,000

Each Friday during the year, the payroll has been debited to the Wages Expense account and credited to the Cash account. As a result, Wages Expense has a debit balance of $51,400. Here is the adjusting entry in T account form.

Wages Expense		Wages Payable	
+	−	−	+
Bal. 51,400			Dec. 31 Adj. 600
Dec. 31 Adj. 600			

As part of the closing process, the accountant clears the Wages Expense account, which yields a zero balance. However, the Wages Payable account continues to have a credit balance. In this case, there is only one way out. The $1,000 payroll on January 2 must be recorded as a debit of $600 to Wages Payable, a debit of $400 to Wages Expense, and a credit of $1,000 to Cash. The employee who records the payroll not only has to record this particular payroll differently from all other weekly payrolls for the year, but also has to refer back to the adjusting entry to determine what portion of the $1,000 is debited to Wages Payable and what portion is debited to Wages Expense. In many companies, however, the employee who records the payroll does not have access to the adjusting entries.

There is a solution to this problem. The need to refer to the earlier entry and divide the debit total between the two accounts is eliminated *if a reversing entry is made on the first day of the following fiscal period.* One makes an entry that is the exact reverse of the adjusting entry, as follows.

GENERAL JOURNAL   PAGE 118

	DATE		DESCRIPTION	POST. REF.	DEBIT	CREDIT	
1			*Reversing Entries*				1
2	19– Jan.	1	Wages Payable		6 0 0 00		2
3			Wages Expense			6 0 0 00	3
4							4

Let us now bring the T accounts up to date.

Wages Expense			
+		**−**	
Bal.	51,400	Dec. 31 Clos.	52,000
Dec. 31 Adj.	600		
		Jan. 1 Rev.	600

Wages Payable			
−		**+**	
Jan. 1 Rev.	600	Dec. 31 Adj.	600

The reversing entry has the effect of transferring the $600 liability from Wages Payable to the credit side of Wages Expense. Wages Expense will temporarily have a credit balance until the next payroll is recorded in the routine manner. In our example this occurs on January 2, for $1,000. Here are the T accounts.

Wages Expense			
+		**−**	
Bal.	51,400	Dec. 31 Clos.	52,000
Dec. 31 Adj.	600		
Jan. 2	1,000	Jan. 1 Rev.	600

Wages Payable			
−		**+**	
Jan. 1 Rev.	600	Dec. 31 Adj.	600

There is now a *net debit balance* of $400 in Wages Expense. To see this, look at the following ledger accounts:

ACCOUNT **Wages Expense**   ACCOUNT NO. **514**

	DATE		ITEM	POST. REF.	DEBIT	CREDIT	BALANCE DEBIT	BALANCE CREDIT	
1	19– Dec.	26		CP16	1 0 0 0 00		51 4 0 0 00		1
2		31	Adjusting	J116	6 0 0 00		52 0 0 0 00		2
3		31	Closing	J117		52 0 0 0 00	— — — —	— — — —	3
4	19– Jan.	1	Reversing	J118		6 0 0 00		6 0 0 00	4
5		2		CP17	1 0 0 0 00		4 0 0 00		5
6									6

ACCOUNT **Wages Payable**   ACCOUNT NO. **213**

	DATE		ITEM	POST. REF.	DEBIT	CREDIT	BALANCE DEBIT	BALANCE CREDIT	
1	19– Dec.	31	Adjusting	J116		6 0 0 00		6 0 0 00	1
2	19– Jan.	1	Reversing	J118	6 0 0 00		— — —	— — —	2
3									3

The reversing entry for accrued salaries or wages applies to service companies as well as to merchandising ones. You can see that a reversing entry simply switches around an adjusting entry. The question is, Which adjusting entries should be reversed? Here's a handy rule of thumb that will help you decide.

If an adjusting entry increases an asset account or liability account that does not have a previous balance, then reverse the adjusting entry.

Objective 5

Determine which adjusting entries should be reversed.

With the exception of the first year of operations, Merchandise Inventory and contra accounts—such as Accumulated Depreciation—always have previous balances. Consequently, adjusting entries involving these accounts should never be reversed.

Let's apply this rule to the adjusting entries for C. L. Frederickson Plumbing Supply.

Income Summary	
Adj. 63,000	

Merchandise Inventory	
+	−
Bal. 63,000	Adj. 63,000

(Do not reverse; Merchandise Inventory is an asset, but it has a previous balance.)

Merchandise Inventory	
+	−
Bal. 63,000	Adj. 63,000
Adj. 58,800	

Income Summary	
Adj. 63,000	Adj. 58,800

(Do not reverse; Merchandise Inventory is an asset, but it has a previous balance.)

Course Fees Income	
−	+
	Adj. 600

Unearned Course Fees	
−	+
Adj. 600	Bal. 900

(Do not reverse; Unearned Course Fees is a liability, but it was decreased. Also, it had a previous balance.)

Supplies Expense	
+	−
Adj. 1,028	

Supplies	
+	−
Bal. 1,440	Adj. 1,028

(Do not reverse; Supplies is an asset account, but it was decreased. Also, it had a previous balance.)

Insurance Expense			Prepaid Insurance		
+	−		+	−	
Adj. 320			Bal. 960	Adj. 320	

(Do not reverse; Prepaid Insurance is an asset account, but it was decreased. Also, it had a previous balance.)

Depreciation Expense, Equipment			Accumulated Depreciation, Equipment		
+	−		−	+	
Adj. 4,800				Bal. 16,400	
				Adj. 4,800	

(Do not reverse; Accumulated Depreciation is a contra asset, and it always has a previous balance after the first year.)

Depreciation Expense, Building			Accumulated Depreciation, Building		
+	−		−	+	
Adj. 4,000				Bal. 32,000	
				Adj. 4,000	

(Do not reverse; Accumulated Depreciation is a contra asset, and it always has a previous balance after the first year.)

Wages Expense			Wages Payable		
+	−		−	+	
Bal. 45,800				Adj. 1,220	
Adj. 1,220					

(Reverse; Wages Payable is a liability account. It was increased and it had no previous balance.)

Whenever we introduce additional adjusting entries, we'll make it a point to state whether they should be reversed.

OTHER WAYS OF RECORDING ADJUSTING ENTRIES

Recording Prepaid Expenses Originally as Expenses

In order to enlarge your experience in bookkeeping practices, it should be mentioned that some accountants record certain prepaid expenses (items that will be eventually used up or expire) originally as expenses. Examples are payments for supplies and insurance. Look at the following examples.

On May 2, a firm bought $265 of supplies, paying cash.

Supplies Expense			Cash		
+	–		+	–	
May 2 265				May 2 265	

On July 1, paid $360 as a premium on liability insurance policy for thirty-six months.

Insurance Expense			Cash		
+	–		+	–	
Jul. 1 360				Jul. 1 360	

By December 31, the end of the fiscal period, $130 of supplies are left over, and $300 of insurance is unexpired. Consequently, the following adjusting entries are required.

Supplies Expense			Supplies		
+	–		+	–	
May 2 265	Dec. 31 Adj. 130		Dec. 31 Adj. 130		

Insurance Expense			Prepaid Insurance		
+	–		+	–	
Jul. 1 360	Dec. 31 Adj. 300		Dec. 31 Adj. 300		

Since these adjusting entries open up new balance sheet accounts, reversing entries are required. However, in this text, we will follow the policy of recording prepaid expenses originally as assets. In other words, record the buying of supplies as a debit to Supplies and then adjust for the amount of supplies used up. Also, record the purchase of insurance as a debit to Prepaid Insurance and then adjust for the amount of insurance expired.

Recording Unearned Revenue Originally as Revenue

Some accountants record unearned revenue (revenue received in advance) originally as revenue. Look at the following example.

An ice skating rink sold $14,320 of season tickets in advance.

Cash			Season Ticket Sales	
+	−		−	+
Sep. 30 14,320				Sep. 30 14,320

By December 31, the end of the fiscal period, $10,080 of the season ticket sales are unearned. Consequently, the adjusting entry is

Season Ticket Sales			Unearned Season Tickets	
−	+		−	+
Dec. 31 Adj. 10,080	Sep. 30 14,320			Dec. 31 Adj. 10,080

Since the adjusting entry opens up a new balance sheet account, a reversing entry is required. Nevertheless, we will follow the policy of recording unearned revenue as a liability. In other words, record the revenue received in advance as a credit to an unearned revenue account and then adjust for the amount earned.

GLOSSARY

Cost of Merchandise Sold Merchandise Inventory at beginning of fiscal period, plus net purchases, minus Merchandise Inventory at end of fiscal period. Terms often used to describe the same thing are *cost of goods sold* and *cost of sales*.

Merchandise Inventory (beginning)
Plus Net Purchases

Merchandise Available for Sale
Less Merchandise Inventory (ending)

Cost of Merchandise Sold

Current assets Cash and any other assets or resources that are expected to be realized in cash or sold or consumed during the normal operating cycle of the business (or one year if the normal operating cycle is less than twelve months).

Current liabilities Debts that are due within the normal operating cycle of a business, usually within one year, and that are normally paid from current assets.

Current ratio A firm's current assets divided by its current liabilities. Portrays a firm's short-term-debt-paying ability.

General expenses Expenses incurred in the administration of a business, including office expenses and any expenses that are not wholly classified as Selling Expenses or Other Expenses.

Gross profit Net Sales minus Cost of Merchandise Sold, or profit before deducting expenses.

Net Sales
Less Cost of Merchandise Sold

Gross Profit

Liquidity The ability of an asset to be quickly turned into cash, either by selling it or by putting it up as security for a loan.

Long-term liabilities Debts that you don't have to pay right away; they can be paid over a comparatively long period, usually more than one year.

Net income The final figure on an income statement after all expenses have been deducted from revenues. Also called *net profit*.

Net purchases Total purchases minus both Purchases Returns and Allowances and Purchases Discount.

Purchases
Less Purchases Returns and Allowances
Less Purchases Discount

Net Purchases

Net sales Sales, minus Sales Returns and Allowances and minus Sales Discount.

Sales
Less Sales Returns and Allowances
Less Sales Discount

Net Sales

Notes receivable (current) Written promises to pay received from customers and due in a period of less than one year.

Plant and equipment Long-lived assets that are held for use in the production or sale of other assets or services. They may also be called *fixed assets*.

Reversing entries The reverse of certain adjusting entries, recorded as of the first day of the following fiscal year.

Selling expenses Expenses directly related to the sale of merchandise, such as salaries of sales staff, advertising expenses, and delivery expenses.

Temporary-equity accounts Accounts whose balances apply to one fiscal period only, such as revenues, expenses, and the Drawing account. Temporary-equity accounts are also called *nominal accounts*.

Working capital The excess of a firm's current assets over its current liabilities. Portrays the amount of capital a firm has to work with during a normal operating cycle.

QUESTIONS, EXERCISES, AND PROBLEMS

Discussion Questions

1. In the closing procedure, what happens to Purchases Discount?
2. What is the difference between current liabilities and long-term liabilities? Give an example of each.
3. In this chapter, the Adjusted Trial Balance columns of a work sheet have been omitted. Does this affect the use of the work sheet? Explain.
4. Describe how to calculate the cost of merchandise sold.
5. What is the correct order for listing accounts in the Current Assets section of the balance sheet?
6. What is the correct order for listing accounts in the Plant and Equipment section of a balance sheet?
7. What rule is used to recognize whether or not an adjusting entry should be reversed?

Exercises

Exercise 15-1 Identify each of the following as (1) a current asset, (2) plant ,property and equipment, (3) a current liability, (4) a long-term liability, (5) an owner's equity item.

a. Land - 2
b. Wages Payable - 3
c. Mortgage Payable (due June 30, 1994) - 4
d. Store Equipment - 2
e. Notes Payable (current) - 3

f. Accounts Receivable - 1
g. Building - 2
h. Darlene Foss, Capital - 5
i. Cash - 1
j. Mortgage Payable (current portion) - 3

Exercise 15-2 Organize the following as they appear in the Cost of Merchandise Sold section of an income statement. Determine the cost of merchandise sold.

Purchases Returns and Allowances	$ 4,000
Ending Merchandise Inventory	63,000
Purchases Discount	3,000
Purchases	190,000
Beginning Merchandise Inventory	60,000

Exercise 15-3 On June 30, the following selected accounts and amounts appeared in the balance sheet. Determine the amount of the working capital and the current ratio.

Accounts Payable	$ 8,000	Wages Payable	$ 4,000
Store Supplies	900	Merchandise Inventory	46,000
Henry Drew, Capital	52,000	Notes Payable	10,000
Store Equipment	16,000	Accumulated Depreciation,	
Prepaid Insurance	600	Store Equipment	12,000
Cash	3,000		

Exercise 15-4 From the following T accounts, record the closing entries.

Sales		Salary Expense		Sales Returns and Allowances	
	100,000	16,000		2,000	

Rent Expense		Purchases		Miscellaneous Expense	
6,000		60,000		6,300	

Purchases Returns and Allowances		J. Cole, Drawing		Purchases Discount	
	1,500	16,000			1,800

J. Cole, Capital		Income Summary	
	87,000	22,000	26,000

Exercise 15-5 Calculate the missing items in the following.

	Sales	Sales Returns and Allowances	Net Sales	Beginning Inventory	Net Purchases	Merchandise Available	Ending Inventory	Cost of Merchandise Sold	Gross Profit
a	$62,000	$1,500	60,500	$37,000	$42,500	$ 79,500	$34,000	$45,500	15,000
b	76,000	2,000	$ 74,000	36,000	65,000	101,000	49,000	52,000	13,000
c	160,000	3,000	157,000	21,000	103,000	124,000	23,000	101,000	$56,000

Exercise 15-6 From the following information, present a statement of owner's equity.

D. C. Collier, Capital			D. C. Collier, Drawing		
16,500	Bal.	60,000	Bal.	16,500	Closing 16,500
		18,000			

Income Summary			
Adj.	48,000	Adj.	51,000
	105,000		120,000
Closing	18,000		

Exercise 15-7 Arrange the following accounts as they would appear in the Current Assets section of the balance sheet.

Supplies	$ 410	Prepaid Insurance	$ 360
Accounts Receivable	18,000	Notes Receivable (current)	2,400
Merchandise Inventory	36,000	Prepaid Advertising	220
Cash	6,900		

Exercise 15-8 The Income Statement columns of the December 31 (year end) work sheet for the Conroy Company appear below. From the information given, prepare an income statement for the company.

ACCOUNT NAME	INCOME STATEMENT	
	DEBIT	CREDIT
Income Summary	26 0 0 0 00	22 0 0 0 00
Sales		284 0 0 0 00
Sales Returns and Allowances	11 0 0 0 00	
Sales Discount	4 2 0 0 00	
Purchases	122 9 0 0 00	
Purchases Returns and Allowances		1 8 0 0 00
Purchases Discount		2 2 0 0 00
Selling Expenses	48 5 0 0 00	
General Expenses	37 2 0 0 00	
	249 8 0 0 00	310 0 0 0 00
Net Income	60 2 0 0 00	
	310 0 0 0 00	310 0 0 0 00

Problem Set A

Problem 15-1A A partial work sheet for Sinclair Craft and Hobby Shop is presented below. The merchandise inventory at the beginning of the fiscal period is $24,792. C. A. Sinclair, the owner, withdrew $16,400 during the year.

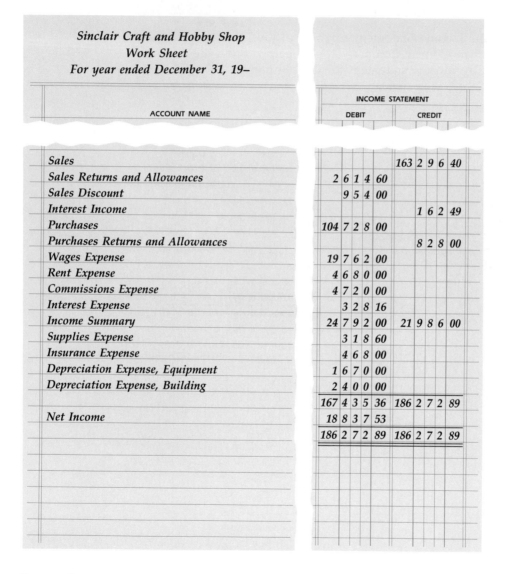

ACCOUNT NAME	INCOME STATEMENT	
	DEBIT	CREDIT
Sales		163 2 9 6 40
Sales Returns and Allowances	2 6 1 4 60	
Sales Discount	9 5 4 00	
Interest Income		1 6 2 49
Purchases	104 7 2 8 00	
Purchases Returns and Allowances		8 2 8 00
Wages Expense	19 7 6 2 00	
Rent Expense	4 6 8 0 00	
Commissions Expense	4 7 2 0 00	
Interest Expense	3 2 8 16	
Income Summary	24 7 9 2 00	21 9 8 6 00
Supplies Expense	3 1 8 60	
Insurance Expense	4 6 8 00	
Depreciation Expense, Equipment	1 6 7 0 00	
Depreciation Expense, Building	2 4 0 0 00	
	167 4 3 5 36	186 2 7 2 89
Net Income	18 8 3 7 53	
	186 2 7 2 89	186 2 7 2 89

Instructions

1. Prepare an income statement.
2. Journalize the closing entries.

Problem 15-2A The following partial work sheet is for Randolph Fine Shoes.

Randolph Fine Shoes
Work Sheet
For year ended December 31, 19–

ACCOUNT NAME	BALANCE SHEET DEBIT	BALANCE SHEET CREDIT
Cash	6 4 8 2 00	
Notes Receivable	2 4 0 0 00	
Accounts Receivable	28 5 8 6 40	
Merchandise Inventory	37 7 9 8 00	
Supplies	3 1 6 00	
Prepaid Taxes	4 0 9 00	
Prepaid Insurance	4 2 0 00	
Delivery Equipment	3 7 1 0 00	
Accumulated Depreciation, Delivery Equipment		2 8 7 0 00
Store Equipment	4 3 8 0 00	
Accumulated Depreciation, Store Equipment		3 3 3 0 00
Office Equipment	3 6 1 6 00	
Accumulated Depreciation, Office Equipment		2 7 8 0 00
Building	42 0 0 0 00	
Accumulated Depreciation, Building		14 4 0 0 00
Land	5 6 0 0 00	
Notes Payable		3 6 2 0 00
Accounts Payable		19 7 2 7 80
Mortgage Payable (current portion)		1 8 0 0 00
Mortgage Payable		37 1 4 2 00
L. P. Randolph, Capital		43 3 7 2 60
L. P. Randolph, Drawing	16 7 9 6 00	
Wages Payable		8 5 2 00
	152 5 1 3 40	129 8 9 4 40
Net Income		22 6 1 9 00
	152 5 1 3 40	152 5 1 3 40

Instructions

1. Prepare a statement of owner's equity (no additional investment).
2. Prepare a balance sheet.
3. Determine the amount of working capital.
4. Determine the current ratio (carry to one decimal place).

The following partial work sheet covers the affairs of Padrow and Company for the year ended June 30.

Padrow and Company
Work Sheet
For year ended June 30, 19–

	ACCOUNT NAME	INCOME STATEMENT DEBIT	INCOME STATEMENT CREDIT	BALANCE SHEET DEBIT	BALANCE SHEET CREDIT	
1	Cash			16 192 17		1
2	Accounts Receivable			52 317 27		2
3	Merchandise Inventory			59 728 00		3
4	Supplies			516 00		4
5	Prepaid Insurance			660 00		5
6	Delivery Equipment			6 460 00		6
7	Accumulated Depreciation, Delivery					7
8	Equipment				3 240 00	8
9	Store Equipment			18 250 00		9
10	Accumulated Depreciation, Store					10
11	Equipment				5 180 00	11
12	Accounts Payable				33 718 67	12
13	Salaries Payable				426 00	13
14	T. L. Padrow, Capital				99 961 29	14
15	T. L. Padrow, Drawing			20 720 72		15
16	Income Summary	57 613 00	59 728 00			16
17	Sales		268 176 20			17
18	Purchases	208 640 00				18
19	Purchases Returns and Allowances		3 914 00			19
20	Purchases Discount		2 873 00			20
21	Salary Expense	25 700 00				21
22	Truck Expense	4 671 00				22
23	Supplies Expense	1 282 00				23
24	Depreciation Expense, Delivery					24
25	Equipment	1 350 00				25
26	Depreciation Expense, Store					26
27	Equipment	1 448 00				27
28	Insurance Expense	960 00				28
29	Miscellaneous Expense	709 00				29
30		302 373 00	334 691 20	174 844 16	142 525 96	30
31	Net Income	32 318 20			32 318 20	31
32		334 691 20	334 691 20	174 844 16	174 844 16	32
33						33
34						34
35						35
36						36
37						37
38						38

Instructions

1. Journalize the adjusting entries.
2. Journalize the closing entries.
3. Journalize the reversing entry.

Problem 15-4A The following accounts appear in the ledger of the Andrczi Company as of December 31, the end of this fiscal year.

Cash	$ 2,900	Sales	$148,420
Accounts Receivable	9,940	Sales Returns and Allowances	1,760
Merchandise Inventory	34,320	Purchases	97,540
Store Supplies	490	Purchases Returns and	
Prepaid Insurance	650	Allowances	2,930
Store Equipment	19,760	Purchases Discount	1,710
Accumulated Depreciation,		Wages Expense	15,400
Store Equipment	1,920	Advertising Expense	2,100
Accounts Payable	6,990	Depreciation Expense,	
Wages Payable	—	Store Equipment	—
P. A. Andrezi, Capital	48,130	Store Supplies Expense	—
P. A. Andrezi, Drawing	18,840	Rent Expense	6,400
Income Summary	—	Insurance Expense	—

The data needed for adjustments on December 31 are as follows.

a–b. Merchandise inventory, December 31, $32,160
  c. Store supplies inventory, December 31, $180
  d. Insurance expired for the year, $420
  e. Depreciation for the year, $860
  f. Accrued wages on December 31, $110

Instructions

1. Prepare a work sheet for the fiscal year ended December 31.
2. Prepare an income statement.
3. Prepare a statement of owner's equity.
4. Prepare a balance sheet.
5. Journalize the adjusting entries.
6. Journalize the closing entries.
7. Journalize the reversing entry.

PROBLEM SET B

Problem 15-1B A partial work sheet for Sturgis Garden Shop is presented below. The merchandise inventory at the beginning of the fiscal period is $26,600. R. E. Sturgis, the owner, withdrew $12,200 during the year.

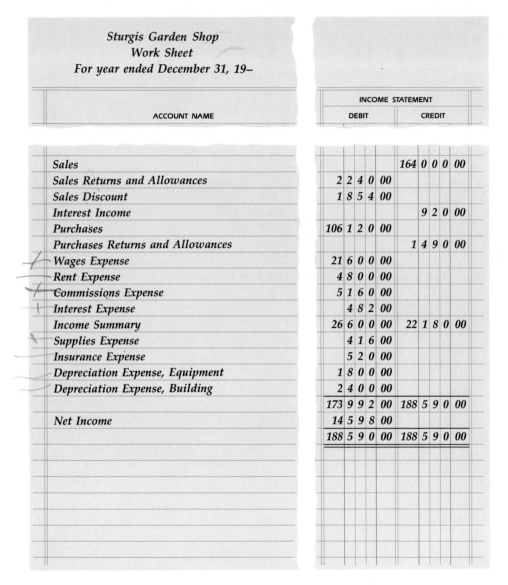

Sturgis Garden Shop
Work Sheet
For year ended December 31, 19–

ACCOUNT NAME	INCOME STATEMENT	
	DEBIT	CREDIT
Sales		164 0 0 0 00
Sales Returns and Allowances	2 2 4 0 00	
Sales Discount	1 8 5 4 00	
Interest Income		9 2 0 00
Purchases	106 1 2 0 00	
Purchases Returns and Allowances		1 4 9 0 00
Wages Expense	21 6 0 0 00	
Rent Expense	4 8 0 0 00	
Commissions Expense	5 1 6 0 00	
Interest Expense	4 8 2 00	
Income Summary	26 6 0 0 00	22 1 8 0 00
Supplies Expense	4 1 6 00	
Insurance Expense	5 2 0 00	
Depreciation Expense, Equipment	1 8 0 0 00	
Depreciation Expense, Building	2 4 0 0 00	
	173 9 9 2 00	188 5 9 0 00
Net Income	14 5 9 8 00	
	188 5 9 0 00	188 5 9 0 00

Instructions

1. Prepare an income statement.
2. Journalize the closing entries.

Problem 15-2B A partial work sheet for Heinrich Garden Supply appears below.

ACCOUNT NAME	BALANCE SHEET			
	DEBIT		CREDIT	
Cash	8 6 1 0 00			
Notes Receivable	4 2 0 0 00			
Accounts Receivable	22 1 8 0 00			
Merchandise Inventory	36 8 9 6 00			
Supplies	2 8 0 00			
Prepaid Taxes	4 2 0 00			
Prepaid Insurance	3 6 0 00			
Delivery Equipment	3 6 0 0 00			
Accumulated Depreciation, Delivery Equipment			2 9 8 0 00	
Testing Equipment	4 8 2 0 00			
Accumulated Depreciation, Testing Equipment			3 6 1 6 00	
Store Equipment	2 9 2 8 00			
Accumulated Depreciation, Store Equipment			1 1 1 6 00	
Building	40 0 0 0 00			
Accumulated Depreciation, Building			12 6 0 0 00	
Land	5 2 0 0 00			
Notes Payable			2 8 1 0 00	
Accounts Payable			18 7 6 0 00	
Mortgage Payable (current portion)			1 2 0 0 00	
Mortgage Payable			36 8 0 0 00	
D. L. Heinrich, Capital			44 8 7 6 00	
D. L. Heinrich, Drawing	14 9 6 0 00			
Wages Payable			6 5 6 00	
	144 4 5 4 00		125 4 1 4 00	
Net Income			19 0 4 0 00	
	144 4 5 4 00		144 4 5 4 00	

Heinrich Garden Supply
Work Sheet
For year ended December 31, 19–

Instructions

1. Prepare a statement of owner's equity (no additional investment).
2. Prepare a balance sheet.
3. Determine the amount of working capital.
4. Determine the current ratio (carry to one decimal place).

Problem 15-3B The partial work sheet for Ralston and Company for the year ended June 30 is as follows.

Ralston and Company
Work Sheet
For year ended June 30, 19–

	ACCOUNT NAME	INCOME STATEMENT		BALANCE SHEET		
		DEBIT	CREDIT	DEBIT	CREDIT	
1	Cash			14 1 0 0 00		1
2	Accounts Receivable			46 0 0 0 00		2
3	Merchandise Inventory			56 2 0 0 00		3
4	Supplies			4 2 0 00		4
5	Prepaid Insurance			6 1 0 00		5
6	Delivery Equipment			6 2 0 0 00		6
7	Accumulated Depreciation, Delivery					7
8	Equipment				2 9 0 0 00	8
9	Store Equipment			16 7 0 0 00		9
10	Accumulated Depreciation, Store					10
11	Equipment				4 8 0 0 00	11
12	Accounts Payable				30 1 0 0 00	12
13	Salaries Payable				6 2 0 00	13
14	M. A. Ralston, Capital				83 9 1 0 00	14
15	M. A. Ralston, Drawing			14 0 0 0 00		15
16	Income Summary	54 6 0 0 00	56 2 0 0 00			16
17	Sales		260 0 0 0 00			17
18	Purchases	202 0 0 0 00				18
19	Purchases Returns and Allowances		3 8 0 0 00			19
20	Purchases Discount		2 4 0 0 00			20
21	Salary Expense	24 0 0 0 00				21
22	Truck Expense	4 3 0 0 00				22
23	Supplies Expense	1 1 0 0 00				23
24	Depreciation Expense, Delivery					24
25	Equipment	1 2 0 0 00				25
26	Depreciation Expense, Store					26
27	Equipment	1 4 0 0 00				27
28	Insurance Expense	9 2 0 00				28
29	Miscellaneous Expense	9 8 0 00				29
30		290 5 0 0 00	322 4 0 0 00	154 2 3 0 00	122 3 3 0 00	30
31	Net Income	31 9 0 0 00			31 9 0 0 00	31
32		322 4 0 0 00	322 4 0 0 00	154 2 3 0 00	154 2 3 0 00	32
33						33

Instructions

1. Journalize the seven adjusting entries.
2. Journalize the closing entries.
3. Journalize the reversing entry.

Problem 15-4B The following accounts appear in the ledger of the Simmons Company on December 31, the end of this fiscal year.

Cash	$ 3,600	Sales	$156,000
Accounts Receivable	9,400	Sales Returns and Allowances	2,000
Merchandise Inventory	37,000	Purchases	98,000
Store Supplies	460	Purchases Returns	
Prepaid Insurance	720	and Allowances	2,300
Store Equipment	18,600	Purchases Discount	1,600
Accumulated Depreciation,		Wages Expense	16,000
Store Equipment	1,800	Advertising Expense	2,600
Accounts Payable	7,200	Depreciation Expense,	
Wages Payable	—	Store Equipment	—
C. R. Simmons, Capital	49,080	Store Supplies Expense	—
C. R. Simmons, Drawing	24,000	Rent Expense	5,600
Income Summary	—	Insurance Expense	—

The data needed for adjustments on December 31 are as follows.

a–b. Merchandise inventory, December 31, $35,600
  c. Store supplies inventory, December 31, $260
  d. Insurance expired, $410
  e. Depreciation for the year, $930
  f. Accrued wages on December 31, $180

Instructions

1. Prepare a work sheet for the fiscal year ended December 31.
2. Prepare an income statement.
3. Prepare a statement of owner's equity.
4. Prepare a balance sheet.
5. Journalize the adjusting entries.
6. Journalize the closing entries.
7. Journalize the reversing entry.

APPENDIX C

Financial Statement Analysis

An important function of accounting is to provide tools for interpreting the financial statements or the results of operations. This appendix presents a number of percentages and ratios that are frequently used for analyzing financial statements.

Midwest Clothiers will serve as our example (see comparative income statement at top of next page).

For each year, net sales is the base (100 percent). Every other item on the income statement can be expressed as a percentage of net sales for the particular year involved. For example, let's look at the following percentages:

Midwest Clothiers
Comparative Income Statement
For years ended January 31, 19x6 and January 31, 19x5

	19x6		19x5	
	AMOUNT	PERCENT	AMOUNT	PERCENT
Revenue from Sales:				
Sales	$ 453 6 0 0 00	106	$ 420 0 0 0 00	105
Less Sales Returns and Allowances	25 6 0 0 00	6	20 0 0 0 00	5
Net Sales	$ 428 0 0 0 00	100	$ 400 0 0 0 00	100
Cost of Merchandise Sold:				
Merchandise Inventory, February 1	$ 116 0 0 0 00	27	$ 64 0 0 0 00	16
Purchases (net)	320 0 0 0 00	75	300 0 0 0 00	75
Merchandise Available for Sale	$ 436 0 0 0 00	102	$ 364 0 0 0 00	91
Less Merchandise Inventory,				
January 31	158 0 0 0 00	37	116 0 0 0 00	29
Cost of Merchandise Sold	$ 278 0 0 0 00	65	$ 248 0 0 0 00	62
Gross Profit	$ 150 0 0 0 00	35	$ 152 0 0 0 00	38
Operating Expenses:				
Sales Salary Expense	$ 63 6 0 0 00	14.86	$ 58 0 0 0 00	14.5
Rent Expense	24 0 0 0 00	5.61	24 0 0 0 00	6
Advertising Expense	21 4 0 0 00	5	16 0 0 0 00	4
Office Salary Expense	20 0 0 0 00	4.61	18 0 0 0 00	4.5
Insurance Expense	2 0 0 0 00	.46	2 0 0 0 00	.5
Store Supplies Expense	1 0 0 0 00	.23	1 0 0 0 00	.25
Miscellaneous Expense	1 0 0 0 00	.23	1 0 0 0 00	.25
Total Operating Expenses	$ 133 0 0 0 00	31	$ 120 0 0 0 00	30
Net Income	$ 17 0 0 0 00	4	$ 32 0 0 0 00	8

$$\text{Gross profit \% (19x6)} = \frac{\text{Gross profit for 19x6}}{\text{Net sales for 19x6}} = \frac{\$150,000}{\$428,000} = .35 = 35\%$$

$$\text{Gross profit \% (19x5)} = \frac{\text{Gross profit for 19x5}}{\text{Net sales for 19x5}} = \frac{\$152,000}{\$400,000} = .38 = 38\%$$

$$\text{Sales salary expense (19x6)} = \frac{\text{Sales salary expense for 19x6}}{\text{Net sales for 19x6}}$$

$$= \frac{\$63,600}{\$428,000} = .1486 = 14.86\%$$

$$\text{Sales salary expense (19x5)} = \frac{\text{Sales salary expense for 19x5}}{\text{Net sales for 19x6}}$$

$$= \frac{\$58,000}{\$400,000} = .145 = 14.5\%$$

Here's how one might interpret a few of the percentages.

19x6

- For every $100 in net sales, gross profit amounted to $35.
- For every $100 in net sales, sales salary expense amounted to $14.86.
- For every $100 in net sales, net income amounted to $4.

19x5

- For every $100 in net sales, gross profit amounted to $38.
- For every $100 in net sales, sales salary expense amounted to $14.50.
- For every $100 in net sales, net income amounted to $8.

Merchandise Inventory Turnover

Merchandise inventory turnover is the number of times a firm's average inventory is sold during a given year.

$$\text{Merchandise inventory turnover} = \frac{\text{Cost of merchandise sold}}{\text{Average merchandise inventory}}$$

Average merchandise inventory

$$= \frac{\text{Beginning merchandise inventory} + \text{Ending merchandise inventory}}{2}$$

19x6

$$\text{Average merchandise inventory} = \frac{\$116{,}000 + \$158{,}000}{2}$$

$$= \frac{\$274{,}000}{2} = \$137{,}000$$

$$\text{Merchandise inventory turnover} = \frac{\$278{,}000}{\$137{,}000} = 2.03 \text{ times per year}$$

19x5

$$\text{Average merchandise inventory} = \frac{\$64{,}000 + \$116{,}000}{2}$$

$$= \frac{\$180{,}000}{2} = \$90{,}000$$

$$\text{Merchandise inventory turnover} = \frac{\$248{,}000}{\$90{,}000} = 2.76 \text{ times per year}$$

With each turnover of merchandise, the company makes a gross profit; so the higher the turnover the better.

Accounts Receivable Turnover

Accounts receivable turnover is the number of times charge accounts are turned over (paid off) during a given year. A turnover implies a sales on account followed by payment of the debt.

$$\text{Accounts receivable turnover} = \frac{\text{Net sales on account}}{\text{Average accounts receivable}}$$

Average accounts receivable

$$= \frac{\text{Beginning accounts receivable} + \text{Ending accounts receivable}}{2}$$

Going back to Midwest Clothiers, let's assume the following information for 19x6 and 19x5:

	19x6	19x5
Net sales on account (from the sales journal)	$330,000	$302,000
Beginning accounts receivable (from Accounts Receivable account)	$39,680	$37,500
Ending accounts receivable (from Accounts Receivable account)	$45,840	$39,680

19x6

$$\text{Average accounts receivable} = \frac{\$39,680 + \$45,840}{2} = \frac{\$85,520}{2} = \$42,760$$

$$\text{Accounts receivable turnover} = \frac{\$330,000}{\$42,760} = 7.72 \text{ times per year}$$

19x5

$$\text{Average accounts receivable} = \frac{\$37,500 + \$39,680}{2} = \frac{\$77,180}{2} = \$38,590$$

$$\text{Accounts receivable turnover} = \frac{\$302,000}{\$38,590} = 7.83 \text{ times per year}$$

A lower turnover rate indicates greater difficulty in collecting charge accounts. In addition, more investment capital is tied up in accounts receivable.

Return on Investment (Yield)

Return on investment represents the earning power of the owner's investment in the business.

$$\text{Return on investment} = \frac{\text{Net income for the year}}{\text{Average capital}}$$

$$\text{Average capital} = \frac{\text{Beginning capital} + \text{Ending capital}}{2}$$

Getting back to Midwest Clothiers, let's assume the following information for 19x6 and 19x5:

	19x6	19x5
Beginning balance of owner's Capital account	$176,920	$181,440
Ending balance of owner's Capital account	$184,780	$176,920

19x6

$$\text{Average capital} = \frac{\$176{,}920 + \$184{,}780}{2} = \frac{\$361{,}700}{2} = \$180{,}850$$

$$\text{Return on investment} = \frac{\$17{,}000}{\$180{,}850} = .094 = 9.4\%$$

19x5

$$\text{Average capital} = \frac{\$181{,}440 + \$176{,}920}{2} = \frac{\$358{,}360}{2} = \$179{,}180$$

$$\text{Return on investment} = \frac{\$32{,}000}{\$179{,}180} = .179 = 17.9\%$$

As a result, we can state the following:

- In 19x6, for an average investment of $100, the business earned $9.40.
- In 19x5, for an average investment of $100, the business earned $17.90.

Problems

Problem C-1 Grabo Company's abbreviated comparative income statement for years 19x6 and 19x5 is as follows.

Grabo Company
Comparative Income Statement
For years ended December 31, 19x6, and December 31, 19x5

	19x6	19x5
Net Sales	$ 232 0 0 0 00	$ 220 0 0 0 00
Cost of Merchandise Sold	136 8 8 0 00	132 0 0 0 00
Gross Profit	$ 95 1 2 0 00	$ 88 0 0 0 00
Total Operating Expenses	69 6 0 0 00	61 6 0 0 00
Net Income	$ 25 5 2 0 00	$ 26 4 0 0 00

Instructions

a. For the years 19x6 and 19x5, determine gross profit as a percentage of sales.
b. For the years 19x6 and 19x5, determine net income as a percentage of sales.

Problem C-2 Grabo Company's merchandise inventory figures are:

	19x6	19x5
Beginning merchandise inventory (January 1)	$31,580	$37,894
Ending merchandise inventory (December 31)	$36,860	$31,580

Determine the merchandise inventory turnover for the years 19x6 and 19x5.

Problem C-3 N. C. Grabo, Capital account balances are as follows.

January 1, 19x5	$134,168
January 1, 19x6	$176,420
December 31, 19x6	$188,152

Determine the return on capital for the years 19x6 and 19x5.

REVIEW OF T-ACCOUNT PLACEMENT AND REPRESENTATIVE TRANSACTIONS CHAPTERS 11–15

Review of T-Account Placement

The following sums up the placement of T accounts covered in Chapters 11 through 15 in relation to the fundamental accounting equation. Color indicates those accounts that are treated as deductions from the related accounts above them.

Assets		=	Liabilities		+	Owner's Equity		+	Revenue		–	Expenses	
+	–		–	+		–	+		–	+		+	–
Debit	Credit		Debit	Credit		Debit	Credit		Debit	Credit		Debit	Credit

Merchandise Inventory									Sales			and Purchases	
+	–								–	+		+	–

Sales Returns and Allowances — Purchases Returns and Allowances

									Sales Returns and Allowances			Purchases Returns and Allowances	
									+	–		–	+

Sales Discount — Purchases Discount

									Sales Discount			Purchases Discount	
									+	–		–	+

Credit Card Expense

												Credit Card Expense	
												+	–

Review of Representative Transactions

The following table summarizes the recording of transactions covered in Chapters 11 through 15, along with a classification of the accounts involved.

Transaction	Accounts Involved	Class.	Increase or Decrease	Therefore Debit or Credit	Financial Statement
Sold merchandise on account	Accounts Receivable Sales	CA S	I I	Debit Credit	Bal. Sheet Inc. State.
Sold merchandise on account involving sales tax	Accounts Receivable Sales Sales Tax Payable	CA S CL	I I I	Debit Credit Credit	Bal. Sheet Inc. State. Bal. Sheet
Issued credit memo to customer for merchandise returned	Sales Returns and Allowances Accounts Receivable	S CA	I D	Debit Credit	Inc. State. Bal. Sheet
Summarizing entry for the total of sales invoices for sales on account for the month	Accounts Receivable Sales	CA S	I I	Debit Credit	Bal. Sheet Inc. State.
Bought merchandise on account	Purchases Accounts Payable	CMS CL	I I	Debit Credit	Inc. State. Bal. Sheet
Received credit memo from supplier for merchandise returned	Accounts Payable Purchases Returns and Allowances	CL CMS	D I	Debit Credit	Bal. Sheet Inc. State.
Summarizing entry for the total of purchases of all types of goods on account	Purchases Store Supplies Office Supplies Store Equipment Accounts Payable	CMS CA CA P&E CL	I I I I I	Debit Debit Debit Debit Credit	Inc. State. Bal. Sheet Bal. Sheet Bal. Sheet Bal. Sheet
Paid for transportation charges on incoming merchandise	Purchases Cash	CMS CA	I D	Debit Credit	Inc. State. Bal. Sheet

Transaction	Accounts Involved	Class.	Increase or Decrease	Therefore Debit or Credit	Financial Statement

Sold merchandise, involving sales tax, for cash	Cash
	  Sales
	  Sales Tax Payable
		CA
		S
		CL
			I
			I
			I
				Debit
				Credit
				Credit
					Bal. Sheet
					Inc. State.
					Bal. Sheet

Sold merchandise involving a sales tax and the customer used a bank charge card	Cash
	Credit Card Expense
	  Sales
	  Sales Tax Payable
		CA
		SE
		S
		CL
			I
			I
			I
			I
				Debit
				Debit
				Credit
				Credit
					Bal. Sheet
					Inc. State.
					Inc. State.
					Bal. Sheet

Charge customer paid bill within the discount period	Cash Sales Discount Accounts Receivable	CA S CA	I I D	Debit Debit Credit	Bal. Sheet Inc. State. Bal. Sheet

Paid invoice for the purchase of merchandise within the discount period	Accounts Payable
	  Cash
	  Purchases Discount
		CL
		CA
		CMS
			D
			D
			I
				Debit
				Credit
				Credit
					Bal. Sheet
					Bal. Sheet
					Inc. State.

First adjusting entry for merchandise inventory	Income Summary
	  Merchandise
	    Inventory
		—
		CA&
		CMS
			—
			D
				Debit
				Credit
					—
					Bal. Sheet &
					Inc. State.

Second adjusting entry for merchandise inventory	Merchandise
	  Inventory
	  Income Summary
		CA&
		CMS
		—
			I
			—
				Debit
				
				Credit
					Bal. Sheet &
					Inc. State.

Adjusting entry for rent earned (Rent Income)	Unearned Rent Rent Income	CL OI	D I	Debit Credit	Bal. Sheet Inc. State.
Reversing entry for adjustment for accrued wages	Wages Payable Wages Expense	CL SE or GE	D D	Debit Credit	Bal. Sheet Inc. State.

16 Accounting for Notes Payable

Learning Objectives

After you have completed this chapter, you will be able to do the following:

1. Recognize a promissory note.

2. Calculate the interest on promissory notes.

3. Determine the due dates of promissory notes.

4. Make journal entries for
   a. Notes given to secure an extension of time on an open account.
   b. Payment of an interest-bearing note at maturity.
   c. Notes given in exchange for merchandise or other property purchased.
   d. Notes given to secure a cash loan, when the borrower receives full face value of the note.
   e. Notes given to secure a cash loan, when the bank discounts the note.
   f. Renewal of a note at maturity.
   g. Adjustment for accrued interest on notes payable.
   h. Adjustment for prepaid interest on notes payable.

Credit plays an extremely important role in the operation of most business enterprises. We have seen that credit may be extended on a charge-account basis, with payment generally due in 30 days. This type of credit involves the Accounts Payable and Accounts Receivable accounts. Credit may also be granted on the basis of giving or receiving notes for specific transactions. This sort of credit involves the Notes Payable and Notes Receivable accounts. The notes, which represent formal instruments of credit, are known as *promissory notes*. They are customarily used as evidence of credit transactions for periods longer than 60 days. For example, promissory notes may be used in sales of equipment on the installment plan and for transactions involving large amounts of money.

Promissory notes are also used to grant extensions of credit beyond the regular credit terms. For example, suppose that the Smith Company buys merchandise from Parker Brothers on the basis of 2/10, n/30. The Smith Company finds that it can't pay its bill within the 30-day period. To preserve its credit standing, the Smith Company offers a note. The advantages to Parker Brothers are as follows: (1) they now have specific evidence of the transaction, (2) the note may carry interest, and (3) they can borrow from the bank by pledging the note as security for a loan. Business concerns may also borrow from banks by issuing their own promissory notes.

In general, then, most companies at one time or another become involved with notes, either by issuing notes to creditors, receiving notes from customers, or issuing notes to banks in order to borrow money. Consequently, an accountant must be acquainted with the procedures for the handling of promissory notes. In this chapter we shall discuss transactions involving notes payable. Chapter 17 will describe transactions involving notes receivable.

PROMISSORY NOTES

A **promissory note**—usually referred to simply as a *note*—is a written promise to pay a certain sum at a fixed or determinable future time. Like a check, it must be payable to the order of a particular person or firm, known as the **payee.** It must also be signed by the person or firm making the promise, known as the **maker.** In Figure 16-1 Alman Manufacturing Company is the payee, and C. L. Frederickson Plumbing Supply is the maker.

Objective 1

Recognize a promissory note.

Figure 16-1

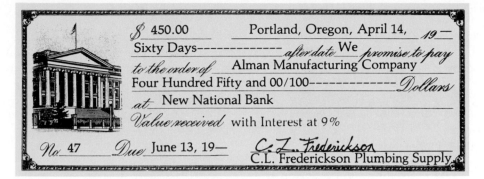

CALCULATING INTEREST

Interest is a charge made for the use of money. To the maker of the note, interest is an expense. The amount of interest a maker pays is expressed as a certain percentage of the principal of the note for a period of one year (or less). The following formula is used to calculate interest.

Interest (in dollars)	=	**Principal** of note (in dollars)	×	**Rate** of interest (as a percentage) of the principal)	×	**Time** of note (expressed as a year or fraction of a year)

Objective 2

Calculate the interest on promissory notes.

The **principal** is the face amount of the note. The *rate of interest* is a percentage of the principal, such as 8 percent or 9 percent. Since 1 percent equals $\frac{1}{100}$ or .01, then 8 percent equals $\frac{8}{100}$ or .08.

Time, or the length of life of the note, is expressed in terms of days or months. It is the period between the date of issue of the note (starting date) and the **maturity date** of the note (the due date or interest payment date). It is stated in terms of a year or fraction of a year. Examples are

$$1 \text{ year} = 1$$
$$6 \text{ months} = \frac{6}{12}$$
$$3 \text{ months} = \frac{3}{12}$$
$$90 \text{ days} = \frac{90}{360}$$
$$24 \text{ days} = \frac{24}{360}$$

The usual commercial practice is to use a 360-day year, thus making the denominator of the fraction 360. However, agencies of the federal government use the actual number of days in the year.

Example 1 $2,000, 8 percent, 1 year.

Interest = Principal × Rate × Time

Interest = $2,000 × .08 × 1 = $160

Example 2 $4,000, 9 percent, 3 months.

Interest = Principal × Rate × Time

Interest = $4,000 × .09 × $\dfrac{3}{12}$

Interest = $4,000 × .09 × 3 ÷ 12 = $90

Example 3 $6,000, 11 percent, 60 days.

Interest = Principal × Rate × Time

Interest = $6,000 × .11 × $\dfrac{60}{360}$

Interest = $6,000 × .11 × 60 ÷ 360 = $110

Example 4 $3,640, 12 percent, 45 days.

Interest = Principal × Rate × Time

Interest = $3,640 × .12 × $\dfrac{45}{360}$

Interest = $3,640 × .12 × 45 ÷ 360 = $54.60

Example 5 $5,684, 8 percent, 23 days.

Interest = Principal × Rate × Time

Interest = $5,684 × .08 × $\dfrac{23}{360}$

Interest = $5,684 × .08 × 23 ÷ 360 = $29.05

Example 6 $6,000, 6 percent, 60-day (shortcut). A variation of the third example, $6,000 at 6 percent for 60 days, shows the following.

Interest = Principal × Rate × Time

Interest = $6,000 × .06 × $\dfrac{60}{360}$

Interest = $6,000 × .06 × 60 ÷ 360 = $60

$60 is 1% of $6,000, or .01 of $6,000.

The interest on any note that runs exactly 60 days and earns interest at exactly 6 percent is always *1 percent of the principal of the note.*

Why have we bothered learning this shortcut? To compute the interest on any given principal for exactly 60 days at exactly 6 percent, one has only to multiply the principal by 1 percent, or .01, or move the decimal point two places to the left: $6,000 \times .01 = 6,0.00 = 60$. The rule also applies to fractions of 60 days, as long as the 6 percent element is held constant. For example,

60 days at 6% interest = 1% of principal
30 days at 6% interest = ½% of principal
45 days at 6% interest = ¾% of principal
90 days at 6% interest = 1½% of principal

Take the case of $8,000 at 6 percent for 90 days.

1% of $8,000	= $ 80.00	(move decimal point two places to the left)
+½% of $8,000	= $ 40.00	(½ of 80)
1½% of $8,000	= $120.00	

The rule also applies to fractions of 6 percent, as long as the 60-day element is held constant. For example,

60 days at 6% interest = 1% of principal
60 days at 12% interest = 2% of principal
60 days at 4% interest = ⅔% of principal
60 days at 7½% interest = 1¼% of principal

Take the case of $12,000 at 7½ percent for 60 days.

1% of $12,000	= $120.00	(move decimal point two places to the left)
+¼% of $12,000	= $ 30.00	(¼ of 120)
1¼% of $12,000	= $150.00	

The rule is also useful in estimating interest, as in the following example.

Suppose we have $9,000 at 6 percent for 32 days. Now, 32 days at 6 percent interest is approximately equal to ½ percent of the principal.

1% of $9,000	= $90.00	(move decimal point two places to the left)
+½% of $9,000	= $45.00	(½ of 90)

Obviously the answer should be in the neighborhood of $45. If you work out the problem by the long method and the answer varies greatly from $45, then it must surely be incorrect.

DETERMINING DUE DATES

Objective 3

Determine the due dates of promissory notes.

As we have said, the period of time a note has to run may be expressed in either days or months. If the time of the note is expressed in months, the maturity date is the corresponding day in the month after the specified number of months have elapsed. For example, a note dated March 12 with a time period of three months has a due date of June 12. In those cases in which there is no date in the month of maturity that corresponds to the issuance date, the due date becomes the last day of the month. For example, a three-month note dated January 31 would be due on April 30.

But suppose that the period of time a note has to run is expressed in days. In counting the number of days, begin counting with the day after the date the note was issued, since the note states "after date." The last day, however, is counted. Let us say that the due date of a promissory note is specified as 60 days after April 14. The calendar shows that the due date is June 13 (see Figure 16-2 below).

In summary, the due date is determined by the following steps.

1. Determine the number of days remaining in the month of issue by subtracting the date of the note from the number of days in the month in which it is dated.
2. Add as many full months as possible without exceeding the number of days in the note, counting the full number of days in these months.
3. Determine the number of days remaining in the month in which the note matures by subtracting the total days counted so far from the number of days in the note, as shown here.

April (30 − 14)	= 16 days left in April
May	= 31 days
Total days so far	= 47 days
June (60 − 47)	= 13th day of June (due date)

Figure 16-2

April						
S	M	T	W	T	F	S
		1	2	3	4	5
6	7	8	9	10	11	12
13	14	15	16	17	18	19
20	21	22	23	24	25	26
27	28	29	30			

16 days
15th through the 30th
30 − 14 = 16 days left

May						
S	M	T	W	T	F	S
				1	2	3
4	5	6	7	8	9	10
11	12	13	14	15	16	17
18	19	20	21	22	23	24
25	26	27	28	29	30	31

+ 31 days

June						
S	M	T	W	T	F	S
1	2	3	4	5	6	7
8	9	10	11	12	13	14
15	16	17	18	19	20	21
22	23	24	25	26	27	28
29	30					

= 47 days have passed
60 − 47 = 13 days remaining after May 31
June 13 due date

In another example, suppose you have a 120-day note dated May 27.

May (31 − 27)	= 4 days left in May
June	= 30 days
July	= 31 days
August	= 31 days
Total days so far	= 96 days
September (120 − 96)	= 24th day of September (due date)

TRANSACTIONS INVOLVING NOTES PAYABLE

The following types of transactions involve the issuance and payment of notes payable:

1. Note given to a supplier in return for an extension of time for payment of an open account (charge account)
2. Note given in exchange for merchandise or other property purchased
3. Note given as evidence of a loan
4. Note renewed at maturity

The accounts particularly involved are Notes Payable (classified under Current Liabilities on the balance sheet in our examples, although they could be classified as long-term liabilities if the due date is more than a year away) and Interest Expense (classified as Other Expense on the income statement).

Note Given to Secure an Extension of Time on an Open Account

When a firm wishes to obtain an extension of time for the payment of an account, the firm may ask a supplier to accept a note for all or part of the amount due. For example, let's say that C. L. Frederickson Plumbing Supply prefers to not pay its open account with Alman Manufacturing Company when it becomes due. Alman agrees to accept a 60-day, 9 percent, $450 note from C. L. Frederickson in settlement of the charge account. The entry that caused the account to be put on Alman's books in the first place came about when C. L. Frederickson bought merchandise on account on March 15, with terms 2/10, n/30. C. L. Frederickson recorded the transaction as a debit to Purchases for $450 and a credit to Accounts Payable, Alman Manufacturing Company, for $450. Now C. L. Frederickson records the issuance of the note in its general journal with the entry shown on the next page.

Objective 4

Make journal entries for
a. Notes given to secure an extension of time on an open account.

	19– Apr.	14	Accounts Payable, Alman												1
1			Accounts Payable, Alman												1
2			Manufacturing Company	4	5	0	00								2
3			Notes Payable						4	5	0	00			3
4			Gave a 60-day, 9 percent note												4
5			in settlement of our open												5
6			account.												6
7															7

By T accounts, the transactions look like this:

Purchases		Accounts Payable		Notes Payable	
+	−	−	+	−	+
Mar. 15 450		Apr. 14 450	Mar. 15 450		Apr. 14 450

Observe that the above entry cancels out the Accounts Payable, Alman Manufacturing Company account and substitutes Notes Payable. The note does not *pay* the debt, it merely changes the account from Accounts Payable to Notes Payable. Alman prefers the note to the open account because, in the case of default and a subsequent lawsuit to collect, the possession of the note improves Alman's legal position. The note is written evidence of the debt and the amount owed. In addition, Alman is, in this case, entitled to 9 percent interest.

Payment of an Interest-bearing Note at Maturity

When a note payable falls due, payment may be made directly to the holder, or it may be made to a bank in which the note was left for collection. The maker of course knows the identity of the original payee, but he or she may not know who the holder of the note is at maturity. The payee may have transferred the note by endorsement to another party or may have left it with a bank for collection. When a note is left with a bank for collection, the bank usually mails the maker a **notice of maturity** specifying the details of the note. For example, Alman Manufacturing Company turned the note over to its bank, the New National Bank, for collection. Accordingly, the bank sent C. L. Frederickson a notice of maturity of the note.

C. L. Frederickson Plumbing Supply pays the note on June 13. In general journal form, the entry is as follows.

b. Payment of an interest-bearing note at maturity.

	19–Jun.	13	Notes Payable		4	5	0	00							1
1			Notes Payable		4	5	0	00								1
2			Interest Expense				6	75								2
3			Cash							4	5	6	75			3
4			Paid note to Alman													4
5			Manufacturing Company.													5
6																6

Because Interest = Principal × Rate × Time, we perform these calculations:

Interest = $450 × .09 × 60 ÷ 360 = $6.75

Or

60 days at 9% Interest = $1\frac{1}{2}$% of Principal

$$
\begin{aligned}
1\% \text{ of Principal} &= 450 \times .01 &= \$4.50 \\
+\tfrac{1}{2}\% \text{ of Principal} &= (\tfrac{1}{2} \times 4.50) &= 2.25 \\
\hline
1\tfrac{1}{2}\% \text{ of Principal} &= &\$6.75
\end{aligned}
$$

The organization for the entry is shown by T accounts.

Cash		Notes Payable		Interest Expense	
+	−	−	+	+	−
	456.75	450.00		6.75	

In practice, transactions such as this one are recorded directly in the cash payments journal rather than in the general journal. However, to simplify the discussion of the entries, all transactions will be presented here in general journal form. As stated earlier, Notes Payable is listed in the Current Liabilities section of a balance sheet. Interest Expense is listed in the Other Expense section of an income statement.

Note Given in Exchange for Assets Purchased

Occasionally, when the price of an item is high or the credit period is long, a buyer gives a note instead of buying the item on account. For example, C. L. Frederickson Plumbing Supply issues a 60-day, 8 percent interest-bearing note for $2,400 to the Dundee Equipment Company in exchange for equipment purchased May 3 and records the transaction in the general journal as follows.

c. Notes given in exchange for merchandise or other property purchased.

1	19– May	3	Store Equipment		2	4	0	0	00						1
2			Notes Payable							2	4	0	0	00	2
3			Acquired shelves and counters												3
4			from Dundee Equipment												4
5			Company, 60 days, 8 percent.												5
6															6

By T accounts, it looks like this.

Store Equipment		Notes Payable	
+	–	–	+
2,400			2,400

When C. L. Frederickson pays the note at maturity, the entry in its books is the same as the entry it makes for the payment of any interest-bearing note. In general journal form, the entry looks like this.

1	19– Jul.	2	Notes Payable		2	4	0	0	00						1
2			Interest Expense				3	2	00						2
3			Cash							2	4	3	2	00	3
4			Paid note to Dundee Equipment												4
5			Company.												5
6															6

May (31 − 3) = 28 days left in May
June   = 30 days
_____
Total days so far = 58 days
July (60 − 58) = 2nd day of July (due date)

And since Interest = Principal × Rate × Time,
Interest = \$2,400 × .08 × 60 ÷ 360 = \$32

Or

8% for 60 days = $1\frac{1}{3}$% of Principal
      Interest = $1\frac{1}{3}$% of Principal

   1% of principal = \$24
+$\frac{1}{3}$% of principal =   8
_____
$1\frac{1}{3}$% of principal = \$32

Note Given to Secure a Cash Loan

Businesses frequently need to stock up on merchandise in large amounts in order to meet seasonal demands. Sometimes their usual receipts from customers aren't enough to cover the sudden volume of purchases. During such periods, business firms customarily borrow money from banks, through the medium of short-term notes, in order to finance their operations.

Borrowing from a Bank When Borrower Receives Full Face Value of Note

In one type of bank loan, a business firm signs an interest-bearing note and receives the full face value of the note. The borrower repays the principal plus interest. For example, on May 11 C. L. Frederickson Plumbing Supply borrows $1,200 from Valley National Bank for 120 days with interest of 7 percent payable at maturity. The entry to record the transaction is as follows.

d. Notes given to secure a cash loan, when the borrower receives full face value of the note.

	19– May	11	Cash	1 2 0 0 00		1
2			Notes Payable		1 2 0 0 00	2
3			Gave Valley National Bank a			3
4			120-day, 7 percent note.			4
5						5

May (31 − 11)	= 20 days left in May
June	= 30 days
July	= 31 days
August	= 31 days
Total days so far	= 112 days
September (120 − 112)	= 8th day of September (due date)

Note Paid to the Bank at Maturity

After C. L. Frederickson has paid the note and interest, its accountant makes the following entry on the books.

	19– Sep.	8	Notes Payable	1 2 0 0 00		1
2			Interest Expense	2 8 00		2
3			Cash		1 2 2 8 00	3
4			Paid note to Valley National			4
5			Bank.			5
6						6

Interest = Principal × Rate × Time

Interest = $1,200 × .07 × 120 ÷ 360 = $28

Borrowing from a Bank When Bank Discounts Note (Deducts Interest in Advance)

In another type of bank loan, the bank deducts the interest in advance, which is called **discounting a note payable.** For example, on May 19 C. L. Frederickson Plumbing Supply borrows $6,000 for 60 days from Northwest National Bank; the bank requires C. L. Frederickson to sign a note. From the face value of the note, the bank deducts 9 percent interest for 60 days, so C. L. Frederickson actually gets only $5,910. This interest deducted in advance by a bank is called the **discount.** The principal of the loan left after the discount has been subtracted is called the **proceeds,** which is the amount the borrower has available to use. The calculations are as follows.

Interest = Principal × Rate × Time

Interest = $6,000 × .09 × 60 ÷ 360 = $90

Or

Interest = 1½% of Principal = 6,000 × .015 = $90

As we said, the bank deducts the discount from the face amount of the note, before making the money available to the borrower.

Principal	$6,000
− Discount	90
Proceeds	$5,910

Entry When Note Discounted at Bank Matures Before End of Fiscal Period

As long as a note begins and matures during the same fiscal period, the borrower may debit all the interest (or discount) to Interest Expense. The 60-day note that C. L. Frederickson Plumbing Supply submits to the bank is dated May 19 and therefore matures July 18. Since C. L. Frederickson's fiscal period is from January 1 to December 31, C. L. Frederickson can include the entire amount of interest in Interest Expense. Accordingly, C. L. Frederickson records the transaction as follows.

e. Notes given to secure a cash loan, when the bank discounts the note.

1	19– May 19	Cash	5 9 1 0 00		1
2		Interest Expense	9 0 00		2
3		Notes Payable		6 0 0 0 00	3
4		Discounted our 60-day			4
5		non-interest-bearing note at the			5
6		Northwest National Bank,			6
7		discount rate 9 percent.			7
8					8

Note Paid to the Bank at Maturity

When the note becomes due, C. L. Frederickson Plumbing Supply pays the bank just the *face value of the note,* and records the transaction as follows.

1	19– Jul. 18	Notes Payable	6 0 0 0 00		1
2		Cash		6 0 0 0 00	2
3		Paid Northwest National Bank			3
4		on our note payable discounted.			4
5					5

May (31 − 19)   = 12 days left in May
June   = 30 days
_____
Total days so far = 42 days
July (60 − 42)   = 18th day of July (due date)

Entry When Note Discounted at Bank Matures After End of Fiscal Period

Now suppose that the time period of the note extends into the next fiscal period. C. L. Frederickson Plumbing Supply must then record the discount as a debit to Discount on Notes Payable. Discount on Notes Payable is a contra liability account; in other words, it is a deduction from Notes Payable. Recall that we defined the Accumulated Depreciation account as a contra asset—for example, a deduction from Equipment with the plus and minus signs switched. Since Discount on Notes Payable is a deduction from Notes Payable, its plus and minus signs will also be switched around. In T account form, using hypothetical amounts, the accounts look like this:

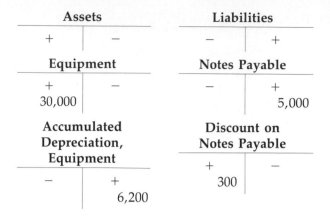

Assets		Liabilities	
+	–	–	+

Equipment		Notes Payable	
+	–	–	+
30,000			5,000

Accumulated Depreciation, Equipment		Discount on Notes Payable	
		+	–
–	+	300	
	6,200		

Also, on a balance sheet, the contra account is deducted as shown below:

Assets		
Equipment	$ 30 0 0 0 00	
Less Accumulated Depreciation	6 2 0 0 00	$ 23 8 0 0 00

Liabilities		
Notes Payable	$ 5 0 0 0 00	
Less Discount on Notes Payable	3 0 0 00	$ 4 7 0 0 00

At the end of the fiscal period, an adjusting entry must be made to record the amount of interest expense for the time between the date the note is issued until the end of the fiscal period.

Let's say that on December 1 C. L. Frederickson Plumbing Supply borrows $1,800 from a bank for 120 days. The bank deducts 8 percent interest (in advance) for 120 days, $48, and gives C. L. Frederickson $1,752. C. L. Frederickson's fiscal period is from January 1 through December 31, so its accountant's entry in the general journal is like this:

1	19– Dec.	1	Cash	1 7 5 2 00	
2			Discount on Notes Payable	4 8 00	
3			Notes Payable		1 8 0 0 00
4			Borrowed $1,800 at 8 percent		
5			for 120 days with interest		
6			deducted in advance.		
7					
8					

As an alternative method, some accountants prefer to record the interest deducted in advance as Interest Expense. This method requires an adjusting entry debiting Prepaid Interest and crediting Interest Expense. A reversing entry is also required.

In a discounted-note transaction, since all the interest is deducted at the time the loan is made, the note must state that only the face amount is to be paid at maturity.

Renewal of Note at Maturity

What if the maker (or borrower) is unable to pay a note in full at maturity? Then he or she may arrange to renew all or part of the note. At this time, he or she usually pays the interest on the old note. For example, assume that on May 27 C. L. Frederickson Plumbing Supply issues a 60-day note to Darvik, Inc., for $1,500, with interest at 8 percent. The original entry in general journal form is as follows.

f. Renewal of a note at maturity.

1	19– May	27	Accounts Payable, Darvik, Inc.	1 5 0 0 00		1
2			Notes Payable		1 5 0 0 00	2
3			Issued a 60-day, 8 percent			3
4			note.			4
5						5

Renewal of Note with Payment of Interest

When a firm renews an interest-bearing note, the accountant first makes an entry to pay the interest on the existing note, up to the present date. This entry occurs on July 26, the maturity date of the note.

1	19– Jul.	26	Interest Expense	2 0 00		1
2			Cash		2 0 00	2
3			Interest payment on note to			3
4			Darvik, Inc.			4
5						5

ACCOUNTING FOR NOTES PAYABLE   485

May (31 − 27) = 4 days left in May
June = 30 days
_____
Total days so far = 34 days
July (60 − 34) = 26th day of July (due date)

Interest = Principal × Rate × Time

Interest = $1,500 × .08 × 60 ÷ 360 = $20

The accountant then makes a separate entry for the issuance of the new note, to run for 30 days at 9 percent (the interest rate has been increased) as follows.

1		26	Notes Payable				1	5	0	0	00						1
2			Notes Payable									1	5	0	0	00	2
3			Canceled note to Darvik, Inc.,														3
4			by issuing 30-day, 9 percent														4
5			note.														5
6																	6

Renewal of Note with Payment of Interest and Part Payment of Principal

Now, what if the maker decides to pay *part* of a note at maturity? Let us assume that, instead of taking the course of action we have just described, C. L. Frederickson pays $500 on the principal of the note that is due (the old note), and also pays the entire interest on it. In other words, the maker pays the interest up to the present date for the old note, plus $500 to reduce the principal from $1,500 to $1,000, and issues a *new* note for $1,000.

1		26	Notes Payable				5	0	0	00							1
2			Interest Expense					2	0	00							2
3			Cash									5	2	0	00		3
4			Interest payment on note to														4
5			Darvik, Inc., and part payment														5
6			on the principal.														6
7																	7
8		26	Notes Payable				1	0	0	0	00						8
9			Notes Payable									1	0	0	0	00	9
10			Canceled note to Darvik, Inc.,														10
11			by issuing 30-day, 9 percent														11
12			note.														12
13																	13

END-OF-FISCAL-PERIOD ADJUSTMENTS

In the case of notes that start in one fiscal period and mature in the next, adjusting entries must be made both for accrued interest and for discounts on notes payable. Otherwise, neither the expenses incurred by the business firm during a fiscal period nor its liabilities at the end of the fiscal period would be correctly stated.

Accrued Interest on Notes Payable

On all interest-bearing notes, interest expense *accrues*, or *accumulates*, daily. Consequently, if any notes payable are outstanding at the end of a fiscal period, the **accrued interest on notes payable** (that is, the interest due but not yet paid) should be calculated and recorded. For example, assume that a firm has two notes payable outstanding as of December 31, the end of the current fiscal period.

$2,000, 90 days, 9%, dated December 5
$3,600, 60 days, 7%, dated December 16

We can diagram the period of each note like this.

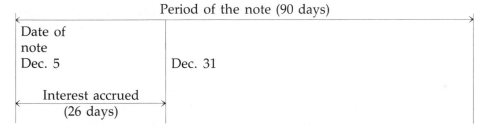

Interest = Principal × Rate × Time

Interest = $2,000 × .09 × 26 ÷ 360 = $13

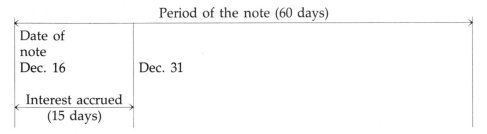

Interest = Principal × Rate × Time

Interest = $3,600 × .07 × 15 ÷ 360 = $10.50

Obviously both notes extend into the next fiscal period; if they didn't, there would be no need for an adjustment. When one is paying interest on notes—except for notes discounted at a bank—one usually pays the principal and interest together, on the day the note matures, or falls due. But since *these* notes have not matured, naturally the interest expense has been neither paid nor recorded. Therefore the firm has to make an adjustment, since the accountant tries to portray the firm's expenses and liabilities for the current fiscal period as accurately as possible. In general journal form, the adjusting entry for the interest expense accrued on the two notes is as follows.

g. Adjustment for accrued interest on notes payable.

	19– Dec.	31	Adjusting Entry					
2			Interest Expense		2 3 50			2
3			Interest Payable			2 3 50		3
4								4

Like all other adjustments, this one is first recorded in the Adjustments columns of the work sheet. By T accounts, it looks like this, assuming a balance of $724 before adjustment of Interest Expense:

Interest Expense			Interest Payable	
+	–		–	+
Dec. 31 Bal. 724.00				Dec. 31 Adj. 23.50
Dec. 31 Adj. 23.50				(13 + 10.50)
(13 + 10.50)				

On the balance sheet, Interest Payable is classified as a current liability.

This situation parallels that of the adjustment for accrued salaries, in which the objective is to record the extra amount of salaries owed at the end of the year.

Salary Expense			Salaries Payable	
+	–		–	+
Dec. 31 Adj. xxx				Dec. 31 Adj. xxx

There is another similarity between the adjustment for accrued interest and the adjustment for accrued salaries: Both require reversing entries (recall Chapter 15). The rule for reversing entries is: If an adjusting entry increases an asset or liability account that does not have a previous balance, then reverse the adjusting entry. Entries involving contra accounts are never reversed. The credits to Interest Payable and Salaries Payable both represent increases to liability accounts. The reversing entry enables one to make the routine entry for the payment of an interest-bearing note at maturity as a debit to Notes Payable, a debit to Interest Expense, and a credit to Cash.

Discount on Notes Payable

Recall that when a note payable is discounted at a bank, the bank deducts the interest (based on the principal of the note) in advance. If the note begins and ends during one fiscal period, the interest is recorded as Interest Expense and no adjustment is needed. But if the note extends into the next fiscal period, the interest is recorded as Discount on Notes Payable. An adjusting entry will be needed to record the interest from the day the note started until the last day of the fiscal period.

Now let us recall our original entry made on December 1, in which the firm discounted its note at the bank. The note is to run for 120 days, and the bank discounts it at 8 percent. C. L. Frederickson's fiscal period, remember, is from January 1 through December 31.

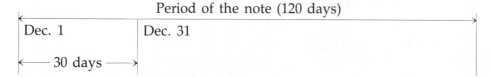

Period of the note (120 days)

Dec. 1   Dec. 31

←—— 30 days ——→

Interest = Principal × Rate × Time

Interest = $1,800 × .08 × 30 ÷ 360 = $12

Since 30 days elapse between December 1 and December 31, C. L. Frederickson's accountant has to make an adjusting entry to record the Interest Expense.

<table>
<tr><td>1</td><td>19–
Dec.</td><td>31</td><td>Adjusting Entry</td><td></td><td></td><td></td><td></td><td></td><td></td><td></td><td></td><td>1</td></tr>
<tr><td>2</td><td></td><td></td><td>Interest Expense</td><td></td><td>1</td><td>2</td><td>00</td><td></td><td></td><td></td><td></td><td>2</td></tr>
<tr><td>3</td><td></td><td></td><td>Discount on Notes Payable</td><td></td><td></td><td></td><td></td><td>1</td><td>2</td><td>00</td><td></td><td>3</td></tr>
<tr><td>4</td><td></td><td></td><td></td><td></td><td></td><td></td><td></td><td></td><td></td><td></td><td></td><td>4</td></tr>
</table>

In T accounts, it looks this way.

Interest Expense		Discount on Notes Payable	
+	−	+	−
Dec. 31 Adj. 12		Dec. 1 48	Dec. 31 Adj. 12

In addition to recording Interest Expense, the adjusting entry also serves to reduce the balance of Discount on Notes Payable to its correct amount.

Both accounts now reflect true balances for the end of the fiscal year, and the Interest Expense account is closed along with all the other expense accounts.

h. Adjustment for prepaid interest on notes payable.

ACCOUNT NAME	TRIAL BALANCE		
	DEBIT		CREDIT
Discount on Notes Payable	4 8 00		
Interest Expense	7 2 4 00		
Interest Payable			

Now let us proceed one step further, and make the entries for the final payment of the note to the bank. These may be separated into two entries; the first is like the payment of any discounted note.

	19— Mar.	31	Notes Payable	1 8 0 0 00		
1						1
2			Cash		1 8 0 0 00	2
3			Paid the bank the 120-day			3
4			non-interest-bearing note, dated			4
5			December 1, and discounted at			5
6			8 percent.			6
7						7

The Discount on Notes Payable that was on the books has now become entirely an expense, so it is converted into Interest Expense.

8		31	Interest Expense	3 6 00		8
9			Discount on Notes Payable		3 6 00	9
10			To expense the discount for the			10
11			current year for the 120-day			11
12			note, dated December 1, and			12
13			discounted at 8 percent.			13
14						14
15						15

In T accounts, it looks like this.

Interest Expense		Discount on Notes Payable	
+	−	+	−
Dec. 31 Adj. 12	Dec. 31 Clos. 12	Dec. 1 48	Dec. 31 Adj. 12
Mar. 31 36			Mar. 31 36

Figure 16-3

ADJUSTMENTS		INCOME STATEMENT		BALANCE SHEET	
DEBIT	CREDIT	DEBIT	CREDIT	DEBIT	CREDIT
	(b) 12 00			36 00	
(a) 23 50		759 50			
(b) 12 00					
	(a) 23 50				23 50

Effect on Financial Statements

In this section we have discussed two kinds of year-end adjustments: accrued interest on notes payable and discount on notes payable. Taking a hypothetical example, let's look at the effect of these two year-end adjustments on the income statement and the balance sheet.

1. Accrued interest on notes payable. Suppose that the amount of the adjustment is $23.50. The entry is like the adjusting entry for accrued salaries.
2. Discount on notes payable. Assume that the amount of the adjustment is $12.

These adjustments and their effects on the income statement and the balance sheet are shown in Figure 16-3 above.

USE OF SPECIAL JOURNALS

Until now, in this chapter, we have concentrated on analyzing the debits and credits for each transaction. The entries were shown in general journal form to portray the debits and credits in a clear manner. However, if a firm is using a cash receipts journal and a cash payments journal, any entries involving cash should be recorded in one of these journals. They should not be recorded in a general journal.

To illustrate the use of the cash journals, we will show the related entries again. To conserve space in showing the general journal, we omit explanations.

April 14: Issued a 60-day, 9 percent note for $450, payable to Alman Manufacturing Company, in place of the open-book account.

1	Apr.	14	Accounts Payable, Alman		1
2			Manufacturing Company	4 5 0 00	2
3			Notes Payable	4 5 0 00	3
4					4

June 13: Paid at maturity the note given to Alman Manufacturing Company.

CASH PAYMENTS JOURNAL PAGE _____

	DATE	CK. NO.	ACCOUNT NAME	POST. REF.	SUNDRY ACCOUNTS DEBIT	ACCOUNTS PAYABLE DEBIT	PURCHASES DISCOUNT CREDIT	CASH CREDIT	
1	19–Jun. 13		Notes Payable		4 5 0 00			4 5 6 75	1
2			Interest Expense		6 75				2
3									3
4									4

May 3: Issued a 60-day, 8 percent note for $2,400, payable to the Dundee Equipment Company, for equipment.

	DATE		ACCOUNT NAME		SUNDRY ACCOUNTS DEBIT			
1	19–May 3		Store Equipment		2 4 0 0 00			1
2			Notes Payable			2 4 0 0 00		2
3								3
4								4

July 2: Paid at maturity the note given to Dundee Equipment Company.

CASH PAYMENTS JOURNAL PAGE _____

	DATE	CK. NO.	ACCOUNT NAME	POST. REF.	SUNDRY ACCOUNTS DEBIT	ACCOUNTS PAYABLE DEBIT	PURCHASES DISCOUNT CREDIT	CASH CREDIT	
1	19–Jul. 2		Notes Payable		2 4 0 0 00			2 4 3 2 00	1
2			Interest Expense		3 2 00				2
3									3
4									4

May 11: Borrowed $1,200 from the Valley National Bank, giving in exchange a 120-day, 7 percent note (received full face amount).

CASH RECEIPTS JOURNAL PAGE _____

	DATE	ACCOUNT CREDITED	POST. REF.	SUNDRY ACCOUNTS CREDIT	ACCOUNTS RECEIVABLE CREDIT	SALES CREDIT	CASH DEBIT	
1	19–May 11	Notes Payable		1 2 0 0 00			1 2 0 0 00	1
2								2
3								3

September 8: Paid loan in full, at maturity, to the Valley National Bank.

CASH PAYMENTS JOURNAL   PAGE _____

	DATE	CK. NO.	ACCOUNT NAME	POST. REF.	SUNDRY ACCOUNTS DEBIT	ACCOUNTS PAYABLE DEBIT	PURCHASES DISCOUNT CREDIT	CASH CREDIT	
1	19– Sep.	8	*Notes Payable*		1 2 0 0 00			1 2 2 8 00	1
2			*Interest Expense*		2 8 00				2
3									3
4									4

May 19: Borrowed $6,000 from Northwest National Bank for 90 days; discount rate is 6 percent; issued a note for $6,000.

CASH RECEIPTS JOURNAL   PAGE _____

	DATE	ACCOUNT CREDITED	POST. REF.	SUNDRY ACCOUNTS DEBIT	SUNDRY ACCOUNTS CREDIT	SALES CREDIT	CASH DEBIT	
1	19– May 19	*Interest Expense*		9 0 00			5 9 1 0 00	1
2		*Notes Payable*			6 0 0 0 00			2
3								3
4								4

July 18: Paid bank when loan matured.

CASH PAYMENTS JOURNAL   PAGE _____

	DATE	CK. NO.	ACCOUNT NAME	POST. REF.	SUNDRY ACCOUNTS DEBIT	ACCOUNTS PAYABLE DEBIT	PURCHASES DISCOUNT CREDIT	CASH CREDIT	
1	19– Jul.	18	*Notes Payable*		6 0 0 0 00			6 0 0 0 00	1
2									2
3									3

May 27: Issued a 60-day note payable to Darvik, Inc., for $1,500, with interest at 8 percent, in place of open-book account.

1	*May*	27	*Accounts Payable, Darvik, Inc.*	1 5 0 0 00		1
2			*Notes Payable*		1 5 0 0 00	2
3						3
4						4

July 26: Paid interest up to the present date on note given to Darvik, Inc., and issued a new 30-day note for $1,500 with interest at 9 percent.

	DATE	CK. NO.	ACCOUNT NAME	POST. REF.	SUNDRY ACCOUNTS DEBIT	ACCOUNTS PAYABLE DEBIT	PURCHASES DISCOUNT CREDIT	CASH CREDIT	
			CASH PAYMENTS JOURNAL					PAGE _____	
1	19— Jul. 26		*Interest Expense*		2 0 00			2 0 00	1
2									2

Also we would have:

1	Jul. 26	*Notes Payable*		1 5 0 0 00		1
2		*Notes Payable*			1 5 0 0 00	2
3						3

GLOSSARY

Accrued interest on notes payable For notes payable beginning in one fiscal period and maturing in the following fiscal period, accrued interest is the unpaid interest expense from the date of issue of the note until the last day of the fiscal period.

Discount Interest deducted in advance by a bank that makes a loan.

Discounting a note payable The procedure by which a bank collects interest in advance when it loans money.

Interest A charge made for the use of money.

Maker An individual or firm that signs a promissory note.

Maturity date The due date of a promissory note.

Notice of maturity A notice specifying the terms and due date of a promissory note that has been left with a bank for collection; mailed by the bank to the maker.

Payee The party receiving payment.

Principal The face amount of a note.

Proceeds The principal of a loan less the discount.

Promissory note A written promise to pay a certain sum at a fixed and determinable future time.

QUESTIONS, EXERCISES, AND PROBLEMS

Discussion Questions

1. Name three characteristics of a promissory note.
2. Identify the two parties to a promissory note.

3. What is the basic formula for the calculation of interest?
4. Describe the 60-day, 6 percent method of calculating interest.
5. Explain the situation whereby a firm obtains a discounted note at a bank.
6. When a business borrows from a bank and the bank discounts the note, why is the effective rate of interest higher than the discount rate charged by the bank?
7. Explain why it is necessary to make an adjusting entry for accrued interest on an interest-bearing note payable. Should the entry be reversed?

Exercises

Exercise 16-1   Determine the interest on the following notes.

	Principal	Number of Days	Interest Rate
(a)	$1,800	60	9%
(b)	1,200	60	8%
(c)	8,000	90	10%
(d)	7,200	63	12%
(e)	960	45	7½%

Exercise 16-2   Determine the maturity dates on the following notes.

	Date of Issue	Time Period
(a)	March 25	60 days
(b)	October 15	90 days
(c)	December 15	3 months
(d)	June 30	30 days
(e)	July 2	120 days

Exercise 16-3   On March 12, L. O. Phipps gives a 90-day, 9 percent note for $8,600 to Mitchell Company.

a. What is the due date of the note?
b. How much interest is to be paid on the note at maturity?
c. On Phipps's books, show entries in general journal form to record (1) issuance of the note by the maker, and (2) payment of the note at maturity.

Exercise 16-4   As the result of a loan from the Mason State Bank, the Mueller Company signed a 90-day note for $14,000 that the bank discounted at 11 percent. Present the entries for the maker in general journal form to record the following, assuming that the note is paid in the same fiscal period:

a. Issuance of the note
b. Payment of the note at maturity

Exercise 16-5   In arranging for a 60-day loan from a bank, Harbor Machinery Company has the option of either (1) giving a $48,000, 9 percent interest-bearing note that will be accepted at face value, or (2) giving a $48,000 note that will be discounted at 9 percent.

a. What is the amount of interest in each case?
b. What is the amount Harbor Machinery Company actually receives in each case?
c. Which of the two alternatives is more favorable to Harbor Machinery Company?

Exercise 16-6   On August 1, Gilmore Automotive bought the land and building that it was formerly renting. The terms of sale are: land, $8,000; building, $27,000; cash downpayment, $11,000; and the balance in the form of an 8 percent note, secured by a ten-year mortgage on the property. The terms of the note provide for 120 monthly payments of $200 each on the principal plus interest on the unpaid balance. Give entries in general journal form to record the following.

a. The transaction on August 1
b. The payment of the first installment on September 1
c. The payment of the second installment on October 1

Exercise 16-7   On October 5 Mary Lou Prentice issued a 90-day, 12 percent note to Melton Supply Company, a creditor, for $6,600. Present the entries in general journal form to record the following.

a. Issuance of the note on October 5
b. Adjusting entry for accrued interest on December 31, the end of the fiscal year

Exercise 16-8   On December 2 Henry Lucas borrowed $8,400 from Pioneer National Bank for 60 days, with a discount rate of 8 percent. Accordingly, Henry Lucas signed a discounted note for $8,400. The end of the fiscal year is December 31. Give entries in general journal form to record the following:

a. Issuance of the note on December 2
b. Adjusting entry on December 31
c. Payment of the note at maturity (two entries) on January 31

Problem Set A

Problem 16-1A The following were among the transactions of the F. J. Fowler Company during this year.

Jan.   14 Bought merchandise on account from J. C. Conrad Company, $3,200.
         22 Paid J. C. Conrad Company for the invoice of January 14, less 2 percent discount.
Feb.   18 Bought merchandise on account from Costigan and Company, $3,800.
Mar.   20 Gave a 60-day, 9 percent note for $3,800 to Costigan and Company to apply on account.
May   19 Paid Costigan and Company the amount owed on the note of March 20.
Jun.   3 Borrowed $4,800 from Midwest National Bank, giving a 90-day, 10 percent note for that amount (received full face value).
Sep.   1 Paid Midwest National Bank the amount due on the note of June 3.

Instructions

Record these transactions in general journal form.

Problem 16-2A The following were among the transactions of Hanson Motors and Machine during this year (January 1 through December 31).

Feb.   12 Bought merchandise on account from John T. Cox Company, $2,640.
Mar.   13 Gave a 30-day, 9 percent note for $2,640 to John T. Cox Company to apply on account.
Apr.   12 Paid John T. Cox Company amount owed on note of March 13.
May   2 Bought merchandise on account from Rasmussen Company, $6,900.
Jun.   3 Gave a 30-day, 8 percent note for $6,900 to Rasmussen Company to apply on account.
Jul.   3 Paid Rasmussen Company interest due on note of June 3 and renewed obligation by issuing a new 60-day, 10 percent note for $6,900.
Sep.   1 Paid Rasmussen Company amount owed on note of July 3.
         24 Borrowed $9,000 from Shadle National Bank for 90 days; discount rate is 10 percent. Accordingly, signed a discounted note for $9,000.
Dec.   23 Paid Shadle National Bank at maturity of loan.

Instructions

Record these transactions in general journal form.

Problem 16-3A The following were among the transactions of Doolittle Cycle during this year (January 1 through December 31).

Jan.   16 Bought merchandise on account from J. P. Evans Company, $3,200.

Feb. 15 Gave a 30-day, 7 percent note to J. P. Evans Company, dated February 15, to apply on account, covering purchase of January 16.

Mar. 17 Paid $800 as part payment of principal and paid full interest on the note given to J. P. Evans Company; issued new 60-day, 8 percent note, dated March 17, for $2,400.

May 12 Borrowed $4,400 from the Texas National Bank for 90 days; discount rate is 7 percent. Accordingly, signed a discounted note for $4,400.

16 Paid amount owed on the note issued to J. P. Evans Company, dated March 17.

Aug. 10 Paid amount owed on the note issued to the Texas National Bank, dated May 12.

Nov. 25 Bought a microcomputer for $5,600 from Sperry Office Supply; issued a 60-day, 8 percent note.

Dec. 31 Made the adjusting entry to record accrued interest on the note given to Sperry Office Supply.

Instructions

Using the cash receipts journal, the cash payments journal, and the general journal, record these transactions in the appropriate journal.

Problem 16-4A The following were among the transactions of the Taylor Restaurant Supply Company during the year ended December 31.

May 29 Gave a 60-day, 8 percent note for $16,800, dated May 29, to A. C. Antonelli, for an addition to the building.

Jun. 26 Borrowed $5,600 from New York Exchange Bank, signing a three-month, 8 percent note for that amount, dated June 26 (received full face value).

Jul. 20 Gave note to Ramsey Office Equipment for data processing equipment, $9,640, at 9 percent for 90 days, dated July 20. The invoice was not previously recorded.

28 Paid amount due on note given to A. C. Antonelli.

Sep. 26 Paid interest on note issued to New York Exchange Bank; renewed loan, issuing new 60-day, 8 percent note, dated September 26.

Oct. 18 Paid amount owed on the note given to Ramsey Office Equipment.

29 Gave two notes to Roberts Machine Company in settlement of October 29 invoice for merchandise, as follows: $5,400 note for 30 days at 8 percent, dated October 29; $5,400 note for 60 days at 8 percent, dated October 29. The invoice was not previously recorded.

Nov. 25 Paid note given to New York Exchange Bank.

28 Paid amount owed on the 30-day note given to Roberts Machine Company.

Dec. 11 Issued 60-day, 9 percent note, dated December 11, to Gonzales and McGuire Company in settlement of November 21 invoice for merchandise, $4,600. The invoice was previously recorded.

Dec. 21 Borrowed $7,500 from Jacobs National Bank for 60 days; discount rate is 10 percent; signed a discounted note for $7,500 (debit Discount on Notes Payable, since note extends into next fiscal period).

28 Paid amount owed on 60-day note given to Roberts Machine Company.

Instructions

1. Record these transactions in a general journal.
2. Make the adjusting entries, dated December 31, to record interest expense on notes issued to Gonzales and McGuire Company and Jacobs National Bank.

Problem Set B

Problem 16-1B   The following were among the transactions of the Palmer Company.

Jan. 12 Bought merchandise on account from S. T. Oliver Company, $2,250.

Feb. 15 Bought merchandise on account from Parsons and Company, $2,400.

Mar. 17 Gave a 30-day, 9 percent note for $2,400 to Parsons and Company to apply on account.

Apr. 16 Paid Parsons and Company the amount owed on the note of March 17.

May 24 Borrowed $6,000 from First National Bank, giving a 60-day, 10 percent note for that amount (received full face value).

Jul. 23 Paid First National Bank the amount due on the note of May 24.

Instructions

Record these transactions in general journal form.

Problem 16-2B   The following were among the transactions of Waterbury and Company during this year (January 1 through December 31).

Jan. 26 Bought merchandise on account from Simpson and Adler, $2,700.

Feb. 27 Gave a 30-day, 8 percent note for $2,700 to Simpson and Adler to apply on account.

Mar. 29 Paid Simpson and Adler the amount owed on the note of February 27.

Apr. 3 Bought merchandise on account from Paine Hardware Company, $6,300.

May 4 Gave a 30-day, 9 percent note for $6,300 to Paine Hardware Company to apply on account.

Jun. 3 Paid Paine Hardware Company the interest due on the note of May 4, and renewed the obligation by issuing a new 60-day, 10 percent note for $6,300.

Aug.   2 Paid Paine Hardware Company the amount owed on the note of
           June 3.
        18 Borrowed $7,500 from Patrick National Bank for 90 days; discount
           rate is 9 percent. Accordingly, signed a discounted note for $7,500.
Nov.   16 Paid Patrick National Bank at maturity of loan.

Instructions

Record these transactions in general journal form.

Problem 16-3B   The following were among the transactions of Witten and
Company during this year (January 1 through December 31).

Jan.   29 Bought merchandise on account from Cole and Richards; terms
           2/10, n/30; $2,600.
Feb.   28 Gave a 30-day, 9 percent note to Cole and Richards, dated February
           28, to apply on account, covering purchase of January 29.
Mar.   30 Paid $900 as part payment of principal and paid the full interest on
           note given to Cole and Richards, issued a new 60-day, 9 percent
           note, dated March 30, for $1,700.
May   29 Paid amount owed on note dated March 30.
Jul.   20 Borrowed $3,000 from Tucson Trust Bank for 90 days, discount rate
           is 10 percent. Accordingly, signed a discounted note for $3,000.
Oct.   18 Paid amount owed on note given to Tucson Trust Bank, dated
           July 20.
Nov.   16 Bought a cash register and display shelves for $3,300 from Rogers
           Supply Company. Issued a 90-day, 10 percent note, dated November 16.
Dec.   31 Made the adjusting entry to record accrued interest on the note
           given to Rogers Supply Company.

Instructions

Using the cash receipts journal, the cash payments journal, and the general
journal, record these transactions in the appropriate journal.

Problem 16-4B   The following were among the transactions of Koski Boats
and Motors during the year ended December 31.

Jun.   6 Gave a 60-day, 8 percent note, dated June 6, to Price Construction
           Company, $18,000, for an addition to the showroom.
        28 Borrowed $6,400 from Kalamazoo Mutual Bank signing a three-
           month, 8 percent note for that amount, dated June 28 (received full
           face value).
Jul.   18 Gave a note to Jenkins Equipment Company for data processing
           equipment, $8,900, at 9 percent for 90 days, dated July 18. The
           invoice was not previously recorded.
Aug.   5 Paid the amount owed on the note given to Price Construction
           Company.

Sep. 28 Paid interest on note given to Kalamazoo Mutual Bank; renewed loan by issuing note for 60 days at 8 percent, dated September 28.

Oct. 16 Paid amount owed on note given to Jenkins Equipment Company.

27 Gave two notes to Patton Manufacturing Company in settlement of their October 26 invoice for merchandise, as follows: $3,600, 30 days, 8 percent, dated October 27; $3,600, 60 days, 8 percent, dated October 27. The invoice was not previously recorded.

Nov. 26 Paid amount owed on 30-day note given to Patton Manufacturing Company.

27 Paid note given to Kalamazoo Mutual Bank.

Dec. 11 Issued 60-day, 10 percent note, dated December 11, payable to Palmer and Ross Company, in settlement of November 11 bill for merchandise, $6,900. The invoice was previously recorded.

16 Borrowed $9,600 from Manor National Bank for 60 days; discount rate is 9 percent; issued a discounted note for $9,600 (debit Discount on Notes Payable, as the note extends into the next fiscal period).

26 Paid amount owed on the 60-day note given to Patton Manufacturing Company.

Instructions

1. Record these transactions in a general journal.
2. Make the adjusting entries, dated December 31, to record the interest expense on notes issued to Palmer and Ross Company and Manor National Bank.

17 Accounting for Notes Receivable

Learning Objectives

After you have completed this chapter, you will be able to write journal entries to record these transactions:

1. Receipt of a note from a charge customer.

2. Receipt of payment of an interest-bearing note at maturity.

3. Receipt of a note as a result of granting a personal loan.

4. Receipt of a note in exchange for merchandise or other property.

5. Renewal of a note at maturity.

6. Dishonored notes receivable.

7. Collection on a note receivable formerly dishonored.

8. Discounting an interest-bearing note.

9. Dishonoring of a discounted note receivable.

10. Adjustment for accrued interest on notes receivable.

Business firms receive promissory notes for a variety of reasons, either regularly or occasionally. Sometimes a business firm accepts a promissory note from a customer at the time of sale. Companies frequently accept promissory notes from charge-account customers who request an extension of time to settle past-due accounts. In effect, they substitute notes receivable for open accounts. The net result is that the charge customer gets an extension of time for the payment of a debt.

Obviously, getting a note receivable is not as good as having cash in hand. However, it offers several advantages to the company: (1) the note represents proof of the original transaction, (2) the note may bear interest, and (3) the note may be pledged as security for a loan from a bank. Banks, in fact, loan a higher proportion of the face value on notes (Notes Receivable) than on open accounts (Accounts Receivable). For example, banks may grant loans for 100 percent of the face value of notes but only 60 percent of the face value of open accounts.

Notes receivable also come into being when a company grants loans to employees or preferred customers or suppliers. In some business fields, the credit period is often longer than 30 days; here, the transactions are frequently evidenced by notes rather than by open accounts. Examples are sales of farm machinery, construction equipment, and trucks.

Let us now see how one journalizes transactions involving notes receivable. The accounts particularly involved are Notes Receivable (classified as a current asset on the balance sheet in our examples, although they could be classified as a long-term asset if the repayment period is longer than a year) and Interest Income (classified as other income on the income statement).

TRANSACTIONS FOR NOTES RECEIVABLE

First, let us say that all notes received are recorded in a single current asset account, Notes Receivable. Second, throughout this chapter we are going to use C. L. Frederickson Plumbing Supply to illustrate such transactions. Now let's begin with a simple example.

Notes from Charge Customers to Extend Time on Their Accounts

On March 6, C. L. Frederickson Plumbing Supply sold $480 worth of merchandise to Henning's Plumbing, with the customary terms of 2/10, n/30, and made the original entry in its sales journal. On April 6, Henning's sent C. L. Frederickson a note for $480, payable within 30 days, at 8 percent interest; the note, dated April 6, was in settlement of the transaction of March 6. C. L. Frederickson Plumbing Supply recorded this new development in its general journal as follows.

	DATE		DESCRIPTION	POST. REF.	DEBIT	CREDIT	
			GENERAL JOURNAL			PAGE _____	
1	19– Apr.	6	Notes Receivable		4 8 0 00		1
2			Accounts Receivable, Henning's				2
3			Plumbing			4 8 0 00	3
4			Received a 30-day, 8 percent note,				4
5			dated April 6, in settlement of				5
6			open account.				6
7							7

T accounts for the transactions look like this.

Accounts Receivable		Sales		Notes Receivable	
+	−	−	+	+	−
Mar. 6 480	Apr. 6 480		Mar. 6 480	Apr. 6 480	

Receipt of Payment of an Interest-bearing Note at Maturity

On May 6 Henning's paid C. L. Frederickson in full: principal plus interest. C. L. Frederickson recorded the transaction in the general journal as follows.

1	19– May	6	Cash		4 8 3 20		1
2			Notes Receivable			4 8 0 00	2
3			Interest Income			3 20	3
4			Received full payment of				4
5			Henning's note.				5
6							6

Let's look at the T accounts for this entry.

Cash		Notes Receivable		Interest Income	
+	−	+	−	−	+
483.20			480.00		3.20

In practice, this transaction would be recorded directly in the cash receipts journal rather than in the general journal. But, for the sake of simplicity and clarity, we'll use the general journal format to illustrate entries throughout this chapter.

Notes Received as a Result of Granting Personal Loans

Sometimes employees, preferred customers, or suppliers may want to borrow cash from the business. When that is the case, the business often accepts a note receivable. Let's say that James Hudson, an employee of C. L. Frederickson Plumbing Supply, borrows $336 from his employer, for three months at 6 percent. His note is dated April 8. In general journal form, the entry is as shown below.

Objective 3

Receipt of a note as a result of granting a personal loan.

1	19– Apr.	8	Notes Receivable		3 3 6	00					1
2			Cash					3 3 6	00		2
3			Granted a loan to James Hudson,								3
4			three months, 6 percent, dated								4
5			April 8.								5
6											6

When the loan reaches maturity, Hudson pays the principal plus interest.

1	19– Jul.	8	Cash		3 4 1	04					1
2			Notes Receivable					3 3 6	00		2
3			Interest Income					5	04		3
4			Received full payment of								4
5			James Hudson's note, dated								5
6			April 8.								6
7											7
8											8
9											9

Note Received in Exchange for Merchandise or Other Property

Business firms that sell high-priced durable goods in which the credit period is longer than the normal 30 days may fairly regularly accept notes from their customers. (This does not include installment sales; they are discussed separately in Appendix F.)

On April 9, C. L. Frederickson Plumbing Supply sold merchandise to Maxwell Heating and Air Conditioning for $900. Maxwell gave C. L. Frederickson a promissory note, promising to pay the full amount within 60 days; the note specified 7 percent interest. When this type of transaction occurs occasionally, the transaction is recorded in the general journal as follows.

Objective 4

Receipt of a note in exchange for merchandise or other property.

	19– Apr.	9	Notes Receivable		9	0	0	00						1
2			Sales							9	0	0	00		2
3			Maxwell Heating and Air												3
4			Conditioning, 60-day, 7 percent												4
5			note, dated April 9.												5
6															6
7															7

However, if this type of transaction were to occur frequently, C. L. Frederickson would use a Notes Receivable Debit column in the sales journal to record such transactions.

Renewal of Note at Maturity and Payment of Interest

If the maker of a note is unable to pay the entire principal at maturity, he or she may be allowed to renew all or a part of the note.

Now suppose that Maxwell Heating and Air Conditioning is not able to pay the note at maturity and offers to pay the interest on the current note and to issue a new note, for 30 days at 8 percent. C. L. Frederickson makes the entries in the general journal as follows.

Objective 5

Renewal of a note at maturity.

	19– Jun.	8	Cash			1	0	50						1
2			Interest Income								1	0	50		2
3			Received payment of interest												3
4			on Maxwell Heating and Air												4
5			Conditioning note, dated												5
6			April 9.												6
7															7
8		8	Notes Receivable		9	0	0	00							8
9			Notes Receivable							9	0	0	00		9
10			Maxwell Heating and Air												10
11			Conditioning renewal of note,												11
12			dated April 9, new note is dated												12
13			June 8, 30 days, 8 percent.												13
14															14

Note that, in actuality, there is only one Notes Receivable ledger account. When a firm renews a note, it is customary for the debtor or maker to pay the interest on the old note and issue a new one.

Renewal of Note with Payment of Interest and Partial Payment of Principal

Sometimes the maker of a note cancels the original note by paying the interest, plus part of the principal, and issuing a new note. Suppose that as a substitute for the $900 note described above, Maxwell gives C. L. Frederickson $300 toward the principal and a new note for $600, in addition to the interest on the old note.

C. L. Frederickson records the transactions in the general journal as follows:

1	19– Jun.	8	Cash	3 1 0 50		1
2			Notes Receivable		3 0 0 00	2
3			Interest Income		1 0 50	3
4			Maxwell Heating and Air			4
5			Conditioning note, dated April 9,			5
6			partial payment of the principal			6
7			and interest payment			7
8						8
9		8	Notes Receivable	6 0 0 00		9
10			Notes Receivable		6 0 0 00	10
11			Maxwell Heating and Air			11
12			Conditioning renewal of note			12
13			dated April 9; the new note is			13
14			dated June 8, 30 days, 8 percent.			14
15						15
16						16
17						17

DISHONORED NOTES RECEIVABLE

When the maker of a note fails to pay the principal amount or to renew the note at maturity, the note is said to be a **dishonored note receivable.** The maker of the note is still obligated to pay the principal plus interest, and the creditor should take legal steps to collect the debt. However, the balance of the Notes Receivable account shows only the principal of notes that have not yet matured. A note that is past due, or dishonored, should be removed from the Notes Receivable account and returned to the Accounts Receivable account; the amount listed should be the principal plus interest.

For example, C. L. Frederickson Plumbing Supply holds a 60-day, 7 percent note for $800, dated April 20, from Baker Building Supplies, which fails to pay by the due date. Thus the note is dishonored at maturity. Accordingly, C. L. Frederickson makes the following entry in its general journal to remove the dishonored note from the Notes Receivable account.

Objective 6

Dishonored notes receivable.

	DATE		DESCRIPTION		DEBIT		CREDIT		
1	19– Jun.	19	Accounts Receivable, Baker Building						1
2			Supplies		8 0 9 33				2
3			Notes Receivable				8 0 0 00		3
4			Interest Income				9 33		4
5			Baker Building Supplies dis-						5
6			honored their 60-day, 7 percent						6
7			note for $800, dated April 20.						7
8									8

Baker Building Supplies owes both the principal and the interest, and the account should reflect the full amount owed. Note particularly that C. L. Frederickson credits the Interest Income account, even though Baker didn't pay the interest. This is consistent with the accrual basis of accounting: Revenue is recorded when it is *earned*, rather than when it is received. If Baker Building Supplies should ever ask C. L. Frederickson to act as a credit reference, or if Baker ever asks for credit in the future, subsidiary records will show all past dealings, including the dishonored note.

Collection of a Dishonored Note

Now suppose that 30 days after its note has been dishonored, Baker Building Supplies pays up the balance of its account, plus an additional 30 days' interest at 7 percent on the amount owed. The entry in C. L. Frederickson's general journal is as follows.

Objective 7

Collection on a note receivable formerly dishonored.

GENERAL JOURNAL   PAGE _____

	DATE		DESCRIPTION	POST. REF.	DEBIT		CREDIT		
1	19– Jul.	19	Cash		8 1 4 05				1
2			Accounts Receivable, Baker						2
3			Building Supplies				8 0 9 33		3
4			Interest Income				4 72		4
5			Baker Building Supplies paid the						5
6			dishonored note, plus interest						6
7			for 30 days at 7 percent.						7
8									8

C. L. Frederickson gets its money in the long run anyway, and it can now consider the matter closed.

DISCOUNTING NOTES RECEIVABLE

Instead of keeping notes receivable until they come due, a firm can raise cash by selling its notes receivable to a bank or finance company. This type of financing is usually called **discounting,** because the bank deducts the interest from the maturity value of the note to determine the proceeds (that is, the amount of money received by the firm). The **maturity value** is the principal (face value) of the note plus interest from the date of the note until due date.

In the process of discounting a note receivable, the firm endorses the note (as in a check) and delivers it to the financial institution. The financial institution gives out cash now for the privilege of collecting the principal and interest when the note comes due. The discount rate is the annual rate (percentage of maturity value) charged by the financial institution for buying the note.

A Discounted Note: Example 1   C. L. Frederickson Plumbing Supply granted an extension on an open account by accepting a 60-day, 8 percent note for $540, dated April 20, from Craig and Fraser Hardware. To raise cash to buy additional merchandise, C. L. Frederickson sold the note to Valley National Bank on May 5. The bank charged a discount rate of 7 percent. A diagram of the situation looks like this.

Period of the note (60 days)	
Date of note Apr. 20	Date discounted May 5
C. L. Frederickson holds note	Bank holds note (discount period)

The discount period of the note consists of the interval between the date the note is given to the bank and the maturity date of the note. This is referred to as the **discount period.** (In other words, the discount period is the time the note has left to run.) Now we ask: How many days are there in the discount period? For emphasis, let us repeat the diagram in abbreviated form.

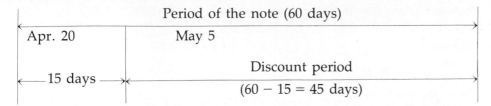

Period of the note (60 days)

Apr. 20	May 5

15 days

Discount period

(60 − 15 = 45 days)

Next we determine the value of the note at maturity and deduct the amount of the bank's discount from it, using the following listing or formula.

Principal ($540)
+ Interest to maturity date (8%, 60 days)

Value at maturity
− Discount (7%, 45 days)

Proceeds

After we set up the problem, we can complete the calculation.

Principal	$540.00
+ Interest (8%, 60 days)	7.20
Value at maturity	$547.20
− Discount (7%, 45 days)	4.79
Proceeds	$542.41

Interest = Principal × Rate × Time

$$\text{Interest} = 540 \times .08 \times \frac{60}{360} = \$7.20$$

Interest = Principal × Rate × Time

$$\text{Interest} = 547.20 \times .07 \times \frac{45}{360} = \$4.788$$

Note that in our calculations we figure the discount on the value of the note at maturity ($547.20, 7 percent, 45 days). The proceeds are the amount that C. L. Frederickson Plumbing Supply receives from the bank; this amount is therefore debited to Cash. If the amount of the proceeds is greater than the amount of the principal, the difference represents Interest Income, since C. L. Frederickson Plumbing Supply made money on the deal. If the amount of the proceeds is less than the principal, on the other hand, the deficiency represents Interest Expense. Look at the entry in C. L. Frederickson's general journal (next page).

Objective 8

Discounting an interest-bearing note.

	19– May	5	Cash			5	4	2	41						1
2			Notes Receivable								5	4	0	00		2
3			Interest Income										2	41		3
4			Discounted at the bank Craig													4
5			and Fraser Hardware's note,													5
6			dated April 20. The bank													6
7			discount rate is 7 percent.													7
8																8
9																9
10																10
11																11
12																12

Contingent Liability

At the time C. L. Frederickson Plumbing Supply discounted Craig and Fraser's note at the bank, C. L. Frederickson had to endorse the note. By this endorsement, C. L. Frederickson was agreeing to pay the note when it became due if the maker did not pay it. Therefore the endorser has a **contingent liability** for payment of the note. If the maker dishonors the note, the endorser is liable. In other words, the liability of the endorser is contingent on the possible dishonoring of the note by the maker. It follows that if the credit rating of the endorser of the note is good, a bank is usually willing to accept and discount a note. The endorser, by virtue of his or her endorsement or guarantee, agrees to pay the note at maturity *if* it is not paid by the maker. The fact that the note receivable is pledged as security, along with the amount of the contingent liability, should be shown as a footnote to the endorser's balance sheet.

Payment of a Discounted Note
by the Maker

The bank collects the principal plus the interest on a discounted note directly from the maker. When the maker pays the bank, the endorser no longer has any contingent liability; the footnote to the endorser's balance sheet can be eliminated when the note is paid. A journal entry is not required.

A Discounted Note: Example 2   On April 25 C. L. Frederickson Plumbing Supply received a 90-day, 6 percent $600 note, dated April 24, from Manning Service Company. On May 4 C. L. Frederickson discounted the note at the bank. The discount rate charged by the bank is 7 percent. In handling discounted notes receivable, you should by all means follow a definite step-by-step procedure.

1. Diagram the situation.

```
                 Period of the note (90 days)
|←─────────────────────────────────────────────────────→|
| Date of | Date        |
| note    | discounted  |
| Apr. 24 | May 4       |
|                   Discount period
|←10 days→|←──────────────────────────────────────────→|
|                   (90 − 10 = 80 days)
```

2. Determine the discount period. Endorser holds the note, April 24 through May 4.

April (30 − 24) = 6 days left in April
May   = 4 days
_____
Days held   = 10 days

Discount period (bank holds note)
90 days − 10 days = 80 days

3. Record the formula.

   Principal ($600)
+ Interest (6%, 90 days)
_____
   Value at maturity
− Discount (7%, 80 days)
_____
   Proceeds

4. Complete the formula.

Principal	$600.00
Plus interest (6%, 90 days)	9.00
Value at maturity	$609.00
Less discount (7%, 80 days)	9.47
Proceeds	$599.53

Interest = Principal × Rate × Time

$$\text{Interest} = 600 \times .06 \times \frac{90}{360} = \$9.00$$

Interest = Principal × Rate × Time

$$\text{Interest} = 609 \times .07 \times \frac{80}{360} = \$9.473$$

5. Make the entry, recognizing that the amount of the proceeds is a debit to Cash. If the amount of the proceeds is less than the principal, debit Interest Expense for the difference.

19– May	4	Cash		5 9 9 53		
		Interest Expense		47		
		Notes Receivable			6 0 0 00	
		Discounted at the bank Manning				
		Service Company's note, dated				
		April 24. The bank discount				
		rate is 7 percent.				

Dishonor of a Discounted Note by the Maker

Suppose that the bank cannot get the maker of the note to pay the principal plus the interest on a pledged note. The bank immediately notifies the firm that endorsed and discounted the note. To take legal advantage of the contingent-liability relationship of the endorser, the bank must formally protest the note. It does so by preparing and mailing to each endorser a Notice of Dishonor and Protest. This statement, signed by a notary public, identifies the note and affirms that the note was duly presented to the maker for payment and that payment was refused. The fee levied by the bank, known as a **protest fee,** is charged initially to the endorser, who passes this fee along to the maker. In essence, any amount that the endorser must pay on behalf of the maker is charged to the maker.

For example, let's say that Manning Service Company dishonors its note that was discounted at the bank by C. L. Frederickson Plumbing Supply. The bank issues a formal Notice of Dishonor and Protest and charges a protest fee of $3. As a consequence, the bank deducts $612 from the account of C. L. Frederickson Plumbing Supply ($600 principal + $9 interest + $3 protest fee). C. L. Frederickson Plumbing Supply makes the entry in its general journal as follows.

Objective 9

Dishonoring of a discounted note receivable.

	19– Jul.	23	Accounts Receivable, Manning Service													1
1																1
2			Company		6	1	2	00								2
3			Cash							6	1	2	00			3
4			Dishonor of Manning Service													4
5			Company's note, dated April 24,													5
6			90 days, 6 percent, principal													6
7			$600, interest $9, and protest													7
8			fee $3.													8
9																9

It's only fair that the protest fee be charged against the maker, and as a result the maker's account at C. L. Frederickson is increased by this amount. *There is no account called "Protest Fee."*

Maker Pays Dishonored Note Plus Additional Interest

Now assume that Manning Service Company finally comes through. On July 31 it pays the note, dated April 24 and dishonored on July 23, plus 7 percent interest from July 23 until July 31. In C. L. Frederickson's general journal, the entry looks like this.

	19– Jul.	31	Cash			6	1	2	95							1
1																1
2			Accounts Receivable, Manning													2
3			Service Company								6	1	2	00		3
4			Interest Income											95		4
5			Received payment on the													5
6			Manning Service Company note,													6
7			dated April 24, discounted at													7
8			the bank on May 4, dishonored													8
9			on July 23; received additional													9
10			interest at 7 percent for period													10
11			July 23 through 31.													11
12																12

A Discounted Note: Example 3   On May 10 McCready and Son gave C. L. Frederickson Plumbing Supply a 60-day, 8 percent note for $2,640, dated May 9. On June 2 C. L. Frederickson Plumbing Supply discounted the note at the bank. The bank charges a discount rate of 7½ percent.

1. Diagram the situation.

2. Determine the discount period. Endorser holds note through June 2.

May (31 − 9) = 22 days left in May
June   = 2 days
_____
Days held   = 24 days

Discount period (bank holds note)
60 days − 24 days = 36 days

3. Record the formula.

   Principal ($2,640)
 + Interest (8%, 60 days)
 _____
   Value at maturity
 − Discount (7½%, 36 days)
 _____
   Proceeds

4. Complete the formula.

Principal	$2,640.00
Plus interest (8%, 60 days)	35.20
Value at maturity	$2,675.20
Less discount (7½%, 36 days)	20.06
Proceeds	$2,655.14

Interest = Principal × Rate × Time

$$\text{Interest} = 2{,}640 \times .08 \times \frac{60}{360} = \$35.20$$

Interest = Principal × Rate × Time

$$\text{Interest} = 2{,}675.20 \times .075 \times \frac{36}{360} = \$20.064$$

5. Record the entry as shown. If the amount of the proceeds is greater than the principal, credit Interest Income for the difference.

	19– Jun.	2	Cash		2	6	5	5	14							1
2			Notes Receivable								2	6	4	0	00	2
3			Interest Income										1	5	14	3
4			Discounted at bank the note													4
5			received from McCready and Son													5
6			dated May 9; discount rate, 7½													6
7			percent.													7

END-OF-FISCAL-PERIOD ADJUSTMENTS: ACCRUED INTEREST ON NOTES RECEIVABLE

Accrued interest income on notes receivable runs parallel to accrued interest expense on notes payable (Chapter 16). Whenever a firm receives *or* issues an interest-bearing note, the interest accrues or accumulates daily. As a result, any interest-bearing notes that overlap two or more fiscal periods require adjusting entries in order for the financial statements to present a true picture of the firm's net income and financial condition.

For example, let's say that a firm has two notes receivable on December 31, the end of the fiscal period:

$4,000, 90 days, 8%, dated November 28
$5,200, 60 days, 7%, dated December 20

We can diagram the situation as follows.

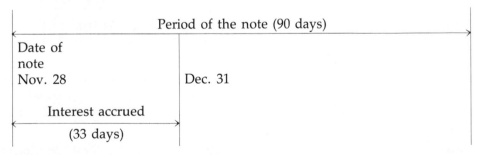

Interest = Principal × Rate × Time

$$\text{Interest} = 4{,}000 \times .08 \times \frac{33}{360} = \$29.33$$

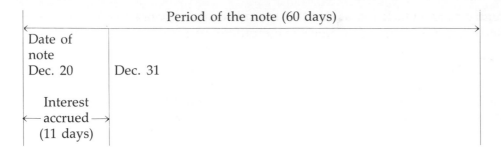

Period of the note (60 days)

Date of note
Dec. 20   Dec. 31

Interest accrued → (11 days)

Interest = Principal × Rate × Time

$$\text{Interest} = 5{,}200 \times .07 \times \frac{11}{360} = \$11.12$$

The maker doesn't ordinarily pay the interest until the note comes due. Since these notes have not matured, the interest income has been neither paid nor recorded ($29.33 + $11.12 = $40.45).

In the firm's general journal, the adjusting entry for the interest income accrued on the two notes looks like this.

Objective 10

Adjustment for accrued interest on notes receivable.

1	19– Dec.	31	*Adjusting Entry*			1
2			*Interest Receivable*	4 0 45		2
3			*Interest Income*		4 0 45	3
4						4

Like all other adjustments, the entry should first be recorded in the Adjustments columns of the work sheet. Here is a T account picture of the situation, assuming a balance in Interest Income of $619.70 before adjustment.

Interest Receivable			Interest Income		
+		–	–		+
Dec. 31 Adj. 40.45					Dec. 31 Bal. 619.70
					Dec. 31 Adj. 40.45

ACCOUNT NAME	TRIAL BALANCE	
	DEBIT	CREDIT
Interest Income		6 1 9 70
Interest Receivable		

Remember that the interest accompanying notes receivable is Interest Income. On the balance sheet, Interest Receivable is classified as a current asset if it is to be received during the coming year.

The accountant reverses this adjusting entry as of the first day of the next fiscal period, because it increases a balance sheet account. When the note matures, the reversing entry makes it possible for the accountant to make the routine entry for the receipt of payment of an interest-bearing note: a debit to Cash, a credit to Notes Receivable, and a credit to Interest Income. This procedure is most convenient, especially when a significant number of notes are involved.

In summary, when a firm has notes that extend from one fiscal period into the next, an adjusting entry is required. Since the interest is not collected until the note becomes due, it is necessary to record the interest income for the first fiscal period. The adjusting entry is this: debit Interest Receivable and credit Interest Income. In the work sheet shown below in Figure 17-1, you can also see the effect of this adjustment on the financial statements.

USE OF SPECIAL JOURNALS

Up to now, in this chapter, we have concentrated on analyzing the debits and credits for each transaction. The entries were shown in general journal form to portray the debits and credits in a clear manner. However, if a firm is using a cash receipts journal and a cash payments journal, any entries involving cash should be recorded in one of these journals. They should not be recorded in a general journal.

To illustrate the use of the cash journals, we will show the related entries again. To conserve space in showing entries in the general journal, we omit explanations.

Figure 17-1

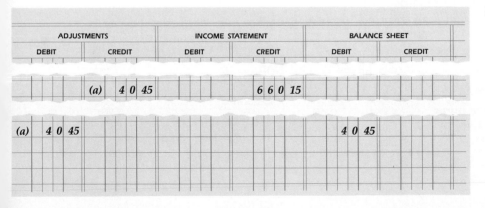

April 6: Received a note for $480 from Henning's Plumbing Company, in settlement of the sale of March 6, 30 days, 8 percent.

	DATE		ACCOUNT								
1	*Apr.*	*6*	*Notes Receivable*		4 8 0 00						1
2			*Accounts Receivable, Henning's*								2
3			*Plumbing*					4 8 0 00			3
4											4

May 6: Received payment at maturity of principal plus interest on the Henning's Plumbing Company's note.

CASH RECEIPTS JOURNAL   PAGE _____

	DATE		ACCOUNT CREDITED	POST. REF.	SUNDRY ACCOUNTS CREDIT	ACCOUNTS RECEIVABLE CREDIT	SALES CREDIT	CASH DEBIT	
1	*19– May*	*6*	*Notes Receivable*		4 8 0 00			4 8 3 20	1
2			*Interest Income*		3 20				2
3									3
4									4

April 8: Granted a loan to James Hudson, an employee, $336, for three months, 6 percent, dated April 8.

CASH PAYMENTS JOURNAL   PAGE _____

	DATE	CK. NO.	ACCOUNT DEBITED	POST. REF.	SUNDRY ACCOUNTS DEBIT	ACCOUNTS PAYABLE DEBIT	CASH CREDIT	
1	*19– Apr.*	*8*	*Notes Receivable*		3 3 6 00		3 3 6 00	1
2								2
3								3

July 8: Received payment from James Hudson of principal plus interest on the three-month, 6 percent loan granted him on April 8.

CASH RECEIPTS JOURNAL   PAGE _____

	DATE		ACCOUNT CREDITED	POST. REF.	SUNDRY ACCOUNTS CREDIT	ACCOUNTS RECEIVABLE CREDIT	SALES CREDIT	CASH DEBIT	
1	*19– Jul.*	*8*	*Notes Receivable*		3 3 6 00			3 4 1 04	1
2			*Interest Income*		5 04				2
3									3

April 9: Received a note for $900 from Maxwell Heating and Air Conditioning for merchandise, 60 days, 7 percent, dated April 9.

	DATE		DESCRIPTION	POST. REF.	DEBIT	CREDIT	
1	19– Apr.	9	Notes Receivable		9 0 0 00		1
2			Sales			9 0 0 00	2

June 8: Received interest from Maxwell Heating and Air Conditioning on its note of April 9.

CASH RECEIPTS JOURNAL   PAGE _____

	DATE		ACCOUNT CREDITED	POST. REF.	SUNDRY ACCOUNTS CREDIT	ACCOUNTS RECEIVABLE CREDIT	SALES CREDIT	CASH DEBIT	
1	19– Jun.	8	Interest Income		1 0 50			1 0 50	1

Then it agreed to renewal of the note by issuance of a new note, 30 days, 8 percent, dated June 8.

	DATE		DESCRIPTION	POST. REF.	DEBIT	CREDIT	
1	19– Jun.	8	Notes Receivable		9 0 0 00		1
2			Notes Receivable			9 0 0 00	2

June 19: Baker Building Supplies dishonored its note of April 20 for $800, at 7 percent, for 60 days.

GENERAL JOURNAL   PAGE _____

	DATE		DESCRIPTION	POST. REF.	DEBIT	CREDIT	
1	19– Jun.	19	Accounts Receivable		8 0 9 33		1
2			Notes Receivable			8 0 0 00	2
3			Interest Income			9 33	3
4							4

July 19: Baker Building Supplies paid its dishonored note, plus additional interest for 30 days at 7 percent.

CASH RECEIPTS JOURNAL

	DATE		ACCOUNT CREDITED	POST. REF.	SUNDRY ACCOUNTS CREDIT	ACCOUNTS RECEIVABLE CREDIT	SALES CREDIT	CASH DEBIT	
1	19– Jul.	19	Accounts Receivable, Baker						1
2			Building Supplies			8 0 9 33		8 1 4 05	2
3			Interest Income		4 72				3

May 5: Discounted at Valley National Bank the note received from Craig and Fraser Hardware, dated April 20, $540, 8 percent, 60 days. The discount rate is 7 percent.

CASH RECEIPTS JOURNAL

	DATE		ACCOUNT CREDITED	POST. REF.	SUNDRY ACCOUNTS CREDIT	ACCOUNTS RECEIVABLE CREDIT	SALES CREDIT	CASH DEBIT	
1	19– May	5	Notes Receivable		5 4 0 00			5 4 2 41	1
2			Interest Income		2 41				2
3									3
4									4

May 4: Discounted at Valley National Bank the note received from Manning Service Company, dated April 24, $600, 6 percent, 90 days. The discount rate is 7 percent.

CASH RECEIPTS JOURNAL

	DATE		ACCOUNT CREDITED	POST. REF.	SUNDRY ACCOUNTS DEBIT	SUNDRY ACCOUNTS CREDIT	SALES CREDIT	CASH DEBIT	
1	19– May	4	Notes Receivable			6 0 0 00		5 9 9 53	1
2			Interest Expense		47				2
3									3
4									4
5									5
6									6

July 23: Notified by Valley National Bank that Manning Service Company dishonored its note previously discounted on May 4. Paid bank the principal, $600, plus interest, $9, plus protest fee, $3.

CASH PAYMENTS JOURNAL PAGE _____

	DATE	CK. NO.	ACCOUNT DEBITED	POST. REF.	SUNDRY ACCOUNTS DEBIT	ACCOUNTS PAYABLE DEBIT	CASH CREDIT	
1	19– Jul.	23	*Accounts Receivable,*					1
2			*Manning Service*					2
3			*Company*		6 1 2 00		6 1 2 00	3
4								4
5								5

July 31: Manning Service Company paid the note dated April 24, previously discounted at the bank and dishonored, plus $.95 interest from July 23 through 31. The same entry in a cash receipts journal looks like this:

CASH RECEIPTS JOURNAL PAGE _____

	DATE	ACCOUNT CREDITED	POST. REF.	SUNDRY ACCOUNTS CREDIT	ACCOUNTS RECEIVABLE CREDIT	SALES CREDIT	CASH DEBIT	
1	19– Jul. 31	*Accounts Receivable, Manning*						1
2		*Service Company*			6 1 2 00		6 1 2 95	2
3		*Interest Income*		95				3
4								4
5								5

June 2: Discounted at Valley National Bank the note received from McCready and Son, dated May 9, $2,640, 8 percent, 60 days. The discount rate is 7½ percent.

CASH RECEIPTS JOURNAL PAGE _____

	DATE	ACCOUNT CREDITED	POST. REF.	SUNDRY ACCOUNTS CREDIT	CASH DEBIT	
1	19– Jun. 2	*Notes Receivable*		2 6 4 0 00	2 6 5 5 14	1
2		*Interest Income*		1 5 14		2
3						3

GLOSSARY

Accrued interest income on notes receivable   When a note receivable begins in one fiscal period and matures in the following one, accrued interest represents interest income earned but not yet received—for example, from the date of the note until the last day of the fiscal period.

Contingent liability   A liability that may develop—for example, if a note receivable is discounted at a bank and then the maker does not pay.

Discounting a note receivable   The process by which a firm may raise cash by selling a note receivable to a bank or finance company. The bank deducts the interest from the maturity value of the note to determine the proceeds (amount of money) that the firm receives.

Discount period   The time between the date a note receivable is discounted and the date it matures.

Dishonored note receivable   When the maker of a note fails to pay the principal and interest at the maturity date, the maker is said to be dishonoring the note.

Maturity value   The principal (face value) of a note plus interest from date of note until due date.

Protest fee   If the maker of a note receivable that has been discounted by a bank dishonors the note (fails to pay the bank by the due date), the bank charges a protest fee for compiling and mailing a Notice of Dishonor and Protest.

QUESTIONS, EXERCISES, AND PROBLEMS

Discussion Questions

1. Why is a note receivable considered to be superior to an account receivable?
2. Describe possible situations in which notes receivable may come into existence.
3. What is meant by dishonoring a note receivable, and what happens to a dishonored note receivable?
4. What is the formula for discounting an interest-bearing note receivable?
5. Explain what *contingent liability* means in relation to the endorser of a note.
6. Where are Notes Receivable due within a year and Interest Income placed in classified financial statements?
7. Why is it necessary to make an adjusting entry for accrued interest on an interest-bearing note receivable. Should the adjusting entry be reversed?

Exercises

Exercise 17-1   The Marcia Thompson Company received a 90-day, 9 percent note for $1,200, dated March 5, from Howard A. Hansen, a charge customer.

a. What is the due date of the note?
b. How much interest is due at maturity?

Exercise 17-2 Given the data in Exercise 17-1, write entries in general journal form on the books of the Marcia Thompson Company to record the following.

a. Receipt of the note from Hansen.
b. Receipt of the principal and interest at maturity.

Given the data in Exercise 17-1, write entries in general journal form on Howard A. Hansen's books to record the following.

c. Issuance of the note by Hansen.
d. Payment of the note at maturity.

Exercise 17-3 On May 4 the Robert Hendricks Company received a 90-day, 9 percent note for $6,000, dated May 4, for merchandise sold to the Blivens Company. Hendricks Company endorsed the note in favor of its bank on May 28. The bank discounted the note at 8 percent, paying Hendricks $6,045.02. Determine the following facts.

a. Number of days the Robert Hendricks Company held the note
b. Number of days in the discount period
c. Face value
d. Maturity value
e. Proceeds
f. Interest income or expense recorded by the payee (the Robert Hendricks Company)

Exercise 17-4 Prepare entries in general journal form to record the following.

Jun.   8 Sold merchandise on account to Norman Schultz; terms 2/10, n/30; $1,060.
Jul.   8 Received $160 in cash from Norman Schultz, and a 60 day, 10 percent note for $900, dated July 8.
Aug. 13 Discounted note at the bank at 9 percent.

Exercise 17-5 A discounted note receivable is dishonored by the maker, the Tredder Company. The endorser pays the bank the face value of the note, $600; the interest, $9; plus a protest fee, $3. In general journal form, journalize the entry to record the payment by the endorser.

Exercise 17-6 Prepare entries in general journal form to record the following transactions for the Colt Company.

Mar.   3 The Colt Company received from Amalgamated Stores a $3,000, 90-day, 12 percent note, dated March 3, as an extension of a charge account.
      13 Discounted the note at the bank at 10 percent.

Jun.   1 Amalgamated Stores dishonored the note; Colt paid the bank the amount due on the note, plus a protest fee of $3.

Jul.   1 Colt received from Amalgamated Stores the amount due on the dishonored note, plus interest for 30 days at 12 percent on the total amount owed.

Exercise 17-7   The T accounts below show a series of six transactions concerning a sale of merchandise on account and subsequent payment of the amount owed. Describe the nature of each transaction.

Cash		Accounts Receivable		Sales	Interest Income
(d) 894	**(e)** 909	**(a)** 930	**(b)** 30	**(a)** 930	**(f)** 4
(f) 913		**(e)** 909	**(c)** 900		
			(f) 909		

Sales Returns and Allowances	Notes Receivable		Interest Expense
(b) 30	**(c)** 900	**(d)** 900	**(d)** 6

Exercise 17-8   Journalize the following transactions incurred by the Cooper Company.

Year 1

Nov.   1 Received a 90-day, 12 percent note receivable in the amount of $6,000 from the Baxter Company, a charge customer.

Dec.   31 Made the adjusting entry and the closing entry.

Year 2

Jan.   1 Made the reversing entry.

Jan.   30 Received full payment on the note issued by the Baxter Company.

PROBLEM SET A

Problem 17-1A   The Swanson Paint Company carried out the following transactions this year.

Jan.   19 Sold merchandise on account to C. L. Conway Company; 2/10, n/30; $1,800.

29 Received check from C. L. Conway Company for the sale on January 19.

Feb.   23 Sold merchandise on account to P and M Construction Company; 2/10, n/30; $2,100.

Mar.   24 Received a 60-day, 9 percent note, dated this day, for $2,100 from P and M Construction Company for the amount owed on account.

May   23 Received a check from P and M Construction Company for the amount owed on the note of March 24.

Jun.   8 Sold merchandise on account to Radach and Son for $2,600, receiving its 90-day, 10 percent note.

Sep.   6 Received payment from Radach and Son for the amount owed on its note of June 8.

Instructions

Record the above transactions in general journal form.

Problem 17-2A   The Cobb Distributing Company carried out the following transactions this year.

Jan.   14 Sold merchandise on account to Clark Service Company; 1/10, n/30; $1,920.

Feb.   13 Received a 30-day, 9 percent note, dated this day, for $1,920 from Clark Service Company on account.

Mar.   15 Clark Service Company paid the amount due on its note of February 13.

Apr.   29 Sold merchandise on account to Taylor Arcade; 1/10, n/30; $2,400.

May   29 Received a 60-day, 10 percent note, dated this day, for $2,400 from Taylor Arcade on account.

Jul.   28 Taylor Arcade paid the interest on its note of May 29 and renewed the obligation by issuing a new 60-day, 11 percent note for $2,400.

Sep.   26 Received check from Taylor Arcade for the amount owed on its note of July 28.

Oct.   2 Sold merchandise to A. B. Signer Company for $3,600, receiving a 30-day, 7 percent note dated this day.

        22 Discounted the note received from A. B. Signer Company at the Randolph State Bank; discount rate, 8 percent.

Instructions

Record these transactions in a general journal.

Problem 17-3A   Here are some selected transactions carried out by the Bates Hotel Supply Company this year.

Jan.   11 Sold merchandise on account to Cape Mallon Motor Lodge; 2/10, n/30; $2,980.

Feb.   10 Received a 30-day, 9 percent note from Cape Mallon Motor Lodge for $2,980, dated February 10.

Mar.   12 Received $1,502.35 from Cape Mallon Motor Lodge as payment on its note dated February 10: $1,480 as part payment on the principal, $22.35 as interest on $2,980 for 30 days at 9 percent. Received a new 30-day, 10 percent note for $1,500, dated March 12.

Apr.   11 Sold merchandise to Jerry's Motel, receiving its 60-day, 10 percent note, dated April 11, in the amount of $2,000.

        11 Received a check from Cape Mallon Motor Lodge for the amount owed on the note of March 12.

        19 Discounted the note received from Jerry's Motel at the Mountain State Bank; discount rate, 8 percent.

May   27 Sold merchandise on account to Fifth Avenue Motor Inn; 2/10, n/30; $1,590.

Jun. 26 Received a $1,590 note from Fifth Avenue Motor Inn for 90 days at 10 percent, dated June 26.

Sep. 24 Fifth Avenue Motor Inn dishonored its note dated June 26.

Instructions

Use a sales journal, a cash receipts journal, and a general journal to record the above transactions. Record each transaction in the appropriate journal.

Problem 17-4A The Kozack Machinery Company completed the following transactions during the year ended December 31.

Jun. 8 Received a 60-day, 7 percent note, dated June 8, for $1,800 from Peerless Building Maintenance Company for the sale of merchandise. (The sale was not previously recorded.)

21 Received a 30-day, 7 percent note, dated June 20, for $2,700, from Kline and Kline, a charge customer.

Jul. 6 Received a 90-day, 8 percent note, dated July 6, for $3,000, from Sargent Tool Company, a charge customer.

20 Received a check from Kline and Kline in payment of principal and interest on its note.

Aug. 7 Received payment of interest from Peerless Building Maintenance Company for its note of June 8 and also a new 30-day, 8 percent note, dated August 7, for $1,800.

22 Received a 60-day, 7 percent note, dated August 22, for $1,500, from Midwest Equipment Company, a charge customer.

Sep. 6 Peerless Building Maintenance paid its note dated August 7, principal plus interest.

11 Discounted the note received from Midwest Equipment Company, dated August 22, at the Morton State Bank; discount rate, 6 percent.

Oct. 4 Sargent Tool Company dishonored its note dated July 6.

Dec. 16 Received a 60-day, 7 percent note, dated December 16, for $4,500, from Callas Machine Tool Company, a charge customer.

Instructions

1. Record the above transactions in a general journal.
2. Make the adjusting entry.

Problem Set B

Problem 17-1B Here are selected transactions carried out by Hunter and Company this year.

Jan. 14 Sold merchandise on account to T. R. Vaughn Company; 2/10, n/30; $1,600.

24 Received check from T. R. Vaughn Company for the sale of January 14.

Feb. 18 Sold merchandise on account to Steele and Stacy; 2/10, n/30; $2,850.

Mar. 19 Received a 30-day, 9 percent note, dated this day, for $2,850 from Steele and Stacy on account.

Apr. 18 Received a check from Steele and Stacy for the amount owed on the note of March 19.

Jun. 2 Sold merchandise to Riddle Refrigeration, $3,750, receiving a 90-day, 10 percent note, dated this day. (This sale was not previously recorded.)

Aug. 31 Received payment from Riddle Refrigeration for the amount owed on the note of June 2.

Instructions

Record the above transactions in a general journal.

Problem 17-2B Here are some of the transactions carried out by Randolph and Company this year.

Jan. 9 Sold merchandise on account to Shaw Electrical Supply; 2/10, n/30; $2,260.

Feb. 8 Received a 30-day, 9 percent note, dated this day, for $2,260 from Shaw Electrical Supply on account.

Mar. 10 Shaw Electrical Supply paid the amount due on its note of February 8.

Apr. 27 Sold merchandise on account to Hanford Electric; 2/10, n/30; $2,200.

May 27 Received a 45-day, 11 percent note, dated this day, for $2,200 from Hanford Electric on account.

Jul. 11 Hanford Electric paid the interest on its note of May 27 and renewed the obligation by issuing a new 60-day, 12 percent note for $2,200, dated July 11.

Sep. 9 Received check from Hanford Electric for the amount owed on its note of July 11.

12 Sold merchandise on account to Peart Service Company, $4,200, receiving its 30-day, 10 percent note. (The sale was not previously recorded.)

22 Discounted the note received from Peart Service Company at the Northern State Bank; discount rate, 9 percent.

Instructions

Record these transactions in a general journal.

Problem 17-3B Selected transactions of the Romano Restaurant Supply Company carried out this year are as follows.

Jan. 8 Sold merchandise on account to Paragon Palace; 2/10, n/30; $3,630.

Feb. 7 Received a 30-day, 7 percent note from Paragon Palace, $3,630, dated February 7.

Mar. 9 Received $1,651.18 from Paragon Palace as part payment on the note dated February 7: $1,630 as part payment on the principal and $21.18 as interest on $3,630 for 30 days at 7 percent. Received a new 30-day, 8 percent note, dated March 9, for $2,000.

Apr.   2 Sold merchandise to Tony's Pizza, $1,800, receiving their 90-day, 9 percent note, dated April 2.

    8 Received a check from Paragon Palace for the amount owed on the note of March 9.

    10 Discounted the note received from Tony's Pizza at the Rocky Mountain National Bank; discount rate, 8 percent.

May   6 Sold merchandise on account to Hagen's Steak House; 2/10, n/30; $960.

Jun.   5 Received a 45-day, 9 percent note for $960 from Hagen's Steak House, dated June 5.

Jul.   20 Hagen's Steak House dishonored its note dated June 5.

Instructions

Using a sales journal, a cash receipts journal, and a general journal, record the above transactions in the appropriate place.

Problem 17-4B   Here are some selected transactions of Pinter Lumber Supply carried out during the year ended December 31.

Jun.   3 Received a 60-day, 8 percent note, dated June 3, for $1,750 from Sutherlin Fibre Company for merchandise. (The sale was not previously recorded.)

    14 Received a 30-day, 8 percent note, dated June 14, for $2,200 from Smithson and Francis, a charge customer.

Jul.   1 Received a 90-day, 7 percent note, dated July 1, for $2,800 from Johnson Equipment Company, a charge customer.

    14 Received a check from Smithson and Francis in payment of principal and interest on its note.

Aug.   2 Received payment of interest from Sutherlin Fibre Company for its note of June 3 and a new 30-day, 8 percent note, for $1,750, dated August 2.

    15 Received a 60-day, 8 percent note, dated August 15, from Philmore Lumber Company, a charge customer, $1,600.

Sep.   1 Sutherlin Fibre Company paid its note dated August 2, principal plus interest.

    4 Discounted the note received from Philmore Company, dated August 15, at the Pinkerton State Bank; discount rate, 6 percent.

    29 Johnson Equipment Company dishonored its note dated July 1.

Dec.   4 Received a 60-day, 7 percent note, dated December 4, from Tedford Machinery Company, a charge customer, $1,590.

Instructions

1. Record the transactions in general journal form.
2. Make the adjusting entry.

18 Accounting for Valuation of Receivables

Learning Objectives

After you have completed this chapter, you will be able to do the following:

1. Make the adjusting entry to record estimated bad-debt losses by using the allowance method of handling bad debts.

2. Determine the amount of the adjusting entry by aging Accounts Receivable or by using a percentage of Accounts Receivable.

3. Calculate the amount of the adjusting entry by using a percentage of sales or net sales.

4. Journalize the entries to write off Accounts Receivable as being uncollectible using the allowance method of accounting for bad-debt losses.

5. Journalize entries to reinstate Accounts Receivable previously written off.

6. Journalize the entries to write off Accounts Receivable as being uncollectible using the direct write-off method of accounting for bad-debt losses.

The use of credit for both buying and selling goods and services has become standard practice for business firms of all types and levels: retailers, wholesalers, and manufacturers. By now, you have learned to record sales of merchandise on account as a debit to Accounts Receivable and a credit to Sales. You have also learned to debit Cash and credit Accounts Receivable when the account is collected.

Business firms selling goods or services on credit inevitably find that not all the Accounts Receivable are collected in full. Consequently, the unpaid accounts must eventually be written off as uncollectible, or as a bad debt. In other words, a firm that grants credit "can't win 'em all," so the firm is obliged to provide for the anticipated losses. In this chapter we'll discuss ways to provide for losses as well as to write off charge accounts that are no longer collectible.

We shall examine two methods of accounting for uncollectible accounts; both are acceptable to the federal income tax authorities. The allowance-for-bad-debts method is more popular because it enables the firm to match up sales of one year with bad-debt losses of the same year. It portrays revenue and expense more accurately. Large firms, or firms selling primarily on a credit basis, use this method; we shall place our main emphasis on this method because of its relative importance. Small firms use the direct write-off method. We'll talk about this method in the last part of the chapter.

THE CREDIT DEPARTMENT

Because it governs the extension of credit to charge customers, the Credit Department has to keep a watchful eye on present customers, evaluate the debt-paying ability of prospective customers, and determine the maximum amount of credit to be extended to each. Retail stores selling to individuals rely on reports from local retail credit bureaus. When wholesalers and manufacturers grant credit to customers, they utilize reports of national credit-rating institutions such as Dun and Bradstreet, wholesale credit bureaus, and the financial statements of prospective customers. Business firms that make many sales on credit find it worthwhile to subscribe to credit bureaus or credit-rating agencies. These credit-reporting organizations maintain files of current financial information on charge customers, establish credit ratings for each charge customer, and conduct special investigations on request.

It's always bad, of course, if a business firm has high credit losses, since any firm needs to be paid for its sales on account. Surprisingly, it may be bad if a firm has no credit losses. Such a record indicates that the firm must be turning down applications for credit, even though most applicants would indeed pay their bills. In this last situation, the firm not only loses many immediate sales but reaps considerable ill will as well, because it turns down so many prospective customers. A sound credit policy should provide for a limited amount of credit losses; it is the function of the Credit Department to keep the losses within acceptable limits.

MATCHING BAD-DEBT LOSSES WITH SALES

A basic principle of the accrual basis of accounting is that revenue for a fiscal period must be matched by the expenses incurred during that same period to earn that revenue. This principle is consistent with our earlier presentation of adjusting entries. As you recall, depreciation represents the loss in usefulness of, say, equipment for a particular year. In making the adjustment, we allocate this expense to one year of operations. For example, we debit Depreciation Expense, Equipment and credit Accumulated Depreciation, Equipment. By the same token, when a firm sells merchandise on account to a customer who may eventually default on the obligation, the firm has a bad-debt loss potential. The firm must try to match the loss with the revenue earned for the year in which the sale is made. Consequently, the firm should anticipate this bad-debt loss or expense in the year in which the sale is made.

At the time of making the sale, the firm does not *know* that it has incurred a loss, because it anticipates that the customer will pay the obligation (otherwise it would not have extended credit to that particular customer). In other words, the firm making the credit sale has increased its revenue account, but it does not know at the time of the sale whether or not the revenue will be received. As a matter of fact, the firm will not be certain of the loss until it has repeatedly failed in attempts to collect the bill. So the final recognition of the loss will probably occur many months after the sale. In order to match up the bad-debt losses of the year with the sales of the same year, the firm must make an estimate of the losses as a means of providing for them in advance. The allowance method of accounting for bad debts provides the means for matching bad-debt losses with the applicable sales.

THE ALLOWANCE METHOD OF ACCOUNTING FOR BAD DEBTS

Most business firms use the **allowance method of accounting for bad-debt losses.** An adjusting entry is recorded first in the Adjustment columns of the work sheet—much like the adjustment for depreciation, which was described in Chapter 5. In general journal and T account form, the adjusting entry for the estimated bad-debt losses is shown in the following examples.

				Adjusting Entry											
1				Adjusting Entry											1
2	19– Dec.	31	Bad Debts Expense			7	0	0	00						2
3			Allowance for Doubtful Accounts								7	0	0	00	3
4															4

Bad Debts Expense			Allowance for Doubtful Accounts		
+		–	–		+
Adj.	700			Bal.	1,100
				Adj.	700

The purpose of the adjusting entry is to increase Bad Debts Expense by the amount of the estimated loss, and also to show a realistic figure for the book value of Accounts Receivable. Allowance for Doubtful Accounts is classified as a deduction from Accounts Receivable. As such, it is a contra account, similar to Accumulated Depreciation. Just as the book value of Equipment equals the cost of Equipment minus Accumulated Depreciation, Equipment, the book value of Accounts Receivable equals Accounts Receivable minus Allowance for Doubtful Accounts. Accountants also refer to the book value of Accounts Receivable as the *expected realizable value*.

Because a firm cannot know with certainty which accounts won't be fully collected, it's not possible to credit Accounts Receivable directly. Think of a life insurance company that insures 1,000 newborn infants. The insurance company doesn't know *who* will be alive at age 21, but on the basis of experience, it can estimate *how many* will be alive at age 21. Simi-

Objective 1

Make the adjusting entry to record estimated bad-debt losses by using the allowance method of handling bad debts.

ACCOUNT NAME	TRIAL BALANCE				
	DEBIT		CREDIT		
Accounts Receivable	60 0 0 0 00				
Allowance for Doubtful Accounts			1 1 0 0 00		
Equipment	74 0 0 0 00				
Accumulated Depreciation, Equipment			22 0 0 0 00		
Bad Debts Expense					
Depreciation Expense, Equipment					

larly, on the basis of its experience, a business firm is able to estimate what this year's bad-debt losses will be. The firm bases its estimate on a year's sales, but it can't designate with certainty *which* credit sales will not be paid.

Prior to the adjustments, the *Bad Debts Expense account has no previous balance, as the account is not used during the fiscal period.* The firm's accountant makes an adjusting entry to increase Bad Debts Expense and immediately closes the account along with all other expense accounts. Allowance for Doubtful Accounts, on the other hand, has a balance that is carried over from previous years and is not closed. Notice where these accounts appear in the partial worksheet shown below.

Note that Accounts Receivable is recorded in the debit column, and Allowance for Doubtful Accounts is recorded in the credit column. The $700 adjustment is added to the previous credit balance of $1,100, resulting in $1,800 being recorded in the Balance Sheet Credit column. As you can see, Allowance for Doubtful Accounts is handled much like Accumulated Depreciation. Both are recorded as credits in the Adjustments and Balance Sheet columns of the work sheet; also, the adjustments are never reversed because both accounts have previous balances after the first year of operations.

Bad Debts Expense and Allowance for Doubtful Accounts on Financial Statements

The Bad Debts Expense account appears on the income statement as an operating expense. Some firms subdivide operating expenses into selling expenses and general expenses, in which case they list Bad Debts Expense in the category of general expenses. (*Reason:* The decision to grant credit is usually a function of the administrative rather than the sales staff.)

ADJUSTMENTS		INCOME STATEMENT		BALANCE SHEET	
DEBIT	CREDIT	DEBIT	CREDIT	DEBIT	CREDIT
				60 0 0 0 00	
	a) 7 0 0 00				1 8 0 0 00

				74 0 0 0 00	
	b) 6 0 0 0 00				28 0 0 0 00

a) 7 0 0 00		7 0 0 00			
b) 6 0 0 0 00		6 0 0 0 00			

Figure 18-1

R. A. Simpson and Company
Balance Sheet
December 31, 19–

Assets					
Current Assets:					
Cash			$ 12 0 0 0 00	
Notes Receivable			8 0 0 0 00	
Accounts Receivable	$60 0 0 0 00			
Less Allowance for Doubtful				
Accounts	1 8 0 0 00		58 2 0 0 00	
Merchandise Inventory			96 0 0 0 00	
Supplies			4 0 0 00	
Total Current Assets			$ 174 6 0 0 00	
Plant and Equipment:				
Equipment	$74 0 0 0 00			
Less Accumulated Depreciation	28 0 0 0 00		$ 46 0 0 0 00	

Allowance for Doubtful Accounts is listed immediately below Accounts Receivable in the Current Assets section of the balance sheet, as in Figure 18-1.

The $58,200 represents the anticipated net realizable value of Accounts Receivable; this is also known as the **book value of Accounts Receivable.** Again, one classifies Allowance for Doubtful Accounts as a *valuation* or *contra account,* since it is a deduction from an asset. Sometimes accountants use other names for this account, such as Allowance for Bad Debts, Allowance for Uncollectible Accounts, and Estimated Uncollectible Accounts.

Estimating the Amount of Bad Debts Expense

Objective 2

Determine the amount of an adjusting entry by aging Accounts Receivable or by using a percentage of Accounts Receivable.

Management—on the basis of its judgment and past experience—has to make a reasonable estimate of the amount of its uncollectible accounts. Of course, it stands to reason that any such estimate is modified by business trends. In a period of prosperity and high employment, one can expect fewer losses due to uncollectible accounts than in a period of recession.

There are two alternative approaches commonly used to estimate the amount of the adjustment for Bad Debts Expense: (1) base the estimate on an analysis or aging of Accounts Receivable, and (2) base the estimate on a percentage of Accounts Receivable.

Estimating Bad Debts on the Basis of an Analysis of Accounts Receivable In this method, each charge customer's account is examined to estimate the proportion of the total amount of Accounts Receivable that is likely to be uncollectible. Since this figure should be the new balance of Allowance for Doubtful Accounts, *one makes an adjusting entry large enough to make the balance of the Allowance for Doubtful Accounts the same as the estimated uncollectible amount.*

For example, the Clarise Stanley Company has a present credit balance in the Allowance for Doubtful Accounts of $410. The company estimates that $3,580 of Accounts Receivable are uncollectible. We make the adjusting entry for $3,170 ($3,580 − $410). This situation is illustrated by T accounts as follows.

Bad Debts Expense		Allowance for Doubtful Accounts	
+	−	−	+
Adj. 3,170			Bal. 410
			Adj. 3,170
			3,580

The new balance of Allowance for Doubtful Accounts is $3,580, the amount of receivables that the firm now estimates to be uncollectible.

Aging the Accounts Receivable

The most common technique for estimating the total uncollectible amount of Accounts Receivable is to **age** each charge customer's account, by (1) determining the number of days old each account is, and (2) determining the number of days the account is past due. One then makes out a working paper, dividing the ages of the accounts into categories or age groups, as shown below. One can then think of this as an aging schedule.

ANALYSIS OF ACCOUNTS RECEIVABLE BY AGE

CUSTOMER'S NAME	BALANCE	NOT YET DUE	DAYS PAST DUE					
			1–30	31–60	61–90	91–180	181–365	OVER 365
A. B. Allen	722.00	722.00						
B. N. Baker	464.00				464.00			
C. L. Chase	136.90			136.90				
D. R. Dalton	914.00	914.00						
E. V. Early	593.10			593.10				
Total	78,200.00	4,030.00	3,280.00	1,975.00	1,260.00	834.00	421.00	

All the accounts in the accounts receivable ledger are listed by both name and amount. The older an account, the more likely it is to be uncollectible. On the basis of its past experience, a firm can estimate that a given percentage of each age group of accounts is uncollectible. The firm can then multiply the total amount for each age group by the appropriate percentage for that group to determine the amount that is estimated to be uncollectible for that age group. Here is an example.

Age Interval	Amount	Estimated Percentage Uncollectible	Allowance for Doubtful Accounts
Not yet due	$78,200	2	$78,200 × .02 = $1,564.00
1 to 30 days past due	4,030	4	4,030 × .04 = 161.20
31 to 60 days past due	3,280	10	3,280 × .10 = 328.00
61 to 90 days past due	1,975	20	1,975 × .20 = 395.00
91 to 180 days past due	1,260	30	1,260 × .30 = 378.00
181 to 365 days past due	834	50	834 × .50 = 417.00
More than 365 days past due	421	80	421 × .80 = 336.80
	$90,000		$3,580.00

To sum up: The firm estimates that $3,580 of Accounts Receivable is uncollectible. *It now has to bring the balance of Allowance for Doubtful Accounts up to the desired figure of $3,580.* Allowance for Doubtful Accounts has a present credit balance of $410, so the firm adjusts for the difference, $3,170. After the accountant posts the adjusting entry, the footing of Al-

Clarise Stanley Company
Work Sheet
For year ended December 31, 19—

ACCOUNT NAME	TRIAL BALANCE	
	DEBIT	CREDIT
Accounts Receivable	90 0 0 0 00	
Allowance for Doubtful Accounts		4 1 0 00
Bad Debts Expense		
	641 5 0 0 00	641 5 0 0 00

lowances for Doubtful Accounts indicates the desired balance, as determined by the aging procedure. The adjusting data and their effect on the accounts are illustrated in Figure 18-2.

Bad Debts Expense ($3,170) will appear in the income statement in the general-expense portion of Operating Expenses. Like all expenses, it will be closed at the end of the year into Income Summary. For emphasis, let's repeat the placement of the accounts in the balance sheet.

Assets			
Current Assets:			

Accounts Receivable	90 0 0 0 00		
Less Allowance for Doubtful Accounts	3 5 8 0 00	86 4 2 0 00	

Estimating Bad Debts as a Percentage of Accounts Receivable

Some business firms feel that the aging procedure is too time-consuming; they prefer a quicker but less exact method for estimating the amount of uncollectible Accounts Receivable. These firms take an average of the actual bad-debt losses of previous years as a percentage of Accounts Receivable. For example, the William Bush Company calculated the amount of the adjustment for uncollectible accounts as follows (top of next page).

Figure 18-2

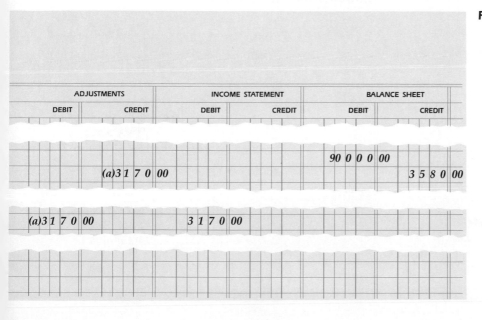

ADJUSTMENTS		INCOME STATEMENT		BALANCE SHEET	
DEBIT	CREDIT	DEBIT	CREDIT	DEBIT	CREDIT
				90 0 0 0 00	
	(a)3 1 7 0 00				3 5 8 0 00
(a)3 1 7 0 00		3 1 7 0 00			

End of Year	Balance of Accounts Receivable	Total Actual Losses from Accounts Receivable (Accounts Receivable Written Off)
19x1	$22,000	$ 770
19x2	28,000	764
19x3	24,000	686
	$74,000	$2,220

The firm's average loss over three consecutive years was 3 percent.

$$\frac{2,220}{74,000} = .03 = 3\%$$

Assume that, at the end of 19x4, the balance of Accounts Receivable was $29,200 and the credit balance of Allowance for Doubtful Accounts was $172. The amount of Accounts Receivable the company estimated to be uncollectible was $876 ($29,200 × .03 = $876). Since $876 was the desired figure, the amount of the adjustment was $704 ($876 − $172 = $704). As in the case of aging Accounts Receivable, when you figure the adjustment for bad debts as a percentage of Accounts Receivable, *you make an adjusting entry to change the balance of Allowance for Doubtful Accounts to the desired figure.* Notice how the adjusting entry looks in the following T accounts.

Bad Debts Expense		Allowance for Doubtful Accounts	
+	−	−	+
Adj. 704			Bal. 172
			Adj. 704
			876

William Bush Company
Work Sheet
For year ended December 31, 19x4

ACCOUNT NAME	TRIAL BALANCE	
	DEBIT	CREDIT
Cash	16 8 9 1 00	
Notes Receivable	1 6 0 0 00	
Accounts Receivable	29 2 0 0 00	
Allowance for Doubtful Accounts		1 7 2 00
Bad Debts Expense		

You would then record the adjustment in the work sheet (Figure 18-3). Let's examine a portion of the balance sheet derived from the work sheet.

William Bush Company
Balance Sheet
December 31, 19x4

Assets				
Current Assets:				
Cash			$16 8 9 1 00	
Notes Receivable			1 6 0 0 00	
Accounts Receivable	$29 2 0 0 00			
Less Allowance for Doubtful				
Accounts		8 7 6 00	28 3 2 4 00	

In this statement, the book value of Accounts Receivable is shown as $28,324.

Estimating Bad Debts as a Percentage of Sales   Some business firms prefer a simplified method for determining the amount of the adjustment for Bad Debts Expense. They multiply the current year's sales by a set percentage rate and then record the adjusting entry for the exact amount.

For example, the actual losses from sales on account for the J. P. Downey Company have averaged approximately 1 percent of net sales (Sales less Sales Returns and Allowances and less Sales Discount). The firm makes virtually all sales on credit. On the basis of this information, the company computes the amount of the adjustment as 1 percent of net sales.

Objective 3

Calculate the amount of the adjusting entry by using a percentage of sales or net sales.

Figure 18-3

ADJUSTMENTS		INCOME STATEMENT		BALANCE SHEET	
DEBIT	CREDIT	DEBIT	CREDIT	DEBIT	CREDIT
				16 8 9 1 00	
				1 6 0 0 00	
				29 2 0 0 00	
	(a) 7 0 4 00				8 7 6 00

(a) 7 0 4 00			7 0 4 00		

Here is the figure for net sales, as shown in the income statement.

Revenue from Sales:			
Sales		$ 640 0 0 0 00	
Less: Sales Returns and Allowances	$ 26 0 0 0 00		
Sales Discount	1 2 0 0 00	27 2 0 0 00	
Net Sales		$ 612 8 0 0 00	

Now 1 percent of net sales is $6,128 ($612,800 × .01), *so the firm uses this amount directly for the adjusting entry,* adding it to both accounts, as shown below.

Bad Debts Expense		Allowance for Doubtful Accounts	
+	−	−	+
Adj. 6,128			Bal. 216
			Adj. 6,128
			6,344

Figure 18-4 below shows how to record the adjustment in the work sheet. A portion of the balance sheet is shown at the top of the next page.

Many companies that sell on both a cash and a charge-account basis compute the amount of their adjustment for bad debts on net credit sales. For example, assume that the Fenwick Company sells merchandise on both a cash and a charge-account basis. Charge sales, recorded in a sales journal, total $490,000. Sales Returns and Allowances and Sales Discounts

J. P. Downey Company
Work Sheet
For year ended June 30, 19–

ACCOUNT NAME	TRIAL BALANCE	
	DEBIT	CREDIT
Accounts Receivable	48 0 0 0 00	
Allowance for Doubtful Accounts		2 1 6 00
Sales		640 0 0 0 00
Sales Returns and Allowances	26 0 0 0 00	
Sales Discount	1 2 0 0 00	
Bad Debts Expense		

J. P. Downey Company
Balance Sheet
June 30, 19–

Assets		
Current Assets:		

Accounts Receivable	$48 0 0 0 00	
Less Allowance for Doubtful		
Accounts	6 3 4 4 00	$41 6 5 6 00

relating to credit sales are $18,000 and $2,900, respectively. The Fenwick Company records the adjustment for bad debts at ¾ percent of net credit sales. Look at the adjustment and the calculation that follows.

Credit (charge) sales		$490,000
Less: Sales Returns and Allowances	$18,000	
Sales Discounts	2,900	20,900
Net credit sales		$469,100

$469,100
× .0075

$3,518.25

Figure 18-4

ADJUSTMENTS			INCOME STATEMENT			BALANCE SHEET		
DEBIT		CREDIT	DEBIT		CREDIT	DEBIT		CREDIT
						48 0 0 0 00		
	(a)6 1 2 8 00							6 3 4 4 00

					640 0 0 0 00			
			26 0 0 0 00					
			1 2 0 0 00					

(a)6 1 2 8 00			6 1 2 8 00					

By T accounts, the adjustment looks like this.

Bad Debts Expense			Allowance for Doubtful Accounts		
	+	−		−	+
Adj.	3,518.25			Bal.	220.32
				Adj.	3,518.25
					3,738.57

Note that a firm using this simplified method multiplies net sales or net sales on credit by the given percentage in order to determine the amount of the adjustment. *The present balance of Allowance for Doubtful Accounts is not involved in the calculation.* If the given percentage does not adequately provide for the firm's losses (that is, if it yields either too little or too much), the firm merely changes the percentage.

WRITING OFF UNCOLLECTIBLE ACCOUNTS

Up to now, we have seen that the firm's accountant first records the adjusting entry for bad debts in the appropriate columns of the work sheet. For the sake of additional clarification, the relevant accounts are illustrated in T accounts.

Bad Debts Expense			Allowance for Doubtful Accounts		
	+	−		−	+
Adj.	3,518.25			Bal.	220.32
				Adj.	3,518.25
					3,738.57

Next the firm's accountant closes Bad Debts Expense, along with all expenses, into the Income Summary account. The company in our example never uses the Bad Debts Expense account during the year, so the only entries in it are the adjusting entry and the closing entry. This represents the beginning and the end of Bad Debts Expense for the fiscal period. In other words, the only entry in Bad Debts Expense is the adjusting entry, and, as we said, this account is immediately closed out. After the adjusting entry and closing entry have been posted, the accounts look like this:

Bad Debts Expense				Allowance for Doubtful Accounts		
	+		−		−	+
Adj.	3,518.25	Clos.	3,518.25		Bal.	220.32
					Adj.	3,518.25

Allowance for Doubtful Accounts

It is apparent that Allowance for Doubtful Accounts remains open. Rather than have the balance continually increase because of the successive adjustments on the credit side of the account, the accountant uses the debit side of the account to write off charge accounts that are considered to be definitely uncollectible.

We can consider Allowance for Doubtful Accounts as a reservoir: We fill it up at the end of the year through the medium of the adjusting entry by crediting the account. During the following year, we drain off the reservoir through the medium of write-offs by debiting the account. To avoid the possibility of the reservoir's "running dry," the accountant should make the adjusting entry large enough to provide for all possible write-offs and still have a balance left over with which to begin the next year.

Entry to Write Off a Charge Account in Full

Suppose that a firm decides, after all attempts to collect a customer's debt have failed, that the account is definitely uncollectible. In such a case, the firm should write off the amount due. Assume that on March 12, the J. P. Downey Company decides that the account of a customer, Ronald D. Oakes, is uncollectible. The accountant records the write-off by making the following entry.

Objective 4

Journalize the entries to write off Accounts Receivable as being uncollectible using the allowance method.

GENERAL JOURNAL　　　　　　　　　　　　　　　PAGE __116__

	DATE	DESCRIPTION	POST. REF.	DEBIT	CREDIT	
1	19– Mar. 12	Allowance for Doubtful Accounts		7 1 40		1
2		Accounts Receivable, Ronald D.				2
3		Oakes			7 1 40	3
4		Wrote off the account as				4
5		uncollectible.				5
6						6

By T accounts, the entry looks like this:

Accounts Receivable				Allowance for Doubtful Accounts			
+		–		–		+	
Bal.	48,000.00	Mar. 12	71.40	Mar. 12 (Oakes write-off)	71.40	Bal.	6,344.00

The accountant also posts the entry to the account of Ronald D. Oakes in the accounts receivable subsidiary ledger.

NAME Ronald D. Oakes
ADDRESS 217 Barclay Road
Boston, MA 02101

DATE		ITEM	POST. REF.	DEBIT	CREDIT	BALANCE
19x2 May	1	Balance	✓			7 1 40
19x5 Mar.	12		J116		7 1 40	———

Note that the above entry does not change the net realizable value or book value of the Accounts Receivable.

Account Name	Balances Before Write-offs	Balances After Write-offs
Accounts Receivable	$48,000.00	$47,928.60
Less Allowance for Doubtful Accounts	6,344.00	6,272.60
Book value (net realizable value)	$41,656.00	$41,656.00

Also note that *the entry to write off an account does not involve an expense account.* The adjusting entry, which was made long before this time, provides for the expense. The estimated expense was recorded *during the year in which the sale was made,* even though the account is written off in a later year.

Compound Entry to Write Off a Number of Accounts as Uncollectible

Rather than writing off each uncollectible account separately during the year, a firm may write off a number of accounts at the end of the year by using a compound entry. For example, assume that on December 31 the McNair Company writes off the following accounts of charge customers as being uncollectible: C. D. Davis, $72.00; M. R. Franklin, $29.00; O. C. Hillier, $18.00; and M. A. Tilden, $93.00. The accountant records the write-offs by making the following entry.

	Date	Account	Debit	Credit	
1	19— Dec.	Allowance for Doubtful Accounts	2 1 2 00		1
2		Accounts Receivable, C. D. Davis		7 2 00	2
3		Accounts Receivable, M. R. Franklin		2 9 00	3
4		Accounts Receivable, O. C. Hillier		1 8 00	4
5		Accounts Receivable, M. A. Tilden		9 3 00	5
6		Wrote off the accounts as			6
7		uncollectible.			7
8					8

Entry to Write Off a Charge Account Paid in Part

Sometimes a part payment is involved in a write-off of an account. When this happens, it may be due to a bankruptcy settlement. The federal laws governing **bankruptcy** legally excuse a debtor from paying off certain obligations. For example, on April 21 the J. P. Downey Company received 10 cents on the dollar in settlement of a $364 account owed by its customer, M. A. Smythe, a bankrupt. In general journal form, the entry is as follows.

	Date	Account	Debit	Credit	
1	19— Apr.	21 Cash	3 6 40		1
2		Allowance for Doubtful Accounts	3 2 7 60		2
3		Accounts Receivable, M. A. Smythe		3 6 4 00	3
4		Settlement in bankruptcy, wrote			4
5		off account balance as			5
6		uncollectible.			6
7					7

Write-offs Seldom Agree with Previous Estimates

The total amount of Accounts Receivable written off during a given year does not ordinarily agree with the estimates of uncollectible accounts previously debited to Bad Debts Expense and credited to Allowance for Doubtful Accounts. In the usual situation, the amounts written off as uncollectible turn out to be less than the estimated amount. At the end of a given year there is normally a credit balance in Allowance for Doubtful Accounts. However, if (as sometimes happens) the amounts written off are greater than the estimated amounts, Allowance for Doubtful Accounts temporarily has a debit balance. The debit balance will be eliminated by the adjusting entry at the end of the year, which results in a credit to, or increase in, Allowance for Doubtful Accounts.

COLLECTION OF ACCOUNTS PREVIOUSLY WRITTEN OFF

Every now and then the sun shines when you least expect it, and an account previously written off as uncollectible may later be recovered, either in part or in full. In such cases, the firm's accountant restores the account to the books, or reinstates it, by an entry that is the exact opposite of the write-off entry.

As an example, the J. P. Downey Company sells merchandise on account to Cecil E. Dowell for $405, on May 5, 19x4. Here is the entry in general journal form.

1	19x4 May	5	Accounts Receivable, Cecil E. Dowell		4 0 5 00				1
2			Sales				4 0 5 00		2
3			Sold merchandise on account,						3
4			2/10, n/30.						4
5									5
6									6
7									7
8									8

The Downey Company makes many futile attempts to collect, and the **statute of limitations** finally expires. Since the statute of limitations is set at three years in many states, let's say that the Downey Company has not been able to collect any money at all from Dowell during a three-year period and that Dowell has remained within the jurisdiction of the court. This means that the debt is outlawed by the statute of limitations. In other words, the firm cannot use the courts to force the debtor to pay up. Accordingly, three years later in 19x7, the accountant for the J. P. Downey Company writes off the account of Cecil E. Dowell as uncollectible.

1	19x7 Jun.	10	Allowance for Doubtful Accounts		4 0 5 00				1
2			Accounts Receivable, Cecil E.						2
3			Dowell				4 0 5 00		3
4			Wrote off the account as						4
5			uncollectible.						5
6									6
7									7

But on September 15, 19x7, Cecil E. Dowell suddenly pays his account in full! The entry to reinstate the account is the reverse of the entry used to write off the account.

	19x7							
1	Sep.	15	Accounts Receivable, Cecil E. Dowell	4 0 5 00				1
2			Allowance for Doubtful Accounts			4 0 5 00		2
3			Reinstated the account.					3
4								4
5								5

The way is now clear to record the collection of the account.

	19x7							
1	Sep.	15	Cash	4 0 5 00				1
2			Accounts Receivable, Cecil E.					2
3			Dowell			4 0 5 00		3
4			Collection in full of account.					4
5								5
6								6

Now suppose that Cecil E. Dowell had gone into bankruptcy and settled his account with the J. P. Downey Company by paying it 5 cents on the dollar. The Downey Company would realize that there was no hope of collecting any more, so the accountant would reinstate the account only for the amount collected, like this.

1		Accounts Receivable, Cecil E. Dowell	2 0 25				1
2		Allowance for Doubtful Accounts			2 0 25		2
3		Settlement in bankruptcy,					3
4		5 percent of $405; reinstated					4
5		the account to the extent of					5
6		the settlement.					6
7							7

The subsequent entry to record the cash payment would be as follows.

1		Cash	2 0 25				1
2		Accounts Receivable, Cecil E.					2
3		Dowell			2 0 25		3
4		Settlement in bankruptcy,					4
5		5 percent of $405.					5
6							6

DIRECT WRITE-OFF OF BAD DEBTS

The **direct write-off method of accounting for bad-debt losses** is a simpler system for writing off charge accounts determined to be uncollectible. No adjusting entry is made, since there is no attempt to provide for bad-debt losses in advance or to match revenue with related expenses. Instead, when a firm decides that a charge account is never going to be paid, the accountant makes an entry in the general journal debiting Bad Debts Expense and crediting Accounts Receivable. As we said before, this method is used primarily for a small business or a professional enterprise. The account called Allowance for Doubtful Accounts does not exist in the firm's chart of accounts.

Objective 6

Journalize the entries to write off Accounts Receivable as being uncollectible using the direct write-off method.

For example, on April 16, 19x3, the Sloan Company sold merchandise on account to C. T. Slocum for $44.20, making the following entry in the general journal.

	19x3						
1	Apr.	16	Accounts Receivable, C. T. Slocum		4 4 20		1
2			Sales			4 4 20	2
3			Sale of merchandise on account,				3
4			n/30.				4
5							5

Slocum never pays his bill. Finally, three years later, on September 1, the account is written off as follows.

	19x6						
1	Sep.	1	Bad Debts Expense		4 4 20		1
2			Accounts Receivable, C. T. Slocum			4 4 20	2
3			To write off an uncollectible				3
4			account.				4
5							5

By T accounts, the entries look like this.

Accounts Receivable		Sales		Bad Debts Expense	
+	−	−	+	+	−
19x3	19x6	19x3	19x3	19x6	
Apr. 16 44.20	Sep. 1 44.20	Dec. 31 Closed	Apr. 16 44.20	Sep. 1 44.20	

The entry to reinstate an account previously written off is a debit to Accounts Receivable and a credit to Bad Debts Expense.

The entry to reinstate an account previously written off is a debit to Accounts Receivable and a credit to Bad Debts Expense.

You can see that revenue does not match expenses for a particular year. The Sloan Company counted the original sale of $44.20 in 19x3, thereby overstating true revenue for that year. It counted Bad Debts Expenses three years later in 19x6, thereby overstating expenses for that year. Note that the Sloan Company did not use the account titled Allowance for Doubtful Accounts. In other words, if you wait until you consider an account to be a bad debt and then write it off, with no provision for realistically estimating the losses in advance, you are operating in a rather precarious situation. In the balance sheet, Accounts Receivable is stated at the gross amount only; there is no book value or net realizable value.

GLOSSARY

Age (Accounts Receivable) To analyze the composition of Accounts Receivable by classifying the outstanding balance of each charge customer's account according to the amount of time it has been outstanding. One can then multiply the totals for each time period by a percentage deemed to be uncollectible.

Allowance method of accounting for bad-debt losses This requires an adjusting entry debiting Bad Debts Expense and crediting Allowance for Doubtful Accounts. Write-offs of uncollectible accounts are debited to Allowance for Doubtful Accounts and credited to Accounts Receivable.

Bankruptcy A federal law excusing a debtor from certain obligations incurred.

Book value of Accounts Receivable The balance of Accounts Receivable after one has deducted the balance of Allowance for Doubtful Accounts; also called the *net realizable value* of Accounts Receivable.

Direct write-off method of accounting for bad-debt losses This method, used by small business firms, requires no adjusting entry. The accountant debits write-offs of uncollectible accounts to Bad Debts Expense and credits them to Accounts Receivable.

Statute of limitations Laws that limit the period of time during which the courts may force a debtor to pay a debt; usually three years for charge accounts.

QUESTIONS, EXERCISES, AND PROBLEMS

Discussion Questions

1. Where are Allowance for Doubtful Accounts and Bad Debts Expense placed in classified financial statements?
2. Explain the nature of Allowance for Doubtful Accounts, how it comes into existence, and what happens to it.
3. Describe the process of aging accounts receivable.

4. In what situation would Allowance for Doubtful Accounts have a debit balance?
5. How is the book value of Accounts Receivable figured?
6. When an account is written off under the allowance method of accounting for bad debts, why doesn't the book value of Accounts Receivable decrease?
7. Why is the allowance method of handling bad debts considered to be more effective than the direct write-off method?

Exercises

Exercise 18-1   The Damon Company analyzed its Accounts Receivable balances on December 31 and determined the following aged balances.

Age Interval	Balance	Estimated Percentage Uncollectible
Not yet due	$50,000	1
30 to 60 days past due	10,000	2
61 to 120 days past due	4,000	5
121 to 365 days past due	1,000	30
More than 1 year past due	2,000	60
	$67,000	

The credit balance of Allowance for Doubtful Accounts is $1,100. What is the adjusting entry for estimated credit losses on December 31?

Exercise 18-2   The Buckner Company uses the allowance method of handling losses due to bad debts. They consider estimated losses to be 3 percent of Accounts Receivable. On December 31 the Accounts Receivable balance was $80,000, and Allowance for Doubtful Accounts had a credit balance of $200. Journalize the adjusting entry to record the estimated bad-debt losses.

Exercise 18-3   The Ruth Brown Company uses the allowance method of handling losses due to bad debts. On December 31, before any adjustments have been recorded, the ledger contains the following balances.

Sales	$110,000
Sales Returns and Allowances	10,000

The company estimates that bad-debt losses will be ½ percent of net sales. Journalize the adjusting entry to record the estimated bad-debt losses. The present balance of Allowance for Doubtful Accounts is $150.

Exercise 18-4   The Kingwell Paint Company had the following transactions this year. Assuming that the Kingwell Paint Company uses the allowance method of accounting for bad-debt losses, record the three transactions in general journal form. The present balance of Allowance for Doubtful Accounts is $350.

a. Wrote off the account of A. Adkins as uncollectible, $200.
b. Reinstated the account of B. Brody that had been written off during the preceding year, $60; received $60 cash in full payment.
c. Estimated bad-debt losses to be 1 percent of credit sales of $40,000.

Exercise 18-5   With reference to Exercise 18-4, assume that the Kingwell Company uses the direct write-off method of accounting for bad-debt losses. Record transactions **a** and **b** in general journal form.

Exercise 18-6   At the end of this year, the Kimble Company's Accounts Receivable account has a balance of $80,000. Net sales for the year total $960,000. Determine the amount of the adjusting entry to record the estimated bad-debt losses under each of the following conditions. Assume that Allowance for Doubtful Accounts had a credit balance of $620.

a. Analysis of the charge accounts in the accounts receivable ledger indicates doubtful accounts of $5,160.
b. Bad-debt losses are estimated at ½ percent of net sales.

Exercise 18-7   With reference to Exercise 18-6, determine the amount of the Kimble Company's entry to record the estimated bad-debt losses under each of the following conditions.

a. Analysis of the charge accounts in the accounts receivable ledger indicates doubtful accounts of $4,920.
b. Bad-debt losses are estimated at ¾ percent of net sales.

Exercise 18-8   Record the following transactions in general journal form for the Sever Company; these transactions occurred during this fiscal year.

Jan.   11 Sold merchandise to Janine Odom on account, $4,500.
        19 Received a check from Janine Odom in settlement of her account.
Mar.   20 Sold merchandise to Robert Carlson on account, $3,000.
Apr.   20 Received a 90-day, 6 percent note dated this day from Robert Carlson in settlement of his account, $3,000.
May   20 Discounted Carlson's note at the bank; the bank levied a discount rate of 9 percent.
Jul.   19 Carlson dishonored his note previously discounted. The Sever Company paid the bank the principal, plus interest, plus a protest fee of $4.
Dec.   30 Wrote off the account of Robert Carlson as worthless.

Problem Set A

Problem 18-1A   On December 31 of last year, the accountant for Pierce and Son prepared a balance sheet that included $128,000 in Accounts Receivable and $11,960 in Allowance for Doubtful Accounts. Selected transactions **a** through **f** occurred during January of this year.

a. Sales of merchandise on account, $118,000.
b. Sales Returns and Allowances related to sales of merchandise on account, $5,123.68.
c. Cash payments by charge customers (no cash discounts), $110,761.20.
d. The Hunter Company account was written off as uncollectible, $753.
e. By the process of aging Accounts Receivable, on January 31, the accountant for Pierce and Son decided that Allowance for Doubtful Accounts should be adjusted to a balance of $12,526.
f. The accountant closed Bad Debts Expense.

Instructions

1. Record the entries in general journal form.
2. Post the appropriate entries to the accounts for Allowance for Doubtful Accounts and Bad Debts Expense.

Problem 18-2A Crowell Company uses the aging method of estimating bad debts as of December 31, the end of the fiscal year. Terms of sales are net 30 days. While preparing the aging schedule, the accountant became very ill and was unable to finish the job. The accountant's report, as complete as he left it, appears as follows:

Customer Accounts	Total	Not Yet Due	1–30 Days Past Due	31–60 Days Past Due	61–90 Days Past Due	More than 90 Days Past Due
Balance Forward	$176,146	$96,400	$47,200	$18,726	$7,480	$6,340

The accountant had the following accounts still to analyze:

Account	Amount	Due Date
S. Waters	$1,740	January 12 (next year)
T. Wong	1,180	December 22
C. Wyreski	3,910	November 2
T. Yates	4,140	August 18
C. Young	760	December 3
L. Zimmerman	580	January 22 (next year)

From past experience, the company has found that the following rates of estimated uncollectible accounts produce an adequate balance for Allowance for Doubtful Accounts:

Time Past Due	Estimated Percentage Uncollectible
Not yet due	2
1–30 days	4
31–60 days	20
61–90 days	30
Over 90 days	50

Prior to aging the accounts receivable, Allowance for Doubtful Accounts has a credit balance of $3,624.

Instructions

1. Complete a table for aging the accounts, and estimate an allowance for uncollectible accounts.
2. Write the adjusting entry in general journal form.

Problem 18-3A   On January 1 of this year Finley Wholesale Grocery had a credit balance of $2,170 in Allowance for Doubtful Accounts. During the year Finley completed the following selected transactions.

Feb.   7 Wrote off as uncollectible a $216 account of Foster Grocery, which had gone out of business, leaving no assets.

May   4 Wrote off the account of Baker and Gilman as uncollectible, $125.40.

   17 Collected 5 percent of the $722 owed by Sharon Whaley, a bankrupt. Wrote off the remainder as worthless.

Aug.   2 Received $214.20 unexpectedly from the Donald Whiting Company, whose account had been written off two years earlier. Reinstated the account for $214.20 and recorded the collection.

Sep.   11 Received $75 from Baker and Gilman as part of the account written off on May 4. They wrote a letter stating that they expect to pay the balance soon. Accordingly, reinstated the account for the amount of the original obligation, $125.40.

Dec.   30 Journalized a compound entry to write off the following accounts as uncollectible: Thomas Wilder, $192.16; Quillan Restaurant, $136.41; Northside Drive-In, $283.15.

   31 Made the adjusting entry to record estimated bad-debt losses at ½ percent of charge sales of $268,000.

   31 Closed the Bad Debts Expense account.

Instructions

1. Record the opening balance in the ledger account of Allowance for Doubtful Accounts.
2. Record entries in general journal form.
3. Post entries to the ledger accounts for Allowance for Doubtful Accounts and Bad Debts Expense.

Problem 18-4A   The following transactions were among those completed by Storlie Restaurant Supply this year.

Jan.   6 Sold merchandise on account to Quincy Cafe, $820.

Feb. 15 Wrote off as uncollectible the account of Trowbridge Hotel, $692.15. This company had gone out of business, leaving no assets to attach.

      17 Received a 60-day, 9 percent note, dated February 17, for $820, from Quincy Cafe, in payment of account.

Mar. 15 Reinstated the account of Trudy's Drive-In that had been written off in the preceding year; received $193.16 in full payment.

Apr. 18 Quincy Cafe dishonored its note due today. Charged principal plus interest to Accounts Receivable.

Aug.   3 Received $74 unexpectedly from Morton Watson, whose account had been written off last year in the amount of $74. Reinstated the account and recorded the collection of $74.

Sep. 17 Received 10 percent of the $832.30 balance owed by Quincy Cafe from the referee in bankruptcy and wrote the remainder off as worthless.

Oct. 14 Reinstated the account of Trujillo's Fine Foods that had been written off two years earlier; received $291 in full payment.

Dec. 29 Journalized a compound entry to write off as uncollectible the following accounts: Trotter Motel, $159.00; Cecil Thornton, $118.60; Lucille's Coffee Shop, $472.50; Goodrich Drive-In, $743.16.

      31 On the basis of an analysis of Accounts Receivable balance of $91,511.18, estimated that $2,745.00 will be uncollectible. Made the adjusting entry.

      31 Made the entry to close the appropriate account to Income Summary.

Instructions

1. Open the following accounts, recording the credit balance as of January 1 of this fiscal year.

   114 Allowance for Doubtful Accounts $2,529.00
   313 Income Summary   —
   627 Bad Debts Expense   —

2. Record in general journal form the transactions as well as the adjusting and closing entries described above. After each entry, post to the three selected ledger accounts.

3. Prepare the Current Assets section of the balance sheet. Other pertinent accounts are: Cash, $5,691.87; Notes Receivable, $897.76; Merchandise Inventory, $197,711; Supplies, $849.12; Prepaid Insurance, $418.

Problem Set B

Problem 18-1B   The balance sheet prepared by Rodgers Associates for December 31 of last year included $256,000 in Accounts Receivable and

$11,960 in Allowance for Doubtful Accounts. The following transactions occurred during January of this year.

a. Sales of merchandise on account, $228,000.
b. Sales returns and allowances related to sales of merchandise on account, $6,236.
c. Cash payments by charge customers (no cash discounts), $217,252.
d. Account receivable from L. A. Johnson Company written off as uncollectible, $1,484.
e. By the aging process, at January 31, it was decided that Allowance for Doubtful Accounts should be adjusted to a balance of $14,272.
f. Closed Bad Debts Expense account.

Instructions

1. Record the entries in general journal form. (Record the letter in the Date column.)
2. Post the appropriate journal entries to the accounts for Allowance for Doubtful Accounts and Bad Debts Expense.

Problem 18-2B Stafford Company uses the aging method of estimating bad debts as of December 31, the end of the fiscal year. Terms of sales are net 30 days. While in the process of completing the aging schedule, the accountant became very ill and was unable to finish the job. The accountant's report, as far as she had done it, appears as follows:

Customer Accounts	Total	Not Yet Due	1–30 Days Past Due	31–60 Days Past Due	61–90 Days Past Due	More than 90 Days Past Due
Balance Forward	$194,950	$124,600	$38,140	$19,424	$7,516	$5,270

The accountant had the following accounts left to analyze.

Account	Amount	Due Date
D. Turner	$1,920	November 28
L. Tuttle	460	January 16 (next year)
C. Van Dyke	3,240	November 6
N. Walker	4,710	January 27 (next year)
F. Warner	1,850	September 20
B. Yeager	580	October 16

From past experience, the company has found that the following rates of estimated uncollectible accounts produce an adequate balance for Allowance for Doubtful Accounts:

Time Past Due	Estimated Percentage Uncollectible
Not yet due	2
1–30 days	4
31–60 days	20
61–90 days	30
Over 90 days	50

Prior to aging Accounts Receivable, Allowance for Doubtful Accounts has a credit balance of $2,173.

Instructions

1. Complete the table for aging the accounts, and estimate an allowance for uncollectible accounts.
2. Record the adjusting entry in general journal form.

Problem 18-3B On January 1 of this year, Wade Company's Allowance for Doubtful Accounts had a $961 credit balance. During the year Wade completed the following selected transactions.

Feb. 11 Wrote off the $327 account of Southside Company; the company had gone out of business leaving no assets.
May   6 Wrote off the account of John Boling as uncollectible, $174.16.
      19 Received $91 unexpectedly from Stella Biles. The account had been written off two years earlier. Reinstated the account for $91, and recorded the collection of $91.
Aug. 3 Collected 10 percent of the $126 owed by Douglas Boman, a bankrupt. Wrote off the remainder as uncollectible.
Sep. 21 Received $90 from John Boling as part payment of the account written off on May 6. Boling stated in a letter that he expects to pay the balance in the near future. Accordingly, reinstated the account for the amount of the original obligation, $174.16.
Dec. 29 Journalized a compound entry to write off the following accounts: Nathan Bigelow, $176.20; Rachel Kelley, $124.36; Todd Kimball, $114.
      31 Recorded the adjusting entry for estimated bad-debt losses at ½ percent of charge sales of $148,000.
      31 Closed the Bad Debts Expense account.

Instructions

1. Record the opening balance in the ledger account of Allowance for Doubtful Accounts.
2. Make the entries in general journal form.
3. Post the entries to ledger accounts for Allowance for Doubtful Accounts and Bad Debts Expense.

Problem 18-4B The following are among the transactions completed by Pemberton Pool Supply this year.

Jan.   8 Sold merchandise on account to Empire Motel, $740.
Feb.   6 Wrote off the account of Walter Daniels, Inc., $686. The company went out of business, leaving no assets to attach.
       7 Received a 60-day, 9 percent note, for $740, from Empire Motel, in settlement of the sale of January 8. The note is dated February 7.
Mar. 12 Reinstated the account of Delaney Apartments that had been written off in the preceding year; received $158 in full payment.
Apr.   8 Empire Motel dishonored their note due today. Charged principal plus interest to Accounts Receivable.
Aug. 17 Received $69 unexpectedly from Jana Colson. The account had been written off last year in the amount of $69. Reinstated the account and recorded the collection of $69.
Sep. 28 Received 10 percent of the $751.10 balance owed by Empire Motel from the referee in bankruptcy and wrote the remainder off as worthless.
Oct. 15 Reinstated the account of Eggers Manor that had been written off two years earlier and received $326 in full payment.
Dec. 29 Journalized a compound entry to write off the following accounts as uncollectible: Gardner Lodge, $164; Norman Henning, $76.14; Anderson Construction Company, $984; Hilliard Terrace, $793.20.
      31 On the basis of an analysis of Accounts Receivable, which amounted to $43,201.27, estimated that $2,296 will be uncollectible. Made the adjusting entry.
      31 Closed the appropriate account to Income Summary.

Instructions

1. Open the following accounts, recording the credit balance as of January 1 of this fiscal year.

   114 Allowance for Doubtful Accounts $3,176.00
   313 Income Summary   —
   627 Bad Debts Expense   —

2. Journalize in general journal form the transactions as well as the adjusting and closing entries described above. After each entry, post to the three selected ledger accounts.
3. Prepare the Current Assets section of the balance sheet. Other pertinent accounts are: Cash, $6,820.16; Notes Receivable, $971; Merchandise Inventory, $89,625; Supplies, $925; Prepaid Insurance, $348.

19 Accounting for Valuation of Inventories

Learning Objectives

After you have completed this chapter, you will be able to do the following:

1. Determine unit cost, the value of the ending inventory, and the cost of merchandise sold by the following methods: (a) specific identification, (b) weighted-average cost, (c) first-in, first-out, and (d) last-in, first-out.

2. Journalize transactions relating to perpetual inventories.

3. Complete a perpetual inventory record card.

One of the most important aspects of the operation of any merchandising business is the accounting for, and valuation of, the merchandise in stock. Let us look back briefly at what we've said so far. We defined *merchandise inventory* as goods purchased by the company and held for resale to customers in the ordinary course of business. We have pictured Merchandise Inventory and related T accounts as follows.

Assets		Revenue		Expenses	
+	–	–	+	+	–

Merchandise Inventory		Sales		Purchases	
+	–	–	+	+	–
Only when a physical inventory has been taken			Selling of merchandise, recorded at selling price	Buying of merchandise, recorded at cost, including transportation costs	

Sales Returns and Allowances		Purchases Returns and Allowances	
+	–	–	+
Return of merchandise previously sold, recorded at selling price			Return of merchandise previously purchased, recorded at cost

Sales Discount		Purchases Discount	
+	–	–	+
Cash discounts offered to customers			Cash discounts on buying merchandise

We have assumed that firms take a physical inventory periodically and include the most up-to-date figure in the Adjustments columns of the work sheet. We have also assumed that firms make two adjustments:

1. They close off or "reverse out" the beginning merchandise inventory.
2. They add the ending merchandise inventory.

Assume that a firm has a beginning merchandise inventory amounting to $84,000. The cost of the ending merchandise inventory is $92,000. The adjustment was first described by T accounts as follows.

Merchandise Inventory				Income Summary			
+		−		(a)	84,000	(b)	92,000
Bal. 84,000	(a)	84,000					
(b) 92,000							

The same adjustments appear in the work sheet.

In this example, the ending inventory figure of $92,000 is given. However, in a practical business situation, the cost of the ending inventory must be determined. Counting the goods on hand is a relatively easy but time consuming procedure compared with the more difficult task of assigning a dollar amount to them in a time of changing prices. We'll talk mainly about the Merchandise Inventory account because of its relative importance. However, the same principle applies to other assets, such as supplies for a service business or raw materials for a manufacturer.

We're going to tackle the valuation of inventories in two ways: First, some merchandising firms take a physical inventory of merchandise on hand and then attach a value to it. This is known as a **periodic inventory system.** Second, some merchandising firms keep running records of inventories by recording all transactions, so that at any given time they know what they have on hand and the current cost of each item. This is known as **perpetual inventory.**

THE IMPORTANCE OF INVENTORY VALUATION

Merchandise Inventory is the only account that can appear on both major financial statements. On the balance sheet, it appears under Current Assets. On the income statement, it is listed under Cost of Merchandise Sold. Why is the valuation of merchandise inventory so important? In many business firms merchandise inventory is the asset with the largest dollar amount. Likewise, as a part of Cost of Merchandise Sold, it vitally affects the net income, because the Cost of Merchandise Sold is the largest deduction from Sales. As a result, inventory determination plays an important role in matching costs with revenue for a given period.

Differing costs of ending merchandise inventory have a dramatic effect on net income. We can see this in the partial income statements that follow (Figures 19-1 through 19-4).

Figure 19-1

YEAR 1

Sales (net)							$ 203	0	0	0	00
Cost of Merchandise Sold:											
Merchandise Inventory											
(beginning)	$	84	0	0	0	00					
Purchases (net)		160	0	0	0	00					
Merchandise Available for Sale	$	244	0	0	0	00					
Less Merchandise Inventory											
(ending)		92	0	0	0	00					
Cost of Merchandise Sold							152	0	0	0	00
Gross Profit							$ 51	0	0	0	00
Expenses							30	0	0	0	00
Net Income							$ 21	0	0	0	00

Now assume that instead of setting $92,000 as the value for ending merchandise inventory, one could quite legally set its value at $82,000. The result would be a net income of only $11,000 (Figure 19-2), instead of $21,000. Of course, this would result in lower income taxes as well.

From Figures 19-1 and 19-2 we can see that if the ending merchandise inventory is overstated (too high) by $10,000, the net income will be overstated (too high) by $10,000, because the two are directly proportional to each other. Similarly, **if the ending merchandise inventory is understated (too low), net income will be understated (too low).**

But there's something else you have to take into account. Since the *ending* inventory of one year becomes the *beginning* inventory of the following year, the net income of the following year is also affected, but in

Figure 19-2

YEAR 1

Sales (net)							$ 203	0	0	0	00
Cost of Merchandise Sold:											
Merchandise Inventory											
(beginning)	$	84	0	0	0	00					
Purchases (net)		160	0	0	0	00					
Merchandise Available for Sale	$	244	0	0	0	00					
Less Merchandise Inventory											
(ending)		82	0	0	0	00					
Cost of Merchandise Sold							162	0	0	0	00
Gross Profit							$ 41	0	0	0	00
Expenses							30	0	0	0	00
Net Income							$ 11	0	0	0	00

Figure 19-3

YEAR 2

Sales (net)			$ 236 0 0 0 00
Cost of Merchandise Sold:			
Merchandise Inventory			
(beginning)	$ 92 0 0 0 00		
Purchases (net)	184 0 0 0 00		
Merchandise Available for Sale	$ 276 0 0 0 00		
Less Merchandise Inventory			
(ending)	100 0 0 0 00		
Cost of Merchandise Sold		176 0 0 0 00	
Gross Profit		$ 60 0 0 0 00	
Expenses		35 0 0 0 00	
Net Income		$ 25 0 0 0 00	

an opposite manner. Let's continue with our example into year 2. The $92,000 *ending* inventory of year 1 becomes the *beginning* inventory of year 2 (Figure 19-3).

Look at Figure 19-4 to see what happens when the $82,000 ending inventory of year 1 becomes the beginning inventory of year 2.

We can see that if the beginning merchandise inventory is overstated by $10,000, the net income will be understated by $10,000, because the two are *in*directly proportional to each other. Similarly, **if the beginning merchandise inventory is understated, net income will be overstated.**

In other words, over a two-year period, the net income will be correct, since the overstatement of one year cancels out the understatement of the following year, and vice versa. We can summarize all this as shown in the tables on the next page.

Figure 19-4

YEAR 2

Sales (net)			$ 236 0 0 0 00
Cost of Merchandise Sold:			
Merchandise Inventory			
(beginning)	$ 82 0 0 0 00		
Purchases (net)	184 0 0 0 00		
Merchandise Available for Sale	$ 266 0 0 0 00		
Less Merchandise Inventory			
(ending)	100 0 0 0 00		
Cost of Merchandise Sold		166 0 0 0 00	
Gross Profit		$ 70 0 0 0 00	
Expenses		35 0 0 0 00	
Net Income		$ 35 0 0 0 00	

Year	Ending Inventory of $92,000		Ending Inventory of $82,000	
		Net Income		Net Income
1		$21,000		$11,000
2		25,000		35,000
	Total	$46,000	Total	$46,000

If the *Ending* Inventory Is	Net Income for the Period Will Be
Overstated	Overstated
Understated	Understated

If the *Beginning* Inventory Is	Net Income for the Period Will Be
Overstated	Understated
Understated	Overstated

THE NEED FOR INVENTORIES

Firms that want to satisfy their customers have to maintain large and varied inventories, because naturally all of us would rather shop in stores that offer a wide selection. This assumes, of course, that the firm does not run out of goods at the end of the year. The successful firm has to buy enough merchandise in advance to satisfy the demands of its customers. Efficient purchasing also dictates that the firm take advantage of quantity discounts as well as special buys of seasonal or distressed goods. So, well-run business firms keep fairly large stocks of merchandise on hand at all times.

TAKING A PHYSICAL INVENTORY

Many merchandising firms, at a given moment in time, possess no record that shows the exact quantity and cost of merchandise on hand. They do make spot checks from time to time as part of inventory control, but they can determine *exact* amounts only by physically counting the goods on hand. Even stores that use computers or other means to maintain a perpetual inventory system need to take a physical inventory from time to time. Stores that carry a particularly wide array of merchandise in large amounts wait until their stock is reasonably low before they attempt to count it. Many department stores, for example, take a physical inventory of their stock toward the end of January, after the holiday rush and the postholiday special sales.

When they do take inventory, firms use various procedures and internal checks to be certain that they don't miss any items or include any items more than once. Usually employees work in pairs, with one person counting the items and the other recording the information on inventory tickets or schedules. Some firms use an electronic recorder. As part of internal control, people from the management level may make spot checks on the inventory counts. Most firms take inventory after regular business hours and record data on inventory sheets, such as the one shown in Figure 19-5 for C. L. Frederickson Plumbing Supply.

When people take inventory, they must be careful to count only goods belonging to the firm. They must exclude goods that have been sold and are awaiting shipment, as well as goods held on a consignment basis.

Figure 19-5

INVENTORY

DATE _January 2, 19–_   SHEET NO. _326_
CALLED BY _Jack Lyon_   COSTED BY _H.H.C._
ENTERED BY _Tom Peterson_   METHOD OF COSTING _LIFO_
DEPARTMENT _Copper Tubing and Fittings_   EXTENDED BY _J.C._
LOCATION _Store & Warehouse_   EXAMINED BY _M. R._

DESCRIPTION	QUANTITY	UNIT	UNIT COST	EXTENSIONS
90° street elbow (copper to fitting)				
½"	273	ea.	67 @ .19 206 @ .23	$ 60.11
¾"	319	ea.	146 @ .32 173 @ .38	112.46
90° drop ear elbow (copper to inside thread)				
½" to ⅜"	194	ea.	194 @ .42	81.48
½" to ½"	222	ea.	222 @ .46	102.12
45° elbow (copper to copper)				
½"	976	ea.	200 @ .14 400 @ .16 376 @ .17	155.92
¾"	818	ea.	600 @ .31 218 @ .32	255.76
1"	149	ea.	149 @ .59	87.91
Tee (copper to copper inside thread)				
⅜"	733	ea.	140 @ .33 593 @ .37	265.61
				$1,121.37

Merchandise sold on the basis of FOB destination should be included in the ending inventory of the seller, since the seller is paying the freight charges and thus still has title. Sometimes a firm must also count goods that it does not have on hand. This situation occurs when the supplier has turned the goods over to a transportation company, and the goods are shipped FOB shipping point. Remember, this means that the buyer is paying the freight charges and as a result normally has title to the goods.

METHODS OF ASSIGNING COSTS TO ENDING INVENTORY

After the items are described and counted, the unit costs are inserted in the inventory sheet and the total costs are extended. How does one determine unit cost? You might think that this would be rather elementary. Indeed, it would be—*if* all the purchases of a given article had been made at the same price per unit. To determine the total unit cost, you'd only need to look up one invoice, check the unit price, then multiply it by the number of items present. Simple! But nothing is ever that simple, unfortunately. Usually a firm buys a number of batches of a given item during the year, and—especially these days—the unit cost varies. A can of shoe polish that cost 50 cents in January may cost 60 cents in October. So which unit cost should one assign to the goods on hand?

There are four main methods of assigning costs to goods in the ending inventory: (1) specific identification, (2) weighted-average cost, (3) first-in, first-out, and (4) last-in, first-out.

Inventory Evaluation: Example 1 C. L. Frederickson Plumbing Supply keeps an inventory of electric water heaters (1,400-watt, 52-gallon capacity) purchased from Alman Manufacturing Company. This year C. L. Frederickson sells 80 of these heaters, and has 26 remaining in stock. C. L. Frederickson started out the year with 22 in stock, and bought more as the year went by, as follows.

Jan. 1	Beginning inventory	22 units @ $57 each = $1,254
Mar. 16	Purchase	30 units @ 62 each = 1,860
Jul. 29	Purchase	36 units @ 65 each = 2,340
Nov. 18	Purchase	18 units @ 68 each = 1,224
	Total available	106 units $6,678

Now let's compute the cost of merchandise sold (80 water heaters) and the value of the ending inventory (26 water heaters). We'll use four different methods.

Objective 1

Determine unit cost, the value of the ending inventory, and the cost of merchandise sold by the following methods: (a) specific identification, (b) weighted-average cost, (c) first-in, first-out, and (d) last-in, first-out.

Specific Identification

When a firm sells "big-ticket" items (cars, appliances, furniture, and so forth), it can keep track of the purchase price of each individual article and determine the exact cost of the merchandise sold. Such a firm uses the **specific-identification method** of inventory control. Because the water heaters have separate serial numbers, C. L. Frederickson can identify each heater with a separate purchase invoice listing the unit cost. When C. L. Frederickson takes inventory at the end of the year, it finds that there are 26 water heaters left in stock; 12 of these were bought in November, 10 were bought in July, and 4 were bought back in March. Costs are assigned to the ending inventory as follows.

12 units @ $68 each =	$ 816
10 units @ 65 each =	650
4 units @ 62 each =	248
26 units	$1,714

C. L. Frederickson Plumbing Supply determines the cost of merchandise sold by subtracting the value of the ending inventory from the total available for sale.

Total water heaters available (106 units)	$6,678
Less ending inventory (26 units)	1,714
Cost of merchandise sold (80 units)	$4,964

Weighted-Average Cost

An alternative to keeping track of the cost of each item purchased is to find the **weighted-average cost** per unit of all like articles available for sale during the period. First, C. L. Frederickson finds the total cost of the water heaters it had on hand during the year by multiplying the number of units by their respective purchase costs.

22 units @ $57 each =	$1,254
30 units @ 62 each =	1,860
36 units @ 65 each =	2,340
18 units @ 68 each =	1,224
106 units	$6,678

Next C. L. Frederickson finds the average cost per heater.

$6,678 ÷ 106 units = $63 average cost per unit
Value of ending inventory = 26 units × $63 each = $1,638
Cost of merchandise sold = 80 units × $63 each = $5,040

According to this method, the beginning inventory is *weighted* (that is, multiplied by the number of units it comprises). Each purchase thereafter is weighted by the number of units involved in that purchase. In other words, the more you buy at a time, the more that purchase influences the average cost.

First-In, First-Out (FIFO) Method

The **first-in, first-out (FIFO)** method is based on the flow-of-cost assumption that merchandise sold should be charged against revenue in the order in which the costs were incurred. To determine the cost of merchandise sold, the accountant records the first (oldest) cost first, then the next-oldest cost, and so on. First-in, first-out is a logical way for a firm to rotate its stock of merchandise. Think of a grocery store selling milk. Because milk will sour, the oldest milk is moved up to the front of the shelf. As a result, the ending inventory consists of the freshest milk.

Again, let us return to C. L. Frederickson's water heaters. To repeat, 106 water heaters were available for sale during the year.

22 units @ $57 each =	$1,254
30 units @ 62 each =	1,860
36 units @ 65 each =	2,340
18 units @ 68 each =	1,224
106 units	$6,678

C. L. Frederickson sold 80 units. The accountant calculates the total cost of the heaters on a first-in, first-out (FIFO) basis, like this.

22 units @ $57 each =	$1,254
30 units @ 62 each =	1,860
28 units @ 65 each =	1,820
80 units	$4,934

C. L. Frederickson has the 26 newest or freshest units on hand in the ending inventory. The accountant records the ending inventory at the most recent costs, like this.

```
18 units @ $68 each = $1,224
 8 units @  65 each =    520
─────────────────────────────
26 units              $1,744
```

The accountant now verifies the total cost of the 80 units sold.

Total available − Ending inventory = Cost of merchandise sold
$$\$6,678 - \$1,744 = \$4,934$$

Last-In, First-Out (LIFO) Method

The **last-in, first-out (LIFO)** method is based on the flow-of-cost assumption that the most recently purchased articles are sold first and the articles remaining in the ending inventory are the oldest items. As an example, think of a coal yard selling coal. When the coal yard buys coal from its supplier, the new coal is added to the top of the pile. When the coal yard sells coal to its customers, coal is taken off the top of the pile. Consequently, the ending inventory consists of those first few tons at the bottom of the pile. And unless the pile is exhausted, they will never be sold.

Meanwhile, back at C. L. Frederickson, the firm sold 80 units. The accountant calculates the cost of the heaters on a last-in, first-out (LIFO) basis.

```
18 units @ $68 each = $1,224
36 units @  65 each =  2,340
26 units @  62 each =  1,612
─────────────────────────────
80 units              $5,176
```

C. L. Frederickson has the 26 oldest units (or the units at the bottom of the pile) on hand in the ending inventory. The accountant records the ending inventory at the earliest costs, like this.

```
22 units @ $57 each = $1,254
 4 units @  62 each =    248
─────────────────────────────
26 units              $1,502
```

The accountant now verifies the total cost of the 80 units sold.

Total available − Ending inventory = Cost of merchandise sold
$$\$6,678 - \$1,502 = \$5,176$$

Comparison of Methods

If prices don't change very much, all inventory methods give just about the same results. However, in a dynamic market where prices are constantly rising and falling, each method may yield different amounts. Here is a comparison of the results of the sale of the water heaters using the four methods we have described.

Method	Cost of Merchandise Sold (80 Units)	Ending Inventory (26 Units)
Specific identification	$4,964	$1,714
Weighted-average cost	5,040	1,638
First-in, first-out	4,934	1,744
Last-in, first-out	5,176	1,502

Assume that C. L. Frederickson sells the 80 water heaters for $90 apiece. The four methods yield the following gross profits.

	Specific Identification	Weighted-Average Cost	First-In, First-Out	Last-In, First-Out
Sales	$7,200	$7,200	$7,200	$7,200
Cost of merchandise sold	4,964	5,040	4,934	5,176
Gross profit	$2,236	$2,160	$2,266	$2,024

We can see from all this that the effects of the methods are as follows:

1. Specific identification matches costs exactly with revenues.
2. Weighted-average cost is a compromise between LIFO and FIFO, both for the amount of the ending inventory and for the cost of merchandise sold.
3. FIFO portrays the most realistic figure for ending merchandise inventory in the Current Assets section of the balance sheet. The ending inventory is evaluated at the most recent costs.
4. LIFO portrays the most realistic figure for the Cost of Merchandise Sold section of the income statement because the items that have been sold will have to be replaced at the most recent costs.

Tax Effect of LIFO

In a period of rising prices, LIFO yields the smallest gross profit and hence the smallest income tax because the most recent costs are assigned to the cost of merchandise sold. For the past thirty years prices have just kept going up in most industries, and there has been a built-in tax advantage for users of LIFO. If prices were ever to start falling, LIFO would be disadvantageous from the standpoint of taxes.

Consistency

We have seen that a firm can increase or decrease its gross profit, and likewise its net income and income tax, by changing the flow-of-cost assumption from one method to another—from FIFO to LIFO, for example. Although a firm may change its method of assigning inventory costs, it may not change back and forth repeatedly. Consistency in the method of determining cost of merchandise sold and the related cost of the ending inventory is necessary. For one thing, the government has said that a firm can't switch back and forth in order to evade some of its income tax. In addition, the firm must stick to a single method of reporting in financial statements to the owners and creditors of a firm. Consistency is a fundamental principle of accounting!

Bear in mind that the cost figure determined by the different methods may have nothing to do with the physical flow of the goods. By physical flow, we mean the way that specific items are taken out of inventory and sold.

LOWER-OF-COST-OR-MARKET RULE

All the above methods for determining the cost of the ending inventory are based on the cost per unit. In our examples prices were generally rising. However, sometimes the replacement cost of items in stock is *less* than the original market cost. The word *market* refers to the current price charged in the market. It is the price at which, *at the time of taking the inventory*, the items could be bought through the usual channels and in the usual quantities. The current prices may be quoted in catalogs or reflect contract quotations.

The **lower-of-cost-or-market rule** says that if the replacement or market cost is lower than the original cost, the inventory should be valued at the lowest cost. For example, the inventory of a store consists of 20 ski coats purchased originally for $22 each (total, $440). At the time of taking the inventory, the same type of ski coats may be purchased (replaced) for $18 each (total, $360). Under the lower-of-cost-or-market rule, the inventory is valued at $360. In this example, the original cost of $22 may have been determined by either the specific-identification method, the weighted-average-cost method, or the FIFO method. Under the tax law, the cost may *not* be determined by the LIFO method, because this method already offers tax advantages.

PERPETUAL INVENTORIES

Business firms such as equipment or appliance dealers that sell a limited variety of products of relatively high value maintain book records of their inventories on hand. They record additions to or deductions from their inventories *directly* in Merchandise Inventory accounts. This is known as the perpetual-inventory system, because the firms perpetually (or continually) *know* the *amount* of goods on hand. With computers, many other firms have also adopted the perpetual-inventory system. This system involves the following accounts, as illustrated by T accounts.

Objective 2

Journalize transactions relating to perpetual inventories.

Merchandise Inventory		Cost of Merchandise Sold		Sales	
+	−	+	−	−	+
Buying Merchandise recorded at cost	Selling Merchandise recorded at cost	Cost of merchandise sold			Amount received for merchandise sold

The adjusting entries at the end of the year are the only entries firms using the periodic system make in Merchandise Inventory. But firms using the perpetual-inventory system make entries directly in the Merchandise Inventory account throughout the year. One virtue of this system is that it enables the firm to do away with the Purchases and Purchases Returns and Allowances accounts. Firms using the perpetual-inventory system may record transactions at either the purchase price (gross) or at the purchase price less the cash discount (net).

To illustrate the perpetual-inventory system, let's look at a series of entries in general journal form, with transactions recorded at the gross amount.

Feb. 14 Bought merchandise on account, from Dever, Inc.; 2/10, n/30; $800.

	19–						
1	Feb.	14	Merchandise Inventory	8 0 0 00			1
2			Accounts Payable, Dever, Inc.		8 0 0 00		2
3			Terms: 2/10, n/30.				3
4							4

	Merchandise Inventory			Accounts Payable	
+		−	−		+
800					800

Feb. 24 Paid the invoice within the discount period.

	19– Feb.	24	Accounts Payable	8 0 0 00		1
1			Accounts Payable	8 0 0 00		1
2			Cash		7 8 4 00	2
3			Purchases Discount		1 6 00	3
4			Paid invoice within discount			4
5			period.			5
6						6

	Accounts Payable			Cash			Purchases Discount	
−		+	+		−	−		+
800					784			16

Mar. 5 Sold the merchandise on account to S. T. Dunn for $900. (The cost of the merchandise is $800. Two entries are required to record a sale under a perpetual-inventory system.)

	19– Mar.	5	Accounts Receivable, S. T. Dunn	9 0 0 00		1
1			Accounts Receivable, S. T. Dunn	9 0 0 00		1
2			Sales		9 0 0 00	2
3			Sold merchandise on account.			3
4						4
5		5	Cost of Merchandise Sold	8 0 0 00		5
6			Merchandise Inventory		8 0 0 00	6
7			Relating to $900 sale to			7
8			S. T. Dunn.			8
9						9

	Accounts Receivable			Sales	
+		−	−		+
900					900

	Cost of Merchandise Sold			Merchandise Inventory	
+		−	+		−
800			Bal. 800		800

For a firm using the perpetual-inventory system, one can compare the Cost of Merchandise Sold account to an expense account: both are increased by debits, and both are closed at the end of the year.

Firms may take physical inventories both during and at the end of the year to verify the book balance of the perpetual inventory and to adjust any discrepancy between the book balance and the actual count by adjusting the Merchandise Inventory and the Cost of Merchandise Sold accounts. Suppose the book figure for Merchandise Inventory is $16,250 and the physical count shows $16,140 of merchandise on hand. The adjusting entry looks like this.

1		*Adjusting Entry*			1
2	Jun. 30	*Cost of Merchandise Sold*	1 1 0 00		2
3		*Merchandise Inventory*		1 1 0 00	3
4					4

When a firm uses the perpetual-inventory system, Merchandise Inventory is a controlling account. The firm maintains an individual record in the subsidiary ledger for each kind of product, recording the number of units received as "units received" and the number of units sold as "units sold." The firm records the remaining balance after each receipt or sale. Companies may keep perpetual inventories by any of the four methods we talked about. For example, assume that C. L. Frederickson Plumbing Supply maintains a perpetual inventory on pumps, on a LIFO basis, as shown in Figure 19-6.

The ending balance of 26 units amounts to $1,920 ($720 + $1,200). Assuming that the 18 units were sold at $120 each, then total sales are $2,160, and gross profit is $822.

Objective 3

Complete a perpetual inventory record card.

Figure 19-6

INVENTORY RECORD CARD

ITEM __Self-priming centrifugal pump (1/2 hp)__   LOCATION __Warehouse Pump Section__

MAXIMUM __40__   MINIMUM __8__   METHOD __LIFO__

	PURCHASED AT COST			COST OF MERCHANDISE SOLD			INVENTORY AT COST		
DATE	UNITS	COST	TOTAL	UNITS	COST	TOTAL	UNITS	COST	TOTAL
1/2							14	$72	$1,008
2/6				4	$72	$288	10	72	720
2/22	30	$75	$2,250				⎰10	72	720
							⎱30	75	2,250
3/14				6	75	450	⎰10	72	720
							⎱24	75	1,800
3/29				8	75	600	⎰10	72	720
							⎱16	75	1,200
Total	30	—	$2,250	18	—	$1,338	—	—	

Sales (from sales journal)	$2,160
Less Cost of Merchandise Sold	1,338
Gross profit	$ 822

The weighted-average-cost flow can be used with a perpetual-inventory system. Rather than computing the average price for each inventory item at the end of a period, a new average is calculated each time a purchase is made. This average method is called a **moving average.** When goods are sold, their cost is determined by multiplying the number of units sold by the moving-average cost existing at that time. Further discussion of moving averages is reserved for more advanced accounting texts.

Perpetual-Inventory Records in Electronic Data Processing Accounting Systems

Several years ago, perpetual-inventory systems were most appropriate only for firms selling a limited variety of products of relatively high value. This was true because they had to depend on hand-operated techniques. However, electronic computers—which have large data storage capacities and can retrieve an item of stored information in fractions of a second—have enabled business firms to maintain perpetual inventories involving a wide variety of products, and with a large volume of transactions. Let's take as an example an automobile parts distribution center.

Each item of stock in the inventory is assigned a code number. Whenever the amounts of the items change, information concerning the changes is fed into the computer by means of an on-line data entry terminal. The computer performs the arithmetic operations and determines the new balance in accordance with the inventory method in use: LIFO, FIFO, or moving average. Thus the firm can determine the current status of any given item instantaneously. Whenever desired, the computer can list the balances of all the items in the inventory, in terms of both units and dollars. Some firms get such a listing or printout daily.

Our discussion of perpetual inventories has been geared to merchandising firms. However, manufacturing concerns use perpetual inventories almost exclusively. A lumber mill, for example, uses the balances of daily inventories as a basis for deciding which sizes of lumber to cut: $2'' \times 4'' \times 8'$, $1'' \times 3'' \times 6'$, and so on.

GLOSSARY

First-in, first-out (FIFO) Process of assigning costs to merchandise sold, based on the flow-of-cost assumption that units are sold in the order in which they were acquired. Unsold units on hand at date of inventory are assumed to be valued at the most recent costs.

Last-in, first-out (LIFO) Process of assigning costs to merchandise sold, based on the flow-of-cost assumption that units sold are recorded at the costs of the most recently acquired units. Unsold units on hand at date of inventory are assumed to be valued at the earliest costs.

Lower-of-cost-or-market rule When there is a difference between the cost price and the market price of goods, the lower price is used for determining the value of the ending inventory. The term *market price* means current replacement price.

Moving average A modification of the weighted-average-cost method, used for computing the average cost of a perpetual inventory. The firm determines the moving-average unit price each time it buys more units.

Periodic-inventory system Determining the amount of goods on hand by periodically taking a physical count.

Perpetual inventory A book record of the ending inventory showing the unit costs of the items received and the items sold. This gives the firm a running balance of the inventory on hand.

Specific-identification method Counting the actual cost of each individual item in the ending inventory.

Weighted-average cost A method of determining the cost of the ending inventory by multiplying the weighted-average cost per unit by the number of remaining units.

QUESTIONS, EXERCISES, AND PROBLEMS

Discussion Questions

1. Name the four methods of assigning costs to ending inventory.
2. Identify an advantage and a disadvantage of LIFO.
3. During periods of inflation, which inventory method will result in the lowest reported profits?
4. Due to an error, merchandise costing $2,000 was omitted from the ending inventory. What effect does the omission have on the company's gross profit?
5. What is the difference between the periodic (physical) system and the perpetual system of accounting for inventories?
6. When a perpetual inventory system is in use, what are the necessary journal entries for buying merchandise on account and selling merchandise on account?
7. In a perpetual inventory system, what happens to the Cost of Merchandise Sold account at the end of the fiscal period?

Exercises

Exercise 19-1 Condensed income statements for Peerless Company for two years are presented below.

	19x7		19x8	
Sales (net)		$88 0 0 0 00		$80 0 0 0 00
Cost of Merchandise Sold:				
Beginning Merchandise Inventory	$14 0 0 0 00		$12 0 0 0 00	
Purchases (net)	48 0 0 0 00		46 0 0 0 00	
Merchandise Available for Sale	$62 0 0 0 00		$58 0 0 0 00	
Less Ending Merchandise Inventory	12 0 0 0 00		13 0 0 0 00	
Cost of Merchandise Sold		50 0 0 0 00		45 0 0 0 00
Gross Profit		$38 0 0 0 00		$35 0 0 0 00
Operating Expenses		18 0 0 0 00		17 0 0 0 00
Net Income		$20 0 0 0 00		$18 0 0 0 00

After the end of 19x8, it was discovered that an error had been made in 19x7. Ending inventory in 19x7 should have been $9,000 instead of $12,000. Determine the corrected net income for 19x7 and 19x8. What is the amount of the total net income for the two-year period both without the correction and with the correction?

Exercise 19-2 Morris Irrigation maintains an inventory of pumps, #A321. The beginning inventory of #A321 and the purchases of them during the year were as follows. (Round all computations to two decimal places.)

Jan.   1 Inventory of 22 units @ $72 each
Mar.   12 Purchased 32 units @ $72 each
Aug.   16 Purchased 18 units @ $76 each
Oct.   27 Purchased 12 units @ $78 each

The ending inventory, by physical count, is 26 units. Determine the value of the ending inventory and the cost of merchandise sold by the following methods: weighted-average cost; first-in, first-out; last-in, first-out.

Exercise 19-3 The J. P. Pierson Company's fiscal year is from January 1 through December 31. The following figures are available.

Inventory, January 1 $176,000 (by physical count)
Inventory, December 31   192,000 (by physical count)

a. Record the adjusting entries, assuming that the company uses the periodic-inventory system.
b. Record the adjusting entry, assuming that the company uses the perpetual-inventory system and that the book balance of the ending inventory is $192,300.

Exercise 19-4 The accounts of the Phelan Hobby Shop, which uses the periodic-inventory method, contain the following balances at the end of the first month of this fiscal year.

Merchandise Inventory	$ 62,000
Purchases	96,000
Purchases Discounts	2,000
Purchases Returns and Allowances	8,000
Sales	139,000
Sales Discounts	1,500
Sales Returns and Allowances	8,500

Assuming that the ending inventory, determined by physical count, is $51,000, determine the cost of merchandise sold and the gross profit, using an income statement outline.

Exercise 19-5 Sylvan Wholesale Jewelers keeps perpetual inventories on ring mountings, using the first-in, first-out method. Determine the cost of merchandise sold in each sale and the inventory balance after each sale for the following purchases and sales of ring mounting #67.

Jan.	1 Inventory of 30 units @ $45 each
	20 Sold 16 units
Feb.	4 Purchased 20 units @ $48 each
	17 Sold 17 units
Mar.	4 Sold 10 units
	20 Purchased 16 units @ $50 each

Exercise 19-6 The records of Sherman Appliance show the following data as of June 30, the end of the fiscal year. Determine the value of the ending merchandise inventory.

a. Cost of merchandise on hand, based on a physical count, $98,000.
b. Cost of defective merchandise (to be thrown away) included in **a** above, $140.
c. Merchandise purchased June 27, FOB shipping point, delivered to the transportation company on June 28, $360.
d. Cost of merchandise sold to a customer on June 29, which is paid for in full and is awaiting shipping instructions, $420; not included in **a** above.
e. Cost of merchandise shipped out FOB destination on June 28, with an expected delivery date of approximately four days, $600; not included in **a** above.

Exercise 19-7 An abbreviated income statement for the Walter Granger Company for this fiscal year is shown at the top of the next page.

An accountant discovers that the ending inventory is overstated by $6,000. What effect does this have on cost of merchandise sold, gross profit, and net income in this fiscal year?

Sales (net)							$	160	0 0 0	00
Cost of Merchandise Sold										
Merchandise Inventory,										
January 1	$	37	0 0 0	00						
Purchases (net)		128	0 0 0	00						
Merchandise Available for Sale	$	165	0 0 0	00						
Merchandise Inventory,										
December 31		42	0 0 0	00						
Cost of Merchandise Sold								123	0 0 0	00
Gross Profit							$	37	0 0 0	00
Expenses								20	0 0 0	00
Net Income							$	17	0 0 0	00

Exercise 19-8 Manning Equipment Company's beginning inventory for May consisted of 3,200 units at $2 each. Purchases and sales during May were as follows.

May 3 Sold 1,100 units
  9 Purchased 1,600 units @ $2.00 each
  14 Sold 2,000 units
  21 Purchased 1,800 units @ $2.10 each
  30 Sold 700 units

Calculate the cost of the ending inventory under each of the following pricing methods: weighted-average cost; first-in, first-out; last-in, first-out.

Problem Set A

Problem 19-1A Waterton Company's inventory of MC509 on January 1 of one year was 16,000 gallons, which cost them $.25 per gallon. In addition to the beginning inventory, the firm bought more MC509 during the next six months, as follows.

Date	Quantity (Gallons)	Cost per Gallon	Total Cost
Jan. 1 inventory	16,000	$.25	$4,000
23	10,000	.25½	2,550
Feb. 5	12,000	.26	3,120
22	9,000	.26	2,340
Mar. 6	11,000	.25½	2,805
29	8,000	.27	2,160
Apr. 17	9,000	.27	2,430
May 19	6,000	.27	1,620
Jun. 18	4,000	.28	1,120

Waterton Company's inventory on June 30 was 9,000 gallons. During this six-month period, the firm sold all its MC509 at $.30 per gallon. Assume that no liquid was lost through evaporation or leakage. (Round all computations to four decimal places.)

Instructions

1. Find the cost of the ending inventory by the following methods:
   a. Weighted-average cost
   b. First-in, first-out
   c. Last-in, first-out
2. Determine the cost of merchandise sold according to the three methods of costing inventory.
3. Determine the amount of the gross profit according to the three methods of costing inventory.

Problem 19-2A Stewart Appliance uses the periodic-inventory system. Data for their inventories on January 1, the beginning of their fiscal year, as well as purchases during the year and the inventory count at December 31 are as follows.

	Model		
	JB11	**GG24**	**7216**
Inventory, January 1	6 @ $218 each	4 @ $346 each	17 @ $168 each
First purchase	9 @ 225 each	7 @ 361 each	21 @ 172 each
Second purchase	11 @ 230 each	8 @ 361 each	33 @ 172 each
Third purchase	8 @ 230 each	6 @ 368 each	14 @ 174 each
Fourth purchase	7 @ 233 each		
Inventory, December 31	8	7	23

Instructions

Round all computations to two decimal places.
1. Determine the cost of the inventory on December 31 by the first-in, first-out method.
2. Determine the cost of the inventory on December 31 by the last-in, first-out method.
3. Determine the cost of the inventory on December 31 by the weighted-average-cost method.

Problem 19-3A The Drew Company's beginning inventory of item 164C and dates of purchases and sales for a three-month period are as follows.

Date	Number of Units	Purchase Price per Unit	Selling Price per Unit
Jan. 1	Inventory 160	$22.00	
16	Purchase 220	22.10	
18	Sale 70		$26.00
29	Sale 140		26.00

Feb.	6	Purchase	240	22.80	
	8	Sale	130		26.50
	19	Sale	190		26.50
	26	Purchase	220	23.10	
Mar.	3	Sale	70		27.00
	15	Purchase	150	24.00	
	21	Sale	80		27.00
	30	Sale	145		28.00

Drew Company maintains a perpetual inventory record using the first-in, first-out method. Data for the month of January are recorded in the *Working Papers.*

Instructions

1. Record the data for purchases of item 164C and for cost of merchandise sold in a perpetual-inventory record using the first-in, first-out method for the three months.
2. Determine the total cost of merchandise sold during the three-month period.
3. Determine the total sales for the three-month period.
4. Determine the gross profit from sales of item 164C for the period.

Problem 19-4A The Patterson Company carried out the following transactions during the year.

Jan. 2 Bought merchandise on account from Berquist Machine Products; terms 2/10, n/30; $8,400.

5 Received credit memo no. 2768 from Berquist Machine Products for the return of merchandise bought on January 2, $600.

11 Issued check no. 9014, payable to Berquist Machine Products, in payment of the invoice dated January 2, $7,644.

22 Sold merchandise on account to Bennham School District, $5,760; the cost of the merchandise was $4,692.

30 Sold merchandise on account to Henson Health Spa, $3,648; the cost of the merchandise was $2,952.

Dec. 31 Made the adjusting entry for the ending merchandise inventory determined by physical count, $192,768. The beginning inventory was $192,658. The balance in the inventory account under the perpetual-inventory system is $192,814.

Instructions

1. Assuming that Patterson uses the perpetual-inventory system, record the transactions in general journal form, with purchases recorded at the gross amount.
2. Assuming that Patterson uses the periodic-inventory system, record the transactions in general journal form, with purchases recorded at the gross amount.

Problem Set B

Problem 19-1B Koch and Wagner Company, on January 1 of one year, had an inventory of RL628 of 1,200 gallons, which cost $.21 per gallon. In addition to this beginning inventory, purchases during the next six months were as follows.

Date	Quantity (Gallons)	Cost per Gallon	Total Cost
Jan. 1 inventory	1,200	$.21	$ 252
21	9,000	.22	1,980
Feb. 17	8,000	.23	1,840
Mar. 8	6,000	.23⅓	1,400
Apr. 16	11,000	.23	2,530
May 2	8,000	.22	1,760
Jun. 1	9,000	.23½	2,115
28	7,000	.24	1,680

The inventory on June 30 was 15,000 gallons. During this six-month period, Koch and Wagner sold RL628 for $.27 per gallon. Assume that no liquid was lost through evaporation or leakage.

Instructions

1. Find the value of the ending inventory by the following methods. (Round all computations to three decimal places.)
   a. Weighted-average cost
   b. First-in, first-out
   c. Last-in, first-out
2. Determine the cost of merchandise sold according to the three methods of taking inventory.
3. Determine the gross profit according to the three methods of taking inventory.

Problem 19-2B Watkins Appliance uses the periodic-inventory system. Data pertaining to the inventory on January 1, the beginning of the fiscal year, as well as purchases during the year and the inventory count on December 31, are as follows.

	Model		
	JB11	GG24	7Z16
Inventory, January 1	11 @ $216 each	3 @ $393 each	21 @ $159 each
First purchase	17 @ 222 each	7 @ 391 each	28 @ 161 each
Second purchase	22 @ 226 each	9 @ 394 each	30 @ 161 each
Third purchase	16 @ 226 each	6 @ 398 each	32 @ 165 each
Fourth purchase	12 @ 229 each		26 @ 166 each
Inventory, December 31	14	8	32

Instructions

Round all computations to two decimal places.
1. Determine the cost of the inventory on December 31 by the first-in, first-out method.
2. Determine the cost of the inventory on December 31, by the last-in, first-out method.
3. Determine the cost of the inventory on December 31 by the weighted-average-cost method.

Problem 19-3B The Drew Company's beginning inventory of item 164C and dates of purchases and sales for a three-month period are as follows.

Date		Number of Units		Purchase Price per Unit	Selling Price per Unit
Jan.	1	Inventory	160	$22.00	
	16	Purchase	220	22.10	
	18	Sale	70		$26.00
	29	Sale	140		26.00
Feb.	4	Purchase	180	23.00	
	9	Sale	120		26.50
	16	Purchase	200	24.00	
	27	Sale	170		28.00
Mar.	11	Sale	90		28.00
	19	Purchase	120	24.30	
	23	Sale	75		28.00
	29	Sale	80		28.20

Drew Company maintains a perpetual-inventory record using the first-in, first-out method. Data for the month of January are recorded in the *Working Papers*.

Instructions

1. Record the data for purchases of item 164C and for cost of merchandise sold in a perpetual-inventory record using the first-in, first-out method for the three months.
2. Determine the total cost of merchandise sold during the three-month period.
3. Determine the total sales for the three-month period.
4. Determine the gross profit from sales of item 164C for this period.

Problem 19-4B The Underwood Company made the following transactions during the year.

Jan. 3 Bought merchandise on account from Van Dyke Manufacturing Company; terms 2/10, n/30; $6,000.

Jan. 6 Received credit memo no. 1911 from Van Dyke Manufacturing Company for the return of merchandise bought on January 3, $400.

12 Issued check no. 7618, payable to Van Dyke Manufacturing Company, in payment of invoice dated January 3, $5,488.

15 Sold merchandise on account to Crawford and Sanders, $2,700; the cost of the merchandise was $2,442.

30 Sold merchandise on account to Currier and Son, $3,664; the cost of the merchandise was $3,046.

Dec. 31 Made the adjusting entry for ending merchandise inventory determined by physical count, $80,926. The beginning inventory was $81,050. The balance in the inventory account under the perpetual-inventory system is $81,162.

Instructions

1. Record the above transactions in general journal form, assuming that Underwood uses the perpetual-inventory system and records purchases at the gross amount.
2. Record the above transactions in general journal form, assuming that Underwood uses the periodic-inventory system and records purchases at the gross amount.

APPENDIX D

Estimating the Value of Inventories

In Chapter 1, we described accounting as the eyes and ears of management. Management sees and hears through the medium of financial reports that summarize the results of business operations. Management, in order to function efficiently, must have interim income statements and balance sheets prepared monthly. Management needs a physical inventory at the end of the year because inventory balance figures are an integral element of financial statements. However, because it is both time-consuming and expensive to take a physical inventory, management finds it more expedient to estimate the value of the ending inventories each month and to use these estimates on the monthly financial statements. Let's take a look at the two most frequently used methods of estimating the value of inventories—the retail method and the gross-profit method.

Retail Method of Estimating the Value of Inventories

As the name implies, this method is widely used by retail concerns, particularly department stores. The retailer buys merchandise at cost, then adds the normal markup, and prices the goods at the retail level. The **normal markup**—which is the normal amount, or percentage, that you add to the cost of an item to arrive at its selling price—covers operating expenses and profit. When a firm uses the retail method of estimating inventories, it must record the Purchases-related accounts at both cost and retail values. The firm's accountant records retail values in supplementary records; he or she also records the physical inventory taken at the end of the previous year at both cost and retail values.

Example 1 Henderson Company takes a physical inventory at the end of each year and estimates the value of the ending inventory at the end of each month for its monthly financial statements.

The accountant for Henderson Company needs to determine the following information to estimate the value of the ending merchandise inventory at cost.

- Cost value and retail value of merchandise on hand at the beginning of the month. (The inventory at the beginning of a given month is the same as the inventory at the end of the preceding month.)

	AT COST	AT RETAIL
Merchandise Inventory (beginning)	41 2 0 0 00	68 6 0 0 00

- Net purchases of merchandise during the month, both cost value and retail value. To obtain the retail figures, the accountant adds the normal markup to the cost figures, as shown.

	AT COST		AT RETAIL	
Purchases		83 0 0 0 00		138 4 1 0 00
Less: Purchases Returns and Allowances	3 2 0 0 00			
Purchases Discounts	1 0 0 0 00	4 2 0 0 00		7 0 1 0 00
Net Purchases		78 8 0 0 00		131 4 0 0 00

- Net sales for the month. All sales are recorded at retail price levels, as listed on sales slips and cash register tapes.

	AT RETAIL	
Sales		151 6 5 0 00
Less: Sales Returns and Allowances	7 0 0 0 00	
Sales Discounts	2 6 5 0 00	9 6 5 0 00
Net Sales		142 0 0 0 00

The accountant can determine this information by following these four steps:

1. Determine the dollar value of merchandise available for sale, at cost and at retail. The cost figures are the same as the Merchandise Available for Sale, which is part of the Cost of Merchandise Sold section of the income statement.

	At Cost	At Retail
Beginning inventory	$ 41,200	$ 68,600
Plus net purchases	78,800	131,400
Merchandise available for sale	$120,000	$200,000

2. Find the ratio of the cost value of merchandise available to the retail value of merchandise available.

$$\frac{\text{Cost value of merchandise available for sale}}{\text{Retail value of merchandise available for sale}} = \frac{\$120,000}{\$200,000} = 60\%$$

3. Determine the retail value of ending inventory.

Retail value of merchandise available	$200,000
Less net sales	142,000
Retail value of ending inventory	$ 58,000

Think of the retail value of the ending inventory this way: If the firm had $200,000 of merchandise available for sale, and $142,000 was actually sold, then the amount left over should be $58,000.

4. Convert the retail value of the ending inventory into the cost value of the ending inventory by using this formula.

$58,000 \times 60\% = \$58,000 \times .6 = \$34,800$

Therefore, on its income statement for the month, Henderson Sporting Goods records the value of the ending inventory as $34,800. If the retail value is $58,000 and 40 percent of this figure represents markup, the remaining 60 percent must be the cost.

Example 2 N. R. Gallaher Company had the following account balances, as shown by T accounts.

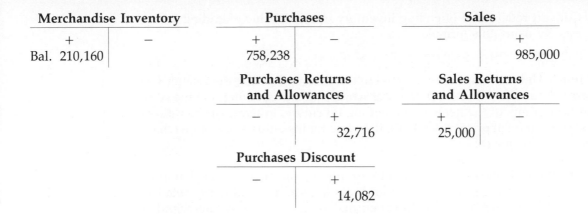

Merchandise Inventory			Purchases			Sales	
+	−		+	−		−	+
Bal. 210,160			758,238				985,000

	Purchases Returns and Allowances			Sales Returns and Allowances	
−	+		+	−
	32,716		25,000	

	Purchases Discount	
−	+
	14,082

Retail value of beginning inventory, $296,000 (the accountant picks up this figure from a report dated the end of the preceding month).

Net Purchases = Purchases − Purchases Returns and Allowances
− Purchases Discount

$= \$758,238 - \$32,716 - \$14,082$

$= \$711,440$

Retail value of net purchases, $984,000 (the normal markup is added to the cost figure).

Net Sales = Sales − Sales Returns and Allowances

$= \$985,000 - \$25,000$

$= \$960,000$

Again, the information is obtained by following the four steps:

1. Determine the dollar value of merchandise available for sale, at cost and at retail.

	At Cost	At Retail
Beginning inventory	$210,160	$ 296,000
Plus net purchases	711,440	984,000
Merchandise available for sale	$921,600	$1,280,000

2. Find the ratio of the cost value of merchandise available to the retail value of merchandise available.

$$\frac{\text{Cost value of merchandise available for sale}}{\text{Retail value of merchandise available for sale}} = \frac{\$921,600}{\$1,280,000} = 72\%$$

3. Find the retail value of ending inventory, as follows.

Retail value of merchandise available	$1,280,000
Less net sales	960,000
Retail value of ending inventory	$ 320,000

4. Convert retail value of ending inventory into cost value of ending inventory by using this formula.

$320,000 × 72% = $320,000 × .72 = $230,400

In the above examples, there is a built-in assumption that the retailer will maintain the normal markup. In other words, we are assuming that the composition or mix of the items in the ending inventory, in terms of the ratio of cost price to retail price, will remain the same for the entire stock of merchandise available for sale.

Markups and Markdowns In our examples, the retailers used normal markups, but some stores use additional markups and markdowns. Retailers impose additional markups on top of normal markups when the merchandise involved is in great demand. Because of the highly desirable nature of the goods (for example, up-to-the minute fashion in clothes), a store may feel that it can get higher-than-normal prices for the goods. Conversely, a store uses markdowns to sell slow-moving merchandise during a clearance sale.

When a store using the retail inventory method imposes additional markups and markdowns, it must keep track of them, so that it can calculate the ratio of the cost value of merchandise available to the retail value of merchandise available. Look at the following example of how a store keeps track of markups and markdowns.

Step 1 Merchandise available for sale, at cost and at retail.

	At Cost	At Retail
Beginning inventory	$ 60,000	$ 90,000
Plus net purchases	110,000	165,000
Plus additional markups		4,000
Merchandise available for sale	$170,000	$259,000

Step 2 Ratio of cost value of merchandise available to retail value of merchandise available is as follows.

$$\frac{\text{Cost value of merchandise available for sale}}{\text{Retail value of merchandise available for sale}} = \frac{\$170,000}{\$259,000} = 66\%$$

Step 3 Retail value of ending inventory.

Retail value of merchandise available for sale	$259,000
Less net sales	200,000
Less markdowns	3,000
Retail value of ending inventory	$ 56,000

Step 4 Convert retail value of ending inventory into cost value of ending inventory.

$56,000 × .66 = $36,960

The accountant adds any additional markups in the retail column of his or her working paper, because such markups result in an increase in the retail value of the merchandise available for sale. For example, let's say that the price of a popular item is $40, so a store seizes the opportunity and marks it up to $49; this is a $9 increase in the retail value of the merchandise available for sale. On the other hand, when a store marks down the price of an item, the accountant deducts the amount of the markdown from the retail value of the merchandise available for sale (step 3) to obtain the retail value of the merchandise inventory at the end of a given month. For example, say that the price tag of an item is $389, but nobody's buying. So the store marks it down to $359. This means that there has been a $30 decrease in the retail value of this merchandise available for sale.

End-of-Year Procedure

As we have said, it is very important to take a physical inventory at the end of the year. Physical inventories may also be taken periodically during the year to spot-check the estimated inventories. Most retail stores record items in stock on the inventory sheets at retail prices (in other words, they take the total of all the price tags). It is then necessary to convert the total of the retail values into the total of the cost values, as in step 4. For example, suppose that the total retail value of the merchandise on all the inventory sheets is $96,000, and the ratio of cost value to retail value is

$$\frac{\text{Cost value of merchandise available}}{\text{Retail value of merchandise available}} = 70\%$$

The cost value of the merchandise is $96,000 \times .7 = \$67,200$. The only difference between the steps taken to prepare the end-of-the-year statement and the steps taken to prepare the interim or monthly statements is that, at the end of the year, there is a physical count of the merchandise, and consequently one begins with step 4.

However, to find out the magnitude of shoplifting, or to verify the accuracy of the evaluation of the physical inventory, some firms go through the full procedure of estimating the value of the inventory at the end of the year, then they take a physical count of the goods on hand and compare this value with the value of the estimated inventory.

Gross-Profit Method of Estimating the Value of Inventories

Sometimes a firm may find that the total of the retail prices of the beginning inventory and purchases isn't readily available; in such cases, the firm naturally can't use the retail method of estimating the value of the ending inventory. The **gross-profit method** is an alternative procedure that achieves the same objective. As the name implies, the key element in this method of estimating the value of inventories is the percentage of gross profit the firm makes over a given period of time.

The term *gross profit,* as used on income statements, represents net sales less cost of merchandise sold.

Net sales	$60,000
Less cost of merchandise sold	45,000
Gross profit	$15,000

You arrive at the figure for the percentage of gross profit by dividing the gross profit by the net sales, like this.

$$\text{Percentage of gross profit} = \frac{\text{Gross profit}}{\text{Net sales}} = \frac{\$15,000}{\$60,000} = 25\%$$

A 25 percent gross-profit rate means that there is 25¢ of gross profit for every $1 of net sales. *Gross profit* is the profit earned on the sale of merchandise *before* expenses are deducted. You can compute the gross-profit rate or percentage by using figures from a recent income statement. Alternatively, you may compute the percentage of gross profit from income statements from past years, using averages of figures. The variation from year to year is usually relatively minor, unless marked changes have taken place in the buying and selling policies of the firm.

You need the following information for the current year.

- Sales (balance of account to date)
- Sales Returns and Allowances (balance of account to date)
- Sales Discounts (balance of account to date, if any)
- Beginning Merchandise Inventory (ending inventory of the previous period)
- Purchases (balance of account to date)
- Purchases Returns and Allowances (balance of account to date)
- Purchases Discount (balance of account to date)

Example 1   On the night of April 29, the Underwood Variety Store was destroyed by fire. However, a heroic sales clerk ran into the building and rescued the company's books and records of transactions. For insurance purposes, the owner must estimate the value of the inventory by the gross-profit method. The owner knows that the average gross-profit percentage for the past five years is 32 percent. By journalizing and posting the transactions of the current month, the company's accounts can be brought up to date from these sources.

- Sales (from sales journal, cash receipts journal, and invoices for April 29)
- Sales Returns and Allowances (from cash receipts and general journal)
- Merchandise Inventory, December 31 (ending inventory of last fiscal period)
- Purchases (from purchases journal and invoices for April 29)
- Purchases Returns and Allowances (from general journal)
- Purchases Discount (from cash payments journal)

The owner of Underwood Variety arranges these figures in the customary income statement format, extending from Sales to Gross Profit (see Figure D-1).

Underwood Variety Store
Income Statement
For period January 1 through April 29, 19–

Revenue from Sales:				
Sales				$ 217 0 0 0 00
Less Sales Returns and Allowances				17 0 0 0 00
Net Sales				$ 200 0 0 0 00
Cost of Merchandise Sold:				
Merchandise Inventory, January 1, 19–			$ 72 0 0 0 00	
Purchases		$ 143 4 0 0 00		
Less: Purchases Returns and Allowances	$14 0 0 0 00			
Purchases Discount	2 4 0 0 00	16 4 0 0 00		
Net Purchases			127 0 0 0 00	
Merchandise Available for Sale			$ 199 0 0 0 00	
Less Merchandise Inventory, April 29, 19–				
Cost of Merchandise Sold				$
Gross Profit				$

Figure D-1

Underwood Variety Store
Income Statement
For period January 1 through April 29, 19–

Revenue from Sales:				
Sales				$ 217 0 0 0 00
Less Sales Returns and Allowances				17 0 0 0 00
Net Sales				$ 200 0 0 0 00
Cost of Merchandise Sold:				
Merchandise Inventory, January 1, 19–			$ 72 0 0 0 00	
Purchases		$ 143 4 0 0 00		
Less: Purchases Returns and Allowances	$14 0 0 0 00			
Purchases Discount	2 4 0 0 00	16 4 0 0 00		
Net Purchases			127 0 0 0 00	
Merchandise Available for Sale			$ 199 0 0 0 00	
Less Merchandise Inventory, April 29, 19–				
Cost of Merchandise Sold				$ 64 0 0 0 00
Gross Profit				

Figure D-2

$$\text{Percentage of gross profit} = \frac{\text{Gross profit}}{\text{Net sales}} = \frac{\text{Gross profit}}{\$200,000} = 32\%$$

Gross Profit = .32 × $200,000 = $64,000

Now we fill in the Gross Profit blank in the income statement (see Figure D-2).

Obviously, in order to find the value of the merchandise at the end (April 29), we should work backward. The cost of merchandise sold is the difference between net sales and gross profit, or $136,000 ($200,000 − $64,000). The equation is as shown here.

Cost of Merchandise Sold = Net Sales − Gross Profit

$$= \$200,000 - \$64,000$$

$$= \$136,000$$

Now that we have filled in the figures for Gross Profit and Cost of Merchandise Sold, the partial income statement (from Merchandise Available for Sale through Gross Profit) looks like this.

Merchandise Available for Sale	$199,000.00	
Less Merchandise Inventory, Apr. 29, 19–		
Cost of Merchandise Sold		136,000.00
Gross Profit		$ 64,000.00

The value of the merchandise inventory on April 29 is the difference between the value of the merchandise available for sale and the cost of merchandise sold, or $63,000 ($199,000 − $136,000). The equation is as follows.

Value of ending inventory = Value of merchandise available for sale
− Cost of merchandise sold

$$= \$199,000 - \$136,000$$

$$= \$63,000$$

Merchandise Available for Sale	$199,000.00	
Less Merchandise Inventory, Apr. 29, 19–	63,000.00	
Cost of Merchandise Sold		136,000.00
Gross Profit		$ 64,000.00

The income statement is a very useful device in the box of tools that you have been accumulating. That is why we suggested earlier that you memorize the form initially in order to implant it firmly in your mind; then it will always be at your fingertips when you need it to do a specific job.

Example 2   Woodward Oxygen Supply has an average gross-profit rate of 34 percent. Their account balances on May 31 of this year are shown by the T accounts on page 597 and by the partial income statement in Figure D-3.

Woodward Oxygen Supply
Income Statement
For period January 1 through May 31, 19—

Revenue from Sales:				
Sales				$314 7 1 9 00
Less: Sales Returns and Allowances			$ 12 4 9 1 00	
Sales Discount			6 2 2 8 00	18 7 1 9 00
Net Sales				$ 296 0 0 0 00
Cost of Merchandise Sold:				
Merchandise Inventory, January 1, 19—			$ 83 1 1 8 00	
Purchases		$ 213 9 0 1 00		
Less: Purchases Returns and Allowances	$11 2 2 8 00			
Purchases Discount	3 7 1 5 00	14 9 4 3 00		
Net Purchases			198 9 5 8 00	
Merchandise Available for Sale			$ 282 0 7 6 00	
Less Merchandise Inventory, May 31, 19—			86 7 1 6 00	
Cost of Merchandise Sold				195 3 6 0 00
Gross Profit				$ 100 6 4 0 00

Figure D-3

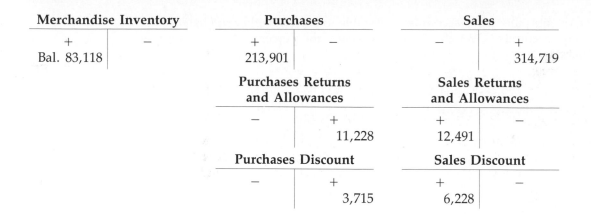

Merchandise Inventory		Purchases		Sales	
+	−	+	−	−	+
Bal. 83,118		213,901			314,719

Purchases Returns and Allowances		Sales Returns and Allowances	
−	+	+	−
	11,228	12,491	

Purchases Discount		Sales Discount	
−	+	+	−
	3,715	6,228	

$$\text{Percentage of gross profit} = \frac{\text{Gross profit}}{\text{Net sales}} = \frac{\text{Gross profit}}{\$296,000} = 34\%$$

Gross profit = .34 × $296,000 = $100,640

The cost of merchandise sold is equal to net sales minus gross profit, or $195,360 ($296,000 − $100,640). The ending merchandise inventory is the value of the merchandise available for sale minus the cost of merchandise sold, or $86,716 ($282,076 − $195,360).

Problems

Problem D-1   You are given the following information for Buckner's Tackle Shop at the end of its fiscal year, October 31.

	At Cost	At Retail
Sales		$88,263
Sales Returns and Allowances		3,553
Purchases	$53,616	88,376
Purchases Returns and Allowances	2,342	2,748
Merchandise Inventory, Beginning	19,724	32,708

Instructions

1. Determine the cost value of the ending merchandise inventory as of October 31, presenting details of your computations.
2. At the end of the year, Buckner's Tackle Shop takes a physical inventory at marked selling prices and finds that the retail stock totals $32,984. There is a possibility that the difference between the estimated ending inventory and the actual physical inventory is due to shoplifting. Convert the value of the physical inventory at retail into its value at cost and determine the amount of the loss.

Problem D-2   On May 10 of this year, a fire in the night destroyed the entire stock of merchandise of the Jessup Health Store. Most of the accounting records were destroyed also. However, from assorted statements and documents, the firm's accountant was able to piece together the balances of several accounts. Over the past three years, the percentage of gross profit averaged 40 percent.

Merchandise Inventory, January 1 (beginning of fiscal year)	$41,729
Account balances, as of May 10	
Purchases	57,292
Purchases Returns and Allowances	328
Sales	71,140
Sales Returns and Allowances	220

Instructions

Determine the cost value of the ending merchandise inventory as of May 10, giving details of your computations.

Problem D-3 On the morning of July 27, the owner of Nancy's Sewing Center opened her store and discovered that a robbery had taken place over the weekend. A large part of the stock had been stolen. However, the following information for the period January 1 through July 27 was available. Each year during the past four years, the store had earned an average 34 percent gross profit on sales.

Merchandise Inventory, January 1 (beginning of fiscal year)	$63,419
Account balances, as of July 27	
Purchases	144,465
Purchases Returns and Allowances	3,662
Purchases Discounts	2,748
Sales	198,746
Sales Returns and Allowances	2,146

Instructions

1. Determine the cost value of the ending merchandise inventory as of July 27, giving details of your computations.
2. By physical count, the cost value of the remaining inventory on hand is $26,980. What is the amount of the loss to be claimed for insurance purposes?

20 Accounting for Valuation of Plant and Equipment

Learning Objectives

After you have completed this chapter, you will be able to do the following:

1. Allocate costs to Land, Land Improvements, and Buildings accounts.

2. Calculate depreciation by the straight-line method, units-of-production method, double-declining-balance method, and sum-of-the-years'-digits method.

3. Differentiate between capital expenditures and revenue expenditures.

4. Differentiate between expenditures for ordinary and for extraordinary repairs.

5. Prepare journal entries for discarding of assets fully depreciated, discarding of assets not fully depreciated, sale of assets involving a loss, sale of assets involving a gain, exchange of assets involving a loss on the trade, and exchange of assets involving a gain on the trade.

6. Maintain a plant and equipment subsidiary ledger.

We described plant and equipment as an account classification in Chapter 15, in connection with the classified balance sheet. Assets in this category have a useful life longer than one year, and so are often referred to as long-lived or fixed assets. Such assets are originally purchased for use in the business, as opposed to merchandise, which is bought for the purpose of resale. Items most frequently classified as plant and equipment are equipment, furniture, machinery, tools, buildings, land improvements, and land.

INITIAL COSTS OF PLANT AND EQUIPMENT

The original cost of plant and equipment includes all normal expenditures necessary to acquire and install them. For example, the cost of a cash register includes not only its invoice price (less any discount for paying cash), but sales tax, freight charges, insurance costs while it is being transported, and costs of unpacking and assembling. Assuming that the buyer of the cash register pays these additional charges in cash, the accountant for the buyer debits Store Equipment and credits Cash. Suppose the firm bought a second-hand cash register and had to have it repaired before it could be used. The cost of the repairs would be debited to the relevant asset account, in this case Store Equipment.

The accountant should debit only normal and necessary costs to the asset accounts, which rules out expenditures that result from carelessness, vandalism, or other abnormal causes. For example, suppose that an employee dropped the cash register while unpacking it. The cost of the repair is not part of the cost of the cash register; that cost is charged to an expense account, such as Repair Expense or Miscellaneous Expense. The cost is charged as an expense and not as an asset because the repair does not *add* to the usefulness of the cash register—it simply restores its usefulness.

DIFFERENTIATING COSTS OF LAND, LAND IMPROVEMENTS, AND BUILDINGS

Objective 1

Allocate costs to Land, Land Improvements, and Buildings accounts.

There is no legal recognition for the depreciation of land. Yet a buyer usually buys a package including the land, land improvements, and the building. In other words, the buyer pays one price for one package. So the question is: How should the price be allocated among the three elements?

When there is no qualified appraisal available, then one accepts the ratio established by the county or municipal assessor. For example, suppose that someone buys some real property, including land and a building, for $500,000. The assessor evaluated this property for tax purposes at $300,000, valuing the land at $60,000 and the building at $240,000. The percentage the assessor allocated to the land is $60,000/$300,000 = 20 percent. The percentage the assessor allocated to the building is $240,000/$300,000 = 80 percent. Therefore, the value that the buyer should allocate to the land is $500,000 × .2 = $100,000; to the building, $500,000 × .8 = $400,000. For bookkeeping purposes, one separates land improvements from buildings because of the different lengths of life involved.

Land

Suppose that someone buys a piece of land—just land, no building. The cost of the land includes the amount paid for the land plus incidental charges connected with the sale: real estate agents' commissions, escrow and legal fees, delinquent taxes paid by the buyer, plus any costs of surveying, clearing, draining, or grading the land. In addition, the municipality or county—either at the time of purchase or later—may assess the buyer for such improvements as the installation of paved streets, curbs, sidewalks, and sewers. The buyer debits these items to the Land account, since they are considered to be as permanent as the land. If a business entity buys land for a building site and the land happens to have old buildings standing on it, the firm debits the cost of the structures as well as the costs of demolishing them to the Land account.

Land Improvements

An accountant uses the account **Land Improvements** to record expenditures for improvements that are (1) not as permanent as the land, or (2) not directly associated with a building. Examples are driveways, parking lots, trees and shrubs, fences, and outdoor lighting systems.

Buildings

The cost of a building includes not only money spent for labor and materials, but architectural and engineering fees, money spent for insurance premiums during construction, and all other necessary and normal expenditures applicable to the project.

THE NATURE AND RECORDING
OF DEPRECIATION

The usefulness of assets declines as a result of physical wear and exhaustion, inadequacy, obsolescence, and a multitude of other causes. As we said in Chapter 5, depreciation represents a systematic procedure for allocating the cost of plant and equipment to the periods in which the firm receives services from the assets. An item of supplies is bought and used up in one fiscal period; its cost is charged to the same fiscal period. In contrast, a plant asset is used over several fiscal periods. In order to follow the matching principle, the cost of the plant asset must be spread out over the several periods.

The firm treats depreciation as a debit to Depreciation Expense and a credit to Accumulated Depreciation. It treats Accumulated Depreciation as a deduction from the related asset account; in other words, depreciation is a contra account. We referred to this entry earlier as an *internal transaction*, because no outside business or person is involved. One can record depreciation as an adjusting entry at the end of each month or postpone recording it until the end of the fiscal year except when there is a change in the assets, such as a sale or a trade-in. In that case, one first records depreciation of the asset from the beginning of the fiscal year until the date of the change *before* making any other accounting entries.

Determining the Amount
of Depreciation

To determine the depreciation of a long-lived asset one must take into account three elements.

1. The **depreciation base:** cost less trade-in or salvage value
2. The length of the useful life of the asset
3. The method of depreciation chosen to allocate the depreciation base over the useful life of the asset

Depreciation Base

When a business entity first puts an asset into service, it's hard to predict the amount of the trade-in or salvage value, especially when such a trade-in will not take place for many years. Many firms make estimates based on their own experience or on data supplied by trade associations or government agencies. If the firm expects the salvage value to be insignificant in comparison with the cost of the asset, the accountant often assumes the salvage value to be zero.

Useful Life

The length of an asset's useful life is affected not only by physical wear and exhaustion but also by technological change and innovation. For accounting purposes, the useful life of an asset is based on the expected use of the asset, in keeping with the company's replacement policy. An average car, for example, may have a useful life of five years. However, for reasons of competition, a car rental company may replace its cars every year in order to offer customers the latest models. And a company operating a fleet of cars for its sales force may replace the cars every three years.

CALCULATING DEPRECIATION

The objective of recording depreciation is to spread out systematically the cost of a long-lived asset over the length of the asset's useful life. However, a firm need not use the same method of depreciation for all its assets.

The four most common methods of computing depreciation are (1) the straight-line method, (2) the units-of-production method, (3) the double-declining-balance method, and (4) the sum-of-the-years'-digits method. The last three methods allow a firm to calculate **accelerated depreciation.** If relatively large amounts of depreciation are recorded early in an asset's life, less depreciation is taken in later years. The Accelerated Cost Recovery System of depreciation, which must be used for certain assets for income tax purposes, is discussed in Appendix E.

Objective 2

Calculate depreciation by the straight-line method, units-of-production method, double-declining-balance method, and sum-of-the-years'-digits method.

Straight-line Method

A firm that uses the straight-line method of calculating depreciation charges an equal amount of depreciation for each year of service anticipated. The accountant computes the annual depreciation by dividing the depreciation base (cost minus trade-in value, if any) by the number of years of useful life predicted for the asset. This is the type of depreciation we illustrated in Chapter 5. The percentage rate of depreciation per year is determined by dividing the number of years of useful life into 1. For instance, take an asset with a life of eight years:

$$\frac{1}{8 \text{ years}} = .125 = 12\tfrac{1}{2}\%$$

One always applies the depreciation rate against the depreciation base (cost less trade-in value).

$$\text{Depreciation per year} = \frac{\text{Cost} - \text{Trade-in value}}{\text{Useful life (in years)}}$$

Now let's look at two examples.

Example 1   A truck costs $9,000 and has a useful life of six years. The estimated trade-in value at end of six years is $1,200.

$$\text{Depreciation per year} = \frac{\$9,000 - \$1,200}{6} = \frac{\$7,800}{6} = \$1,300$$

$$\text{Depreciation rate per year} = \frac{1}{6 \text{ years}} = .16\tfrac{2}{3} = 16\tfrac{2}{3}\%$$

Example 2   A neon sign costs $1,600 and has a useful life of eight years. The estimated trade-in value at end of eight years is zero.

$$\text{Depreciation per year} = \frac{\$1,600 - 0}{8} = \frac{\$1,600}{8} = \$200$$

$$\text{Depreciation rate per year} = \frac{1}{8 \text{ years}} = .125 = 12\tfrac{1}{2}\%$$

Units-of-Production Method

The units-of-production method enables one to allow for an asset that is used a great deal more in one year than in another. You can obtain the depreciation charge per unit of production by dividing the depreciation base by the total estimated units of production.

$$\text{Depreciation per unit of production} = \frac{\text{Cost} - \text{Trade-in value}}{\text{Estimated units of production}}$$

Example 1   A salesperson's car costs $10,800 and has a useful life of 60,000 miles. Estimated trade-in value at end of 60,000 miles is $2,400. The car is driven 18,000 miles this year.

$$\frac{\text{Depreciation}}{\text{per mile}} = \frac{\$10,800 - \$2,400}{60,000 \text{ miles}} = \frac{\$8,400}{60,000 \text{ miles}} = \$.14 \text{ per mile } (14¢)$$

Depreciation for 18,000 miles = 18,000 miles × $.14 per mile = $2,520

Example 2   A bulldozer costs $70,000 and has a useful life of 4,000 hours. Estimated salvage value after 4,000 hours is $6,000. The firm uses the bulldozer for 380 hours this year.

$$\text{Depreciation per hour} = \frac{\$70,000 - \$6,000}{4,000 \text{ hours}} = \frac{\$64,000}{4,000 \text{ hours}} = \$16 \text{ per hour}$$

Depreciation for 380 hours = 380 hours × $16 per hour = $6,080

Double-Declining-Balance Method

The double-declining-balance method is popular because it allows larger amounts for depreciation to be taken during the early life of the asset. Some accountants reason that the amount charged to depreciation of an asset should be higher during the asset's early years so as to offset the higher repair and maintenance expenses of the asset's later years. The total annual expense would then tend to be equalized over the entire life of the asset.

For an asset that has a life of three years or more, the method allows a firm to calculate depreciation by multiplying the book value (cost less accumulated depreciation) at the beginning of the year by *twice* the straight-line method. (This method applies only to new equipment and certain real estate. For used equipment, the maximum allowable rate is 1½ times the straight-line rate. This method is called the *declining-balance method*.) Trade-in or salvage value is not considered in determining depreciation by the declining balance methods until the very last year. As with other methods, an asset may not be depreciated below a reasonable salvage value.

To compute depreciation by the double-declining-balance method, follow these steps:

1. Calculate the straight-line depreciation rate.
2. Multiply the straight-line rate by 2.
3. Multiply the book value of the asset at the beginning of the year by double the straight-line rate.

Example 1   A firm's word processing equipment costs $20,000 and has a useful life of five years. Estimated trade-in value at end of five years is zero.

1. Compute the straight-line depreciation rate.

$$\text{Straight-line depreciation rate} = \frac{1}{5 \text{ years}} = .2 = 20\%$$

2. Twice the straight-line rate = $.2 \times 2 = .4$.
3. Depreciation per year = Book value at beginning of year $\times$ .4.

Year	Book Value at Beginning of Year	Depreciation Expense	Book Value at End of Year
1	$20,000.00	$20,000 × .4 = $8,000.00	$20,000 − $8,000.00 = $12,000.00
2	12,000.00	12,000 × .4 = 4,800.00	12,000 − 4,800.00 = 7,200.00
3	7,200.00	7,200 × .4 = 2,880.00	7,200 − 2,880.00 = 4,320.00
4	4,320.00	4,320 × .4 = 1,728.00	4,320 − 1,728.00 = 2,592.00
5	2,592.00	2,592 × .4 = 1,036.80	2,592 − 1,036.80 = 1,555.20

(Under the double-declining-balance method, book value never reaches zero. Therefore, a company typically switches over to the straight-line basis at the point where straight-line depreciation exceeds double-declining-balance.)

Example 2   A delivery truck costs $6,000 and has a useful life of six years. Estimated trade-in value at end of six years is $1,000.

1. Compute the straight-line depreciation rate.

$$\text{Straight-line depreciation rate} = \frac{1}{6 \text{ years}} = .1667 = \frac{1}{6}$$

Since the decimal equivalent of $\frac{1}{6}$ has a remainder (.1667), it is more accurate to use the fraction.
2. Twice the straight-line rate = $\frac{1}{6} \times 2 = \frac{2}{6} = \frac{1}{3}$.
3. Depreciation per year = Book value at beginning of year $\times \frac{1}{3}$.

Year	Book Value at Beginning of Year	Depreciation Expense	Book Value at End of Year
1	$6,000.00	$6,000.00 × ⅓ = $2,000.00	$6,000.00 − $2,000.00 = $4,000.00
2	4,000.00	4,000.00 × ⅓ = 1,333.33	4,000.00 − 1,333.33 = 2,666.67
3	2,666.67	2,666.67 × ⅓ = 888.89	2,666.67 − 888.89 = 1,777.78
4	1,777.78	1,777.78 × ⅓ = 592.59	1,777.78 − 592.59 = 1,185.19
5	1,185.19	1,185.19 − 1,000 = 185.19	1,185.19 − 185.19 = 1,000.00
6	1,000.00	0	1,000.00 − 0 = 1,000.00
		Total $5,000.00	

Observe carefully that the trade-in or salvage value is not counted until the last year. When one uses the double-declining-balance method and there is a trade-in value involved, the book value gradually declines until it reaches the amount of the trade-in value. This is the end of the depreciation schedule; no further depreciation is allowable. For example, take the delivery truck. During the fifth year, the normal depreciation would be one-third of the book value at the beginning of the year. One would determine depreciation for the year and the ending book value as follows.

$1,185.19 \times \frac{1}{3} = $395.06 =$ Depreciation expense

$1,185.19 − 395.06 = $790.13 =$ Book value at end of year

Obviously if one calculates depreciation in this manner the book value of the truck dips below its established trade-in value. Consequently one must make an adjustment during this year so that the truck's ending book value will be the same as its trade-in value. Even though its useful life was set at six years, in actuality the truck is depreciated to the limit in five years. Remember, the double-declining-balance method is the only method in which one figures in the trade-in value at the *end* of the depreciation schedule.

Sum-of-the-Years'-Digits Method

The sum-of-the-years'-digits method yields a large proportion of depreciation during the early years of an asset's life. It does this on a reducing-fraction basis. To compute depreciation by this method, follow these steps:

1. Decide how many years the asset is likely to last. Then find the sum of the years' digits. For example, suppose the asset has an expected life of three years. Then add to find the sum of year 1, year 2, and year 3.

   $$1 + 2 + 3 = 6$$

   One can also determine the sum of the years by the following formula.

   $$\frac{\text{Life}^2 + \text{Life}}{2}$$

   For example, a life of three years would be

   $$\frac{3^2 + 3}{2} = \frac{9 + 3}{2} = \frac{12}{2} = 6$$

2. Record the years in reverse (or descending) order as the numerator (top) of the fraction and the sum of the years' digits as the denominator (bottom) of the fraction:

   $$\tfrac{3}{6} + \tfrac{2}{6} + \tfrac{1}{6} = \tfrac{6}{6}$$

3. Multiply the decreasing fractions by the depreciation base (cost less trade-in value).

Example 1   A printing press costs $11,200 and has a useful life of five years. Estimated salvage value at end of five years is $400. The depreciation base is $10,800 ($11,200 − $400).

Step 1	Step 2		Step 3	
			Year	Depreciation Expense
1	5	$\tfrac{5}{15}$	1	$\tfrac{5}{15} \times \$10,800 = \$\ 3,600$
2	4	$\tfrac{4}{15}$	2	$\tfrac{4}{15} \times\ \ \ 10,800 =\ \ \ \ 2,880$
3	3 and	$\tfrac{3}{15}$	3	$\tfrac{3}{15} \times\ \ \ 10,800 =\ \ \ \ 2,160$
4	2	$\tfrac{2}{15}$	4	$\tfrac{2}{15} \times\ \ \ 10,800 =\ \ \ \ 1,440$
5	1	$\tfrac{1}{15}$	5	$\tfrac{1}{15} \times\ \ \ 10,800 =\ \ \ \ \ \ \ 720$
15		$\tfrac{15}{15}$		$\$10,800$

Example 2 A fork-lift truck costs $4,500 and has a useful life of six years. Estimated salvage value at end of six years is $300.

Step 1	Step 2			Year	Depreciation Expense
1	6		$6/21$	1	$6/21 \times \$4,200 = \$1,200$
2	5		$5/21$	2	$5/21 \times \ 4,200 = \ 1,000$
3	4	and	$4/21$	3	$4/21 \times \ 4,200 = \ 800$
4	3		$3/21$	4	$3/21 \times \ 4,200 = \ 600$
5	2		$2/21$	5	$2/21 \times \ 4,200 = \ 400$
6	1		$1/21$	6	$1/21 \times \ 4,200 = \ 200$
21			$21/21$		$\$4,200$

Comparison of Three Methods

You can see in the following charts that the double-declining-balance method and the sum-of-the-years'-digits method yield relatively large amounts of depreciation during the early years of use of an asset. For this reason they are examples of *accelerated depreciation*. In the example shown, assume that a hoist costs $6,000 and has a useful life of four years. Estimated value at the end of four years is $400.

Straight-line Method

Year	Depreciation per Year	Accumulated Depreciation	Book Value at End of Year
1	$\dfrac{\$6,000 - \$400}{4 \text{ years}} =$ $1,400	$1,400	$6,000 - $1,400 = $4,600
2	1,400	$1,400 + $1,400 = 2,800	6,000 - 2,800 = 3,200
3	1,400	2,800 + 1,400 = 4,200	6,000 - 4,200 = 1,800
4	1,400	4,200 + 1,400 = 5,600	6,000 - 5,600 = 400
	Total $5,600		

Double-declining-balance Method (based on twice the straight-line rate)

Year	Beginning Book Value	Depreciation per Year	Accumulated Depreciation	Book Value at End of Year
1	$6,000	$6,000 × .5 = $3,000	$3,000	$6,000 - $3,000 = $3,000
2	3,000	3,000 × .5 = 1,500	$3,000 + $1,500 = 4,500	6,000 - 4,500 = 1,500
3	1,500	1,500 × .5 = 750	4,500 + 750 = 5,250	6,000 - 5,250 = 750
4	750	750 - 400 = 350	5,250 + 350 = 5,600	6,000 - 5,600 = 400
		Total $5,600		

Sum-of-the-years'-digits Method

Year	Depreciation per Year	Accumulated Depreciation	Book Value at End of Year
1	$\frac{4}{10} \times \$5,600 = \$2,240$	$\$2,240$	$\$6,000 - \$2,240 = \$3,760$
2	$\frac{3}{10} \times 5,600 = 1,680$	$\$2,240 + \$1,680 = 3,920$	$6,000 - 3,920 = 2,080$
3	$\frac{2}{10} \times 5,600 = 1,120$	$3,920 + 1,120 = 5,040$	$6,000 - 5,040 = 960$
4	$\frac{1}{10} \times 5,600 = 560$	$5,040 + 560 = 5,600$	$6,000 - 5,600 = 400$
10	$\frac{10}{10} \qquad \$5,600$		

A firm may calculate its regular depreciation by any of these methods: straight-line, double-declining-balance, or sum-of-the-years'-digits. Or it may use other available methods.

DEPRECIATION FOR PERIODS OF LESS THAN A YEAR

Businesses don't acquire (or get rid of) all their depreciable assets on the first and last days of their fiscal period. They buy and sell assets throughout the year. How, then, do they calculate depreciation?

When a business entity acquires a depreciable asset during the year, the accountant usually figures depreciation to the nearest whole month. If the firm held the asset for *less* than half a given month, the accountant doesn't count that month. But if the firm has held it for *more* than half of a given month, the accountant counts it as a whole month.

Suppose a firm buys an asset on June 11. Depreciation is computed from June 1, counting the entire month. But if the firm bought that asset on June 17, no depreciation would be computed for the month of June.

Here are other examples (assume that the fiscal year ends on December 31).

Date Acquired	Cost	Trade-in Value	Method	Useful Life	Depreciation for First Year
April 12	$9,000	$1,000	Straight line	5 years	$\dfrac{\$9,000 - \$1,000}{5 \text{ years}} = \$1,600 \text{ per year}$ $\$1,600 \times \frac{9}{12} = \$1,200$ for 9 months
October 19	6,000	200	Double declining balance	8 years	$\$6,000 \times \frac{1}{4} = \$1,500$ for first year $\$1,500 \times \frac{2}{12} = \$250$ for 2 months
August 8	6,800	500	Sum of the years' digits	6 years	$\$6,300 \times \frac{6}{21} = \$1,800$ for first year $\$1,800 \times \frac{5}{12} = \$750$ for 5 months

CAPITAL AND REVENUE EXPENDITURES

The term *expenditure* refers to spending, either by paying cash now or by promising to pay in the future for services received or assets purchased. After paying the initial price for an asset, one often has to pay out more, either to maintain the asset's operating efficiency or to increase its capacity. So there are two classifications of expenditures: capital and revenue.

Capital expenditures include the initial costs of plant and equipment; they also include any costs of increasing the capacity or prolonging the life of assets. You reap the benefits of capital expenditures during more than one accounting period. Examples are expenditures for buying a building, enlarging it, putting in air conditioning, and replacing a stairway with an elevator. All these expenditures result in debits to an asset account.

Revenue expenditures include the costs of maintaining the operation of an asset, such as the expense of making normal repairs. Examples are expenditures for painting, plumbing repairs, fuel, property taxes, and so on. These expenditures provide benefit only during the current accounting period and are recorded as debits to expense accounts.

Objective 3

Differentiate between capital expenditures and revenue expenditures.

EXTRAORDINARY-REPAIRS EXPENDITURES

In accounting, **extraordinary-repairs expenditures** refer to a major overhaul or reconditioning that extends the useful life of an asset beyond its original estimated life. An accountant usually records expenditures for extraordinary repairs as debits to Accumulated Depreciation and credits to Cash or Accounts Payable.

For example, a firm buys a used car for $6,000; the car's estimated useful life is four years, and its trade-in value is $1,600; straight-line annual depreciation expense is $1,100. After three years the firm puts in a new engine and has other major repairs done, for which it spends $1,400 in cash. The entry in general journal form is as follows.

Objective 4

Differentiate between expenditures for ordinary and for extraordinary repairs.

	19x7 Jan.	6	Accumulated Depreciation, Automobile	1 4 0 0 00		
1				1 4 0 0 00		1
2			Cash		1 4 0 0 00	2
3			New engine installed in			3
4			company car.			4
5						5

This extraordinary repair extends the life of the car from the present one additional year to three additional years. Here are relevant balances, together with the $1,400 payment as shown by T accounts.

Automobile

+		−
Jan. 3, 19x4	6,000	

Accumulated Depreciation, Automobile

−		+	
Jan. 6, 19x7	1,400	Dec. 31, 19x4	1,100
		Dec. 31, 19x5	1,100
		Dec. 31, 19x6	1,100

The car's book value before the extraordinary repair was $2,700 ($6,000 − $3,300). The accountant debits the Accumulated Depreciation account (rather than the asset account) to preserve the original cost figure in the asset account. In this example, the car that the firm bought cost $6,000, not $7,400. We can see this in the balance sheet as follows.

Plant and Equipment:		
Automobile	$6 0 0 0 00	
Less Accumulated Depreciation	1 9 0 0 00	$4 1 0 0 00

When it comes to recording the remaining depreciation of the asset, the accountant now has a new cost base, which he or she uses to determine the new depreciation base. Assume that the trade-in value is still $1,600.

New book value	$4,100
Less trade-in value	1,600
New depreciation base	$2,500

$2,500 ÷ 3 years = $833.33

The adjusting entry for depreciation of the car at the end of 19x7 is:

1		*Adjusting Entry*			1
2	19x8 Dec.	31	*Depreciation Expense, Automobile*	8 3 3 33	2
3			*Accumulated Depreciation,*		3
4			*Automobile*	8 3 3 33	4
5					5

Assuming that no additional expenditures are made for extraordinary repairs, the adjusting entries for the remaining two years (19x8 and 19x9) will be $833.33 for 19x8 and $833.34 for 19x9.

DISPOSITION OF PLANT AND EQUIPMENT

Sooner or later a business entity disposes of its long-lived assets by (1) discarding or retiring them, (2) selling them, or (3) trading them in for other assets. If the assets are not fully depreciated, the accountant must first make an entry to bring the depreciation up to date. Let's look at some examples. (Ordinarily entries involving Cash would be recorded in the cash journals; however, for simplification and clarity, we shall present all the following entries in general journal form.)

Objective 5

Prepare journal entries for discarding of assets fully depreciated, discarding of assets not fully depreciated, sale of assets involving a loss, sale of assets involving a gain, exchange of assets involving a loss on the trade, and exchange of assets involving a gain on the trade.

Discarding or Retiring Plant and Equipment

When long-lived assets are no longer useful to the business and have no market value, a firm discards them.

Discarding of Fully Depreciated Assets   A display case that cost $1,400 and has been fully depreciated is given away as junk. The present status of the accounts is as follows.

Store Equipment			Accumulated Depreciation, Store Equipment		
+		−	−		+
Bal. 1,400				Bal. 1,400	

The journal entry to record the disposal of the asset looks like this.

1	Accumulated Depreciation, Store			1
2	Equipment	1 4 0 0 00		2
3	Store Equipment		1 4 0 0 00	3
4	Discarded a fully depreciated			4
5	display case.			5
6				6

Although fully depreciated assets are retained on the books as long as they remain in use, the firm may not take any additional depreciation on them.

Discarding an Asset Not Fully Depreciated A firm discards a time clock that cost $1,600. No salvage value is realized. Accumulated Depreciation up to the end of the previous year is $1,450; depreciation for the current year is $90. The present balances of the accounts are as follows.

Office Equipment		Accumulated Depreciation, Office Equipment	
+	−	−	+
Bal. 1,600			Bal. 1,450

Record the entry to depreciate the asset up to date.

1		Depreciation Expense, Office		1
2		Equipment	9 0 00	2
3		Accumulated Depreciation, Office		3
4		Equipment		9 0 00	4
5		Depreciation on time clock for		5
6		the partial year.		6
7				7
8				8

The T accounts look like this.

Depreciation Expense, Office Equipment		Accumulated Depreciation, Office Equipment	
+	−	−	+
90			Bal. 1,450
			90

The journal entry to record the disposal of the asset is as follows.

1		Accumulated Depreciation, Office		1
2		Equipment	1 5 4 0 00	2
3		Loss on Disposal of Plant and		3
4		Equipment	6 0 00	4
5		Office Equipment		1 6 0 0 00	5
6		Discarded a time clock.		6
7				7
8				8

The T accounts look like this.

Accumulated Depreciation, Office Equipment		Loss on Disposal of Plant and Equipment		Office Equipment	
−	+	+	−	+	−
1,540	Bal. 1,450	60		Bal. 1,600	1,600
	90				

The book value of the asset is $60 ($1,600 − $1,540). Because the firm realized nothing from the disposal of the asset, the loss is for the same amount as the book value.

Loss on Disposal of Plant and Equipment is an expense account that appears under Other Expense in the income statement.

Selling of Plant and Equipment

Naturally it's very hard to estimate the exact trade-in or salvage value of a long-lived asset. It's quite likely that when a firm sells or trades in such an asset, the amount realized will differ from the estimated amount.

Sale of an Asset at a Loss   Suppose that a firm sells a drill press for $135. This drill press originally cost $1,900; accumulated depreciation up to the end of the previous year was $1,560. Yearly depreciation is $180. The drill press is sold on August 21.

The present balances of the accounts are as follows:

Factory Equipment		Accumulated Depreciation, Factory Equipment	
+	−	−	+
Bal. 1,900			Bal. 1,560

We record the depreciation of the asset to the present date.

1	Depreciation Expense, Factory			1
2	Equipment	1 2 0 00		2
3	Accumulated Depreciation, Factory			3
4	Equipment		1 2 0 00	4
5	Depreciation on drill press for			5
6	8 months. ($180 × 8/12 = $120)			6
7				7

By T accounts, the situation looks like this.

Depreciation Expense, Factory Equipment			Accumulated Depreciation, Factory Equipment		
+		−	−	+	
120				Bal.	1,560
					120

The entry, in general journal form, to record the sale of the drill press is as follows.

1		Cash			1 3 5	00					1
2		Accumulated Depreciation, Factory									2
3		Equipment			1 6 8 0	00					3
4		Loss on Disposal of Plant and									4
5		Equipment			8 5	00					5
6		Factory Equipment						1 9 0 0	00		6
7		Sold a drill press for $135, having									7
8		an original cost of $1,900 and									8
9		accumulated depreciation									9
10		of $1,680.									10
11											11

For purposes of illustration, let us record the above entry in the T accounts as follows.

Cash			Accumulated Depreciation, Factory Equipment		
+		−	−	+	
135			1,680	Bal.	1,560
					120

Loss on Disposal of Plant and Equipment			Factory Equipment		
+		−	+		−
85			Bal.	1,900	1,900

Note that the book value of the drill press is $220 ($1,900 − $1,680). When the firm sells it for $135, the loss is $85.

Sale of an Asset at a Gain   Suppose that a firm sells a printing press for $310. The firm had originally paid $4,200; accumulated depreciation up to the end of the previous year was $3,960. Yearly depreciation is $120. The printing press is sold on October 18. The present balances of the accounts are as follows.

	Printing Equipment			Accumulated Depreciation, Printing Equipment		
	+		−	−		+
Bal.	4,200				Bal.	3,960

We record the depreciation of the asset to the present date.

1	$\frac{19-}{Oct.}$	18	*Depreciation Expense, Printing*								1
2			*Equipment*	1 0 0 00							2
3			*Accumulated Depreciation, Printing*								3
4			*Equipment*					1 0 0 00			4
5			*Recorded depreciation through*								5
6			*October 18. Depreciation for 10*								6
7			*months is $100*								7
8			*($120 × 10/12 = $100).*								8
9											9

By T accounts, the situation looks like this.

	Depreciation Expense, Printing Equipment			Accumulated Depreciation, Printing Equipment		
	+		−	−		+
	100				Bal.	3,960
						100

The general journal entry to record the sale of the printing press is as follows.

1	$\frac{19-}{Oct.}$	18	*Cash*	3 1 0 00							1
2			*Accumulated Depreciation, Printing*								2
3			*Equipment*	4 0 6 0 00							3
4			*Printing Equipment*					4 2 0 0 00			4
5			*Gain on Disposal of Plant and*								5
6			*Equipment*					1 7 0 00			6
7			*Sold a printing press for $310,*								7
8			*having an original cost of*								8
9			*$4,200 and accumulated depreci-*								9
10			*ation of $4,060.*								10
11											11

The T accounts look like this.

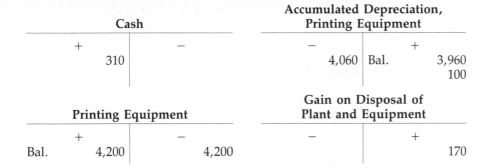

Cash				Accumulated Depreciation, Printing Equipment			
+		−		−		+	
	310				4,060	Bal.	3,960
							100

Printing Equipment				Gain on Disposal of Plant and Equipment			
+		−		−		+	
Bal.	4,200		4,200				170

The revenue account **Gain on Disposal of Plant and Equipment** appears under Other Income in the income statement.

The book value of the printing press is $140 ($4,200 − $4,060). When the firm sells the press for $310, the firm's gain is $170.

Exchange of Long-lived Assets for Other Assets Without Recognition of Gain or Loss

Often a business trades in one asset for another, using the old item as part payment for the new one. The trade-in allowance may differ from the book value of the asset. If the trade-in allowance is greater than the book value, the firm has a gain; if less than the book value, it has a loss. However, federal income tax laws state that when assets held for productive use are exchanged for other assets acquired for similar use, *no gain or loss is recognized.* In effect, the gain or loss is absorbed into the recorded cost of the new asset.

Depreciation of assets acquired after 1980 is accounted for by a different method for income tax purposes. See Appendix E, "Accelerated Cost Recovery System of Depreciation." Many firms use one schedule of depreciation for their own company financial statements and another schedule of depreciation for their income tax returns. This procedure is entirely legal.

Exchange When Trade-in Value Is Less Than Book Value   Suppose that a firm bought a delivery truck for $4,900. Four years later, the truck has an accumulated depreciation of $4,200. The firm buys a new truck, with a list price of $5,600, trading in the old one, for which they are allowed only $400, and paying the difference in cash. Assume that the depreciation for the year is already up to date. The present status of the accounts is as follows.

	Delivery Equipment		Accumulated Depreciation, Delivery Equipment	
	+	−	−	+
Bal.	4,900		Bal.	4,200

The firm's accountant records the transaction by the following steps.

1. Credit cash, $5,200 (quoted price of new truck, $5,600, minus $400, which is the trade-in allowance on old truck).
2. Close or clear the account of the old asset: credit Delivery Equipment, $4,900.
3. Close or clear the account of the Accumulated Depreciation of the old asset: debit Accumulated Depreciation, $4,200.
4. Debit the account of the new asset for the difference between total debits and total credits, $5,900 ($5,200 + $4,900 − $4,200 = $5,900), which is the book value of the old asset plus the amount of cash or notes given.

Here are the entries in general journal form.

(4)	Delivery Equipment	5 9 0 0 00		1
(3)	Accumulated Depreciation, Delivery			2
	Equipment	4 2 0 0 00		3
(1)	Cash		5 2 0 0 00	4
(2)	Delivery Equipment		4 9 0 0 00	5
	Bought a new delivery truck			6
	having a list price of $5,600.			7
	Received a trade-in allowance			8
	of $400 on old delivery truck,			9
	having an original cost of			10
	$4,900 and accumulated depreci-			11
	ation of $4,200.			12
				13
				14

You can see from this that when you use the income tax method of accounting, the loss is absorbed in the cost of the new equipment. In this case the accountant added the loss of $300 to the price of the new equipment, as follows.

Cost of old equipment	$4,900
Less accumulated depreciation	4,200
Book value	$ 700
Less trade-in allowance	400
Loss	$ 300
Quoted price of new equipment	$5,600
Plus loss absorbed in recorded cost of new equipment	300
Recorded cost of new equipment	$5,900

You can also use this technique to verify the cost recorded for the new equipment. For income tax purposes, the firm cannot count the $300 loss at this time; however, the firm does have an additional $300 that it can count as depreciation in the future.

Exchange When Trade-in Value Is Greater Than Book Value A business bought an automated file for $2,600. After some years the business decides to trade it in on a new model. The old one has an accumulated depreciation of $2,480 *on the date of the trade-in,* leaving a net book value of $120. The new file has a list price of $3,350; however, the salesperson gives the firm a generous trade-in allowance of $310 on the old equipment, and the firm pays the difference in cash. The present status of the accounts is shown in the following T accounts.

Office Equipment		Accumulated Depreciation, Office Equipment	
+	−	−	+
Bal. 2,600			Bal. 2,480

The firm's accountant records the transaction by the following steps.

1. Credit Cash, $3,040 (quoted price of new file, $3,350, minus $310, which is the trade-in allowance on old model).
2. Close or clear the account of the old asset: credit Office Equipment, $2,600.
3. Close or clear the account of the Accumulated Depreciation on the old asset: debit Accumulated Depreciation, $2,480.
4. Debit the account of the new asset for the difference between the total debits and credits, $3,160 ($3,040 + $2,600 − $2,480 = $3,160), which is the book value of the old asset plus the amount of cash or notes given.

Here's how one records the entries in general journal form.

(4)	Office Equipment		3 1 6 0 00					1
(3)	Accumulated Depreciation, Office							2
	Equipment		2 4 8 0 00					3
(1)	Cash				3 0 4 0 00			4
(2)	Office Equipment				2 6 0 0 00			5
	Bought a new automated file							6
	having a list price of $3,350.							7
	Received a trade-in allowance							8
	of $310 on old file, which had							9
	an original cost of $2,600 and							10
	accumulated depreciation of							11
	$2,480.							12
								13

The accountant records the cost of the new equipment at less than the list price, which indicates that a gain is involved. This gain has been absorbed in the price of the new equipment.

Cost of old equipment	$2,600
Less accumulated depreciation	2,480
Book value	$ 120
Less trade-in allowance	310
Gain	$ 190
Quoted price of new equipment	$3,350
Less gain absorbed in recorded cost of new equipment	190
Recorded cost of new equipment	$3,160

For income tax purposes, the firm does not count the gain at this time. However, the amount that the firm can count as depreciation in the future has been reduced by $190.

PLANT AND EQUIPMENT RECORDS

Depreciation, which is regarded as an expense, vitally affects the net income of any business. Because net income is affected, the amount of income taxes owed is likewise affected. And not only Depreciation Expense, but also Loss (or Gain) on Disposal can affect net income. For income tax purposes, the business must be able to justify the amount of depreciation taken, as well as the gain or loss on disposal of assets.

Objective 6

Maintain a plant and equipment subsidiary ledger.

We have discussed Plant and Equipment as a category on a classified balance sheet. Now let's look at an example.

Plant and Equipment:					
Delivery Equipment	$20 0 0 0 00				
Less Accumulated Depreciation	12 0 0 0 00	$ 8 0 0 0 00			
Store Equipment	$18 0 0 0 00				
Less Accumulated Depreciation	14 0 0 0 00	4 0 0 0 00			
Office Equipment	$ 6 0 0 0 00				
Less Accumulated Depreciation	4 5 0 0 00	1 5 0 0 00			
Building	$40 0 0 0 00				
Less Accumulated Depreciation	28 0 0 0 00	12 0 0 0 00			
Land Improvements	$ 3 0 0 0 00				
Less Accumulated Depreciation	2 3 0 0 00	7 0 0 00			
Land		6 0 0 0 00			
Total Plant and Equipment			$32 2 0 0 00		

The asset accounts represent functional groups. When you are listing asset accounts, a common practice is to list the asset with the shortest life first, then the next shortest, and so on. Immediately after you list an asset account that is subject to depreciation, write its respective Accumulated Depreciation account.

The Store Equipment account is an asset that represents a functional group. Store Equipment includes all types of equipment used in the operation of a store: display cases, cash registers, counters, storage shelves, and the like. To account for the depreciation of each item of store equipment, accountants maintain a separate record card for each item in the plant and equipment ledger. Store Equipment is a controlling account; the plant and equipment ledger is a subsidiary ledger. This relationship is like that of Accounts Receivable, which is a controlling account, and the accounts receivable ledger, which is a subsidiary ledger with an account for each individual charge customer. Figure 20-1 shows a record card in a firm's plant and equipment ledger. Posting to the subsidiary ledger will also be marked by a check mark in the journal's Post. Ref. column when the asset accounts and the related accumulated depreciation accounts are debited or credited.

Account 122 is the number of the general ledger account for Store Equipment. Account 122-1 is the first piece of equipment classified under Store Equipment. One determines the adjusting entry for Depreciation Expense, Store Equipment by adding the current depreciation for each piece of equipment within the classification.

The plant and equipment record enables the accountant to determine the amount of the adjusting entry for depreciation as well as to keep a record of the accumulated depreciation and book value. Plant and equipment records are invaluable when a business has to submit insurance claims in the event of insured losses.

PLANT AND EQUIPMENT RECORD

ITEM *Cash Register*   ACCOUNT NO. *122-1*

SERIAL NO. *ND37-4163*   MAKER *Security, Inc.*

FROM WHOM PURCHASED *Rogers Equipment Company*   EST. SALVAGE

ESTIMATED LIFE *5*   VALUE *$50*

DEPRECIATION METHOD *Straight line*   DEPRECIATION PER YEAR *$150.00*   DEPRECIATION PER MONTH *$12.50*   RATE OF DEPRECIATION *20%*

DATE	EXPLANATION	ASSET			ACCUMULATED DEPRECIATION			BOOK VALUE
		DEBIT	CREDIT	BALANCE	DEBIT	CREDIT	BALANCE	
7/3/82		800		800				800
12/31/82						75	75	725
12/31/83						150	225	575
12/31/84						150	375	425

Figure 20-1

GLOSSARY

Accelerated depreciation Relatively large amounts of depreciation recorded during the early years of an asset's use; decreasing in later years.

Capital expenditures Costs incurred for the purchase of plant and equipment, as well as the cost of increasing the capacity of assets; the firm receives services or benefits from this plant and equipment for more than one accounting period.

Depreciation base Cost of plant and equipment less trade-in or salvage value.

Extraordinary-repairs expenditures Costs incurred for major overhauls or reconditioning of assets; repairs that significantly prolong the life of the asset.

Gain on Disposal of Plant and Equipment When a firm sells or trades in an asset and receives an amount in excess of the book value for that asset, the gain is recorded in this account, which appears under Other Income in the income statement.

Land Improvements An asset account covering the cost of expenditures for improvements that are (1) not as permanent as the land, or (2) not directly associated with a building. These include driveways, parking lots, trees and shrubs, fences, and outdoor lighting systems.

Loss on Disposal of Plant and Equipment When a firm sells or trades in an asset and receives an amount less than the book value for that asset, the loss is recorded in this account.

Revenue expenditures Costs incurred to maintain the operation of assets, such as normal repair expenses and fuel expenses.

QUESTIONS, EXERCISES, AND PROBLEMS

Discussion Questions

1. How does the accountant's meaning of the term *depreciation* differ from the nonaccountant's meaning of the term?
2. Name four things that an accountant must know about an asset, classified as plant and equipment, in order to calculate its depreciation expense.
3. Which methods of depreciation are classified as accelerated depreciation?
4. Distinguish between capital expenditures and revenue expenditures.
5. Which of the following would be listed under Plant and Equipment?

   a. a truck held for sale by a truck dealer
   b. a typewriter used by a secretary of a company
   c. a parking lot for company employees
   d. pollution-control equipment that does not reduce the cost or improve the efficiency of the factory
   e. a machine that is used in the manufacturing operations but is now fully depreciated

6. Distinguish between expenditures for ordinary repairs and expenditures for extraordinary repairs.
7. Describe the use and operation of a plant and equipment ledger. What items are listed on each card in the ledger?

Exercises

Exercise 20-1   Wright Manufacturing purchased land adjacent to its factory for the installation of a parking lot. Expenditures incurred by the company were as follows: purchase price, $100,000; broker's fees, $7,000; title search and other fees, $500; demolition of a shack on the property, $2,000; grading, $1,500; parking lots, $15,000; lighting, $10,000; signs, $800.
    Determine the amount that should be debited to the Land account.

Exercise 20-2   Streetman Plywood bought a dry kiln for $36,000; terms 2/10, n/30, FOB factory. Streetman paid the invoice within the discount period, along with $460 transportation charges. Streetman also paid installation costs of $970 and power connection costs of $612. How much should Streetman debit to its Plant and Equipment account?

Exercise 20-3   At the beginning of the fiscal year, Cindy's Drive In bought cooking equipment for $4,920, with an estimated salvage value of $420, and an estimated useful life of six years. Determine the amount of the depreciation for the first year by the following methods.

a. Straight-line method
b. Double-declining-balance method at twice the straight-line rate
c. Sum-of-the-years'-digits method

Exercise 20-4   On May 13 of this year, Nancy's Clothes and Things discarded a display case; there was no salvage value. The following details are taken from the subsidiary ledger: cost, $294; accumulated depreciation as of December 31, the end of last year, was $294. Journalize the necessary entry.

Exercise 20-5   On April 4, City Cab Company sold a taxicab for cash, $260. The following details are taken from the subsidiary ledger: cost, $4,450; accumulated depreciation as of the previous December 31, $3,840; monthly depreciation, $65. Make entries in general journal form to record the depreciation up to the present date and the sale of the asset.

Exercise 20-6   On August 18, Springer and Valdez discarded a carpet (Office Equipment) with no salvage value. The following details are taken from the subsidiary ledger: cost, $620; accumulated depreciation as of the previous December 31, $482; monthly depreciation, $8. Journalize entries to record the depreciation of the carpet to date and to record the disposal of the carpet.

Exercise 20-7   On October 19, Meadow-green Dairy traded in its old delivery truck on a new one, which cost $4,940. Meadow-green got a trade-in allowance of $420 on the old truck and paid the difference in cash. The subsidiary account shows the following: cost (of old truck), $3,790; accumulated depreciation as of last December 31, $3,218; monthly depreciation, $48. Without recognizing gains or losses, make entries in general journal form to record the depreciation of the old truck to date and to record the exchange of assets.

Exercise 20-8   On May 13, Richardson Company, a machine shop, trades in a lathe (Machinery) on a new one priced at $3,846, receiving a trade-in allowance of $410 on the old lathe. Richardson makes a downpayment of $500 in cash, and issues a 60-day, 8 percent note for the remainder. The subsidiary account shows the following: cost, $2,782; accumulated depreciation as of last December 31, $2,276; monthly depreciation, $34. Without recognizing gains or losses, make entries in general journal form to record the depreciation of the lathe to date and to record the exchange of assets.

Problem Set A

Problem 20-1A   At the beginning of a fiscal year, the Dow Paper Products Company buys a truck for $12,000. The truck's estimated life is five years, and its estimated trade-in value is $1,200.

Instructions

Determine the annual depreciation for each of the estimated five years of life, the accumulated depreciation at the end of each year, and the book value of the truck at the end of each year, using the columns provided by:

a. Straight-line method
b. Double-declining-balance method
c. Sum-of-the-years'-digits method

Problem 20-2A During a three-year period the L and C Chemical Company completed the following transactions related to its delivery truck.

Year 1

Jan. 6 Bought a used delivery truck for cash, $12,400.
Oct. 21 Paid garage for maintenance repairs to the truck, $126.
Dec. 31 Recorded the adjusting entry for depreciation for the fiscal year. The estimated life of the truck is four years, with a trade-in value of $2,600. L and C Chemical uses the straight-line method of depreciation.
     31 Closed the expense accounts to the Income Summary account.

Year 2

Mar. 9 Paid garage for tune-up of truck, $52.
Aug. 27 Paid for tire recaps, $240.
Dec. 31 Recorded the adjusting entry for depreciation for the fiscal year.
     31 Closed the expense accounts to the Income Summary account.

Year 3

Apr. 21 Paid garage for maintenance repairs to truck, $316.
Jun. 27 Traded in the used truck on a new truck, which cost $19,600, receiving a trade-in allowance of $7,800, and paying the difference in cash. Made the entry to record the depreciation on the truck up to the present date. Made the entry to record the exchange, assuming gain or loss is not recognized.
Dec. 31 Recorded the adjusting entry for depreciation of the new truck for the fiscal year. The estimated life of the truck is six years, with a trade-in value of $1,275. L and C Chemical uses the straight-line method of depreciation.
     31 Closed the expense accounts to the Income Summary account.

Instructions

1. Record the transactions in general journal form.
2. After journalizing each entry, post to the following ledger accounts: Delivery Equipment; Accumulated Depreciation, Delivery Equipment; Truck Repair Expense; Depreciation Expense, Delivery Equipment.

Problem 20-3A During a three-year period, Copy-Cat Printers completed the following transactions pertaining to its printing press.

Year 1

Jun. 30 Bought a printing press, $20,400, paying $4,400 in cash and issuing a series of four notes for $4,000 each, to come due at six-month intervals; payments to include principal plus interest of 9 percent to maturity on each note.
Jul. 3 Paid transportation charges for the press, $280.
      8 Paid installation charges for the press, $920.

Dec.	31	Paid the principal, $4,000, plus interest of $180 on the first note.
	31	Made the adjusting entry to record depreciation for the fiscal year. The estimated life of the press is four years; it has a salvage value of $2,000. Copy-Cat's accountant uses the double-declining-balance method, at twice the straight-line rate ($5,400; verify this figure).
	31	Closed the expense accounts to the Income Summary account.

Year 2

May	4	Paid for normal mechanical repairs, $624.
Jun.	30	Paid the principal, $4,000, plus interest of $360 on the second note.
Dec.	31	Paid the principal, $4,000, plus interest of $540 on the third note.
	31	Recorded the adjusting entry for the fiscal year ($8,100; verify this figure).
	31	Closed the expense accounts to the Income Summary account.

Year 3

May	11	Paid for normal mechanical repairs, $719.
Jun.	30	Paid the principal, $4,000, plus interest of $720 on the fourth note.
Sep.	21	Copy-Cat Printers decides to get rid of its press and use the services of another printer in the future. Sold the press for $4,200 cash. Made the entry to depreciate the press up to date ($3,037.50). Made the entry to account for the sale of the press.
Dec.	31	Closed the expense accounts to the Income Summary account.

Instructions

1. Record the transactions in general journal form.
2. After making each journal entry, post to the following ledger accounts: Equipment; Accumulated Depreciation, Equipment; Depreciation Expense, Equipment; Equipment Maintenance Expense; Interest Expense; Loss on Disposal of Plant and Equipment.

Problem 20-4A The general ledger of the Care-free Travel Agency includes controlling accounts for Office Equipment and Accumulated Depreciation, Office Equipment. Care-free's accountant also records the details of each item of office equipment in a subsidiary ledger. During a three-year period the following transactions affecting office equipment took place.

Year 1

Jan.	8	Bought the following items from Modern Office Furniture Company for cash:

Filing cabinet, $120, account no. 122-1, expected life fifteen years, trade-in value zero.
Executive desk, $480, account no. 122-2, expected life twelve years, trade-in value zero.
Executive chair, $180, account no. 122-3, expected life twelve years, trade-in value zero.

(The above assets are depreciated on the basis of the straight-line method.)

Jan. 9 Paid Hiller Cabinet Shop $640 for a custom-made counter, account no. 122-4; expected life ten years, trade-in value zero; straight-line method.

  11 Bought for cash a Servo typewriter, serial no. PA-17361, account no. 122-5, from Grigsby Equipment Company for $360; estimated life five years, estimated trade-in value $60; sum-of-the-years'-digits method.

Dec. 31 Made the adjusting entry to record depreciation of office equipment for the fiscal year.

  31 Closed the Depreciation Expense, Office Equipment account into the Income Summary account (total depreciation, $227; verify this figure).

Year 2

Jun. 24 Bought a rug from Girard Carpet Company on account, account no. 122-6, price $640, estimated life eight years, trade-in value zero; double-declining-balance method at twice the straight-line rate.

Dec. 31 Made the adjusting entry to record depreciation of office equipment for the fiscal year (depreciation for six months on the rug; total depreciation, $287; verify this figure).

  31 Closed the Depreciation Expense, Office Equipment account into the Income Summary account.

Year 3

Jun. 29 Traded in the executive chair for a new one from Rodriguez Office Supplies, account no. 122-7. The new chair cost $260, has an estimated life of eight years, and a zero trade-in value. Care-free received a trade-in allowance of $115 on the old chair and paid the balance in cash (straight-line method of depreciation). Recorded the entry to depreciate the old chair up to date. Made the entry to record the exchange of assets, without recognizing gain or loss.

Dec. 31 Made the adjusting entry to record depreciation of office equipment for the fiscal year (depreciation for six months on the chair; total depreciation, $329.97; verify this figure).

  31 Closed the Depreciation Expense, Office Equipment account into the Income Summary account.

Instructions

1. Record the transactions in general journal form.
2. Each time Care-free buys a new asset, open an account in the subsidiary ledger.
3. After each entry, post to the two controlling accounts and to the subsidiary ledger.
4. Make a list of the balances at the end of year 3 in the subsidiary ledger accounts and compare the totals with the balances of the two controlling accounts.

Problem Set B

Problem 20-1B   The Sturdivant Company, at the beginning of a fiscal year, buys a machine for $20,000. The machine has an estimated life of five years and an estimated trade-in value of $2,000.

Instructions

Determine the annual depreciation of the machine for each of the expected five years of its life, the accumulated depreciation at the end of each year, and the book value of the machine at the end of each year, using the columns provided by:

a. Straight-line method
b. Double-declining-balance method
c. Sum-of-the-years'-digits method

Problem 20-2B   During a three-year period, Overman Auto Parts completed the following transactions pertaining to its delivery truck.

Year 1

Jan.   8 Bought a used pick-up truck for cash, $1,340.
Nov. 16 Paid garage for maintenance repairs to truck, $119.
Dec.   31 Made the adjusting entry to record depreciation for the fiscal year, using the straight-line method of depreciation. The estimated life of the truck is four years, with a trade-in value of $540.
Dec.   31 Closed the expense accounts to the Income Summary account.

Year 2

Apr.   3 Paid garage for tune-up and minor repairs, $43.
Jul.   16 Bought a tire, $41.
Dec.   31 Recorded the adjusting entry for depreciation.
         31 Closed the expense accounts to the Income Summary account.

Year 3

May   19 Paid garage for maintenance repairs to truck, $214.
Jun.   19 Traded in the truck for another truck, priced at $2,420, receiving a trade-in allowance of $860; paid the difference in cash. Recorded the entry to depreciate the old truck up to date. Made the entry to record the exchange, assuming gain or loss is not recognized.
Dec.   31 Recorded adjusting entry for depreciation of the new truck for the fiscal year, using the straight-line method of depreciation. The estimated life of the new truck is six years, with a trade-in value of $300.
         31 Closed the expense accounts to the Income Summary account.

Instructions

1. Record all these transactions in general journal form.
2. After journalizing each entry, post to the following ledger accounts: Delivery Equipment; Accumulated Depreciation, Delivery Equipment; Truck Repair Expense; Depreciation Expense, Delivery Equipment.

Problem 20-3B   During a three-year period, the Piedmont Electric Company completed the following transactions connected with its electronic computer.

Year 1

Jun.   30 Bought an electronic computer, $60,200, paying $20,200 in cash, and issuing a series of four notes for $10,000 each, to come due at six-month intervals, payments to include principal plus 9 percent interest to maturity on each note.

Jul.   1 Paid installation charges for the computer, $1,800.

Dec.   31 Paid the principal, $10,000, plus interest of $450 on the first note.

        31 Made the adjusting entry to record depreciation on the computer for the fiscal year, using the double-declining-balance method at twice the straight-line rate ($12,400; verify this figure). The estimated life of the computer is five years, with a trade-in value of $5,800.

        31 Closed the expense accounts to the Income Summary account.

Year 2

Mar.   16 Paid for maintenance repairs to the computer, $2,918.

Jun.   30 Paid the principal, $10,000, plus interest of $900 on the second note.

Dec.   31 Paid the principal, $10,000, plus interest of $1,350 on the third note.

        31 Made the adjusting entry to record depreciation for the fiscal year ($49,600 × ⅖ = $19,840; verify this figure).

        31 Closed the expense account to the Income Summary account.

Year 3

Jun.   21 Paid for maintenance repairs to the computer, $1,696.

        30 Paid the principal, $10,000, plus interest of $1,800 on the fourth note.

Sep.   26 Piedmont Electric Company decides to get rid of its computer and use the services of a data processing firm in the future. Sold the computer for $12,000, receiving cash. Made the entry to depreciate the computer up to date ($8,928; verify this figure). Made the entry accounting for the sale of the machine.

Dec.   31 Closed the expense accounts to the Income Summary account.

Instructions

1. Record the transactions in general journal form.
2. After journalizing each entry, post to the following ledger accounts: Equipment; Accumulated Depreciation, Equipment; Depreciation Expense, Equipment; Equipment Maintenance Expense; Interest Expense; Loss on Disposal of Plant and Equipment.

Problem 20-4B The general ledger of the Rhoades Advertising Agency includes controlling accounts for Office Equipment and for Accumulated Depreciation, Office Equipment. Rhoades's accountant also records the details of each item of office equipment in a subsidiary ledger. The following transactions affecting office equipment occurred during a three-year period.

Year 1

Jan. 11 Bought the following items from Engley Office Supplies, for cash:

Executive desk, $540, account no. 122-1, estimated life ten years, trade-in value zero.
Executive chair, $190, account no. 122-2, estimated life ten years, trade-in value zero.
Filing cabinet, metal, $120, account no. 122-3, estimated life fifteen years, trade-in value zero.

(The above assets are depreciated on the basis of the straight-line method.)

12 Paid Coe Cabinet Shop $720 for a custom-made counter, account no. 122-4, estimated life ten years, trade-in value zero; depreciation by straight-line method.

14 Purchased a Paton and Rose electric typewriter for cash from Reiman Equipment Company, $380, serial no. TE-98519, account no. 122-5, estimated life five years, estimated trade-in value, $50; depreciation by sum-of-the-years'-digits method.

Dec. 31 Made the adjusting entry to record depreciation of Office Equipment for the fiscal year (total depreciation, $263; verify this figure).

31 Closed the Depreciation Expense, Office Equipment account into the Income Summary account.

Year 2

Jun. 29 Bought a rug from Sherwood Furniture on account, $480, account no. 122-6; estimated life eight years, trade-in value zero; depreciation by double-declining-balance method at twice the straight-line rate.

Dec. 31 Recorded the adjusting entry for depreciation of office equipment for the fiscal year (depreciation for six months on the rug; total depreciation, $301; verify this figure).

31 Closed the Depreciation Expense, Office Equipment account into the Income Summary account.

Year 3

Jun. 21 Traded in the executive desk for a new one, which cost $680, from Simmons Stationery and Supply, account no. 122-7, receiving a trade-in allowance of $320 on the old desk and paying the balance in cash. Expected life of the new desk is eight years, with zero trade-in value. Use straight-line method of depreciation. Made the entry to depreciate the old desk up to date. Made the entry to record the exchange of assets, without recognizing gain or loss.

Dec. 31 Made the adjusting entry to record depreciation of office equipment for the fiscal year (depreciation for six months on the desk; total depreciation, $317.81; verify this figure).

31 Closed the Depreciation Expense, Office Equipment account into the Income Summary account.

Instructions

1. Record the transactions in general journal form.
2. With the purchase of each new asset, open an account in the subsidiary ledger.
3. After each entry, post to the two controlling accounts and to the subsidiary ledger.
4. Make a list of balances at the end of year 3 in the subsidiary ledger accounts and compare the totals with the balances of the two controlling accounts.

APPENDIX E

Accelerated Cost Recovery System of Depreciation

The Economic Recovery Tax Act of 1981 introduced a new method of depreciation *for income-tax purposes* called the Accelerated Cost Recovery System, commonly referred to as ACRS. (The Deficit Reduction Act of 1984 changed some of the ACRS benefits enacted in 1981, and there may be other changes in future.) ACRS property includes new and used equipment and buildings used in a trade or business or held for the production of income, such as rental property. ACRS pertains to property placed in service after December 31, 1980.

Categories of Assets

In effect, this new law allows a company to write off or deduct on its tax return a percentage of the asset's cost at a more rapid rate than was previously allowed. The amount that can be written off depends on the category in which the asset falls. **Note, however, that under the ACRS, the trade-in or salvage value is not counted at all.**

- **Three-year property** Automobiles, light-trucks, certain manufacturing tools, tractor units for use over the road
- **Five-year property** Most equipment, office furniture and fixtures, and property not included in any other category
- **Ten-year property** Certain public utility property, such as telephone poles and power transmission lines; mobile homes
- **Fifteen-year property** Buildings acquired between January 1, 1981, and March 15, 1984, and low-income housing
- **Eighteen-year property** Buildings acquired after March 15, 1984, and improvements to buildings acquired before that date

Year	Three-Year Property	Five-Year Property	Ten-Year Property
1	25	15	8
2	38	22	14
3	$\dfrac{37}{100}$	21	12
4		21	10
5		$\dfrac{21}{100}$	10
6			10
7			9
8			9
9			9
10			$\dfrac{9}{100}$

Figure E-1

Percentage of cost allocated (written off or depreciated) each year

The amount of cost that can be written off, or depreciated, depends, of course, on the depreciation base, which is intimately tied to the investment tax credit. Tangible personal property, such as equipment, machinery, and office furniture, qualifies for investment tax credit. Investment tax credit is a reduction of the income tax liability. The reduction is generally 6 percent of the cost of three-year property and 10 percent of the cost of five-year property. As of January 1, 1983, the depreciation base of an asset must be reduced by 50 percent of the investment tax credit. Suppose for example, that a company buys office furniture for $1,000. Since office furniture is classified as five-year property, the investment tax credit (reduction of the tax liability) is 10 percent of $1,000, or $100. The depreciation base is $950: [$1,000 − ($100 × 50%)]. Consequently, the depreciation for the first year amounts to $144.50 ($950 × 15 percent). (Or a taxpayer may elect to reduce the investment tax credit and maintain the full depreciation base of an asset.)

The investment tax credit has been changed a number of times.

Cost Allocations of Three-, Five-, and Ten-Year Property

Three-, five-, or ten-year property placed in service at any time during the first year is eligible to claim depreciation for the full year. In other words the depreciation base is multiplied by the percentages shown in Figure E-1 no matter whether the truck has been in service one month or eleven.

Let's look at one example. A company buys a pick-up truck for $8,000 on November 15, 1983. Although the company's fiscal period runs from January

1 through December 31, 1983, the company takes a full year's depreciation for 1983 because the truck qualifies as three-year property. Here is a breakdown of the cost written off for income tax purposes.

- **First year** $2,000 ($8,000 × .25)
- **Second year** $3,040 ($8,000 × .38)
- **Third year** $2,960 ($8,000 × .37)

After the third year, no more depreciation may be taken, even if the company continues to use the truck.

Although the cost of the truck is entirely written off at the end of three years, *its asset account and accumulated depreciation account should be kept on the company's books until the truck is sold or traded.* Let's say that the company sells the truck for $2,300 after five years of use. Since the cost has been entirely written off, the $2,300 must be recorded as a gain.

1	*Cash*	2 3 0 0 00		1
2	*Accumulated Depreciation, Truck*	8 0 0 0 00		2
3	*Truck*		8 0 0 0 00	3
4	*Gain on Disposal of Plant and*			4
5	*Equipment*		2 3 0 0 00	5
6	*Sold pick-up truck that was*			6
7	*fully depreciated.*			7
8				8

Cash		Truck		Accumulated Depreciation, Truck		Gain on Disposal of Plant and Equipment	
+	−	+	−	−	+	−	+
2,300		Bal. 8,000	8,000	8,000	Bal. 8,000		2,300

Incidentally, *if an asset is sold before it is fully depreciated, under ACRS no depreciation may be taken during the year of sale.*

Cost Allocation of Buildings

As we stated earlier, buildings are classified under ACRS as fifteen-year or eighteen-year property. As with the other asset categories, trade-in value is not counted.

Unlike depreciation of three-, five-, and ten-year property, the amount of depreciation that can be claimed depends on when during the company's fiscal year the building is placed into service. The IRS tables for cost allocation break down depreciation for buildings *by month,* as shown in Figure E-2.

Example 1 Adams Company constructs a building at a total cost of $220,000. The building is placed in service on August 27, 1983. The firm's fiscal period is the same as the calendar year. Since August is the eighth

Year	\multicolumn{12}{c}{Month Placed in Service}

Year	1	2	3	4	5	6	7	8	9	10	11	12
1	12%	11%	10%	9%	8%	7%	6%	5%	4%	3%	2%	1%
2	10%	10%	11%	11%	11%	11%	11%	11%	11%	11%	11%	12%
3	9%	9%	9%	9%	10%	10%	10%	10%	10%	10%	10%	10%
4	8%	8%	8%	8%	8%	8%	9%	9%	9%	9%	9%	9%
5	7%	7%	7%	7%	7%	7%	8%	8%	8%	8%	8%	8%
6	6%	6%	6%	6%	7%	7%	7%	7%	7%	7%	7%	7%
7	6%	6%	6%	6%	6%	6%	6%	6%	6%	6%	6%	6%
8	6%	6%	6%	6%	6%	6%	5%	6%	6%	6%	6%	6%
9	6%	6%	6%	6%	5%	6%	5%	5%	5%	6%	6%	6%
10	5%	6%	5%	6%	5%	5%	5%	5%	5%	5%	6%	5%
11	5%	5%	5%	5%	5%	5%	5%	5%	5%	5%	5%	5%
12	5%	5%	5%	5%	5%	5%	5%	5%	5%	5%	5%	5%
13	5%	5%	5%	5%	5%	5%	5%	5%	5%	5%	5%	5%
14	5%	5%	5%	5%	5%	5%	5%	5%	5%	5%	5%	5%
15	5%	5%	5%	5%	5%	5%	5%	5%	5%	5%	5%	5%
16			1%	1%	2%	2%	3%	3%	4%	4%	4%	5%
	100%	100%	100%	100%	100%	100%	100%	100%	100%	100%	100%	100%

Figure E-2

Fifteen-year real property table (other than low-income housing)

month of the fiscal period, we use column 8 of the Fifteen-Year Real Property Table for the entire life of the building as determined by ACRS (stay in column 8). The depreciation expense for the first three years is calculated as follows.

- **First year** $11,000 ($220,000 × .05).
- **Second year** $24,200 ($220,000 × .11).
- **Third year** $22,000 ($220,000 × .10).

Example 2 On March 18, 1983, Berquist Motel buys a building for $400,000. The company's fiscal period extends from October 1 through September 30. Since March is the sixth month of the fiscal period, we use column 6 of the Fifteen-Year Real Property Table (stay in the column headed 6). Depreciation for the first three years is shown below.

- **First year** $28,000 ($400,000 × .07).
- **Second year** $44,000 ($400,000 × .11).
- **Third year** $40,000 ($400,000 × .10).

ACRS Versus Depreciation Methods Used for the Company's Books

Since lives of property under ACRS may differ from the actual useful lives of assets, a company may use ACRS for its income-tax return and other methods of depreciation for financial-reporting purposes. Many firms use ACRS for taxes and straight-line depreciation for computing net income. Assuming that the dollar amount of property acquisitions is about the same from year to year, these two methods would show the highest net income to the owner(s) and the lowest net income to the IRS. Firms that follow this procedure maintain a double set of accounts for Depreciation Expense and Accumulated Depreciation.

When an asset is sold or traded, the gain or loss must be computed under ACRS. (Refer to the example of the pick-up truck at the beginning of this appendix.) In addition, the gain or loss must also need to be calculated under the straight-line method. When the asset is traded in on a similar asset, any loss or gain is absorbed into the recorded cost of the new asset (see Chapter 20).

Alternative Method of Depreciation

Rather than using the tax tables, a company may use an alternative method of figuring the deduction for depreciation under ACRS. This approach utilizes the straight-line method, but offers a choice of three different useful lives for each class of property, as follows:

Three-year property	3, 5, or 12 years
Five-year property	5, 12, or 25 years
Ten-year property	10, 25, or 35 years
Fifteen-year property	15, 35, or 45 years
Eighteen-year property	18, 35, or 45 years

Some companies find it easier to use the alternative method because depreciation is the same for book and tax purposes. In addition, the choice of depreciation method will have significant tax consequences in the event that a building is sold. For example, if a building has been fully depreciated under the ACRS fifteen-year tables, the owner may find that an alternative method, based on an asset life of thirty-five or forty-five years, would have resulted in substantially lower taxes.

Problems

Problem E-1 On April 1, 1984, Blume Company bought a computer for $5,600.

Instructions

Determine the annual depreciation for each year during the ACRS life of the computer, the accumulated depreciation at the end of each year, and the book value at the end of each year. In calculating depreciation, do not consider any investment tax credit.

Problem E-2   During a three-year period, Donovan Electric completed the following transactions pertaining to its service truck:

Year 1

Nov.   21 Bought a truck for cash, $10,400.
      23 Bought storage bins for the truck, paying cash, $514.
Dec.   31 Recorded the adjusting entry for depreciation for the fiscal year using the ACRS method. (In calculating depreciation, do not consider any investment tax credit.)
      31 Closed the appropriate account to the Income Summary account.

Year 2

Dec.   31 Made the adjusting entry to record depreciation for the fiscal year using the ACRS method.
      31 Closed the appropriate account to the Income Summary account.

Year 3

Dec.   31 Made the adjusting entry to record depreciation for the fiscal year using the ACRS method.
      31 Closed the appropriate account to the Income Summary account.

Instructions

Record the transactions in general journal form.

Problem E-3   During a four-year period, Santiago Company completed the following transactions related to its company car:

Year 1

Sep.   15 Bought an automobile for $10,600 from JB Motors, paying $2,000 in cash with the remainder due in 30 days.
Oct.   15 Paid the balance due on the purchase of the automobile.
Dec.   31 Made the adjusting entry to record depreciation for the fiscal year using the ACRS method. (Do not consider any investment tax credit.)
      31 Closed the appropriate account to the Income Summary account.

Year 2

Dec.   31 Made the adjusting entry to record depreciation for the fiscal year using the ACRS method.
      31 Closed the appropriate account to the Income Summary account.

Year 3

Dec.   31 Made the adjusting entry to record depreciation for the fiscal year using the ACRS method.
      31 Closed the appropriate account to the Income Summary account.

Year 4

Jun.   28 Sold the automobile for cash, $3,950.

Instructions

1. Record the transactions in general journal form.
2. Post to the following ledger accounts after journalizing each entry: Automobile; Accumulated Depreciation, Automobile; Gain on Disposal of Plant and Equipment; Depreciation Expense, Automobile.

REVIEW OF T-ACCOUNT PLACEMENT AND REPRESENTATIVE TRANSACTIONS CHAPTERS 16–20

Review of T-Account Placement

The following sums up the placement of T accounts covered in Chapters 16 through 20 in relation to the fundamental accounting equation. Color indicates that an account is treated as a deduction from the account above it.

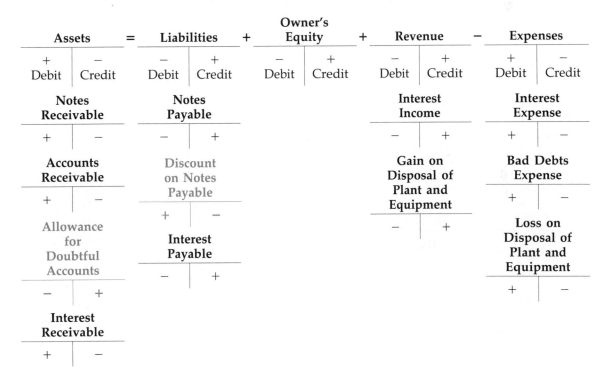

Review of Representative Transactions

The following table summarizes the recording of transactions covered in Chapters 16 through 20, along with the classification of the accounts involved. Note that, in this table, OE stands for Other Expenses.

Transaction	Accounts Involved	Class.	Increase or Decrease	Therefore Debit or Credit	Financial Statement
Gave a note to secure an extension of time on an open account.	Accounts Payable Notes Payable	CL CL	D I	Debit Credit	Bal. Sheet Bal. Sheet
Paid an interest-bearing note at maturity.	Notes Payable Interest Expense Cash	CL OE CA	D I D	Debit Debit Credit	Bal. Sheet Inc. State. Bal. Sheet
Borrowed from a bank; bank deducted interest in advance. Time period of note does not extend into next fiscal period.	Cash Interest Expense Notes Payable	CA OE CL	I I I	Debit Debit Credit	Bal. Sheet Inc. State. Bal. Sheet
Paid the bank at maturity of loan, previously discounted.	Notes Payable Cash	CL CA	D D	Debit Credit	Bal. Sheet Bal. Sheet
Borrowed from a bank; bank deducted interest in advance. Time period of note expires next fiscal period.	Cash Discount on Notes Payable Notes Payable	CA CL CL	I I I	Debit Debit Credit	Bal. Sheet Bal. Sheet Bal. Sheet
Adjusting entry for interest expired.	Interest Expense Discount on Notes Payable	OE CL	I D	Debit Credit	Inc. State. Bal. Sheet
Renewed a note and paid interest up to date.	Notes Payable Interest Expense Notes Payable Cash	CL OE CL CA	D I I D	Debit Debit Credit Credit	Bal. Sheet Inc. State. Bal. Sheet Bal. Sheet
Adjusting entry for accrued interest on notes payable.	Interest Expense Interest Payable	OE CL	I I	Debit Credit	Inc. State. Bal. Sheet
Reversing entry for accrued interest on notes payable.	Interest Payable Interest Expense	CL OE	D D	Debit Credit	Bal. Sheet Inc. State.

Transaction	Accounts Involved	Class.	Increase or Decrease	Therefore Debit or Credit	Financial Statement
Received a note from a charge customer to gain an extension of time.	Notes Receivable Accounts Receivable	CA CA	I D	Debit Credit	Bal. Sheet Bal. Sheet
Received amount due on an interest-bearing note.	Cash Notes Receivable Interest Income	CA CA OI	I D I	Debit Credit Credit	Bal. Sheet Bal. Sheet Inc. State.
Maker dishonored an interest-bearing note at maturity.	Accounts Receivable Notes Receivable Interest Income	CA CA OI	I D I	Debit Credit Credit	Bal. Sheet Bal. Sheet Inc. State.
Discounted an interest-bearing note receivable; proceeds are less than the principal.	Cash Interest Expense Notes Receivable	CA OE CA	I I D	Debit Debit Credit	Bal. Sheet Inc. State. Bal. Sheet
Maker dishonored a note receivable previously discounted, involving a protest fee.	Accounts Receivable Cash	CA CA	I D	Debit Credit	Bal. Sheet Bal. Sheet
Adjusting entry for accrued interest on notes receivable.	Interest Receivable Interest Income	CA OI	I I	Debit Credit	Bal. Sheet Inc. State.
Reversing entry for accrued interest on notes receivable.	Interest Income Interest Receivable	OI CA	D D	Debit Credit	Inc. State. Bal. Sheet
Adjusting entry for estimated bad-debt losses.	Bad Debts Expense Allowance for Doubtful Accounts	GE CA	I I	Debit Credit	Inc. State. Bal. Sheet
Wrote off an account as uncollectible.	Allowance for Doubtful Accounts Accounts Receivable	CA CA	D D	Debit Credit	Bal. Sheet Bal. Sheet
Received part payment in bankruptcy settlement of amount owed by charge customer.	Cash Allowance for Doubtful Accounts Accounts Receivable	CA CA CA	I D D	Debit Debit Credit	Bal. Sheet Bal. Sheet Bal. Sheet
Reinstated an account previously written off.	Accounts Receivable Allowance for Doubtful Accounts	CA CA	I I	Debit Credit	Bal. Sheet Bal. Sheet

Transaction	Accounts Involved	Class.	Increase or Decrease	Therefore Debit or Credit	Financial Statement
Using the perpetual-inventory method, bought merchandise on account.	Merchandise Inventory	CA	I	Debit	Bal. Sheet
	Accounts Payable	CL	I	Credit	Bal. Sheet
Adjusting entry for merchandise inventory under a perpetual-inventory system; physical count is less than book value.	Cost of Merchandise Sold	CMS	I	Debit	Inc. State.
	Merchandise Inventory	CA	D	Credit	Bal. Sheet
Adjusting entry for depreciation of building housing general office.	Depreciation Expense, Building	GE	I	Debit	Inc. State.
	Accumulated Depreciation, Building	P & E	I	Credit	Bal. Sheet
Discarded equipment that was fully depreciated.	Accumulated Depreciation, Equipment	P & E	D	Debit	Bal. Sheet
	Equipment	P & E	D	Credit	Bal. Sheet
Sold for cash, equipment having a book value that is less than the amount received.	Cash	CA	I	Debit	Bal. Sheet
	Accumulated Depreciation, Equipment	P & E	D	Debit	Bal. Sheet
	Equipment	P & E	D	Credit	Bal. Sheet
	Gain on Disposal of Plant and Equipment	OI	I	Credit	Inc. State.
Sold for cash, equipment having a book value that is greater than the amount received.	Cash	CA	I	Debit	Bal. Sheet
	Accumulated Depreciation, Equipment	P & E	D	Debit	Bal. Sheet
	Loss on Disposal of Plant and Equipment	OE	I	Debit	Inc. State.
	Equipment	P & E	D	Credit	Bal. Sheet
Traded in old equipment, receiving a trade-in allowance that is less than the book value.	Equipment (new)	P & E	I	Debit	Bal. Sheet
	Accumulated Depreciation, Equipment	P & E	D	Debit	Bal. Sheet
	Cash	CA	D	Credit	Bal. Sheet
	Equipment (old)	P & E	D	Credit	Bal. Sheet
Paid for extraordinary repairs to equipment, prolonging life of equipment three years.	Accumulated Depreciation, Equipment	P & E	D	Debit	Bal. Sheet
	Cash	CA	D	Credit	Bal. Sheet

21 The Voucher System of Accounting

Learning Objectives

After you have completed this chapter, you will be able to do the following:

1. Prepare vouchers.

2. Record vouchers in a voucher register.

3. Record payment of vouchers in a check register.

4. Record transactions involving canceling or altering an original voucher.

5. Record the receipt and payment of invoices by the net amount method.

We have often used the term *internal control* in connection with cash receipts and payments. The objectives of internal control are (1) to prevent errors, (2) to prevent the stealing of cash or other assets by employees and customers, and (3) to provide for the efficient management of the owner's investment. To meet these objectives, business transactions should be recorded in such a way that one person acts as a check or verification on another person. In other words, no one person is "out on a limb" by himself or herself. As the size of the economic unit increases, the owner becomes less directly involved in the transactions, and internal control becomes more important. The voucher system has been devised as a means of achieving internal control and enabling the owner or manager to maintain contact with day-by-day transactions.

OBJECTIVES OF THE VOUCHER SYSTEM

The objective of the **voucher system** is to *control the incurring of all liabilities and the making of all expenditures*—in other words, to control the purchase of (1) merchandise or materials, (2) other assets, and (3) services. An owner or chief executive who uses the voucher system can delegate authority while maintaining control over these transactions through the medium of signatures. An executive who signs a voucher has presumably read it and signifies that he or she approves the incurring of an obligation or the making of a payment. That is why the voucher system provides for the efficient management of the owner's investment. This feature is of vital importance, especially when large sums of money are involved.

The following four steps all involve the efficient management of resources. They aren't, of course, exclusive to the voucher system. However, when a firm is using the voucher system, these four steps are implied.

1. All expenditures must be backed up by purchase orders or other authorizations.
2. Goods and services received must be inspected and approved.
3. Invoices from suppliers must be checked against their respective purchase orders and verified as to accuracy of the computations of the amounts listed, shipping costs, and credit terms. Computation of amounts listed on the invoices, such as unit prices multiplied by the number of units purchased, are called **price extensions.**
4. All payments must be made by check, except for payments made from petty cash.

The voucher system focuses on the four steps listed and includes the following component parts, each of which we shall describe in detail.

- Vouchers
- Voucher register
- Check register
- Unpaid Voucher file
- Paid Voucher file
- General journal

At the outset, bear in mind that the voucher system is appropriate only for medium- to large-sized businesses. The volume of transactions must be big enough to make the extra paperwork economically feasible, and the firm must customarily pay its bills when they are due rather than making part payments or installment payments. Also bear in mind that the voucher system has fixed channels in which to record routine types of transactions. Nonroutine transactions do not fit into these channels and therefore require special entries in the general journal.

VOUCHERS

The dictionary defines a **voucher** as a piece of paper that serves as proof of a transaction. Recall that we used the word in Chapter 8 in connection with petty cash. The petty cash voucher not only describes the transaction, but also provides for signatures of the employee in charge of the fund and of the person receiving payment.

When a business is using the voucher system, a voucher must be filled out for *every* invoice or bill received, *whether it is to be paid immediately or in the future.* The voucher describes the terms of the transaction, and the invoice or bill is attached (usually stapled) to the voucher. If a business is buying merchandise, the voucher lists the name and address of the supplier, the date of the invoice, the amount, and the credit terms. There are always blanks for the necessary signatures, signifying approval of amounts, terms, and so forth.

Characteristics of Vouchers

Just as the form of *invoices* varies from one company to another, so too the form of *vouchers* varies from one company to another. In some enterprises, the voucher is in the form of a jacket and has a pocket or envelope, so that the invoice can be included with the voucher.

Although vouchers for different business firms or government units do vary a bit from one to another, the following characteristics are usually present.

- Vouchers must be prepared for every incoming bill, and are numbered consecutively.
- Name and address of the payee or creditor appear on vouchers.

- Amount and credit terms of the invoice appear on vouchers.
- Vouchers state due dates so that firms can take advantage of possible cash discounts.
- For internal control, vouchers require signatures (1) approving payment and (2) showing that payment has been recorded in the account books.
- Vouchers record payment: date paid and check number.

A completed voucher, with the invoice or bill stapled to it, describes an entire transaction, as well as the procedure for processing the voucher.

Preparation and Approval of Vouchers

Each voucher bears an identification number, which appears both inside and outside the voucher. To cite a familiar example, let us assume that C. L. Frederickson Plumbing Supply has now achieved such a volume of business that it is using a voucher system, and that it has received from its supplier, Darvik, Inc., the invoice shown in Figure 21-1.

C. L. Frederickson's accountant, using the invoice as the source of information, fills out the voucher shown in Figure 21-2. The inside or face of the voucher lists the particulars of the transaction.

The accountant staples the invoice to the voucher and circulates the two for the required approval signatures. When the voucher and the at-

Objective 1

Prepare vouchers.

Figure 21-1

DARVIK, INC.
1616 Madera Ave.
Los Angeles, CA 90026

INVOICE

Sold To: *C. L. Frederickson Plumbing Supply*
1968 N.E. Allen St.
Portland, OR 97201

Date: *October 1, 19–*
Invoice No.: *3394*
Order No.: *9764*
Shipped By: *Western Freight Line*
Terms: *2/10, n/30*

Quantity	Description	Unit Price	Total
2,600'	Galv. steel pipe (10' lengths) ¾"	.275	715.00

Figure 21-2

C. L. FREDERICKSON PLUMBING SUPPLY
1968 N.E. Allen Street
Portland, OR 97201

VOUCHER
No. 117

Pay
To: Darvik, Inc.
1616 Madera Ave.
Los Angeles, CA 90026   Date _____10/1_____

Date of Invoice	Terms	Description	Amount
10/1	2/10, n/30	Invoice No. 3394 Less discount Net amount payable	715.00 14.30 700.70

APPROVAL	DATES	APPROVED BY
Extensions and footings verified	10/2	M C L
Prices in agreement with purchase order	10/2	J. T.
Credit terms in agreement with purchase order	10/2	J. T.
Quantities in agreement with receiving report	10/2	QDS
Approved for payment	10/7	ALR

tached invoice get back to the accounting department, the accountant fills in the following required information on the outside of the voucher: the accounts to be debited and credited, the due date, the name and address of the payee, and the payment information (see Figure 21-3).

The Account Distribution section is used to record the account titles and amounts to be debited, the total amount to be credited to Vouchers Payable, and the initials of the person authorized to determine the distribution. The accounts to be debited depend, of course, on the types of goods and services purchased.

The *due date* represents the last day on which one can take advantage of the cash discount (taking into consideration the time required for mail delivery). For example, the invoice of Darvik, Inc., was dated October 1, with terms of 2/10, n/30. The discount period ends on October 11. However, if three days are necessary for mail delivery, the due date is moved back from October 11 to October 8, so that the cash will be in the hands of the creditor by October 11.

Figure 21-3

ACCOUNT DISTRIBUTION

ACCOUNT DEBITED	AMOUNT
Purchases	715.00
Supplies	
Wages Expense	
Miscellaneous Expense	
Total Vouchers Payable Cr.	715.00

ACCOUNT DISTRIBUTION by _RRH_

VOUCHER NO. _117_

Due Date   10/8

Pay To   Darvik, Inc.
1616 Madera Ave.
Los Angeles, CA 90026

SUMMARY OF CHARGES

Amount of invoice	$715.00
Less cash discount	14.30
Net amount	$700.70

RECORD OF PAYMENT

Paid by check no.	390
Date of check	10/8
Amount of check	700.70

ENTERED IN VOUCHER REG. by _M.C.L_

THE VOUCHERS PAYABLE ACCOUNT

When you use a voucher system, you substitute the Vouchers Payable account for Accounts Payable. For example, as we saw before, when a firm buys merchandise on account, the accountant enters it as a debit to Purchases and a credit to Vouchers Payable. Similarly, when a firm buys store equipment on account, the accountant records it as a debit to Store Equipment and a credit to Vouchers Payable. The voucher now represents the amount of the invoice or bill. When the obligation is paid, the payment is recorded as a debit to Vouchers Payable and a credit to Cash.

THE VOUCHER SYSTEM AND EXPENSES

We have stressed the fact that when you're using a voucher system, you have to write out a voucher *every time you incur a liability*, and this includes liabilities incurred for expenses as well as those incurred for acquiring assets. For example, suppose that when the telephone bill comes in, you notice some long-distance toll charges. First verify that these were business calls, then make out a voucher and attach the telephone bill to the inside of it. In the column headed Account Distribution, record the bill as a debit to Telephone Expense and a credit to Vouchers Payable. When a check is issued in payment of the voucher, record the entry in the check register as a debit to Vouchers Payable and a credit to Cash. Again let us emphasize that *all* liabilities are recorded in the Vouchers Payable account.

THE VOUCHER REGISTER

Objective 2

Record vouchers in a voucher register.

The **voucher register** has the status of a journal; it is a book of original entry. All vouchers must be recorded in it, in numerical order. Think of it as an expanded purchases journal. The voucher register has only one credit column, Vouchers Payable Credit, but a number of debit columns. Headings for the debit columns are selected on the basis of their frequency of use. A merchandising business, for example, would always have a Purchases Debit column because a merchant naturally buys a great volume of merchandise on account. The voucher register may vary widely, of course, depending on the size of the business and the number of accounts. In addition to the money columns, the voucher register also has space for recording the voucher number, name of creditor, date of payment, and check number. The voucher register for C. L. Frederickson Plumbing Supply is shown in Figure 21-4 (next two pages).

When you first record the voucher, leave the Payment Date and Check Number columns blank. After you've recorded the payment in the check register, go back to the voucher register and enter the date of payment and the number of the check. In Figure 21-4, vouchers no. 123 and 149 have not been paid yet; voucher no. 126 was "paid" by issuing a note (this transaction will be discussed later in this chapter); voucher no. 122 was issued payable to a payroll account. (It is assumed that this payroll entry was previously recorded in the general journal, crediting Wages Payable.)

Posting from the Voucher Register

The entries in the Sundry Accounts columns are posted *daily* to the general ledger, just as the Sundry Accounts columns of the other special journals are posted daily. The check mark ($\sqrt{}$) under the column total means "do not post." At the end of the month, total all the columns, and prove the equality of the debit and credit entries by comparing the combined total of the debit columns with the total of the Vouchers Payable Credit column. After you have proved the voucher register to be in balance, post the special-column totals to the general ledger. To show that

	DATE	VOU. NO.	CREDITOR	PAYMENT		VOUCHERS PAYABLE CREDIT	PURCHASES DEBIT	SUPPLIES DEBIT	WAGES PAYABLE DEBIT
				DATE	CK. NO.				
1	19– Oct.	1 117	Darvik, Inc.	10	8 390	7 1 5 00	7 1 5 00		
2		1 118	Reliable Express Co.	10	1 383	4 2 00	4 2 00		
3		3 119	Davenport Of. Sup.	10	3 384	4 8 72		4 8 72	
4		5 120	Rockland Insurance						
5			Company	10	5 387	7 4 00			
6		9 121	Reiter & Simon Co.	10	18 404	3 2 8 00	3 2 8 00		
7		10 122	Payroll Bank Acc.	10	10 393	1 6 9 0 00			1 6 9 0 00
8		12 123	Northwest Journal			7 6 00			
9		12 124	Dundee Equip. Co.	10	12 395	1 1 6 00			
10		15 125	C. L. Frederickson	10	15 399	5 0 0 00			
11		15 126	True-Fit Valve, Inc.	10	18 By note	4 2 1 00	4 2 1 00		
13									
14		29 149	Alman Mfg. Co.			7 1 4 00	7 1 4 00		
15		30 150	Safety National Bank	10	30 412	1 5 0 7 50			
16									
17		31				10 6 9 8 68	4 5 5 3 20	1 2 1 79	3 3 1 4 00
18						(2 1 2)	(5 1 1)	(1 1 5)	(2 1 3)
19									
20									

each total has been posted, write the account number in parentheses immediately below the column total. In the ledger accounts write the letters VR and the page number to show that the posting came from the voucher register.

THE CHECK REGISTER

Any economic unit using a voucher system uses the check register (see Chapter 13 for a discussion of it) as a book of original entry, in conjunction with the voucher register. It works this way: Since checks are issued only in payment of approved and recorded vouchers, the entry in the check register is always a debit to Vouchers Payable and a credit to Cash. A Vouchers Payable Debit column in the check register offsets the Vouchers Payable Credit column in the voucher register. Recall that after you record the entry in the check register, you enter the notation of the payment on the appropriate line in the voucher register and on the outside of the voucher in the Record of Payment section. First prove the column totals of the check register to see that the debits equal the credits, then post the amounts as totals, as shown in Figure 21-5.

Objective 3

Record payment of vouchers in a check register.

Figure 21-4

ADVERTISING EXPENSE DEBIT	MISCELLANEOUS EXPENSE DEBIT	SUNDRY ACCOUNTS DEBIT			
		ACCOUNT	POST. REF.	AMOUNT	
					1
					2
					3
					4
		Prepaid Insurance	116	74 00	5
					6
					7
76 00					8
		Sales Returns and Allowances	412	116 00	9
		C. L. Frederickson, Drawing	312	500 00	10
					11
					13
					14
		Notes Payable	211	1500 00	15
		Interest Expense	521	7 50	16
112 00	83 69			2514 00	17
(518)	(519)			(✓)	18
					19
					20

Figure 21-5

CHECK REGISTER

	DATE	CK. NO.	PAYEE	VOU. NO.	VOUCHERS PAYABLE DEBIT	PURCHASES DISCOUNT CREDIT	CASH CREDIT	
1	19– Oct. 1	383	Reliable Express Company	118	42 00		42 00	1
2	3	384	Davenport Office Supplies	119	48 72		48 72	2
3	3	385	Sullivan Manufacturing Company	114	206 00	2 06	203 94	3
4	4	386	Alman Manufacturing Company	115	540 00	10 80	529 20	4
5	5	387	Rockland Insurance Company	120	74 00		74 00	5
6	6	388	Void					6
7	6	389	Reiter and Simon Company	116	464 00	9 28	454 72	7
8	8	390	Darvik, Inc.	117	715 00	14 30	700 70	8
10	30	412	Safety National Bank	150	1507 50		1507 50	10
11	31				6404 98	75 84	6329 14	11
12					(212)	(512)	(111)	12
13								13

HANDLING OF UNPAID VOUCHERS

Business firms usually prepare vouchers in duplicate. In the system used by C. L. Frederickson Plumbing Supply, invoices are attached to the original copy of the voucher and it is circulated within the company for the necessary signatures. After a voucher is recorded in the voucher register, it is filed under the name of the creditor. (Other companies prepare only one voucher and file it only under the date on which it is supposed to be paid.) At C. L. Frederickson, the Unpaid Voucher file also contains any other outstanding vouchers or credit memos. This file, listed by names of creditors, now comprises a subsidiary ledger. In fact, at C. L. Frederickson this file substitutes for the accounts payable ledger.

The *second* copy of the voucher goes to the treasurer, who files it chronologically by due date. This Unpaid Voucher file helps the treasurer to forecast the amount of cash that will be needed to pay outstanding bills and to take advantage of cash discounts.

At the end of the month, the accountant lists all the vouchers payable, taking the information directly from the Unpaid Voucher file. She or he writes the amount owed, as well as the name of each creditor. This same procedure was used to prepare the schedule of accounts payable, as you recall.

C. L. Frederickson Plumbing Supply		
Schedule of Vouchers Payable		
October 31, 19–		

VOU. NO.	NAME OF CREDITOR	
123	*Northwest Journal*	$ 76 00
149	*Alman Manufacturing Company*	714 00
	Total Vouchers Payable	$ 790 00

FILING PAID VOUCHERS

Now let's assume that the firm has paid its bill. The vouchers with their attached invoices are first removed from the Unpaid Voucher files, and the payment is recorded in the check register and in the Payment column of the voucher register. Then the two vouchers are combined, marked paid, and filed in numerical order in a Paid Vouchers file. Many firms staple a copy of the check to the paid voucher, which means that the Paid Vouchers file contains complete documents for every cash payment.

SITUATIONS REQUIRING SPECIAL TREATMENT

When a firm is using the voucher system, it inevitably runs into an occasional nonroutine type of transaction that does not fit into the fixed channels of the voucher system and therefore requires an entry in the general journal. One can consider such treatment as an adjustment to the voucher system. Let us now look at four such types of transactions.

Objective 4

Record transactions involving canceling or altering an original voucher.

Return of a Purchase Before Original Voucher Has Been Recorded

Normally if a firm with an efficient purchasing department is going to return any merchandise, it returns the merchandise before the vouchers are recorded in the voucher register. The accountant records the deduction right on the invoice and records the invoice in the voucher register for the net amount. For example, C. L. Frederickson Plumbing Supply buys $1,200 worth of merchandise on account. Before its accountant records the voucher, C. L. Frederickson returns $100 worth of the merchandise to the supplier and receives a credit memorandum. The accountant staples the credit memorandum to the invoice, deducts $100 from the face amount, and records the invoice in the voucher register as a debit to Purchases for $1,100 and a credit to Vouchers Payable for $1,100.

Return of a Purchase After Original Voucher Has Been Recorded

Now what happens when a firm returns an item after the accountant has recorded the voucher listing its purchase in the voucher register?

On September 29, C. L. Frederickson Plumbing Supply bought $566 worth of merchandise from Alman Manufacturing Company. C. L. Frederickson's accountant recorded the transaction in the voucher register as a debit to Purchases for $566 and a credit to Vouchers Payable for $566, as shown.

			VOUCHER REGISTER			PAGE 2		
				PAYMENT		VOUCHERS PAYABLE CREDIT	PURCHASES DEBIT	
	DATE	VOU. NO.	CREDITOR	DATE	CK. NO.			
3	Sep. 29	115	Alman Mfg. Co.			5 6 6 00	5 6 6 00	
4								
5								
6								

A few days later, C. L. Frederickson returned $26 worth of defective merchandise to Alman and got a credit memorandum from Alman. C. L. Frederickson's accountant recorded this transaction in the general journal as follows.

	DATE		DESCRIPTION	POST. REF.	DEBIT	CREDIT	
1	19– Oct.	1	Vouchers Payable		26 00		1
2			Purchases Returns and Allowances			26 00	2
3			Returned defective merchandise to				3
4			Alman Manufacturing Company,				4
5			receiving their credit memo no.				5
6			4611, voucher no. 115.				6
7							7
8							8
9							9

GENERAL JOURNAL — PAGE 37

You will recognize that this entry is like a normal entry for the return of merchandise, except that here one uses Vouchers Payable instead of Accounts Payable and doesn't have to post anything to the accounts payable ledger. C. L. Frederickson's accountant deducts the amount of the return ($26) on voucher no. 115, and staples Alman's credit memorandum to it; then the accountant makes a notation in the Payment column of the voucher register, on the upper half of the line used to record the original voucher. C. L. Frederickson pays the invoice on October 4, and the accountant records the issuance of check no. 386 in the check register as a debit to Vouchers Payable for $540.00, a credit to Purchases Discount for $10.80, and a credit to Cash for $529.20. The notations in the Payment column of the voucher register look like this:

VOUCHER REGISTER — PAGE 2

	DATE	VOU. NO.	CREDITOR	PAYMENT DATE	CK. NO.	VOUCHERS PAYABLE CREDIT	PURCHASES DEBIT	
3	Sep. 29	115	Alman Mfg. Co.	10 10	1 Ret. 4 386	566 00	566 00	3
4								4
5								5
6								6

By T accounts, the entries look like this:

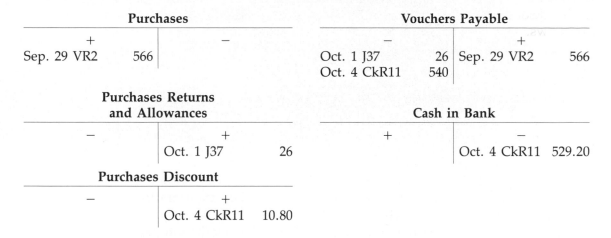

Purchases			Vouchers Payable		
+		−	−		+
Sep. 29 VR2	566		Oct. 1 J37	26	Sep. 29 VR2 566
			Oct. 4 CkR11	540	

Purchases Returns and Allowances			Cash in Bank		
−		+	+		−
	Oct. 1 J37	26			Oct. 4 CkR11 529.20

Purchases Discount		
−		+
	Oct. 4 CkR11	10.80

Issuing a "Note Payable" After Original Voucher Has Been Recorded

Suppose that someone in the firm issues a note canceling a voucher; then an entry is made in the general journal debiting Vouchers Payable and crediting Notes Payable. For example, let's say that on October 15 C. L. Frederickson Plumbing Supply bought $421 worth of merchandise from True-Fit Valve, Inc., and issued voucher no. 126, which was recorded in the voucher register. On October 18, C. L. Frederickson issued a 30-day, 8 percent note for $421, canceling the original voucher. C. L. Frederickson's general journal entry is as follows:

	DATE		DESCRIPTION	POST. REF.	DEBIT	CREDIT	
1	19– Oct.	18	Vouchers Payable		4 2 1 00		1
2			Notes Payable			4 2 1 00	2
3			Canceled voucher no. 126, payable				3
4			to True-Fit Valve, Inc., and				4
5			issued a 30-day, 8 percent note,				5
6			dated October 18.				6
7							7
8							8

GENERAL JOURNAL   PAGE 37

In the Payment columns of the voucher register, on the line on which voucher no. 126 is recorded, the accountant writes "10/18" in the Date column and "By note" in the Check Number column.

	DATE	VOU. NO.	CREDITOR	PAYMENT		VOUCHERS PAYABLE CREDIT	PURCHASES DEBIT	SUPPLIES DEBIT
				DATE	CK. NO.			
1								
3	Oct. 15	126	*True-Fit Valve, Inc.*	10 18	*By note*	4 2 1 00	4 2 1 00	
4								
5								

The accountant makes a notation on the voucher as well, indicating that it has been canceled by the issuance of a note, then transfers the voucher from the Unpaid Voucher file to the Paid Voucher file.

On November 17, when the note comes due, C. L. Frederickson prepares a new voucher and records it in the voucher register as a debit to Notes Payable for $421 in the Sundry Accounts Debit column, a debit to Interest Expense for $2.81 in the Sundry Accounts Debit column ($421, 8 percent, 30 days), and a credit to Vouchers Payable for $423.81 in the Vouchers Payable Credit column. Next, the voucher is paid; C. L. Frederickson's accountant records the payment in the check register in the usual manner as a debit to Vouchers Payable for $423.81 and a credit to Cash for $423.81. By T accounts, the entries appear as follows.

Purchases				Vouchers Payable			
+		−		−		+	
Oct. 15 VR3	421.00			Oct. 18 J37	421.00	Oct. 15 VR3	421.00
				Nov. 17 CkR17	423.81	Nov. 17 VR4	423.81

Interest Expense				Notes Payable			
+		−		−		+	
Nov. 17 VR4	2.81			Nov. 17 VR4	421.00	Oct. 18 J37	421.00

Cash			
+		−	
		Nov. 17 CkR17	423.81

Installment Payments Planned at Time of Original Purchase

In a voucher system, invoices generally are paid in full. Sometimes, however, management prefers to pay for an item in installments. When this happens, the company's accountant prepares a separate voucher and records it in the voucher register for each installment. As an illustration, assume that on November 2 C. L. Frederickson bought an office safe for $750 from Newell Office Equipment Company, with a down payment of $250, and two installments of $250 each, payable on November 17 and December 2. C. L. Frederickson's accountant prepares three vouchers and records each of them in the voucher register.

			VOUCHER REGISTER				PAGE 4		
DATE	VOU. NO.	CREDITOR		VOUCHERS PAYABLE CREDIT	SUNDRY ACCOUNTS DEBIT				
					ACCOUNT	POST. REF.	AMOUNT		
Nov. 2	154	*Newell Office Equip-*							3
		ment Co.		2 5 0 00	*Office Equipment*		7 5 0 00		4
2	155	*Newell Office Equip-*							5
		ment Co.		2 5 0 00					6
2	156	*Newell Office Equip-*							7
		ment Co.		2 5 0 00					8

Each voucher's due date corresponds to the date that installment is to be paid. Voucher no. 154 is paid immediately; voucher no. 155 is filed according to its due date, November 17; voucher no. 156 is filed according to *its* due date, December 2.

Installment Payments Planned After Original Voucher Has Been Recorded

However, suppose that the buyer records the entire amount of the invoice on one voucher, and *later* decides to pay the invoice in installments. The accountant must now cancel the original voucher by means of a general journal entry and issue new vouchers for each installment.

Suppose that C. L. Frederickson buys merchandise from Donaldson and Farr and records the transaction in the voucher register as follows except that the information in the Payment columns, which appears in color, is not included at this time.

	DATE	VOU. NO.	CREDITOR	PAYMENT		VOUCHERS PAYABLE CREDIT	PURCHASES DEBIT	SUPPLIES DEBIT
				DATE	CK. NO.			
3	Sep.	21 103	*Donaldson and Farr*	10	16 V127, 128,9	9 0 0 00	9 0 0 00	
4								
5								

Remember, when C. L. Frederickson's accountant originally records the transaction, he or she leaves the Payment column blank. On October 16, C. L. Frederickson arranges to pay the $900 debt in three installments of $300 each, with due dates of October 21, November 5, and November 21. Accordingly, the accountant makes an entry in the general journal as follows.

1	Oct.	16	*Vouchers Payable*	9 0 0 00	1
2			*Purchases*	9 0 0 00	2
3			*Canceled voucher no. 103 payable*		3
4			*to Donaldson and Farr, the*		4
5			*amount to be paid in three equal*		5
6			*installments, due October 21,*		6
7			*November 5, and November 21.*		7
8					8
9					9

The accountant then notes "10/16" and the voucher numbers for the installments in the Payment column of the voucher register and makes entries in the voucher register for three new vouchers, as shown.

VOUCHER REGISTER

PAGE __3__

	DATE	VOU. NO.	CREDITOR	PAYMENT		VOUCHERS PAYABLE CREDIT	PURCHASES DEBIT	SUPPLIES DEBIT
				DATE	CK. NO.			
3	Oct.	16 127	*Donaldson and Farr*			3 0 0 00	3 0 0 00	
4		16 128	*Donaldson and Farr*			3 0 0 00	3 0 0 00	
5		16 129	*Donaldson and Farr*			3 0 0 00	3 0 0 00	
6								

C. L. Frederickson then puts voucher no. 103—the original voucher that was canceled—in the Paid Voucher file, and puts vouchers no. 127, 128, and 129 in the Unpaid Voucher file, in the usual manner.

Correcting an Amount After Original Voucher Has Been Recorded

The required approvals and verifications of records demanded by the voucher system will not entirely eliminate errors. However, these procedures should reduce errors to a minimum. If an error is discovered *after* a voucher has been recorded in the voucher register, the accountant can correct it by means of a general journal entry. The purpose of the entry is to cancel the original voucher by reversing the original entry. Since this has the effect of clearing the accounts, it paves the way for the issuance of a new voucher for the correct amount. For example, C. L. Frederickson Plumbing Supply bought merchandise from Alman Manufacturing Company for $546 and issued voucher no. 102, as follows.

			VOUCHER REGISTER					PAGE __2__

DATE	VOU. NO.	CREDITOR	PAYMENT DATE	CK. NO.	VOUCHERS PAYABLE CREDIT	PURCHASES DEBIT	SUPPLIES DEBIT
Sep. 20	102	Alman Mfg. Co.	10 19	V130	5 4 6 00	5 4 6 00	

When C. L. Frederickson's accountant recorded the voucher, he or she left the Payment columns of the voucher register blank. On October 19 someone discovered an error in the price extensions; the correct amount of the invoice should have been $518. The entry necessary to correct the situation is as follows: first, cancel out the original voucher; next, record a new voucher for the correct amount.

Oct. 19	Vouchers Payable		5 4 6 00		
	Purchases			5 4 6 00	
	Canceled voucher no. 102 payable				
	to Alman Manufacturing Company				
	because of error in amount of				
	invoice.				

				PAYMENT		VOUCHERS PAYABLE CREDIT	PURCHASES DEBIT	SUPPLIES DEBIT
	DATE	VOU. NO.	CREDITOR	DATE	CK. NO.			

VOUCHER REGISTER — PAGE 3

	DATE	VOU. NO.	CREDITOR			VOUCHERS PAYABLE CREDIT	PURCHASES DEBIT	SUPPLIES DEBIT
3	Oct. 19	130	Alman Mfg. Co.			5 1 8 00	5 1 8 00	
4								
5								
6								
7								
8								

The accountant makes a notation in the Payment columns of the voucher register that voucher no. 102 has been canceled by writing "10/19" and the new voucher number, "130." He or she makes a similar notation on voucher no. 102 itself, then places it in the Paid Voucher file. If he or she discovers the error during the same month that the voucher was issued, he or she can handle the correction in this way or make the correction directly on the original voucher and in the voucher register by drawing a line through the incorrect amount and inserting the correct one. The accountant can do this because the transaction has not yet been posted.

THE VOUCHER SYSTEM AS A MANAGEMENT TOOL

The voucher system illustrates how well the accounting procedure implements internal control, and also how the voucher system helps organizations manage financial resources efficiently. In this respect, it has the following advantages. (Computers can also serve these functions.)

1. Vouchers supply up-to-date information on due dates and amounts owed. The financial manager is more interested in knowing *when* payment is due than in knowing to whom the amount is payable; she or he needs to plan for cash requirements. This information is provided in the **tickler file** (unpaid vouchers filed by due dates).
2. Vouchers systematize the taking of cash discounts. A firm that takes cash discounts saves a lot of money. The tickler file helps to ensure that a business will save this money, by informing the firm about the last day to take advantage of cash discounts.

3. Payments cover specific invoices. Each check issued covers a specific invoice, which eliminates confusion about amounts owed to creditors.
4. Authority may be delegated and responsibility fixed. This advantage stems from the system of required approval signatures. Because the approval is given when the goods arrive or the service is received, if something is not satisfactory, it is given immediate attention.

RECORDING PURCHASES AT THE NET AMOUNT

Objective 5

Record the receipt and payment of invoices by the net amount method.

Until now, even when we were discussing the voucher system, we have always assumed that the firm's accountant records the cost of purchases at the gross amount. For example, Figure 21-1 showed an invoice from Darvik, Inc., for $715; terms 2/10, n/30. C. L. Frederickson's accountant recorded the invoice as a debit of $715 to Purchases and a credit of $715 to Vouchers Payable. (If C. L. Frederickson had not been using the voucher system, Accounts Payable would have been credited.) As an alternative, firms that try to take advantage of all cash discounts use the **net-amount system.** They record all purchases at the net amount, which would be $700.70 ($715 less the 2 percent cash discount of $14.30).

Recording purchases at the net amount means recording the amount of a purchase after the cash discount has been deducted.

A company that records purchases at the net amount does not necessarily have to use a voucher system. However, since firms that use voucher systems are usually medium- to large-sized business operations that take advantage of cash discounts whenever possible, many of these concerns do record purchases at the net amount.

To compare the gross-amount procedure versus the net-amount procedure, let's look at some sample transactions in general journal form, using both methods side by side.

Transaction (a) Bought merchandise on account from Skinner and Roe, terms 2/10, n/30; $6,000. Issued voucher no. 2811.

Transaction (b) Issued check no. 3748 in payment of voucher no. 2811, less the cash discount.

Gross-Amount Procedure			Net-Amount Procedure		
(a) *In voucher register:*			(a) *In voucher register:*		
Purchases	6,000		Purchases	5,880	
Vouchers Payable		6,000	Vouchers Payable		5,880
(b) *In check register:*			(b) *In check register:*		
Vouchers Payable	6,000		Vouchers Payable	5,880	
Purchases Discount		120	Cash		5,880
Cash		5,880			

Using the net-amount procedure to record purchases eliminates the Purchases Discount account. But both methods yield the same net purchase that appears in the Cost of Merchandise Sold section of the income statement, because when you use the Purchases Discount account, you deduct it from Gross Purchases in order to arrive at Net Purchases.

Enterprises using the net-amount system naturally take advantage of all cash discounts available to them. However, sometimes, because of carelessness or oversight, one may miss out on the cash discount. In this case, one uses the account Purchases Discounts Lost, as illustrated here.

Transaction (c) Bought merchandise on account from J. H. Thomas Company; terms 2/10, n/30; $3,200. Issued voucher no. 3092, May 17.

Transaction (d) Issued check no. 4167 in payment of voucher no. 3092, $3,200, June 17.

Gross-Amount Procedure			Net-Amount Procedure		
(c) *In voucher register:*			(c) *In voucher register:*		
Purchases	3,200		Purchases	3,136	
Vouchers Payable		3,200	Vouchers Payable		3,136
(d) *In check register:*			(d) *In check register:*		
Vouchers Payable	3,200		Vouchers Payable	3,136	
Cash		3,200	Purchases Discounts Lost	64	
			Cash		3,200

When the net-amount procedure is used in conjunction with a voucher system, a notation in the Payment column of the voucher register indicates any discounts lost, as shown here.

DATE	PAYMENT	CHECK NO.
Jun. 17	DISCOUNT LOST	

Under such a system, the check register contains a Purchases Discounts Lost Debit column. Purchases Discounts Lost is classified as an expense account:

**Purchases
Discounts Lost**

+	−

This account is closed into Income Summary along with all other expense accounts in the one large compound entry. On the income statement,

Purchases Discounts Lost appears under Other Expenses. Additional accounts in this classification are Interest Expense and Loss on Disposal of Plant and Equipment (recall Chapter 15). For internal control, the prime advantage of using the net-amount procedure is that if a firm fails to take discounts, this fact is apparent to management, since it stands out as an exception. If this loss is due to someone's carelessness, management can take steps to see that the oversight doesn't recur. As an alternative, some accountants put the balance of Purchases Discounts Lost in the Cost of Merchandise Sold section of the income statement.

GLOSSARY

Net-amount system   A procedure by which incoming invoices are recorded at the net amount (gross amount less cash discount).

Price extensions   Computations of amounts listed on an invoice; unit prices multiplied by the number of units purchased, for example.

Tickler file   A file of unpaid vouchers arranged chronologically by due dates.

Voucher   A paper or document summarizing the terms of a transaction. It includes signatures or initials that vouch for its correctness, authorize its entry in the books, and approve its payment at the appropriate time.

Voucher register   A book of original entry in which all vouchers are recorded as credits to Vouchers Payable and debits to other accounts.

Voucher system   A procedure for the recording and payment of all liabilities incurred through the issuance of vouchers. It involves a voucher register and check register, Unpaid Voucher files, and Paid Voucher files.

QUESTIONS, EXERCISES, AND PROBLEMS

Discussion Questions

1. When a business is using a voucher system, what types of transactions require the filling out of a voucher?
2. Describe each of the two Unpaid Voucher files.
3. Regarding the purchase of merchandise, describe what must be done when a credit memorandum is received after the original voucher has been recorded.
4. When a voucher system is in use, is it necessary to have an accounts payable ledger?
5. Explain briefly how the voucher system serves as a management tool.
6. Regarding the purchase of merchandise, what happens when installment payments are decided upon after the original voucher has been recorded?
7. Describe the net-amount procedure for recording purchases.

Exercises

Exercise 21-1   Record the following transactions in general journal form, indicating, above the entry, the title of the book of original entry in which each should be recorded. Assume that a voucher register and a check register are being used.

May   1 Prepared voucher no. 616 for $620, in favor of Nolan Real Estate, for rent for the month.

       3 Prepared voucher no. 617, in favor of Richards Company, for merchandise purchased; terms 2/10, n/30; $2,600.

       4 Issued check no. 738 in payment of voucher no. 616.

    14 Issued check no. 739 in payment of voucher no. 617.

    14 Prepared voucher no. 618 in favor of Polson Office Supply for typewriter ribbons and carbon paper purchased, $63.72.

    14 Issued check no. 740 in payment of voucher no. 618.

Exercise 21-2   Using the gross-amount procedure, record in general journal form the following related transactions.

Apr.   6 Bought merchandise on account from Norman Denton Company; terms 2/10, n/30; $6,400. Issued voucher no. 3842.

      9 Received credit memo no. A319 from Norman Denton Company for return of defective merchandise purchased April 6, $280.

   15 Issued check no. 4915 in payment of voucher no. 3842 less the return and less the discount.

Exercise 21-3   Enter the following in general journal form.

a. Issued voucher no. 683 to establish a Petty Cash Fund, $90.
b. Prepared check no. 712 in payment of voucher no. 683, $90.
c. The present balance in the Petty Cash Fund is $11.18. Petty cash receipts indicate the following expenditures.

Store supplies	$21.60
Office supplies	19.84
Miscellaneous general expense	37.38

Issued voucher no. 741 to reimburse the Petty Cash Fund, $78.82.
d. Issued check no. 856 in payment of voucher no. 741.

Exercise 21-4   Assuming that invoices are recorded by the net-amount procedure, prepare general journal entries to record the following:

Oct.   2 Received from Johnson and Son an invoice for merchandise, dated October 1; terms 2/10, n/30; $6,200. Issued voucher no. 7662 authorizing payment, and filed voucher for payment on last day of discount period.

   14 Discovered that voucher no. 7662 had been filed in error for payment on this date. Refiled it for payment on last day of credit period, November 1.

Nov.   1 Issued check no. 8592, in payment of voucher no. 7662.

Exercise 21-5 Using the gross-amount procedure, record the following related transactions in general journal form.

Jan.   6 Bought merchandise on account from C. C. Dewey Company; terms 1/10, n/30; $3,720. Issued voucher no. 7934.
          9 Gave a 60-day, 8 percent note to C. C. Dewey Company, dated January 9; canceled voucher no. 7934.
Mar.   7 Issued voucher no. 9961, $3,769.60, in favor of C. C. Dewey Company for our note: principal $3,720, interest $49.60.
          7 Prepared check no. 1172 in payment of voucher no. 9961.

Exercise 21-6 Make entries for the following transactions in general journal form.

Jun.   2 Bought display equipment on account from Rutherford Supply Company, terms 30 days, $840. Issued voucher no. 921.
Jul.   1 Rutherford Supply Company agreed to accept payment on an installment basis as follows: one-third immediately, one-third by July 31, and one-third by August 30. Canceled voucher no. 921 and issued voucher no. 1112 for $280, voucher no. 1113 for $280, and voucher no. 1114 for $280.
          1 Issued check no. 1373 in payment of voucher no. 1112.
         31 Issued check no. 1498 in payment of voucher no. 1113.
Aug.   30 Issued check no. 1619 in payment of voucher no. 1114.

Exercise 21-7 Record in general journal form the following transactions.

a. Issued voucher no. 3 to establish a change fund, $200.
b. Issued check no. 2 in payment of voucher no. 3.
c. Determined cash sales for the day according to the cash register tapes to be $714.55, and cash on hand to be $912.95. A bank deposit was prepared for $712.95.

Exercise 21-8 At the suggestion of the accountant, S. T. Anscott borrowed $20,000 from the bank for 30 days at 12 percent. Anscott then used the proceeds to take advantage of discount terms of 2/10, n/30 offered by her suppliers of merchandise. Anscott had not previously been taking advantage of the available cash discount terms because the cash needed was not always available and because she was not convinced that it was worthwhile to borrow money for this purpose.

Instructions

1. State briefly the specific advantage of the loan.
2. What kind of accounting controls should Anscott put into use to make sure that discounts are not overlooked?

Problem Set A

Problem 21-1A Montgomery and Sons, which uses a voucher system, has the following vouchers that were issued during June and that were unpaid on July 1.

Voucher Number	Company	For	Date of Voucher	Amount
933	Timmins and Company	Merchandise	Jun. 25	$1,426.00
936	Rollick and Stanford	Merchandise	Jun. 29	2,380.00
				$3,806.00

The following transactions were completed during July.

Jul. 1 Issued voucher no. 938 in favor of Pennard Land Company for July rent, $820.

2 Issued check no. 1116 in payment of voucher no. 938, $820.

5 Bought merchandise on account from Allen Manufacturing Company; terms 2/10, n/30; $4,960. Issued voucher no. 939. (Invoices are recorded at the gross amount.)

5 Issued check no. 1117 in payment of voucher no. 933, $1,411.74 ($1,426.00 less 1 percent cash discount).

8 Issued voucher no. 940 in favor of United Telephone Company for telephone bill, $84.

8 Issued check no. 1118 in payment of voucher no. 940.

8 Issued check no. 1119 in payment of voucher no. 936, $2,332.40 ($2,380.00 less 2 percent cash discount).

13 Issued check no. 1120 in payment of voucher no. 939, less the cash discount.

16 Bought merchandise on account from Tolliver Products Company; terms 2/10, EOM; $3,950. Issued voucher no. 941.

24 Issued voucher no. 942 for a note payable, previously recorded in the general journal: principal $4,500, plus interest of $52. The note is payable to the Citizens State Bank.

24 Paid voucher no. 942 by issuing check no. 1121.

25 Issued check no. 1122 in payment of voucher no. 941, less the cash discount.

31 Issued voucher no. 943 for Wages Payable, $2,694, in favor of the payroll bank account. (Assume that the payroll entry was previously recorded in the general journal.)

31 Paid voucher no. 943 by issuing check no. 1123.

Instructions

1. Under the date of the original purchase, enter the unpaid invoices in the voucher register, beginning with voucher no. 933. Then draw double lines across all columns to separate the vouchers of June from those of July.
2. Enter the transactions for July in the voucher register at the gross amount. Also record the appropriate transactions in the check register.

Problem 21-2A The S. T. Nielson Company, which uses a voucher system, has the following unpaid vouchers on April 30.

Voucher Number	Company	For	Date of Invoice	Amount
3618	Forsgren Supply Company	Merchandise	Apr. 15	$ 1,942.50
3634	Baker and Thomas	Merchandise	Apr. 28	3,730.00
3636	R. L. Peters and Company	Merchandise	Apr. 29	4,800.00
				$10,472.50

The company made the following transactions during May.

May 1 Issued voucher no. 3649 in favor of Fidelity Insurance Company for three-year premium on fire insurance policy, $390.
  1 Paid voucher no. 3618 by issuing check no. 7118, $1,903.65 ($1,942.50 less 2 percent cash discount).
  2 Issued check no. 7119 in payment of voucher no. 3649.
  4 Issued voucher no. 3650 in favor of Trojan Fast Freight for transportation charges on merchandise purchases, $56.
  5 Paid voucher no. 3650 by issuing check no. 7120.
  7 Issued check no. 7121 in payment of voucher no. 3634, $3,692.70 ($3,730.00 less 1 percent cash discount).
  8 Issued check no. 7122 in payment of voucher no. 3636, $4,752 ($4,800 less 1 percent cash discount).
  11 Established a Petty Cash Fund of $125. Issued voucher no. 3651.
  11 Paid voucher no. 3651 by issuing check no. 7123.
  13 Issued voucher no. 3652 in favor of Adams and Bleighton for merchandise; terms 2/10, n/30; $6,940.
  16 Bought advertising space for two weeks in the *Daily Times*. Issued voucher no. 3653 in the amount of $150.
  17 Received a credit memorandum for $326 from Adams and Bleighton for merchandise returned to them, credit memorandum no. 299.
  19 Issued voucher no. 3654 in favor of Queen County for six months' property taxes, $1,080.
  20 Paid voucher no. 3654 by issuing check no. 7124.
  21 Issued check no. 7125 in payment of voucher no. 3652, $6,481.72 ($6,940.00 less $326 return, less cash discount).
  23 Bought merchandise on account from Baker and Thomas; terms 1/10, n/30; $2,964. Issued voucher no. 3655.
  28 Received a credit memorandum for $516 from Baker and Thomas for damaged merchandise, credit memorandum no. 261C.

May   31 Issued voucher no. 3656 to reimburse Petty Cash Fund. The
          charges were as follows:

             Store Supplies $40.50
             Office Supplies   15.16
             S. T. Nielson, Drawing   24.00
             Miscellaneous Expense   14.28

      31 Issued check no. 7126 in payment of voucher no. 3656.
      31 Issued voucher no. 3657 for Wages Payable, $2,970, in favor of
         payroll bank account. (Assume that the payroll entry was previ-
         ously recorded in the general journal.)
      31 Paid voucher no. 3657 by issuing check no. 7127, payable to payroll
         bank account.

Instructions

1. Under the date of the original purchase, enter the unpaid invoices in the
   voucher register, beginning with voucher no. 3618. Then draw double
   lines across all columns to separate the vouchers of April from those of
   May.
2. Enter the transactions for May in the voucher register at the gross amount.
   Also record the appropriate transactions in the check register and general
   journal.
3. Total and rule the voucher register and check register for the transactions
   recorded for May.

Problem 21-3A   Pounder Sales Company uses a voucher system in which
it records invoices at the gross amount. During July it completed the following transactions affecting Vouchers Payable.

Jul.   1 Prepared voucher no. 1481 in favor of Thompson and Rand for the
         purchase of merchandise having an invoice price of $3,200, terms 30
         days.
       3 Prepared voucher no. 1482 for $720, voucher no. 1483 for $720, and
         voucher no. 1484 for $720. The debt arose because Pounder Sales
         bought an electronic calculator from Sterling Office Supply. The
         terms are $720 cash on delivery, $720 in 30 days, and $720 in 60
         days. (Use three lines.)
       5 Issued check no. 1614 in payment of voucher no. 1482.
       8 Issued voucher no. 1485 in favor of Crawford Supply Company for
         the purchase of store supplies; terms n/30, $173.
       9 Prepared voucher no. 1486 in favor of Girard Motor Freight for
         freight charges on merchandise purchased, $46.
       9 Issued check no. 1615 in payment of voucher no. 1486.
      14 Prepared voucher no. 1487 in favor of Rolland Realty for rent for the
         month, $860.
      14 Issued check no. 1616 in payment of voucher no. 1487.

Jul. 15 Prepared voucher no. 1488 in favor of Underwood Products Company for the purchase of merchandise having an invoice price of $3,600 with a 25 percent trade discount (record voucher for $2,700); terms 2/10, n/30.

16 Canceled voucher no. 1481 due to the fact that the invoice will be paid in two installments as follows: voucher no. 1489, payable August 1, $1,600; voucher no. 1490, payable August 15, $1,600. Prepared vouchers no. 1489 and no. 1490.

18 Received a credit memorandum from Underwood Products Company for merchandise returned, $160, voucher no. 1488, credit memo no. 326.

21 Prepared voucher no. 1491 in favor of Amalgamated Telephone Company for telephone bill, $84.16.

21 Issued check no. 1617 in payment of voucher no. 1491.

23 Issued check no. 1618 in payment of voucher no. 1488, $2,489.20 ($2,700.00 less $160 return, less cash discount).

31 Prepared voucher no. 1492 for Wages Payable, $1,842, in favor of payroll bank account. (Assume that the payroll entry was recorded previously in the general journal.)

31 Issued check no. 1619 in payment of voucher no. 1492.

31 Prepared voucher no. 1493 in favor of R. T. Pounder, the owner, for a personal withdrawal, $1,060.

31 Issued check no. 1620 for the payment of voucher no. 1493.

Instructions

1. Record the transactions for July in the voucher register, the check register, and the general journal.
2. Total and rule the voucher register and the check register.
3. Post the amounts from the registers and the general journal to the Vouchers Payable account.
4. Prepare a schedule of Vouchers Payable. Compare the total with the balance of the Vouchers Payable account.

Problem 21-4A   The Simpson Sales Company uses a voucher system by which they record invoices at the net amount. They have the following unpaid vouchers on October 31.

Voucher Number	Company	For	Date of Invoice	Amount
5139	Norman Supply Company	Store Equipment	Oct. 25	$ 4,800.00
5145	Raymond Equipment Company	Office Equipment	Oct. 27	5,350.00
				$10,150.00

The company made the following transactions during November.

Nov. 1 Prepared voucher no. 5151 in favor of Universal Power and Light for electric bill, $109.

Nov. 1 Paid voucher no. 5151 by issuing check no. 6872.
2 Bought merchandise on account from Sherman Manufacturing Company; terms 2/10, n/30; $5,850. Prepared voucher no. 5152 (record invoice for $5,733, using the net amount).
3 Canceled voucher no. 5139 because the invoice is to be paid in three installments, as follows: voucher no. 5153, due November 15, $1,600; voucher no. 5154, due December 1, $1,600; and voucher no. 5155, due December 15, $1,600.
6 Louella Simpson, the owner, withdrew $590 for personal use. Issued voucher no. 5156.
7 Issued check no. 6873 in payment of voucher no. 5156.
8 Raymond Equipment Company agreed to accept 60-day, 8 percent note, dated November 8. Accordingly, canceled voucher no. 5145.
12 Issued check no. 6874 in payment of voucher no. 5152.
14 Issued check no. 6875 in payment of voucher no. 5153.
15 Prepared voucher no. 5157 for $514 for sales commissions expense, in favor of salespersons. The expense was not previously recorded.
15 Issued check no. 6876 in payment of voucher no. 5157, payable to O. T. Freund for sales commission.
21 Bought merchandise on account from S. T. Tolliver Company; terms 1/10, EOM; $6,720. Issued voucher no. 5158 (record the invoice for $6,652.80).
23 Prepared voucher no. 5159 in favor of Drexel Freight Company for freight bill on the purchase from S. T. Tolliver Company, $59.
23 Issued check no. 6877 in payment of voucher no. 5159.
25 Discovered an error in the computations on the invoice from S. T. Tolliver, reducing amount due by $220. Canceled voucher no. 5158 and issued voucher no. 5160, $6,435.
28 Prepared voucher no. 5161, $359, in favor of Newton Savings and Loan, for mortgage payment: principal, $176; interest, $183.
28 Issued check no. 6878 in payment of voucher no. 5161.
30 Prepared voucher no. 5162 for Wages Payable, $2,069, in favor of payroll bank account. (Assume that the payroll entry was previously recorded in the general journal.)
30 Paid voucher no. 5162 by issuing check no. 6879.

Instructions

1. Under the date of the original purchases, enter the unpaid invoices in the voucher register, beginning with voucher no. 5139. Then draw double lines to separate the vouchers of October from those of November. Record the total of the two vouchers as a balance in the Vouchers Payable account.
2. Record the transactions for November in the voucher register, the check register, and the general journal.
3. Total and rule the voucher register and the check register.
4. Post the amounts from the registers and the general journal to the Vouchers Payable account.
5. Prepare a schedule of Vouchers Payable. Compare this total with the balance of the Vouchers Payable account.

Problem Set B

Problem 21-1B   The Westerman Company, which uses a voucher system, issued the following vouchers during February that were unpaid on March 1.

Voucher No.	Company	For	Date of Voucher	Amount
716	Robbins and Company	Merchandise	Feb. 24	$1,550.00
719	Stevens and Turner	Merchandise	Feb. 28	2,400.00
				$3,950.00

The Westerman Company made the following transactions during March.

Mar. 1 Issued voucher no. 721 in favor of Grangeville Realty Company for March rent, $740.

1 Issued check no. 926 in payment of voucher no. 721, $740.

2 Bought merchandise on account from Drexel Manufacturing Company; terms 2/10, n/30; $1,900. Issued voucher no. 722. (Invoices are recorded for the gross amount.)

3 Issued check no. 927 in payment of voucher no. 716, $1,534.50 ($1,550.00 less 1 percent cash discount).

7 Issued voucher no. 723 in favor of National Telephone Company for telephone bill, $72.

7 Issued check no. 928 in payment of voucher no. 723.

9 Issued check no. 929 in payment of voucher no. 719, $2,352 ($2,400 less 2 percent cash discount).

11 Issued check no. 930 in payment of voucher no. 722, less the cash discount.

14 Bought merchandise on account from Great Lakes Products Company; terms 2/10, EOM; $3,420. Issued voucher no. 724.

23 Issued voucher no. 725 for note payable previously recorded in the general journal: principal, $2,000, plus interest of $24. The note is payable to the First National Bank.

23 Paid voucher no. 725 by issuing check no. 931.

23 Issued check no. 932 in payment of voucher no. 724 less the cash discount.

31 Issued voucher no. 726 for Wages Payable, $1,950, in favor of the payroll bank account. (Assume that the payroll entry was previously recorded in the general journal.)

31 Paid voucher no. 726 by issuing check no. 933.

Instructions

1. Under the date of the original purchase, enter the unpaid invoices in the voucher register, beginning with voucher no. 716. Then draw double lines across all columns to separate the vouchers of February from those of March.

2. Record the transactions for March in the voucher register at the gross amount. Also record the appropriate transactions in the check register.

Problem 21-2B The J. R. Mitchell Company, which uses a voucher system, has the following unpaid vouchers on April 30.

Voucher No.	Company	For	Date of Invoice	Amount
7219	Owens and Porter	Merchandise	Apr. 22	$ 5,840.00
7222	Stanton Supply Company	Store Equipment	Apr. 24	2,272.50
7223	Feldman and Company	Merchandise	Apr. 27	3,200.00
				$11,312.50

The J. R. Mitchell Company made the following transactions during May.

May 1 Issued voucher no. 7226 in favor of Security Insurance Company as a one-year premium on a fire insurance policy, $216.

1 Paid voucher no. 7219 by issuing check no. 9626, $5,723.20 ($5,840.00 less 2 percent cash discount).

3 Issued check no. 9627 in payment of voucher no. 7226.

5 Issued voucher no. 7227 in favor of Eller Motor Freight for transportation charges on merchandise purchases, $42.

5 Paid voucher no. 7227 by issuing check no. 9628.

6 Issued check no. 9629 in payment of voucher no. 7223, $3,136 ($3,200 less 2 percent cash discount).

10 Established a Petty Cash Fund of $120. Issued voucher no. 7228.

10 Paid voucher no. 7228 by issuing check no. 9630.

12 Issued voucher no. 7229 in favor of Randolph and Womack for the purchase of merchandise; terms 2/10, n/30; $5,120.

14 Bought office stationery from Storley Envelope Company, terms n/30, $620. Issued voucher no. 7230.

16 Received credit memorandum for $520 from Randolph and Womack for merchandise returned to them, credit memorandum no. 719.

19 Issued voucher no. 7231 in favor of Aragon County for six months' property taxes, $900.

19 Paid voucher no. 7231 by issuing check no. 9631.

21 Issued check no. 9632 in payment of voucher no. 7229, $4,508 ($5,120 less $520 return, less cash discount).

24 Bought merchandise on account from Owens and Porter; terms 2/10, n/30; $4,816. Issued voucher no. 7232.

24 Paid voucher no. 7222 by issuing check no. 9633.

27 Received credit memorandum for $472 from Owens and Porter for damaged merchandise, credit memorandum no. 1176.

31 Issued voucher no. 7233 to reimburse Petty Cash Fund. The charges were as follows:

Store Supplies	$42.00
Office Supplies	37.46
J. R. Mitchell, Drawing	20.00
Miscellaneous Expense	12.15

May 31 Issued check no. 9634 in payment of voucher no. 7233.

31 Issued voucher no. 7234 for Wages Payable, $3,860, in favor of payroll bank account. (Assume that the payroll entry was previously recorded in the general journal.)

31 Paid voucher no. 7234 by issuing check no. 9635, payable to payroll bank account.

Instructions

1. Under the date of the original purchase, enter the unpaid invoices in the voucher register, beginning with voucher no. 7219. Then draw double lines across all columns to separate the vouchers of April from those of May.
2. Enter the transactions for May in the voucher register at the gross amount. Also record the appropriate transactions in the check register and general journal.
3. Total and rule the voucher register and check register for the transactions recorded for May.

Problem 21-3B The Puckett Company uses a voucher system to record invoices at the gross amount. During August of this year it completed the following transactions affecting Vouchers Payable.

Aug. 1 Issued voucher no. 1079 in favor of Townsend Company for the purchase of merchandise having an invoice price of $2,600, terms 30 days.

4 Prepared voucher no. 1080 for $650, voucher no. 1081 for $650, and voucher no. 1082 for $650. The Puckett Company incurred this debt because it bought an electronic calculator from Reed Office Supply, with terms of $650 cash on delivery, $650 in 30 days, and $650 in 60 days. (Use three lines.)

4 Issued check no. 1426 in payment of voucher no. 1080.

7 Issued voucher no. 1083 in favor of Rockford Supply Company for store supplies, terms n/30; $162.

9 Prepared voucher no. 1084 in favor of Wonderlich Products Company for the purchase of merchandise having an invoice price of $4,000 with a 25 percent trade discount (record voucher for $3,000); terms 2/10, n/30.

11 Prepared voucher no. 1085 in favor of Jankowski Real Estate for rent for the month, $950.

11 Issued check no. 1427 in payment of voucher no. 1085.

14 Issued voucher no. 1086 in favor of Acme Transportation Company for freight charges on merchandise purchased, $56.

14 Prepared check no. 1428 in payment of voucher no. 1086.

15 Canceled voucher no. 1079 due to the fact that the invoice is to be paid in two installments, as follows: voucher no. 1087 for $1,300,

Aug.   payable September 1, and voucher no. 1088, payable September 15, $1,300. Issued vouchers no. 1087 and no. 1088.

16 Received a credit memorandum from Wonderlich Products Company for merchandise returned, $120, credit memo no. 218.

17 Issued check no. 1429 in payment of voucher no. 1084, $2,822.40 ($3,000.00, less $120 return, less cash discount).

22 Issued voucher no. 1089 in favor of Universal Telephone Company for telephone bill, $71.42.

22 Prepared check no. 1430 in payment of voucher no. 1089.

31 Prepared voucher no. 1090 for Wages Payable, $1,960, in favor of a payroll bank account. (Assume that the payroll entry was recorded previously in the general journal.)

31 Issued check no. 1431 in payment of voucher no. 1090.

31 Issued voucher no. 1091 in favor of T. C. Puckett, the owner, for a personal withdrawal, $980.

31 Prepared check no. 1432 in payment of voucher no. 1091.

Instructions

1. Record the transactions for August in the voucher register, the check register, and the general journal.
2. Total and rule the voucher register and the check register.
3. Post the amounts from the registers and the general journal to the Vouchers Payable account.
4. Prepare a schedule of vouchers payable. Compare this total with the balance of the Vouchers Payable account.

Problem 21-4B   The Sara Montgomery Company, which uses a voucher system, has the following unpaid vouchers on September 30. The firm records invoices at the net amount.

Voucher No.	Company	For	Date of Invoice	Amount
4993	Roberts and Eaton	Store Equipment	Aug. 26	$4,500.00
4998	Seton Equipment Company	Office Equipment	Aug. 28	5,270.00
				$9,770.00

The company made the following transactions during September.

Sep.   1 Issued voucher no. 5003 in favor of Consolidated Power and Light for electric bill, $116.

1 Paid voucher no. 5003 by issuing check no. 6815.

3 Canceled voucher no. 4993 because the invoice is to be paid in three installments, as follows: voucher no. 5004, payable September 15, $1,500; voucher no. 5005, payable October 1, $1,500; and voucher no. 5006, payable October 15, $1,500.

4 Bought merchandise on account from Snelling Products Company

Sep.   for $5,400; terms 2/10, n/30. Issued voucher no. 5007 (record invoice at $5,292, using the net amount).

7 S. Montgomery, the owner, withdrew $640 for personal use. Issued voucher no. 5008.

8 Prepared check no. 6816 in payment of voucher no. 5008.

9 Seton Equipment Company agreed to accept a 60-day, 8 percent note, dated September 9. Accordingly, canceled voucher no. 4998.

13 Issued check no. 6817 in payment of voucher no. 5007.

15 Prepared check no. 6818 in payment of voucher no. 5004.

15 Prepared voucher no. 5009 for $490 to P. G. Perigo for sales commissions.

15 Issued check no. 6819 in payment of voucher no. 5009.

20 Bought merchandise on account from R. D. Trager Company; terms 1/10, EOM; $6,400. Issued voucher no. 5010 (record the invoice as $6,336).

22 Issued voucher no. 5011 in favor of Western Express Company for freight bill on the purchase from R. D. Trager Company, $56.

24 Discovered an error in the computations on the invoice from R. D. Trager Company, reducing the amount due by $240. Canceled voucher no. 5010; issued voucher no. 5012 for $6,098.40.

27 Prepared voucher no. 5013, $374, in favor of Security Savings and Loan for mortgage payment: principal, $180; interest, $194.

28 Issued check no. 6820 in payment of voucher no. 5013.

30 Prepared voucher no. 5014 for Wages Payable, $2,082, in favor of a payroll bank account. (Assume that the payroll entry was previously recorded in the general journal.)

30 Paid voucher no. 5014 by issuing check no. 6821.

Instructions

1. Under the date of the original purchase, enter the unpaid invoices in the voucher register, beginning with voucher no. 4993. Then draw double lines to separate the vouchers of August from those of September. Record the total of the two vouchers as a balance in the Vouchers Payable account.
2. Record the transactions for September in the voucher register, the check register, and the general journal.
3. Total and rule the voucher register and the check register.
4. Post the amounts from the registers and the general journal to the Vouchers Payable account.
5. Prepare a schedule of Vouchers Payable. Compare the total with the balance of the Vouchers Payable account.

22 Accounting for Partnerships

Learning Objectives

After you have completed this chapter, you will be able to do the following:

1. Prepare a section of an income statement relating to division of net income for a partnership involving division of income on the basis of fractional shares, on the basis of ratio of capital investments, and on the basis of salary and interest allowances.

2. Journalize the closing entries for a partnership.

3. Prepare a statement of owners' equity for a partnership.

4. Journalize entries involving the sale of a partnership interest or withdrawal of a partner.

5. Journalize entries pertaining to the liquidation of a partnership involving the immediate sale of the assets for cash.

Up to this time, we have been dealing entirely with sole proprietorships. In this chapter and the ones that follow, we shall deal with two other forms of business organizations: partnerships and corporations. In the professions and in firms that stress personal service, partnerships are widely used. Each professional practitioner can maintain her or his own clientele, yet share with colleagues the expenses of operating an office or clinic. Partnerships are also popular in manufacturing and trade because they afford a means of combining the capital and abilities of two or more persons.

CHARACTERISTICS OF A PARTNERSHIP

A **partnership,** as defined by the Uniform Partnership Act, is an association of two or more persons to carry on, as co-owners, a business for profit. It is a voluntary association, entered into by the parties without compulsion. Certain features of a partnership affect just the partners; other features affect the partners as well as others who are not members of the partnership. Let us examine some of these features.

Co-ownership of Partnership Property

All partners are co-owners of the assets of the partnership. For example, Deats and Mullin formed a 50-50 partnership to run a fuel oil business. The partnership owns two tank trucks of equal value. According to the **co-ownership** concept, each partner owns half of each truck, as well as half of the other assets of the firm.

Limited Life

A partnership may be ended by the death or withdrawal of any partner. Other factors that may bring about the dissolution of a partnership include the bankruptcy or incapacity of a partner, the expiration of the period of time specified in the partnership agreement, or the completion of the project for which the partnership was formed.

Unlimited Liability

Each partner is personally liable to creditors for all the debts the partnership incurs during his or her membership in the firm. When a new partner joins an existing firm, he or she may or may not assume liability for debts incurred by the firm prior to admission. When a partner withdraws from a firm, he or she must give adequate public notice of withdrawal, or he or she may be held liable for debts the partnership incurs after withdrawal.

Mutual Agency

Each partner can enter into binding contracts in the name of the firm for the purchase or sale of goods or services within the normal scope of the firm's business. When the partners agree among themselves to limit the right of any partner to enter into certain contracts in the name of the firm, this agreement is not binding on outsiders who are unaware of its existence.

ADVANTAGES OF A PARTNERSHIP

Here are some advantages of a partnership:

1. Partnerships offer the opportunity to pool the abilities and capital of two or more persons.
2. It is easy to form a partnership, the only requirement being an agreement or mutual understanding by the partners.
3. Legal restrictions are minimal. Although a partnership must have a legal purpose, there are no other limitations on types of business activities.
4. Federal income taxes are not levied against a partnership as an entity, although a partnership must file an information return (Form 1065), containing an income statement, balance sheet, and report of the distributive shares of income (the shares of the year's net income allocated to each partner). A partner has to pay taxes on his or her share of the net income, whether this share is taken out of the business or not.

DISADVANTAGES OF A PARTNERSHIP

Here are some disadvantages of a partnership:

1. **General partners** (those who actively and publicly participate in transactions of the firm) have unlimited liability.
2. A partnership has limited life.
3. The actions of one partner are binding on the other partners; this relationship is known as **mutual agency.**

4. The raising of investment capital depends entirely on the partners themselves.
5. It is hard to transfer a partial or entire partnership interest to another person, as the transfer must be agreed to by all partners.

PARTNERSHIP AGREEMENTS

Although generally a partnership may be formed on the basis of an oral understanding, it is much better to have the partnership agreement based on a written contract. Although there is no standard form of partnership agreement, the following provisions are usually included.

- Effective date of the agreement
- Names and addresses of the partners
- Name, location, and nature of the business
- Duration of the agreement
- Investment of each partner
- Withdrawals to be allowed each partner
- Procedure for sharing profits and losses
- Provision for division of assets upon dissolution

Let us now look at a typical partnership agreement (Figure 22-1).

ACCOUNTING ENTRIES FOR PARTNERSHIPS

The only difference between accounting for a sole proprietorship and accounting for partnerships is in the owners' equity accounts. Otherwise, the accountant uses the same types of assets, liabilities, revenues, and expenses that we have discussed before. But because there is more than one owner, it is necessary to have one capital account and one drawing account for each partner. As in the case of sole proprietorships, the capital accounts are involved only when there is a change in investments or when the Income Summary account and the Drawing accounts are closed.

Recording Investments

The accountant makes a separate entry for the investment of each partner. All assets contributed by a given partner are debited to the appropriate asset accounts. If the partnership assumes liabilities, the accountant credits the proper liability accounts, and credits the partner's capital account for the net amount.

Let's take a case of recording initial investments in a partnership: Frances A. Noble and Mary C. Reynolds decide to form a partnership for the

Figure 22-1

PARTNERSHIP AGREEMENT

C. L. Reitz of San Diego, California, and J. O. Stoddard of the same city and state agree as follows:

Recitals of Fact: The parties have this day formed a partnership for the purpose of engaging in and conducting a retail women's wear business in the city of San Diego under the following stipulations, which are a part of this contract:

First: The partnership is to continue for a term of 20 years from January 1 of this year.

Second: The business is to be conducted under the firm name of Hi Fashion Shop, at 1424 West Sixth Street, San Diego, California.

Third: The investments are as follows: C. L. Reitz, cash, $50,000; J. O. Stoddard, cash, $50,000. These invested assets are partnership property in which the equity of each partner is the same.

Fourth: Each partner is to devote his or her entire time and attention to the business and to engage in no other business enterprise without the written consent of the other partner.

Fifth: During the operation of this partnership, neither partner is to become surety or bondsman for anyone without the written consent of the other partner.

Sixth: Each partner is to receive a salary of $12,000 a year, payable $500 in cash on the fifteenth and $500 on the last business day of each month. At the end of each annual fiscal period, the net income or the net loss shown by the income statement, after the salaries of the two partners have been allowed, is to be shared as follows: C. L. Reitz, 50 percent: J. O. Stoddard, 50 percent.

Seventh: Neither partner is to withdraw assets in excess of his or her salary, any part of the assets invested, or assets in anticipation of net income to be earned, without the written consent of the other partner.

Eighth: In the case of the death or the legal disability of either partner, the other partner is to continue the operations of the business until the close of the annual fiscal period on the following December 31. At that time the continuing partner is to be given an option to buy the interest of the deceased or incapacitated partner at the value of the deceased or incapacitated partner's proprietary interest as determined by the agreement of the continuing partner and the legal representative of the deceased or incapacitated partner. In the event they are unable to agree, then the determination of such value shall be submitted to arbitration in accordance with the rules of the American Arbitration Association. It is agreed that this purchase price is to be paid one half in cash and the balance in four equal installments payable quarterly.

Ninth: At the conclusion of this contract, unless it is mutually agreed to continue the operation of the business under a new contract, the assets of the partnership, after the liabilities are paid, are to be divided in proportion to the net credit to each partner's capital account on that date.

Dated December 28, 19– C. L. Reitz (Seal)

J. O. Stoddard (Seal)

operation of a jewelry store. Noble presently owns and operates Noble's Jewelry Store; she is contributing the assets and liabilities of her store to the new firm. Reynolds's investment is $20,000 in cash; the following is the entry to record this investment.

		DATE		DESCRIPTION	POST. REF.	DEBIT	CREDIT	
				GENERAL JOURNAL			PAGE 1	
1	19– Feb.	2		Cash		20 0 0 0 00		1
2				Mary C. Reynolds, Capital			20 0 0 0 00	2
3				To record the original investment				3
4				of Mary C. Reynolds.				4
5								5

Both partners have to agree on the monetary amounts at which Noble's noncash assets are to be recorded. Assume that Noble's Jewelry Store has the following account balances.

Cash	$ 2,900
Accounts Receivable	18,000
Allowance for Doubtful Accounts	200
Merchandise Inventory	20,400
Equipment	16,000
Accumulated Depreciation, Equipment	4,500
Notes Payable	1,600
Accounts Payable	8,400

Furthermore, $400 of the Accounts Receivable have been definitely ascertained to be uncollectible; the $400 should not be recorded on the books of the new partnership. Of the remaining $17,600 of Accounts Receivable, there is some doubt as to the collectibility of $500. The present appraised value of Noble's merchandise is $21,000. The present appraised value of Noble's equipment is $9,000. Therefore, the accountant records Noble's investment as follows.

					DEBIT	CREDIT	
1	19– Feb.	2		Cash	2 9 0 0 00		1
2				Accounts Receivable	17 6 0 0 00		2
3				Merchandise Inventory	21 0 0 0 00		3
4				Equipment	9 0 0 0 00		4
5				Allowance for Doubtful Accounts		5 0 0 00	5
6				Notes Payable		1 6 0 0 00	6
7				Accounts Payable		8 4 0 0 00	7
8				Frances A. Noble, Capital		40 0 0 0 00	8
9				To record the original investment			9
10				of Frances A. Noble.			10
11							11

The accountant debits Accounts Receivable for the face amount of the accounts taken over by the new partnership and credits Allowance for Doubtful Accounts for the amount estimated to be uncollectible. Any definitely uncollectible customer accounts are excluded from those being taken over by the new business.

The accountant debits the new firm's Merchandise Inventory and Equipment accounts for the amount of their appraised present values. The accumulated depreciation is not recorded, because the appraised value represents the new book value for the partnership.

Additional Investments

Now let's say that eight months have gone by and the new partnership needs more cash. On October 1, the partners each invest an additional $4,000. The entry is as follows.

GENERAL JOURNAL
PAGE __28__

	DATE		DESCRIPTION	POST. REF.	DEBIT	CREDIT	
1	19– Oct.	1	Cash		8 0 0 0 00		1
2			Frances A. Noble, Capital			4 0 0 0 00	2
3			Mary C. Reynolds, Capital			4 0 0 0 00	3
4			To record additional investments.				4
5							5
6							6
7							7
8							8

At the end of the year, before the books are closed, the capital accounts of the partners appear as shown here.

GENERAL LEDGER

ACCOUNT _Frances A. Noble, Capital_   ACCOUNT NO. __301__

	DATE	ITEM	POST. REF.	DEBIT	CREDIT	BALANCE DEBIT	BALANCE CREDIT	
1	19– Feb. 2		J1		40 0 0 0 00		40 0 0 0 00	1
2	Oct. 1		J28		4 0 0 0 00		44 0 0 0 00	2
3								3
4								4
5								5
6								6

GENERAL LEDGER

ACCOUNT _Mary C. Reynolds, Capital_   ACCOUNT NO. _303_

	DATE	ITEM	POST. REF.	DEBIT	CREDIT	BALANCE DEBIT	BALANCE CREDIT	
1	19– Feb. 2		J1		20 0 0 0 00		20 0 0 0 00	1
2	Oct. 1		J28		4 0 0 0 00		24 0 0 0 00	2
3								3

Drawing Accounts

Drawing accounts of partners serve the same purpose as the Drawing account of the owner of a sole proprietorship. Debits to the Drawing accounts originate through transactions like those listed below and illustrated in Figure 22-2.

- Withdrawal of cash by a partner, $200.
- Withdrawal of merchandise by a partner, $148.

Figure 22-2

	DATE	DESCRIPTION	POST. REF.	DEBIT	CREDIT	
1	19– Mar. 17	Frances A. Noble, Drawing		2 0 0 00		1
2		Cash			2 0 0 00	2
3		To record a cash withdrawal.				3

	DATE	DESCRIPTION	POST. REF.	DEBIT	CREDIT	
5	May 4	Mary C. Reynolds, Drawing		1 4 8 00		5
6		Purchases			1 4 8 00	6
7		To record a merchandise				7
8		withdrawal at cost.				8
9						9

DIVISION OF NET INCOME OR NET LOSS

Recall that the closing entries for a sole proprietorship require the following steps.

1. Close the revenue accounts into Income Summary.
2. Close the expense accounts into Income Summary (the expense accounts do not include any payments to partners).

3. Close Income Summary into the Capital account by the amount of the net income or loss.
4. Close the Drawing account into the Capital account.

Objective 1

Prepare a section of an income statement relating to division of net income for a partnership.

The only differences between closing entries for a partnership and those for a sole proprietorship pertain to steps 3 and 4. Instead of a single capital account and a single drawing account, in a partnership there are as many accounts of each type as there are partners. Income Summary is closed into the capital accounts by the amount of the net income or loss, and the drawing accounts are closed into the respective capital accounts.

Let's look at step 3, which deals with the division of net income. The partnership agreement should specify the arrangement for the division of net income. However, suppose the partnership agreement fails to do this. Then, from a legal standpoint, the partners should share any net income or loss equally. This is true regardless of differences in amounts invested, in special skills provided, or in time devoted to the business. The share of net income (or net loss) allocated to each partner is known as his or her **distributive share.**

Partners may use any one of a number of alternative methods of sharing partnership earnings, or they may use a combination of methods. The variety of methods reflects the different value of the services or investments contributed by individual partners. We shall discuss four methods for sharing partnership earnings:

1. Division of income on a fractional-share basis
2. Division of income based on the ratio of capital investments
3. Division of income based on salary allowances
4. Division of income based on interest allowances

We shall look at two examples of each.

In our first example, the partnership of Dunn and Easely has a net income of $48,000. In the second, the partnership of Dunn and Easely has a net *loss* of $2,000. We shall use the same balances in the capital and drawing accounts for each example, and consider that each method used for dividing net income represents a separate partnership agreement.

The balances of the capital accounts represent the partners' individual investments at the beginning of the year. The balances of the drawing accounts represent the total personal withdrawals during the year. These are shown by T accounts as follows.

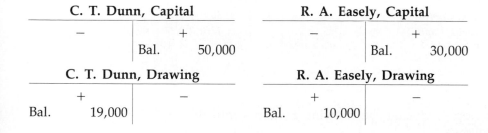

DIVISION OF INCOME ON A FRACTIONAL-SHARE BASIS

The simplest way to divide net income or loss is to allot each partner a stated fraction of the total. One can establish the size of the fraction by taking into consideration (1) the amount of investment of each partner, and (2) the value of services rendered by each partner. Assume that the partnership agreement stipulates that profits and losses are to be divided this way: three-fourths for Dunn and one-fourth for Easely.

The accountant may present a report of the division of net income as a separate statement or record it on the income statement, immediately below Net Income.

Net Income of $48,000 If the accountant adopts the latter procedure, the division of net income appears as follows.

Objective 2

Journalize the closing entries for a partnership.

Dunn and Easely			
Income Statement			
For year ended December 31, 19–			

Revenue from Sales:			

Net Income			$48 0 0 0 00
Division of Net Income:	*C. T. Dunn*	*R. A. Easely*	*Total*
Fractional Share	$36 0 0 0 00	$12 0 0 0 00	$48 0 0 0 00

The division of net income is recorded as a closing entry in step 3 of the closing procedure whether or not the partner has withdrawn his or her share. The entry looks like this.

	DATE	DESCRIPTION	POST. REF.	DEBIT	CREDIT	
1		*Closing Entry*				1
2	19– Dec. 31	Income Summary		48 0 0 0 00		2
3		C. T. Dunn, Capital			36 0 0 0 00	3
4		R. A. Easely, Capital			12 0 0 0 00	4
5						5
6						6

The entries for step 4, closing the drawing accounts into the capital accounts, are as follows.

	DATE		DESCRIPTION	POST. REF.	DEBIT	CREDIT	
1			*Closing Entries*				1
2	19– Dec.	31	*C. T. Dunn, Capital*		19 0 0 0 00		2
3			*C. T. Dunn, Drawing*			19 0 0 0 00	3
4							4
5		31	*R. A. Easely, Capital*		10 0 0 0 00		5
6			*R. A. Easely, Drawing*			10 0 0 0 00	6
7							7

Now let's see what these entries look like by means of T accounts, with steps 3 and 4 labeled.

Income Summary

(3) Closing	48,000	Bal.	48,000

C. T. Dunn, Capital

–		+	
(4)	19,000	Bal.	50,000
		(3)	36,000

R. A. Easely, Capital

–		+	
(4)	10,000	Bal.	30,000
		(3)	12,000

C. T. Dunn, Drawing

+		–	
Bal.	19,000	(4) Closing	19,000

R. A. Easely, Drawing

+		–	
Bal.	10,000	(4) Closing	10,000

Note that step 4 is the same for partnerships as for sole proprietorships.

Net Loss of $2,000 The lower portion of the following income state-
ment reflects the net loss. (The parentheses around the totals indicate that
the figures are minus numbers.)

Revenue from Sales:				

	C. T. Dunn	R. A. Easely	Total	
Net Loss				$(2 0 0 0 00)
Division of Net Loss:				
Fractional Share	$(1 5 0 0 00)	$(5 0 0 00)	$(2 0 0 0 00)	

The closing entries and posting to the ledger accounts are shown in Figure 22-3 and the T accounts that follow.

Figure 22-3

	DATE		DESCRIPTION	POST. REF.	DEBIT	CREDIT	
1			*Closing Entries*				1
2	19–Dec.	31	*C. T. Dunn, Capital*		1 5 0 0 00		2
3			*R. A. Easely, Capital*		5 0 0 00		3
4			*Income Summary*			2 0 0 0 00	4
5							5
6		31	*C. T. Dunn, Capital*		19 0 0 0 00		6
7			*C. T. Dunn, Drawing*			19 0 0 0 00	7
8							8
9		31	*R. A. Easely, Capital*		10 0 0 0 00		9
10			*R. A. Easely, Drawing*			10 0 0 0 00	10
11							11

Income Summary

Bal.	2,000	(3) Closing	2,000

C. T. Dunn, Capital

–		+	
(3)	1,500	Bal.	50,000
(4)	19,000		

R. A. Easely, Capital

–		+	
(3)	500	Bal.	30,000
(4)	10,000		

C. T. Dunn, Drawing

+		–	
Bal.	19,000	(4) Closing	19,000

R. A. Easely, Drawing

+		–	
Bal.	10,000	(4) Closing	10,000

When partners share net income on a fractional basis, this basis is often expressed as a ratio. We can express Dunn's three-fourths and Easely's one-fourth as a 3:1 (3-to-1) ratio.

When you list the division of net income as a ratio and want to turn the ratio into a fraction, do it this way. First add the figures; then use the total as the denominator of the fraction:

3:1   (3 + 1 = 4)   ¾ and ¼

or (in the case of three partners):

5:3:1   (5 + 3 + 1 = 9)   ⁵⁄₉ and ³⁄₉ and ¹⁄₉

or (in the case of four partners):

3:2:1:1 $(3 + 2 + 1 + 1 = 7)$ ³⁄₇ and ²⁄₇ and ½⁷ and ½⁷

Division of Income Based on Ratio of Capital Investments

Allocating earnings to partners on the basis of the amounts of their investment often works well for enterprises whose earnings are closely related to the amount of money invested, such as real estate ventures, cattle feeding operations, and the like. Suppose that Dunn and Easely have agreed to share earnings or losses according to the ratio of their investments at the beginning of the year. Let's say that Dunn put in $50,000 and Easely $30,000. One can calculate their respective shares as follows.

Dunn	$50,000
Easely	30,000
Total	$80,000

$$\text{Dunn's share} = \frac{\$50,000}{\$80,000} = \frac{5}{8} \text{ or .625 (62.5\%)}$$

$$\text{Easely's share} = \frac{\$30,000}{\$80,000} = \frac{3}{8} \text{ or .375 (37.5\%)}$$

Net Income of $48,000   When the partnership has a net income of $48,000, the accountant determines the distribution like this.

Dunn's share of earnings $48,000 × ⅝ (or $48,000 × .625) = $30,000
Easely's share of earnings $48,000 × ⅜ (or $48,000 × .375) − $18,000

The section of the income statement showing the division of net income looks like this.

Revenue from Sales:				

	C. T. Dunn	R. A. Easely	Total	
Net Income				$48 0 0 0 00
Division of Net Income:	C. T. Dunn	R. A. Easely	Total	
Capital investment ratio	$30 0 0 0 00	$18 0 0 0 00	$48 0 0 0 00	

The accompanying closing entries are as follows.

	DATE		DESCRIPTION	POST. REF.	DEBIT	CREDIT	
1			*Closing Entries*				1
2	19– Dec.	31	*Income Summary*		48 0 0 0 00		2
3			*C. T. Dunn, Capital*			30 0 0 0 00	3
4			*R. A. Easely, Capital*			18 0 0 0 00	4
5							5
6		31	*C. T. Dunn, Capital*		19 0 0 0 00		6
7			*C. T. Dunn, Drawing*			19 0 0 0 00	7
8							8
9		31	*R. A. Easely, Capital*		10 0 0 0 00		9
10			*R. A. Easely, Drawing*			10 0 0 0 00	10
11							11
12							12
13							13
14							14
15							15
16							16
17							17

Net Loss of $2,000   When the partnership has a net loss of $2,000, the accountant calculates the sharing of the loss as follows.

Dunn's share of the loss $2,000 \times \frac{5}{8}$ (or $2,000 \times .625) = $1,250
Easely's share of the loss $2,000 \times \frac{3}{8}$ (or $2,000 \times .375) = $750

The section of the income statement showing the division of net loss and the accompanying closing entries looks like this.

Revenue from Sales:			

	C. T. Dunn	R. A. Easely	Total
Net Loss			$(2 0 0 0 00)
Division of Net Loss:			
Capital investment ratio	$(1 2 5 0 00)	$(7 5 0 00)	$(2 0 0 0 00)

	DATE		DESCRIPTION	POST. REF.	DEBIT	CREDIT	
1			*Closing Entries*				1
2	19– Dec.	31	C. T. Dunn, Capital		1 2 5 0 00		2
3			R. A. Easely, Capital		7 5 0 00		3
4			Income Summary			2 0 0 0 00	4
5							5
6		31	C. T. Dunn, Capital		19 0 0 0 00		6
7			C. T. Dunn, Drawing			19 0 0 0 00	7
8							8
9		31	R. A. Easely, Capital		10 0 0 0 00		9
10			R. A. Easely, Drawing			10 0 0 0 00	10
11							11

Note that the entries for step 4—closing the drawing accounts into the capital accounts—are always the same, regardless of whether the firm finishes the year with a net income or a net loss.

Division of Income Based on Salary Allowances

Salary allowances are purely allocations of net income. They are used as a means of recognizing and rewarding differences in ability and in the amount of time devoted to the business. **Salary allowances are different from payments to the partners, which are recorded in the drawing accounts.** They are also different from remuneration to employees, which is recorded as Salaries or Wages Expense. They may be thought of as guaranteed amounts determined without regard to the income of the partnership.

Suppose that Dunn and Easely's partnership agreement provides for yearly salaries of $12,000 and $8,000, respectively, with the remainder of the net income to be divided equally. (It would also be possible to divide the remainder on the basis of the ratio of investments or any other ratio agreed on by the partners.)

Net Income of $48,000   The Division of Net Income section of the income statement when there is a net income of $48,000 is as follows.

Revenue from Sales:					

	C. T. Dunn	R. A. Easely	Total
Net Income			$48 0 0 0 00
Division of Net Income:	*C. T. Dunn*	*R. A. Easely*	*Total*
Salary allowances	$12 0 0 0 00	$ 8 0 0 0 00	$20 0 0 0 00
Remainder allocated equally	14 0 0 0 00	14 0 0 0 00	28 0 0 0 00
Net Income	$26 0 0 0 00	$22 0 0 0 00	$48 0 0 0 00

The firm's accountant determines the allocation of the remainder as follows.

Net income	$48,000
Less amount allocated as salaries ($12,000 + $8,000)	20,000
Remainder	$28,000

$$\text{Remainder} \div 2 = \frac{\$28,000}{2} = \$14,000$$

Look at the closing entries.

	DATE		DESCRIPTION	POST. REF.	DEBIT	CREDIT	
1			*Closing Entries*				1
2	19– Dec.	31	*Income Summary*		48 0 0 0 00		2
3			*C. T. Dunn, Capital*			26 0 0 0 00	3
4			*R. A. Easely, Capital*			22 0 0 0 00	4
5							5
6		31	*C. T. Dunn, Capital*		19 0 0 0 00		6
7			*C. T. Dunn, Drawing*			19 0 0 0 00	7
8							8
9		31	*R. A. Easely, Capital*		10 0 0 0 00		9
10			*R. A. Easely, Drawing*			10 0 0 0 00	10
11							11
12							12
13							13
14							14
15							15

Net Loss of $2,000   When salary allowances are stipulated in the partnership agreement, they must be allocated (not necessarily paid) regardless of whether there is enough net income to take care of them.

The accountant determines the remainder as follows.

Net Loss	$ 2,000
Add amount allocated as salaries ($12,000 + $8,000)	20,000
Remainder	($22,000)

$$\text{Remainder} \div 2 = \frac{(\$22,000)}{2} = (\$11,000)$$

The income statements and closing entries appear as follows.

Revenue from Sales:						

		C. T. Dunn	R. A. Easely	Total
Net Loss				$ (2 0 0 0 00)
Division of Net Loss:		C. T. Dunn	R. A. Easely	Total
Salary allowances		$12 0 0 0 00	$ 8 0 0 0 00	$20 0 0 0 00
Excess of allowances over income allocated equally		(11 0 0 0 00)	(11 0 0 0 00)	(22 0 0 0 00)
Net Loss		$ 1 0 0 0 00	$(3 0 0 0 00)	$ (2 0 0 0 00)

	DATE	DESCRIPTION	POST. REF.	DEBIT	CREDIT	
1		Closing Entries				1
2	19– Dec. 31	R. A. Easely, Capital		3 0 0 0 00		2
3		Income Summary			2 0 0 0 00	3
4		C. T. Dunn, Capital			1 0 0 0 00	4
5						5
6	31	C. T. Dunn, Capital		19 0 0 0 00		6
7		C. T. Dunn, Drawing			19 0 0 0 00	7
8						8
9	31	R. A. Easely, Capital		10 0 0 0 00		9
10		R. A. Easely, Drawing			10 0 0 0 00	10
11						11

After posting, the owners' equity accounts look like this.

Income Summary

Bal.	2,000	(3) Closing	2,000

C. T. Dunn, Capital				R. A. Easely, Capital			
−		+		−		+	
(4)	19,000	Bal.	50,000	(3)	3,000	Bal.	30,000
		(3)	1,000	(4)	10,000		

C. T. Dunn, Drawing				R. A. Easely, Drawing			
+		−		+		−	
Bal.	19,000	(4) Closing	19,000	Bal.	10,000	(4) Closing	10,000

As a result of the $2,000 net loss for the year and the activity in the drawing accounts, Dunn's capital account decreased by $18,000 (credit $1,000 and debit $19,000); Easely's capital account decreased by $13,000 (debit $3,000 and debit $10,000).

Division of Income Based on Interest Allowances

Sometimes a partnership agreement stipulates an allowance for interest on the capital investment of the partners. This clause acts as an incentive for partners not only to leave their investments in the business but even to increase them. For example, suppose that Dunn and Easely, in addition to their salary allowances of $12,000 and $8,000, are allowed 8 percent interest on their capital balances at the beginning of the fiscal year, and the remainder is to be divided equally. Interest allowances, like salary allowances, are just allocations of net income.

Net Income of $48,000   The section of the income statement relating to the division of a $48,000 net income appears as follows.

	C. T. Dunn	R. A. Easely	Total
Revenue from Sales:			
Net Income			$48 0 0 0 00
Division of Net Income:			
Salary allowances	$12 0 0 0 00	$ 8 0 0 0 00	$20 0 0 0 00
Interest allowances	4 0 0 0 00	2 4 0 0 00	6 4 0 0 00
Remainder allocated equally	10 8 0 0 00	10 8 0 0 00	21 6 0 0 00
Net Income	$26 8 0 0 00	$21 2 0 0 00	$48 0 0 0 00

The accountant figures out the remainder in the following way.

Net Income		$48,000
Less:		
Amount allocated as salaries		
($12,000 + $8,000)	$20,000	
Amount allocated as interest		
($4,000 + $2,400)	6,400	26,400
Remainder		$21,600

$$\text{Remainder} \div 2 = \frac{\$21,600}{2} = \$10,800$$

And the closing entries look like this.

	DATE		DESCRIPTION	POST. REF.	DEBIT	CREDIT	
1			*Closing Entries*				1
2	19– Dec.	31	*Income Summary*		48 0 0 0 00		2
3			*C. T. Dunn, Capital*			26 8 0 0 00	3
4			*R. A. Easely, Capital*			21 2 0 0 00	4
5							5
6		31	*C. T. Dunn, Capital*		19 0 0 0 00		6
7			*C. T. Dunn, Drawing*			19 0 0 0 00	7
8							8
9		31	*R. A. Easely, Capital*		10 0 0 0 00		9
10			*R. A. Easely, Drawing*			10 0 0 0 00	10
11							11
12							12
13							13

Net Loss of $2,000   The accountant handles interest allowances the same way he or she handles salary allowances: Both must be allocated, whether or not there is enough net income to take care of them. The section of the income statement relating to the division of a $2,000 net loss appears as follows.

	C. T. Dunn	R. A. Easely	Total
Revenue from Sales:			
Net Loss			$ (2 0 0 0 00)
Division of Net Loss:	C. T. Dunn	R. A. Easely	Total
Salary allowances	$12 0 0 0 00	$ 8 0 0 0 00	$20 0 0 0 00
Interest allowances	4 0 0 0 00	2 4 0 0 00	6 4 0 0 00
Excess of allowances over income allocated equally	(14 2 0 0 00)	(14 2 0 0 00)	(28 4 0 0 00)
Net Loss	$ 1 8 0 0 00	$(3 8 0 0 00)	$ (2 0 0 0 00)

The accountant computes the remainder as follows.

Net Loss		$ 2,000
Add:		
Amount allocated as salaries		
($12,000 + $8,000)	$20,000	
Amount allocated as interest		
($4,000 + $2,400)	6,400	26,400
Remainder		($28,400)

$$\text{Remainder} \div 2 = \frac{(\$28,400)}{2} = (\$14,200)$$

And the closing entries look like this.

	DATE	DESCRIPTION	POST. REF.	DEBIT	CREDIT	
1		*Closing Entries*				1
2	19– Dec. 31	*R. A. Easely, Capital*		3 8 0 0 00		2
3		*Income Summary*			2 0 0 0 00	3
4		*C. T. Dunn, Capital*			1 8 0 0 00	4
5						5
6	31	*C. T. Dunn, Capital*		19 0 0 0 00		6
7		*C. T. Dunn, Drawing*			19 0 0 0 00	7
8						8
9	31	*R. A. Easely, Capital*		10 0 0 0 00		9
10		*R. A. Easely, Drawing*			10 0 0 0 00	10
11						11
12						12

After posting, the owner's equity accounts look like this.

Income Summary

Bal.	2,000	(3) Closing	2,000

C. T. Dunn, Capital

	−		+	
(4)	19,000	Bal.	50,000
		(3)	1,800

R. A. Easely, Capital

	−		+	
(3)	3,800	Bal.	30,000
(4)	10,000		

C. T. Dunn, Drawing

	+		−	
Bal.	19,000	(4) Closing	19,000

R. A. Easely, Drawing

	+		−	
Bal.	10,000	(4) Closing	10,000

FINANCIAL STATEMENTS FOR A PARTNERSHIP

We have already talked about how an income statement for a partnership looks with the section on Division of Net Income inserted immediately below Net Income.

Objective 3

Prepare a statement of owners' equity for a partnership.

Changes in the balances of the partners' capital accounts are recorded in the statement of owners' equity, which is just like a statement of owner's equity for a sole proprietorship, except that there is a separate column for each partner.

Dunn and Easely
Statement of Owners' Equity
For year ended December 31, 19–

	C. T. Dunn	R. A. Easely	Total
Capital, January 1, 19–	$50 0 0 0 00	$30 0 0 0 00	$ 80 0 0 0 00
Net Income for the year	26 8 0 0 00	21 2 0 0 00	48 0 0 0 00
Total	$76 8 0 0 00	$51 2 0 0 00	$128 0 0 0 00
Less withdrawals during the year	19 0 0 0 00	10 0 0 0 00	29 0 0 0 00
Capital, December 31, 19–	$57 8 0 0 00	$41 2 0 0 00	$ 99 0 0 0 00

When a partner makes any additional permanent investment after the beginning of the fiscal period, the accountant records this amount right below the beginning balances of the capital accounts.

Partners have to pay federal income taxes on the basis of each partner's distributive share (his or her share of net income) in the business. For example, C. T. Dunn's taxable income is $26,800, even though he withdrew only $19,000. He lists $26,800 on his personal income tax return. The Internal Revenue Code decrees that details of the distributive shares of each partner must be recorded on a U.S. Partnership Return of Income (Form 1065).

DISSOLUTION OF A PARTNERSHIP

As we said earlier in this chapter, one disadvantage of a partnership is its limited life. Any change in the personnel of the membership formally ends the partnership. Whenever a partnership dissolves, the main visible result is a change in the names listed in the partnership agreement and a change in the division of net income. However, the routine transactions of the business go on as usual. For example, suppose that a partnership originally consists of A, B, and C. Then C withdraws his or her investment from the firm, and a new partnership emerges: A and B. During the transition, business is carried on as usual. In other words, in a **dissolution,** the original partnership is dissolved by either the sale of one partner's interest in the firm to a new partner or the withdrawal of a partner, but the firm continues to operate as before.

Sale of a Partnership Interest

When a partner retires, he or she may sell his or her interest to a person outside the firm who is acceptable to the remaining partners. Let's say that at the end of a given year R. A. Easely has a capital balance of $31,760, and decides to sell his interest to P. E. Falkner for $40,000. The accountant makes the following entry to account for the transfer of ownership.

Objective 4

Journalize entries involving the sale of a partnership interest or withdrawal of a partner.

	DATE	DESCRIPTION	POST. REF.	DEBIT	CREDIT	
1		R. A. Easely, Capital		31 7 6 0 00		1
2		P. E. Falkner, Capital			31 7 6 0 00	2
3		To transfer Easely's equity in				3
4		the partnership to Falkner.				4
5						5
6						6
7						7
8						8

The difference between $40,000 and $31,760 represents a personal profit to *Easely,* not to the firm. There has been no change in the partnership's assets or liabilities, and consequently there is no change in the total owners' equity. However, if the firm is to continue, Dunn (the other original partner) must be willing to accept Falkner as a new partner.

Withdrawal of a Partner

The partnership agreement should outline a set procedure to be followed when one of the partners withdraws. Such a procedure usually entails an audit of the books and a revaluation of the partnership's assets to reflect current market values.

Partner Withdraws Book Value of His or Her Equity After Revaluation

Suppose that S. T. Hogan is retiring from the partnership of Boyd, Hogan, and Insell. The partnership agreement stipulates that net income and net loss shall be shared on an equal basis; it also provides for an audit and revaluation of assets in the event that a partner retires. Figure 22-4 shows the firm's balance sheet, immediately prior to the audit and revaluation.

At this point, an accountant (usually someone from an outside firm) audits the books and makes a fresh appraisal of the firm's assets. This

Figure 22-4

Boyd, Hogan, and Insell						
Balance Sheet						
September 30, 19–						

Assets				
Current Assets:				
Cash			$28 0 0 0 00	
Accounts Receivable	$8 0 0 0 00			
Less Allowance for Doubtful Accounts	5 0 0 00	7 5 0 0 00		
Merchandise Inventory		47 5 0 0 00		
Total Current Assets			$83 0 0 0 00	
Plant and Equipment:				
Equipment		$27 0 0 0 00		
Less Accumulated Depreciation		11 0 0 0 00	16 0 0 0 00	
Total Assets			$99 0 0 0 00	
Liabilities				
Accounts Payable			$ 7 0 0 0 00	
Owners' Equity				
R. L. Boyd, Capital		$46 0 0 0 00		
S. T. Hogan, Capital		24 0 0 0 00		
D. J. Insell, Capital		22 0 0 0 00		
Total Owners' Equity			92 0 0 0 00	
Total Liabilities and Owners' Equity			$99 0 0 0 00	

audit and appraisal indicate that Merchandise Inventory is undervalued by $9,800, that Allowances for Doubtful Accounts should be increased by $200, and that Equipment is overvalued by $2,400. The accountant allocates the net difference between debits and credits to the partners' capital accounts, according to their basis for sharing profits and losses, as shown.

	DATE		DESCRIPTION	POST. REF.	DEBIT	CREDIT	
1	19– Sep.	30	Merchandise Inventory		9 8 0 0 00		1
2			Allowance for Doubtful Accounts			2 0 0 00	2
3			Equipment			2 4 0 0 00	3
4			R. L. Boyd, Capital			2 4 0 0 00	4
5			S. T. Hogan, Capital			2 4 0 0 00	5
6			D. J. Insell, Capital			2 4 0 0 00	6
7			To record the revaluation of the				7
8			assets; net increase in owners'				8
9			equity is $7,200.				9
10							10

After the entry has been posted, the owners' equity accounts look like this.

R. L. Boyd, Capital

−	+
	Bal. 46,000
	Sep. 30 2,400

S. T. Hogan, Capital

−	+
	Bal. 24,000
	Sep. 30 2,400

D. J. Insell, Capital

−	+
	Bal. 22,000
	Sep. 30 2,400

After the accountant has recorded the revaluation of the firm's assets, S. T. Hogan withdraws cash from the partnership equal to her equity, which leads to the following entry.

	DATE		DESCRIPTION	POST. REF.	DEBIT	CREDIT	
1	19– Sep.	30	S. T. Hogan, Capital		26 4 0 0 00		1
2			Cash			26 4 0 0 00	2
3			To record the withdrawal of				3
4			S. T. Hogan.				4
5							5

Partner Withdraws More Than Book Value of His or Her Equity

Sometimes it happens that a partner may withdraw more cash than the amount of his or her capital account. There are two possible reasons for this: (1) The business is prosperous and shows excellent potential for growth. (2) The remaining partners are so anxious for the partner to retire that they are willing to buy him or her out.

When Hogan announced she was going to retire, for example, Boyd and Insell agreed to pay her $27,000 for her interest in the partnership. Because the balance of her capital account after the revaluation is $26,400, the excess of $600 must be deducted from the capital accounts of the remaining partners, in accordance with their basis for sharing profits and losses. The general journal entry appears as follows.

	DATE		DESCRIPTION	POST. REF.	DEBIT	CREDIT	
1	19– Sep.	30	S. T. Hogan, Capital		26 4 0 0 00		1
2			R. L. Boyd, Capital		3 0 0 00		2
3			D. J. Insell, Capital		3 0 0 00		3
4			Cash			27 0 0 0 00	4
5			To record the withdrawal of				5
6			S. T. Hogan.				6
7							7
8							8
9							9
10							10

Partner Withdraws Less Than Book Value of His or Her Equity

Sometimes a partner may be so anxious to retire that he or she is willing to take less than the current value of his or her equity just to get out of the partnership, or out of the business. In the firm of Boyd, Hogan, and Insell, let's say that Hogan is willing to withdraw if she gets just $21,000 cash out of it all. Because the balance of her capital account after the revaluation is $26,400, the difference ($5,400) represents a profit to the remaining partners. The entry to record this situation is as follows.

	DATE		DESCRIPTION	POST. REF.	DEBIT	CREDIT	
1	19– Sep.	30	S. T. Hogan, Capital		26 4 0 0 00		1
2			R. L. Boyd, Capital			2 7 0 0 00	2
3			D. J. Insell, Capital			2 7 0 0 00	3
4			Cash			21 0 0 0 00	4
5			To record the withdrawal of				5
6			S. T. Hogan.				6
7							7
8							8
9							9

Death of a Partner

The death of a partner automatically ends the partnership, and his or her estate is entitled to receive the amount of his or her equity. Such a death makes it necessary to close the books immediately, so that the accountant can determine the firm's net income for the current fiscal period. Partnership agreements usually provide for an audit and revaluation of the assets at this time. After the accountant has determined the current value of the deceased partner's capital account, the remaining partners and the executor of the deceased partner's estate must agree on the method of payment. The journal entries are similar to those the accountant makes for the withdrawal of a partner. To be certain of having enough cash to meet such a demand, partnerships often carry life insurance policies.

Liquidation of a Partnership

A **liquidation** means an end of the partnership as well as of the business itself. This final winding-up process involves selling assets, paying off liabilities, and distributing the remaining cash to the partners. The closing entries are journalized and posted prior to the liquidation.

The accountant makes the necessary journal entries in four steps, as follows.

1. Sale of the assets, using the Loss or Gain from Realization account. The accountant debits this account for losses and credits it for gains. In this respect the account is comparable to the Cash Short and Over account. The word **realization** refers to the sale of the assets for cash.
2. Allocation of loss or gain. The accountant closes the Loss or Gain from Realization account into the partners' capital accounts according to the profit and loss ratio. It must be closed as a separate account because it came into being after the regular closing entries had been recorded.

Objective 5

Journalize entries pertaining to the liquidation of a partnership involving the immediate sale of the assets for cash.

3. Payment of liabilities. The firm makes a final settlement with all creditors.
4. Distribution of remaining cash to the partners, in accordance with the balances of their capital accounts.

Occasionally it takes a long time to convert merchandise inventory and other assets into cash; on the other hand, things can move quickly. It is impossible to predict how long liquidation operations may take. In the process, several things may happen. We shall discuss only two possibilities here, though you can find more complex situations set forth in more advanced books.

Our first example concerns the partnership of Jacobs, King, and Lowell. The partners share profits and losses as follows: Jacobs, one-half; King, one-fourth; Lowell, one-fourth.

Let's look at an abbreviated balance sheet for this firm (Figure 22-5).

Figure 22-5

Jacobs, King, and Lowell
Balance Sheet
June 30, 19–

Assets				
Cash			$10 0 0 0 00	
Merchandise Inventory			20 0 0 0 00	
Other Assets			40 0 0 0 00	
Total Assets			$70 0 0 0 00	
Liabilities				
Accounts Payable			$ 7 0 0 0 00	
Owners' Equity				
R. C. Jacobs, Capital	$27 0 0 0 00			
M. L. King, Capital	24 0 0 0 00			
C. C. Lowell, Capital	12 0 0 0 00		63 0 0 0 00	
Total Liabilities and Owners' Equity			$70 0 0 0 00	

Assets Are Sold at a Profit

Assume that the firm sells its merchandise inventory for $26,000, and the other assets for $48,000. Figure 22-6 shows the journal entries to cover this transaction.

Figure 22-6

		DATE		DESCRIPTION	POST. REF.	DEBIT	CREDIT	
(1)	1	19– Jun.	30	Cash		74 0 0 0 00		1
	2			Merchandise Inventory			20 0 0 0 00	2
	3			Other Assets			40 0 0 0 00	3
	4			Loss or Gain from Realization			14 0 0 0 00	4
	5			Sold the assets at a gain.				5
	6							6
(2)	7		30	Loss or Gain from Realization		14 0 0 0 00		7
	8			R. C. Jacobs, Capital			7 0 0 0 00	8
	9			M. L. King, Capital			3 5 0 0 00	9
	10			C. C. Lowell, Capital			3 5 0 0 00	10
	11			To allocate the net gain to the				11
	12			partners' capital accounts				12
	13			according to the profit and loss				13
	14			ratio.				14
	15							15
(3)	16		30	Accounts Payable		7 0 0 0 00		16
	17			Cash			7 0 0 0 00	17
	18			To pay the claims of creditors.				18
	19							19
(4)	20		30	R. C. Jacobs, Capital		34 0 0 0 00		20
	21			M. L. King, Capital		27 5 0 0 00		21
	22			C. C. Lowell, Capital		15 5 0 0 00		22
	23			Cash			77 0 0 0 00	23
	24			To distribute the remaining cash				24
	25			to the partners according to				25
	26			their account balances.				26
	27							27

The T accounts for the Cash and capital accounts look like this.

	Cash		
	+		−
Bal.	10,000	(3)	7,000
(1)	74,000	(4)	77,000

R. C. Jacobs, Capital			
−		+	
(4)	34,000	Bal.	27,000
		(2)	7,000

M. L. King, Capital			
−		+	
(4)	27,500	Bal.	24,000
		(2)	3,500

C. C. Lowell, Capital			
−		+	
(4)	15,500	Bal.	12,000
		(2)	3,500

Assets Are Sold at a Loss: Partners' Capital Accounts Sufficient to Absorb Loss

Now suppose that Jacobs, King, and Lowell sells its merchandise inventory for only $16,000 and its other assets for $32,000. The journal entries would look like Figure 22-7 at the bottom of the page. The T accounts for the Cash and the capital accounts look like this.

	Cash					R. C. Jacobs, Capital			
	+		−			−		+	
Bal.	10,000	(3)	7,000		(2)	6,000	Bal.	27,000
(1)	48,000	(4)	51,000		(4)	21,000		

	M. L. King, Capital					C. C. Lowell, Capital			
	−		+			−		+	
(2)	3,000	Bal.	24,000		(2)	3,000	Bal.	12,000
(4)	21,000					(4)	9,000		

Figure 22-7

		DATE	DESCRIPTION	POST. REF.	DEBIT	CREDIT	
(1)	1	19– Jun. 30	Cash		48 0 0 0 00		1
	2		Loss or Gain from Realization		12 0 0 0 00		2
	3		Merchandise Inventory			20 0 0 0 00	3
	4		Other Assets			40 0 0 0 00	4
	5		Sold the assets at a loss.				5
	6						6
(2)	7	30	R. C. Jacobs, Capital		6 0 0 0 00		7
	8		M. L. King, Capital		3 0 0 0 00		8
	9		C. C. Lowell, Capital		3 0 0 0 00		9
	10		Loss or Gain from Realization			12 0 0 0 00	10
	11		To allocate the net loss to the				11
	12		partners' capital accounts				12
	13		according to the profit and loss				13
	14		ratio.				14
	15						15
(3)	16	30	Accounts Payable		7 0 0 0 00		16
	17		Cash			7 0 0 0 00	17
	18		To pay the claims of creditors.				18
	19						19
(4)	20	30	R. C. Jacobs, Capital		21 0 0 0 00		20
	21		M. L. King, Capital		21 0 0 0 00		21
	22		C. C. Lowell, Capital		9 0 0 0 00		22
	23		Cash			51 0 0 0 00	23
	24		To distribute the remaining cash				24
	25		to the partners according to				25
	26		their account balances.				26
	27						27

GLOSSARY

Co-ownership   A situation in which each party owns a fractional share of all the assets.

Dissolution   The ending of a partnership because of a change in the personnel of the membership and the forming of a new partnership. The transition results primarily in changes in the capital accounts, with routine business being carried on as usual.

Distributive share   The share of the net income allocated to each partner.

General partners   Partners who actively and publicly participate in the transactions of the firm and have unlimited liability.

Liquidation   The ending of a partnership, involving the sale of the assets, payment of the liabilities, and distribution of the remaining cash to the partners.

Mutual agency   Each partner may act as an agent of the firm, thereby committing the entire firm to a binding contract.

Partnership   An association of two or more persons to carry on, as co-owners, a business for profit.

Realization   Conversion into cash, as happens in the case of the sale of assets.

QUESTIONS, EXERCISES, AND PROBLEMS

Discussion Questions

1. What is meant by the concept of co-ownership of partnership property?
2. What do you consider to be the greatest advantage and the greatest disadvantage of the partnership form of business organization?
3. Is it possible for one partner to lose a greater amount than the amount of his or her investment in the partnership? Why?
4. Alber, Baker, and Latham are partners. Latham dies, and her daughter claims the right to take her mother's place in the partnership. Explain why Latham's daughter either does or does not have the right to do this.
5. Rowe and Pence are considering forming a partnership. What do you consider to be the three most important factors to include in their partnership agreement?
6. Describe how a dissolution of a partnership differs from a liquidation of a partnership.
7. When assets other than cash are invested in a partnership by one of the partners, at what value are these assets recorded on the books of the partnership?

Exercises

Exercise 22-1   Schneider, a partner in the firm of Roland, Schneider, and Turner, sells her share in the partnership (capital balance of $32,000) to Carter for $26,000. Assuming that Roland and Turner are willing to admit Carter to the firm, give the entry on the firm's books to record the change in ownership. Does the withdrawal of Schneider dissolve the firm?

Exercise 22-2   Gene Taylor, as his original investment in the firm of Taylor and Weiler, contributes equipment that had been recorded on the books of his own business as costing $40,000, with accumulated depreciation of $26,000. The partners agree on a valuation of $19,000. They also agree to accept Taylor's Accounts Receivable of $20,000, collectible to the extent of 80 percent. Give the journal entry to record Taylor's investment in the partnership of Taylor and Weiler.

Exercise 22-3   The partnership agreement of Adams and Brown provides for salary allowances of $14,000 per year for Adams and $12,000 per year for Brown. They share the remaining balance of net income on the basis of three-fifths for Adams and two-fifths for Brown. The net income amounts to $29,000; calculate the total share for each partner.

Exercise 22-4   Akers and Beidler share profits and losses in the ratio of the balances of their capital accounts at the beginning of the year. The net income for a given year is $35,000, and the balances of the capital accounts for Akers and Beidler are $40,000 and $30,000, respectively. What is each partner's share of the net income?

Exercise 22-5   Nelson is retiring from the partnership of Lang, Morgan, and Nelson. The profit and loss ratio is 2:2:1. After the accountant has posted the revaluation and closing entries, the balances in the capital accounts are: Lang, $27,000; Morgan, $22,000; and Nelson, $11,000. Journalize the entries to record the retirement of Nelson under each of the following unrelated assumptions.

a. Nelson retires, taking $11,000 of partnership cash for her equity.
b. Nelson retires, taking $13,000 of partnership cash for her equity.

Exercise 22-6   Berry is the senior member of the partnership of Berry, Collins, and Dowell. When Berry dies, the firm's accountant revalues the assets. The following assets are increased in value by these amounts: Merchandise Inventory, $12,000; Building, $32,000. The value of the asset Equipment is decreased by $4,000. Assuming that the partnership profit and loss ratio is 2:2:1, write the journal entry to show the revaluation of the assets prior to dissolution of the firm.

Exercise 22-7 The partners Pomeroy, Quinn, and Rogers have a profit and loss ratio of 2:2:1. They decide to liquidate the firm and to sell off all its assets. After distribution of the firm's loss from realization, the credit balances of the capital accounts are as follows: Pomeroy, $42,000; Quinn, $31,000; Rogers, $37,000. The balance of Cash is $110,000. Write the entry the accountant would make on the books to record the distribution of cash.

Exercise 22-8 Stillman and Thomas are partners who share profits and losses equally. The balances of their capital accounts are $30,000 and $40,000, respectively. When they liquidate their partnership, they sell the noncash assets and pay all the partnership's liabilities, leaving a balance of $60,000 in cash. What is the amount of the gain or loss on realization? How much cash should be distributed to each partner?

Problem Set A

Problem 22-1A The firm of C. C. Green, L. E. Johannsen, and M. C. Lewis has a net income of $72,000 for this year. Balances in the capital accounts of the partners at the beginning of the year were $28,000, $31,000, and $36,000, respectively. At the end of the year, the balances of the drawing accounts are $14,000, $16,800, and $13,500, respectively. The partnership agreement stipulates salary allowances as follows: Green, $14,000; Johannsen, $17,000; Lewis, $13,500. It also allows 10 percent interest on the balances of the partners' capital accounts at the beginning of the year. The remainder of the net income, after salary and interest allowances, is divided equally.

Instructions

1. Prepare the section of the income statement on the division of net income for the current year.
2. Prepare entries to close the firm's Income Summary and drawing accounts.
3. Assuming that the net income of the firm is $30,000, prepare the section of the income statement that deals with division of net income.

Problem 22-2A C. T. Gilbert and B. R. Jordan, interior decorators, are forming a partnership. Both plan to work in the firm on a full-time basis. Gilbert's initial investment is $18,000, Jordan's investment $26,000. They are considering the following plans for the division of net income.

a. Division in the same ratio as the balances of their capital accounts.
b. Interest of 9 percent on the balances of their capital accounts at the beginning of the year and the remainder of the net income to be divided equally.
c. Salary allowances of $12,000 to Gilbert and $10,000 to Jordan (according to value of services), interest of 9 percent on the balances of their capital accounts at the beginning of the year, and the remainder of the net income to be divided equally.

Instructions

1. Using the form provided in the *Working Papers,* record the distribution of net income for each of the partners, assuming (a) a net income of $22,000, and (b) a net income of $11,000.
2. Which plan is the fairest? Give reasons for your opinion.

Problem 22-3A The following are the account balances of Albertson and Stewart as of December 31, the end of this fiscal year.

Accounts Payable	$ 34,708
Accounts Receivable	29,482
Accumulated Depreciation, Equipment	23,410
Norman C. Albertson, Capital	32,000
Norman C. Albertson, Drawing	14,800
Allowance for Doubtful Accounts	1,074
Cash	1,871
Equipment	39,564
General Expenses (control)	7,106
Interest Expense	1,471
Merchandise Inventory	63,118
Notes Payable	8,000
Prepaid Insurance	345
Purchases	268,340
Purchases Discount	2,214
Purchases Returns and Allowances	12,845
Sales	342,418
Sales Returns and Allowances	17,936
Selling Expense (control)	17,781
Beverly R. Stewart, Capital	26,000
Beverly R. Stewart, Drawing	14,400

The merchandise inventory at the beginning of the year was $69,573, and there were no changes in the partners' capital accounts during the year. The partnership agreement provides for salary allowances of $15,600 for Albertson and $14,400 for Stewart and interest of 10 percent on invested capital at the beginning of the year. The remainder of the net income is to be divided equally.

Instructions

1. Prepare an income statement for the year.
2. Prepare a statement of owners' equity for the year.
3. Prepare a classified balance sheet at the end of the year.

Problem 22-4A The partnership of Dill, Garber, and Pickering is to be liquidated as of September 30 of this year. The partners share profits and losses in the ratio of 2 : 2 : 1. The firm's post-closing trial balance looks like this.

ACCOUNT NAME	DEBIT	CREDIT
Cash	18 7 0 0 00	
Merchandise Inventory	33 6 2 0 00	
Other Assets	24 0 8 0 00	
Accounts Payable		7 8 6 0 00
Marcia A. Dill, Capital		26 9 0 0 00
Donna C. Garber, Capital		21 8 4 0 00
Nina D. Pickering, Capital		19 8 0 0 00
	76 4 0 0 00	76 4 0 0 00

The firm's realization and liquidation transactions are as follows.

a. The merchandise inventory sold for $32,000; the other assets sold for $24,000.
b. The accountant allocated the loss or gain from realization to the partners' capital accounts according to the profit and loss ratio.
c. The firm paid its creditors in full.
d. The firm distributed the remaining cash to the partners in accordance with the balances in their capital accounts.

Instructions

1. Record the balances in the selected ledger accounts.
2. Record the liquidating transactions in general journal form.
3. Post the entries to the ledger accounts.

Problem Set B

Problem 22-1B The partnership of F. A. Dennis, R. E. Easter, and D. L. Forsberg has a net income of $61,900 for the current year. The balances in the capital accounts of the partners at the beginning of the year were $23,000, $26,000, and $32,000, respectively. At the end of the year the balances of the drawing accounts are $11,000, $13,200, and $12,000, respectively. The partnership agreement stipulates salary allowances as follows: Dennis, $11,000; Easter, $14,000; Forsberg, $12,000. The partnership agreement also allows interest of 10 percent on the balances of the capital accounts at the beginning of the year. The remainder (after salary and interest allowances) is divided equally among the three.

Instructions

1. Prepare the section of the income statement for the current year that deals with division of net income.

2. Prepare the entries to record the closing of the firm's Income Summary and drawing accounts.
3. Assuming a net income of $27,100, prepare the section of the income statement that deals with division of net income.

Problem 22-2B   Agnes Doty and Marcia Hall, who are forming a partnership for an interior decorating business, plan to work full time in the firm. Doty will make an initial investment of $20,000 and Hall $30,000. They are considering the following plans for the division of net income.

a. Division in the same ratio as the balances of their capital accounts.
b. Interest of 10 percent on the balances of their capital accounts at the beginning of the year, and the remainder of the net income to be divided equally.
c. Salary allowances of $10,000 to Doty and $9,000 to Hall (according to value of services); interest of 8 percent on the balances of their capital accounts at the beginning of the year; and the remainder of the net income to be divided equally.

Instructions

1. Using the form provided in the *Working Papers,* record the distributive shares of net income for each of the partners, assuming (a) a net income of $30,000, and (b) a net income of $16,000.
2. Which plan is the fairest? Give reasons for your opinion.

Problem 22-3B   The following are the account balances of Adams and Wentz as of December 31, the end of the current fiscal year.

Accounts Payable	$ 33,716
Accounts Receivable	26,719
Accumulated Depreciation, Equipment	22,690
Malcolm C. Adams, Capital	30,000
Malcolm C. Adams, Drawing	16,000
Allowance for Doubtful Accounts	921
Cash	1,829
Equipment	36,919
General Expenses (control)	7,323
Interest Expense	1,716
Merchandise Inventory	64,726
Notes Payable	10,000
Prepaid Insurance	360
Purchases	275,590
Purchases Discount	2,110
Purchases Returns and Allowances	12,726
Sales	350,245
Sales Returns and Allowances	18,419
Selling Expenses (control)	18,916
Sandra L. Wentz, Capital	24,000
Sandra L. Wentz, Drawing	12,000

There were no changes in the partners' capital accounts during the year. The merchandise inventory at the beginning of the year was $70,617. The partnership agreement provides for salary allowances of $16,000 for Adams and $14,000 for Wentz, and also stipulates an interest allowance of 9 percent on invested capital at the beginning of the year, with the remainder of the net income to be divided equally.

Instructions

1. Prepare an income statement for the year.
2. Prepare a statement of owners' equity for the year.
3. Prepare a classified balance sheet for the partnership at the end of the year.

Problem 22-4B The partnership of Dill, Garber, and Pickering is to be liquidated as of April 30 of this year. The partners share profits and losses in the ratio of 2:2:1. The firm's post-closing trial balance looks like this.

Dill, Garber, and Pickering
Post-Closing Trial Balance
April 30, 19–

ACCOUNT NAME	DEBIT	CREDIT
Cash	26 8 7 0 00	
Merchandise Inventory	39 2 5 0 00	
Other Assets	30 3 0 0 00	
Accounts Payable		8 4 2 0 00
Marcia A. Dill, Capital		36 0 0 0 00
Donna C. Garber, Capital		28 0 0 0 00
Nina D. Pickering, Capital		24 0 0 0 00
	96 4 2 0 00	96 4 2 0 00

The firm's realization and liquidation transactions are as follows.

a. The merchandise inventory sold for $36,000; the other assets sold for $28,000.
b. The accountant allocated the loss or gain from realization to the partners' capital accounts according to the profit and loss ratio.
c. The firm paid its creditors in full.
d. The firm distributed the remaining cash to the partners in accordance with the balances in their capital accounts.

Instructions

1. Record the balances in the selected ledger accounts.
2. Record the liquidating transactions in general journal form.
3. Post the entries to the ledger accounts.

23 Corporations: Organization and Capital Stock

Learning Objectives

After you have completed this chapter, you will be able to do the following:

1. Define a corporation.

2. Name at least two advantages and two disadvantages of a corporation compared to a sole proprietorship or partnership.

3. Journalize entries for the issuance of par-value stock.

4. Journalize entries for the issuance of no-par stock.

5. Journalize entries for the sale of stock on the basis of subscriptions.

6. Prepare a balance sheet for a corporation, including Subscriptions Receivable, Organization Costs, Paid-in Capital accounts, and Retained Earnings.

Business organizations are usually classified as sole proprietorships, partnerships, or corporations. Corporations are fewest in number, but they account for more business transactions than the other two combined. Frequently a firm that begins as a sole proprietorship or a partnership needs more investment capital as it grows and prospers. To raise additional investment capital, the firm incorporates. In other cases, businesses are organized as corporations at the outset. Because of the predominance of corporations, everyone entering the business world should be familiar with the corporate form of organization and its financial structure. We shall be dealing with corporations that issue stock and carry out business activities for the purpose of making profits and distributing the profits to their owners. Nonprofit corporations are those that do not issue stock or distribute profits, but carry out activities for charitable, educational, or other philanthropic purposes.

DEFINITION OF A CORPORATION

In 1818 Chief Justice John Marshall defined a **corporation** as "an artificial being, invisible, intangible, and existing only in contemplation of the law." A corporation does indeed act as an artificial legal being, deriving its existence from its charter. In every respect it is a separate legal entity, having a continuous existence apart from that of its owners, the stockholders. As an entity, a corporation may own property, enter into contracts, sue in the courts, be sued, and so forth.

Objective 1

Define a corporation.

ADVANTAGES OF THE CORPORATE FORM

The corporation offers a number of advantages over the sole proprietorship and the partnership.

Objective 2

Name at least two advantages and two disadvantages of a corporation compared to a sole proprietorship or partnership.

1. **Limited liability**   As a separate legal entity, a corporation is responsible for its own debts. All that a stockholder can lose is the amount of his or her investment. Since the stockholders are the owners, this is the most important advantage. In contrast, the owners of sole proprietorships and partnerships are personally liable for the entire debt of the business.
2. **Ease of raising capital**   A corporation can accumulate more investment capital than a sole proprietorship or partnership because a corporation can sell stock. Some corporations have more than 1 million stockholders. Sole proprietorships and partnerships are limited to the wealth of the few individual owners.

3. **Ease of transferring ownership rights**   Ownership rights in a corporation are represented by shares of stock, which can readily be transferred from one person to another without the permission of other stockholders. (Compare this with a partnership, in which the other partners have to give permission for changes in ownership in order for the business to continue.)

4. **Continuous existence**   The length of life of a corporation is stipulated in its charter; when the charter expires, it may be renewed. The death, incapacity, or withdrawal of an owner does not affect the life of a corporation, but such a circumstance would cause a partnership to be dissolved or liquidated.

5. **No mutual agency**   Stockholders do not have the power to bind the corporation to contracts, unless a given stockholder is an officer. Since owners need not participate in management, the corporation is free to employ the managerial talent it believes can best accomplish its objectives.

DISADVANTAGES OF THE CORPORATE FORM

The corporation also has a number of disadvantages.

1. **Additional taxation**   In addition to the usual property and payroll taxes, corporations must pay income taxes and charter fees. Since corporations are separate legal entities, they pay federal and state income taxes in their own names. Part of the corporation's net income goes to the stockholders in the form of dividends; this money is personal income to the stockholders, and consequently the stockholders have to pay personal income taxes on it. This state of affairs is known as the **double taxation** of corporations. It represents their greatest disadvantage. Charter fees (which are fees paid for the corporation's right to exist) may be considered additional taxes, because they are paid to a state in return for the issuance of a charter.

2. **Government regulation**   Since states create corporations by granting charters, states can exercise closer control and supervision over corporations than over sole proprietorships and partnerships. States often regulate even the amount of net income that a corporation may retain, the extent to which it may buy back its own stock, and the amount of real estate it may own. By contrast, sole proprietorships need only have legal purposes; states impose no further regulations.

FORMING A CORPORATION

To organize a corporation, a person or persons must submit an application for a **charter** to the appropriate official (corporation commissioner or secretary of state) of the state in which the company is to be incorporated. The application is called the **articles of incorporation.** Generally the application for the charter must include at least the following points of information:

- Name and address of the corporation
- Nature of the business to be conducted
- Amount and description of the capital stock to be issued
- Names and addresses of the subscribers and the amount of stock subscribed by each
- Names of the promoters (or temporary officers) who will serve until the first stockholders' meeting is held

The application must be signed by three of the promoters. The articles of incorporation must be accompanied by a charter fee, based on the dollar amount of maximum stock investment, or **authorized capital.**

When the state officials approve the articles of incorporation, these articles become the charter of the corporation. Shortly after receiving the charter, the stock subscribers hold an initial meeting to elect an acting board of directors and formulate bylaws. The charter plus the bylaws provide the basic rules for conducting the corporation's affairs. Next, the directors meet to appoint officers to serve as active managers of the business. Then the corporation issues **capital stock** to the subscribers who have paid in full. The shares of stock are in the form of certificates. Since stockholders have come into existence at this point, they now elect a permanent board of directors.

The size of the corporation may vary as to number of stockholders and amount of investment. It may be a small corporation with only a few owners and a minimum investment of $1,000; or it may be a giant corporation, consisting of more than a million owners, with an investment amounting to more than a billion dollars. In the small corporation, the stockholders may also be the directors and officers. A corporation whose ownership is confined to a small group of stockholders is called a **closely held corporation.** A corporation whose ownership is widely distributed through a stock exchange or through over-the-counter markets to a large number of stockholders is called an **open** or **public corporation.**

Organization Costs

Let us suppose that a new corporation is forming, starting from scratch, and the organizers call in an accountant to set up the books. The accountant debits the costs of organizing the corporation—such as fees paid to the state, attorneys' fees, promotional costs, travel outlays, costs of printing stock certificates, and so on—to an account entitled **Organization Costs.** This account is classified as an **intangible asset.** The Intangible Assets section of the balance sheet appears as a separate category, below Plant and Equipment. The account Organization Costs is like a prepaid expense account, such as Prepaid Insurance, in that it will eventually be written off by means of adjusting entries over a period of years. Organization costs are paid only once, although they benefit the corporation during its entire life; so it seems unfair to list them entirely as expenses of the first year. Income tax laws allow a company to write off its organization costs over a period of five years or more. The adjusting entry is a debit to Organization Cost Expense or Miscellaneous General Expense and a credit to Organization Costs.

Stock Certificate Book

One necessary element of organization costs is the printing of **stock certificates.** In a small corporation the certificates often have stubs attached, and certificates and stubs are bound in a stock certificate book, rather like a checkbook. The corporation issues the stock certificates only when the stockholder has paid for them in full. Each blank certificate must have written on it the name of the owner, the number of shares issued, and the date of issuance. The stub must show the name and address of the stockholder, the number of shares listed on the stock certificate, and the date of issuance. Both certificates and stubs are numbered consecutively.

When a transfer of ownership takes place, the stockholder surrenders the stock certificate to the corporation, and the corporation cancels it; the corporation also cancels the matching stub and issues one or more new certificates in the place of these documents. This procedure enables the corporation to maintain an up-to-date record of the name of each stockholder and the number of shares owned by each. A corporation needs this information when it pays out dividends and when it sends out notices of annual meetings or other information.

The law requires large corporations whose stocks are listed on major stock exchanges to have independent registrars and transfer agents maintain their records of stock ownership. Banks and trust companies perform this service.

STRUCTURE OF A CORPORATION

The stockholders own the corporation; they delegate authority to the board of directors, which manages the corporation's affairs. (Generally the directors are also stockholders, although this is not always so.) The board of directors, in turn, delegates authority to the officers, who do the actual work of running the business. The officers themselves may also be members of the board of directors.

Dividends are the share of the corporation's earnings distributed to stockholders. The sources of dividends are the current year's net income after income taxes and the retained earnings of prior years.

Suppose the corporation issues some new stock. Each original stockholder then has the right to subscribe to additional shares in proportion to his or her present holding. This feature is known as **preemptive right.** For example, assume that the corporation's new issue consists of 1,000 shares. The present amount of stock outstanding is 10,000 shares, of which Ruth Cowen owns 2,000. Her proportion of stock held to stock outstanding is one-fifth (2,000/10,000). Therefore she has the right to subscribe to 200 shares (one-fifth of 1,000 shares) of the new issue.

Stockholders' Equity

The owners' equity in a corporation is called **stockholders' equity,** or **capital.** Just as in sole proprietorships and partnerships, the equity of the owners represents the excess of assets over liabilities. Of the five major classifications of accounts, the main difference with corporations occurs in the Stockholders' Equity classification, in which capital stock accounts replace owners' capital accounts, and **Retained Earnings** is used to record earnings plowed back into the business.

The following T accounts compare accounts for a sole proprietorship with those for a corporation.

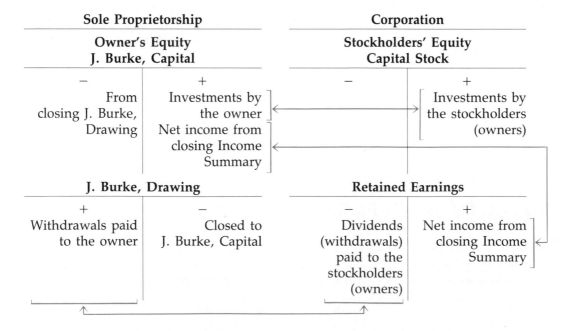

CAPITAL STOCK

Capital stock refers to shares of ownership in a corporation. *Authorized capital stock* is the maximum number of shares designated in the charter. **Issued stock** refers to the shares apportioned out to the stockholders. Stock that is actually in the hands of stockholders is called **outstanding stock.** Occasionally, a corporation may reacquire some of the stock it has issued by buying back its own stock or by receiving it as a donation. This reacquired stock is known as **treasury stock;** consequently the number of shares that have been issued may differ from the number outstanding.

Classes of Capital Stock

In order to appeal to as many investors as possible, a corporation may issue more than one kind of stock, just as a manufacturer of refrigerators, say, makes different models in order to please different groups of potential buyers. The two main types of stock are *common* and *preferred.* Each type may have a variety of characteristics. Some may be **par-value stock,** in which a uniform face value of each share is printed on the stock certificate. Some may be **no-par stock,** in which no value is printed on the stock certificates.

Common Stock

When a corporation issues only one type of stock, it is called **common stock** and may be either par or no-par stock. Holders of common stock have all the rights listed above, with voting privilege of one vote for each share of stock.

Preferred Stock

Preferred stock, which is generally par-value stock, is preferred in two ways: (1) the corporation pays dividends on preferred stock before it pays them on common stock, and (2) it pays them at a uniform rate. A company is allowed to omit dividend payments altogether. However, if it does pay dividends, it must meet the requirements on preferred stock before paying anything on common stock. The dividend on preferred stock consists of a percentage of the par value of the stock. In the event that the corporation is liquidated, holders of preferred stock are paid off before holders of common stock. In most circumstances, however, holders of preferred stock do not have voting privileges. There are several specific types of preferred stock, so let's discuss each of them briefly.

Cumulative and Noncumulative Preferred Stock   Suppose that a corporation has a bad year and finds that it is not able to pay the dividend on its preferred stock. In this case the dividend is said to be *passed*. Stockholders who own **cumulative preferred stock** get to accumulate the dividends passed in former years (that is, the dividends in arrears). The corporation has to pay these dividends in full before it can pay any dividends to common stockholders. If stockholders own **noncumulative preferred stock,** their dividends in arrears do not accumulate. In other words, if the corporation passes dividends, they are gone forever. Since preferred stockholders naturally want a regular dividend, most preferred stock is cumulative.

Participating and Nonparticipating Preferred Stock   Recall that the dividend on preferred stock consists of an established percentage of the par value of that stock. Some preferred stock, however, provides for the possibility of dividends in excess of this established amount; this kind of preferred stock is called **participating preferred stock.** Holders of participating preferred stock first get the regular dividend that is due them. Then the corporation allocates a stipulated amount to holders of its common stock. And *then* the stockholders who own participating preferred stock are allowed to participate or share in the extra earnings, which are distributed as cash dividends. The dividends of **nonparticipating preferred stock,** on the other hand, are limited to the regular rate. Most preferred stock is nonparticipating.

ISSUING STOCK

Stock is issued when the buyer has paid for it in full or when the corporation has received noncash assets in exchange for its stock. Let us first discuss the issuance of par-value stock and then the issuance of no-par stock. [*Note:* A corporation may issue par-value stock at a figure equal to, above, or below its par value.]

Issuing Stock at Par for Cash

There is a separate ledger account for each class of stock. The accountant records investments of cash as debits to Cash and credits to the stock accounts for the total amount of the par value. Later we shall deal with sales of stock in which the cash received is greater than or less than the par value of the shares issued. Remember that par value is the face value printed on each stock certificate. This designation of par value is a convenient means of dividing the corporation's capital into units, with the ownership of each unit known.

Objective 3

Journalize entries for the issuance of par-value stock.

For example, the Catalano Corporation is organized on July 16 with an authorized capital of 4,000 shares of $100-par preferred stock and 20,000 shares of $50-par common stock. On August 1 Catalano issues 1,000 shares of preferred 8 percent stock at par and 10,000 shares of common stock at par. In general journal form, the entry looks like this.

GENERAL JOURNAL   PAGE ___1___

	DATE		DESCRIPTION	POST. REF.	DEBIT	CREDIT	
1	19– Aug.	1	Cash		600 0 0 0 00		1
2			Preferred 8 Percent Stock			100 0 0 0 00	2
3			Common Stock			500 0 0 0 00	3
4			Issued 1,000 shares of preferred				4
5			8 percent stock at par and 10,000				5
6			shares of common stock at par.				6
7							7

According to T accounts, the situation looks like this.

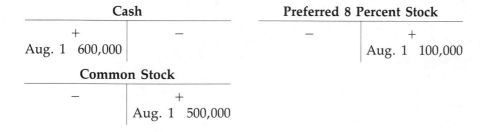

The capital stock accounts (Preferred 8 Percent Stock and Common Stock) are controlling accounts. The subsidiary ledger may consist of the stock certificate book, or it may be a supplementary record showing the name and address of each stockholder and the number of shares owned. This is known as a **stockholders' ledger.**

Issuing Stock at Par for Noncash Assets

Corporations often accept assets other than cash in exchange for their stock. The Catalano Corporation received equipment, a building, and land in exchange for common stock, as we see in the following journal entry (next page).

1	Aug.	1	Equipment		6 0 0 0 00						1
2			Building		50 0 0 0 00						2
3			Land		10 0 0 0 00						3
4			Common Stock				66 0 0 0 00				4
5			Exchanged 1,320 shares of common								5
6			stock for equipment, building,								6
7			and land.								7
8											8

When a corporation accepts an asset other than cash, the accountant records the asset at its fair market value, in order to present an accurate balance sheet and have a realistic base on which to calculate future depreciation.

Now let's take the case of a corporation that gives shares of its stock to its organizers in exchange for their services in organizing the corporation. In this instance, the corporation receives the intangible asset, Organization Costs. Suppose that the Catalano Corporation issues 100 shares of common stock to its organizers. The accountant handles it this way.

1	Aug.	1	Organization Costs		5 0 0 0 00					1
2			Common Stock				5 0 0 0 00			2
3			Issued 100 shares to the pro-							3
4			moters in exchange for their							4
5			services in organizing the							5
6			corporation.							6
7										7

Issuing Stock at a Premium or Discount

A newly organized corporation, such as the Catalano Corporation, generally issues its stock at par. However, after the business has been operating for some time the directors may realize that they need additional investment capital. Perhaps the business has been so successful that they want to expand it. Or perhaps they need to cover losses suffered during the early years of the business. So the directors decide to issue some new stock. The present market price of the original stock affects the price they can secure for the new shares. The market price of the stock of a corporation is usually influenced by the following factors:

1. The earnings record, financial condition, and dividend record of the corporation

2. The potential for growth in earnings of the corporation
3. The supply of and demand for money for investment purposes in the money market as a whole
4. General business conditions and prospects for the future

When a corporation issues stock at a price above par value, the stock is said to be issued at a **premium;** the premium is the amount by which the selling price of the new stock exceeds the par value. The premium price may be due to the fact that the corporation has performed successfully in the past and has good prospects for growth in earnings in the future. Conversely, when a corporation sells its stock at a price below par value, the stock is said to be issued at a **discount;** the discount is the amount by which the selling price of the new stock falls below the par value. This discount may be due to the fact that the corporation incurred losses during its early period, or perhaps its prospects for the future are not too promising.

Premium on Stock

When a corporation issues stock at a price *above* its par value, the accountant debits Cash or other noncash assets for the amount received, credits the stock account for the par value, and credits a premium account for the difference between the amount received and the par value.

Let's take an example. The Garrison Corporation issues 500 shares of $100-par preferred 9 percent stock at $103. In general journal form, the entry looks like this.

1	Cash	51 5 0 0 00		1
2	Preferred 9 Percent Stock		50 0 0 0 00	2
3	Premium on Preferred 9 Percent			3
4	Stock		1 5 0 0 00	4
5	Issued 500 shares at $103 per			5
6	share.			6
7				7
8				8
9				9
10				10
11				11
12				12
13				13

According to T accounts, the entry looks like this.

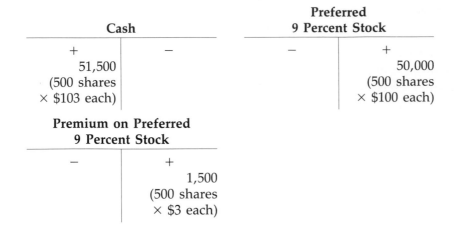

In the case of par-value stock, the stock account contains only the total par value of the stock issued. Why would buyers be willing to pay a premium for Garrison's 9 percent preferred stock? The 9 percent rate may be higher than the current market rate for the same type of stock. For example, other companies in comparable financial condition may be paying only 8 percent dividends on their stock.

Discount on Stock

When a corporation issues stock at a price *below its par value*, the accountant debits Cash or other assets for the amount received, credits the stock account for the par value, and debits a discount account for the difference between the amount received and the par value.

Suppose that the Garrison Corporation issues 4,000 shares of $20-par common stock at $19. In general journal form, the entry is as follows.

1	Cash	76 0 0 0 00		1
2	Discount on Common Stock	4 0 0 0 00		2
3	Common Stock		80 0 0 0 00	3
4	Issued 4,000 shares at $19 per			4
5	share.			5
6				6
7				7
8				8

According to T accounts, the entry looks like this.

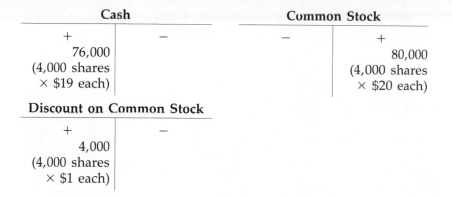

Cash		Common Stock	
+	−	−	+
76,000			80,000
(4,000 shares			(4,000 shares
× $19 each)			× $20 each)

Discount on Common Stock	
+	−
4,000	
(4,000 shares	
× $1 each)	

As in the case of par-value stock, the accountant records in the stock account the total *par* value of the stock issued and treats the discount on the stock as a deduction from stockholders' equity. It is a contra account. The total par value of a corporation's stock represents its **legal capital.** In some states, the stockholders have a contingent liability for the amount of the discount, because the amount they paid for the stock does not cover the legal capital. Other states do not permit corporations to issue stock at a discount.

Let's review the placement of the major accounts presented thus far in the fundamental accounting equation.

Assets	=	Liabilities	+	Stockholders' Equity	+	Revenue	−	Expenses
+ −		− +		− +		− +		+ −

Organization Costs
+   −

Preferred Stock
−   +

Premium on Preferred Stock
−   +

Common Stock
−   +

Discount on Common Stock
+   −

Retained Earnings
−   +

The Stockholder's Equity section of the balance sheet of the Garrison Corporation—showing the stock, premium, and discount accounts—looks like this.

Stockholder's Equity			
Paid-in Capital:			
Preferred 9 Percent Stock, cumulative, $100 par			
(1,000 shares authorized, 500 shares issued)	$50 0 0 0 00		
Premium on Preferred 9 Percent Stock	1 5 0 0 00	$ 51 5 0 0 00	
Common Stock, $20 par (10,000 shares authorized,			
4,000 shares issued)	$80 0 0 0 00		
Less Discount on Common Stock	4 0 0 0 00	76 0 0 0 00	
Total Paid-in Capital		$127 5 0 0 00	
Retained Earnings		45 0 0 0 00	
Total Stockholders' Equity			172 5 0 0 00

Notice that the listing of the stock states the par value, the number of shares authorized, and the number of shares issued. The record also describes preferred stock as cumulative and participating; if the stock is noncumulative or nonparticipating, the record doesn't mention it. Preferred stock is assumed to be noncumulative and nonparticipating unless otherwise stated. **Paid-in Capital** is a main caption under Stockholders' Equity. Preferred stock, and related premium or discount accounts, are always listed before common stock. (A corporation can also issue preferred stock at a discount or common stock at a premium.)

Concerning the Retained Earnings account, note that the amount is not necessarily in the form of cash. The surplus would probably be reinvested in the corporation's assets, such as merchandise inventory or plant and equipment.

No-Par Stock

Preferred stock generally has a par value. However, common stock may or may not have one; if it doesn't, it is referred to as *no-par stock*. It used to be the law that all stock had to have par value. Today, corporations in all the fifty states can issue no-par stock. The main advantages claimed for no-par stock are as follows.

1. No-par stock, since it does not have a par value, may be issued without a discount contingent liability.
2. No-par stock prevents misconception on the part of naive stockholders as to the value of the stock. In the case of par stock, investors might believe that the stock is worth the amount printed on the face of the

stock certificate. Actually, the market value of the stock may differ markedly from the par value, due to ups and downs of the corporation's past earnings and future prospects.

Stated Value and No-Par Stock

We have said that when all of a company's stock is of the par-value type, the par value of the shares represents the company's legal capital, which stockholders cannot withdraw. This law protects creditors. When various state legislatures passed laws permitting corporations to issue no-par stock, they tried to continue to protect creditors by stipulating that all or part of the amount the corporation receives for its no-par shares be exempt from withdrawal by stockholders. This amount is known as the stock's **stated value.** The minimum stated value per share of no-par stock varies from state to state. In addition, in some states the board of directors of the corporation, if it wishes, may choose a stated value for the company's no-par stock that is higher than the minimum required by the state law.

Established Amount of Stated Value

Houston Modern Homes is located in a state that allows the board of directors of a corporation to designate a stated value for its stock. Accordingly, the board of directors of Houston Modern Homes chooses a stated value of $25 per share for its common stock. On June 20, Houston issues 1,000 shares at $28 per share, receiving cash. On September 10, it issues 1,000 shares at $30 per share, receiving cash. The accountant uses the account entitled Paid-in Capital in Excess of Stated Value to record the amounts of the excess over stated value.

Objective 4

Journalize entries for the issuance of no-par stock.

The accountant's entries, in general journal form, are as follows.

1	19– Jun. 20	Cash	28 0 0 0 00		1
2		Common Stock		25 0 0 0 00	2
3		Paid-in Capital in Excess of			3
4		Stated Value		3 0 0 0 00	4
5		Issued 1,000 shares at $28 per			5
6		share.			6
7					7

	19–Sep.	10	Cash	30 0 0 0 00		
1						1
2			Common Stock		25 0 0 0 00	2
3			Paid-in Capital in Excess of			3
4			Stated Value		5 0 0 0 00	4
5			Issued 1,000 shares at $30 per			5
6			share.			6
7						7
8						8
9						9
10						10
11						11
12						12
13						13
14						14

According to T accounts, the entries look like this.

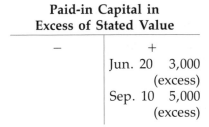

Cash

+	−
Jun. 20 28,000	
Sep. 10 30,000	

Common Stock

−	+
	Jun. 20 25,000
	(total stated)
	Sep. 10 25,000
	(total stated)

Paid-in Capital in Excess of Stated Value

−	+
	Jun. 20 3,000
	(excess)
	Sep. 10 5,000
	(excess)

Now let's compare the accounting for no-par stock having a stated value and the accounting for par stock. When a firm issues no-par stock with a stated value, the accountant substitutes the Paid-in Capital in Excess of Stated Value account for the premium account used for par-value stock. Although the pattern is similar, there is a definite distinction between par value and stated value. The corporation's charter stipulates the par value of its stock, and the corporation can change this value only with the approval of the state. On the other hand, the board of directors of a corporation can change the stated value of no-par stock merely by passing a resolution. In our problems involving no-par stock, however, we shall assume that there is an established stated value, as in our previous examples.

Subscriptions and Stock Issuance

We've been talking about corporations that issue stock for which investors pay in full, either by giving cash or by giving noncash assets or organizational services. However, a corporation often sells its stock directly to investors on a subscription contract (installment) basis. This means that the investor enters into a contract with the corporation, promising to pay at a later date for a specified number of shares at an agreed price. The corporation agrees to issue the shares when the investor has paid for them in full.

The accountant records the amount of the subscription, which is an asset, in the Subscriptions Receivable account, and credits the par or stated value of the stock to Stock Subscribed, a stockholders' equity account. The accountant then records the difference between the subscription price and the par value under either premium or discount, and the difference between the subscription price and the stated value under Paid-in Capital in Excess of Stated Value.

As the investor sends in payments, the accountant records them as debits to Cash and credits to Subscriptions Receivable. When the investor finishes paying for all the shares, the accountant records the issuance of the stock as a debit to Stock Subscribed and a credit to Common Stock or Preferred Stock. When investors want subscriptions to both common and preferred stock, the accountant uses separate accounts for each. We can best describe the procedure with some examples.

Objective 5

Journalize entries for the sale of stock on the basis of subscriptions.

Subscription Transactions: No-Par Stock   The Sempert Manufacturing Corporation, a newly organized company, sets up its books with the following transactions involving its own stock.

May 1 Received subscriptions to 10,000 shares of common stock (stated value $10 per share) from various subscribers at $16 per share, with a downpayment of 50 percent of the subscription price.

Jun. 1 Received an additional 30 percent of the subscription price from all subscribers.

Jul. 1 Received an additional 20 percent of the subscription price from all subscribers; then issued the stock.

The general journal entries are shown in Figure 23-1. The items in parentheses are just explanations; they would not actually appear in the journal.

Figure 23-1

			Description	Debit	Credit	
1	19–May	1	Subscriptions Receivable, Common			1
2			Stock (10,000 shares at $16 per			2
3			share)	160 0 0 0 00		3
4			Common Stock Subscribed (10,000			4
5			shares at $10 per share)		100 0 0 0 00	5
6			Paid-in Capital in Excess of Stated			6
7			Value ($160,000 – $100,000)		60 0 0 0 00	7
8			Received subscriptions to 10,000			8
9			shares at $16 per share.			9
10						10
11		1	Cash (10,000 shares × $16 per share			11
12			× .5)	80 0 0 0 00		12
13			Subscriptions Receivable, Common			13
14			Stock		80 0 0 0 00	14
15			Received 50 percent of the sub-			15
16			scription of May 1 on 10,000			16
17			shares.			17
18						18
19	Jun.	1	Cash (10,000 shares × $16 per share			19
20			× .3)	48 0 0 0 00		20
21			Subscriptions Receivable, Common			21
22			Stock		48 0 0 0 00	22
23			Received 30 percent of the sub-			23
24			scription of May 1 on 10,000			24
25			shares.			25
26						26
27	Jul.	1	Cash (10,000 shares × $16 per share			27
28			× .2)	32 0 0 0 00		28
29			Subscriptions Receivable, Common			29
30			Stock		32 0 0 0 00	30
31			Received 20 percent of the sub-			31
32			scription of May 1 on 10,000			32
33			shares.			33
34						34
35		1	Common Stock Subscribed	100 0 0 0 00		35
36			Common Stock (10,000 shares × $10			36
37			per share)		100 0 0 0 00	37
38			Issued 10,000 shares.			38
39						39
40						40
41						41
42						42
43						43

After the accountant has posted these transactions, the T accounts appear as follows.

	Cash		
+		−	
May 1	80,000		
Jun. 1	48,000		
Jul. 1	32,000		

	Common Stock		
−		+	
		Jul. 1	100,000
			(10,000 shares)

	Subscriptions Receivable, Common Stock		
+		−	
May 1	160,000	May 1	80,000
		Jun. 1	48,000
		Jul. 1	32,000

	Common Stock Subscribed		
−		+	
Jul. 1	100,000	May 1	100,000
			(10,000 shares)

	Paid-In Capital In Excess of Stated Value		
−		+	
		May 1	60,000

Common Stock Subscribed represents the total par value or stated value of the shares subscribed. It is considered to be a temporary account to handle subscribed shares that have not yet been paid for in full. When the investors finish paying for all the shares, the accountant records the issuance of stock by debiting the Stock Subscribed account and crediting the Stock account.

Subscription Transactions: Par-Value Stock Security Service Corporation, a newly organized company, has the following transactions involving its own stock.

Jun. 15 Received subscriptions to **2,000** shares of preferred 9 percent stock ($100 par value) from various subscribers at $103 per share, with a down payment of 40 percent of the subscription price.

Jul. 1 Received 30 percent of the subscription price from all subscribers (2,000 shares).

Jul. 15 Received 30 percent of the subscription price from subscribers to 500 shares, and issued **500** shares.

The general journal is shown in Figure 23-2. The items in parentheses are explanations. They would not actually appear in the journal.

All this goes to show that Preferred 9 Percent Stock Subscribed represents the total par value of the shares subscribed. It also points up the fact that a firm does not issue stock until the investor has paid for it in full. Since only 500 shares were paid for in full, the firm issued only 500 shares.

Figure 23-2

1	19— Jun.	15	Subscriptions Receivable, Preferred																1
2			9 Percent Stock (2,000 shares at																2
3			$103 per share)	206	0	0	0	00										3
4			Preferred 9 Percent Stock Sub-																4
5			scribed (2,000 shares at $100																5
6			per share)							200	0	0	0	00		6
7			Premium on Preferred 9 Percent																7
8			Stock								6	0	0	0	00	8
9			Received subscription to 2,000																9
10			shares at $103 per share.																10
11																			11
12		15	Cash (2,000 shares × $103 per share																12
13			× .4)	82	4	0	0	00										13
14			Subscriptions Receivable, Pre-																14
15			ferred 9 Percent Stock							82	4	0	0	00		15
16			Received 40 percent of the sub-																16
17			scription of June 15 on 2,000																17
18			shares.																18
19																			19
20	Jul.	1	Cash (2,000 shares × $103 × .3)	61	8	0	0	00										20
21			Subscriptions Receivable, Pre-																21
22			ferred 9 Percent Stock							61	8	0	0	00		22
23			Received 30 percent of the sub-																23
24			scription of June 15 on 2,000																24
25			shares.																25
26																			26
27		15	Cash (500 shares × $103 per share																27
28			× .3)	15	4	5	0	00										28
29			Subscriptions Receivable, Pre-																29
30			ferred 9 Percent Stock							15	4	5	0	00		30
31			Received 30 percent, the final																31
32			installment of the subscription																32
33			of June 15, on 500 shares.																33
34																			34
35		15	Preferred 9 Percent Stock Subscribed	50	0	0	0	00										35
36			Preferred 9 Percent Stock (500																36
37			shares × $100 per share)							50	0	0	0	00		37
38			Issued 500 shares.																38

Controlling Accounts and Subsidiary Ledgers

Investors may finish paying for subscriptions at different times, and a firm issues stock only when the individual subscriber has paid in full; therefore, the firm's accountant has to maintain an account for each individual subscriber. As a result, the books exhibit the following relationships between controlling accounts and subsidiary ledgers.

Controlling Account	Subsidiary Ledger
Subscriptions Receivable, Preferred 9 Percent Stock Subscriptions Receivable, Common Stock	Preferred 9 Percent Stock Subscribers' ledger Common Stock Subscribers' ledger

These records are similar to the Accounts Receivable controlling account and the accounts receivable ledger.

The firm's accountant has to keep an accurate record of the number of shares owned by each stockholder. Consequently, each stock account is a controlling account.

Controlling Account	Subsidiary Ledger
Preferred 9 Percent Stock	Preferred 9 Percent Stockholders' ledger
Common Stock	Common Stockholders' ledger

As we have said, a small corporation may use its stock certificate book as a subsidiary ledger. Naturally, the accountant must see to it that the information is complete, so that the company can declare and pay dividends correctly. Cash dividends are paid on outstanding stock only.

ILLUSTRATION OF A CORPORATE BALANCE SHEET

In order to reinforce your understanding of the accounts introduced in this chapter, examine the balance sheet shown in Figure 23-3 to see where each account is placed. Because this balance sheet covers so many of the concepts just discussed, you'll probably want to refer back to it in the future.

Objective 6

Prepare a balance sheet for a corporation, including Subscriptions Receivable, Organization Costs, Paid-in Capital accounts, and Retained Earnings.

Mid-City Service Corporation
Balance Sheet
June 30, 19–

Assets				
Current Assets:				
Cash			$ 27 0 0 0 00	
Notes Receivable			50 0 0 0 00	
Accounts Receivable	$ 419 0 0 0 00			
Less Allowance for Doubtful Accounts	12 0 0 0 00		407 0 0 0 00	
Subscriptions Receivable, Preferred				
9 Percent Stock			14 0 0 0 00	
Subscriptions Receivable, Common Stock			30 0 0 0 00	
Merchandise Inventory			279 0 0 0 00	
Supplies			3 0 0 0 00	
Prepaid Insurance			5 0 0 00	
Total Current Assets				$ 810 5 0 0 00
Plant and Equipment:				
Delivery Equipment	$ 60 0 0 0 00			
Less Accumulated Depreciation	40 0 0 0 00	$ 20 0 0 0 00		
Store Equipment	$ 82 0 0 0 00			
Less Accumulated Depreciation	19 0 0 0 00	63 0 0 0 00		
Total Plant and Equipment				83 0 0 0 00
Investments:				
Friedman Equipment Company				
8 Percent Bonds				16 0 0 0 00
Intangible Assets:				
Organization Costs				8 0 0 0 00
Total Assets				$ 917 5 0 0 00
Liabilities				
Current Liabilities:				
Notes Payable			$ 20 0 0 0 00	
Accounts Payable			281 5 0 0 00	
Salaries Payable			3 0 0 0 00	
Interest Payable			1 0 0 0 00	
Total Liabilities				$ 305 5 0 0 00

Figure 23-3

	Stockholders' Equity																		
Paid-in Capital:																			
Preferred 7 Percent Stock, $50 par (2,000																			
shares authorized and issued)	$ 100	0	0	0	00														
Less Discount on Preferred 7 Percent Stock	1	0	0	0	00	$ 99	0	0	0	00									
Preferred 9 Percent Stock, $50 par																			
(4,000 shares authorized, 1,500 shares issued)	$ 75	0	0	0	00														
Preferred 9 Percent Stock Subscribed																			
(500 shares)	25	0	0	0	00														
Premium on Preferred 9 Percent Stock	3	0	0	0	00	103	0	0	0	00									
Common Stock, no-par, stated value																			
$10 per share (20,000 shares author-																			
ized, 14,000 shares issued)	$ 140	0	0	0	00														
Common Stock Subscribed (2,000 shares)	20	0	0	0	00														
Paid-in Capital in Excess of Stated Value	80	0	0	0	00	240	0	0	0	00									
Total Paid-in Capital						$ 442	0	0	0	00									
Retained Earnings						170	0	0	0	00									
Total Stockholders' Equity											612	0	0	0	00				
Total Liabilities and Stockholders' Equity											$ 917	5	0	0	00				

Figure 23-3
(continued)

NEW ACCOUNTS AND THE FUNDAMENTAL ACCOUNTING EQUATION

The placement and use of the accounts we have introduced in this chapter with respect to the fundamental accounting equation are shown on the next page in Figure 23-4.

GLOSSARY

Articles of incorporation Application for a charter.

Authorized capital The maximum number of shares that may be issued for each class of stock (common and preferred).

Capital stock General term referring to shares of ownership in a corporation; subdivided into common stock and preferred stock.

Charter Written right, issued by a state government, for a corporation to exist; approved articles of incorporation.

Closely held corporation A corporation having a relatively small group of owners.

Common stock Stock whose owners are paid dividends only after owners of preferred stock have been paid (residual share); holders of common stock have voting privileges.

Corporation "An artificial being, invisible, intangible, and existing only in contemplation of the law." As such, it is a separate legal entity.

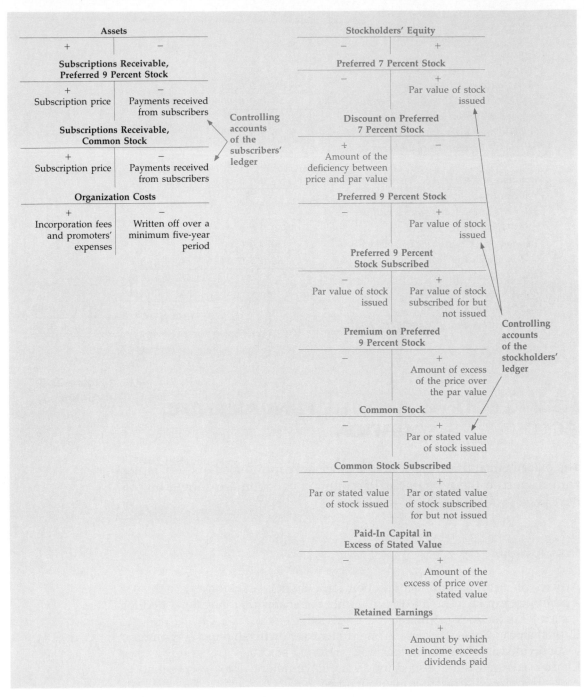

Figure 23-4

Cumulative preferred stock   When a firm fails to pay dividends during certain years, these dividends may be said to accumulate. When the firm finally pays the accumulated dividends, holders of cumulative preferred stock must be paid these dividends before any dividends can be paid to holders of common stock.

Discount   The amount by which the issuing price of a stock falls below the par value.

Dividends   Distributions of earnings of a corporation, in the form of either cash or additional shares of stock.

Double taxation   The net income of the corporation is taxed first, since the corporation is a separate entity. When the net income is distributed as dividends to stockholders, it becomes part of the personal income of the individual stockholder and is taxed a second time.

Intangible asset   An asset with no physical attributes; this classification includes such accounts as Organization Costs, Patents, and Goodwill.

Issued stock   Stock issued by a corporation.

Legal capital   Minimum capital stock investment that a corporation must maintain; capital that is not subject to withdrawal by stockholders; usually equal to par or stated value.

Noncumulative preferred stock   Preferred stock in which dividends in arrears do not accumulate; once they are passed, they are gone forever.

Nonparticipating preferred stock   Stock in which the dividends are limited to the regular rate.

No-par stock   Stock that has no value printed on the stock certificates.

Open or **public corporation**   A corporation having a large group of owners, ordinarily with shares traded on a stock exchange or in over-the-counter markets.

Organization Costs   An intangible asset account; used to record the cost of organizing a corporation, such as fees paid to the state, attorneys' fees, promotional costs, travel expenses, costs of printing stock certificates, and so on.

Outstanding stock   Stock actually in the possession of stockholders (issued stock less the number of shares reacquired by the company).

Paid-in Capital   A caption in the balance sheet listed immediately under stockholders' equity. The Paid-in Capital section includes the stock accounts and their related premium or discount accounts.

Participating preferred stock   Holders of preferred stock share in any extra dividends distributed by the corporation after the regular dividend has been paid to holders of preferred stock and a stipulated dividend to holders of common stock.

Par-value stock   Stock in which a uniform face value, indicating the amount per share to be entered in the capital stock account, is printed on the stock certificates.

Preemptive right   A stockholder who has a preemptive right, in order to maintain the same proportionate ownership in a corporation in the future as he or she does originally, has the privilege of subscribing to a new issue of stock in the same proportion as his or her present ownership.

Preferred stock   Stock whose holders are paid dividends at a regular rate before any dividends are paid to a holder of common stock. The holder of preferred stock also has preference in the distribution of assets in the event of a liquidation.

Premium   The amount by which the issuing price of a stock exceeds the par value.

Retained earnings A stockholders' equity account representing capital generated by the corporation's earnings that remains in the firm; the amount by which net income exceeds dividends paid.

Stated value The amount per share of no-par stock that is recorded in the corporation's stock accounts; an amount designated by the law as being not subject to withdrawal by stockholders.

Stock certificates Documents giving evidence of ownership of shares of stock; issued only when the stockholder has paid for the shares in full.

Stockholders' equity The owners' equity in a corporation. Also referred to as *capital*.

Stockholders' ledger A record showing the name and address of each stockholder and the number of shares owned.

Treasury stock A corporation's own stock, which it has issued and which was at one time outstanding, that the firm reacquires; the firm does not intend to cancel the stock.

QUESTIONS, EXERCISES, AND PROBLEMS

Discussion Questions

1. In what respect is a corporation a separate legal entity?
2. Identify four advantages and two disadvantages of the corporate form of business organization over sole proprietorship and partnership forms. In your opinion, which is the greatest advantage and which is the greatest disadvantage?
3. Name three types of organization costs. How is Organization Costs classified on a balance sheet? What eventually happens to Organization Costs?
4. If a corporation sells its stock at a premium, does the amount of the premium represent revenue to the firm?
5. In regard to common stock, what is the difference between par value and stated value?
6. What is a stock subscription?
7. What is the purpose of Common Stock Subscribed, and what happens to the account?

Exercises

Exercise 23-1 Describe the transactions recorded in the following ledger accounts of the Templeton Company.

Cash				Common Stock		
(1)	205,000	(2)	4,000		(1)	200,000

Organization Costs			Premium on Common		
(2)	4,000			(1)	5,000

Exercise 23-2 The T. R. Thompson Corporation is authorized to issue 20,000 shares of $50 par-value common stock. Record the following transactions in general journal form.

Jan. 16 Sold 4,000 shares of common stock at $51 per share; received cash.
    21 Issued 2,100 shares of common stock in exchange for land and building valued at $20,000 and $90,000, respectively.
Feb. 25 Sold 1,000 shares of common stock at $52 per share; received cash.

Exercise 23-3 Standerford, Inc., organized on February 5 of this year, was authorized to issue 500 shares of cumulative preferred 8 percent stock, $100 par value, and 5,000 shares of common stock, $25 par value. Record in general journal form the following transactions, completed during Standerford's first year of operations.

Feb. 5 Sold 2,000 shares of common stock at par for cash.
    5 Issued 50 shares of common stock to an attorney in return for legal services pertaining to incorporation.
May 6 Sold 400 shares of preferred stock at $101 per share; received cash.
Aug. 6 Issued 2,200 shares of common stock in exchange for land with a fair market value of $55,000.

Exercise 23-4 The outstanding stock of Tate Investment Corporation consists of 3,000 shares of preferred 6 percent stock, $100 par value, and 10,000 shares of common stock, $50 par value. Tate's board of directors declares a dividend of $60,000 for this year. How much of the dividend is allocated to holders of preferred stock and how much to holders of common stock?

Exercise 23-5 The Sanderson Electric Corporation is authorized to issue 100,000 shares of no-par common stock, $10 stated value. Record the following transactions in general journal form.

May 14 Sold 20,000 shares of common stock at $12 per share for cash.
Jun. 9 Sold 10,000 shares of common stock at $11 per share for cash.

Exercise 23-6 St. John's Motors has authorized capital consisting of 1,000 shares of cumulative preferred 7 percent stock, $100 par value, and 10,000 shares of common stock, $20 par value. Record the following transactions in general journal form.

a. Received subscriptions to 500 shares of preferred 7 percent stock at $102 per share, with a downpayment of 50 percent of the subscription price.
b. Received 30 percent of the subscription price from all subscribers.
c. Received 20 percent of the subscription price from all subscribers, and issued the stock certificates.

Exercise 23-7 Describe the transactions recorded in the following ledger accounts of Evans Oil Company, Inc.

Cash		Common Stock	
(a) 12,000			(a) 10,000
(c) 16,800			(e) 20,000
(d) 11,200			

Subscriptions Receivable, Common Stock		Common Stock Subscribed	
(b) 28,000	(c) 16,800	(e) 20,000	(b) 20,000
	(d) 11,200		

Paid-in Capital in Excess of Stated Value	
	(a) 2,000
	(b) 8,000

Exercise 23-8 The A. P. Higgins Corporation's charter authorized it to issue 1,000 shares of $50 par-value preferred 9 percent stock and 10,000 shares of no-par common stock (stated value $15). The following account balances are from the Balance Sheet columns of the work sheet.

Retained Earnings (credit balance)	$29,000
Common Stock Subscribed (2,000 shares)	30,000
Discount on Preferred 9 Percent Stock	1,600
Common Stock	90,000
Preferred 9 Percent Stock	40,000
Paid-in Capital in Excess of Stated Value	24,000

Instructions

Prepare the Stockholders' Equity section of the balance sheet.

Problem Set A

Problem 23-1A The Sea Fare Restaurant, organized on April 4 of this year, has a charter that stipulates the following authorized capital.

a. 4,000 shares of preferred 7 percent stock, $50 par value
b. 20,000 shares of common stock, $20 par value

During the first year of its operations, Sea Fare completed the following transactions.

Apr. 12 Received subscriptions to 6,000 shares of common stock at $20 per share, collecting 50 percent of the subscription price.

May 18 Sold 1,000 shares of preferred 7 percent stock for $49 per share, receiving cash.

Jun. 12 Subscribers to 6,000 shares of common stock paid an additional 30 percent of the subscription price.

Jul.   12 Subscribers to 6,000 shares of common stock paid an additional 20 percent of the subscription price; the Sea Fare Restaurant then issued the 6,000 shares of stock.

Sep.   9 Sold 1,200 shares of preferred 7 percent stock for $48 per share, receiving cash.

Nov.   29 Received subscriptions to 1,000 shares of common stock at $21 per share, collecting 25 percent of the subscription price.

Dec.   18 Received subscriptions to 800 shares of preferred 7 percent stock for $49 per share, collecting 10 percent of the subscription price.

Instructions

Record the above transactions in general journal form.

Problem 23-2A   Three people—Beasley, Poe, and Russell—organized City Van and Storage, Inc., with a charter providing for the following authorized capital.

a. 1,000 shares of preferred 9 percent stock, $50 par value
b. 10,000 shares of common stock, $10 par value

During its first year of operations, City Van and Storage completed the following transactions that affected stockholders' equity.

Apr.   3 Issued 2,400 shares of common stock to Beasley, at par, for cash.
         4 Paid an attorney $2,650 for paying state fees and for performing services needed for incorporating the firm.
         4 Bought equipment from Russell for $28,600. Russell accepted 2,860 shares of common stock in exchange for the equipment.
         4 Bought land and a building from Poe. It was agreed that the land would be valued at $10,600 and the building at $32,500. There is an outstanding mortgage on the property of $19,000, held by First Federal Savings and Loan Association. The corporation assumed responsibility for paying the mortgage. Poe accepted common stock at par for his equity.
         6 Issued 40 shares of common stock to Beasley for organizational services.

May   4 Issued 300 shares of preferred 9 percent stock at $53 per share to investors for cash.
        30 Issued 200 shares of preferred 9 percent stock at $52 per share to investors for cash.

Instructions

1. Record the above transactions in general journal form.
2. Post the entries to the following accounts: Common Stock, Preferred 9 Percent Stock, Premium on Preferred 9 Percent Stock.
3. Prepare the Stockholders' Equity section of the balance sheet as of December 31, the end of the first year of operations. Net income after taxes for the year was $22,900, and no dividends were declared during the year. As a result, Retained Earnings has a credit balance of $22,900.

Problem 23-3A The Franklin Company was organized on February 1 of this year, with a charter providing for the following authorized capital.

a. 2,000 shares of preferred 7 percent stock, $25 par value
b. 10,000 shares of no-par common stock, $15 stated value

During the first year of its operations, the Franklin Company completed the following transactions.

Feb. 1 Bought land from Franklin for $26,000. Franklin accepted 1,000 shares of common stock for the land (credit Paid-in Capital in Excess of Stated Value $11,000).

2 Received subscriptions to 3,000 shares of common stock at $26 per share, collecting 40 percent of the subscription price.

3 Issued 50 shares of common stock to Franklin, at $26 per share, in return for organizational services.

5 Subscribers to 3,000 shares of common stock paid an additional 30 percent of the subscription price.

26 Paid an attorney $1,840 for paying state fees and for performing services needed for incorporating the firm.

28 Received subscriptions to 500 shares of preferred 7 percent stock at $24 per share, collecting 20 percent of the subscription price.

28 Subscribers to 3,000 shares of common stock paid the remaining 30 percent of the subscription price; Franklin Company then issued the stock.

Mar. 6 Received subscriptions to 2,500 shares of common stock at $27 per share, collecting 50 percent of the subscription price.

14 Subscribers to 500 shares of preferred 7 percent stock paid an additional 40 percent of the subscription price.

20 Sold 200 shares of preferred 7 percent stock at $22 per share for cash.

26 Subscribers to 2,500 shares of common stock paid the remaining 50 percent of the subscription price; Franklin Company then issued the stock.

Instructions

Record these transactions in general journal form.

Problem 23-4A Broadway Fabrics, Inc., has an authorized capital of 1,000 shares of preferred 8 percent stock, $100 par value, and 10,000 shares of no-par common stock, stated value $20. The following account balances are from the Balance Sheet columns of the work sheet for the fiscal year ended March 31 of this year.

Cash	$ 29,960
Preferred 8 Percent Stock	83,000
Equipment	96,450
Subscriptions Receivable, Preferred 8 Percent Stock	6,400
Accounts Payable	192,720
Common Stock Subscribed	30,000
Retained Earnings	93,000

Subscriptions Receivable, Common Stock	$ 16,200
Building	132,000
Mortgage Payable (long-term liability)	46,000
Paid-in Capital in Excess of Stated Value	37,500
Accounts Receivable	234,780
Accumulated Depreciation, Equipment	43,730
Notes Payable	18,200
Preferred 8 Percent Stock Subscribed	17,000
Allowance for Doubtful Accounts	7,420
Organization Costs	7,120
Common Stock	120,000
Accumulated Depreciation, Building	26,900
Land	34,000
Merchandise Inventory	158,640
Supplies	1,920
Premium on Preferred 8 Percent Stock	2,000

Instructions

1. Determine the number of shares of preferred 8 percent stock issued and subscribed.
2. Determine the number of shares of common stock issued and subscribed.
3. Prepare a classified balance sheet.

Problem Set B

Problem 23-1B Don's Heating and Boiler Service, Inc., which was organized on May 5 of this year, has a charter that stipulates the following authorized capital.

a. 2,000 shares of preferred 8 percent stock, $100 par value
b. 25,000 shares of common stock, $25 par value

Don's Heating and Boiler Service completed the following transactions during this first year of operations.

May   6 Received subscriptions to 8,000 shares of common stock at $25 per share; collected 60 percent of the subscription price.
       12 Sold 800 shares of preferred 8 percent stock for $96 per share, receiving cash.
Jun.   6 Subscribers to 8,000 shares of common stock paid an additional 20 percent of the subscription price.
Jul.   6 Subscribers to 8,000 shares of common stock paid an additional 20 percent of the subscription price; Don's Heating and Boiler Service issued the 8,000 shares of stock.
Aug.   3 Sold 400 shares of preferred 8 percent stock for $94 per share, receiving cash.
Sep.   11 Received subscriptions to 2,000 shares of common stock at $26 per share; collected 50 percent of the subscription price.

Oct. 19 Received subscriptions to 200 shares of preferred 8 percent stock for $97 per share; collected 20 percent of the subscription price.

Instructions

Record the above transactions in general journal form.

Problem 23-2B Three people—Burke, Stacy, and Thomas—organized Central Beauty Supply, Inc. The charter of this corporation authorizes capital consisting of the following.

a. 1,000 shares of preferred 7 percent stock, $50 par value
b. 10,000 shares of common stock, $10 par value

During its first year of operations, Central Beauty Supply completed the following transactions that affected stockholders' equity.

Mar. 1 Issued to Burke 2,000 shares of common stock, at par, for cash.
1 Bought equipment from Stacy for $26,000. Stacy accepted 2,600 shares of common stock in exchange for the equipment.
1 Bought land and building from Thomas. It was agreed that the land would be valued at $9,500 and the building at $38,500. There is an outstanding mortgage on the property of $16,000, held by Commercial Savings and Loan Association. The corporation assumed responsibility for paying the mortgage. Thomas accepted common stock at par for her equity.
4 Paid an attorney $2,400 for paying state fees and for performing services needed for incorporating the firm.
6 Issued 50 shares of common stock at par to Burke for organizational services.
Apr. 9 Issued 400 shares of preferred 7 percent stock at $52 per share to investors for cash.
May 27 Issued 300 shares of preferred 7 percent stock at $51 per share to investors for cash.

Instructions

1. Record the above transactions in general journal form.
2. Post the entries to the following accounts: Common Stock, Preferred 7 Percent Stock, Premium on Preferred 7 Percent Stock.
3. Prepare the Stockholders' Equity section of the balance sheet as of December 31, the end of the first year of operations. Net income after taxes for the year was $24,000, and no dividends were declared during the year. As a result, Retained Earnings has a credit balance of $24,000.

Problem 23-3B The Sterling Dairy was organized on October 1 of this year, with a charter providing for authorized capital as follows.

a. 1,000 shares of preferred 8 percent stock, $50 par value
b. 20,000 shares of no-par common stock ($5 stated value)

During the first year of operations, the Sterling Dairy completed the following transactions.

Oct.   2 Received subscriptions to 4,000 shares of common stock at $12 per share, collecting 30 percent of the subscription price.

2 Bought equipment from Sterling, one of the promoters, for $24,000. Sterling accepted 2,000 shares of common stock in return for the equipment. (Credit Paid-in Capital in Excess of Stated Value $14,000).

14 Subscribers to 4,000 shares of common stock paid an additional 30 percent of the subscription price.

16 Issued 100 shares of common stock to Sterling at $12 per share in return for promotional services valued at $1,200.

20 Received subscriptions to 400 shares of preferred 8 percent stock at $53 per share, collecting 40 percent of the subscription price.

23 Paid an attorney $1,960 for paying state fees and for performing services needed for incorporating the firm.

30 Subscribers to 4,000 shares of common stock paid the remaining 40 percent of the subscription price; the Sterling Dairy then issued the 4,000 shares.

Nov.   5 Received subscriptions to 2,000 shares of common stock at $14 per share, collecting 50 percent of the subscription price.

10 Subscribers to 400 shares of preferred 8 percent stock paid an additional 30 percent of the subscription price.

16 Sold 100 shares of preferred 8 percent stock at $51 per share for cash.

25 Subscribers to 2,000 shares of common stock paid the remaining 50 percent of the subscription price; the Sterling Dairy then issued the 2,000 shares.

Instructions

Record these transactions in general journal form.

Problem 23-4B   Pietro Produce, Inc., has an authorized capital of 1,000 shares of preferred 7 percent stock, $100 par value, and 10,000 shares of no-par common stock, stated value $20. The following account balances for the fiscal year ending December 31 of this year are taken from the Balance Sheet columns of the work sheet for the year.

Cash	$ 27,600
Equipment	92,000
Notes Payable	16,400
Preferred 7 Percent Stock	80,000
Accounts Receivable	221,840
Accumulated Depreciation, Equipment	41,650
Land	30,000
Subscriptions Receivable, Preferred 7 Percent Stock	5,100
Premium on Preferred 7 Percent Stock	1,800
Merchandise Inventory	144,500
Building	128,000

Accounts Payable	$187,640
Accumulated Depreciation, Building	20,600
Organization Costs	6,420
Allowance for Doubtful Accounts	6,920
Common Stock	120,000
Subscriptions Receivable, Common Stock	8,700
Preferred 7 Percent Stock Subscribed	10,000
Common Stock Subscribed	20,000
Mortgage Payable (long-term liability)	42,000
Paid-in Capital in Excess of Stated Value	35,000
Retained Earnings	84,000
Supplies	1,850

Instructions

1. Determine the number of shares of preferred 7 percent stock subscribed and issued.
2. Determine the number of shares of common stock issued and subscribed.
3. Prepare a classified balance sheet.

24 Corporations: Work Sheet, Taxes, and Dividends

Learning Objectives

After you have completed this chapter, you will be able to do the following:

1. Journalize entries for corporate income taxes.

2. Journalize closing entries for a corporation.

3. Complete a work sheet for a corporation.

4. Journalize entries for the appropriation of Retained Earnings.

5. Journalize entries for the declaration and issuance of cash dividends.

6. Journalize entries for the declaration and issuance of stock dividends.

7. Complete a corporate statement of retained earnings and a balance sheet, including the following types of accounts: Appropriated Retained Earnings, Stock Dividend Distributable, Dividends Payable, and Income Tax Payable.

Chapter 23 described the entries the accountant makes during the initial organization of a corporation. Now let's assume that the corporation is established and turn our attention to the year-to-year entries for taxes, dividends, and retained earnings.

PROCEDURE FOR RECORDING AND PAYING INCOME TAXES

Determining the net income of a corporation is simply a matter of

Revenue − Expenses = Net income

One could compare most aspects of the revenue and expense accounts of a corporation to the revenue and expense accounts of sole proprietorships and partnerships. The net income of a sole proprietorship and the distributive shares of net income of a partnership are taxable as part of the owners' personal incomes. Since the corporation is a separate legal entity, however, it must pay income taxes in its own name. Corporations are subject to federal income taxes; many states and cities also impose an income tax on them. We'll only talk about the income tax levied by the federal government, but the same basic principles apply to state and city income taxes as well.

In order to place corporations on a pay-as-you-go basis, the law requires most of them to estimate in advance the amount of their federal income taxes for the forthcoming fiscal year. The corporations then pay the estimated amounts in four installments during the year. The firm's accountant records each entry as a debit to Income Tax and a credit to Cash. The Income Tax account is handled like an expense account, except that the accountant usually makes a separate entry closing Income Tax into Income Summary.

At the end of the fiscal year, after the corporation determines the exact amount of its income, it calculates how much income tax it owes. If the amount of income tax the corporation has paid in advance exceeds its tax liability for the year, the accountant debits the amount of the overpayment to Income Tax Paid in Advance, a current-asset account, and credits it to Income Tax. Usually, however, the amount of income tax paid in advance is less than the amount of the tax liability. In this case, the accountant debits the amount of the underpayment to Income Tax and credits it to Income Tax Payable, a current-liability account. The corporation is required to make full payment of its final tax with its income tax return. (The tax return is filed two and a half months after the close of the fiscal year.) The entry is a debit to Income Tax Payable and a credit to Cash.

Income Tax Entries for a Corporation: First Year

Los Angeles Pool Supply, Inc., begins operations on January 5. The corporation's fiscal year extends from January 1 through December 31. Its authorized capital consists of 200,000 shares of $20 par-value common stock. For the fiscal year, the corporation estimates that its net income will be $100,000 and that its income tax will be $40,000, as calculated below. Throughout this text, we shall assume that the federal corporation income tax rates are 22 percent of the first $25,000 of taxable income and 46 percent of taxable income over $25,000. Incidentally, the official tax rate changes from time to time.

Objective 1

Journalize entries for corporate income taxes.

$$\begin{array}{rl} \$25,000 \times .22 = & \$\ 5,500 \\ 75,000 \times .46 = & \underline{\ 34,500} \\ & \$40,000 \end{array}$$

Here is the way the accountant for Los Angeles Pool Supply records the payment of this tax.

1	Apr.	15	Income Tax	10 0 0 0 00	1
2			Cash		10 0 0 0 00	2
3			Paid first quarterly installment		3
4			of estimated federal income tax		4
5			for the year (one-fourth of		5
6			$40,000).		6
7					7
8					8

1	Jun.	15	Income Tax	10 0 0 0 00	1
2			Cash		10 0 0 0 00	2
3			Paid second quarterly installment		3
4			of estimated federal income tax		4
5			for the year.		5
6					6
7					7

1	Sep.	15	Income Tax		10	0	0	0	00								1
2			Cash								10	0	0	0	00		2
3			Paid third quarterly installment														3
4			of estimated federal income tax														4
5			for the year.														5
6																	6
7																	7
8																	8

1	Dec.	15	Income Tax		10	0	0	0	00								1
2			Cash								10	0	0	0	00		2
3			Paid fourth quarterly installment														3
4			of estimated federal income tax														4
5			for the year.														5
6																	6
7																	7
8																	8

At the end of the year, the accountant prepares a work sheet and determines that the net income of the corporation for the year is $120,000 ($980,000 in revenues minus $860,000 in costs and expenses). Since the estimated net income was $100,000, the additional amount of taxable income is $20,000 ($120,000 − $100,000). The corporation therefore owes the government additional income tax of $9,200 (.46 × $20,000). The following entry appears first as an adjusting entry on the work sheet.

1			Adjusting Entry												1
2	Dec.	31	Income Tax		9	2	0	0	00						2
3			Income Tax Payable								9	2	0	0	00	3
4															4
5															5
6															6
7															7
8															8
9															9

The accountant now records the closing entries. In this example, to save time, we have used "Revenues" to represent all temporary-equity accounts having a credit balance and "Expenses" to represent all accounts having a debit balance.

Objective 2

Journalize closing entries for a corporation.

1			*Closing Entries*													1
2	*Dec.*	*31*	*Revenues*	980	0	0	0	00								2
3			*Income Summary*						980	0	0	0	00			3
4																4
5		*31*	*Income Summary*	860	0	0	0	00								5
6			*Expenses*						860	0	0	0	00			6
7																7
8		*31*	*Income Summary*	49	2	0	0	00								8
9			*Income Tax*						49	2	0	0	00			9
10																10
11		*31*	*Income Summary*	70	8	0	0	00								11
12			*Retained Earnings*						70	8	0	0	00			12
13																13
14																14
15																15
16																16
17																17
18																18
19																19
20																20
21																21
22																22
23																23

Now let's summarize the steps for journalizing the closing entries of a corporation.

1. Close revenue accounts into Income Summary.
2. Close expense accounts into Income Summary.
3. Close Income Tax into Income Summary, by the amount of the actual income tax for the year.
4. Close Income Summary into Retained Earnings, by the amount of the net income after income tax.

As we have said, the Retained Earnings account is classified as a stockholders' equity account. It is a permanent or real account, as opposed to a temporary-equity account. After the accountant has finished posting to the Retained Earnings account, the account represents accumulated earnings if it has a credit balance. Conversely, if the Retained Earnings account has a debit balance, it represents a **deficit.** The accountant posts the entries for the year to the T accounts, as follows.

	Cash		
+		−	
		Apr. 15	10,000
		Jun. 15	10,000
		Sep. 15	10,000
		Dec. 15	10,000

	Income Tax		
+		−	
Apr. 15	10,000	Dec. 31 Clos.	49,200
Jun. 15	10,000		
Sep. 15	10,000		
Dec. 15	10,000		
Dec. 31 Adj.	9,200		

	Revenues		
−		+	
Dec. 31 Clos.	980,000	Bal.	980,000

	Expenses		
+		−	
Bal.	860,000	Dec. 31 Clos.	860,000

	Income Tax Payable		
−		+	
		Dec. 31 Adj.	9,200

	Income Summary		
Dec. 31	860,000	Dec. 31	980,000
Dec. 31	49,200		
Dec. 31 Clos.	70,800		

	Retained Earnings		
−		+	
		Bal.	—
		Dec. 31	70,800

Income taxes are considered to be a necessary expense of conducting a business, and—as stated earlier—the accountant handles the Income Tax account much like any other expense account. However, it is common practice to make a separate entry closing Income Tax into Income Summary and not to include the amount for income tax with the total amounts for all the other expenses. This procedure makes the amount of taxable income more evident from a quick analysis of Income Summary. Notice in the Income Summary T account illustrated above that the balance of the account prior to transferring the Income Tax balance is $120,000 ($980,000 − $860,000), the taxable income. If the amount of income tax is closed into Income Summary with all the other expenses, the amount of taxable income is not as obvious.

Income Tax Entries for a Corporation: Second Year

The next year begins with a carry-over of the income tax liability for the previous year. Los Angeles Pool Supply estimates that its net income will be $110,000 and that the related income tax will be $44,600. The entries are shown on the right.

1	Mar.	15	Income Tax Payable	9 2 0 0 00			1
2			Cash		9 2 0 0 00		2
3			Paid tax liability for last				3
4			year, due two and one-half				4
5			months after the close of the				5
6			fiscal year.				6
7							7
8							8
9							9
10							10
11							11
12							12
13							13

1	Apr.	15	Income Tax	11 1 5 0 00			1
2			Cash		11 1 5 0 00		2
3			Paid first quarterly installment				3
4			of estimated federal income tax				4
5			for the year (one-fourth of				5
6			$44,600).				6
7							7
8							8
9							9
10							10
11							11
12							12
13							13

1	Jun.	15	Income Tax	11 1 5 0 00			1
2			Cash		11 1 5 0 00		2
3			Paid second quarterly installment				3
4			of estimated federal income tax				4
5			for the year.				5
6							6
7							7
8							8
9							9
10							10
11							11
12							12
13							13

1	Sep.	15	Income Tax		11	1	5	0	00									1
2			Cash								11	1	5	0	00			2
3			*Paid third quarterly installment*															3
4			*of estimated federal income tax*															4
5			*for the year.*															5
6																		6
7																		7
8																		8
9																		9
10																		10
11																		11
12																		12

1	Dec.	15	Income Tax		11	1	5	0	00									1
2			Cash								11	1	5	0	00			2
3			*Paid fourth quarterly installment*															3
4			*of estimated federal income tax*															4
5			*for the year.*															5
6																		6
7																		7
8																		8
9																		9
10																		10
11																		11

At the end of the year, the accountant determines the actual net income on the work sheet: $142,000. The net income in excess of the advance estimate is $32,000 ($142,000 − $110,000), and the amount of the adjustment for additional income tax is $14,720.

WORK SHEET FOR A CORPORATION

The second-year work sheet for Los Angeles Pool Supply, Inc., is shown in Figure 24-1.

When the accountant is completing the work sheet, he or she must give special treatment to the adjusting entry for the additional income tax. Before recording the adjustment for income tax, the accountant must do the following.

Objective 3

Complete a work sheet for a corporation.

1. Record and total the Trial Balance columns.
2. Record all adjustments except the adjustment for income tax.
3. Extend account balances into the Income Statement columns and tentatively determine the net income before taxes, as shown below. (The

accountant's objective, naturally, is to determine the net income in advance, and then to calculate the exact amount of the income tax.)

ACCOUNT NAME		INCOME STATEMENT	
		DEBIT	CREDIT
	2		
3 Sales			1,062 0 0 0 00
4 Purchases		762 0 0 0 00	
5 Purchases Discount			4 8 0 0 00
6 Selling Expenses (control)		130 7 5 0 00	
7 General Expenses (control)		37 7 1 0 00	
8 Interest Expense		3 7 2 0 00	
9 Income Summary		180 5 0 0 00	189 8 8 0 00
10		1,114 6 8 0 00	1,256 6 8 0 00
11 Net Income before Income Tax		142 0 0 0 00	
12		1,256 6 8 0 00	1,256 6 8 0 00

4. The accountant calculates the additional income tax this way. (We present two methods; take your choice.)

Method 1

Actual net income	$142,000
Estimated net income	− 110,000
Income not yet taxed	$ 32,000
Tax rate (46%)	× .46
Additional income tax	$ 14,720

Method 2

Income tax on net income of $142,000

On first $25,000 ($25,000 × .22)	$ 5,500
On next $117,000 ($117,000 × .46)	53,820
Total income tax	$59,320
Income tax already paid	− 44,600
Additional income tax	$14,720

5. The accountant records the adjusting entry of $14,720 in the Adjustments columns of the work sheet.

	ACCOUNT NAME	TRIAL BALANCE	
		DEBIT	CREDIT
1	Cash	3 4 9 0 00	
2	Accounts Receivable	106 6 8 0 00	
3	Allowance for Doubtful Accounts		1 8 2 0 00
4	Subscriptions Receivable, Common Stock	24 5 0 0 00	
5	Merchandise Inventory	180 5 0 0 00	
6	Prepaid Insurance	1 2 2 0 00	
7	Store Equipment	54 7 2 0 00	
8	Accumulated Depreciation, Store Equipment		27 2 5 0 00
9	Office Equipment	28 9 2 0 00	
10	Accumulated Depreciation, Office Equipment		8 4 1 0 00
11	Organization Costs	5 0 0 0 00	
12	Notes Payable		16 0 0 0 00
13	Accounts Payable		62 7 5 0 00
14	Common Stock		100 0 0 0 00
15	Common Stock Subscribed		20 0 0 0 00
16	Premium on Common Stock		2 4 0 0 00
17	Retained Earnings		69 0 0 0 00
18	Sales		1,062 0 0 0 00
19	Purchases	762 0 0 0 00	
20	Purchases Discount		4 8 0 0 00
21	Selling Expenses (control)	126 4 5 0 00	
22	General Expenses (control)	32 7 5 0 00	
23			
24			
25	Interest Expense	3 6 0 0 00	
26	Income Tax	44 6 0 0 00	
27		1,374 4 3 0 00	1,374 4 3 0 00
28	Income Summary		
29	Interest Payable		
30	Income Tax Payable		
31			
32	Net Income after Income Tax		
33			
34			
35			
36			
37			
38			
39			
40			

Figure 24-1

	ADJUSTMENTS		INCOME STATEMENT		BALANCE SHEET		
	DEBIT	CREDIT	DEBIT	CREDIT	DEBIT	CREDIT	
					3 4 9 0 00		1
					106 6 8 0 00		2
		(e) 1 6 8 0 00				3 5 0 0 00	3
					24 5 0 0 00		4
	(b)189 8 8 0 00	(a)180 5 0 0 00			189 8 8 0 00		5
		(f) 5 2 0 00			7 0 0 00		6
					54 7 2 0 00		7
		(c) 4 3 0 0 00				31 5 5 0 00	8
					28 9 2 0 00		9
		(d) 2 7 6 0 00				11 1 7 0 00	10
					5 0 0 0 00		11
						16 0 0 0 00	12
						62 7 5 0 00	13
						100 0 0 0 00	14
						20 0 0 0 00	15
						2 4 0 0 00	16
						69 0 0 0 00	17
				1,062 0 0 0 00			18
			762 0 0 0 00				19
				4 8 0 0 00			20
	(c) 4 3 0 0 00		130 7 5 0 00				21
	(d) 2 7 6 0 00						22
	(e) 1 6 8 0 00						23
	(f) 5 2 0 00		37 7 1 0 00				24
	(g) 1 2 0 00		3 7 2 0 00				25
	(h) 14 7 2 0 00		59 3 2 0 00				26
							27
	(a)180 5 0 0 00	(b)189 8 8 0 00	180 5 0 0 00	189 8 8 0 00			28
		(g) 1 2 0 00				1 2 0 00	29
		(h) 14 7 2 0 00				14 7 2 0 00	30
	394 4 8 0 00	394 4 8 0 00	1,174 0 0 0 00	1,256 6 8 0 00	413 8 9 0 00	331 2 1 0 00	31
			82 6 8 0 00			82 6 8 0 00	32
			1,256 6 8 0 00	1,256 6 8 0 00	413 8 9 0 00	413 8 9 0 00	33
							34
							35
							36
							37
							38
							39
							40

6. The accountant records the amount of the entire income tax in the Income Statement Debit column and completes the Income Statement columns by determining the net income after taxes: $82,680.
7. The accountant extends all remaining figures, including Income Tax Payable and Net Income after Taxes, into the Balance Sheet columns, and completes the Balance Sheet columns.

Financial Statements

Here is an abbreviated income statement for the second year.

Los Angeles Pool Supply, Inc.
Income Statement
For year ended December 31, 19–

Revenue from Sales:	
Sales	$1 062 0 0 0 00

Net Income before Income Tax	142 0 0 0 00
Income Tax	59 3 2 0 00
Net Income after Income Tax	$ 82 6 8 0 00

The balance sheet includes Income Tax Payable as a current liability. It also includes the final balance of Retained Earnings. We'll look at a complete balance sheet later in this chapter.

Adjusting and Closing Entries

The next step in the accounting cycle is to take the adjusting entries and closing entries directly from the Adjustments columns of the work sheet and record them in the general journal (Figure 24-2).

Income Statement Net Income Versus Taxable Income

In our example, we've been assuming that the accountant for Los Angeles Pool Supply determined the income tax for the year as a matter of course by multiplying the corporation's net income for the year (as shown on the income statement) by the tax rate. The accountant maintained that the corporation's net income was its taxable income. Well, in real life, things

				Debit					Credit					
1				*Adjusting Entries*										1
2	19– Dec.	31	Income Summary	180	5	0	0	00						2
3			Merchandise Inventory						180	5	0	0	00	3
4														4
5		31	Merchandise Inventory	189	8	8	0	00						5
6			Income Summary						189	8	8	0	00	6
7														7
8		31	Selling Expenses (control)	4	3	0	0	00						8
9			Accumulated Depreciation, Store Equipment						4	3	0	0	00	9
10														10
11		31	General Expenses (control)	2	7	6	0	00						11
12			Accumulated Depreciation, Office Equipment						2	7	6	0	00	12
13														13
14		31	General Expenses (control)	1	6	8	0	00						14
15			Allowance for Doubtful Accounts						1	6	8	0	00	15
16														16
17		31	General Expenses (control)		5	2	0	00						17
18			Prepaid Insurance							5	2	0	00	18
19														19
20		31	Interest Expense		1	2	0	00						20
21			Interest Payable							1	2	0	00	21
22														22
23		31	Income Tax	14	7	2	0	00						23
24			Income Tax Payable						14	7	2	0	00	24
25														25
26			*Closing Entries*											26
27		31	Sales	1,062	0	0	0	00						27
28			Purchases Discount	4	8	0	0	00						28
29			Income Summary						1,066	8	0	0	00	29
30														30
31		31	Income Summary	934	1	8	0	00						31
32			Purchases						762	0	0	0	00	32
33			Selling Expenses (control)						130	7	5	0	00	33
34			General Expenses (control)						37	7	1	0	00	34
35			Interest Expense						3	7	2	0	00	35
36														36
37		31	Income Summary	59	3	2	0	00						37
38			Income Tax						59	3	2	0	00	38
39														39
40		31	Income Summary	82	6	8	0	00						40
41			Retained Earnings						82	6	8	0	00	41
42														42

Figure 24-2

aren't quite that simple. The net income shown on the income statement may differ quite a lot from the income reported for tax purposes. Here are some of the reasons why.

1. The depreciation method used for income statement purposes may differ from the method used for tax statement purposes. For example, the firm might use the straight-line method of depreciation for its income statement but the Accelerated Cost Recovery System (Appendix E) for its tax statement.
2. A firm may include certain types of revenue in the income statement but not in the tax statement. For example, in the income statement, the firm may count in the total of installment sales, but on the tax statement the firm may list only the cash actually received from installment sales (see Appendix F). Also, some items listed in the income statement, such as interest on state and municipal bonds, are not taxable; and some revenues, such as capital gains on the sale of property, are taxed at different rates.
3. A corporation may list certain types of expenditures as assets, and consequently not put them on the income statement. These same expenditures may be listed on the tax statement as expenses. For example, a company might not list prepaid advertising on its income statement, whereas it would list it as an expense on its tax statement.

REASONS FOR APPROPRIATING RETAINED EARNINGS

Since a corporation declares dividends out of its Retained Earnings, the *amount* of dividends is necessarily limited by the amount of Retained Earnings. However, rather than using the entire balance of Retained Earnings for cash or stock dividends (we'll discuss cash and stock dividends later), the board of directors may wish to earmark part of Retained Earnings for some specific purpose.

Such a restriction constitutes an **appropriation of retained earnings.** Let us say that the directors decide they want to provide for future expansion. The board passes a resolution, which is recorded in the minutes of a meeting, restricting or appropriating a certain amount of Retained Earnings for future expansion. The minutes of the meeting represent the source document for the accounting entry. For example, Los Angeles Pool Supply, Inc., plans to erect its own building. To finance the project, it decides to restrict Retained Earnings for a total amount of $500,000, at the rate of $50,000 per year, for ten years. The accountant makes the following type of entry at the end of each year, after the closing entries.

Objective 4

Journalize entries for the appropriation of Retained Earnings.

	1985 Feb.	5	Retained Earnings	50	0	0	0	00						1
2			Retained Earnings Appropriated for											2
3			Building						50	0	0	0	00	3
4			To appropriate Retained Earn-											4
5			ings, as ordered by the board											5
6			of directors in meeting of											6
7			February 5, 1985.											7
8														8

This appropriation of Retained Earnings does *not* represent a separate kitty or cash fund of $50,000. Let's look at cash dividends for a moment: If we consider the Retained Earnings account as a well or reservoir from which cash dividends are declared, then this reservoir has dried up by $50,000. **If the corporation does not declare and pay out these dividends, then the firm is preserving its net assets, particularly cash.**

At the end of the ten-year period, although there is *not* an actual $500,000 fund of cash, there is an additional $500,000 accumulated in net assets (assets minus liabilities). The corporation can now formulate plans to convert the $500,000 increase in net assets into cash in order to put a downpayment on the building.

When the objective—buying or erecting the building—has been accomplished, the corporation no longer needs to restrict Retained Earnings. The accountant may then make the following entry, reversing the ten previous entries.

	1995 Mar.	18	Retained Earnings Appropriated for											1
2			Building	500	0	0	0	00						2
3			Retained Earnings						500	0	0	0	00	3
4			To return to Retained Earnings											4
5			the balance in the Retained Earn-											5
6			ings Appropriated for Building											6
7			account, as ordered by the board											7
8			of directors in the meeting of											8
9			March 18, 1995.											9
10														10

Other examples of appropriated Retained Earnings accounts include:

- Retained Earnings Appropriated for Plant Expansion (no specific objective stated)
- Retained Earnings Appropriated for Bonded Indebtedness (an obligation imposed by contract)
- Retained Earnings Appropriated for Self-Insurance (planning for casualty losses)

- Retained Earnings Appropriated for Inventory Losses (in the event of getting caught in a price drop)
- Retained Earnings Appropriated for Contingencies (in the event of a rainy day)

Each appropriated Retained Earnings account is labeled "Retained Earnings Appropriated for _____." Therefore the account Retained Earnings represents unappropriated retained earnings. These accounts appear in a statement of retained earnings, an example of which is illustrated in Figure 24-3 (page 766).

DECLARATION AND PAYMENT OF DIVIDENDS

A dividend is a distribution—of cash, shares of stock, or other assets—which a corporation makes to its stockholders. Dividends are allocated to persons who own stock according to the number of shares they own and according to whether the stock is preferred or common. We shall discuss three types of dividends: cash dividends, stock dividends, and liquidating dividends. Cash dividends and stock dividends reduce Retained Earnings; liquidating dividends reduce Paid-in Capital.

Cash Dividends

A dividend payable in cash—or **cash dividend**—is the most usual form of dividend. It ordinarily represents a share of the current earnings paid to the stockholders as a reward for their investment. The board of directors declares dividends, generally paying cash dividends up to a certain percentage of the firm's net income after income tax. The cash dividend is expressed as a specific amount per share—for example, $1.12 per share. A stockholder who owns 100 shares is thus entitled to $112.

Before a corporation can pay a cash dividend, three things are needed.

1. **Retained Earnings** The company must have a sufficient balance in the unappropriated Retained Earnings account.
2. **An adequate amount of cash** A corporation may have earned large profits, but not all profits are in cash. For example, the revenue may be in the form of charge accounts, such as Accounts Receivable. Cash comes in only when the company receives payments from charge customers.
3. **Formal declaration by the board of directors** The payment of dividends, although it may be a matter of policy, is not automatic. The board of directors must pass the declaration in the form of a motion and record it in the minute book. This minute book is the source document for the accounting entry.

Dividend Dates

Three significant dates are involved in the declaration and payment of a dividend.

1. **Date of declaration** Date on which the board of directors votes to declare dividends. The entry recorded as of this date debits Retained Earnings and credits Dividends Payable.
2. **Date of record** Date as of which the ownership of shares is set. This date determines a person's eligibility for dividends, and ordinarily is about three weeks after the date of declaration.
3. **Date of payment** The date payment is made; on this date, the accountant debits the amount to Dividends Payable and credits it to Cash.

For example, on January 20, the board of directors of Los Angeles Pool Supply declares a quarterly cash dividend of $.72 per share (5,000 shares × $.72 = $3,600) to stockholders of record as of February 11, payable on March 2. (Dividends Payable is classified as a current liability.) The entries, in general journal form, are as follows.

Objective 5

Journalize entries for the declaration and issuance of cash dividends.

1	Jan.	20	Retained Earnings		3 6 0 0 00			1
2			Dividends Payable			3 6 0 0 00		2
3			To record declaration of quar-					3
4			terly cash dividend on common					4
5			stock at the rate of $.72 per					5
6			share to stockholders of record					6
7			as of February 11, payable					7
8			March 2, as ordered by board					8
9			of directors in meeting of					9
10			January 20.					10
11								11

1	Mar.	2	Dividends Payable		3 6 0 0 00			1
2			Cash			3 6 0 0 00		2
3			Payment of quarterly dividend					3
4			declared on January 20 to stock-					4
5			holders of record as of					5
6			February 11.					6
7								7

Stock Dividends

A **stock dividend** is a distribution, on a pro rata (proportional) basis, of additional shares of a company's stock to the stockholders. In other words, the dividend consists of shares of stock rather than cash. One could describe it as a dividend payable in stock. Generally, stock dividends consist of common stock distributed to holders of common stock. Stock dividends are usually issued by corporations that plow back (retain) earnings in order to finance future expansion.

Suppose that the board of directors of Los Angeles Pool Supply, Inc., declared a 20 percent stock dividend on October 11 to stockholders of record as of November 1, payable on November 16. The ledger sheet for the Common Stock account on October 11 looks like this in T account form.

Objective 6

Journalize entries for the declaration and issuance of stock dividends.

Common Stock
	Bal. 100,000
	$20 per share
	(5,000 shares)

Number of shares in the stock dividend:
20 percent of 5,000 shares = 1,000 shares

The present market value of the shares is $23 per share. The entries, in general journal form, are as follows. (We have put in the calculations just by way of explanation.)

1	Oct.	11	*Retained Earnings (1,000 shares ×*					1
2			*$23 each)*	23 0 0 0 00				2
3			*Stock Dividend Distributable*					3
4			*(1,000 shares × $20 each)*		20 0 0 0 00			4
5			*Premium on Common Stock*		3 0 0 0 00			5
6			*To record the declaration of*					6
7			*a 20 percent stock dividend to*					7
8			*stockholders of record as of No-*					8
9			*vember 1; payable November 16,*					9
10			*as ordered by board of directors*					10
11			*in meeting of October 11.*					11
12								12

1	Nov.	16	*Stock Dividend Distributable*	20 0 0 0 00				1
2			*Common Stock*		20 0 0 0 00			2
3			*Issuance of a stock dividend*					3
4			*(1,000 shares) declared on October*					4
5			*11 to stockholders of record as*					5
6			*of November 1.*					6
7								7

Stock Dividend Distributable is a stockholders' equity account, representing the total par value of the shares of stock to be issued. If the account is on the books at the time of the preparation of a balance sheet, the accountant lists it in the Paid-in Capital section, just below Common Stock.

The stock dividend—unlike the cash dividend—does *not* result in a reduction of assets. It merely reshuffles the stockholders' equity accounts. The stock dividend increases the Capital Stock accounts and decreases the Retained Earnings account, without making any change in the total stockholders' equity.

The stock dividend has no effect on the proportionate share of ownership of an individual stockholder. For example, Rosemary Baker owns 500 shares of the corporation's stock, which represents a one-tenth share in the corporation, since the total number of shares issued was 5,000. The corporation declares a 20 percent stock dividend. As her part of this dividend, Baker receives 100 shares (20 percent of 500 shares). Her total stock now amounts to 600 shares; the corporation's total stock is now 6,000 shares. Consequently, Rosemary Baker still has a one-tenth share in the ownership (600 shares/6,000 shares).

For accounting purposes, corporations make a distinction between a stock dividend of 25 percent or less (small) and a stock dividend of 26 percent or more (large). The above example represented a small stock dividend, in which the accountant debited Retained Earnings for the fair market value of the shares issued. If the stock dividend had been large, the accountant would have debited Retained Earnings for the par or stated value of the shares to be issued.

Reasons for Issuing Stock Dividends

In view of the fact that a stockholder's proportionate share or equity in a company does not change when the company issues a stock dividend, why does a corporation bother with stock dividends? Here are a few reasons.

1. Stock dividends appease stockholders by giving them paper to hold onto. The corporation can conserve its cash, and the stockholders feel partially satisfied. They didn't get cash, but at least they got something.
2. Stock dividends tend to reduce the market price of the stock. The supply of the stock increases with no immediate commensurate change in the demand for it. Stock with a lower price per share is more easily sold to the public.
3. Stock dividends enable stockholders to avoid income tax liability, since the recipients of stock dividends do not have to consider them as income and, therefore, don't have to pay any income tax on them.

Liquidating Dividends

A corporation pays **liquidating dividends** when (1) it is going out of existence or (2) it is permanently reducing the size of its operations. It returns to the stockholders all or a part of their investment. For example, in the situation shown here, a corporation has returned all stockholders' investments.

1	Common Stock	240 0 0 0 00			1
2	Premium on Common Stock	10 0 0 0 00			2
3	Cash		250 0 0 0 00		3
4	To end the business affairs of				4
5	the corporation, the board of				5
6	directors during meeting of				6
7	August 12 authorized a 100				7
8	percent liquidation dividend.				8
9					9
10					10

STOCK SPLIT

When there is a **stock split,** a corporation deliberately splits its stock, on the basis of its par or stated value, and issues a proportionate number of additional shares. For example, a corporation with 10,000 shares of $50 par-value stock outstanding may reduce the par value to $25 and increase the number of shares to 20,000. If you own 200 shares before the split, you will own 400 shares after it. The company may call in all the old shares and issue certificates for new ones on a 2-for-1 basis, or it may issue an additional share for each old share. The accountant records a stock split by the following entry. (We list the par values by way of explanation.)

1	Common Stock ($50 par value)	500 0 0 0 00			1
2	Common Stock ($25 par value)		500 0 0 0 00		2
3	The board of directors have this				3
4	day ordered a 2-for-1 stock				4
5	split, increasing the outstanding				5
6	shares from 10,000 to 20,000,				6
7	and reducing the par value from				7
8	$50 to $25.				8
9					9
10					10

This 2-for-1 stock split reduces the market price per share by approximately half, thereby increasing the stock's salability, because each share now costs less.

There is no change in Retained Earnings. The accountant changes the headings of the Capital Stock accounts in the ledger to show the new par or stated value per share and revises the stockholders' ledger to show the new distribution of shares. (As an alternative, some accountants record stock splits with a memorandum entry.)

Minute Book

We have said that the **minute book** is an important source document for any accounting entries involving the declaration of dividends and the appropriation of Retained Earnings. The minute book is just like the minute book of a club; it is a written, narrative record of all actions taken at official meetings. A corporation's minute book may also contain details relating to the purchase of plant and equipment, the obtaining of bank loans, the establishing of officers' salaries, and so on.

STATEMENT OF RETAINED EARNINGS AND A BALANCE SHEET FOR A CORPORATION

In this chapter, we have discussed a number of possible situations that would affect the status of retained earnings within a given period of time. These changes are reported on a separate financial statement, called a *statement of retained earnings.* Generally, this statement lists only those items that represent significant changes. For example, in the statement of retained earnings of the Fessenden Distributing Company (Figure 24-3, next page), specific appropriations for plant expansion and possible price declines are listed.

So that you can better visualize the relationship of the statement of retained earnings to the balance sheet, Figure 24-4 (pages 767-768) presents the balance sheet for Fessenden Distributing Company.

The accountant may use the account Paid-in Capital from Donation to record a situation in which the corporation receives a material gift. For example, the city of Loganville gives the Fessenden Distributing Company one acre of land, valued at $11,650, as an incentive to locate a processing plant there. The accountant for Fessenden debits Land and credits Paid-in Capital from Donation for $11,650 each.

Objective 7

Complete a corporate statement of retained earnings and a balance sheet, including the following types of accounts: Appropriated Retained Earnings, Stock Dividend Distributable, Dividends Payable, and Income Tax Payable.

Fessenden Distributing Company
Statement of Retained Earnings
For year ended December 31, 19—

Unappropriated Retained Earnings:				
Unappropriated Retained Earnings,				
Jan. 1, 19—	$ 112 7 0 0 00			
Net income for the year	73 0 0 0 00	$ 185 7 0 0 00		
Less: Cash dividends declared	$ 20 0 0 0 00			
Stock dividends declared	39 5 0 0 00			
Transfer to Appropriation for Plant				
Expansion (see below).	4 0 0 0 00			
Transfer to Appropriation for				
Possible Price Declines (see below)	3 0 0 0 00	66 5 0 0 00		
Unappropriated Retained Earnings,				
Dec. 31, 19—				$ 119 2 0 0 00
Appropriated Retained Earnings:				
Appropriated for Plant Expansion,				
Jan. 1, 19—	$ 16 0 0 0 00			
Add appropriation for the year (see above)	4 0 0 0 00			
Appropriated for Plant Expansion,				
Dec. 31, 19—		$ 20 0 0 0 00		
Appropriated for Possible Price Declines,				
Jan. 1, 19—	$ 15 0 0 0 00			
Add appropriation for the year (see above)	3 0 0 0 00			
Appropriated for Possible Price Declines,				
Dec. 31, 19—		18 0 0 0 00		
Retained Earnings Appropriated,				
Dec. 31, 19—				$ 38 0 0 0 00
Total Retained Earnings, Dec. 31, 19—				$ 157 2 0 0 00

Figure 24-3

GLOSSARY

Appropriation of retained earnings A portion of Retained Earnings designated for a specific purpose; the amount appropriated may not be used for cash or stock dividends.

Cash dividends Distribution of a corporation's earnings to stockholders in the form of cash.

Deficit Debit or negative balance in the Retained Earnings account.

Liquidating dividends Distribution of assets to stockholders when a corporation is going out of existence or is permanently reducing its size.

Fessenden Distributing Company
Balance Sheet
December 31, 19–

Assets				
Current Assets:				
Cash			$ 6 4 2 0 00	
Accounts Receivable	$ 163 3 9 0 00			
Less Allowance for Doubtful Accounts	4 2 9 0 00		159 1 0 0 00	
Subscriptions Receivable, Common Stock			3 5 0 0 00	
Merchandise Inventory			320 2 2 0 00	
Supplies			1 2 5 0 00	
Total Current Assets				$ 490 4 9 0 00
Plant and Equipment:				
Equipment	$ 80 7 6 0 00			
Less Accumulated Depreciation	26 7 5 0 00		$ 54 0 1 0 00	
Building	$ 160 0 0 0 00			
Less Accumulated Depreciation	78 0 0 0 00		82 0 0 0 00	
Land			40 0 0 0 00	
Total Plant and Equipment				176 0 1 0 00
Intangible Assets:				
Organization Costs			$ 7 2 0 0 00	
Patents			7 0 0 0 00	
Total Intangible Assets				14 2 0 0 00
Total Assets				$ 680 7 0 0 00
Liabilities				
Current Liabilities:				
Notes Payable	$ 16 0 0 0 00			
Accounts Payable	85 6 9 0 00			
Income Tax Payable	9 2 0 0 00			
Dividends Payable	4 0 0 0 00			
Interest Payable	9 6 0 00			
Total Current Liabilities			$ 115 8 5 0 00	
Long-term Liabilities:				
Mortgage Payable (due July 1, 19–)			54 0 0 0 00	
Total Liabilities				$ 169 8 5 0 00

Figure 24-4
(continued on next page)

Minute book A written narrative of all actions taken at official meetings of the board of directors.

Stock dividend Distribution of corporation retained earnings to stockholders in the form of shares of the corporation's own stock.

Stock split A deliberate reduction of the par value or stated value of a corporation's stock and the issuing of a proportionate number of additional shares.

Stockholders' Equity						
Paid-in Capital:						
Preferred 7 Percent Stock, $25 par						
(5,000 shares authorized and issued)	$ 125 0 0 0 00					
Less Discount on Preferred						
7 Percent Stock	10 0 0 0 00	$ 115 0 0 0 00				
Common Stock, no-par, stated value $10						
per share (20,000 shares authorized,						
16,000 shares issued)	$ 160 0 0 0 00					
Stock Dividend Distributable (3,950 shares)	39 5 0 0 00					
Common Stock Subscribed (500 shares)	5 0 0 0 00					
Paid-in Capital in Excess of Stated Value	22 5 0 0 00	227 0 0 0 00				
Paid-in Capital from Donation		11 6 5 0 00				
Total Paid-in Capital		$ 353 6 5 0 00				
Retained Earnings:						
Unappropriated Retained Earnings		119 2 0 0 00				
Appropriated:						
Appropriated for Plant Expansion	$ 20 0 0 0 00					
Appropriated for Possible Price Declines	18 0 0 0 00	38 0 0 0 00				
Total Retained Earnings		$ 157 2 0 0 00				
Total Stockholders' Equity				510 8 5 0 00		
Total Liabilities and Stockholders' Equity				$ 680 7 0 0 00		

Figure 24-4
(continued)

QUESTIONS, EXERCISES, AND PROBLEMS

Discussion Questions

1. Describe the difference between a stock dividend and a stock split.
2. Explain why an appropriation of retained earnings is not the same as setting aside cash.
3. How does a corporation dispose of a retained earnings appropriated account, such as Retained Earnings Appropriated for Building?
4. Why aren't stock dividends considered to be taxable income to the receivers of the dividends?
5. If the Retained Earnings account has a debit balance, what is it called? How is it presented in the balance sheet?
6. What journal entry is made for cash dividends for the following dates: date of declaration, date of record, date of payment?
7. How does one write journal entries to eliminate the following accounts: Income Tax Payable, Income Tax?

Exercises

Exercise 24-1   Describe the entries recorded by letters in the T accounts below.

Income Tax		Cash		Revenues		Retained Earnings	
(a)	(e)		(a)	(c)			(f)
(b)							

Income Summary		Income Tax Payable		Expenses	
(d)	(c)		(b)	(d)	
(e)					
(f)					

Exercise 24-2   The dates connected with a cash dividend of $98,000 on a corporation's common stock are March 10, March 27, and April 6. Present the entries, in general journal form, required on each date.

Exercise 24-3   The stockholders of Savich and Wentworth, Inc., donated 2,000 shares of no-par common stock to the corporation. Later the corporation sold the stock for $8 per share. Give the journal entries for the receipt and sale of the stock.

Exercise 24-4   A corporation's balance sheet includes the following.

Preferred 8 Percent Stock	$ 90,000
Preferred 8 Percent Stock Subscribed	30,000
Subscriptions Receivable, Preferred 8 Percent Stock	14,860
Discount on Preferred 8 Percent Stock	1,200
Common Stock	150,000
Paid-in Capital in Excess of Stated Value	40,000
Retained Earnings (credit balance)	55,000

a. How much of the paid-in capital is the result of the preferred 8 percent stock?
b. How much of the paid-in capital is the result of the common stock?
c. What is the total stockholders' equity?

Exercise 24-5   On December 31, the stockholders' equity of AZ Transmission Repair Company, Inc., is as follows.

Paid-in Capital:																		
Common Stock, no par, stated value $20																		
per share (20,000 shares authorized, 17,000																		
shares issued)	$	340	0	0	0	00												
Paid-in Capital in Excess of Stated Value		51	0	0	0	00												
Total Paid-in Capital							$	391	0	0	0	00						
Retained Earnings:																		
Appropriated:																		
For contingencies	$	60	0	0	0	00												
Unappropriated		134	0	0	0	00												
Total Retained Earnings								194	0	0	0	00						
Total Stockholders' Equity													$	585	0	0	0	00	

On December 31, when the stock was selling at $32 per share, the board of directors voted a 20 percent stock dividend, distributable on February 5, to stockholders of record on January 16. Give the entries to record the declaration and distribution of the dividend.

Exercise 24-6 On December 31, the board of directors of Coast Fish Company, Inc., votes to appropriate $40,000 of the corporation's unappropriated retained earnings to Retained Earnings Appropriated for Plant Expansion. This is the fourth such appropriation; it gives a balance of $160,000 in Retained Earnings Appropriated for Plant Expansion. On January 20, the corporation buys a warehouse for $172,000 (building, $158,000; land, $14,000), paying $72,000 down and financing the remainder on a mortgage note. Write the entries to record the following.

a. The appropriation of retained earnings on December 31
b. The purchase of the building and land
c. The release of $160,000 of the Retained Earnings Appropriated for Plant Expansion

Exercise 24-7 Prepare the Stockholders' Equity section of the balance sheet from the following account balances.

Retained Earnings	$ 70,000
Subscriptions Receivable Preferred 9 Percent Stock	20,000
Common Stock, $50 par (10,000 shares authorized)	300,000
Preferred 9 Percent Stock, $100 par (500 shares authorized)	20,000
Premium on Common Stock	24,000
Preferred 9 Percent Stock Subscribed	20,000

Exercise 24-8 Indicate the effect, if any, of each of the following transactions on total retained earnings of Victor Company, Inc.

a. Wrote off accounts receivable against the allowance for doubtful accounts.
b. Paid accounts payable.

c. Issued 2,000 shares of $10 par-value common stock, receiving $14 per share.
d. The board of directors declared a 10 percent stock dividend to be issued 30 days from the present date.
e. Bought equipment on account, $25,000.
f. Issued the stock dividend declared in **d**.
g. The board of directors voted to appropriate $96,000 for future expansion.

Problem Set A

Problem 24-1A   Some of the transactions of the Precision Lock Corporation during this fiscal year are as follows.

Mar.   15 Paid balance due on previous year's federal income tax, $14,980.
Apr.   15 Paid $20,700 for the first quarterly installment of estimated federal income tax for current year.
Jun.   15 Paid $20,700 for the second quarterly installment of estimated federal income tax for this year.
Jul.   18 Declared a cash dividend of $22,800 ($2.28 per share on 10,000 shares, $25 par value) to stockholders of record as of July 31, payable on August 12.
Aug.   12 Paid cash dividend.
Sep.   15 Declared a 10 percent stock dividend on common stock outstanding to stockholders of record as of September 28, payable October 8. Fair market value of stock: $40 per share (10,000 shares outstanding before stock dividend).
       15 Paid $20,700 for the third quarterly installment of estimated federal income tax for this year.
Oct.   8 Issued stock comprising stock dividend.
Nov.   18 Declared a cash dividend of $26,400 ($2.40 per share on 11,000 shares) to stockholders of record as of November 30, payable December 12.
Dec.   12 Paid cash dividend.
       15 Paid $20,700 for fourth quarterly installment of estimated federal income tax for this year.
       31 Recorded $14,640 additional federal income tax allocable to net income for the year.
       31 The board of directors authorized the appropriation of retained earnings for plant expansion, $9,800.

Instructions

Record the above transactions in general journal form.

Problem 24-2A   The trial balance for Tate Jewelers, Inc., dated May 31 of this year, is as follows.

Tate Jewelers, Inc.
Trial Balance
May 31, 19–

ACCOUNT NAME	DEBIT	CREDIT
Cash	3 9 1 6 00	
Accounts Receivable	115 4 1 0 00	
Allowance for Doubtful Accounts		1 8 6 6 00
Subscriptions Receivable, Common Stock	26 0 0 0 00	
Merchandise Inventory	189 6 7 0 00	
Store Supplies	6 3 0 00	
Store Equipment	72 6 8 0 00	
Accumulated Depreciation, Store Equipment		11 6 2 0 00
Organization Costs	5 4 2 0 00	
Notes Payable		10 0 0 0 00
Accounts Payable		51 0 4 0 00
Preferred 8 Percent Stock ($100 par)		40 0 0 0 00
Premium on Preferred 8 Percent Stock		2 0 0 0 00
Common Stock ($20 stated value)		110 0 0 0 00
Common Stock Subscribed		30 0 0 0 00
Paid-in Capital in Excess of Stated Value		14 0 0 0 00
Retained Earnings		51 6 0 0 00
Sales		1 016 3 0 0 00
Purchases	729 1 0 0 00	
Purchases Discount		5 3 2 0 00
Selling Expenses (control)	134 3 0 4 00	
General Expenses (control)	38 2 6 6 00	
Interest Expense	1 5 4 0 00	
Income Tax	26 8 1 0 00	
	1 343 7 4 6 00	1 343 7 4 6 00

To reduce the number of accounts in the trial balance, Selling Expenses (control) is used in place of all selling expenses. Likewise, General Expenses (control) is used in place of all general expenses.

Data for adjustments are as follows:

a. Merchandise Inventory, May 31 (ending inventory), $194,220.
b. Additional depreciation of store equipment for the year amounts to $4,130; record depreciation expense under Selling Expenses (control).
c. Inventory of store supplies at May 31, $434. Use Selling Expenses (control).
d. Analysis of Accounts Receivable indicates $3,490 is uncollectible; record estimated bad-debt losses under General Expenses (control).
e. Accrued interest on Notes Payable, $140.
f. Additional income tax due for the current year, $9,420.
g. No dividends were declared during the year.

Instructions

1. Record the trial balance in the work sheet (leave two lines for Selling Expenses control) and complete the work sheet for the year.
2. Prepare an income statement.
3. Prepare a statement of retained earnings.
4. Prepare a classified balance sheet.

Problem 24-3A The Stockholders' Equity section of the balance sheet of the Dundee Fabrics, Inc., as of December 31 is as follows.

Stockholders' Equity			
Paid-in Capital:			
Preferred 9 Percent Stock, $100 par (3,750			
shares authorized, 2,250 shares issued)	$225 0 0 0 00		
Premium on Preferred 9 Percent Stock	9 0 0 0 00		
Common Stock, no par, stated value			
$20 per share (30,000 shares authorized,			
18,000 shares issued)	360 0 0 0 00		
Paid-in Capital in Excess of Stated Value	108 0 0 0 00		
Total Paid-in Capital		$702 0 0 0 00	
Retained Earnings:			
Unappropriated Retained Earnings	$210 0 0 0 00		
Appropriated:			
Retained Earnings Appropriated for			
Expansion	42 0 0 0 00		
Total Retained Earnings		252 0 0 0 00	
Total Stockholders' Equity			954 0 0 0 00

Some of the transactions that took place during the next year are:

Apr. 12 Declared the regular semiannual $4.50 per share dividend on the preferred stock and a $1.25 per share dividend on the common stock to stockholders of record on May 1, payable on May 10.

May 3 Received subscriptions to 3,000 shares of common stock at $29 per share, collecting 70 percent of the subscription price.

10 Paid cash dividends declared on April 12.

28 Subscribers to 3,000 shares of common stock paid the remaining 30 percent of the subscription price; Dundee Fabrics then issued the 3,000 shares.

Aug. 12 Declared the regular semiannual $4.50 per share dividend on the preferred stock and a $1.50 per share dividend on the common stock to stockholders of record on September 1, payable September 21.

Sep. 21 Paid cash dividends declared on August 12.

Dec.   29 Declared a 10 percent stock dividend on common stock outstanding to stockholders of record on January 16, payable January 28.
Fair market value of the stock is $30 per share.

31 After the accountant has closed all revenue, expense, and Income
Tax accounts, the Income Summary account has a credit balance of
$111,000. Closed the Income Summary account.

31 Increased the appropriation for plant expansion by $24,000.

Instructions

1. Enter in the ledger accounts the balances appearing in the Stockholders'
Equity section of the balance sheet as of December 31.
2. Journalize entries in general journal form to record the transactions that
occurred during the next year and post to the stockholders' equity accounts.
3. Prepare Stockholders' Equity section of balance sheet as of December 31 of
the next year.

Problem 24-4A   Here are the account balances taken from the general
ledger and statement of retained earnings for Angie's Fine Fashions:

a. Preferred 8 percent stock: 1,000 shares authorized, 760 shares issued
b. Common stock: 15,000 shares authorized, 12,000 shares issued

Prepaid Insurance	$ 960
Organization Costs	8,000
Allowance for Doubtful Accounts	5,640
Accounts Payable	112,760
Accumulated Depreciation, Equipment	34,200
Paid-in Capital in Excess of Stated Value	36,000
Retained Earnings	106,700
Common Stock, $15 stated value, 15,000 shares authorized	180,000
Equipment	72,900
Merchandise Inventory	342,510
Retained Earnings Appropriated for Inventory Losses	8,400
Paid-in Capital from Donation	7,200
Premium on Preferred 8 Percent Stock	2,000
Cash	8,710
Subscriptions Receivable, Preferred 8 Percent Stock	12,240
Preferred 8 Percent Stock Subscribed (240 shares)	24,000
Income Tax Payable	20,600
Retained Earnings Appropriated for Plant Expansion	16,000
Preferred 8 Percent Stock, $100 par, 1,000 shares authorized	76,000
Notes Receivable	12,600
Accumulated Depreciation, Building	62,400
Land	25,000
Dividends Payable	8,200
Stock Dividend Distributable (1,110 shares)	16,650
Mortgage Payable (due April 10, 1991)	48,600
Building	120,000
Accounts Receivable	162,430

Instructions

Prepare a classified balance sheet dated December 31.

Problem Set B

Problem 24-1B   Some of the transactions of Waterhouse, Inc., during this fiscal year are as follows.

Mar.   15 Paid balance due on previous year's federal income tax, $3,750.
Apr.   15 Paid $6,420 for the first quarterly installment of estimated federal income tax for this year.
Jun.   15 Paid $6,420 for the second quarterly installment of estimated federal income tax for this year.
Jul.   15 Declared a cash dividend of $8,400 ($.84 per share on 10,000 shares, $10 par value) to stockholders of record as of July 30, payable on August 10.
Aug.   10 Paid the cash dividend.
Sep.   15 Paid $6,420 for the third quarterly installment of estimated federal income tax for this year.
         20 Declared a 5 percent stock dividend on the common stock outstanding, to stockholders of record as of September 30, payable on October 10. Fair market value of stock: $14 per share.
Oct.   10 Issued stock comprising the stock dividend.
Nov.   15 Declared a cash dividend of $8,820 ($.84 per share on 10,500 shares) to stockholders of record as of November 30, payable on December 10.
Dec.   10 Paid the cash dividend.
         15 Paid $6,420 for the fourth quarterly installment of estimated federal income tax for this year.
         31 Recorded $7,320 additional federal income tax allocable to net income for the year.
         31 The board of directors authorized the appropriation of retained earnings for plant expansion, $2,400.

Instructions

Record these transactions in general journal form.

Problem 24-2B   The trial balance of Sinclair Surgical Supply, Inc., dated December 31 of this year, is shown on the next page.

To reduce the number of accounts in the trial balance, Selling Expenses (control) is used in place of all selling expenses. Likewise, General Expenses (control) is used in place of all general expenses.

Sinclair Surgical Supply, Inc.
Trial Balance
December 31, 19–

ACCOUNT NAME	DEBIT	CREDIT
Cash	4 6 8 0 00	
Notes Receivable	9 6 4 0 00	
Accounts Receivable	105 0 1 6 00	
Allowance for Doubtful Accounts		1 7 9 4 00
Subscriptions Receivable, Preferred 7 Percent		
Stock	8 6 0 0 00	
Merchandise Inventory	186 7 4 0 00	
Prepaid Insurance	8 6 4 00	
Delivery Equipment	56 7 4 0 00	
Accumulated Depreciation,		
Delivery Equipment		10 7 3 0 00
Organization Costs	6 4 0 0 00	
Accounts Payable		48 7 6 6 00
Preferred 7 Percent Stock ($100 par)		50 0 0 0 00
Preferred 7 Percent Stock Subscribed		10 0 0 0 00
Premium on Preferred 7 Percent Stock		2 2 0 0 00
Common Stock ($20 stated value)		100 0 0 0 00
Paid-in Capital in Excess of Stated Value		12 0 0 0 00
Retained Earnings		52 0 0 0 00
Sales		1 178 4 0 0 00
Purchases	895 3 4 0 00	
Purchases Discount		5 2 0 0 00
Selling Expenses (control)	132 6 3 0 00	
General Expenses (control)	37 4 0 0 00	
Income Tax	28 1 8 0 00	
Interest Income		1 1 4 0 00
	1 472 2 3 0 00	1 472 2 3 0 00

Data for the adjustments are as follows.

a. Merchandise Inventory, December 31 (ending inventory), $192,190.
b. Additional depreciation of delivery equipment for the year amounts to $4,290; record depreciation under Selling Expenses (control).
c. Insurance expired during the year, $514; record insurance expired under General Expenses (control).
d. Analysis of Accounts Receivable indicates $3,520 is uncollectible; record estimated bad-debt losses under General Expenses (control).
e. Accrued interest on Notes Receivable, $120.
f. Additional income tax due for this year, $8,560.
g. No dividends were declared during the year.

Instructions

1. Record the trial balance in the work sheet (leave two lines for General Expenses control) and complete the work sheet for the year.
2. Prepare an income statement.
3. Prepare a statement of retained earnings.
4. Prepare a classified balance sheet.

Problem 24-3B   The Stockholders' Equity section of the balance sheet of the L and C Construction Company, Inc., as of December 31 is as follows.

Stockholders' Equity				
Paid-in Capital:				
Preferred 9 Percent Stock, $100 par (2,600 shares authorized, 1,500 shares issued)	$ 150 0 0 0 00			
Premium on Preferred 9 Percent Stock	6 0 0 0 00			
Common Stock, no par, stated value $20 per share (23,000 shares authorized, 12,000 shares issued)	240 0 0 0 00			
Paid-in Capital in Excess of Stated Value	120 0 0 0 00			
Total Paid-in Capital		$ 516 0 0 0 00		
Retained Earnings:				
Unappropriated Retained Earnings	$ 127 5 0 0 00			
Appropriated:				
Retained Earnings Appropriated for Expansion	27 0 0 0 00			
Total Retained Earnings		154 5 0 0 00		
Total Stockholders' Equity			$ 670 5 0 0 00	

Some of the transactions that took place during the next year are:

Mar.   26 Declared the regular semiannual $4.50 per share dividend on the preferred stock and a $1.00 per share dividend on the common stock to stockholders of record on April 15, payable on April 21.

Apr.   21 Paid cash dividends declared on March 26.

28 Received subscriptions to 750 shares of common stock at $32 per share, collecting 60 percent of the subscription price.

May   15 Subscribers to 750 shares of common stock paid the remaining 40 percent of the subscription price; L and C Construction then issued the 750 shares.

Sep.   26 Declared the regular semiannual $4.50 per share dividend on the preferred stock and a $1.50 per share dividend on the common stock to stockholders of record on October 15, payable October 22.

Oct.   22 Paid cash dividends declared on September 26.

Dec.   21 Declared a 10 percent stock dividend on common stock outstanding to stockholders of record on January 15, payable January 21. Fair market value of the stock is $34 per share.

31 After the accountant has closed all revenue, expense, and Income Tax accounts, the Income Summary account has a credit balance of $102,000. Closed the Income Summary account.

31 Increased the appropriation for expansion by $13,500.

Instructions

1. Enter in the ledger accounts the balances appearing in the Stockholders' Equity section of the balance sheet as of December 31.
2. Journalize entries in general journal form to record the transactions that occurred during the next year and post to the stockholders' equity accounts.
3. Prepare Stockholders' Equity section of balance sheet as of December 31 of the next year.

Problem 24-4B   The account balances taken from the general ledger and statement of retained earnings for Catu Produce, Inc., are as follows.

a. Preferred 8 percent stock: 1,000 shares authorized, 800 shares issued
b. Common stock: 10,000 shares authorized, 6,800 shares issued

Accounts Receivable	$126,360
Building	90,000
Mortgage Payable (due April 10, 1992)	42,000
Stock Dividend Distributable (620 shares)	9,300
Dividends Payable	4,800
Land	12,000
Accumulated Depreciation, Building	22,800
Notes Receivable	12,000
Preferred 8 Percent Stock, $100 par, 1,000 shares authorized	80,000
Retained Earnings Appropriated for Plant Expansion	8,200
Income Tax Payable	14,600
Preferred 8 Percent Stock Subscribed (200 shares)	20,000
Subscriptions Receivable, Preferred 8 Percent Stock	10,100
Cash	5,820
Premium on Preferred 8 Percent Stock	1,000
Paid-in Capital from Donation	12,000
Retained Earnings Appropriated for Inventory Losses	4,000
Merchandise Inventory	237,870
Equipment	46,600
Common Stock, $15 stated value, 10,000 shares authorized	102,000
Retained Earnings	76,900
Paid-in Capital in Excess of Stated Value	22,260
Accumulated Depreciation, Equipment	24,870
Accounts Payable	98,260
Allowance for Doubtful Accounts	4,620
Organization Costs	6,000
Prepaid Insurance	860

Instructions

Prepare a classified balance sheet dated December 31.

25 Corporations: Long-Term Obligations

Learning Objectives

After you have completed this chapter, you will be able to do the following:

1. Journalize transactions involving the issuance of bonds at a premium or discount.

2. Journalize adjusting entries for amortization of bond premiums and discounts and accrued interest payable.

3. Journalize entries pertaining to the establishment of a bond sinking fund, the receipt of income from sinking fund investments, and the eventual payment of the principal of the bonds.

4. Journalize transactions involving the redemption of bonds.

In our discussions of corporations, we have assumed that the company got the money it needed for building and expansion by selling stock and retaining earnings. There is another possibility: A corporation can borrow money for a long period (five to forty years) by issuing bonds. For all practical purposes, one may consider a bond to be a long-term promissory note. A **bond issue**—the total amount that the corporation promises to pay—is subdivided into denominations of $1,000 or $5,000 each, with $1,000 the most common. You can get a better picture of bonds by comparing them with capital stock.

Bonds	Capital Stock
Bondholders are creditors; they receive interest and are eventually repaid the principal.	Stockholders are owners; they receive dividends.
Bonds Payable is classified as a long-term liability account.	Capital stock is subdivided into Common Stock and Preferred Stock accounts, which are stockholder's equity accounts.
Interest paid on bonds is a valid expense, which must be paid year after year. Otherwise, bondholders may initiate bankruptcy proceedings against the debtor corporation.	Dividends are distributions of net income, rather than expenses.
Interest is deductible as an expense before arriving at net income.	Dividends are not deductible before arriving at net income.

CLASSIFICATION OF BONDS

To appeal to investors, corporations have created a wide variety of bonds, each with slightly different combinations of characteristics, just as automobile manufacturers offer different models with various combinations of accessories.

Bonds Classified as to Time of Payment

- **Term bonds** All term bonds have the same term or time period, the entire issue of bonds coming due at the same time. For example, $1,000,000 worth of 10-year bonds issued January 1, 1979, all mature January 1, 1989.

- **Serial bonds** Serial bonds have a series of maturity dates. *Example:* $1,000,000 worth of bonds issued March 1, 1976, may mature as follows.

$100,000 on March 1, 1981	$100,000 on March 1, 1986
$100,000 on March 1, 1982	$100,000 on March 1, 1987
$100,000 on March 1, 1983	$100,000 on March 1, 1988
$100,000 on March 1, 1984	$100,000 on March 1, 1989
$100,000 on March 1, 1985	$100,000 on March 1, 1990

Bonds Classified as to Ownership

- **Registered bonds** When bonds are registered, the names of the owners are recorded with the issuing corporation. Title to such bonds is transferred when the bonds are sold, just as title to stock is transferred. The corporation pays interest by mailing checks to the registered owners.
- **Coupon bonds** These bonds derive their name from the interest coupons attached to each bond. The interest coupons are payable to bearer, in much the same manner as paper money is. The owners' names may or may not be listed for the amount of the principal. Figure 25-1 shows the format of a coupon bond.

The corporation pays the interest every six months, and each coupon is worth $40. The owner of the bond clips the coupons as they become due, and deposits them with a regular commercial bank for collection.

Figure 25-1

Atlas Corporation Bond $1,000, 20 years, 8 percent Payable semiannually, April 1 and October 1			
$40 Apr. 1, 1996	$40 Oct. 1, 1995	$40 Apr. 1, 1995	$40 Oct. 1, 1994
$40 Apr. 1, 1994	$40 Oct. 1, 1993	$40 Apr. 1, 1993	$40 Oct. 1, 1992
$40 Apr. 1, 1982	$40 Oct. 1, 1981	$40 Apr. 1, 1981	$40 Oct. 1, 1980
$40 Apr. 1, 1980	$40 Oct. 1, 1979	$40 Apr. 1, 1979	$40 Oct. 1, 1978
$40 Apr. 1, 1978	$40 Oct. 1, 1977	$40 Apr. 1, 1977	$40 Oct. 1, 1976

Bonds Classified as to Security

- **Secured bonds** When a bond is secured, it is covered or backed up by mortgages on real estate or by titles to personal property. It may be called a mortgage bond or an equipment trust bond. In case the corporation defaults in its payment of principal or interest, the bondholders, acting through a trustee, may take over the pledged assets.
- **Unsecured bonds** An unsecured bond, also called a **debenture,** is one that is issued just on the corporation's credit standing. Such bonds usually succeed only when issued by financially strong firms.

A bond can have characteristics of all three classifications. For example, if a corporation issues 20-year mortgage bonds with coupons providing for the payment of interest, the bonds are term bonds, coupon bonds, and secured bonds.

WHY A CORPORATION ISSUES BONDS

A corporation that needs money on a long-term basis has the choice of raising the necessary funds by issuing (1) common stock, (2) preferred stock, or (3) bonds. Each choice has advantages and disadvantages. Since the holders of common stock control the corporation through their voting power, the choice of means of financing is up to them. Stockholders think about the pros and cons of bonds as follows.

Advantages of Issuing Bonds

Bonds offer these advantages:

1. The bond-issuing corporation has the prospect of earning a greater return on the money it raises than it has to pay out in interest. This is known as **leverage.** For example, if a firm can borrow money at an interest rate of 8 percent and use this cash in the business to earn a net income of 15 percent after taxes, then the additional earnings of 7 percent (15 percent − 8 percent) are available to pay dividends to the holders of common stock.
2. Interest payments are tax-deductible expenses.
3. Bondholders cannot vote, so common stockholders can retain control of the company's affairs.

Disadvantages of Issuing Bonds

On the other hand, these disadvantages have to be considered:

1. Bondholders are creditors of the corporation, so interest payments are fixed obligations. A corporation pays dividends only when it has enough money to do so.
2. The corporation must eventually pay the principal of the bonds it issues, but it does not have to repay the money it receives from issuing stock.

When a corporation is trying to decide whether to issue additional stock or to issue bonds, an important factor is estimated future earnings and the probable stability of these earnings. The advantages and disadvantages of issuing bonds become apparent in the following example.

Pemberton Chemical, which has 40,000 shares of $50 par-value common stock outstanding ($2,000,000), wishes to raise an additional $1,000,000 for expansion. Pemberton is considering three possible ways of raising the money:

- **Plan 1** Issue an additional $1,000,000 of common stock, thereby increasing the total stock outstanding from 40,000 to 60,000 shares.
- **Plan 2** Issue $1,000,000 of 8 percent cumulative preferred stock.
- **Plan 3** Issue $1,000,000 of 7 percent bonds.

Figure 25-2 shows how Pemberton Chemical comes out (1) if it has a yearly net income from operations of $420,000 and (2) if it has a yearly net income from operations of $60,000. (We assume that the federal corporation income tax is 50 percent.)

You can see that plan 3 offers the greatest advantage to the original holders of common stock, provided that the company's earnings are large enough to pay the bondholders and still leave a sizable share for the holders of common stock. When the company has a *low* level of earnings, plan 1 is most advantageous to the holders of common stock, because there are no prior claims of bondholders or preferred stockholders. The firm can use a combination of the three, but this entails bigger underwriting or financing costs.

ACCOUNTING FOR THE ISSUANCE OF BONDS

Objective 1

Journalize transactions involving the issuance of bonds at a premium or discount.

When a corporation issues bonds at face value, it records the transaction as a debit to Cash and a credit to Bonds Payable. Bonds Payable is a long-term liability account. If there is more than one bond issue, the company keeps a separate account for each. The listing in the balance sheet should identify the issue by stipulating its interest rate and due date.

	Income from Operations: $420,000			Income from Operations: $60,000		
	Plan 1	Plan 2	Plan 3	Plan 1	Plan 2	Plan 3
Common Stock now outstanding (40,000 shares)	$2,000,000	$2,000,000	$2,000,000	$2,000,000	$2,000,000	$2,000,000
Additional Common Stock, $50 par (20,000 shares)	1,000,000			1,000,000		
Preferred Stock, 8%, cumulative		1,000,000			1,000,000	
Bonds, 7%			1,000,000			1,000,000
Total Capitalization	$3,000,000	$3,000,000	$3,000,000	$3,000,000	$3,000,000	$3,000,000
Income from Operations (before income tax)	$ 420,000	$ 420,000	$ 420,000	$ 60,000	$ 60,000	$ 60,000
Deduct bond interest expense	0	0	70,000	0	0	70,000
Net Income or Loss after bond interest	$ 420,000	$ 420,000	$ 350,000	$ 60,000	$ 60,000	$ (10,000)
Deduct federal and state income taxes (50%)	210,000	210,000	175,000	30,000	30,000	0
Net income after income taxes	$ 210,000	$ 210,000	$ 175,000	$ 30,000	$ 30,000	$ (10,000)
Deduct preferred dividends		80,000			80,000	
Net income after income taxes and preferred dividends	$ 210,000	$ 130,000	$ 175,000	$ 30,000	$ (50,000)	$ (10,000)
Net income or loss per share of common stock	$ 210,000	$ 130,000	$ 175,000	$ 30,000	$ (50,000)	$ (10,000)
	60,000 shares	40,000 shares	40,000 shares	60,000 shares	40,000 shares	40,000 shares
	$3.50 per share	$3.25 per share	$4.37 per share	$.50 per share	($1.25) per share	($.25) per share

Figure 25-2

Bonds Sold at a Premium

The corporation may receive a price for its bonds that is above or below their face value, depending on the rate of interest offered and the general credit standing of the company. If a corporation offers a rate of interest that is higher than the market rate for similar securities, investors may be willing to pay a **premium** for the bonds.

For example, on January 1, United Construction Corporation issues $500,000 of 10 percent, 10-year bonds at 104, with interest payable semiannually, on June 30 and December 31. The term "104" refers to the price of the bonds; it is a percentage of the face value of the bonds, with the percent symbol omitted. This is how people record bond prices. In this example, $500,000 of bonds at 104 means 104 percent of $500,000 ($1.04 × $500,000 = $520,000$). [If $1,000,000 worth of bonds, say, had been sold at 106, the price received would have been $1,060,000 ($1.06 × $1,000,000 = $1,060,000$).] United's entry to record the sale of the bonds, in general journal form, is as follows.

	DATE	DESCRIPTION	POST. REF.	DEBIT	CREDIT	
1	19– Jan. 1	Cash		520 0 0 0 00		1
2		Bonds Payable			500 0 0 0 00	2
3		Premium on Bonds Payable			20 0 0 0 00	3
4		Sold 10-year, 10 percent				4
5		bonds, dated January 1,				5
6		19–, at 104.				6
7						7

Premium on Bonds Payable represents the amount received over and above the face value of the bonds. The accountant lists Premium on Bonds Payable right below the bond account in the Long-term Liabilities section of the balance sheet. The corporation will write off or amortize Premium on Bonds Payable over the remaining life of the bond issue. The entries to pay the interest on the bonds, in general journal form, are shown here.

	DATE	DESCRIPTION	POST. REF.	DEBIT	CREDIT	
1	19– Jun. 30	Interest Expense		25 0 0 0 00		1
2		Cash			25 0 0 0 00	2
3		Made semiannual interest payment				3
4		on bonds, face value of $500,000,				4
5		10 percent.				5
6						6

1	*Dec.*	**31**	*Interest Expense*			25 0 0 0 00					1
2			*Cash*					25 0 0 0 00			2
3			*Made semiannual interest payment*								3
4			*on bonds, face value of $500,000,*								4
5			*10 percent.*								5
6											6

Adjusting Entry for Bonds Sold at a Premium

Just what is **amortization?** A company writes off, or *amortizes*, the Premium on Bonds Payable account over the remaining life of the bonds by debiting the account and using Interest Expense as the offsetting credit. The entry appears as an adjusting entry at the end of the fiscal period. It is first recorded in the Adjustments columns of the work sheet, like any other adjusting entry. (The calculation is recorded here purely as a means of explanation.)

Objective 2

Journalize adjusting entries for amortization of bond premiums and discounts and accrued interest payable.

	DATE		DESCRIPTION	POST. REF.	DEBIT	CREDIT	
1			*Adjusting Entry*				1
2	19– *Dec.*	**31**	*Premium on Bonds Payable*		2 0 0 0 00		2
3			*Interest Expense ($20,000 ÷ 10 years)*			2 0 0 0 00	3
4							4

By T accounts, the entries look like this.

	Cash					Bonds Payable			
	+		−			−		+	
Jan. 1	520,000	June 30	25,000				Jan. 1	500,000	
		Dec. 31	25,000						

	Interest Expense					Premium on Bonds Payable			
	+		−			−		+	
Jun. 30	25,000	Dec. 31 Adj.	2,000		Dec. 31 Adj.	2,000	Jan. 1	20,000	
Dec. 31	25,000								

In this illustration, we showed the amortization of the bond premium calculated by the straight-line method on an annual basis, which will also be used in the problems. As you can probably see, this is like calculating depreciation by the straight-line method. One can also record the amortization of the bond premium, just as one can record depreciation, on a monthly basis. It should be mentioned, however, that many corporations amortize premiums and discounts on bonds using the effective interest rate method. This method is covered in more advanced accounting courses.

After the accountant records the adjusting entry, the balance of Interest Expense is $48,000, representing the amount of the annual interest expense on the bonds, as follows.

Cash to be paid		
Face value of the bonds	$500,000	
Interest (10 payments of $50,000 each)	500,000	$1,000,000
Less cash received		
Face value of the bonds	$500,000	
Premium on the bonds	20,000	520,000
Excess of cash to be paid over cash received		
(Interest expense for 10 years)		$ 480,000

$$\text{Interest expense per year} = \frac{\$480,000}{10 \text{ years}} = \$48,000$$

The adjusting entry reduces the balance of the Interest Expense account from $50,000 to $48,000. The accountant then closes Interest Expense into Income Summary in the amount of $48,000.

Bonds Sold at a Discount

When a corporation issues bonds that will pay a rate of interest that is less than the prevailing market rate of interest for comparable bonds, it sells its bonds at less than face value—or at a **discount.**

To demonstrate this, assume that on January 1, Plainview Dairy Products issues 6 percent, 20-year bonds with a face value of $100,000, at 96, with interest to be paid semiannually on June 30 and December 31.

	DATE		DESCRIPTION	POST. REF.	DEBIT	CREDIT	
1	19– Jan.	1	Cash		96 0 0 0 00		1
2			Discount on Bonds Payable		4 0 0 0 00		2
3			Bonds Payable			100 0 0 0 00	3
4			Sold 20-year bonds, 6 percent,				4
5			dated January 1, 19–, at 96.				5
6							6

Discount on Bonds Payable is a **contra-liability account;** it is listed on a classified balance sheet as a deduction from Bonds Payable. The entries, in general journal form, for the payment of interest are as follows.

1	Jun.	30	Interest Expense	3 0 0 0 00				1
2			Cash		3 0 0 0 00			2
3			Paid semiannual interest on					3
4			bonds, face value of $100,000,					4
5			6 percent.					5
6								6

1	Dec.	31	Interest Expense	3 0 0 0 00				1
2			Cash		3 0 0 0 00			2
3			Paid semiannual interest on					3
4			bonds, face value of $100,000,					4
5			6 percent.					5
6								6

Adjusting Entry for Bonds Sold at a Discount

The corporation writes off or amortizes the Discount on Bonds Payable account, as it does the Premium on Bonds Payable account, over the remaining life of the bond issue, as an adjusting entry at the end of the fiscal period. Again, the accountant uses Interest Expense as the offsetting account in the adjusting entry. The adjusting entry, taken from the Adjustments columns of the work sheet, is as follows.

1			Adjusting Entry					1
2	Dec.	31	Interest Expense ($4,000 ÷ 20 years)	2 0 0 00				2
3			Discount on Bonds Payable		2 0 0 00			3
4								4
5								5
6								6

By T accounts, the entries look like this.

Cash				
+		**−**		
Jan. 1	96,000	Jun. 30	3,000	
		Dec. 31	3,000	

Bonds Payable			
−		**+**	
		Jan. 1	100,000

Interest Expense			
+		**−**	
Jun. 30	3,000		
Dec. 31	3,000		
Dec. 31 Adj.	200		

Discount on Bonds Payable			
+		**−**	
Jan. 1	4,000	Dec. 31 Adj.	200

The adjustment for Discount on Bonds Payable results in an increase in the Interest Expense account. Here's how it works.

Cash to be paid

Face value of the bonds	$100,000	
Interest (20 payments of $6,000 each)	120,000	$220,000

Less cash received

Face value of the bonds	$100,000	
Less discount on the bonds	4,000	96,000

Excess of cash to be paid over cash received
(Interest expense for 20 years) $124,000

$$\text{Interest expense per year} = \frac{\$124,000}{20 \text{ years}} = \$6,200$$

The adjusting entry increases the balance of Interest Expense from $6,000 to $6,200. The accountant then closes Interest Expense into Income Summary in the amount of $6,200.

Example: bonds sold at a premium, whose interest payment dates do not coincide with the end of fiscal year On March 1, Ace Fast Freight issues $1,000,000 worth of 20-year, 9 percent bonds, at 103, dated March 1, with interest payable semiannually on September 1 and March 1. The corporation's fiscal year ends on December 31. A diagram of the dates looks like this.

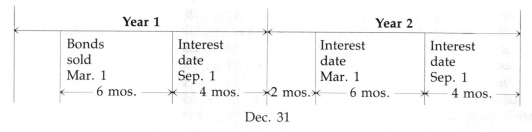

Since the date on which the interest has to be paid does not coincide with the end of the fiscal year, Ace Fast Freight has to make an adjusting entry for the accrued interest for the period from September 1 to December 31. The entries for the first year, in general journal form, are as follows.

	DATE		DESCRIPTION	POST. REF.	DEBIT	CREDIT	
1	19– Mar.	1	*Cash*		1,030 0 0 0 00		1
2			*Bonds Payable*			1,000 0 0 0 00	2
3			*Premium on Bonds Payable*			30 0 0 0 00	3
4			*Sold 20-year bonds, 9 percent,*				4
5			*dated March 1, at 103.*				5
6							6

	DATE		DESCRIPTION	POST. REF.	DEBIT	CREDIT	
1	Sep.	1	*Interest Expense*		45 0 0 0 00		1
2			*Cash*			45 0 0 0 00	2
3			*Paid semiannual interest on*				3
4			*bonds ($1,000,000, 9 percent,*				4
5			*6 months).*				5
6							6

	DATE		DESCRIPTION	POST. REF.	DEBIT	CREDIT	
1			*Adjusting Entries*				1
2	Dec.	31	*Premium on Bonds Payable*		1 2 5 0 00		2
3			*Interest Expense* $\left(\$30,000 \times \frac{10\ months}{240\ months}\right)$			1 2 5 0 00	3
4							4
5		31	*Interest Expense*		30 0 0 0 00		5
6			*Interest Payable*			30 0 0 0 00	6
7			*($1,000,000, 9 percent, 4 months.)*				7
8							8
9			*Closing Entry*				9
10		31	*Income Summary*		73 7 5 0 00		10
11			*Interest Expense*			73 7 5 0 00	11
12							12

The amortization of the premium on December 31 is for only a part of a year. The next year, however, amortization will be for a full year. The adjusting entry for accrued interest on a bond is like the one for accrued interest on an interest-bearing note payable. In T account form the first-year entries look like this.

Cash

	+		–	
Mar. 1	1,030,000	Sep. 1	45,000	

Bonds Payable

–		+	
		Mar. 1	1,000,000

Interest Expense

	+		–	
Sep. 1	45,000	Dec. 31 Adj.	1,250	
Dec. 31 Adj.	30,000	Dec. 31 Clos.	73,750	

Premium on Bonds Payable

–		+	
Dec. 31 Adj.	1,250	Mar. 1	30,000

Interest Payable

–		+	
		Dec. 31 Adj.	30,000

Income Summary

(Int. Exp.)	73,750	Closed	

Because the adjusting entry for accrued interest opened a new balance sheet account, Ace's accountant has to make a reversing entry as of the first day of the next fiscal year. The reversing entry enables the accountant to make the regular entry for the payment of interest on March 1. The other entries for the second year are as follows.

	DATE		DESCRIPTION	POST. REF.	DEBIT	CREDIT	
1			*Reversing Entry*				1
2	19– Jan.	1	Interest Payable		30 0 0 0 00		2
3			Interest Expense			30 0 0 0 00	3
4							4
5							5
6							6

1	Mar.	1	Interest Expense		45 0 0 0 00		1
2			Cash			45 0 0 0 00	2
3			*Paid semiannual interest on bonds*				3
4			*($1,000,000, 9 percent, 6*				4
5			*months).*				5
6							6

1	Sep.	1	Interest Expense		45 0 0 0 00		1
2			Cash			45 0 0 0 00	2
3			*Paid semiannual interest on bonds*				3
4			*($1,000,000, 9 percent, 6*				4
5			*months).*				5
6							6

	DATE		DESCRIPTION	POST. REF.	DEBIT	CREDIT	
1			*Adjusting Entries*				1
2	19– Dec.	31	Premium on Bonds Payable		1 5 0 0 00		2
3			Interest Expense $\left(\$30{,}000 \times \frac{12 \text{ months}}{240 \text{ months}}\right)$			1 5 0 0 00	3
4							4
5		31	Interest Expense		30 0 0 0 00		5
6			Interest Payable ($1,000,000,				6
7			9 percent, 4 months)			30 0 0 0 00	7
8							8
9			*Closing Entry*				9
10		31	Income Summary		88 5 0 0 00		10
11			Interest Expense			88 5 0 0 00	11
12							12

The accountant brings out the relevant T accounts from the previous year and posts them up to date.

Bonds Payable

−		+	
		Mar. 1	1,000,000

Premium on Bonds Payable

−		+	
Dec. 31 Adj.	1,250	Mar. 1	30,000
Dec. 31 Adj.	1,500		

Interest Payable

−		+	
		Dec. 31 Adj.	30,000
Jan. 1 Rev.	30,000	Dec. 31 Adj.	30,000

Interest Expense

+		−	
Sep. 1	45,000	Dec. 31 Adj.	1,250
Dec. 31 Adj.	30,000	Dec. 31 Clos.	73,750
Mar. 1	45,000	Jan. 1 Rev.	30,000
Sep. 1	45,000	Dec. 31 Adj.	1,500
Dec. 31 Adj.	30,000	Dec. 31 Clos.	88,500

Income Summary

(Int. Exp.)	73,750	Closed	
(Int. Exp.)	88,500	Closed	

BOND SINKING FUND

To provide greater security for bondholders, the bond agreement may specify that the issuing corporation make annual deposits of cash into a special fund—called a **sinking fund**—to be used to pay off the bond issue when it comes due. The company keeps the sinking fund separate from its other assets and puts the cash deposited in the sinking fund to work by investing it in income-producing securities. When the bonds mature, the total of the annual deposits, plus the earnings on the investments, should add up to approximately the face value of the bonds. The sinking fund may be controlled by either the corporation or a trustee—usually a bank.

When the corporation deposits cash in its sinking fund, it records the transaction as a debit to Sinking Fund Cash and as a credit to Cash. When the corporation or the trustee invests the sinking fund cash, the transaction is recorded as a debit to Sinking Fund Investments and a credit to Sinking Fund Cash, both of which are classified as investment accounts. When the corporation receives interest or dividend income on the investments, it debits Sinking Fund Cash and credits Sinking Fund Income. Sinking Fund Income is classified as an Other Income account on the income statement.

Objective 3

Journalize entries pertaining to the establishment of a bond sinking fund, the receipt of income from sinking fund investments, and the eventual payment of the principal of the bonds.

For example, the Lockern Furniture Company issues $100,000 worth of 10-year bonds dated January 1, with the provision that at the end of each of the ten years, it make equal annual deposits in a sinking fund. Lockern, which manages its own sinking fund, intends to invest this money in securities that will yield approximately 6 percent per year. Let us assume that, according to compound-interest tables, an annual deposit of $7,040 will accumulate to $100,000 in ten years, given the 6 percent annual interest rate.

The following are a few of the many routine transactions that affect the sinking fund during the ten-year period.

- **Annual deposits of cash in bond sinking fund**

	DATE	DESCRIPTION	POST. REF.	DEBIT	CREDIT	
1		Sinking Fund Cash		7 0 4 0 00		1
2		Cash			7 0 4 0 00	2
3		Annual deposit in bond sinking				3
4		fund, according to bond				4
5		agreement.				5
6						6

- **Purchase of investments** (Time of purchase and amount invested may vary.)

		DESCRIPTION		DEBIT	CREDIT	
1		Sinking Fund Investments		6 9 8 0 00		1
2		Sinking Fund Cash			6 9 8 0 00	2
3		Bought $7,000 of Consolidated				3
4		Steel 7 percent bonds at 99½,				4
5		plus brokerage commission ($15).				5
6						6

- **Receipt of income from investments** (Interest and dividends are received at different times during the year.)

			POST. REF.	DEBIT				CREDIT				
1		*Sinking Fund Cash*				4	2	0	00			1
2		*Sinking Fund Income*								4 2 0	00	2
3		*Received interest and dividends*										3
4		*on sinking fund investments.*										4
5												5

- **Sale of investments** (Investments may be sold and proceeds reinvested.)

			POST. REF.	DEBIT					CREDIT				
1		*Sinking Fund Cash*			18	6	2	0	00				1
2		*Sinking Fund Investments*								18 4 0 0	00		2
3		*Gain on Sale of Sinking Fund*											3
4		*Investments*								2 2 0	00		4
5		*Sold sinking fund investments,*											5
6		*yielding a profit of $220.*											6
7													7

- **Payment of bonds** (Cash available consists of sinking fund after sale of investments, with addition of last annual deposit, to bring sinking fund up to $100,000.)

	DATE	DESCRIPTION	POST. REF.	DEBIT					CREDIT				
1		*Bonds Payable*		100	0	0	0	00					1
2		*Sinking Fund Cash*							100 0 0 0	00			2
3		*Paid bond obligation with sink-*											3
4		*ing fund cash.*											4
5													5

REDEMPTION OF BONDS

To protect itself against a decline in market interest rates, a corporation may issue **callable bonds.** Callable bonds give the corporation the right— as stipulated in the bond **indenture,** or agreement—to **redeem** or buy back the bonds at a specified figure, known as the *call price,* which is ordinarily higher than the face value.

The CP Development Corporation issues $2,000,000 worth of 10 percent, 20-year, callable bonds, with a call price of 104. Later, interest rates in general go down. Under the new market conditions, CP Development could sell $2,000,000 worth of bonds at par, with an interest rate of 7 percent. It would pay CP Development to buy back the bonds, even though it would have to pay $2,080,000 for them ($2,000,000 × 1.04) and then turn around and issue new bonds at 7 percent. The annual savings in interest would amount to $60,000 (3 percent of $2,000,000). Even if a corporation's bonds are not callable, it may still buy its own bonds on the open market if it can find any for sale.

Objective 4

Journalize transactions involving the redemption of bonds.

When a corporation redeems its bonds at a price less than their book value, it realizes a gain. Conversely, if it redeems its bonds at a price that is more than their book value, it incurs a loss. The book value is the sum of the Bonds Payable account and the Premium on Bonds Payable (or Discount on Bonds Payable) account.

For example, Northeast Transit Company has $500,000 worth of callable bonds outstanding, with a call price of 105; there is an unamortized discount of $2,000. Northeast pays the interest up to date on December 31 and exercises its option of calling in or redeeming the bonds on the same date, December 31. The entry is shown in general journal form. The loss represents the difference between the book value and the price paid (also determined by the difference between debits and credits).

	DATE		DESCRIPTION	POST. REF.	DEBIT	CREDIT	
1	Dec.	31	Bonds Payable		500 0 0 0 00		1
2			Loss on Redemption of Bonds		27 0 0 0 00		2
3			Cash			525 0 0 0 00	3
4			Discount on Bonds Payable			2 0 0 0 00	4
5			To record redemption of bonds				5
6			at 105.				6
7							7

Recall that even if a corporation's bonds are not callable, the firm can buy back the bonds—all of them, or as many as it can find on the open market. For example, the Seacoast Paper Company has $1,000,000 worth of 7 percent coupon bonds outstanding, on which there is an unamortized premium of $30,000. On July 15, Seacoast buys $100,000 (one tenth of the original issue) of bonds in the open market at 97, plus 15 days' accrued interest. The entry, in general journal form, is as follows.

1	Jul.	15	Bonds Payable		100 0 0 0 00		1
2			Premium on Bonds Payable		3 0 0 0 00		2
3			Interest Expense ($100,000,				3
4			7 percent, 15 days)		2 9 1 67		4
5			Cash			97 2 9 1 67	5
6			Gain on Redemption of Bonds			6 0 0 0 00	6
7			To record redemption of bonds				7
8			at 97 plus accrued interest.				8
9							9

(text continues, page 798)

C. K. Gill Company, Inc.
Balance Sheet
December 31, 19–

Assets

Current Assets:			
Cash		$ 12 0 0 0 00	
Notes Receivable		30 0 0 0 00	
Accounts Receivable	$ 220 0 0 0 00		
Less Allowance for Doubtful Accounts	4 0 0 0 00	216 0 0 0 00	
Merchandise Inventory		647 0 0 0 00	
Supplies		2 0 0 0 00	
Total Current Assets			$ 907 0 0 0 00
Investments:			
Sinking Fund Cash		$ 5 0 0 0 00	
Sinking Fund Investments		84 0 0 0 00	
Total Investments			89 0 0 0 00
Plant and Equipment:			
Equipment	$ 222 0 0 0 00		
Less Accumulated Depreciation	32 0 0 0 00	$ 190 0 0 0 00	
Building	$ 180 0 0 0 00		
Less Accumulated Depreciation	45 0 0 0 00	135 0 0 0 00	
Land		70 0 0 0 00	
Total Plant and Equipment			395 0 0 0 00
Intangible Assets:			
Goodwill		$ 20 0 0 0 00	
Organization Costs		8 0 0 0 00	
Total Intangible Assets			28 0 0 0 00
Total Assets			$1 419 0 0 0 00

Liabilities

Current Liabilities:			
Accounts Payable		$ 70 0 0 0 00	
Income Tax Payable		8 0 0 0 00	
Dividends Payable		12 0 0 0 00	
Total Current Liabilities			$ 90 0 0 0 00
Long-Term Liabilities:			
6 percent Bonds Payable, due December 31, 1990	$ 100 0 0 0 00		
Less Discount on Bonds Payable	3 0 0 0 00	$ 97 0 0 0 00	
8 percent Bonds Payable, due March 31, 1992	$ 200 0 0 0 00		
Add Premium on Bonds Payable	2 0 0 0 00	202 0 0 0 00	
Total Long-term Liabilities			299 0 0 0 00
Total Liabilities			$ 389 0 0 0 00

Stockholders' Equity

Paid-in Capital:			
Common Stock, $10 par (100,000 shares authorized, 40,000 shares issued)	$ 400 0 0 0 00		
Premium on Common Stock	220 0 0 0 00		
Total Paid-in Capital		$ 620 0 0 0 00	
Retained Earnings:			
Unappropriated Retained Earnings	$ 310 0 0 0 00		
Appropriated For Plant Expansion	100 0 0 0 00		
Total Retained Earnings		410 0 0 0 00	
Total Stockholders' Equity			1 030 0 0 0 00
Total Liabilities and Stockholders' Equity			$1 419 0 0 0 00

Figure 25-3

Redemption, in effect, cancels all or a portion of the Bonds Payable account, as well as the accompanying premium or discount. We shall list Gain (or Loss) on Redemption of Bonds in the income statement under the heading Other Income or Other Expense. If the gains or losses are significant, they are listed (net of any related income tax effect) under the heading of **Extraordinary Items,** a classification of accounts appearing at the bottom of an income statement.

BALANCE SHEET

The balance sheet of the C. K. Gill Company, Inc., shown in Figure 25-3 (previous two pages), is designed to show you how to place the accounts we've introduced in this chapter.

GLOSSARY

Amortization The systematic writing off of bond premium or discount.

Bond issue The total amount a corporation promises to pay to redeem its bonds; subdivided into denominations of $1,000 or $5,000 each.

Callable bonds Bonds that give the corporation the right to redeem or buy back the bonds at a specified figure, known as the *call price.*

Contra-liability account A deduction from a liability, such as Discount on Bonds Payable, which is a deduction from the balance of Bonds Payable.

Coupon bonds Bonds that have interest coupons attached to each bond. These coupons are payable to bearer and may be cashed on interest payment dates.

Debenture Unsecured bond.

Discount Deficiency between the price received and the face value of a bond.

Extraordinary Items Significant transactions that appear at the bottom of an income statement (net of any related income tax effect) because they are unusual in nature and do not recur with any regularity. They may include gains or losses on redemption of bonds, fire losses, expropriation of property by a foreign government, or major revaluation of a foreign currency.

Indenture A bond agreement, or contract between the corporation and its bondholders.

Leverage Debt used as a lever to raise the owner's rate of return, earning income on borrowed money (as, for example, borrowing money at 8 percent and using it to earn a 15 percent rate of return).

Premium Excess between the price received and the face value of a bond.

Redeem Buy back or repurchase bonds from bondholders.

Registered bonds Bonds whose owners' names are registered with the corporation that issued the bonds.

Secured bonds Bonds that are backed up by titles to property that may be claimed by the bondholders in the event that the issuing corporation does not fulfill its obligation.

Serial bonds Bonds of a particular issue that have a series of maturity dates.

Sinking fund A special fund accumulated over the life of a bond issue to enable the issuing corporation to pay off the bonds when they mature (come due).

Term bonds Bonds of a particular issue, all having the same maturity date.

Unsecured bonds Bonds backed only by the credit standing (good name) of the issuing corporation.

QUESTIONS, EXERCISES, AND PROBLEMS

Discussion Questions

1. If the market rate of interest is higher than the rate of interest stated in the bond agreement, will the bonds be sold at a premium or a discount? Why?
2. How is the bond premium reported on the balance sheet?
3. What is the difference between term bonds and serial bonds?
4. What is the difference between a debenture and an indenture?
5. What are two definite obligations incurred by a corporation when it issues bonds?
6. What is a bond sinking fund, and what purpose does it serve?
7. How is a bond sinking fund classified on a balance sheet?

Exercises

Exercise 25-1 Suppose that a corporation sells $1,000,000 of 7 percent, 10-year bonds at 103. What is the amount of annual amortization of the premium?

Exercise 25-2 On January 2 of this year, a corporation issues $500,000 of 9 percent, 20-year bonds at 104. What is the net amount of interest expense for this year?

Exercise 25-3 On February 1 of this year, a corporation sold $1,000,000 of 7½ percent, 10-year bonds at 97. The bonds were dated February 1, and the dates of interest payment are August 1 and February 1. Set forth entries to record the sale and the first interest payment.

Exercise 25-4 Determine the average annual interest cost on the following bond issue: $3,000,000, 6 percent, 20-year bonds sold at 94.

Exercise 25-5 Two companies are financed as follows.

	J. B. Fulton, Inc.	N. C. Wentzel, Inc.
Bonds payable, 7 percent (issued at face value)	$ 400,000	$300,000
Preferred 8 percent stock, $100 par	100,000	400,000
Common stock, $100 par	1,000,000	800,000

Each company had an income of $160,000 before payment of bond interest and income tax. Assuming a federal corporation income tax of 50 percent, determine for each company the earnings per share on common stock.

Exercise 25-6   The United Peach Growers Corporation has outstanding $200,000 of 10-year sinking fund bonds. At the end of the ninth year after it has issued the bonds, the balance of United's Sinking Fund Investments account is $185,600. List the entries to record the following.

a. The sale of the investments for $192,000
b. The final deposit in the sinking fund, bringing the balance of the account up to $200,000
c. The payment of the bonds

Exercise 25-7   The Kay Plumbing Corporation has the following account balances: Bonds Payable, $800,000; Premium on Bonds Payable, $24,000. As a step in redeeming the bond issue, Kay Plumbing buys $100,000 worth of its bonds on the open market at 98. Give the entry to record the redemption.

Exercise 25-8   Describe the entries recorded in the T accounts below.

Cash				Bonds Payable			Interest Expense			
(1)	1,060,000	(2)	45,000		(1)	1,000,000	(2)	45,000	(4)	2,000
							(3)	15,000	(5)	58,000
									(6)	15,000

Premium on Bonds Payable				Interest Payable				Income Summary	
(4)	2,000	(1)	60,000	(6)	15,000	(3)	15,000	(5)	58,000

Problem Set A

Problem 25-1A   During two consecutive years, the Briggs Sanitation Service, Inc., completed the following transactions.

Year 1

Jan.   1 Issued $500,000 worth of 20-year, 8 percent bonds, dated January 1 of this year, at 98. Interest is payable semiannually on June 30 and December 31.
Jun. 30 Paid semiannual interest on bonds.
Dec. 31 Paid semiannual interest on bonds.
      31 Recorded amortization of discount on bonds.
      31 Closed Interest Expense account.

Year 2

Jun. 30 Paid semiannual interest on bonds.
Dec. 31 Paid semiannual interest on bonds.
      31 Recorded amortization of discount on bonds.
      31 Closed the Interest Expense account.

Instructions

Record the transactions in general journal form.

Problem 25-2A Backstrom Company, Inc., completed the following selected transactions.

Year 1

Apr.	1	Issued $1,000,000 worth of 20-year, 9 percent bonds, dated April 1 of this year, at 104. Interest is payable semiannually on October 1 and April 1.
Oct.	1	Paid semiannual interest on bonds.
Dec.	31	Recorded adjusting entry for accrued interest payable.
	31	Recorded amortization of premium on bonds.
	31	Closed Interest Expense account.

Year 2

Jan.	1	Reversed adjusting entry for accrued interest payable.
Apr.	1	Paid semiannual interest on bonds.
Oct.	1	Paid semiannual interest on bonds.
Dec.	31	Made adjusting entry to record accrued interest payable.
	31	Made adjusting entry to record amortization of premium on bonds.
	31	Closed Interest Expense account.

Instructions

1. Record the transactions in general journal form.
2. Post the entries to the Interest Expense account. Label the adjusting, closing, and reversing entries.

Problem 25-3A During two consecutive years the Kekic Manufacturing Corporation completed the following transactions related to its $4,000,000 issue of 25-year, 6 percent bonds, dated May 1 of the first year. Interest is payable on May 1 and November 1. The corporation's fiscal year extends from January 1 through December 31.

Year 1

May	1	Sold bond issue for $3,940,000.
Nov.	1	Paid semiannual interest on bonds.
Dec.	31	Made adjusting entry to record accrued interest payable.
	31	Made adjusting entry to record amortization of bond discount.
	31	Deposited $57,750 in a bond sinking fund.
	31	Closed Interest Expense account.

Year 2

Jan.	1	Reversed adjustment for interest payable.
	4	Bought various securities with sinking fund cash; cost, $56,200.
May	1	Paid semiannual interest on bonds.
Nov.	1	Paid semiannual interest on bonds.

Dec. 31 Recorded receipt of $2,920 of income derived from sinking fund investments, depositing cash in sinking fund.
31 Made adjusting entry to record accrued interest payable.
31 Made adjusting entry to record amortization of bond discount.
31 Deposited $86,000 in bond sinking fund.
31 Closed Interest Expense account.

Instructions

1. Record the transactions in general journal form.
2. Post entries to the Interest Expense account and the Discount on Bonds Payable account. Label the adjusting, closing, and reversing entries.

Problem 25-4A On March 1, the Pembrook Development Corporation issued $6,000,000 worth of 25-year bonds, 9 percent, dated March 1, with interest payable March 1 and September 1. The corporation's fiscal year is the calendar year. The following transactions pertain to the bond issue for the first two years.

Year 1

Mar. 1 Sold bond issue for $6,030,000.
Sep. 1 Paid semiannual interest on bonds.
Dec. 31 Made adjusting entry to record accrued interest payable.
31 Made adjusting entry to record amortization of bond premium.
31 Deposited $108,000 in a bond sinking fund.
31 Closed Interest Expense account.

Year 2

Jan. 1 Reversed adjusting entry for interest payable.
10 Bought various securities with sinking fund cash, $98,000.
Mar. 1 Paid semiannual interest on bonds.
Jul. 1 Recorded receipt of $3,840 of income derived from sinking fund investments, depositing cash in sinking fund.
6 Bought various securities with sinking fund cash, $12,900.
Sep. 1 Paid semiannual interest on bonds.
Dec. 31 Recorded receipt of $4,440 of income derived from sinking fund investments, depositing cash in sinking fund.
31 Made adjusting entry to record accrued interest payable.
31 Made adjusting entry to record amortization of bond premium.
31 Deposited $129,600 in bond sinking fund.
31 Closed Sinking Fund Income account.
31 Closed Interest Expense account.

Instructions

1. Record the transactions in general journal form.
2. Post entries to the Interest Expense account and the Premium on Bonds Payable account. Label the adjusting, closing, and reversing entries.

Problem Set B

Problem 25-1B During two consecutive years, the S. T. Jones Company, Inc., completed the following transactions.

Year 1

Jan.   2 Issued $1,000,000 worth of 20-year, 8½ percent bonds, dated January 1 of this year, at 99. Interest is payable semiannually on June 30 and December 31.

Jun. 30 Paid semiannual interest on bonds.

Dec. 31 Paid semiannual interest on bonds.
      31 Recorded amortization of discount on bonds.
      31 Closed Interest Expense account.

Year 2

Jun. 30 Paid semiannual interest on bonds.

Dec. 31 Paid semiannual interest on bonds.
      31 Recorded amortization of discount on bonds.
      31 Closed the Interest Expense account.

Instructions

Record the transactions in general journal form.

Problem 25-2B Star Auto Parts, Inc., completed the following selected transactions.

Year 1

Mar.   1 Issued $500,000 of 20-year, 9 percent bonds, dated March 1 of this year, at 106. Interest is payable semiannually on September 1 and March 1.

Sep.   1 Paid semiannual interest on bonds.

Dec. 31 Recorded adjusting entry for accrued interest payable.
      31 Recorded amortization of premium on bonds.
      31 Closed Interest Expense account.

Year 2

Jan.   1 Reversed adjusting entry for accrued interest payable.

Mar.   1 Paid semiannual interest on bonds.

Sep.   1 Paid semiannual interest on bonds.

Dec. 31 Made adjusting entry to record accrued interest payable.
      31 Made adjusting entry to record amortization of premium on bonds.
      31 Closed Interest Expense account.

Instructions

1. Record the transactions in general journal form.
2. Post entries to the Interest Expense account. Label the adjusting, closing, and reversing entries.

Problem 25-3B During two consecutive years, the Dietz Tug and Barge Corporation completed the following transactions relating to its $6,000,000 issue of 30-year, 7 percent bonds, dated April 1 of the first year. Interest is payable on April 1 and October 1. The corporation's fiscal year extends from January 1 through December 31.

Year 1

Apr.   1 Sold the bond issue for $5,820,000.
Oct.   1 Paid semiannual interest on bonds.
Dec. 31 Made adjusting entry to record accrued interest payable.
      31 Made adjusting entry to record amortization of bond discount.
      31 Deposited $77,000 in a bond sinking fund.
      31 Closed Interest Expense account.

Year 2

Jan.   1 Reversed adjusting entry for accrued interest payable.
       6 Bought various securities with sinking fund cash; cost, $72,420.
Apr.   1 Paid semiannual interest on bonds.
Oct.   1 Paid semiannual interest on bonds.
Dec. 31 Recorded receipt of $3,893 of income derived from sinking fund investments, depositing the cash in the sinking fund.
      31 Made adjusting entry to record accrued interest payable.
      31 Made adjusting entry to record amortization of bond discount.
      31 Deposited $111,300 in bond sinking fund.
      31 Closed Interest Expense account.

Instructions

1. Record the transactions in general journal form.
2. Post entries to the Interest Expense account and the Discount on Bonds Payable account. Label the adjusting, closing, and reversing entries.

Problem 25-4B On May 1, Kallin, Inc., whose fiscal year is the calendar year, issued $8,000,000 of 20-year, 9 percent bonds, dated April 1, with interest payable on April 1 and October 1. The following transactions pertain to the bond issue for the first two years.

Year 1

Apr.   1 Sold the bond issue for $8,080,000.
Oct.   1 Paid semiannual interest on bonds.
Dec. 31 Made adjusting entry to record accrued interest payable.
      31 Made adjusting entry to record amortization of bond premium.
      31 Deposited $160,000 in a bond sinking fund.
      31 Closed Interest Expense account.

Year 2

Jan.   1 Reversed adjusting entry for accrued interest payable.
      12 Bought various securities with sinking fund cash; cost, $154,600.
Apr.   1 Paid semiannual interest on bonds.

Jul.   1 Recorded receipt of $5,390 of income derived from sinking fund investments, depositing the cash in the sinking fund.
         8 Bought various securities with sinking fund cash; cost, $8,760.
Oct.   1 Paid semiannual interest on bonds.
Dec.   31 Recorded the receipt of $11,130 of income derived from sinking fund investments, depositing the cash in the sinking fund.
        31 Made adjusting entry to record accrued interest payable.
        31 Made adjusting entry to record amortization of bond premium.
        31 Deposited $200,000 in the bond sinking fund.
        31 Closed Sinking Fund Income account.
        31 Closed Interest Expense account.

Instructions

1. Record the transactions in general journal form.
2. Post entries to the Interest Expense account and the Premium on Bonds Payable account. Label the adjusting, closing, and reversing entries.

REVIEW OF T ACCOUNT PLACEMENT
AND REPRESENTATIVE TRANSACTIONS

Review of T Account Placement

The following display sums up the placement of T accounts covered in Chapters 21 through 25 in relation to the fundamental accounting equation.

Review of Representative Transactions

The following table summarizes the recording of transactions covered in Chapters 21 through 25, along with classification of the accounts.

Transaction	Accounts Involved	Class.	Increase or Decrease	Therefore Debit or Credit	Financial Statement
Issued voucher for the purchase of merchandise	Purchases Vouchers Payable	CMS CL	I I	Debit Credit	Inc. State. Bal. Sheet

Paid voucher for purchase of merchandise within discount period	Vouchers Payable
	   Cash
	   Purchases Discount
		CL
		CA
		CMS
			D
			D
			I
				Debit
				Credit
				Credit
					Bal. Sheet
					Bal. Sheet
					Inc. State.

Returned merchandise after original voucher was recorded	Vouchers Payable
	   Purchases Returns
	      and Allowances
		CL
		
		CMS
			D
			
			I
				Debit
				
				Credit
					Bal. Sheet
					
					Inc. State.

Issued a note payable after original voucher was recorded	Vouchers Payable Notes Payable	CL CL	D I	Debit Credit	Bal. Sheet Bal. Sheet
Paid an interest-bearing note under voucher system	Notes Payable Interest Expense Vouchers Payable	CL OE CL	D I I	Debit Debit Credit	Bal. Sheet Inc. State. Bal. Sheet
	Vouchers Payable Cash	CL CA	D D	Debit Credit	Bal. Sheet Bal. Sheet
Recorded cash investment in a partnership	Cash J. Doe, Capital	CA O. Equity	I I	Debit Credit	Bal. Sheet Bal. Sheet
Transferred one partner's equity to a new partner	D. Smith, Capital L. Jones, Capital	O. Equity O. Equity	D I	Debit Credit	Bal. Sheet Bal. Sheet

Partnership assets are sold at a profit	Cash
	   Assets
	   Loss or Gain from
	      Realization
		CA
		Assets
		
		OI
			I
			D
			
			I
				Debit
				Credit
				
				Credit
					Bal. Sheet
					Bal. Sheet
					
					Inc. State.

Allocated net gain to the partners' capital accounts	Loss or Gain from
	   Realization
	   A. Bell, Capital
	   C. Dale, Capital
		OI
		O. Equity
		O. Equity
			D
			I
			I
				Debit
				Credit
				Credit
					Inc. State.
					Bal. Sheet
					Bal. Sheet

Partnership assets are sold at a loss	Cash
	Loss or Gain from
	   Realization
	   Assets
		CA
		
		OE
		Assets
			I
			
			I
			D
				Debit
				
				Debit
				Credit
					Bal. Sheet
					
					Inc. State.
					Bal. Sheet

Sold common stock at par for cash	Cash Common Stock	CA PIC	I I	Debit Credit	Bal. Sheet Bal. Sheet

Transaction	Accounts Involved	Class.	Increase or Decrease	Therefore Debit or Credit	Financial Statement
Sold preferred 12 percent stock for an amount above par	Cash	CA	I	Debit	Bal. Sheet
	Preferred 12 Percent Stock	PIC	I	Credit	Bal. Sheet
	Premium on Preferred 12 Percent Stock	PIC	I	Credit	Bal. Sheet
Paid corporation state charter fees	Organization Costs	IA	I	Debit	Bal. Sheet
	Cash	CA	D	Credit	Bal. Sheet
Sold common stock at less than par value	Cash	CA	I	Debit	Bal. Sheet
	Discount on Common Stock	PIC	I	Debit	Bal. Sheet
	Common Stock	PIC	I	Credit	Bal. Sheet
Received subscription for no-par common stock at an amount over stated value	Subscriptions Receivable, Common Stock	CA	I	Debit	Bal. Sheet
	Common Stock Subscribed	PIC	I	Credit	Bal. Sheet
	Paid-in Capital in Excess of Stated Value	PIC	I	Credit	Bal. Sheet
Received installment on subscription to common stock	Cash	CA	I	Debit	Bal. Sheet
	Subscriptions Receivable, Common Stock	CA	D	Credit	Bal. Sheet
Issued common stock after receiving last installment on subscription	Common Stock Subscribed	PIC	D	Debit	Bal. Sheet
	Common Stock	PIC	I	Credit	Bal. Sheet
Paid installment on corporation income tax	Income Tax	Exp.	I	Debit	Inc. State.
	Cash	CA	D	Credit	Bal. Sheet
Adjusting entry for additional corporation income tax	Income Tax	Exp.	I	Debit	Inc. State.
	Income Tax Payable	CL	I	Credit	Bal. Sheet
Closed the Income Tax account	Income Summary	—	—	Debit	—
	Income Tax	Exp.	D	Credit	Inc. State.
Closed the Income Summary account assuming a net income	Income Summary	—	—	Debit	—
	Retained Earnings	RE	I	Credit	Ret. Earn.

Transaction	Accounts Involved	Class.	Increase or Decrease	Therefore Debit or Credit	Financial Statement
Made an appropriation to retained earnings for contingencies	Retained Earnings	RE	D	Debit	Ret. Earn.
	Retained Earnings Appropriated for Contingencies	RE	I	Credit	Ret. Earn.
Paid interest on corporation bonds	Interest Expense	OE	I	Debit	Inc. State.
	Cash	CA	D	Credit	Bal. Sheet
Sold bonds at an amount over the face value	Cash	CA	I	Debit	Bal. Sheet
	Premium on Bonds Payable	LTL	I	Credit	Bal. Sheet
	Bonds Payable	LTL	I	Credit	Bal. Sheet
Recorded adjusting entry for amortization of bond premium	Premium on Bonds Payable	LTL	D	Debit	Bal. Sheet
	Interest Expense	OE	D	Credit	Inc. State.
Made deposit in bond sinking fund	Sinking Fund Cash	I	I	Debit	Bal. Sheet
	Cash	CA	D	Credit	Bal. Sheet
Sold bonds at an amount less than face value	Cash	CA	I	Debit	Bal. Sheet
	Discount on Bonds Payable	LTL	I	Debit	Bal. Sheet
	Bonds Payable	LTL	I	Credit	Bal. Sheet
Invested bond sinking fund	Sinking Fund Investments	I	I	Debit	Bal. Sheet
	Sinking Fund Cash	I	D	Credit	Bal. Sheet
Sold sinking fund invest-ments at a gain	Sinking Fund Cash	I	I	Debit	Bal. Sheet
	Sinking Fund Investments	I	D	Credit	Bal. Sheet
	Gain on Sale of Sinking Fund Investments	OI	I	Credit	Inc. State.

26 Departmental Accounting

Learning Objectives

After you have completed this chapter, you will be able to do the following:

1. Compile a departmental income statement extended through gross profit.

2. Compile a departmental work sheet.

3. Compile a departmental income statement extended through income from operations.

4. Apportion operating expenses among various operating departments.

5. Compile a departmental income statement extended through contribution margin.

When a company carries on a number of different business activities, the firm should be divided into a number of subdivisions or departments. This enables the company's management to delegate authority to departmental managers, who are held responsible for their respective departments, and to measure the profitability of each department. It is the element of profitability that we're going to discuss in this chapter.

Large companies have greater opportunities to use departmental accounting than small ones. However, even a small business—if it carries on more than one type of business activity—may benefit from departmental accounting. For example, the Neumeister Company deals in insurance and property management and accounts separately for insurance commissions and management fees. At the end of the fiscal year Donna and Irving Neumeister can compare the profitability of each activity with the amount of time and attention they had to devote to it. On the basis of this comparison they may decide to spend more time on one activity and less on the other.

For large business firms—those that engage in service, merchandising, or manufacturing—departmental accounting is a must. The accounting reports consist of several levels of income statements recorded on a departmental basis and extended from sales through gross profit or income from operations or contribution margin.

GROSS PROFIT BY DEPARTMENTS

A department's gross profit depends on its sales volume and its markup on the goods sold.

Net sales − Cost of merchandise sold = Gross profit

Gross profit, in the same context, consists of the items listed in the income statement shown in Figure 26-1.

To determine the gross profit of a given department, one needs a separate departmental set of figures for each element entering into the gross profit. There are two methods of getting these figures.

1. Keep separate general ledger accounts for each item involved in gross profit, such as a Sales account for each department, a Sales Returns and Allowances account for each department, and so on. Then record the balances of these accounts on the income statement.
2. Keep only one general ledger account for each item involved in gross profit and apportion the balance to the various departments. For exam-

Figure 26-1

Revenue from Sales:				
Sales				$120 0 0 0 00
Less: Sales Returns and Allowances		$ 6 0 0 0 00		
Sales Discount		3 0 0 0 00		9 0 0 0 00
Net Sales				$111 0 0 0 00
Cost of Merchandise Sold:				
Merchandise Inventory (beginning)			$ 48 0 0 0 00	
Purchases	$81 0 0 0 00			
Less: Purchases Returns and Allowances	$4 0 0 0 00			
Purchases Discount	2 0 0 0 00	6 0 0 0 00		
Net Purchases			75 0 0 0 00	
Merchandise Available for Sale			$123 0 0 0 00	
Less Merchandise Inventory (ending)			52 0 0 0 00	
Cost of Merchandise Sold				71 0 0 0 00
Gross Profit				$ 40 0 0 0 00

Figure 26-1

SALES JOURNAL

PAGE _____

DATE	INV. NO.	CUSTOMER'S NAME	POST. REF.	ACCOUNTS RECEIVABLE DEBIT	SALES CREDIT DEPT. A	DEPT. B	DEPT. C	DEPT. D	DEPT. E
19— Sep. 1	1698	Carole Barnhart	√	1 6 5 00	1 6 5 00				
Sep. 3	1702	Ralph Muncy	√	3 7 6 00			3 7 6 00		
Sep. 3	1704	Donald Caspar	√	7 1 6 00		7 1 6 00			
				14 9 3 3 00	26 8 1 00	8 6 4 00	47 9 4 00	37 1 6 00	28 7 8 00
				(1114)	(4111)	(4112)	(4113)	(4114)	(4115)

Figure 26-2

813

ple, maintain one Sales account and one Sales Returns and Allowances account for the company, and in addition keep a breakdown of sales and sales returns for each department. Then record the figures for each department on the income statement.

Separate Accounts by Departments

Keeping separate accounts by departments yields the most accurate accounting data. One needs separate accounts for each department for Sales, Sales Returns and Allowances, Sales Discount, Purchases, Purchases Returns and Allowances, Purchases Discount, and Merchandise Inventory. For example, Action Enterprises has five departments and uses five Sales accounts, five Sales Returns and Allowances accounts, five Sales Discount accounts, five Merchandise Inventory accounts, and so forth. The special journals contain columns for each departmental account, as in the sales journal on the previous page (Figure 26-2).

The accountant posts each total to a separate account, as indicated by the ledger account numbers. A company that has many departments and keeps a separate journal column for each may find that the journal becomes quite cumbersome in size. In a situation like this, it is better to post from the sales invoices directly to the departmental sales accounts. (This method is like the process of posting from sales invoices described in Chapter 11.) Another alternative is to establish a controlling account in the general ledger and to record each department in a subsidiary ledger.

Maintaining One General Ledger Account

When a company keeps only one general ledger account for each item involved in gross profit, the accountant has to distribute the total amount among the various departments at the end of the accounting period. To do so, the accountant has to accumulate departmental information on supplementary records. Martin's Grocery, for example, has a produce, a grocery, and a meat department. Martin's records sales by department, by having the checkout clerk punch them separately on the cash register. At the end of each day, the sales are recorded in a journal, taking the totals from the cash register tapes. Sales are also recorded on a departmental analysis sheet.

Businesses also use separate analysis sheets for sales returns, purchases, purchase returns, purchase discounts, and so forth. At the end of the accounting period, these analysis sheets give departmental breakdowns for each item.

Gross Profit by Departments

L. C. Simmons Company, Inc., has two departments, A and B, and keeps separate accounts for each. The income statement for the fiscal year ending December 31, showing departmental reporting only up to Gross Profit, appears in Figure 26-3 (next two pages). A skeleton outline of this process is as follows.

From Sales through Gross Profit

Revenue from Sales   { Based on separate departmental accounts
Less Cost of Merchandise Sold   { or supplementary analysis sheets

Gross Profit
Less Operating Expenses

Income from Operations
Add Other Income
Less Other Expenses

Net Income

INCOME FROM OPERATIONS BY DEPARTMENTS

A company may extend departmental reporting of income to various points, such as Income from Operations or Net Income. The L. C. Simmons Company keeps separate accounts for each item that enters into gross profit and apportions the operating expenses between Gross Profit and Income from Operations to Department A or Department B on a logical basis. (We shall discuss this procedure in detail later.) For emphasis, let us look at the skeleton outline of the income statement.

From Sales Through Income from Operations
Departmentalized

Revenue from Sales   { Separate departmental accounts or supplementary
Less Cost of Merchandise Sold   { analysis sheets

Gross Profit
Less Selling Expenses   { Account balances
Less General Expenses   { are apportioned

Income from Operations

Nondepartmentalized

Add Other Income
Less Other Expense

Net Income

(*text continued on page 820*)

L. C. Simmons Company, Inc.
Income Statement
For year ended December 31, 19–

		DEPARTMENT A		
1	Revenue from Sales:			
2	Sales		$ 560 0 0 0 00	
3	Less Sales Returns and Allowances		14 2 0 0 00	
4	Net Sales			$ 545 8 0 0 00
5	Cost of Merchandise Sold:			
6	Merchandise Inventory, Jan. 1, 19–		$ 96 4 0 0 00	
7	Purchases	$ 325 1 2 0 00		
8	Less: Purchases Returns and Allowances	9 5 8 0 00		
9	Purchases Discount	5 7 4 0 00		
10	Net Purchases		309 8 0 0 00	
11	Merchandise Available for Sale		$ 406 2 0 0 00	
12	Less Merchandise Inventory, Dec. 31, 19–		110 0 0 0 00	
13	Cost of Merchandise Sold			296 2 0 0 00
14	Gross Profit			$ 249 6 0 0 00
15				
16	Operating Expenses:			
17	Selling Expenses:			
18	Sales Salary Expense			
19	Advertising Expense			
20	Depreciation Expense, Store Equipment			
21	Miscellaneous Selling Expense			
22	Total Selling Expenses			
23	General Expenses:			
24	Office Salary Expense			
25	Rent Expense			
26	Utilities Expense			
27	Insurance Expense			
28	Bad Debts Expense			
29	Miscellaneous General Expense			
30	Total General Expenses			
31	Total Operating Expenses			
32	Income from Operations			
33				
34	Other Income:			
35	Interest Income			
36	Other Expenses:			
37	Interest Expense			
38	Net Income before Income Tax			
39				

DEPARTMENT B			TOTAL			
						1
	$ 240 0 0 0 00			$ 800 0 0 0 00		2
	5 8 0 0 00			20 0 0 0 00		3
		$ 234 2 0 0 00			$ 780 0 0 0 00	4
						5
	$ 82 7 4 0 00			$ 179 1 4 0 00		6
$ 167 8 9 0 00			$ 493 0 1 0 00			7
4 7 5 6 00			14 3 3 6 00			8
3 2 7 4 00			9 0 1 4 00			9
	159 8 6 0 00			469 6 6 0 00		10
	$ 242 6 0 0 00			$ 648 8 0 0 00		11
	90 0 0 0 00			200 0 0 0 00		12
		152 6 0 0 00			448 8 0 0 00	13
		$ 81 6 0 0 00			$ 331 2 0 0 00	14
						15
						16
						17
			$ 140 8 2 5 00			18
			17 6 0 0 00			19
			3 3 0 0 00			20
			4 2 7 0 00			21
				$ 165 9 9 5 00		22
						23
			$ 32 1 0 0 00			24
			16 4 0 0 00			25
			4 8 4 0 00			26
			4 4 0 0 00			27
			2 5 7 0 00			28
			9 2 0 00			29
				61 2 3 0 00		30
					227 2 2 5 00	31
				$ 103 9 7 5 00		32
						33
						34
				$ 3 6 2 4 00		35
						36
				2 4 0 0 00	1 2 2 4 00	37
					$ 105 1 9 9 00	38
						39

Figure 26-3

	ACCOUNT NAME	TRIAL BALANCE DEBIT	TRIAL BALANCE CREDIT	ADJUSTMENTS DEBIT	ADJUSTMENTS CREDIT	DEPARTMENT A INCOME STATEMENT DEBIT	DEPARTMENT A INCOME STATEMENT CREDIT
2	Accounts Receivable	82 0 4 0 00					
3	Allowance for						
4	Doubtful Accounts		8 6 2 00		(f) 2 5 7 0 00		
6	Merchandise						
7	Inventory						
8	Department A	96 4 0 0 00		(b)110 0 0 0 00	(a)96 4 0 0 00		
9	Department B	82 7 4 0 00		(d) 90 0 0 0 00	(c)82 7 4 0 00		
10	Prepaid Insurance	5 5 4 0 00			(e) 4 4 0 0 00		
11	Store Equipment	32 4 0 0 00					
12	Accumulated Depre-						
13	ciation, Store						
14	Equipment		21 6 0 0 00		(g) 3 3 0 0 00		
16	Sales						
17	Department A		560 0 0 0 00				560 0 0 0 00
18	Department B		240 0 0 0 00				
19	Sales Returns and						
20	Allowances						
21	Department A	14 2 0 0 00				14 2 0 0 00	
22	Department B	5 8 0 0 00					
23	Purchases						
24	Department A	325 1 2 0 00				325 1 2 0 00	
25	Department B	167 8 9 0 00					
26	Purchases Returns						
27	and Allowances						
28	Department A		9 5 8 0 00				9 5 8 0 00
29	Department B		4 7 5 6 00				
30	Purchases Discount						
31	Department A		5 7 4 0 00				5 7 4 0 00
32	Department B		3 2 7 4 00				
33	Sales Salary						
34	Expense	140 8 2 5 00				88 6 2 5 00	
35	Advertising Expense	17 6 0 0 00				10 3 3 6 00	
36	Misc. Selling						
37	Expense	4 2 7 0 00				2 9 8 9 00	
38	Office Salary						
39	Expense	32 1 0 0 00				22 4 7 0 00	
40	Rent Expense	16 4 0 0 00				10 2 5 0 00	
41	Utility Expense	4 8 4 0 00				3 0 2 5 00	

Figure 26-4

	DEPARTMENT B INCOME STATEMENT		NONDEPARTMENTAL INCOME STATEMENT		BALANCE SHEET		
	DEBIT	CREDIT	DEBIT	CREDIT	DEBIT	CREDIT	
					82 0 4 0 00		2
							3
						3 4 3 2 00	4
							6
							7
					110 0 0 0 00		8
					90 0 0 0 00		9
					1 1 4 0 00		10
					32 4 0 0 00		11
							12
							13
						24 9 0 0 00	14
							16
							17
			240 0 0 0 00				18
							19
							20
							21
	5 8 0 0 00						22
							23
							24
	167 8 9 0 00						25
							26
							27
							28
			4 7 5 6 00				29
							30
							31
			3 2 7 4 00				32
							33
	52 2 0 0 00						34
	7 2 6 4 00						35
							36
	1 2 8 1 00						37
							38
	9 6 3 0 00						39
	6 1 5 0 00						40
	1 8 1 5 00						41

(Continued on next page)

	TRIAL BALANCE		ADJUSTMENTS		DEPARTMENT A INCOME STATEMENT	
ACCOUNT NAME	DEBIT	CREDIT	DEBIT	CREDIT	DEBIT	CREDIT
1 Misc. General						
2 Expense	9 2 0 00				6 4 4 00	
3 Interest Income		3 6 2 4 00				
4 Interest Expense	2 4 0 0 00					
5	1,471 8 6 4 00	1,471 8 6 4 00				
6 Income Summary			(a) 96 4 0 0 00	(b) 110 0 0 0 00	96 4 0 0 00	110 0 0 0 00
7			(c) 82 7 4 0 00	(d) 90 0 0 0 00		
8 Insurance Expense			(e) 4 4 0 0 00		2 5 4 0 00	
9 Bad Debts Expense			(f) 2 5 7 0 00		1 7 9 9 00	
10 Depreciation Ex-						
11 pense, Store						
12 Equipment			(g) 3 3 0 0 00		1 8 4 0 00	
13			389 4 1 0 00	389 4 1 0 00	580 2 3 8 00	685 3 2 0 00
14 Net Income (Loss)						
15 by Department					105 0 8 2 00	
16					685 3 2 0 00	685 3 2 0 00
17 Net Income						
18						
19						
20						
21						

Work Sheet for Departmental Accounting

Each department assumes its share of overhead expenses. Recall once again the sequential steps of the accounting cycle: The accountant records the trial balance in the first columns of the work sheet, formulates and records the adjustments, completes the work sheet, and then uses the work sheet to prepare the income statement. The Income Statement columns of the work sheet for a company that keeps track of income by departments contain debit and credit columns for each department, as well as debit and credit columns entitled Nondepartmental. These last two columns include Other Income and Other Expense accounts that are not directly assigned to a department. By the time the accountant gets to the income statement, she or he has already performed calculations apportioning the expenses, which are accordingly subdivided on the work sheet. A sample portion of the work sheet for the Simmons Company is shown in Figure 26-4. This figure begins on page 818 and continues over to page 821. Various asset, liability, and owners' equity accounts are not shown, but they are included in the totals.

Objective 2

Compile a departmental work sheet.

Figure 26-4
(continued)

	DEPARTMENT B INCOME STATEMENT		NONDEPARTMENTAL INCOME STATEMENT		BALANCE SHEET		
	DEBIT	CREDIT	DEBIT	CREDIT	DEBIT	CREDIT	
1							
2	2 7 6 00						
3				3 6 2 4 00			
4			2 4 0 0 00				
5							
6							
7	82 7 4 0 00	90 0 0 0 00					
8	1 8 6 0 00						
9	7 7 1 00						
10							
11							
12	1 4 6 0 00						
13	339 1 3 7 00	338 0 3 0 00					
14							
15			(1 1 0 7 00)	103 9 7 5 00			
16	339 1 3 7 00	339 1 3 7 00	2 4 0 0 00	107 5 9 9 00	1,118 7 6 1 00	1,013 5 6 2 00	
17			105 1 9 9 00			105 1 9 9 00	
18			107 5 9 9 00	107 5 9 9 00	1,118 7 6 1 00	1,118 7 6 1 00	
19							
20							
21							

Income Statement for Departmental Accounting

Objective 3

Compile a departmental income statement extended through income from operations.

The income statement contains a set of columns for each department, as well as a set of columns for the combined total of all departments. The income statement in Figure 26-5 (next two pages), which is extended through Income from Operations, is a more representative example than the one shown in the previous figure. A discussion of the apportionment of operating expenses between the two departments follows.

Apportionment of Operating Expenses

Objective 4

Apportion operating expenses among various operating departments.

Apportionment of expenses is a crucial element of departmental accounting. It consists of allocating, or dividing, expenses among operating departments. One can readily identify some operating expense as belonging to a given department. For example, suppose that a salesperson makes sales in one department only; the accountant assigns that salesperson's salary or commission directly to that department. However, other

L. C. Simmons Company, Inc.
Income Statement
For year ended December 31, 19–

			DEPARTMENT A	
1	Revenue from Sales:			
2	Sales		$ 560 0 0 0 00	
3	Less Sales Ret. and Allow.		14 2 0 0 00	
4	Net Sales			$ 545 8 0 0 00
5	Cost of Merchandise Sold:			
6	Merchandise Inv., Jan. 1, 19–		$ 96 4 0 0 00	
7	Purchases	$ 325 1 2 0 00		
8	Less: Purch. Ret. and Allow.	9 5 8 0 00		
9	Purch. Discount	5 7 4 0 00		
10	Net Purchases		309 8 0 0 00	
11	Merchandise Available for Sale		$ 406 2 0 0 00	
12	Less Merchandise Inv., Dec. 31, 19–		110 0 0 0 00	
13	Cost of Merchandise Sold			296 2 0 0 00
14	Gross Profit			$ 249 6 0 0 00
15				
16	Operating Expenses:			
17	Selling Expenses:			
18	Sales Salary Expense	$ 88 6 2 5 00		
19	Advertising Expense	10 3 3 6 00		
20	Depr. Expense, Store Equip.	1 8 4 0 00		
21	Misc. Selling Expense	2 9 8 9 00		
22	Total Selling Expenses		$ 103 7 9 0 00	
23	General Expenses:			
24	Office Salary Expense	$ 22 4 7 0 00		
25	Rent Expense	10 2 5 0 00		
26	Utilities Expense	3 0 2 5 00		
27	Insurance Expense	2 5 4 0 00		
28	Bad Debts Expense	1 7 9 9 00		
29	Misc. General Expense	6 4 4 00		
30	Total General Expenses		40 7 2 8 00	
31	Total Operating Expenses			144 5 1 8 00
32	Income (Loss) from Operations			$ 105 0 8 2 00
33				
34	Other Income:			
35	Interest Income			
36	Other Expense:			
37	Interest Expense			
38	Net Income before Income Tax			
39	Income Tax			
40	Net Income after Income Tax			
41				

	DEPARTMENT B		TOTAL		
					1
	$ 240 0 0 0 00		$ 800 0 0 0 00		2
	5 8 0 0 00		20 0 0 0 00		3
		$ 234 2 0 0 00		$ 780 0 0 0 00	4
					5
	$ 82 7 4 0 00		$ 179 1 4 0 00		6
$ 167 8 9 0 00			$ 493 0 1 0 00		7
4 7 5 6 00			14 3 3 6 00		8
3 2 7 4 00			9 0 1 4 00		9
		159 8 6 0 00		469 6 6 0 00	10
		$ 242 6 0 0 00		$ 648 8 0 0 00	11
		90 0 0 0 00		200 0 0 0 00	12
		152 6 0 0 00		448 8 0 0 00	13
		$ 81 6 0 0 00		$ 331 2 0 0 00	14
					15
					16
					17
$ 52 2 0 0 00			$ 140 8 2 5 00		18
7 2 6 4 00			17 6 0 0 00		19
1 4 6 0 00			3 3 0 0 00		20
1 2 8 1 00			4 2 7 0 00		21
		$ 62 2 0 5 00		$ 165 9 9 5 00	22
					23
$ 9 6 3 0 00			$ 32 1 0 0 00		24
6 1 5 0 00			16 4 0 0 00		25
1 8 1 5 00			4 8 4 0 00		26
1 8 6 0 00			4 4 0 0 00		27
7 7 1 00			2 5 7 0 00		28
2 7 6 00			9 2 0 00		29
		20 5 0 2 00		61 2 3 0 00	30
		82 7 0 7 00		227 2 2 5 00	31
		$ (1 1 0 7 00)		$ 103 9 7 5 00	32
					33
					34
			$ 3 6 2 4 00		35
					36
			2 4 0 0 00	1 2 2 4 00	37
				$ 105 1 9 9 00	38
				47 5 8 8 00	39
				$ 57 6 1 1 00	40
					41

Figure 26-5

operating expenses, such as Miscellaneous Selling Expense or Utilities Expense, cannot be restricted to one department and must be divided between the departments on some equitable basis. Let's look at the operating expenses of the L. C. Simmons Company and see what methods it uses to apportion them.

- **Sales salary expense** Simmons allocates the salespersons' salaries to Department A or Department B according to the names on the payroll register, which lists each employee by department. Department A's share is $88,625; Department B's is $52,200.
- **Advertising expense** Simmons advertises itself in three media: billboards, newspapers, and radio. The cost breakdown is like this:

Billboard advertising	$ 1,600
Newspaper advertising	9,600
Radio advertising	6,400
Total	$17,600

The billboard ads display the name of the company and tell where it is, but they don't advertise the products of Department A or Department B. Since no specific department is featured, Simmons's accountant has to apportion the cost of these billboard ads according to gross sales, as follows:

Sales for Department A	$560,000
Sales for Department B	240,000
Total sales	$800,000

Department A's sales as a percentage of the total are

$$\frac{\$560,000}{\$800,000} = 70\%$$

Department B's sales as a percentage of the total are

$$\frac{\$240,000}{\$800,000} = 30\%$$

Department A's share of cost of billboard advertising is

70% of $1,600 = $1,600 × .7 = $1,120

Department B's share of cost of billboard advertising is

30% of $1,600 = $1,600 × .3 = $480

Simmons allocates the cost of its newspaper advertising according to the number of column inches each department uses. In a year, Simmons buys 3,200 inches of newspaper advertising, divided according to departments in the following manner.

Ads for Department A are

$$1{,}920 \text{ column inches or } \frac{1{,}920}{3{,}200} = 60\%$$

Ads for Department B are

$$1{,}280 \text{ column inches or } \frac{1{,}280}{3{,}200} = 40\%$$

Department A's share of cost of newspaper advertising is

$$60\% \text{ of } \$9{,}600 = \$9{,}600 \times .6 = \$5{,}760$$

Department B's share of cost of newspaper advertising is

$$40\% \text{ of } \$9{,}600 = \$9{,}600 \times .4 = \$3{,}840$$

As for radio advertising, Simmons again allocates cost to the two departments according to the amount of air time each department uses. In a year, Simmons buys 1,250 minutes of radio time, divided according to departments, as shown here.

Ads for Department A are

$$675 \text{ minutes or } \frac{675}{1{,}250} = 54\%$$

Ads for Department B are

$$575 \text{ minutes or } \frac{575}{1{,}250} = 46\%$$

Department A's share of cost of radio advertising is

$$54\% \text{ of } \$6{,}400 = \$6{,}400 \times .54 = \$3{,}456$$

Department B's share of cost of radio advertising is

$$46\% \text{ of } \$6{,}400 = \$6{,}400 \times .46 = \$2{,}944$$

Here is a summary of L. C. Simmons Company's allocation of advertising expense.

Expense	Department A	Department B	Total
Billboard advertising	$ 1,120	$ 480	$ 1,600
Newspaper advertising	5,760	3,840	9,600
Radio advertising	3,456	2,944	6,400
	$10,336	$7,264	$17,600

- **Depreciation expense, store equipment** L. C. Simmons keeps a plant and equipment ledger that notes the department in which each piece of equipment is located. The total year's depreciation of the equipment used in Department A is $1,840; the total year's depreciation of the equipment used in Department B is $1,460.
- **Office salary expense** People who work in the office of the L. C. Simmons Company get paid a total of $32,100 per year. Simmons apportions the amount of money that is paid in salaries to office workers on the basis of the amount of time the office personnel has to spend on each department. Management estimates that 70 percent of the office force's time is devoted to Department A, and 30 percent to Department B.

Department A's share is 70% of $32,100 = $32,100 × .7 = $22,470
Department B's share is 30% of $32,100 = $32,100 × .3 = $9,630

- **Rent expense and utilities expense** The Simmons Company rents 40,000 square feet of floor space and allocates the expenses of rent and utilities on the basis of floor space occupied by each department, as follows. (Yearly expense for rent is $16,400; yearly expense for utilities is $4,840.)

Department A occupies 25,000 square feet or

$$\frac{25,000}{40,000} = 62.5\%$$

Department B occupies 15,000 square feet or

$$\frac{15,000}{40,000} = 37.5\%$$

Department A's share of rent is

62.5% of $16,400 = $10,250

Department B's share of rent is

37.5% of $16,400 = $6,150

Department A's share of utilities is

62.5% of $4,840 = $3,025

Department B's share of utilities is

37.5% of $4,840 = $1,815

In this case, for simplicity, we are assuming that all floor space is of equal value. However, when one is apportioning the rent expense in a multistory building, one has to take into account differences in the value of the various floors and locations.

- **Insurance expense** The L. C. Simmons Company carries insurance policies to cover losses that might result from (1) damage to merchandise or equipment (annual cost, $3,600), and (2) injury incurred by customers while on the premises (annual cost, $800). The cost of the insurance on merchandise and equipment is based on the average cost of the assets held by each department. The average is equal to the cost of assets on hand at the beginning of the year plus the cost of assets on hand at the end of the year, divided by 2. The computations are presented in tabular form on the next page.

Department A's percentage is

$$\frac{\$122,640}{\$221,970} = 55\%$$

Department B's percentage is

$$\frac{\$99,330}{\$221,970} = 45\%$$

Department A's share of property insurance is

55% of $3,600 = $1,980

Department B's share of property insurance is

45% of $3,600 = $1,620

Computations for Insurance Expense (see page 827)

Item	Department A		Department B		Total
Merchandise Inventory					
Balance, Jan. 1	$ 96,400		$ 82,740		
Balance, Dec. 31	110,000		90,000		
Total	2)$206,400		2)$172,740		
Average	$103,200	$103,200	$86,370	$86,370	
Store Equipment					
Balance, Jan. 1	$ 19,440		$ 12,960		
Balance, Dec. 31	19,440		12,960		
Total	2)$ 38,880		2)$ 25,920		
Average	$ 19,440	19,440	$ 12,960	12,960	
Total		$122,640		$99,330	$221,970

The cost of liability insurance (in case of personal injury to customers) is based on sales. Using the same percentages as for billboard advertising, L. C. Simmons apportions the cost of liability insurance as follows.

Department A's share of liability insurance is

70% of $800 = $560

Department B's share of liability insurance is

30% of $800 = $240

Here is a summary of the way L. C. Simmons allocates its insurance expense.

Type of Insurance	Department A	Department B	Total
Property insurance	$1,980	$1,620	$3,600
Liability insurance	560	240	800
	$2,540	$1,860	$4,400

- **Bad debts expense, miscellaneous selling expense, and miscellaneous general expense** Bad Debts Expense and the miscellaneous expense accounts vary according to the volume of sales. Accordingly, L. C. Simmons apportions them on this basis, since volume of sales is a reasonable measure of the benefit each department derives from these accounts.

Item	Department A	Department B	Total
Bad Debts Expense	$1,799	$ 771	$2,570
Miscellaneous Selling Expense	2,989	1,281	4,270
Miscellaneous General Expense	644	276	920
	$5,432	$2,328	$7,760

Division of these expense accounts by department is as follows.

Department A's share of bad debts is

70% of $2,570 = $1,799

Department B's share of bad debts is

30% of $2,570 = $771

Department A's share of miscellaneous selling expense is

70% of $4,270 = $2,989

Department B's share of miscellaneous selling expense is

30% of $4,270 = $1,281

Department A's share of miscellaneous general expense is

70% of $920 = $644

Department B's share of miscellaneous general expense is

30% of $920 = $276

CONTRIBUTION MARGIN BY DEPARTMENTS

When a company breaks down its expense figures on a contribution-margin basis, its income statement indicates the contribution each department makes toward the overhead expenses incurred on behalf of the business as a whole. One can divide operating expenses into two classes: (1) **direct expenses,** which are incurred for the sole benefit of a given department and thus are under the control of the department head; (2) **indirect expenses,** which are incurred as overhead expenses of the entire business and thus are not under the control of one department head. For example, Sales Salary Expense is a direct expense, since it is incurred purely for the benefit of one department. Property tax on real estate, on the other hand, is an overhead expense incurred for the business as a whole; it is not directly chargeable to one department.

Some operating expenses may be partially direct and partially indirect. For example, L. C. Simmons Company's Advertising Expense consisted partially of billboard advertising, which stresses the name and location of the company, and partially of newspaper advertising, which directly benefits separate departments of the company. So the part of the advertising budget that went to billboard advertising is an indirect expense, and the part that went to newspaper advertising is a direct expense. Costs of insurance on merchandise inventories and store equipment are a direct expense; costs of liability insurance are indirect or overhead expenses. When you are classifying an expense as being direct or indirect, use this rule of thumb to identify direct expenses: **If the department were not in existence, then the expense would not be in existence.** The expense must be directly related to the department.

Here is a skeleton outline of an income statement that emphasizes contribution margin.

From Sales Through Contribution Margin

Revenue from Sales
Less Cost of Merchandise Sold
_____

Gross Profit
Less Direct Departmental Expenses
_____

Contribution Margin
Less Indirect Expenses
_____

Income from Operations
Add Other Income
Less Other Expense
_____

Net Income

Objective 5

Compile a departmental income statement extended through contribution margin.

The income statement shown in Figure 26-6 (next two pages) presents the same figures that we saw in Figure 26-5 for the L. C. Simmons Company. This time, however, they are in the contribution-margin format. You will find it interesting to compare the two.

The Meaning of Contribution Margin

Contribution margin means the contribution that a given department makes to the net income of the firm, and it is the most realistic portrayal of the profitability of a department. If the company does away with the department, the company's net income will decrease by the amount of the contribution margin. For example, in the case of the L. C. Simmons Company, Department B had a contribution margin of $18,765; if L. C. Simmons eliminated the department, its net income would be reduced by $18,765 (assuming that L. C. Simmons didn't create a new department to take the place of Department B or expand Department A to occupy the void).

In the company's work sheet (Figure 26-4), in which operating expenses were apportioned to departments, Department B showed a net loss from operations of $1,107. Department B sustained this loss because it was assigned a number of indirect expenses. If L. C. Simmons eliminates Department B, these indirect expenses, or overhead, will still exist and will therefore be assigned entirely to Department A, thereby accounting in part for the reduction in net income by $18,765 (the amount of the contribution margin).

L. C. Simmons Company, Inc.

Income Statement

For year ended December 31, 19–

			DEPARTMENT A	
1	Revenue from Sales:			
2	Sales		$ 560 0 0 0 00	
3	Less Sales Returns and Allowances		14 2 0 0 00	
4	Net Sales			$ 545 8 0 0 00
5	Cost of Merchandise Sold:			
6	Merchandise Inventory, January 1, 19–		$ 96 4 0 0 00	
7	Purchases	$ 325 1 2 0 00		
8	Less: Purchases Returns and Allowances	9 5 8 0 00		
9	Purchases Discount	5 7 4 0 00		
10	Net Purchases		309 8 0 0 00	
11	Merchandise Available for Sale		$ 406 2 0 0 00	
12	Less Merchandise Inventory, December 31, 19–		110 0 0 0 00	
13	Cost of Merchandise Sold			296 2 0 0 00
14	Gross Profit			$ 249 6 0 0 00
15				
16	Direct Departmental Expenses:			
17	Sales Salary Expense		$ 88 6 2 5 00	
18	Advertising Expense		9 2 1 6 00	
19	Insurance Expense		1 9 8 0 00	
20	Depreciation Expense, Store Equipment		1 8 4 0 00	
21	Bad Debts Expense		1 7 9 9 00	
22	Total Direct Department Expenses			103 4 6 0 00
23	Contribution Margin			$ 146 1 4 0 00
24				
25	Indirect Expenses:			
26	Office Salary Expense			
27	Rent Expense			
28	Utilities Expense			
29	Advertising Expense (billboard)			
30	Insurance Expense (liability)			
31	Misc. Selling Expense			
32	Misc. General Expense			
33	Total Indirect Expenses			
34	Income from Operations			
35				
36	Other Income:			
37	Interest Income			
38	Other Expense:			
39	Interest Expense			
40	Net Income before Income Tax			
41				

	DEPARTMENT B				TOTAL			
1								
2		$ 240 000 00				$ 800 000 00		
3		5 800 00				20 000 00		
4			$ 234 200 00				$ 780 000 00	
5								
6		$ 82 740 00				$ 179 140 00		
7	$ 167 890 00				$ 493 010 00			
8	4 756 00				14 336 00			
9	3 274 00				9 014 00			
10		159 860 00				469 660 00		
11		$ 242 600 00				$ 648 800 00		
12		90 000 00				200 000 00		
13			152 600 00				448 800 00	
14			$ 81 600 00				$ 331 200 00	
15								
16								
17		$ 52 200 00				$ 140 825 00		
18		6 784 00				16 000 00		
19		1 620 00				3 600 00		
20		1 460 00				3 300 00		
21		771 00				2 570 00		
22			62 835 00				166 295 00	
23			$ 18 765 00				$ 164 905 00	
24								
25								
26						$ 32 100 00		
27						16 400 00		
28						4 840 00		
29						1 600 00		
30						800 00		
31						4 270 00		
32						920 00		
33							60 930 00	
34							$ 103 975 00	
35								
36								
37						$ 3 624 00		
38								
39						2 400 00	1 224 00	
40							$ 105 199 00	
41								

Figure 26-6

833

The Usefulness of Contribution Margin

Income statements that show contribution margin are extremely useful when it comes to controlling a company's direct expenses, because the company can hold the head of a given department accountable for expenses directly chargeable to the department. If a department head reduces direct expenses, this action will have a favorable effect on the contribution margin.

A company that manufactures a number of different products can also use the concept of contribution margin to determine the profitability of a particular product. This, clearly, is one of the most important uses of the contribution margin.

Management can use an income statement portraying contribution margin as a tool for making future plans and analyzing future operations. Sometimes such an income statement may even lead to the elimination of a department. For example, The Peterson Company has five departments; its net income for last year was $120,000, which is about the same as it has been for the past four years. Peterson's income statement, in which all operating expenses are apportioned to the various departments, shows that Department E has a net loss from operations of $9,000. In an abbreviated contribution-margin format, here are the results of the last fiscal year.

Item	Department E (only)	Departments A to D (only)	Total, Departments A to E	Total, Departments A to D (with E eliminated)
Sales	$120,000	$1,480,000	$1,600,000	$1,480,000
Cost of Merchandise Sold	72,000	880,000	952,000	880,000
Gross Profit	$ 48,000	$ 600,000	$ 648,000	$ 600,000
Direct Departmental Expenses	32,000	336,000	368,000	336,000
Contribution Margin	$ 16,000	$ 264,000	$ 280,000	$ 264,000
Indirect Expenses	25,000	135,000	160,000	160,000
Net Income (Loss)	($ 9,000)	$ 129,000	$ 120,000	$ 104,000

Now suppose that Peterson eliminates Department E. Because Department E's contribution margin amounts to $16,000, the net income of the entire firm will decrease by $16,000 ($120,000 − $104,000 = $16,000). Another factor Peterson has to consider is possible "spill-over sales" of Department E; that is, customers of Department E may also buy things in other departments.

BRANCH ACCOUNTING

As a means of increasing sales and income, a firm may open branch operations in different locations. This option applies to both merchandising and service enterprises. You can undoubtedly think of numerous examples of chain store outlets in retail fields, such as grocery stores, drug stores, and variety stores. Examples of branch operations in service fields are restaurants, dry cleaners, motels, and service stations.

With the increasing use of data processing equipment, the accounting for branch operations is generally performed (centralized) at the home office. The accounting system is similar to that for departmental accounting, with each branch treated as a department.

GLOSSARY

Apportionment of expenses Allocating or dividing operating expenses among operating departments.

Contribution margin Gross profit of a department minus its direct expenses.

Direct expenses Expenses that benefit only one department and are controlled by the head of the department.

Indirect expenses Overhead expenses that benefit the business as a whole and are not under the control of any one department.

QUESTIONS, EXERCISES, AND PROBLEMS

Discussion Questions

1. In what ways may departmental accounting information be useful?
2. Assuming that operating expenses are to be allocated to various departments, on what basis would you allocate the following expenses?

   a. Rent
   b. Depreciation of store equipment
   c. Office salaries
   d. Insurance

3. Describe the difference between a direct and an indirect operating expense.
4. You have been employed as the new manager of a clothing store. Previously, the income statement listed total revenue and operating expenses only. The firm can be divided into two departments: clothing and shoes. You want to know the gross profit for each department. Describe the changes in the accounting system that will be required.
5. Referring to question 4, what benefits do you expect to gain from the departmental information?
6. Department A has a positive contribution margin amounting to $35,000. What does this contribution margin mean as far as the firm is concerned?
7. Why does contribution margin provide a more realistic portrayal of the profitability of a department than gross profit?

Exercises

Exercise 26-1 Don's Sporting Goods has annual expenses for salaries of office staff of $9,600, which it allocates to the various departments on the basis of gross sales for each department. Sales by department are as follows.

Women's shoes	$122,000
Girls' shoes	106,000
Accessories	12,000
Total	$240,000

Determine what share of the office salaries expense each of the three operating departments should bear.

Exercise 26-2 For the shoe store in Exercise 26-1, the premium for public liability insurance is $240, and the premium for fire and theft insurance on the inventory is $360. The balances of the inventories at the end of the fiscal period are as follows.

Women's shoes	$40,000
Girls' shoes	30,000
Accessories	10,000

How much of the insurance costs should be allocated to each department, given that the public liability insurance is apportioned on the basis of gross sales and the property insurance is allocated on the basis of the values of the ending inventories?

Exercise 26-3 The Economy Drugstore occupies an area of 10,000 square feet. The departments and the floor space occupied by each are as follows.

Pharmacy	1,200 square feet
Camera supplies	800 square feet
Toiletries and cosmetics	6,700 square feet
Greeting cards	400 square feet
Receiving and storage	900 square feet

Economy leases the building for $14,000 per year. Apportion the rent expense to the five departments.

Exercise 26-4 The pharmacy department of Economy Drugstore has the following account balances.

Sales	$172,000
Purchases	92,000
Purchases Discount	2,000
Sales Returns and Allowances	4,000
Merchandise Inventory (beginning)	29,000
Purchases Returns and Allowances	3,000
Merchandise Inventory (ending)	26,000

Determine the amount of the gross profit.

Exercise 26-5 The following figures apply to Larkin and Turner's sporting goods department.

Sales	$246,000
Direct Departmental Expenses	52,000
Purchases	183,000
Purchases Returns and Allowances	3,000
Interest Expense	2,000
Sales Returns and Allowances	4,000
Merchandise Inventory (ending)	76,000
Indirect Expenses	31,000
Merchandise Inventory (beginning)	66,000

Determine the amount of the contribution margin.

Exercise 26-6 Nickell Hardware is considering eliminating its giftware department. Management does not believe that the indirect expenses and the level of operations in the other departments will be affected if giftware closes. Here is information from Nickell's income statement for the fiscal year ended July 31, which is considered to be a typical year.

	Giftware Department	All Other Departments	Total of All Departments (Including Giftware)
Sales	$74,000	$562,000	$636,000
Cost of Merchandise Sold	48,000	396,000	444,000
Gross Profit	$26,000	$166,000	$192,000
Operating Expenses	30,000	111,000	141,000
Net Income (Loss) from Operations	($ 4,000)	$ 55,000	$ 51,000

Nickell considers that $18,000 of the operating expenses of the giftware department are direct expenses. What is the contribution margin of the giftware department?

Exercise 26-7 For the hardware store in Exercise 26-6, prepare an income statement for the forthcoming year, assuming that Nickell discontinues the giftware department.

Exercise 26-8 McClure Company apportions depreciation on equipment on the basis of the average cost of the equipment. Property tax is apportioned on the basis of the combined total of average cost of the equipment and average cost of the merchandise inventories. Depreciation expense on equipment amounted to $6,000. Property tax expense amounted to $2,400. Determine the apportionment of the depreciation expense and the property tax expense based on the information presented on the next page.

Departments	Average Cost	
	Equipment	Inventories
A	$ 30,000	$100,000
B	60,000	120,000
C	30,000	60,000
	$120,000	$280,000

Problem Set A

Problem 26-1A Overman Appliance has two sales departments: household appliances, and radio and television. Overman's accountant prepared the following adjusted trial balance at the end of the fiscal year, after all adjustments, including adjustments for merchandise inventory, had been recorded and posted.

Overman Appliance
Adjusted Trial Balance
June 30, 19–

ACCOUNT NAME	DEBIT	CREDIT
Cash	3 2 0 8 00	
Accounts Receivable	45 1 8 9 00	
Allowance for Doubtful Accounts		1 6 2 0 00
Merchandise Inventory, Appliance Department	86 1 1 9 00	
Merchandise Inventory, Radio and TV Department	68 1 9 5 00	
Store Supplies	5 1 4 00	
Store Equipment	19 6 7 0 00	
Accumulated Depreciation, Store Equipment		12 7 6 8 00
Accounts Payable		47 9 8 5 00
C. T. Overman, Capital		120 6 2 0 00
C. T. Overman, Drawing	20 4 0 0 00	
Income Summary	78 6 1 6 00	86 1 1 9 00
	72 4 8 2 00	68 1 9 5 00
Sales, Appliance Department		373 5 5 9 00
Sales, Radio and TV Department		315 2 4 0 00
Sales Returns and Allowances, Appliance Dept.	7 1 4 1 00	
Sales Returns and Allowances, Radio and TV Dept.	6 4 7 6 00	
Purchases, Appliance Department	347 6 8 4 00	
Purchases, Radio and TV Department	243 6 7 7 00	
Purchases Returns and Allowances, Appliance Dept.		5 2 8 4 00
Purchases Returns and Allowances, Radio and TV Dept.		4 3 8 4 00
Purchases Discount, Appliance Department		6 8 4 1 00
Purchases Discount, Radio and TV Department		4 9 6 0 00
Sales Salary Expense	28 7 9 0 00	

(continued on page 839)

Depreciation Expense, Store Equipment			4	3	8	2	00							
Miscellaneous Selling Expense				1	7	6	00							
Office Salary Expense			5	8	8	0	00							
Rent Expense			4	8	0	0	00							
Utilities Expense			2	8	8	6	00							
Bad Debts Expense			2	4	2		00							
Miscellaneous General Expense			1	2	0		00							
Interest Expense			9	2	8		00							
		1 047	5	7	5		00	1 047	5	7	5		00	

Instructions

Prepare an income statement to show gross profit for each department and income from operations, as well as net income for the entire business. Beginning balances of merchandise inventories are as follows: appliances, $78,616; radio and television, $72,482.

Problem 26-2A Glenwood Paint and Glass has two departments: a paint department and a glass department. Glenwood's accountant prepares the following adjusted trial balance at the end of the fiscal year, after all adjustments, including the adjustments for merchandise inventory, have been recorded and posted.

Glenwood Paint and Glass
Adjusted Trial Balance
December 31, 19–

ACCOUNT NAME	DEBIT						CREDIT					
Cash		4	8	2	6	00						
Accounts Receivable		46	8	9	0	00						
Allowance for Doubtful Accounts								2	6	2	0	00
Merchandise Inventory, Paint Department		84	1	4	2	00						
Merchandise Inventory, Glass Department		41	1	3	8	00						
Prepaid Insurance			8	4	0	00						
Store Supplies			7	6	2	00						
Store Equipment		53	6	8	2	00						
Accumulated Depreciation, Store Equipment								41	8	1	0	00
Accounts Payable								38	6	8	0	00
Sales Tax Payable								1	2	8	4	00
M. L. Wheeler, Capital								90	4	4	4	00
M. L. Wheeler, Drawing		22	0	0	0	00						
Income Summary		82	7	6	0	00		84	1	4	2	00
		40	7	2	0	00		41	1	3	8	00
Sales, Paint Department								409	8	0	0	00
Sales, Glass Department								273	2	0	0	00
Sales Returns and Allowances, Paint Department		11	6	8	5	00						

(continued on page 840)

	Debit	Credit
Sales Returns and Allowances, Glass Department	1 7 1 6 00	
Purchases, Paint Department	265 1 0 2 00	
Purchases, Glass Department	172 1 2 7 00	
Purchases Returns and Allowances, Paint Dept.		4 6 1 8 00
Purchases Returns and Allowances, Glass Dept.		1 7 9 2 00
Purchases Discount, Paint Department		5 4 9 6 00
Purchases Discount, Glass Department		2 9 6 4 00
Sales Salary Expense	123 2 2 0 00	
Advertising Expense	14 0 0 0 00	
Depreciation Expense, Store Equipment	13 4 3 6 00	
Store Supplies Expense	7 4 2 00	
Miscellaneous Selling Expense	6 8 0 00	
Rent Expense	8 0 0 0 00	
Utilities Expense	3 2 0 0 00	
Insurance Expense	9 0 0 00	
Bad Debts Expense	1 8 0 0 00	
Miscellaneous General Expense	8 2 0 00	
Interest Expense	2 8 0 0 00	
	997 9 8 8 00	997 9 8 8 00

Merchandise inventories at the beginning of the year were as follows: paint department, $82,760; glass department, $40,720. The bases for apportioning expenses and the sources of the figures are as follows.

a. Sales Salary Expense (payroll register): paint department, $74,800; glass department, $48,420

b. Advertising Expense (newspaper column inches): paint department, 1,200 inches; glass department, 800 inches

c. Depreciation Expense, Store Equipment (Plant Asset and Equipment ledger): paint department, $9,616; glass department, $3,820

d. Store Supplies Expense (requisitions): paint department, $418; glass department, $324

e. Rent Expense and Utilities Expense (floor space): paint department, 5,000 square feet; glass department, 3,000 square feet

f. Insurance Expense (average cost of merchandise inventory, rounded off in dollars): paint department, $604; glass department, $296 (verify these figures)

g. Miscellaneous Selling Expense (volume of gross sales): paint department, $408; glass department, $272 (verify these figures)

h. Bad Debts Expense (volume of gross sales): paint department, $1,080; glass department, $720 (verify these figures)

i. Miscellaneous General Expense (volume of gross sales): paint department, $492; glass department, $328 (verify these figures)

Instructions

Prepare an income statement by department to show income from operations, as well as a nondepartmentalized income statement to show net income for the entire company.

Problem 26-3A The Langdon Jewelry Store has two departments: the jewelry department and the watch department. The trial balance, as of December 31, the end of the fiscal year, is as follows.

Langdon Jewelry Store
Trial Balance
December 31, 19–

ACCOUNT NAME	DEBIT	CREDIT
Cash	6 2 0 0 00	
Accounts Receivable	39 6 0 0 00	
Allowance for Doubtful Accounts		1 0 4 0 00
Merchandise Inventory, Jewelry Department	42 0 0 0 00	
Merchandise Inventory, Watch Department	28 0 0 0 00	
Prepaid Insurance	6 0 0 00	
Store Equipment	18 2 0 0 00	
Accumulated Depreciation, Store Equipment		8 1 4 0 00
Accounts Payable		38 7 2 0 00
D. C. Langdon, Capital		66 2 8 0 00
D. C. Langdon, Drawing	14 0 0 0 00	
Sales, Jewelry Department		120 0 0 0 00
Sales, Watch Department		80 0 0 0 00
Purchases, Jewelry Department	60 0 0 0 00	
Purchases, Watch Department	46 0 0 0 00	
Salaries and Commissions Expense	43 0 0 0 00	
Advertising Expense	6 4 0 0 00	
Rent Expense	7 2 0 0 00	
Utilities Expense	1 4 5 0 00	
Miscellaneous Expense	1 0 9 0 00	
Interest Expense	4 4 0 00	
	314 1 8 0 00	314 1 8 0 00

The data for the adjustments are as follows.

a. Merchandise inventories, December 31, the end of the fiscal period: jewelry department, $40,000; watch department, $24,000
b. Insurance expired, $390
c. Estimated uncollectible customer charge accounts (based on an analysis of accounts), $2,500
d. Depreciation of store equipment for the year, $4,820
e. Accrued salaries and commissions, $370
f. Accrued interest payable, $120

The bases for apportioning expenses to the two departments are as follows.

g. Salaries and Commissions Expense (time sheets): jewelry department, $30,360; watch department, $13,010
h. Advertising Expense (space): jewelry department, $5,120; watch department, $1,280
i. Depreciation Expense (equipment ledger): jewelry department, $3,374; watch department, $1,446
j. Rent Expense, Utilities Expense, Miscellaneous Expense, Bad Debts Expense, Insurance Expense (sales): jewelry department, 60 percent; watch department, 40 percent

Instructions

Complete the work sheet.

Problem 26-4A   The Johnson Shoe Store, after it has recorded adjustments, has the following balances of revenue and expense accounts and merchandise inventories for its two departments on December 31, the end of the fiscal year.

Johnson Shoe Store
Work Sheet
For year ended December 31, 19–

ACCOUNT NAME	ADJUSTED TRIAL BALANCE	
	DEBIT	CREDIT
Sales, Women's Shoes		189 8 5 6 00
Sales, Men's Shoes		74 1 4 4 00
Sales Returns and Allowances, Women's Shoes	4 8 1 6 00	
Sales Returns and Allowances, Men's Shoes	2 1 8 4 00	
Merchandise Inventory, Women's Shoes	52 6 6 0 00	
Merchandise Inventory, Men's Shoes	22 9 8 0 00	
Purchases, Women's Shoes	112 1 4 0 00	
Purchases, Men's Shoes	43 2 9 0 00	
Purchases Returns and Allowances, Women's Shoes		1 6 4 8 00
Purchases Returns and Allowances, Men's Shoes		6 7 0 00
Purchases Discount, Women's Shoes		1 1 8 2 00
Purchases Discount, Men's Shoes		7 4 0 00
Sales Salary Expense	46 2 6 0 00	
Advertising Expense	4 2 0 0 00	
Depreciation Expense, Store Equipment	3 2 0 0 00	
Bad Debts Expense	1 9 0 0 00	
Office Salary Expense	8 5 2 0 00	
Rent Expense	8 4 0 0 00	
Utilities Expense	1 2 6 0 00	
Insurance Expense	4 2 0 00	
Miscellaneous Selling Expense	3 9 0 00	
Miscellaneous General Expense	3 4 0 00	
Interest Expense	6 4 0 00	

The values of merchandise inventories on January 1 (beginning) are: women's shoes, $48,710; men's shoes, $24,140.

Essential data for direct expenses (and sources of the figures) are as follows.

a. Sales Salary Expense (sales personnel work in one department only) is allocated as follows: women's shoes, $32,380; men's shoes, $13,880.

b. Advertising: Newspaper advertising is allocated as follows: women's shoes, $3,360; men's shoes, $840.

c. Depreciation: Depreciation of store equipment is apportioned on the basis of the average cost of equipment in each department. The average cost of store equipment is women's shoes, $7,500; men's shoes, $2,500.

d. Bad Debts Expense: Department managers are responsible for granting credit on sales made by their respective departments. Bad Debts Expense is allocated as follows: women's shoes, $1,368; men's shoes, $532.

Instructions

Prepare an income statement to show each department's contribution margin.

Problem Set B

Problem 26-1B The Rocky Mountain Ski Shop has two sales departments: ski equipment and clothing. After recording and posting all adjustments, including the adjustments for merchandise inventory, the accountant prepared the adjusted trial balance at the end of the fiscal year.

Rocky Mountain Ski Shop
Adjusted Trial Balance
April 30, 19–

ACCOUNT NAME	DEBIT	CREDIT
Cash	4 3 3 4 00	
Accounts Receivable	46 5 2 2 00	
Allowance for Doubtful Accounts		1 9 6 0 00
Merchandise Inventory, Ski Equipment	49 9 8 0 00	
Merchandise Inventory, Clothing	35 2 1 7 00	
Store Supplies	6 4 0 00	
Store Equipment	22 7 8 0 00	
Accumulated Depreciation, Store Equipment		14 7 6 0 00
Accounts Payable		30 6 3 7 00
C. C. Van Dusen, Capital		82 0 0 0 00
C. C. Van Dusen, Drawing	22 6 0 0 00	
Income Summary	56 7 1 8 00	49 9 8 0 00
	31 7 8 4 00	35 2 1 7 00
Sales, Ski Equipment		369 8 1 4 00
Sales, Clothing		257 1 4 0 00

(*continued on page 844*)

Sales Returns and Allowances, Ski Equipment	6	8	2	0	00						
Sales Returns and Allowances, Clothing	5	7	9	6	00						
Purchases, Ski Equipment	311	7	2	4	00						
Purchases, Clothing	214	7	9	7	00						
Purchases Returns and Allowances, Ski Equipment						6	7	2	0	00	
Purchases Returns and Allowances, Clothing						4	8	1	4	00	
Purchases Discount, Ski Equipment						4	8	2	8	00	
Purchases Discount, Clothing						3	9	8	8	00	
Sales Salary Expense	26	8	4	0	00						
Depreciation Expense, Store Equipment	3	9	8	4	00						
Miscellaneous Selling Expense		2	2	6	00						
Office Salary Expense	12	0	0	0	00						
Rent Expense	5	6	0	0	00						
Utilities Expense	2	0	9	2	00						
Bad Debts Expense		3	1	6	00						
Miscellaneous General Expense		1	8	4	00						
Interest Expense		9	0	4	00						
	861	8	5	8	00	861	8	5	8	00	

Instructions

Prepare an income statement to show gross profit for each department and income from operations, as well as net income, for the entire business. Beginning balances of merchandise inventories are as follows: ski equipment, $56,718; clothing, $31,784.

Problem 26-2B Sutherland Paint and Glass has two sales departments: a paint and a glass department. After recording and posting all adjustments, including the adjustments for merchandise inventory, the accountant prepared the adjusted trial balance at the end of the fiscal year.

Sutherland Paint and Glass
Adjusted Trial Balance
December 31, 19–

ACCOUNT NAME	DEBIT					CREDIT				
Cash	5	6	4	0	00					
Accounts Receivable	52	3	2	0	00					
Allowance for Doubtful Accounts						2	8	4	0	00
Merchandise Inventory, Paint Department	80	3	3	6	00					
Merchandise Inventory, Glass Department	37	4	8	1	00					
Prepaid Insurance		9	8	4	00					
Store Supplies		7	9	8	00					
Store Equipment	64	2	2	0	00					
Accumulated Depreciation, Store Equipment						48	9	2	8	00

(continued on page 845)

Account	Debit	Credit
Accounts Payable		48 4 2 0 00
Sales Tax Payable		1 3 4 2 00
C. C. Sutherland, Capital		111 9 4 5 00
C. C. Sutherland, Drawing	24 0 0 0 00	
Income Summary	78 9 2 8 00	80 3 3 6 00
	36 2 2 4 00	37 4 8 1 00
Sales, Paint Department		476 0 0 0 00
Sales, Glass Department		204 0 0 0 00
Sales Returns and Allowances, Paint Department	12 2 4 1 00	
Sales Returns and Allowances, Glass Department	8 2 6 00	
Purchases, Paint Department	310 7 1 8 00	
Purchases, Glass Department	148 7 2 2 00	
Purchases Returns and Allowances, Paint Department		4 2 2 6 00
Purchases Returns and Allowances, Glass Department		1 2 9 6 00
Purchases Discount, Paint Department		5 8 8 4 00
Purchases Discount, Glass Department		4 2 8 0 00
Sales Salary Expense	121 7 8 2 00	
Advertising Expense	16 0 0 0 00	
Depreciation Expense, Store Equipment	15 8 0 0 00	
Store Supplies Expense	6 0 6 00	
Miscellaneous Selling Expense	5 2 0 00	
Rent Expense	9 6 0 0 00	
Utilities Expense	3 6 0 0 00	
Insurance Expense	8 4 0 00	
Bad Debts Expense	2 2 0 0 00	
Miscellaneous General Expense	7 8 0 00	
Interest Expense	1 8 1 2 00	
	1 026 9 7 8 00	1 026 9 7 8 00

Merchandise inventories at the beginning of the year were as follows: paint department, $78,928; glass department, $36,224.

The bases (and sources of figures) for apportioning expenses to the two departments are as follows.

a. Sales Salary Expense (payroll register): paint department, $68,338; glass department, $53,444

b. Advertising Expense (newspaper column inches): paint department, 1,200 inches; glass department, 800 inches

c. Depreciation Expense, Store Equipment (Plant Asset and Equipment ledger): paint department, $11,642; glass department, $4,158

d. Store Supplies Expense (requisitions): paint department, $320; glass department, $286

e. Rent Expense and Utilities Expense (floor space): paint department, 5,000 square feet; glass department, 3,000 square feet

f. Insurance Expense (average cost of merchandise inventory, rounded off in dollars): paint department, $574; glass department, $266 (verify these figures)

g. Miscellaneous Selling Expense (volume of gross sales): paint department, $364; glass department, $156 (verify these figures)

h. Bad Debts Expense (volume of gross sales): paint department, $1,540; glass department, $660 (verify these figures)

i. Miscellaneous General Expense (volume of gross sales): paint department, $546; glass department, $234 (verify these figures)

Instructions

Prepare an income statement by department to show income from operations, as well as a nondepartmentalized income statement to show net income for the entire company.

Problem 26-3B The Reliance Jewelry Store has two departments: the jewelry department and the watch department. Its accountant prepares the following trial balance, as of December 31, the end of the fiscal year.

Reliance Jewelry Store
Trial Balance
December 31, 19–

ACCOUNT NAME	DEBIT	CREDIT
Cash	6 1 4 0 00	
Accounts Receivable	40 1 2 0 00	
Allowance for Doubtful Accounts		1 0 6 0 00
Merchandise Inventory, Jewelry Department	41 4 0 0 00	
Merchandise Inventory, Watch Department	28 2 0 0 00	
Prepaid Insurance	5 8 0 00	
Store Equipment	17 9 6 0 00	
Accumulated Depreciation, Store Equipment		8 1 1 0 00
Accounts Payable		38 7 4 0 00
D. R. Justice, Capital		66 0 8 0 00
D. R. Justice, Drawing	15 5 0 0 00	
Sales, Jewelry Department		120 0 0 0 00
Sales, Watch Department		80 0 0 0 00
Purchases, Jewelry Department	59 6 0 0 00	
Purchases, Watch Department	45 8 0 0 00	
Salaries and Commissions Expense	42 1 0 0 00	
Advertising Expense	6 6 0 0 00	
Rent Expense	7 2 0 0 00	
Utilities Expense	1 4 2 0 00	
Miscellaneous Expense	8 9 0 00	
Interest Expense	4 8 0 00	
	313 9 9 0 00	313 9 9 0 00

Here are the data for the adjustments.

a. Merchandise inventories, December 31, the end of the fiscal period: jewelry department, $39,300; watch department, $26,700
b. Insurance expired, $410
c. Estimated uncollectible customer charge accounts (based on an analysis of accounts), $2,440
d. Depreciation of store equipment for the year, $4,860
e. Accrued salaries and commissions, $340
f. Accrued interest payable, $130

The bases for apportioning expenses to the two departments are as follows.

g. Salaries and Commissions Expense (time sheets): jewelry department, $29,700; watch department, $12,740
h. Advertising Expense (column inches of space): jewelry department, $5,280; watch department, $1,320
i. Depreciation Expense (equipment ledger): jewelry department, $3,352; watch department, $1,508
j. Rent Expense, Utilities Expense, Miscellaneous Expense, Bad Debts Expense, Insurance Expense (sales): jewelry, 60 percent; watch, 40 percent

Instructions

Complete the work sheet.

Problem 26-4B On December 31, the end of the fiscal year, the Raymond Shoe Store has the following balances of revenue and expense accounts and merchandise inventory, after adjustments have been recorded. The store has two departments: women's shoes and men's shoes.

ACCOUNT NAME	ADJUSTED TRIAL BALANCE DEBIT	ADJUSTED TRIAL BALANCE CREDIT
Sales, Women's Shoes		187 4 1 6 00
Sales, Men's Shoes		73 9 2 8 00
Sales Returns and Allowances, Women's Shoes	4 7 8 2 00	
Sales Returns and Allowances, Men's Shoes	2 0 0 6 00	
Merchandise Inventory, Women's Shoes	51 0 3 0 00	
Merchandise Inventory, Men's Shoes	21 7 8 2 00	
Purchases, Women's Shoes	111 9 7 4 00	
Purchases, Men's Shoes	43 3 2 4 00	
Purchases Returns and Allowances, Women's Shoes		2 6 4 0 00
Purchases Returns and Allowances, Men's Shoes		6 8 4 00
Purchases Discount, Women's Shoes		1 9 8 0 00
Purchases Discount, Men's Shoes		7 2 0 00
Sales Salary Expense	45 5 0 0 00	

(continued on page 848)

Advertising Expense	4 1 1 0 00				
Depreciation Expense, Store Equipment	3 2 0 0 00				
Bad Debts Expense	1 8 2 0 00				
Office Salary Expense	8 6 0 0 00				
Rent Expense	8 4 0 0 00				
Utilities Expense	1 2 4 0 00				
Insurance Expense	3 9 0 00				
Miscellaneous Selling Expense	3 7 4 00				
Miscellaneous General Expense	3 5 6 00				
Interest Expense	7 2 0 00				

The values of merchandise inventories on January 1 (beginning) are: women's shoes, $47,820; men's shoes, $23,946.

Essential data for direct expenses (and sources of the figures) are as follows.

a. Sales Salary Expense (sales personnel work in one department only) is allocated as follows: women's shoes, $31,860; men's shoes, $13,640.

b. Advertising Expense: Newspaper advertising is allocated as follows: women's shoes, $3,280; men's shoes $830.

c. Depreciation: Depreciation of store equipment is apportioned on the basis of the average cost of equipment in each department. The average cost of store equipment is women's shoes, $7,500; men's shoes, $2,500.

d. Bad Debts Expense: Department managers are responsible for granting credit on sales made by their respective departments. Bad Debts Expense is allocated as follows: women's shoes, $1,296; men's shoes, $524.

Instructions

Prepare an income statement to show each department's contribution margin.

APPENDIX F

COD, Layaway, and Installment Sales

In this appendix we shall talk about COD sales, layaway sales, and installment sales. We'll discuss COD and layaway sales briefly first, because they are relatively simple. However, in terms of volume, installment sales are by far the most important.

COD Sales

COD sales (which means cash-on-delivery sales) enable a business to sell merchandise to customers who do not have established credit. The person who delivers the goods collects the cash from the customer at the time of delivery. This enables the seller to maintain control over the merchandise until cash is received. If the customer cannot pay, the delivering agent returns the goods to the seller.

The accounting procedure is straightforward: The seller prepares a sales invoice marked "COD" and encloses it with the merchandise to be delivered. If the customer pays, the seller then processes the sales invoice as if it had been a cash sale. Conversely, if the customer does not pay, the seller voids the sales invoice and returns the merchandise to stock. When this happens, the accountant lists the delivery charge as a debit to Delivery Expense and a credit to Cash.

Layaway Sales

In the case of a *layaway sale*, also known as a *will-call sale*, the customer deposits some cash toward the purchase of a certain item, and the store puts it aside for the customer. The customer must pay the entire price (usually within a specified time) before the store will release the merchandise. If the customer does not complete the payments within the time allowed, she or he forfeits the money that has been paid. However, to preserve customer goodwill, stores often refund the amount paid or allow it to be used as credit against future purchases.

Most customers do complete their payments on layaway sales. The store can then go ahead and record the sale in the usual manner. For example, Morgan's Fashions sells a coat on layaway to N. D. Williams. The coat costs $80, plus a $4 sales tax. Williams makes a deposit of $14 and then makes two additional payments, of $40 and $30. The entries, in general journal form, are as follows.

Cash	14 00	
Accounts Receivable, N. D. Williams	70 00	
Sales		80 00
Sales Tax Payable		4 00
Layaway sale, initial deposit.		

Cash	40 00	
Accounts Receivable, N. D. Williams		40 00
Deposit received on layaway sale.		

Cash	30 00	
Accounts Receivable, N. D. Williams		30 00
Received final deposit on layaway sale, and		
released the merchandise.		

Morgan's Fashions actually records these entries in the cash receipts journal, not the general journal. If the shop were to give Williams a cash refund, it would have to cancel the original sale.

Installment Sales

Installment sales are common among retailers of automobiles, household appliances, electronic equipment, musical instruments, furniture, and jewelry. The installment plan is a sales arrangement by which the customer makes a cash downpayment and gets possession of the merchandise in return for his or her promise to pay the rest of the money in payments at regular intervals over a period of time. The written agreement between buyer and seller is known as a *conditional sales contract*. The seller keeps title to the merchandise, and will transfer title to the buyer on the condition that the buyer complete all the payments.

Accounting for Installment Sales   A firm may account for sales on the installment plan on either the accrual basis or the installment basis. Each method has its advantages, but the installment basis is used primarily for tax accounting. Let us examine each in turn.

Accrual Basis

A firm that records installment sales on the accrual basis writes them up in the same manner as ordinary charge sales, that is, by debiting Accounts Receivable and crediting Sales. The accounting department makes a notation of the terms of the sale on the customer's individual account in the accounts receivable ledger.

In the event that the customer does not complete the payments, the seller repossesses the merchandise and writes off the unpaid balance by debiting Allowance for Doubtful Accounts and crediting Accounts Receivable.

When the firm sells the repossessed merchandise again, it records this as a separate sale. For example, Ronson Jewelry Store sells a watch for $90 to F. Engels, receiving a $30 cash downpayment. Ronson records the transaction as follows.

Cash			3	0	00							
Accounts Receivable, F. Engels			6	0	00							
Sales								9	0	00		
Sold merchandise on account to F. Engels.												

F. Engels defaults on the payments, so Ronson Jewelry repossesses the watch and writes off F. Engels's account.

Allowance for Doubtful Accounts		6 0 00		
Accounts Receivable, F. Engels			6 0 00	
Wrote off the account of F. Engels as				
uncollectible and repossessed a watch.				

Ronson Jewelry then sells the repossessed watch for $27 cash.

Cash		2 7 00		
Sales			2 7 00	
Sold repossessed merchandise for cash.				

Installment Basis

As mentioned before, the installment basis is used primarily for tax accounting. It is used for book accounting purposes only under exceptional circumstances where collection of the installments is not assured.

If a company uses the installment basis, it assumes that each cash installment payment it receives is a partial recovery of the cost of the merchandise and a portion of the gross profit. In other words, the payment is a combination of part of the cost and part of the gross profit of the sale. For example, Don's Used Cars sells a car for $800. The cost of the car is $600. The gross profit is $200 ($800 − $600). The gross profit as a percentage of the sale is 25 percent ($200/$800). If Don's Used Cars collects $440 during the first year, the gross profit counted is $110 (25 percent of $440); if it collects the remaining $360 during the second year, the gross profit counted during that year is $90 (25 percent of $360).

The installment basis is acceptable for income tax purposes. Firms using this basis pay income tax only on the gross profit counted during the year in which they receive cash. Let's go back to the $800 sale by Don's Used Cars. For income tax purposes the firm reports a gross profit of $110 during the first year (gross profit collected). The firm combines that $110 gross profit with the gross profits it collected during the year from other sales. Next it deducts its operating expenses to determine its net income. To find its income tax, it multiplies its net income by the tax rate.

Let's use this example to compare the installment basis with the accrual basis.

	Installment Basis	Accrual Basis
Gross profit reported for first year	$110	$200
Gross profit reported for second year	90	0

The types of goods sold on the installment basis are mainly the so-called consumer durables, often referred to as "big-ticket items." Since these items have distinguishing features, such as model numbers or serial numbers, the firm is able to account for the cost of each item. This system is similar to accounting for perpetual inventories: When a firm buys merchandise, it debits Merchandise Inventory for the amount of the cost. When a firm sells merchandise, it credits Merchandise Inventory for the amount of the cost.

Companies have a special receivable account for their installment customers: *Installment Accounts Receivable.*

- **An installment sale, beginning and ending in the same year, and paid in full** On February 1, City Furniture Company sells a stereo set to Sonja Powers for $260, with a downpayment of $60, and four monthly payments of $50 each. The cost of the stereo set—that is, the amount that City Furniture paid for it—is $182. The gross profit on the sale is $78 (that is, $260 − $182 = $78) or 30 percent of the sales price ($78 ÷ $260). The entry, in general journal form, to record the sale is as follows.

1	19– Feb.	1	Installment Accounts Receivable,			1
2			Sonja Powers (19–)	2 6 0 00		2
3			Merchandise Inventory		1 8 2 00	3
4			Deferred Installment Sales Income		7 8 00	4
5			To record installment sale of			5
6			CJS stereo, model 1619, cost			6
7			$182.			7
8						8

Note that Deferred Installment Sales Income (a balance sheet account) shows City Furniture Company's gross profit on the sale. Ordinarily a company uses a sales journal with special columns for each of the accounts listed. Installment Accounts Receivable is a controlling account. Note that the accountant lists the year in parentheses after each Installment Accounts Receivable; this information enables management to keep track of installment credit.

When Sonja Powers pays that $60 downpayment, the accountant at City Furniture debits Cash and credits Installment Accounts Receivable. City Furniture handles later cash installment payments the same way, as follows.

1	Feb.	1	Cash	6 0 00		1
2			Installment Accounts Receivable,			2
3			Sonja Powers (19–)		6 0 00	3
4			Downpayment on sale of CJS			4
5			stereo, model 1619.			5
6						6

1	Mar.	1	Cash				5	0	00						1
2			Installment Accounts Receivable,												2
3			Sonja Powers (19–)								5	0	00		3
4			Payment on the sale of												4
5			February 1.												5
6															6

1	Apr.	1	Cash				5	0	00						1
2			Installment Accounts Receivable,												2
3			Sonja Powers (19–)								5	0	00		3
4			Payment on the sale of												4
5			February 1.												5

1	May	1	Cash				5	0	00						1
2			Installment Accounts Receivable,												2
3			Sonja Powers (19–)								5	0	00		3
4			Payment on the sale of												4
5			February 1.												5

1	Jun.	1	Cash				5	0	00						1
2			Installment Accounts Receivable,												2
3			Sonja Powers (19–)								5	0	00		3
4			Final payment on the sale of												4
5			February 1.												5

Ordinarily a merchant makes such entries in a cash receipts journal.

Now let us say that Sonja Powers has completed all the payments. City Furniture makes an entry transferring the gross profit, based on the cash received on the contract during the year, from Deferred Installment Sales Income to Realized Installment Sales Income. The entry and corresponding T accounts are shown here.

1	Jun.	1	Deferred Installment Sales Income				7	8	00						1
2			Realized Installment Sales Income								7	8	00		2
3			Realized gross profit on the col-												3
4			lections during the year based												4
5			on the installment sale to Sonja												5
6			Powers												6

Installment Accounts Receivable					Cash				Deferred Installment Sales Income		
+		−		+		−			−	+	
Feb. 1	260	Feb. 1	60	Feb. 1	60			Jun. 1	78	Feb. 1	78
		Mar. 1	50	Mar. 1	50						
		Apr. 1	50	Apr. 1	50						
		May 1	50	May 1	50						
		Jun. 1	50	Jun. 1	50						

Realized Installment Sales Income	
−	+
	Jun. 1 78

Merchandise Inventory	
+	−
	Feb. 1 182

Notice that Deferred Installment Sales Income has been canceled out. The accountant then closes the balance of Realized Installment Sales Income, representing the firm's gross profit on the transaction, into Income Summary.

The ledger card for City Furniture's installment accounts receivable ledger is shown on the opposite page.

- **An installment sale, beginning in one year and ending the next year, and paid in full**   On October 15, City Furniture sells a refrigerator to Robert A. Hicks for $320, with a downpayment of $110 and five monthly payments of $42 each. The cost of the refrigerator (that is, what City Furniture paid for it) is $240. Here are the entries, in general journal form, to account for the sale.

1	19x1 Oct.	15	Installment Accounts Receivable,			1
2			Robert A. Hicks (19x1)	3 2 0 00		2
3			Merchandise Inventory		2 4 0 00	3
4			Deferred Installment Sales Income		8 0 00	4
5			To record installment sale of			5
6			Prentice Refrigerator, model			6
7			C118, cost $240.			7
8						8
9		15	Cash	1 1 0 00		9
10			Installment Accounts Receivable,			10
11			Robert A. Hicks (19x1)		1 1 0 00	11
12			Downpayment on sale of Prentice			12
13			Refrigerator, model C118.			13
14						14

1	Nov.	15	Cash	4 2 00		1
2			Installment Accounts Receivable,			2
3			Robert A. Hicks (19x1)		4 2 00	3
4			Payment on sale of October 15.			4
5						5

INSTALLMENT ACCOUNTS RECEIVABLE LEDGER

CHARGES

DATE		POST. REF.	ITEM	AMOUNT
19– Feb.	1		CJS stereo, model 1619, cost $182.00, gross profit $78.00, gross profit %, 30%, (78/260 = .3 = 30%).	2 6 0 00

PAYMENTS

DATE		EXPLANATION	POST. REF.	AMOUNT	BALANCE
19– Feb.	1	Downpayment		6 0 00	2 0 0 00
Mar.	1			5 0 00	1 5 0 00
Apr.	1			5 0 00	1 0 0 00
May	1			5 0 00	5 0 00
Jun.	1			5 0 00	

1	Dec.	14	Cash		4 2 00					1
2			Installment Accounts Receivable,							2
3			Robert A. Hicks (19x1)				4 2 00			3
4			Payment on sale of October 15.							4
5										5

1			*Adjusting Entry*							1
2	Dec.	31	Deferred Installment Sales Income		4 8 50					2
3			Realized Installment Sales Income				4 8 50			3
4			Adjusting entry for realized							4
5			gross profit on collections							5
6			during the year based on install-							6
7			ment sale to Robert A. Hicks							7
8			(Gross profit % = 80/320 = 25%;							8
9			$194 × .25 = $48.50).							9
10										10

Note that, by the end of the year, Robert Hicks has paid City Furniture $194, which is his downpayment of $110 plus two $42 payments.

The last entry, an adjusting entry made at the end of the fiscal year, accounts for the gross profit received on all installment contracts that are not paid in full. The accountant can gather the information from the ledger cards by multiplying the collections received for the year on each contract by the rate of gross profit on each item. Instead of the specific percentage of gross profit on each sale, it is possible to use an average percentage.

Here is the entry to close the revenue account, Realized Installment Sales Income.

1			*Closing Entry*							1
2	19x1 Dec.	31	Realized Installment Sales Income		4 8 50					2
3			Income Summary				4 8 50			3
4										4
5										5

At the end of the first year, Deferred Installment Sales Income has a credit balance of $31.50. Deferred Installment Sales Income will appear on the balance sheet under the caption Deferred Credits, a liability category, immediately above Owner's Equity.

During the first three months of the next year, Robert Hicks pays his three remaining installments. Then the accountant converts the remaining balance in Deferred Installment Sales Income into Realized Installment Sales Income. Here are the entries.

		19x2 Jan.	15	Cash				4	2	00					1
2				Installment Accounts Receivable,											2
3				Robert A. Hicks (19x2)							4	2	00		3
4				Payment on the sale of											4
5				October 15, 19x1.											5
6															6
7															7
8															8

		Feb.	14	Cash				4	2	00					1
2				Installment Accounts Receivable,											2
3				Robert A. Hicks (19x2)							4	2	00		3
4				Payment on the sale of											4
5				October 15, 19x1.											5
6															6
7															7
8															8

		Mar.	14	Cash				4	2	00					1
2				Installment Accounts Receivable,											2
3				Robert A. Hicks (19x2)							4	2	00		3
4				Payment on the sale of											4
5				October 15, 19x1.											5
6															6
7															7
8															8

		Mar.	14	Deferred Installment Sales Income				3	1	50					1
2				Realized Installment Sales Income							3	1	50		2
3				To record realized gross profit											3
4				on collections during the year											4
5				on installment sale to Robert A.											5
6				Hicks (Gross profit % = 25%;											6
7				$126 × .25 = $31.50).											7
8															8
9															9

The postings to the T accounts look like this.

Installment Accounts Receivable

+			−	
Oct. 15	320	Oct. 15	110
		Nov. 15	42
		Dec. 14	42
		Jan. 15	42
		Feb. 14	42
		Mar. 14	42

Cash

+		−
Oct. 15	110	
Nov. 15	42	
Dec. 14	42	
Jan. 15	42	
Feb. 14	42	
Mar. 14	42	

Income Summary

Dec. 31 Clos.		Dec. 31	48.50
	48.50		

Merchandise Inventory

+		−	
Bal.	xxx	Oct. 15	240

Deferred Installment Sales Income

−		+	
Dec. 31 Adj.		Oct. 15	80
	48.50		
Mar. 14	31.50		

Realized Installment Sales Income

−		+	
Dec. 31 Clos.		Dec. 31 Adj.	
	48.50		48.50
		Mar. 14	31.50

- **An installment sale beginning in one year and defaulted two years later** On December 5, City Furniture sells a color television set to Ruth C. Bradford for $600, with a downpayment of $60, and fifteen monthly payments of $36 each. The cost of the television set (to City Furniture) is $390. The entries are shown on the next two pages.

		Date	Description	Debit	Credit
1	19x1 Dec.	5	Installment Accounts Receivable,		
2			Ruth C. Bradford (19x1)	6 0 0 00	
3			Merchandise Inventory		, 3 9 0 00
4			Deferred Installment Sales Income		2 1 0 00
5			To record installment sale of		
6			Linton color TV, model DF 912,		
7			cost $390.		
8					
9		5	Cash	6 0 00	
10			Installment Accounts Receivable,		
11			Ruth C. Bradford (19x1)		6 0 00
12			Downpayment on sale of Linton		
13			color TV, model DF 912.		

		Date	Description	Debit	Credit
1			*Adjusting Entry*		
2	Dec.	31	Deferred Installment Sales Income	2 1 00	
3			Realized Installment Sales Income		2 1 00
4			Adjusting entry for realized		
5			gross profit on collections		
6			during the year based on install-		
7			ment sale to Ruth C. Bradford		
8			(Gross profit % = 210/600 =		
9			35%; $60 × .35 = $21).		
10					
11			*Closing Entry*		
12		31	Realized Installment Sales Income	2 1 00	
13			Income Summary		2 1 00

		Date	Description	Debit	Credit
1	19x2 Jan.	4	Cash	3 6 00	
2			Installment Accounts Receivable,		
3			Ruth C. Bradford (19x2)		3 6 00
4			Payment on sale of December 5,		
5			19x1.		

The last entry is repeated on February 5, March 5, April 2, May 3, June 6, July 6, August 5, September 10, October 12, November 21, and December 15.

1			*Adjusting Entry*				1
2	*19x2 Dec.*	31	*Deferred Installment Sales Income*	1 5 1 20			2
3			*Realized Installment Sales Income*		1 5 1 20		3
4			*Adjusting entry for realized*				4
5			*gross profit on collections*				5
6			*during the year based on install-*				6
7			*ment sale to Ruth C. Bradford*				7
8			*(Gross profit % = 35%; $432 ×*				8
9			*.35 = $151.20).*				9
10							10
11			*Closing Entry*				11
12		31	*Realized Installment Sales Income*	1 5 1 20			12
13			*Income Summary*		1 5 1 20		13
14							14

1	*19x3 Jan.*	20	*Cash*	3 6 00			1
2			*Installment Accounts Receivable,*				2
3			*Ruth C. Bradford (19x3)*		3 6 00		3
4			*Payment on sale of December 5,*				4
5			*19x1.*				5
6							6

After January of the second year after the sale, Ruth Bradford stops making payments on the installment contract. Therefore on April 2 of that year, City Furniture repossesses the set. At this time, the wholesale value of the set is $40. The accountant for City Furniture first lists the installments collected during that year, and writes the entry as follows.

1	*19x3 Apr.*	2	*Deferred Installment Sales Income*	1 2 60			1
2			*Realized Installment Sales Income*		1 2 60		2
3			*To record realized gross profit*				3
4			*on installment collected during*				4
5			*the year, prior to the repos-*				5
6			*session based on installment*				6
7			*sale to Ruth C. Bradford*				7
8			*($36 × .35 = $12.60).*				8
9							9
(1) 10		2	*Inventory of Repossessed Merchandise*	4 0 00			10
(3) 11			*Deferred Installment Sales Income*	2 5 20			11
(4) 12			*Loss on Repossession*	6 80			12
(2) 13			*Installment Accounts Receivable,*				13
14			*Ruth C. Bradford (19x3)*		7 2 00		14
15			*Repossessed Linton color TV,*				15
16			*model DF 912, value of set $40.*				16
17							17
18							18

Note: A firm uses a separate account, Inventory of Repossessed Merchandise, to distinguish repossessed goods from new goods (Merchandise Inventory).

The numbers in parentheses indicate the suggested order for recording the debits and credits. Deferred Installment Sales Income and Installment Accounts Receivable, Ruth C. Bradford, are cleared off the books by the last entry. If the debits are *less* than the credits, the difference represents a loss. Conversely, if the debits are *more* than the credits, the difference represents a gain. One can also view the above entry as a loss, since the debits to Inventory of Repossessed Merchandise and Deferred Installment Sales Income are not enough to clear the Installment Accounts Receivable account.

If the reverse had been true—that is, if the total of the debits to Inventory of Repossessed Merchandise and Deferred Installment Sales Income had been greater than the credit to Installment Accounts Receivable—the difference would have represented a gain on repossession. For example, suppose that the wholesale value of the set at the time of repossession had been $120; then the following entry would have been made.

(1)	1	19x3 Apr.	2	Inventory of Repossessed Merchandise	1 2 0 00		1
(3)	2			Deferred Installment Sales Income	2 5 20		2
(2)	3			Installment Accounts Receivable,			3
	4			Ruth C. Bradford (19x3)		7 2 00	4
(4)	5			Gain on Repossession		7 3 20	5
	6			Repossessed Linton color TV,			6
	7			model DF 912, value of set, $120.			7
	8						8
	9						9
	10						10
	11						11
	12						12
	13						13
	14						14
	15						15
	16						16
	17						17
	18						18

Loss on Repossession is classified on the income statement as Other Expense; Gain on Repossession is classified as Other Income.

Here are T accounts to show City Furniture's $6.80 loss on the repossession.

Installment Accounts Receivable

+		−		
Dec. 5	600	Dec. 5	60	
		Jan. 4	36	
		Feb. 5	36	
		Mar. 5	36	
		Apr. 2	36	
		May 3	36	
		Jun. 6	36	
		Jul. 6	36	
		Aug. 5	36	
		Sep. 10	36	
		Oct. 12	36	
		Nov. 21	36	
		Dec. 15	36	
		Jan. 20	36	
		Apr. 2	72	

Cash

+		−
Dec. 5	60	
Jan. 4	36	
Feb. 5	36	
Mar. 5	36	
Apr. 2	36	
May 3	36	
Jun. 6	36	
Jul. 6	36	
Aug. 5	36	
Sep. 10	36	
Oct. 12	36	
Nov. 21	36	
Dec. 15	36	
Jan. 20	36	

Merchandise Inventory

+		−	
Bal.	xxx	Dec. 5	390

Inventory of Repossessed Merchandise

+		−
Apr. 2	40	

Deferred Installment Sales Income

−		+	
Dec. 31 Adj.	21.00	Dec. 5	210.00
Dec. 31 Adj.	151.20		
Apr. 2	12.60		
Apr. 2	25.20		

Realized Installment Sales Income

−		+	
Dec. 31 Clos.	21.00	Dec. 31 Adj.	21.00
Dec. 31 Clos.	151.20	Dec. 31 Adj.	151.20
		Apr. 2	12.60

Income Summary

Closing	Dec. 31	21.00
Closing	Dec. 31	151.20

Loss on Repossession

+		−
Apr. 2	6.80	

You can see from the postings that all the accounts involved in the sale have now been canceled out.

Problems

Problem F-1   On March 15 of this year, James Rossiter bought a suit from Fishbein's Department Store on a layaway plan. The suit cost Rossiter $96, plus $4.80 sales tax. Rossiter made an initial deposit of $20.80 and then made two additional payments, of $50 and $30, on March 30 and April 30.

Instructions

Write the three entries pertaining to the layaway sale in general journal form.

Problem F-2   The books of Johnson Electronics show the following transactions related to installment sales.

Year 1

Sep. 10 Sold a stereo to N. Kennedy, $160, on the installment plan, with a downpayment of $40 and three installments of $40 each. Cost of stereo: $102.40.

$$\left(\text{Gross profit } \% = \frac{\$57.60}{\$160.00} = 36\% \right)$$

10 Recorded downpayment of $40 from Kennedy.

Oct.   9 Sold a computer to T. R. Peters, $182, on the installment plan, with a downpayment of $42 and five installments of $28 each. Cost of computer: $109.20.

$$\left(\text{Gross profit } \% = \frac{\$72.80}{\$182.00} = 40\% \right)$$

9 Recorded downpayment of $42 from T. R. Peters.
11 Received $40 as first installment from N. Kennedy.

Nov.   5 Received $28 as first installment from T. R. Peters.
12 Received $40 as second installment from N. Kennedy.

Dec.   9 Received $28 as second installment from T. R. Peters.
11 Received $40 as third and final installment from N. Kennedy.
11 Recorded the income realized on installments collected during the year from N. Kennedy.
31 Recorded as an adjusting entry the income realized on installments collected during the year from T. R. Peters.
31 Closed the Realized Installment Sales Income account.

Year 2

Jan.   14 Received $28 as third installment from T. R. Peters.
Feb.   10 Received $28 as fourth installment from T. R. Peters.
Mar.   15 Received $28 as fifth and final installment from T. R. Peters.
15 Recorded the income realized on installments collected during the year from T. R. Peters.

Instructions

1. Record these transactions in general journal form.
2. Post the entries to the appropriate accounts.

Problem F-3 The books of the Drummond Furniture Store show the following transactions related to an installment sale.

Year 1

Oct.   21 Sold a dishwasher to C. T. Pierson, $226, on the installment plan, with a downpayment of $26, and ten installments of $20 each. The cost of the dishwasher is $146.90.
21 Recorded downpayment of $26 from C. T. Pierson.

Nov.   28 Received $20 as the first installment from C. T. Pierson.

Dec. 29 Received $20 as the second installment from C. T. Pierson.

31 Recorded as an adjusting entry the income realized on installments collected during the year determined in the installment accounts receivable ledger, $11,726.42 (including $23.10 income realized on the installment sale to C. T. Pierson, using a 35 percent gross profit rate).

31 Closed the Realized Installment Sales Income account.

Year 2

Jan. 30 Received $20 as third installment from C. T. Pierson.

Mar. 20 Received $20 as fourth installment from C. T. Pierson.

Jun. 28 Repossessed the dishwasher sold to C. T. Pierson. Recorded the income realized on installments collected during the year.

28 Recorded the repossession. The wholesale value of the dishwasher as of this date is $60.

Instructions

1. Record the transactions in general journal form.
2. Post the entries to the appropriate accounts.

27 Analyzing and Interpreting Financial Statements

Learning Objectives

After you have completed this chapter, you will be able to do the following:

1. Prepare a comparative income statement and balance sheet involving horizontal analysis.

2. Prepare a comparative income statement and balance sheet involving vertical analysis.

3. Compute the following: working capital, current ratio, quick ratio, accounts receivable turnover, merchandise inventory turnover, ratio of stockholders' equity to liabilities, ratio of the value of plant and equipment to long-term liabilities, equity per share, rate of return on stockholders' equity, earnings per share of common stock, and price-earnings ratio.

As we said in Chapter 1, accounting is the process of analyzing, recording, summarizing, and *interpreting* business transactions. We are now ready to interpret the results: How does one draw conclusions from financial data that have been summarized in financial statements?

The financial condition of a company and the results of operations of business enterprises are of interest not only to owners, employers, and managers, but also to creditors and to prospective owners and creditors. Everybody is interested in two aspects of an enterprise.

1. Its *solvency*, or its ability to pay its debts
2. Its *profitability*, or its ability to earn a reasonable profit on the owners' investment

This chapter will explain the techniques used to determine solvency and profitability.

TYPES OF COMPARISON

To interpret a set of facts, one has to have something else with which to compare it. In other words, a given set of facts by itself is not significant. For example, if you are told that a certain corporation earned a net income of $56,000 during the past year, this figure by itself is not meaningful. Does this net income indicate a successful year or a poor year? Does it compare favorably with other years or unfavorably? Does it represent a reasonable return on sales and investment or not? How does it compare with the net income of other firms in the same industry?

A company's financial statements are meaningful only if you analyze them on a comparative basis. There are three useful bases for making such a comparison:

1. Statements of the same company for one or more prior years
2. Data for other companies in the same industry
3. Previously established standards or objectives

COMPARATIVE STATEMENTS

One technique for analyzing and interpreting financial data is the preparation of comparative statements. Two types of analysis—horizontal and vertical—are commonly used.

Horizontal Analysis

Horizontal analysis compares the same item in a company's financial statements for two or more periods. Let's look at the comparative income statement (Figure 27-1, next two pages) of Benson Athletic Supply Company, Inc., for 19x6 and 19x7. Later we will look at the comparative balance sheet for this firm.

Objective 1

Prepare a comparative income statement and balance sheet involving horizontal analysis.

Note that for each item in the income statement the accountant first expressed the differences—that is, the increases or decreases of 19x7 over 19x6—in dollars and then in percentages. Take the increase in Sales, on the second line, for example. Subtract Sales in 19x6 from Sales in 19x7.

$980,600	Sales for 19x7
− 860,000	Sales for 19x6
$120,600	Increase of 19x7 over 19x6

To calculate the *percentage* of increase in Sales in 19x7 over 19x6, divide the dollar increase by the amount of Sales during the base year, 19x6.

$$\frac{\$120,600}{\$860,000} = 860,000\overline{)120,600}^{\;.1402} = 14.02\%$$

Note: The expression **base year** means the year you are using as a basis for comparison.

As another example, take the change in Sales Returns and Allowances:

$13,700	Sales Returns and Allowances for 19x7
− 11,400	Sales Returns and Allowances for 19x6
$ 2,300	Increase of 19x7 over 19x6

The percentage rate of increase is

$$\frac{\$2,300}{\$11,400} = 11,400\overline{)2,300}^{\;.2018} = 20.18\%$$

People appraising an income statement often use the percentage increase of net sales as a basis for comparison. In other words, they compare all other percentage changes with the percentage change in net sales, to see whether the other percentage changes are out of line. If net sales increased 13.94 percent from 19x6 to 19x7, other percentage changes should amount to approximately 13.94 percent also. If they vary considerably from 13.94 percent, they may be out of line, and one should investigate to find the reasons for the difference.

Benson Athletic Supply Company, Inc.

Comparative Income Statement

For years ended December 31, 19x7, and December 31, 19x6

	19x7	19x6	INCREASE OR DECREASE	
			AMOUNT	PERCENT
Revenue from Sales:				
Sales	$ 980 6 0 0 00	$ 860 0 0 0 00	$ 120 6 0 0 00	14.02
Less Sales Returns and Allowances	13 7 0 0 00	11 4 0 0 00	2 3 0 0 00	20.18
Net Sales	$ 966 9 0 0 00	$ 848 6 0 0 00	$ 118 3 0 0 00	13.94
Cost of Merchandise Sold:				
Merchandise Inventory, January 1	206 5 0 0 00	138 7 0 0 00	$ 67 8 0 0 00	48.88
Purchases	817 1 0 0 00	645 7 0 0 00	171 4 0 0 00	26.54
Less Purchases Returns and Allowances	12 3 0 0 00	9 1 0 0 00	3 2 0 0 00	35.16
Merchandise Available for Sale	$1 011 3 0 0 00	$ 775 3 0 0 00	$ 236 0 0 0 00	30.44
Less Merchandise Inventory, December 31	353 6 0 0 00	206 5 0 0 00	147 1 0 0 00	71.23
Cost of Merchandise Sold	$ 657 7 0 0 00	$ 568 8 0 0 00	$ 88 9 0 0 00	15.63
Gross Profit	$ 309 2 0 0 00	$ 279 8 0 0 00	$ 29 4 0 0 00	10.51
Operating Expenses:				
Selling Expenses:				
Sales Salary Expense	$ 114 6 5 0 00	$ 102 4 0 0 00	$ 12 2 5 0 00	11.96
Delivery Expense	17 7 0 0 00	13 7 0 0 00	4 0 0 0 00	29.20
Advertising Expense	7 9 0 0 00	6 9 0 0 00	1 0 0 0 00	14.49
Depreciation Expense, Equipment	6 8 0 0 00	6 6 0 0 00	2 0 0 00	3.03
Store Supplies Expense	7 5 0 00	6 0 0 00	1 5 0 00	25.00
Total Selling Expenses	$ 147 8 0 0 00	$ 130 2 0 0 00	$ 17 6 0 0 00	13.52

General Expenses:			
Office Salary Expense	$ 33 4 4 0 00	$ 27 6 8 0 00	$ 5 7 6 0 00	20.81
Depreciation Expense, Building	14 2 0 0 00	14 2 0 0 00	0 00	0
Bad Debts Expense	6 2 0 0 00	5 4 0 0 00	8 0 0 00	14.81
Taxes Expense	6 1 0 0 00	5 2 0 0 00	9 0 0 00	17.31
Insurance Expense	1 1 0 0 00	1 0 0 0 00	1 0 0 00	10.00
Miscellaneous General Expense	8 6 0 00	7 2 0 00	1 4 0 00	19.44
Total General Expenses	$ 61 9 0 0 00	$ 54 2 0 0 00	$ 7 7 0 0 00	14.21
Total Operating Expenses	$ 209 7 0 0 00	$ 184 4 0 0 00	$ 25 3 0 0 00	13.72
Income from Operations	$ 99 5 0 0 00	$ 95 4 0 0 00	$ 4 1 0 0 00	4.30
Other Expense:			
Interest Expense	8 5 2 0 00	7 8 6 0 00	6 6 0 00	8.40
Net Income before Income Tax	$ 90 9 8 0 00	$ 87 5 4 0 00	$ 3 4 4 0 00	3.93
Income Tax	36 8 4 0 00	35 5 0 0 00	1 3 4 0 00	3.77
Net Income after Income Tax	$ 54 1 4 0 00	$ 52 0 4 0 00	$ 2 1 0 0 00	4.04

Figure 27-1

Let's look at the main items on the income statement.

Item	Percentage Change
Net Sales	13.94
Cost of Merchandise Sold	15.63
Gross Profit	10.51
Total Operating Expenses	13.72
Net Income after Income Tax	4.04

You can see that gross profit and net income after income tax are considerably less than the percentage change in sales. Since gross profit is determined by subtracting Cost of Merchandise Sold from Net Sales, one should investigate the entire Cost of Merchandise Sold section of the income statement. This is a starting point in accounting for the comparatively small percentage increase in Net Income after Income Tax. The percentage changes of items in the Cost of Merchandise Sold section are as follows.

Item	Percentage Change
Merchandise Inventory, January 1	48.88
Purchases	26.54
Purchases Returns and Allowances	35.16
Merchandise Inventory, December 31	71.23

The merchandise inventory of January 1 was a carry-over from the previous year, but why the large increase in Purchases? Another thing: It costs a great deal to handle Purchases Returns and Allowances; why were so many more purchases returned in 19x7 than in 19x6? And look at the large increase in merchandise inventory at the end of the year; buying all that merchandise took a lot of cash. Also, with such a large increase in merchandise inventory, we would expect a larger increase in sales. Is the increase in sales large enough?

Now look at the balance sheet in Figure 27-2 (pages 872–873), which shows the comparison between 19x7 and 19x6. Again you will see why changes are expressed in both dollars and percentages. Items showing either a large dollar change or a large percentage change stick out like a sore thumb. This time some minus totals show up. Look at the following items.

Item	Dollar Increase or Decrease	Percentage Increase or Decrease
Merchandise Inventory	$147,100	71.23
Accounts Payable	42,600	146.90
Cash	(19,100)	(49.35)

Recall that the comparative income statement already exposed the jump in the Merchandise Inventory account. We should also consider the effects of changes in the balances of other related accounts. For example, the fact that Cash is down by 49 percent while Accounts Payable is up by 147 percent may indicate a pending financial crisis. In order to meet its bills, the firm may be forced to liquidate that big stock of merchandise by selling it off at cost, or even less. That 200 percent increase in Dividends Payable doesn't look good either. One point in their favor, though, is the decrease in Accounts Receivable. The increase in Allowance for Doubtful Accounts, although relatively small in amount, appears to be unreasonable.

Vertical Analysis

Another tool accountants can use to analyze financial statements is **vertical analysis.** To use this method, one needs to see, in a single statement, the relationship of component parts to the whole. In the case of an income statement, *the whole is net sales.* Although each percentage applies to a single item only, one can quickly see the relative importance of each item in the statement. Let us look first at the comparative income statement (Figure 27-3, page 874) and then at the comparative balance sheet for Benson Athletic Supply Company, Inc., this time arranged for vertical analysis.

Objective 2

Prepare a comparative income statement and balance sheet involving vertical analysis.

When you arrange an income statement for vertical analysis, you express each item as a *percentage of net sales.* In other words, you divide the total for each item by the total of net sales. Here's how that works.

Gross Profit % = Gross Profit ÷ Net Sales

$$\text{Gross Profit \% (19x7)} = \frac{\$309,200}{\$966,900} = .3198 = 31.98\%$$

$$\text{Gross Profit \% (19x6)} = \frac{\$279,800}{\$848,600} = .3297 = 32.97\%$$

Income from Operations % = Income from Operations ÷ Net Sales

$$\text{Income from Operations \% (19x7)} = \frac{\$99,500}{\$966,900} = .1029 = 10.29\%$$

(continued on page 875)

Benson Athletic Supply Company, Inc.
Comparative Balance Sheet
December 31, 19x7 and December 31, 19x6

Assets	19x7	19x6	Increase or Decrease Amount	Percent
Current Assets:				
Cash	$ 19 6 0 0 00	$ 38 7 0 0 00	$ (19 1 0 0 00)	(49.35)
Accounts Receivable	76 7 0 0 00	81 4 0 0 00	(4 7 0 0 00)	(5.77)
Less Allowance for Doubtful Accounts	3 3 0 0 00	2 6 0 0 00	7 0 0 00	26.92
Merchandise Inventory	353 6 0 0 00	206 5 0 0 00	147 1 0 0 00	71.23
Prepaid Insurance	2 0 0 0 00	2 1 0 0 00	(1 0 0 00)	(4.76)
Total Current Assets	$ 448 6 0 0 00	$ 326 1 0 0 00	$ 122 5 0 0 00	37.57
Investments:				
Sinking Fund Cash	$ 4 1 0 0 00	$ 5 8 0 0 00	$ (1 7 0 0 00)	(29.31)
Sinking Fund Investments	61 7 0 0 00	59 4 0 0 00	2 3 0 0 00	3.87
Total Investments	$ 65 8 0 0 00	$ 65 2 0 0 00	$ 6 0 0 00	.92
Plant and Equipment:				
Equipment	$ 88 6 0 0 00	$ 86 0 0 0 00	$ 2 6 0 0 00	3.02
Less Accumulated Depreciation	41 0 0 0 00	34 2 0 0 00	6 8 0 0 00	19.88
Building	160 0 0 0 00	160 0 0 0 00	0	0
Less Accumulated Depreciation	56 8 0 0 00	42 6 0 0 00	14 2 0 0 00	33.33
Land	40 0 0 0 00	40 0 0 0 00	0	0
Total Plant and Equipment	$ 190 8 0 0 00	$ 209 2 0 0 00	$ (18 4 0 0 00)	(8.80)
Intangible Assets:				
Organization Costs	3 0 0 0 00	4 0 0 0 00	(1 0 0 0 00)	(25.00)
Total Assets	$ 708 2 0 0 00	$ 604 5 0 0 00	$ 103 7 0 0 00	17.15

Liabilities

Current Liabilities:			
Accounts Payable	$71 6 0 0 00	$29 0 0 0 00	$42 6 0 0 00	146.90
Income Tax Payable	12 8 0 0 00	5 6 0 0 00	7 2 0 0 00	128.57
Dividends Payable	12 0 0 0 00	4 0 0 0 00	8 0 0 0 00	200.00
Salaries Payable	4 2 0 0 00	4 0 0 0 00	2 0 0 0 00	5.00
Total Current Liabilities	$100 6 0 0 00	$42 6 0 0 00	$58 0 0 0 00	136.15
Long-term Liabilities:				
Bonds Payable, 6%, due December 31, 19x9	$100 0 0 0 00	$100 0 0 0 00	0	0
Less Discount on Bonds Payable	2 2 0 0 00	2 4 0 0 00	(2 0 0 00)	(8.33)
Total Long-term Liabilities	$97 8 0 0 00	$97 6 0 0 00	2 0 0 00	.20
Total Liabilities	$198 4 0 0 00	$140 2 0 0 00	$58 2 0 0 00	41.51

Stockholders' Equity

Paid-in Capital:				
Common Stock, $100 par (4,000 shares authorized, 3,000 shares issued)	$300 0 0 0 00	$300 0 0 0 00	0	0
Premium on Common Stock	86 0 0 0 00	86 0 0 0 00	0	0
Total Paid-in Capital	$386 0 0 0 00	$386 0 0 0 00	0	0
Retained Earnings:				
Appropriated:				
Appropriated for Plant Expansion	$20 0 0 0 00	$12 0 0 0 00	$8 0 0 0 00	66.67
Unappropriated	103 8 0 0 00	66 3 0 0 00	37 5 0 0 00	56.56
Total Retained Earnings	$123 8 0 0 00	$78 3 0 0 00	$45 5 0 0 00	58.11
Total Stockholders' Equity	$509 8 0 0 00	$464 3 0 0 00	$45 5 0 0 00	9.80
Total Liabilities and Stockholders' Equity	$708 2 0 0 00	$604 5 0 0 00	$103 7 0 0 00	17.15

Figure 27-2

Benson Athletic Supply Company, Inc.
Comparative Income Statement
For years ended December 31, 19x7 and December 31, 19x6

	19x7		19x6	
	AMOUNT	PERCENT	AMOUNT	PERCENT
Revenue from Sales:				
Sales	$ 980 600 00	101.42	$ 860 000 00	101.34
Less Sales Returns and Allowances	13 700 00	1.42	11 400 00	1.34
Net Sales	$ 966 900 00	100.00	$ 848 600 00	100.00
Cost of Merchandise Sold:				
Merchandise Inventory, Jan. 1	$ 206 500 00	21.36	$ 138 700 00	16.34
Purchases	817 100 00	84.51	645 700 00	76.09
Less Purchases Returns and Allowances	12 300 00	1.27	9 100 00	1.07
Merchandise Available for Sale	$1 011 300 00	104.59	$ 775 300 00	91.36
Less Merchandise Inventory, Dec. 31	353 600 00	36.57	206 500 00	24.33
Cost of Merchandise Sold	$ 657 700 00	68.02	$ 568 800 00	67.03
Gross Profit	$ 309 200 00	31.98	$ 279 800 00	32.97
Operating Expenses:				
Selling Expenses:				
Sales Salary Expense	$ 114 650 00	11.86	$ 102 400 00	12.07
Delivery Expense	17 700 00	1.83	13 700 00	1.61
Advertising Expense	7 900 00	.82	6 900 00	.81
Depreciation Expense, Equipment	6 800 00	.70	6 600 00	.78
Store Supplies Expense	7 50 00	.08	6 00 00	.07
Total Selling Expenses	$ 147 800 00	15.29	$ 130 200 00	15.34
General Expenses:				
Office Salary Expense	$ 33 440 00	3.46	$ 27 680 00	3.26
Depreciation Expense, Building	14 200 00	1.47	14 200 00	1.67
Bad Debts Expense	6 200 00	.64	5 400 00	.64
Taxes Expense	6 100 00	.63	5 200 00	.61
Insurance Expense	1 100 00	.11	1 000 00	.12
Miscellaneous General Expense	8 60 00	.09	7 20 00	.08
Total General Expenses	$ 61 900 00	6.40	$ 54 200 00	6.39
Total Operating Expenses	$ 209 700 00	21.69	$ 184 400 00	21.73
Income from Operations	$ 99 500 00	10.29	$ 95 400 00	11.24
Other Expense:				
Interest Expense	8 520 00	.88	7 860 00	.92
Income before Income Tax	$ 90 980 00	9.41	$ 87 540 00	10.32
Income Tax	36 840 00	3.81	35 500 00	4.18
Net Income after Income Tax	$ 54 140 00	5.60	$ 52 040 00	6.13

Figure 27-3

$$\text{Income from Operations \% (19x6)} = \frac{\$95,400}{\$848,600} = .1124 = 11.24\%$$

$$\text{Net Income after Income Tax \%} = \text{Net Income after Income Tax} \div \text{Net Sales}$$

$$\text{Net Income after Income Tax \% (19x7)} = \frac{\$54,140}{\$966,900} = .0560 = 5.60\%$$

$$\text{Net Income after Income Tax \% (19x6)} = \frac{\$52,040}{\$848,600} = .0613 = 6.13\%$$

One could also interpret the percentages as shown here.

19x7

- For every $100 in net sales, gross profit amounted to $31.98.
- For every $100 in net sales, income from operations amounted to $10.29.
- For every $100 in net sales, income after income tax amounted to $5.60.

19x6

- For every $100 in net sales, gross profit amounted to $32.97.
- For every $100 in net sales, income from operations amounted to $11.24.
- For every $100 in net sales, net income after income tax amounted to $6.13.

Again we see the relative importance assumed by Purchases (84.51 percent of Net Sales) and Merchandise Inventory (36.57 percent of Net Sales). In the area of Selling Expenses the percentage score of Sales Salary Expense declined slightly. Advertising Expense as a percentage of Net Sales remained the same. (Is that necessarily a good sign?)

When you perform a vertical analysis of a comparative balance sheet, you express each item's figure as *a percentage of total assets,* or as a percentage of total liabilities and owners' equity, which is the same figure. (See Figure 27-4, on the next two pages.) For example, suppose you want to find the percentage of total assets represented by Cash, Accounts Receivable, and Merchandise Inventory.

$$\text{Cash \%} = \text{Cash} \div \text{Total Assets}$$

$$\text{Cash \% (19x7)} = \frac{\$19,600}{\$708,200} = .0277 = 2.77\%$$

$$\text{Cash \% (19x6)} = \frac{\$38,700}{\$604,500} = .0640 = 6.40\%$$

$$\text{Accounts Receivable \%} = \text{Net Accounts Receivable} \div \text{Total Assets}$$

$$\text{Accounts Receivable \% (19x7)} = \frac{\$73,400}{\$708,200} = .1036 = 10.36\%$$

$$\text{Accounts Receivable \% (19x6)} = \frac{\$78,800}{\$604,500} = .1304 = 13.04\%$$

(*continued on page 878*)

Benson Athletic Supply Company, Inc.
Comparative Balance Sheet
December 31, 19x7 and December 31, 19x6

Assets	19x7 AMOUNT	PERCENT	19x6 AMOUNT	PERCENT
Current Assets:				
Cash	$ 19 6 0 0 00	2.77	$ 38 7 0 0 00	6.40
Accounts Receivable	76 7 0 0 00	10.83	81 4 0 0 00	13.47
Less Allowance for Doubtful Accounts	3 3 0 0 00	.47	2 6 0 0 00	.43
Merchandise Inventory	353 6 0 0 00	49.93	206 5 0 0 00	34.16
Prepaid Insurance	2 0 0 0 00	.28	2 1 0 0 00	.35
Total Current Assets	$ 448 6 0 0 00	63.34	$ 326 1 0 0 00	53.95
Investments:				
Sinking Fund Cash	$ 4 1 0 0 00	.58	$ 5 8 0 0 00	.96
Sinking Fund Investments	61 7 0 0 00	8.71	59 4 0 0 00	9.83
Total Investments	$ 65 8 0 0 00	9.29	$ 65 2 0 0 00	10.79
Plant and Equipment:				
Equipment	$ 88 6 0 0 00	12.51	$ 86 0 0 0 00	14.23
Less Accumulated Depreciation	41 0 0 0 00	5.79	34 2 0 0 00	5.66
Building	160 0 0 0 00	22.59	160 0 0 0 00	26.47
Less Accumulated Depreciation	56 8 0 0 00	8.02	42 6 0 0 00	7.05
Land	40 0 0 0 00	5.65	40 0 0 0 00	6.62
Total Plant and Equipment	$ 190 8 0 0 00	26.94	$ 209 2 0 0 00	34.61
Intangible Assets:				
Organization Costs	3 0 0 0 00	.42	4 0 0 0 00	.66
Total Assets	$ 708 2 0 0 00	100.00	$ 604 5 0 0 00	100.00

Liabilities				
Current Liabilities:				
Accounts Payable	$ 71 6 0 0 00	10.11	$ 29 0 0 0 00	4.80
Income Tax Payable	12 8 0 0 00	1.81	5 6 0 0 00	.93
Dividends Payable	12 0 0 0 00	1.69	4 0 0 0 00	.66
Salaries Payable	4 2 0 0 00	.59	4 0 0 0 00	.66
Total Current Liabilities	$ 100 6 0 0 00	14.21	$ 42 6 0 0 00	7.05
Long-term Liabilities:				
Bonds Payable, 6%, due Dec. 31, 19x9	$ 100 0 0 0 00	14.12	$ 100 0 0 0 00	16.54
Less Discount on Bonds Payable	2 2 0 0 00	.31	2 4 0 0 00	.40
Total Long-term Liabilities	$ 97 8 0 0 00	13.81	$ 97 6 0 0 00	16.15
Total Liabilities	$ 198 4 0 0 00	28.01	$ 140 2 0 0 00	23.19
Stockholders' Equity				
Paid-in Capital:				
Common Stock, $100 par (4,000 shares authorized, 3,000 shares issued)	$ 300 0 0 0 00	42.36	$ 300 0 0 0 00	49.63
Premium on Common Stock	86 0 0 0 00	12.14	86 0 0 0 00	14.22
Total Paid-in Capital	$ 386 0 0 0 00	54.50	$ 386 0 0 0 00	63.85
Retained Earnings:				
Appropriated for Plant Expansion	$ 20 0 0 0 00	2.82	$ 12 0 0 0 00	1.99
Unappropriated	103 8 0 0 00	14.66	66 3 0 0 00	10.97
Total Retained Earnings	$ 123 8 0 0 00	17.48	$ 78 3 0 0 00	12.95
Total Stockholders' Equity	$ 509 8 0 0 00	71.99	$ 464 3 0 0 00	76.81
Total Liabilities and Stockholders' Equity	$ 708 2 0 0 00	100.00	$ 604 5 0 0 00	100.00

Figure 27-4

Merchandise Inventory % = Merchandise Inventory ÷ Total Assets

$$\text{Merchandise Inventory \% (19x7)} = \frac{\$353,600}{\$708,200} = .4993 = 49.93\%$$

$$\text{Merchandise Inventory \% (19x6)} = \frac{\$206,500}{\$604,500} = .3416 = 34.16\%$$

One could also interpret the above percentages as follows.

19x7
- For every $100 in total assets, $2.77 is in the form of cash.
- For every $100 in total assets, $10.36 is in the form of accounts receivable.
- For every $100 in total assets, $49.93 is in the form of merchandise inventory.

19x6
- For every $100 in total assets, $6.40 was in the form of cash.
- For every $100 in total assets, $13.04 was in the form of accounts receivable.
- For every $100 in total assets, $34.16 was in the form of merchandise inventory.

These percentages accentuate Benson Athletic Supply's poor status with respect to Cash and Merchandise Inventory, as well as their favorable status with respect to Accounts Receivable. Other items that may strike a warning note are

- The percentage value of plant and equipment declined during 19x7.
- The percentage value of Accounts Payable more than doubled during 19x6.

Our illustrations show full income statements and balance sheets. But sometimes accountants give financial statements in condensed form and put the details in supporting schedules. In this case, the figures are taken from the supporting schedules, and the percentages are worked out the same way.

TREND PERCENTAGES

One may also use percentages to indicate trends or general directions that become evident only when one makes a comparison covering a period of years. Here is the way to calculate the percentages.

1. Select a representative year as the **base year.**
2. Label the base year 100 percent.
3. Express all other years as percentages of the base year.

Let us say that you have been able to cull the following figures from the income statements for Benson Athletic Supply for 19x3 through 19x7.

| | Year | | | | |
Item	19x3	19x4	19x5	19x6	19x7
Net Sales	$714,200	$782,380	$806,400	$848,600	$966,900
Cost of Merchandise Sold	466,150	519,180	540,300	568,800	657,700
Gross Profit	248,050	263,200	266,100	279,800	309,200

You establish 19x3 as the base year and calculate the trend percentages for Net Sales by dividing the Net Sales of each year by the Net Sales for 19x3.

For 19x4 $714,200\overline{)782,380} = 1.0954$

For 19x5 $714,200\overline{)806,400} = 1.1290$

For 19x6 $714,200\overline{)848,600} = 1.1881$

For 19x7 $714,200\overline{)966,900} = 1.3538$

You determine trend percentages for Cost of Merchandise Sold and Gross Profit in the same way. Here are the results, with the percentages rounded off to the nearest whole number.

| | Year | | | | |
Item	19x3	19x4	19x5	19x6	19x7
Net Sales	100%	110%	113%	119%	135%
Cost of Merchandise Sold	100%	111%	116%	122%	141%
Gross Profit	100%	106%	107%	113%	125%

Observe that over the five-year period, the trend of Net Sales is upward. However, Cost of Merchandise Sold is going up at a more rapid rate. In other words, over the five years, Cost of Merchandise Sold increased faster than Net Sales, resulting in smaller increases in Gross Profit. This is fine if it's the company's plan to achieve a greater volume of sales accompanied by more moderate profits. But if this shrinking Gross Profit is *not* consistent with company policy, then it may be a sign that the company is not passing along its increased costs to its customers.

INDUSTRY COMPARISONS

Vertical analysis, using percentage figures, is very useful when you wish to compare the figures for one company with the average figures for the given industry. Such comparisons are often referred to as **common-size statements,** since one expresses all items as percentages of a common base. Again, for the income statement, the common base is net sales. Net sales is set at 100 percent, and all other items are expressed as a percentage of net sales. Trade and marketing associations often gather information and publish common-size statements.

ANALYSIS BY CREDITORS AND MANAGEMENT

Because management is vitally interested in increasing the company's solvency and profitability, managers are concerned with all types of analytical tools and techniques. Because creditors want assurance of being repaid, they are concerned first with the company's solvency and second with its profitability.

How Do Short-term Creditors and Management Analyze an Enterprise?

Bankers and other short-term creditors are primarily interested in the *current* position of a given firm: Does the firm have enough money coming in to meet its current operating needs and to pay its current debts promptly? (*Current*, to them, means one year or the operating cycle, whichever is longer. This usage is consistent with the way accountants refer to "current assets" and "current liabilities.") Let us use as an example some calculations derived from the comparative financial statements of Benson Athletic Supply for 19x7 and 19x6.

Working Capital

As we stated previously, **working capital** is the excess of current assets over current liabilities. One determines the working capital for Benson Athletic Supply as shown in the following equations.

Working capital = Current assets − Current liabilities
Working capital (19x7) = $448,600 − $100,600 = $348,000
Working capital (19x6) = $326,100 − $42,600 = $283,500

Objective 3a

Compute working capital.

Benson Athletic Supply has $348,000 of capital available to work with during 19x7 versus $283,500 of capital available to work with during 19x6.

Current Ratio

The relationship of a company's current assets to its current liabilities is known as its **current ratio.** One arrives at this figure by dividing current assets by current liabilities.

$$\text{Current ratio} = \frac{\text{Current assets}}{\text{Current liabilities}}$$

Objective 3b

Compute
current ratio.

$$\text{Current ratio (19x7)} = \frac{\$448,600}{\$100,600} = 4.5:1$$

$$\text{Current ratio (19x6)} = \frac{\$326,100}{\$42,600} = 7.7:1$$

A firm's current ratio reveals its current debt-paying ability. Benson Athletic's current ratio of 4.5:1 in 19x7 indicates that there is $4.50 of cash coming in within a year from now for every dollar Benson Athletic Supply has to pay out within a year. But the firm was better off in 19x6, because in that year it had $7.70 coming in within the year for every dollar to be paid out within the year.

From the points of view of bankers and other credit grantors, the adequacy of a company's current ratio depends on what type of business the firm is in. A favorable ratio for a merchandising business is generally 2 to 1—higher if the type of merchandise the firm sells is subject to abrupt changes in style. But a public utility, which has no inventories other than supplies, is considered solvent even if its current ratio is less than 1 to 1. Due to the stability of the product involved in the athletic-supply business, a ratio of 4.5 to 1 for Benson Athletic Supply is satisfactory. (*Note:* If the company has changed inventory-valuation methods from one year to another—for example, if it has switched from FIFO to LIFO—a correction should be made in the costs of merchandise inventories; otherwise there is no common base for making a comparison.)

Quick Ratio

The relationship of a company's current assets that can be quickly converted into cash to its current liabilities is known as its **quick ratio** or **acid-test ratio. Quick assets** are cash, current notes receivable, net accounts receivable (that is, accounts receivable less allowance for doubtful accounts), interest receivable, and marketable securities. You don't count inventories and prepaid expenses because they are further removed from conversion into cash than are other current assets. You determine the quick ratio by dividing quick assets by current liabilities.

$$\text{Quick ratio} = \frac{\text{Quick assets}}{\text{Current liabilities}}$$

Objective 3c

Compute quick ratio.

$$\text{Quick ratio (19x7)} = \frac{\$19,600 + (\$76,700 - \$3,300)}{\$100,600} = \frac{\$93,000}{\$100,600} = .92:1$$

$$\text{Quick ratio (19x6)} = \frac{\$38,700 + (\$81,400 - \$2,600)}{\$42,600} = \frac{\$117,500}{\$42,600} = 2.76:1$$

Benson Athletic Supply's quick ratio of .92:1 in 19x7 indicates that there are 92 cents in cash coming in quickly—without involving the liquidation of inventory—for every dollar it has to pay out within a year. For 19x6, there was $2.76 that the firm could realize quickly for every dollar it had to pay out within a year.

A quick ratio of 1 to 1 is normally considered satisfactory. Therefore the quick ratio for Benson Athletic Supply exposes a precarious short-term financial position. One has to consider this quick ratio in conjunction with the company's working capital and its current ratio. Although working capital and current ratio are two indicators of a firm's ability to meet its current obligations, they don't reveal the *composition of its current assets*—a very important factor.

Relationship of Each Current Asset to Total Current Assets

Suppose that you are asked to find out the proportionate positions of each item in the list of current assets of Benson Athletic Supply. Your first step is to compile a schedule of each current asset as it relates to total current assets, as shown in the illustration below.

	DECEMBER 31, 19x7		DECEMBER 31, 19x6	
	AMOUNT	PERCENT	AMOUNT	PERCENT
Current Assets:				
Cash	$ 19 6 0 0 00	4.37	$ 38 7 0 0 00	11.87
Accounts Receivable (net)	73 4 0 0 00	16.36	78 8 0 0 00	24.17
Merchandise Inventory	353 6 0 0 00	78.82	206 5 0 0 00	63.32
Prepaid Insurance	2 0 0 0 00	.45	2 1 0 0 00	.64
Total Current Assets	$ 448 6 0 0 00	100.00	$ 326 1 0 0 00	100.00

As an example, the percentage of cash to total current assets is calculated like this:

$$\frac{\$19,600}{\$448,600} = .0437 = 4.37\%$$

We have already commented on the large increase in the proportion of merchandise inventory (it was 63 percent of current assets in 19x6, but amounts to 79 percent of current assets in 19x7). This change, coupled with the decline in the cash position (12 percent of current assets for 19x6, only 4 percent of current assets for 19x7), reinforces the message we got from the decline in the quick ratio, indicating that the firm may have a hard time paying its current debts.

Analysis of Accounts Receivable

Since money tied up in accounts receivable does not yield any revenue, any firm tries to collect accounts receivable promptly and to keep them at a minimum. It can use the cash it gets from collection of accounts receivable to reduce bank loans or to take advantage of cash discounts. This action reduces the amount of interest expense it has to pay and the cost of the merchandise it buys. Prompt collection also reduces the risk of loss from bad debts.

Accounts receivable turnover is the number of times charge accounts are turned over (or paid off) per year. A turnover implies a sale on account followed by payment of the debt in cash. One computes this by *dividing net sales on account by average net accounts receivable.* If possible, use the average of the monthly balances of accounts receivable, since this allows for seasonal fluctuations. If you haven't got figures for monthly balances, use the average of the balances at the beginning and the end of the previous year. Current notes receivable from customers are combined with accounts receivable. Here's how it looks for Benson Athletic Supply. (You would have to take the beginning balance of Accounts Receivable for 19x6 ($58,400) from the 19x5 balance sheet.)

Objective 3d

Compute accounts receivable turnover.

$$\text{Accounts receivable turnover} = \frac{\text{Net Sales on Account}}{\text{Average Accounts Receivable (net)}}$$

$$\frac{\text{Average}}{\text{Accounts Receivable}} = \frac{\text{Beginning Accounts Receivable} + \text{Ending Accounts Receivable}}{2}$$

$$\text{Accounts receivable turnover (19x7)} = \frac{\$773,020}{\dfrac{\$78,800 + \$73,400}{2}} = \frac{\$773,020}{\$76,100} = 10.16 \text{ times/yr.}$$

$$\text{Accounts receivable turnover (19x6)} = \frac{\$678,880}{\dfrac{\$58,400 + \$78,800}{2}} = \frac{\$678,880}{\$68,600} = 9.90 \text{ times/yr.}$$

You can use the accounts receivable turnover to determine the number of days that the receivables were on the books. Calculate this by dividing 365 days by the turnover figure.

$$\text{Year (19x7)} = \frac{365 \text{ days}}{10.16 \text{ times per year}} = 35.93 \text{ or } 36 \text{ days}$$

$$\text{Year (19x6)} = \frac{365 \text{ days}}{9.90 \text{ times per year}} = 36.87 \text{ or } 37 \text{ days}$$

It took an average of one day less in 19x7 to collect accounts receivable than it did in 19x6. This reduction represents a slight improvement in collections for Benson Athletic Supply. Since the company's credit terms are net 30 days, 36 or 37 days is reasonable.

Merchandise inventory turnover is the number of times a company's average inventory is sold during a given year. One calculates this by *dividing Cost of Merchandise Sold by average Merchandise Inventory*. Here is the calculation for Benson Athletic Supply.

Objective 3e

Compute merchandise inventory turnover.

$$\text{Merchandise inventory turnover} = \frac{\text{Cost of Merchandise Sold}}{\text{Average Merchandise Inventory}}$$

$$\begin{array}{l}\text{Average} \\ \text{Merchandise Inventory}\end{array} = \frac{\text{Beginning Merchandise Inventory} + \text{Ending Merchandise Inventory}}{2}$$

$$\text{Merchandise inventory turnover (19x7)} = \frac{\$657,700}{\dfrac{\$206,500 + \$353,600}{2}} = \frac{\$657,700}{\$280,050} = 2.35 \text{ times/yr.}$$

$$\text{Merchandise inventory turnover (19x6)} = \frac{\$568,800}{\dfrac{\$138,700 + \$206,500}{2}} = \frac{\$568,800}{\$172,600} = 3.30 \text{ times/yr.}$$

If possible, one should use the average of the monthly balances of Merchandise Inventory (add them and divide by 12). The figure for merchandise inventory turnover varies depending on the type of product involved. One can compare the figure for merchandise inventory turnover for one company with figures for the rest of the industry to use it as a test of merchandising efficiency. Each turnover yields a gross profit or markup to the company. Note that there has been a serious decline in the rate of merchandise inventory turnover for Benson Athletic Supply. This is something to watch.

One may also use the figure for the merchandise inventory turnover to determine the number of days that the merchandise was kept in stock. One calculates this the same way one calculates accounts receivable turnover, by dividing 365 days by the turnover figure.

$$\text{Year (19x7)} = \frac{365 \text{ days}}{2.35 \text{ times per year}} = 155 \text{ days}$$

$$\text{Year (19x6)} = \frac{365 \text{ days}}{3.30 \text{ times per year}} = 111 \text{ days}$$

Note that Benson Athletic Supply's merchandise remained in stock 44 days longer in 19x7 than it did in 19x6. This fact surely calls for an investigation of the company's sales and purchasing practices.

In addition to yielding a higher gross profit, rapid merchandise inventory turnover has other advantages: The money invested in the inventory is tied up for a shorter period of time; storage costs are lower; there is less risk of spoilage (if the merchandise is perishable); there is less risk of change in demand (if the merchandise is affected by changes in style or in business conditions).

How Do Long-term Creditors and Management Analyze an Enterprise?

Long-term creditors include mortgage holders and bondholders. Whenever specific property has been pledged or mortgaged, they have first claim on the property in the event that the company cannot keep up its payments. Even in the case of debentures (unsecured bonds), the bondholders have a prior claim to the general assets of the company, a claim that takes precedence over that of the stockholders. Management is concerned with the company's taking care of its present obligations, as well as preserving its credit standing, and hence its ability to borrow in the future.

Two ratios are particularly useful from the standpoint of long-term creditors.

- **Ratio of stockholders' equity to liabilities** When we speak of the ratio of stockholders' equity to liabilities, we are talking about the ratio of the stockholders' investment to the creditor's equity.

In calculating any ratio, we mean the ratio *of* one thing *to* something else. When we write the ratio as a fraction, we put the *of* part in the numerator and the *to* part in the denominator. Look at this calculation for Benson Athletic Supply.

$$\text{Ratio of stockholders' equity to liabilities (19x7)} = \frac{\$509,800}{\$198,400} = 2.57:1$$

$$\text{Ratio of stockholders' equity to liabilities (19x6)} = \frac{\$464,300}{\$140,200} = 3.31:1$$

Objective 3f

Compute ratio of stockholders' equity to liabilities.

In 19x7, for every $2.57 of stockholders' investment, the creditors have loaned $1. Benson Athletic Supply's ratio of stockholders' equity to liabilities shows a decline since 19x6, from 3.31:1 to 2.57:1. Creditors like to see a high proportion of stockholders' equity, because stockholders' equity, or owners' equity, acts as a buffer in case the company has to absorb losses. Also, owners often prefer a high proportion of equity to liabilities.

- **Ratio of plant and equipment to long-term liabilities** There is another factor that provides a margin of safety to mortgage holders and bond-holders—the ratio of the value of a firm's total plant and equipment to its long-term liabilities. This ratio also indicates the potential ability of the enterprise to borrow more money on a long-term basis. Let's look at the calculation for Benson Athletic Supply.

Objective 3g

Compute ratio of the value of plant and equipment to long-term liabilities.

$$\text{Ratio of plant and equipment to long-term liabilities} = \frac{\text{Plant and equipment}}{\text{Long-term liabilities}}$$

$$\text{Ratio of plant and equipment to long-term liabilities (19x7)} = \frac{\$190,800}{\$97,800} = 1.95$$

$$\text{Ratio of plant and equipment to long-term liabilities (19x6)} = \frac{\$209,200}{\$97,600} = 2.14$$

In 19x7 there is $1.95 book value of plant and equipment for every dollar of long-term liabilities. But in 19x6, there was $2.14 book value of plant and equipment for every dollar of long-term liabilities. So this figure, too, is less favorable.

As we have seen, a firm's creditors and managers may use eight devices to determine the financial position of a firm:

- Working capital
- Current ratio
- Quick ratio
- Relationship of each current asset to total current assets
- Accounts receivable turnover
- Merchandise inventory turnover
- Ratio of stockholders' equity to liabilities
- Ratio of plant and equipment to long-term liabilities

ANALYSIS BY OWNERS AND MANAGEMENT

In addition to being concerned about the solvency and the profitability of a company, the owners, as well as the managers, are vitally interested in the value and return on investment in the company. In many cases the owners are the managers. However, in other situations, managers are employed by the owners. What diagnostic tools do they use to determine the financial health of their company?

Equity per Share

When you examine the annual report of a corporation, you encounter the term *equity per share*—also referred to as *book value per share*. If a corporation has only one class of common stock outstanding, equity per share is determined by dividing the total stockholders' equity by the number of shares of stock issued. Here are the calculations for Benson Athletic Supply.

$$\text{Equity per share} = \frac{\text{Total stockholders' equity available to a class of stock}}{\text{Number of shares issued and outstanding}}$$

Objective 3h

Compute equity per share.

$$\text{Equity per share (19x7)} = \frac{\$509,800}{3,000 \text{ shares}} = \$169.93 \text{ per share}$$

$$\text{Equity per share (19x6)} = \frac{\$464,300}{3,000 \text{ shares}} = \$154.77 \text{ per share}$$

When there are shares of preferred stock outstanding, one must deduct the liquidation value, including any dividends in arrears on cumulative preferred stock to arrive at the stockholders' equity available to holders of common stock. (Remember that in the event of a firm's liquidation, holders of preferred stock are paid before holders of common stock.)

The term *equity per share* does *not* mean the cash value or market value of a share, but the amount that would be distributed per share of stock *if* the corporation were to **liquidate** (wind up its affairs by paying off its creditors and selling its assets for cash) without incurring any expenses, gains, or losses in selling its assets and paying its liabilities. The equity per share increases as a firm retains net income after taxes. This concept of equity per share is important in contracts involving the sale of stock. For example, a large stockholder might obtain an option to buy the shares of small stockholders at the value of the equity per share as of a certain future date.

Rate of Return on Common Stockholders' Equity

A corporation exists first and foremost to earn a net income for its stockholders. Therefore the rate of return on the common stockholders' equity is important as a means of measuring how good or bad the investment is. This rate is calculated by dividing the net income (after taxes) available to holders of common stock by the *average value* of their equity. Let's look at the calculation for Benson Athletic Supply.

Rate of return on common stockholders' equity

$$= \frac{\text{Net income available to common stock}}{\dfrac{\text{Beginning common stock equity} + \text{Ending common stock equity}}{2}}$$

Rate of return on common stockhold-ers' equity (19x7) $= \dfrac{\$54,140}{\dfrac{\$464,300 + \$509,800}{2}} = \dfrac{\$54,140}{\$487,050} = .1112 = 11.12\%$

Rate of return on common stockhold-ers' equity (19x6) $= \dfrac{\$52,040}{\dfrac{\$422,100 + \$464,300}{2}} = \dfrac{\$52,040}{\$443,200} = .1174 = 11.74\%$

This isn't much of a decline. However, management should look into the matter to uncover the possible causes. Again, one begins by looking hard at merchandise inventory, particularly since in this case it represents 49.93 percent of total assets.

Earnings per Share of Common Stock

You often see earnings per share of stock listed in financial columns of newspapers. If a corporation has no preferred stock outstanding, you compute the earnings per share of common stock by dividing net income (after taxes) by the average number of common stock shares outstanding during the year. When there is preferred stock, you must first deduct any dividends on preferred stock to arrive at the amount available to common stock (again, as you recall, because dividends on preferred are paid before those on common). Here is the calculation of earnings per share of common stock for Benson Athletic Supply.

$$\text{Earnings per share of common stock} = \frac{\text{Net income available to common stock}}{\text{Average number of shares of common stock outstanding}}$$

Earnings per share of common stock (19x7) $= \dfrac{\$54,140}{3,000 \text{ shares}} = \$18.05$

Earnings per share of common stock (19x6) $= \dfrac{\$52,040}{3,000 \text{ shares}} = \$17.35$

Any big change during the year in the *number* of shares outstanding naturally has a vital effect on the amount of earnings per share. That's why a company must consider the average number of shares outstanding and disclose any information relating to stock dividends and stock splits.

Price-Earnings Ratio

The **price-earnings ratio** is a measure commonly used to determine whether the market price of a corporation's stock is reasonable. The way you calculate the price-earnings ratio of a company's stock is to divide the market price per share by the annual earnings per share. Let's say that the market price of a share of common stock of Benson Athletic Supply at the end of 19x7 is $132, and that at the end of 19x6 it was $120. Here is how you figure out the price-earnings ratio.

Objective 3k

Compute price-earnings ratio.

$$\text{Price-earnings ratio} = \frac{\text{Market price per share}}{\text{Earnings per share}}$$

$$\text{Price-earnings ratio (19x7)} = \frac{\$132.00}{\$18.05} = 7.3 = 7.3:1$$

$$\text{Price-earnings ratio (19x6)} = \frac{\$120.00}{\$17.35} = 6.9 = 6.9:1$$

What constitutes a reasonable price-earnings ratio varies from one industry to another. Stocks quoted in the Dow Jones Average usually have about a 15:1 price-earnings ratio. Corporations that have shown a large continued growth in earnings over a period of years may have a ratio of more than 30:1.

You may also use the price-earnings ratio in this manner: If the acceptable price-earnings ratio for a given stock is 15:1 and the earnings per share equal $2.50, it follows that the maximum reasonable price you ought to pay for the stock is $37.50 (that is, $2.50 × 15). But what if the stock is selling for only $20? You may well consider it to be undervalued.

Summary of Ratios

As we have seen, there are many yardsticks with which to analyze and interpret financial statements.

Short-term creditors and management use the following techniques.

$$\text{Working capital} = \text{Current assets} - \text{Current liabilities}$$

$$\text{Current ratio} = \frac{\text{Current assets}}{\text{Current liabilities}}$$

$$\text{Quick ratio} = \frac{\text{Cash} + \text{Receivables} + \text{Marketable securities}}{\text{Current liabilities}}$$

$$\text{Accounts receivable turnover} = \frac{\text{Net Sales on Account}}{\text{Average Accounts Receivable}}$$

$$\text{Merchandise inventory turnover} = \frac{\text{Cost of Merchandise Sold}}{\text{Average Merchandise Inventory}}$$

Long-term creditors and management use the following ratios.

$$\text{Ratio of stockholders' equity to liabilities} = \frac{\text{Stockholders' equity}}{\text{Liabilities}}$$

$$\text{Ratio of plant and equipment to long-term liabilities} = \frac{\text{Plant and equipment}}{\text{Long-term liabilities}}$$

Owners and managers use the following measures.

$$\text{Equity per share} = \frac{\text{Total stockholders' equity available to a class of stock}}{\text{Number of shares issued and outstanding}}$$

$$\text{Rate of return on common stockholders' equity} = \frac{\text{Net income available to common stock}}{\text{Average common stock equity}}$$

$$\begin{array}{l}\text{Earnings per share} \\ \text{of common stock}\end{array} = \frac{\text{Net income available to common stock}}{\text{Average number of shares of common stock outstanding}}$$

$$\text{Price-earnings ratio} = \frac{\text{Market price per share}}{\text{Earnings per share}}$$

GLOSSARY

Accounts receivable turnover The number of times charge accounts are paid off per year; a turnover is a sale on account and subsequent repayment.

Acid-test ratio Same as quick ratio.

Base year The year used as a basis for comparison.

Common-size statements Financial statements using vertical analysis expressed as percentages, showing average industrywide figures for companies of similar size that produce the same product or service.

Current ratio Current assets divided by current liabilities.

Horizontal analysis Comparing the same item in the financial statements of an enterprise for two or more periods.

Liquidate To wind up the affairs of a business by paying off the creditors and selling the assets for cash.

Merchandise inventory turnover The number of times the merchandise inventory is turned over per year; a turnover is the purchase and subsequent sale of merchandise.

Price-earnings ratio Common measure for deciding whether a stock's price is reasonable; calculated by dividing the market price per share by the annual earnings per share.

Quick assets Assets consisting of cash, net accounts receivable, interest receivable, and marketable securities.

Quick ratio Quick assets divided by current liabilities.

Vertical analysis Portraying items in financial statements as percentages (or proportional parts) of a given item on the same financial statement.

Working capital The excess of current assets over current liabilities.

QUESTIONS, EXERCISES, AND PROBLEMS

Discussion Questions

1. What is the difference between a firm's solvency and its profitability?
2. In regard to comparative income statements, describe the difference between horizontal analysis and vertical analysis.
3. A firm has a gross profit percentage of 34 percent. What does this mean?
4. Define *common-size statement*.
5. Why is a high merchandise inventory turnover considered to be beneficial?
6. Which of the following types of business firms would you expect to have a high merchandise inventory turnover?

   a. Supermarket
   b. Jewelry store
   c. Art gallery
   d. Bakery
   e. Camera store

7. What does a decrease in the accounts receivable turnover rate indicate as far as a firm is concerned?

Exercises

Exercise 27-1   Calculate the percentages of increase and decrease for the following items.

	19x6	19x5
Cash	$27,000	$25,500
Notes Receivable	14,000	16,000
Equipment (net)	61,000	66,000
Retained Earnings	38,000	32,000

Exercise 27-2   Using the following revenue and expense data, prepare a comparative income statement, expressing each item for both 19x6 and 19x5 as a percentage of sales. Comment on the results.

	19x6	19x5
Sales (net)	$700,000	$600,000
Cost of Merchandise Sold	540,000	450,000
Selling Expenses	95,000	90,000
General Expenses	21,000	20,000
Income Tax	20,000	18,000

Exercise 27-3   Calculate trend percentages for the following items and comment on the trends. Use 19x2 as the base year.

	19x2	19x3	19x4	19x5
Sales (net)	$400,000	$440,000	$484,000	$516,000
Cost of Merchandise Sold	240,000	282,000	320,000	328,000
Merchandise Inventory	42,000	46,000	52,000	60,000

Exercise 27-4 The following data are taken from the financial statements of the Harris Company.

	19x6	19x5
Sales (net on account)	$450,000	$400,000
Cost of Merchandise Sold	340,000	320,000
Merchandise Inventory (at end of year)	70,000	66,000
Accounts Receivable (at end of year)	60,600	52,000

All sales are on a credit basis. Compute the following for 19x6.

a. Percentage of gross profit
b. Accounts receivable turnover
c. Merchandise inventory turnover

Exercise 27-5 The following items are from the balance sheet of the Jackson Company.

Cash	$ 72,000
Marketable Securities	31,000
Accounts Receivable (net)	236,000
Merchandise Inventory	84,000
Prepaid Expenses	3,000
Accounts Payable	120,000
Notes Payable	11,000
Salaries Payable	1,000

Compute the following.

a. Working capital
b. Current ratio
c. Quick ratio

Exercise 27-6 The following items are taken from the financial statements of the Ireland Company. All sales are made on account.

Sales (net on account)	$1,200,000
Total Assets	1,600,000
Total Liabilities	600,000
Net Income	96,000
Average Accounts Receivable	250,000
Average Merchandise Inventory	170,000
Gross Profit	350,000

Compute the following.

a. Accounts receivable turnover
b. Merchandise inventory turnover
c. Rate earned on total assets
d. Rate earned on stockholders' equity

Exercise 27-7   The following items are from the balance sheets of the C. C. Myerson Company as of December 31, 19x5, and December 31, 19x6.

	19x6	19x5
Current Assets:		
Cash, Marketable Securities, and Receivables (net)	$120,000	$108,000
Merchandise Inventory	180,000	156,000
Total Current Assets	$300,000	$264,000
Current Liabilities	$150,000	$120,000

Calculate the following for each year and comment on the company's comparative financial position.

a. Working capital
b. Current ratio
c. Quick ratio

Exercise 27-8   The Stockholders' Equity section of the balance sheet of the Patrick Corporation is as follows.

Stockholders' Equity			
Paid-in Capital:			
Common Stock, $5 par (50,000			
shares authorized, 40,000 shares			
issued and outstanding)	$ 200 0 0 0 00		
Premium on Common Stock	60 0 0 0 00		
Total Paid-in Capital	$ 260 0 0 0 00		
Retained Earnings	140 0 0 0 00		
Total Stockholders' Equity		400 0 0 0 00	

Net income (after tax) for the year is $64,000. The present market price of the stock is $24 per share. Determine the following.

a. Equity per share
b. Earnings per share
c. Price-earnings ratio
d. Rate of return on stockholders' equity

Problem Set A

Problem 27-1A   During 19x6 Drefus Fabrics put on a big sales promotion campaign that cost them $9,600 more than they usually spent for advertising. Here is the condensed comparative income statement for the fiscal years ended December 31, 19x5, and December 31, 19x6.

Drefus Fabrics
Comparative Income Statement
For years ended December 31, 19x6, and December 31, 19x5

	19x6	19x5
Revenue from Sales:		
Sales	$ 235 2 8 0 00	$ 173 0 0 0 00
Less Sales Returns and Allowances	18 2 0 0 00	13 0 0 0 00
Net Sales	$ 217 0 8 0 00	$ 160 0 0 0 00
Cost of Merchandise Sold	139 0 8 0 00	97 6 0 0 00
Gross Profit	$ 78 0 0 0 00	$ 62 4 0 0 00
Operating Expenses:		
Selling Expenses	$ 44 9 8 0 00	$ 34 6 0 0 00
General Expenses	11 2 2 0 00	10 2 0 0 00
Total Operating Expenses	$ 56 2 0 0 00	$ 44 8 0 0 00
Income from Operations	$ 21 8 0 0 00	$ 17 6 0 0 00
Other Expense	2 8 0 00	2 0 0 00
Net Income	$ 21 5 2 0 00	$ 17 4 0 0 00

Instructions

Using horizontal analysis, prepare a comparative income statement for the two-year period. Round off percentages to the nearest whole percent (two decimal places).

Problem 27-2A   Use the comparative income statement for Drefus Fabrics (Problem 27-1A).

Instructions

Using vertical analysis, prepare a comparative income statement for the two-year period. Round off percentages to the nearest whole percent (two decimal places).

Problem 27-3A   The year-end financial statements of Houston Electric, Inc., are shown on the next two pages.

Houston Electric, Inc.
Income Statement
For year ended December 31, 19x7

Revenue from Sales:				
Sales			$ 540 0 0 0 00	
Cost of Merchandise Sold:				
Merchandise Inventory, Jan. 1, 1987	$ 80 0 0 0 00			
Purchases	336 4 0 0 00			
Merchandise Available for Sale	$ 416 4 0 0 00			
Less Merchandise Inventory, Dec. 31, 1987	88 6 0 0 00			
Cost of Merchandise Sold		327 8 0 0 00		
Gross Profit		$ 212 2 0 0 00		
Operating Expenses:				
Selling Expenses (control)	$ 112 5 0 0 00			
General Expenses (control)	55 3 0 0 00			
Total Operating Expenses		167 8 0 0 00		
Income from Operations		$ 44 4 0 0 00		
Other Expense:				
Interest Expense		7 6 0 0 00		
Net Income before Income Tax		$ 36 8 0 0 00		
Income Tax		10 9 0 0 00		
Net Income after Income Tax		$ 25 9 0 0 00		

Houston Electric, Inc.
Balance Sheet
December 31, 19x7

Assets			
Current Assets:			
Cash	$ 14 2 0 0 00		
Notes Receivable	4 0 0 0 00		
Accounts Receivable (net)	51 8 0 0 00		
Merchandise Inventory	88 6 0 0 00		
Prepaid Expenses	1 2 0 0 00		
Total Current Assets		$ 159 8 0 0 00	
Plant and Equipment:			
Delivery Equipment (net)	$ 49 7 0 0 00		
Store Equipment (net)	30 9 0 0 00		
Office Equipment (net)	9 4 0 0 00		
Total Plant and Equipment		90 0 0 0 00	
Total Assets		$ 249 8 0 0 00	

(continued on next page)

Liabilities				
Current Liabilities:				
Notes Payable	$ 2 4 0 0 00			
Accounts Payable	33 8 0 0 00			
Total Current Liabilities		$ 36 2 0 0 00		
Long-term Liabilities:				
Mortgage Payable (due June 30, 1998)		76 8 0 0 00		
Total Liabilities			$ 113 0 0 0 00	
Stockholder's Equity				
Common Stock, $10 par (10,000 shares				
authorized, issued, and outstanding)		$ 100 0 0 0 00		
Retained Earnings		36 8 0 0 00		
Total Stockholder's Equity			136 8 0 0 00	
Total Liabilities and Stockholders' Equity			$ 249 8 0 0 00	

Instructions

Determine the following, showing the figures you used in your calculations (round off to two decimal places).

1. Working capital
2. Current ratio
3. Quick ratio
4. Merchandise inventory turnover
5. Number of days merchandise inventory kept in stock
6. Rate earned on stockholders' equity
7. Earnings per share of common stock

Problem 27-4A Here is the condensed comparative income statement of the Danville Corporation.

Danville Corporation
Comparative Income Statement
For years ended December 31, 19x5, 19x6, 19x7 (thousands of dollars)

	19x5	19x6	19x7
Sales (net)	$8 0 0 0 00	$8 8 0 0 00	$10 0 0 0 00
Cost of Merchandise Sold	5 7 0 0 00	6 4 0 0 00	7 5 0 0 00
Gross Profit	$2 3 0 0 00	$2 4 0 0 00	$ 2 5 0 0 00
Operating Expenses:			
Selling Expenses	$1 1 8 4 00	$1 2 7 7 00	$ 1 3 4 4 00
General Expenses	7 8 0 00	7 8 0 00	7 8 6 00
Total Operating Expenses	$1 9 6 4 00	$2 0 5 7 00	$ 2 1 3 0 00
Net Income before Income Tax	$ 3 3 6 00	$ 3 4 3 00	$ 3 7 0 00
Income Tax	1 4 9 00	1 5 2 00	$ 1 6 5 00
Net Income after Income Tax	$ 1 8 7 00	$ 1 9 1 00	$ 2 0 5 00

Instructions

1. Express the income statement data in trend percentages.
2. Comment on any significant relationships revealed by the percentages.

Problem Set B

Problem 27-1B   During 19x6 Seaque Marina put on a big sales promotion campaign that cost them $6,000 more than they usually spent for advertising. Here we see the condensed comparative income statement for the fiscal years ended December 31, 19x6, and December 31, 19x5.

Seaque Marina
Comparative Income Statement
For years ended December 31, 19x6, and December 31, 19x5

	19x6	19x5
Revenue from Sales:		
Sales	$ 213 8 4 0 00	$ 162 0 0 0 00
Less Sales Returns and Allowances	17 5 2 0 00	12 0 0 0 00
Net Sales	$ 196 3 2 0 00	$ 150 0 0 0 00
Cost of Merchandise Sold	$ 111 5 1 0 00	$ 88 5 0 0 00
Gross Profit	$ 84 8 1 0 00	$ 61 5 0 0 00
Operating Expenses:		
Selling Expenses	$ 37 4 4 8 00	$ 30 2 0 0 00
General Expenses	11 0 4 0 00	9 6 0 0 00
Total Operating Expenses	$ 48 4 8 8 00	$ 39 8 0 0 00
Income from Operations	$ 36 3 2 2 00	$ 21 7 0 0 00
Other Expense	3 7 5 00	3 0 0 00
Net Income	$ 35 9 4 7 00	$ 21 4 0 0 00

Instructions

Using horizontal analysis, prepare a comparative income statement for the two-year period. Round off percentages to the nearest whole percent (two decimal places).

Problem 27-2B   Use the comparative income statement for Seaque Marina (Problem 27-1B).

Instructions

Using vertical analysis, prepare a comparative income statement for the two-year period. Round off percentages to the nearest whole percent (two decimal places).

Problem 27-3B The year-end financial statements of Bender Company, Inc., are shown on this page and the next.

<table>
<tr><td colspan="4" align="center">*Bender Company, Inc.*
Income Statement
For year ended December 31, 19x7</td></tr>
<tr><td>Revenue from Sales:</td><td></td><td></td><td></td></tr>
<tr><td>Sales</td><td></td><td>$ 470 0 0 0 00</td><td></td></tr>
<tr><td>Cost of Merchandise Sold:</td><td></td><td></td><td></td></tr>
<tr><td>Merchandise Inventory, Jan. 1, 19x7</td><td>$ 76 0 0 0 00</td><td></td><td></td></tr>
<tr><td>Purchases</td><td>306 8 0 0 00</td><td></td><td></td></tr>
<tr><td>Merchandise Available for Sale</td><td>$ 382 8 0 0 00</td><td></td><td></td></tr>
<tr><td>Less Merchandise Inventory,
December 31, 19x7</td><td>81 2 0 0 00</td><td></td><td></td></tr>
<tr><td>Cost of Merchandise Sold</td><td></td><td>301 6 0 0 00</td><td></td></tr>
<tr><td>Gross Profit</td><td></td><td>$ 168 4 0 0 00</td><td></td></tr>
<tr><td>Operating Expenses:</td><td></td><td></td><td></td></tr>
<tr><td>Selling Expenses (control)</td><td>$ 92 7 0 0 00</td><td></td><td></td></tr>
<tr><td>General Expenses (control)</td><td>$ 46 2 0 0 00</td><td></td><td></td></tr>
<tr><td>Total Operating Expenses</td><td></td><td>138 9 0 0 00</td><td></td></tr>
<tr><td>Income from Operations</td><td></td><td>$ 29 5 0 0 00</td><td></td></tr>
<tr><td>Other Expense:</td><td></td><td></td><td></td></tr>
<tr><td>Interest Expense</td><td></td><td></td><td></td></tr>
<tr><td>Net Income before Income Tax</td><td></td><td>5 2 0 0 00</td><td></td></tr>
<tr><td>Income Tax</td><td></td><td>$ 24 3 0 0 00</td><td></td></tr>
<tr><td>Net Income after Income Tax</td><td></td><td>5 5 0 0 00</td><td></td></tr>
<tr><td></td><td></td><td>$ 18 8 0 0 00</td><td></td></tr>
</table>

Instructions

Determine the following, showing the figures you used in your calculations (round off to two decimal places).

1. Working capital
2. Current ratio
3. Quick ratio
4. Merchandise inventory turnover
5. Number of days merchandise inventory kept in stock
6. Rate earned on stockholders' equity
7. Earnings per share of common stock

Bender Company, Inc.
Balance Sheet
December 31, 19x7

Assets			
Current Assets:			
Cash	$ 11 5 0 0 00		
Notes Receivable	4 0 0 0 00		
Accounts Receivable (net)	53 7 0 0 00		
Merchandise Inventory	81 2 0 0 00		
Prepaid Expenses	1 4 0 0 00		
Total Current Assets		$ 151 8 0 0 00	
Plant and Equipment:			
Delivery Equipment (net)	$ 51 4 0 0 00		
Store Equipment (net)	31 2 0 0 00		
Office Equipment (net)	9 1 0 0 00		
Total Plant and Equipment		91 7 0 0 00	
Total Assets		$ 243 5 0 0 00	
Liabilities			
Current Liabilities:			
Notes Payable	$ 2 0 0 0 00		
Accounts Payable	21 5 0 0 00		
Total Current Liabilities		$ 23 5 0 0 00	
Long-term Liabilities:			
Mortgage Payable (due June 30, 1998)		80 0 0 0 00	
Total Liabilities		$ 103 5 0 0 00	
Stockholders' Equity			
Common Stock, $10 par (10,000 shares authorized, issued, and outstanding)		$ 100 0 0 0 00	
Retained Earnings		40 0 0 0 00	
Total Stockholders' Equity		$ 140 0 0 0 00	
Total Liabilities and Stockholders' Equity		$ 243 5 0 0 00	

Problem 27-4B The condensed comparative income statement of the Pitcher Robotics Corporation is shown below.

Pitcher Robotics Corporation
Comparative Income Statement
For years ended December 31, 19x5, 19x6, 19x7 (thousands of dollars)

	19x5	19x6	19x7
Sales (net)	$6 2 0 0 00	$6 8 0 0 00	$7 6 0 0 00
Cost of Merchandise Sold	4 4 0 0 00	4 9 6 0 00	5 6 3 0 00
Gross Profit	$1 8 0 0 00	$1 8 4 0 00	$1 9 7 0 00
Operating Expenses			
Selling Expenses	$ 9 3 0 00	$ 9 4 2 00	$1 0 5 4 00
General Expenses	6 1 0 00	6 2 0 00	6 2 0 00
Total Operating Expenses	$1 5 4 0 00	$1 5 6 2 00	$1 6 7 4 00
Net Income before Income Tax	$ 2 6 0 00	$ 2 7 8 00	$ 2 9 6 00
Income Tax	1 1 4 00	1 2 2 00	1 3 0 00
Net Income after Income Tax	$ 1 4 6 00	$ 1 5 6 00	$ 1 6 6 00

Instructions

1. Express the income statement data in trend percentages.
2. Comment on any significant relationships revealed by the percentages.

28 Statement of Changes in Financial Position

Learning Objectives

After you have completed this chapter, you will be able to do the following:

1. Demonstrate an understanding of the nature and purpose of a statement of changes in financial position.

2. Demonstrate how to collect and organize data to be used in a statement of changes in financial position.

3. Prepare a statement of changes in financial position.

First, let us review the basic financial statements that have been presented.

- **Income statement** Portrays the results of operations of an enterprise during a fiscal period (revenue minus expenses)
- **Statement of owner's equity** Portrays the changes that have taken place in the owner's investment during a fiscal period (beginning investment plus net income minus withdrawals or dividends)
- **Balance sheet** Portrays the financial condition or position of an enterprise at the end of a fiscal period (status of assets, liabilities, and owner's or stockholders' equity)

In this chapter, we introduce another major financial statement, the statement of changes in financial position. According to generally accepted accounting principles, this statement should be presented along with the other principal financial statements.

FINANCIAL POSITION

Financial position is frequently measured by the excess of a firm's current assets over its current liabilities. This excess is also defined as the firm's working capital. In other words, as we stated previously, **working capital equals current assets minus current liabilities.** Recall that current assets represent cash or other items that can be converted into cash within one year, and current liabilities represent debts that must be paid within one year. As a result, working capital is the excess of the amount coming in within one year (collectible) over the amount going out within one year (payable), or the amount of capital that the firm has available to work with or use.

Working capital = Current assets − Current liabilities

- If current assets increase, then working capital increases.
- If current assets decrease, then working capital decreases.
- If current liabilities increase, then working capital decreases.
- If current liabilities decrease, then working capital increases.

STATEMENT OF CHANGES IN FINANCIAL POSITION

The **statement of changes in financial position** explains in detail how working capital has changed between the beginning and the end of the fiscal period. Some accountants refer to the statement of changes in finan-

Objective 1

Demonstrate an understanding of the nature and purpose of a statement of changes in financial position.

cial position as being the "where got, where gone" statement of working capital. The statement is also referred to as a statement of sources and applications of funds; in this case, *funds* is interpreted broadly to mean working capital. (A statement of changes in cash is an alternative format to the working capital format, although it is not specifically addressed in this text.) At any rate, we are concerned with changes in current assets and current liabilities, as opposed to changes in cash only. This concern stems from the fact that in a typical operating cycle the majority of business transactions are completed on a credit basis, as shown in Figure 28-1.

In preparing a statement of changes in financial position, four steps should be followed.

Objective 2

Demonstrate how to collect and organize data to be used in a statement of changes in financial position.

1. Calculate the amount of working capital at the beginning and the end of the fiscal period; next, find the amount of the difference.
2. Prepare a schedule of increases and decreases in current asset and current liability accounts. Verify the amount of the change in working capital determined in step 1.
3. Prepare the Sources and Uses of Working Capital section of the statement of changes in financial position.
4. Prepare the Changes in Components of Working Capital section of the statement of changes in financial position, using as a basis the schedule of increases and decreases in current asset and current liability accounts prepared in step 2.

Figure 28-1

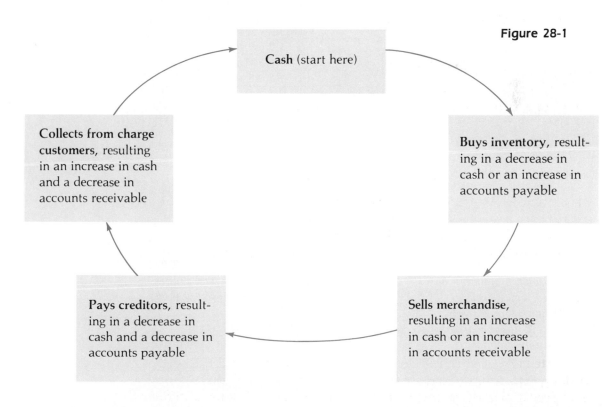

These four steps will be explained in detail in the rest of the chapter.

We will demonstrate how to prepare a statement of changes in financial position through three examples.

Objective 3

Prepare a statement of changes in financial position.

First Example

Suppose that J. Binnion started a business, Binnion Company, on January 1 by originally investing $50,000 in cash. Also assume that later during the year Binnion invested an additional $10,000 in cash. Figure 28-2 presents the financial statements of the business at the end of the year (December 31) in abbreviated form.

Figure 28-2

Binnion Company
Income Statement
For year ended December 31, 19x7

Sales (net)		$85 0 0 0 00
Cost of Merchandise Sold:		
Purchases (net)	$62 0 0 0 00	
Less Merchandise Inventory, December 31	14 0 0 0 00	
Cost of Merchandise Sold		48 0 0 0 00
Gross Profit		$37 0 0 0 00
Operating Expenses		
Wages Expense	$10 0 0 0 00	
Rent Expense	5 0 0 0 00	
Depreciation Expense, Equipment	3 0 0 0 00	
Miscellaneous Expense	2 0 0 0 00	
Total Expenses		20 0 0 0 00
Net Income		$17 0 0 0 00

Binnion Company
Statement of Owner's Equity
For year ended December 31, 19x7

J. Binnion, Capital, January 1		$50 0 0 0 00
Additional Investment, July 1		10 0 0 0 00
Total Investment		$60 0 0 0 00
Net Income for the year	$17 0 0 0 00	
Less Withdrawals during the year	12 0 0 0 00	
Increase in Capital		5 0 0 0 00
J. Binnion, Capital, December 31		$65 0 0 0 00

Figure 28-2
(continued)

Binnion Company
Comparative Balance Sheet
December 31, 19x7

	END OF YEAR	BEGINNING OF YEAR
Assets		
Current Assets:		
Cash	$11 0 0 0 00	$50 0 0 0 00
Accounts Receivable	18 0 0 0 00	
Merchandise Inventory	14 0 0 0 00	
Total Current Assets	$43 0 0 0 00	$50 0 0 0 00
Plant and Equipment:		
Equipment	$30 0 0 0 00	
Less Accumulated Depreciation	3 0 0 0 00	
Total Plant and Equipment	$27 0 0 0 00	
Total Assets	$70 0 0 0 00	$50 0 0 0 00
Liabilities		
Current Liabilities:		
Accounts Payable	$ 5 0 0 0 00	
Owner's Equity		
J. Binnion, Capital	65 0 0 0 00	$50 0 0 0 00
Total Liabilities and Owner's Equity	$70 0 0 0 00	$50 0 0 0 00

Step 1 Determine the amount of the change in working capital between the beginning of the year and the end of the year. Since this is Binnion's first year of operations, the working capital at the beginning of the year happens to be the original investment. The working capital at the end of the year is based on the year-end balance sheet. The change in working capital is calculated as follows.

Beginning of Year

Current assets:	
Cash	$50,000
Total current assets	$50,000
Less current liabilities	0
Working capital	$50,000

End of Year

Current assets:	
Cash	$11,000
Accounts Receivable	18,000
Merchandise Inventory	14,000
Total current assets	$43,000
Less current liabilities:	
Accounts Payable	5,000
Working capital	$38,000

Changes in working capital:

Working capital (ending)	$38,000
Less working capital (beginning)	50,000
Decrease in working capital	$12,000

Step 2   On scratch paper, prepare a schedule of increases and decreases in the current asset and current liability accounts. Then verify the amount of the change in working capital determined in step 1, which was $12,000.

Change in Current Accounts	Balance at End of Year	Balance at Beginning of Year	Increase or (Decrease) in the Account	Increase or (Decrease) in Working Capital
Increase (decrease) in current assets:				
Cash	$11,000	$50,000	($39,000)	($39,000)
Accounts Receivable	18,000	0	18,000	18,000
Merchandise Inventory	14,000	0	14,000	14,000
Increase (decrease) in current liabilities:				
Accounts Payable	5,000	0	5,000	(5,000)
Net increase (decrease) in working capital				($12,000)

At this point, the $12,000 decrease in working capital has been verified.

Figure 28-3 presents a statement of changes in financial position. In the following discussion of the individual sections of the statement, you will recognize that all of our calculations verify the amount of the change in working capital.

Sources of Working Capital

As you know, revenue minus expenses equals net income. On the income statement, revenue takes the form of an increase in cash or an increase in accounts receivable; both result in an increase in working capital. Expenses are in the form either of a decrease in cash or an increase in accounts payable, both resulting in a decrease, or use of, working capital. Therefore, net income represents an increase or source of working capital. **Net income will always be a source of working capital.** It only has to be recognized.

Figure 28-3

Binnion Company
Statement of Changes in Financial Position
For year ended December 31, 19x7

Sources of Working Capital:			
Operations during the year:			
Net income	$ 17 0 0 0 00		
Add expenses not requiring			
decreases in working capital			
Depreciation Expense, Equipment	3 0 0 0 00	$20 0 0 0 00	
Additional investment by owner		10 0 0 0 00	
Total Sources of Working Capital		$30 0 0 0 00	
Uses of Working Capital:			
Purchase of equipment	$ 30 0 0 0 00		
Withdrawals by owner	12 0 0 0 00		
Total Uses of Working Capital		42 0 0 0 00	
Decrease in Working Capital		$ 12 0 0 0 00	
Changes in Components of Working Capital:			
Increases (decreases) in Current Assets:			
Cash	$ (39 0 0 0 00)		
Accounts Receivable	18 0 0 0 00		
Merchandise Inventory	14 0 0 0 00	$(7 0 0 0 00)	
Increases (decreases) in Current Liabilities:			
Accounts Payable	5 0 0 0 00	5 0 0 0 00	
Decrease in Working Capital		$12 0 0 0 00	

Recognizing net income sounds simple, but it is not quite as straightforward as one might think. Certain expenses that reduce net income *do not* reduce working capital. Let's take depreciation. As you know, Depreciation Expense is deducted from revenue along with the other expenses of the business. But does Depreciation Expense reduce working capital? You will recall that we referred to this expense as an internal transaction. *Depreciation Expense was not paid to anyone.* No cash left the business, and no liabilities were increased.

How does this characteristic of Depreciation Expense (and certain other internal transactions) affect our calculation of working capital? After we arrive at Net Income, we must add back the amount of depreciation taken during the year. Remember, also, that while depreciation is listed as a source of working capital, no cash or other assets flow into the business; no liabilities are decreased. The business cannot *pay for* anything with depreciation. Depreciation allows us to match revenues with their related costs, but it does not bring new funds into the business.

Other sources of working capital do increase current assets. One example is an additional investment by the owner. If the owner invests cash, the entry to record the transaction is a debit to Cash and a credit to Capital. A current asset account is increased, but there is no corresponding increase in a current liability.

Uses of Working Capital

If being on the alert for certain kinds of transactions helps us to identify sources of working capital, what can we look for to identify *uses* of working capital? We can look for changes in long-term assets, long-term liabilities, and equity accounts. Let's look at a few typical transactions.

If the purchase of equipment is recorded as a debit to Equipment and a credit to Cash, this transaction results in a decrease in working capital. A current asset was decreased without a corresponding change in a current liability. Recording this transaction as a debit to Equipment and a credit to Accounts Payable also decreases working capital. A current liability was increased without a corresponding increase in a current asset.

A withdrawal by the owner is recorded as a debit to Drawing and a credit to Cash. This transaction decreases working capital. A current asset was decreased, but there was no corresponding change in a current liability.

Please observe that all of the transactions described above have one thing in common: **One side of the transaction (debit or credit) involves a current asset or current liability, and the other side of the transaction (debit or credit) involves a noncurrent asset or noncurrent liability.**

Here are three examples.

a. Bought equipment for cash, $30,000.

Equipment (noncurrent account)	30 0 0 0 00	
Cash (current account)		30 0 0 0 00

b. Bought equipment on account, $30,000.

Equipment (noncurrent account)	30 0 0 0 00	
Accounts Payable (current account)		30 0 0 0 00

c. Owner withdrew cash for personal use, $12,000.

| J. Binnion, Drawing (noncurrent account) | 12 0 0 0 00 | |
| Cash (current account) | | 12 0 0 0 00 |

Changes in Components of Working Capital

On scratch paper you have previously prepared a schedule of increases and decreases in current asset and current liability accounts. This schedule serves as the basis for the lower part of the official statement of changes in financial position.

Second Example

The abbreviated financial statements of Justice Corporation are presented in Figure 28-4.

Figure 28-4

Justice Corporation
Income Statement
For year ended December 31, 19x7

Revenue:			
Sales (net)			$ 900 0 0 0 00
Cost of Merchandise Sold:			
Merchandise Inventory, January 1, 19x7	$ 128 0 0 0 00		
Purchases (net)	698 0 0 0 00		
Merchandise Available for Sale	$ 826 0 0 0 00		
Less Merchandise Inventory,			
December 31, 19x7	126 0 0 0 00		
Cost of Merchandise Sold		700 0 0 0 00	
Gross Profit		$ 200 0 0 0 00	
Operating Expenses:			
Wages Expense	$ 103 2 0 0 00		
Depreciation Expense, Building	8 0 0 0 00		
Depreciation Expense, Equipment	5 2 0 0 00		
Bad Debt Expense	3 0 0 0 00		
Supplies Expense	2 0 0 0 00		
Miscellaneous Expense	4 0 0 0 00		
Total Operating Expenses		125 4 0 0 00	
Income from Operations		$ 74 6 0 0 00	
Other Expenses:			
Interest Expense		15 0 0 0 00	
Net Income		$ 59 6 0 0 00	

Figure 28-4
(continued)

Justice Corporation
Statement of Retained Earnings
For year ended December 31, 19x7

Retained Earnings, January 1, 19x7						$50	4	0 0	00
Net income for the year	$59	6	0 0	00					
Less dividends declared	47	4	0 0	00					
Increase in Retained Earnings						12	2	0 0	00
Retained Earnings, December 31, 19x7						$62	6	0 0	00

Justice Corporation
Comparative Balance Sheet
December 31, 19x7 and December 31, 19x6

	19x7	19x6
Assets		
Current Assets:		
Cash	$ 30 0 0 0 00	$ 19 2 0 0 00
Accounts Receivable	32 0 0 0 00	38 0 0 0 00
Less Allowance for Doubtful		
Accounts	1 1 0 0 00	1 2 0 0 00
Merchandise Inventory	126 0 0 0 00	128 0 0 0 00
Supplies	4 0 0 0 00	4 8 0 0 00
Total Current Assets	$ 190 9 0 0 00	$ 188 8 0 0 00
Plant and Equipment:		
Equipment	$ 116 8 0 0 00	$ 100 0 0 0 00
Less Accumulated Depreciation	24 4 0 0 00	19 2 0 0 00
Building	320 0 0 0 00	320 0 0 0 00
Less Accumulated Depreciation	24 0 0 0 00	16 0 0 0 00
Land	80 0 0 0 00	80 0 0 0 00
Total Plant and Equipment	$ 468 4 0 0 00	$ 464 8 0 0 00
Total Assets	$ 659 3 0 0 00	$ 653 6 0 0 00
Liabilities		
Current Liabilities:		
Notes Payable	$ 9 0 0 0 00	$ 8 0 0 0 00
Mortgage Payable (current portion)	16 0 0 0 00	16 0 0 0 00
Accounts Payable	66 8 0 0 00	78 4 0 0 00
Wages Payable	9 0 0 00	8 0 0 00
Total Current Liabilities	$ 92 7 0 0 00	$ 103 2 0 0 00
Long-term Liabilities:		
Mortgage Payable	184 0 0 0 00	200 0 0 0 00
Total Liabilities	$ 276 7 0 0 00	$ 303 2 0 0 00
Stockholders' Equity		
Common Stock, $100 par (4,000 shares authorized, 3,200 shares issued)	$ 320 0 0 0 00	$ 300 0 0 0 00
Retained Earnings	62 6 0 0 00	50 4 0 0 00
Total Liabilities and Stockholders' Equity	$ 659 3 0 0 00	$ 653 6 0 0 00

Step 1 Determine the amount of the change in working capital between the beginning and the end of the year.

	19x7	19x6
Current assets	$190,900	$188,800
Less current liabilities	92,700	103,200
Working capital	$ 98,200	$ 85,600

Increase in working capital 19x7 over 19x6 = $12,600 ($98,200 − $85,600).

Step 2 On scratch paper, prepare a schedule of increases and decreases in the current asset and current liabilities accounts.

Change in Current Accounts	19x7	19x6	Increase or (Decrease) in the Account	Increase or (Decrease) in Working Capital
Increase (decrease) in current assets:				
Cash	$ 30,000	$ 19,200	$10,800	$10,800
Accounts Receivable (net)	30,900	36,800	(5,900)	(5,900)
Merchandise Inventory	126,000	128,000	(2,000)	(2,000)
Supplies	4,000	4,800	(800)	(800)
Increase (decrease) in current liabilities:				
Notes Payable	9,000	8,000	1,000	(1,000)
Mortgage Payable (current portion)	16,000	16,000	—	—
Accounts Payable	66,800	78,400	(11,600)	11,600
Wages Payable	900	800	100	(100)
Increase in working capital				$12,600

As mentioned previously, the above schedule is used to complete the changes in the components of working capital section (second part) of the statement of changes in financial position, as shown in Figure 28-5.

Step 3 Prepare the sources and uses section of a statement of changes in financial position. In doing this, we can consider net income to be a regular item that is added to the sources of working capital; conversely, a net loss is deducted. Depreciation expense is always added to the sources of working capital. Finally, cash dividends (either declared or paid) or withdrawals are always listed as uses of working capital. In other words, net income, depreciation and dividends are regular recurring items; it is simply a matter of spotting them in the financial statements.

Figure 28-5

Justice Corporation
Statement of Changes in Financial Position
For year ended December 31, 19x7

Sources of Working Capital:			
Operations during the year:			
Net income	$59 600 00		
Add expenses not requiring			
decreases in working capital:			
Depreciation Expense, Building	8 000 00		
Depreciation Expense, Equipment	5 200 00	$72 800 00	
Sale of common stock		20 000 00	
Total Sources of Working Capital		$92 800 00	
Uses of Working Capital:			
Purchase of equipment	$16 800 00		
Decrease in mortgage payable	16 000 00		
Declaration of cash dividend	47 400 00		
Total Uses of Working Capital		80 200 00	
Increases in Working Capital		$12 600 00	
Changes in Components of Working Capital:			
Increases (decreases) in Current Assets:			
Cash	$10 800 00		
Accounts Receivable	(5 900 00)		
Merchandise Inventory	(2 000 00)		
Supplies	(800 00)	$ 2 100 00	
Increases (decreases) in Current Liabilities:			
Notes Payable	$ 1 000 00		
Mortgage Payable (current portion)	— — — —		
Accounts Payable	(11 600 00)		
Wages Payable	100 00	(10 500 00)	
Increase in Working Capital		$12 600 00	

Concerning the possible other items—such as an additional investment, a purchase of equipment, or payment of the principal of a mortgage—the clues to detecting these transactions are found in the changes in the balances of the noncurrent accounts (plant and equipment, long-term liabilities, and stockholders' equity). Next, we look into the specific accounts in the ledger and may trace the transaction back to the journal to determine why the transaction took place as well as its effect on working capital. For example, in the case of the Justice Corporation, the following changes took place in the balances of the noncurrent accounts between the beginning of the year (or end of the previous year) and year end.

- **Equipment increased from $100,000 to $116,800** If we examine the ledger account for Equipment, and trace the transaction back to the journal, we find that the original entry was a debit to Equipment and a credit to Accounts Payable. You recognize that the transaction resulted in a decrease in working capital.

- **Mortgage Payable decreased from $200,000 to $184,000** If we examine the ledger account for Mortgage Payable, and trace the transaction back to the journal, we find that the original entry was a debit to Mortgage Payable and a credit to Cash. You recognize that the transaction resulted in a decrease in working capital.

- **Common Stock increased from $300,000 to $320,000** If we examine the ledger account for Common Stock, and trace the transaction back to the journal, we find that the original entry was a debit to Cash and a credit to Common Stock. You recognize that the transaction resulted in an increase in working capital.

- **Retained Earnings increased from $50,400 to $62,600** Upon examining the ledger account, you recognize the net income being added to the account and dividends being deducted from the account. The information for net income and dividends is also shown in the statement of retained earnings.

Broad Concept of Financing and Investing Activities

The Accounting Principles Board of the American Institute of Certified Public Accountants held that the statement of changes in financial position should list all the important aspects of transactions involving financing and investing even though current assets or current liabilities are not involved. Let's look at two examples.

a. Bought a building and issued a mortgage. Entry: debit Building and credit Mortgage Payable.
b. Received land and issued common stock. Entry: debit Land and credit Common Stock.

Using this broad concept of financing activities, the issuances of the mortgage and common stock are listed on a statement of changes in financial position as sources of working capital; the acquisition of the building and land are listed as uses of working capital. In these cases, the sources cancel out the uses; and there is no net change in the amount of working capital. Further discussion of specific situations involving the broad concept of financing and investing activities will be left to more advanced accounting texts.

Working Capital—A Restatement

Now that you are acquainted with the statement of changes in financial position, let us restate the possible sources and uses of working capital. Some accountants refer to the working capital as funds (in the inclusive sense, cash or items closely related to cash, such as current assets minus current liabilities).

Sources
- **Current operations** Net income plus expenses that do not reduce working capital, such as depreciation
- **Long-term liabilities** Borrowing on a long-term basis that results in an increase in current assets: example, issuing bonds for cash (debit Cash and credit Bonds Payable)
- **Sale of noncurrent assets** For cash or other current asset: example, sale of equipment for cash (debit Cash and credit Equipment)
- **Sale of capital stock** For cash or other current asset: example, issue common stock for cash (debit Cash and credit Common Stock)

Uses
- **Purchase of noncurrent assets** For cash or on a short-term basis: example, buy equipment on account (debit Equipment and credit Accounts Payable)
- **Repayment of long-term liabilities** Such as mortgage or bonds: example, retired (redeemed) bonds, paying cash (debit Bonds Payable and credit Cash)
- **Bought back (canceled) outstanding stock** Bought back our own preferred stock, paying cash (debit Preferred 8 Percent Stock and credit Cash)
- **Declaration of a cash dividend** Results in an increase in a current liability: example, declared a cash dividend to be paid in thirty days (debit Retained Earnings and credit Dividends Payable)

GLOSSARY

Statement of changes in financial position A financial statement that explains in detail how working capital has changed between the beginning and end of the fiscal year.

QUESTIONS, EXERCISES, AND PROBLEMS

Discussion Questions

1. Name the principal sources of working capital. Name the principal uses of working capital.

2. What information is contained in a statement of changes in financial position that is not readily apparent in the other financial statements?
3. Why does an increase in a current liability result in a decrease in working capital?
4. Why is depreciation expense considered to be a source of working capital?
5. What are the necessary sources of information for the preparation of a statement of changes in financial position?
6. Why are noncurrent accounts examined to expose changes in working capital?
7. If a business changed its depreciation method from straight-line to sum-of-the-years'-digits, how would that affect working capital?

Exercises

Exercise 28-1 From the following account balances, determine the amount of the working capital:

Notes Payable (short-term)	$ 3,000
Equipment	18,000
Accounts Receivable	13,500
J. Erdman, Capital	28,500
Cash	9,000
Allowance for Doubtful Accounts	1,500
Accounts Payable	7,500

Exercise 28-2 What is the amount of the increase or decrease (if any) in working capital of each of the following, considered individually?

a. Bought equipment on account, $900.
b. Issued 1,000 shares of common stock for $18 per share ($15 par), receiving cash.
c. Issued a $6,000, 60-day note to a creditor in settlement of a charge account.
d. Received $7,500 from charge customers to apply on account.
e. Sold merchandise on account, $1,200 (cost $900).

Exercise 28-3 Equipment costing $21,000, having an accumulated depreciation of $21,000, is discarded. A junk dealer agrees to remove and dispose of the equipment in exchange for any salvage rights. How does this transaction affect working capital?

Exercise 28-4 For each of the following firms, compute the amount of the increase or decrease in working capital due to operations and transactions.

	A	B	C
Net income (loss) from operations	$30,000	($90,000)	$210,000
Depreciation of plant and equipment	4,500	13,500	30,000
Retired (bought back) bonds payable			90,000
Sold equipment (at cost) for cash		600	

Exercise 28-5   What is the amount of the increase or decrease (if any) in working capital as a result of each of the following transactions?

a. Declared a 10 percent stock dividend on $750,000 of par-value common stock outstanding.
b. Purchased bonds for retirement, having a face value of $3,000,000, at 102. The bonds were originally sold at 100.
c. On January 1, land costing $450,000 was purchased for $150,000 cash downpayment plus four installments of $75,000 due every six months on June 30 and December 31.

Exercise 28-6   For the current year, a company reported a net loss of $16,500 on its income statement and an increase of $7,500 in working capital on its statement of changes in financial position. Explain the seeming contradiction between the net loss and the increase in working capital.

Exercise 28-7   From the following list of transactions completed by Danville Company during 19–, prepare the "sources and uses" section of a statement of changes in financial position for the year.

a. Danville Company reported net income for the year of $450,000.
b. Made payments on the mortgage principal, $150,000.
c. Borrowed cash from the bank, payable in eighteen months, $90,000.
d. Bought equipment on account, payable in three months, $45,000.
e. Depreciation recorded for the year, $180,000.
f. Cash dividends declared and paid, $75,000.

Exercise 28-8   The net income after taxes reported on the income statement of Dodson Corporation for the current year ended December 31 is $120,000. Adjustments required to determine the amount of the increase in working capital provided by operations, as well as some other data used for the year-end adjusting entries, are described below. Prepare the Sources of Working Capital section of the statement of changes in financial position.

a. Wages accrued but not yet paid, $3,000.
b. Depreciation expense, $30,000.
c. Interest accrued on notes receivable, $1,500.
d. Income tax accrued but not yet paid, $4,500.

Problem Set A

Problem 28-1A   Smalley Corporation has the following balances of current asset and current liability accounts at the end of the year.

Item	End of Year	Beginning of Year
Cash	$126,800	$120,000
Notes Receivable	64,000	66,000
Accounts Receivable	148,000	154,000
Merchandise Inventory	308,000	313,000
Prepaid Insurance	12,400	12,000
Accounts Payable	136,000	131,600
Income Tax Payable	22,000	20,000
Dividends Payable	60,000	56,000
Wages Payable	16,200	16,600

Instructions

1. Determine the difference in working capital between the beginning and the end of the year.
2. Prepare the Changes in Components of Working Capital section of the statement of changes in financial position.

Problem 28-2A The comparative balance sheet of the Rolling Company at June 30 of this year and the preceding year appears below.

	THIS YEAR	PRECEDING YEAR
Assets		
Cash	53 0 0 0 00	54 4 0 0 00
Accounts Receivable (net)	66 8 0 0 00	64 2 0 0 00
Merchandise Inventory	169 2 0 0 00	164 8 0 0 00
Supplies	6 4 0 0 00	7 0 0 0 00
Equipment	192 8 0 0 00	160 8 0 0 00
Accumulated Depreciation, Equipment	(82 0 0 0 00)	(77 0 0 0 00)
Total Assets	406 2 0 0 00	374 2 0 0 00
Liabilities and Owner's Equity		
Accounts Payable	89 2 0 0 00	84 4 0 0 00
Mortgage Payable (current portion)	9 6 0 0 00	9 6 0 0 00
Mortgage Payable	36 0 0 0 00	40 0 0 0 00
D. L. Rolling, Capital	271 4 0 0 00	240 2 0 0 00
Total Liabilities and Owner's Equity	406 2 0 0 00	374 2 0 0 00

Additional data for this year obtained from the income statement, the statement of owner's equity, and from an examination of the noncurrent asset and noncurrent liability accounts in the ledger are as follows.

a. Net income (no extraordinary items) reported on the income statement, $75,200.

b. Depreciation reported on the income statement, $5,000.
c. The principal of the mortgage was reduced by $4,000.
d. Additional equipment purchased for cash, $32,000.
e. Withdrawals by Rolling during the year, $44,000.

Instructions

1. Determine the difference in working capital between the beginning and the end of the year.
2. Prepare the Changes in Components of Working Capital section of the statement of changes in financial position.
3. Complete the statement of changes in financial position for year ended June 30.

Problem 28-3A The comparative balance sheet of the Reynolds Corporation at December 31 of this year and of the preceding year appears below in condensed form.

	THIS YEAR	PRECEDING YEAR
Assets		
Cash	38 0 0 0 00	35 2 0 0 00
Accounts Receivable (net)	103 0 0 0 00	101 6 0 0 00
Merchandise Inventory	188 2 0 0 00	184 8 0 0 00
Prepaid Insurance	3 0 0 0 00	2 8 0 0 00
Equipment	150 0 0 0 00	150 0 0 0 00
Accumulated Depreciation, Equipment	(88 0 0 0 00)	(76 0 0 0 00)
Building	200 0 0 0 00	200 0 0 0 00
Accumulated Depreciation, Building	(64 0 0 0 00)	(48 0 0 0 00)
Land	28 0 0 0 00	28 0 0 0 00
Total Assets	558 2 0 0 00	578 4 0 0 00
Liabilities and Stockholders' Equity		
Notes Payable	12 0 0 0 00	8 0 0 0 00
Accounts Payable	49 8 0 0 00	56 0 0 0 00
Dividends Payable	72 0 0 0 00	68 0 0 0 00
Common Stock, $20 par	320 0 0 0 00	300 0 0 0 00
Premium on Common Stock	16 0 0 0 00	15 0 0 0 00
Retained Earnings	88 4 0 0 00	131 4 0 0 00
Total Liabilities and Stockholders' Equity	558 2 0 0 00	578 4 0 0 00

Additional data for this year obtained from the income statement, the statement of retained earnings, and an examination of the noncurrent asset and noncurrent liability accounts in the ledger are as follows.

a. Net income (no extraordinary items) reported on the income statement, $29,000.
b. Depreciation of equipment reported on the income statement, $12,000.
c. Depreciation of building reported on the income statement, $16,000.
d. Issued 1,000 additional shares of common stock for $21 per share, receiving cash.
e. Declared cash dividends, $72,000.

Instructions

1. Determine the difference in working capital between the beginning and end of the year.
2. Prepare the Changes in Components of Working Capital section of the statement of changes in financial position.
3. Complete the statement of changes in financial position for year ended December 31.

Problem 28-4A The comparative balance sheet of the Finley Corporation at December 31 of this year and the preceding year is provided in condensed form.

	THIS YEAR	PRECEDING YEAR
Assets		
Cash	32 0 0 0 00	54 0 0 0 00
Notes Receivable	10 8 0 0 00	30 0 0 0 00
Accounts Receivable (net)	80 0 0 0 00	124 0 0 0 00
Merchandise Inventory	217 0 0 0 00	208 6 0 0 00
Supplies	1 4 0 0 00	1 6 0 0 00
Equipment	132 0 0 0 00	132 0 0 0 00
Accumulated Depreciation, Equipment	(40 0 0 0 00)	(16 0 0 0 00)
Building	240 0 0 0 00	200 0 0 0 00
Accumulated Depreciation, Building	(84 0 0 0 00)	(72 0 0 0 00)
Land	80 0 0 0 00	80 0 0 0 00
Total Assets	669 2 0 0 00	742 2 0 0 00
Liabilities and Stockholders' Equity		
Accounts Payable	86 0 0 0 00	122 0 0 0 00
Income Tax Payable	10 0 0 0 00	9 4 0 0 00
Salaries Payable	6 4 0 0 00	6 0 0 0 00
Preferred 8 Percent Stock, $100 par	200 0 0 0 00	240 0 0 0 00
Common Stock, $50 par	340 0 0 0 00	340 0 0 0 00
Premium on Common Stock	8 8 0 0 00	8 8 0 0 00
Retained Earnings	18 0 0 0 00	16 0 0 0 00
Total Liabilities and Stockholders' Equity	669 2 0 0 00	742 2 0 0 00

Additional data for this year obtained from the income statement, the statement of retained earnings, and an examination of the noncurrent asset and noncurrent liability accounts in the ledger are as follows.

a. Net income (no extraordinary items) reported on the income statement, $46,400.
b. Depreciation of equipment reported on the income statement, $24,000.
c. Depreciation of building reported on the income statement, $12,000.
d. An addition to the building was constructed at a cost of $40,000, paid in cash.
e. Four hundred shares of preferred stock were repurchased and canceled at a cost of $103 per share.
f. Cash dividends of $43,200 were paid during the year.

Instructions

1. Determine the difference in working capital between the beginning and end of the year.
2. Complete the entire statement of changes in financial position for year ended December 31 (with the two sections in proper order).

Problem Set B

Problem 28-1B   Harrow Corporation has the following balances of current asset and current liability accounts at the end of the year.

Item	End of Year	Beginning of Year
Cash	$105,000	$103,000
Notes Receivable	60,000	52,000
Accounts Receivable (net)	142,000	146,000
Merchandise Inventory	292,000	335,000
Prepaid Insurance	11,600	11,000
Accounts Payable	130,000	122,400
Income Tax Payable	20,000	16,000
Dividends Payable	60,000	48,000
Wages Payable	15,200	18,400

Instructions

1. Determine the difference in working capital between the beginning and the end of the year.
2. Prepare the Changes in Components of Working Capital section of the statement of changes in financial position.

Problem 28-2B The comparative balance sheet of the Channing Company at June 30 of this year and the preceding year is given in condensed form.

	THIS YEAR	PRECEDING YEAR
Assets		
Cash	44 0 0 0 00	49 2 0 0 00
Accounts Receivable (net)	64 2 0 0 00	61 8 0 0 00
Merchandise Inventory	166 8 0 0 00	172 4 0 0 00
Supplies	5 4 0 0 00	6 2 0 0 00
Equipment	196 0 0 0 00	144 8 0 0 00
Accumulated Depreciation, Equipment	(84 0 0 0 00)	(73 0 0 0 00)
Total Assets	392 4 0 0 00	361 4 0 0 00
Liabilities and Owner's Equity		
Accounts Payable	94 6 0 0 00	77 8 0 0 00
Mortgage Payable (current portion)	— — — —	8 0 0 0 00
Mortgage Payable	— — — —	32 0 0 0 00
D. R. Channing, Capital	297 8 0 0 00	243 6 0 0 00
Total Liabilities and Owner's Equity	392 4 0 0 00	361 4 0 0 00

Additional data for this year obtained from the income statement, the statement of owner's equity, and an examination of the noncurrent asset and noncurrent liability accounts in the ledger are as follows.

a. Net income (no extraordinary items) reported on the income statement, $92,200.
b. Depreciation reported on the income statement, $11,000.
c. Additional equipment purchased for cash, $51,200.
d. The mortgage note was not due for five years, but the term permitted earlier payment without penalty.
e. Withdrawals by Channing during the year, $38,000.

Instructions

1. Determine the difference in working capital between the beginning and the end of the year.
2. Prepare the Changes in Components of Working Capital section of the statement of changes in financial position.
3. Complete the statement of changes in financial position for year ended June 30.

Problem 28-3B The comparative balance sheet of the Johnson Corporation at December 31 of this year and of the preceding year is given in condensed form.

	THIS YEAR	PRECEDING YEAR
Assets		
Cash	32 0 0 0 00	29 6 0 0 00
Accounts Receivable (net)	98 8 0 0 00	85 2 0 0 00
Merchandise Inventory	186 8 0 0 00	181 4 0 0 00
Prepaid Insurance	2 8 0 0 00	3 2 0 0 00
Equipment	144 0 0 0 00	144 0 0 0 00
Accumulated Depreciation, Equipment	(80 0 0 0 00)	(68 0 0 0 00)
Building	196 0 0 0 00	196 0 0 0 00
Accumulated Depreciation, Building	(48 0 0 0 00)	(42 0 0 0 00)
Land	20 0 0 0 00	20 0 0 0 00
Total Assets	552 4 0 0 00	549 4 0 0 00
Liabilities and Stockholders' Equity		
Notes Payable	6 0 0 0 00	11 0 0 0 00
Accounts Payable	42 0 0 0 00	70 0 0 0 00
Dividends Payable	64 0 0 0 00	60 0 0 0 00
Common Stock, $10 par	300 0 0 0 00	280 0 0 0 00
Premium on Common Stock	4 0 0 0 00	— — — —
Retained Earnings	136 4 0 0 00	128 4 0 0 00
Total Liabilities and Stockholders' Equity	552 4 0 0 00	549 4 0 0 00

Additional data for this year obtained from the income statement, the statement of retained earnings, and an examination of the noncurrent asset and noncurrent liability accounts in the ledger are as follows.

a. Net income (no extraordinary items) reported on the income statement, $72,000.
b. Depreciation of equipment reported on the income statement, $12,000.
c. Depreciation of building reported on the income statement, $6,000.
d. Issued 2,000 additional shares of common stock for $12 per share, receiving cash.
e. Declared cash dividends, $64,000.

Instructions

1. Determine the difference in working capital between the beginning and end of the year.
2. Prepare the section of the statement of changes in financial position entitled Changes in Components of Working Capital.
3. Complete the statement of changes in financial position for year ended December 31.

Problem 28-4B The comparative balance sheet of Bailey Corporation at December 31 of this year and the preceding appears in condensed form.

	THIS YEAR	PRECEDING YEAR
Assets		
Cash	72 0 0 0 00	88 0 0 0 00
Notes Receivable	6 0 0 0 00	8 0 0 0 00
Accounts Receivable (net)	120 0 0 0 00	110 8 0 0 00
Merchandise Inventory	280 0 0 0 00	252 0 0 0 00
Supplies	1 2 0 0 00	1 0 0 0 00
Equipment	138 0 0 0 00	138 0 0 0 00
Accumulated Depreciation, Equipment	(84 0 0 0 00)	(56 0 0 0 00)
Building	200 0 0 0 00	180 0 0 0 00
Accumulated Depreciation, Building	(72 0 0 0 00)	(64 0 0 0 00)
Land	60 0 0 0 00	60 0 0 0 00
Total Assets	721 2 0 0 00	717 8 0 0 00
Liabilities and Stockholders' Equity		
Accounts Payable	82 0 0 0 00	94 0 0 0 00
Income Tax Payable	8 0 0 0 00	6 2 0 0 00
Salaries Payable	4 0 0 0 00	4 8 0 0 00
Preferred 8 Percent Stock, $100 par	160 0 0 0 00	180 0 0 0 00
Common Stock, $100 par	320 0 0 0 00	320 0 0 0 00
Premium on Common Stock	12 8 0 0 00	12 8 0 0 00
Retained Earnings	134 4 0 0 00	100 0 0 0 00
Total Liabilities and Stockholders' Equity	721 2 0 0 00	717 8 0 0 00

Additional data for this year obtained from the income statement, the statement of retained earnings, and an examination of the noncurrent asset and noncurrent liability accounts in the ledger are as follows.

a. Net income (no extraordinary items) reported on the income statement, $89,400.
b. Depreciation of equipment reported on the income statement, $28,000.
c. Depreciation of building reported on the income statement, $8,000.
d. Cash dividends of $54,000 were paid during the year.
e. An addition to the building was built at a cost of $20,000, paid in cash.
f. Two hundred shares of preferred stock were repurchased and canceled at a cost of $105 per share.

Instructions

1. Determine the difference in working capital between the beginning and end of the year.
2. Complete the entire statement of changes in financial position for the year ended December 31 (with the two sections in proper order).

29 Manufacturing Accounting

Learning Objectives

After you have completed this chapter, you will be able to do the following:

1. Prepare financial statements for a manufacturing enterprise.

2. Complete a work sheet for a manufacturing enterprise.

3. Journalize adjusting entries for a manufacturing enterprise.

4. Journalize closing entries for a manufacturing enterprise.

In earlier chapters we dealt with accounting procedures mainly as they apply to service and merchandising enterprises. Now let us turn to another type of business operation: manufacturing.

The accounting principles we have already discussed pertain to manufacturing concerns, but in addition, manufacturers have special procedures to account for manufacturing costs. In this chapter we shall describe how manufacturers determine the total cost of goods manufactured during each accounting period. To acquaint you with the end results, we shall present financial statements of a manufacturer early in the chapter. These statements will enable you to understand the function of the work sheet and its relationship to the financial statements. You may consider this chapter to be an introduction to accounting for manufacturing operations. A discussion of cost accounting systems is beyond the scope of this text.

COMPARISON OF INCOME STATEMENTS FOR MERCHANDISING AND MANUFACTURING ENTERPRISES

Manufacturing and merchandising companies have the same type of revenue accounts. However, a merchant buys goods in a finished condition and later sells them at a higher price in the same condition. A manufacturer, on the other hand, buys raw materials, transforms them into finished goods, and later sells the finished goods.

To see how the two compare, study the following portions of income statements for a merchandising firm and for a manufacturing firm.

Objective 1

Prepare financial statements for a manufacturing enterprise.

A Merchandising Company
Income Statement
For year ended December 31, 19–

Sales (net)		$2 000 00 0 00
Cost of Merchandise Sold:		
Merchandise Inventory, January 1	$ 400 00 0 00	
Purchases (net)	1 200 00 0 00	
Merchandise Available for Sale	$1 600 00 0 00	
Less Merchandise Inventory,		
December 31	250 00 0 00	
Cost of Merchandise Sold		1 350 00 0 00
Gross Profit		$ 650 00 0 00

Lloyd Manufacturing Company
Income Statement
For year ended December 31, 19–

Sales (net)			$2 000 0 0 0 00	
Cost of Goods Sold:				
Finished Goods Inventory, January 1	$ 400 0 0 0 00			
Cost of Goods Manufactured	1 200 0 0 0 00			
Goods Available for Sale	$1 600 0 0 0 00			
Less Finished Goods Inventory,				
December 31	250 0 0 0 00			
Cost of Goods Sold		1 350 0 0 0 00		
Gross Profit		$ 650 0 0 0 00		

The main difference in accounting for a merchandising firm and for a manufacturing firm lies in determining the cost of goods (or merchandise) sold.

Merchandising Firm	**Manufacturing Firm**
Beginning Merchandise Inventory	Beginning Finished Goods Inventory
Plus Purchases (net)	Plus Cost of Goods Manufactured
Merchandise Available	Goods Available
Less Ending Merchandise Inventory	Less Ending Finished Goods Inventory
Cost of Merchandise Sold	Cost of Goods Sold

A manufacturing concern refers to its products as *goods;* a merchandising concern refers to its inventory as *merchandise*. Cost of Goods Manufactured for a manufacturer is the equivalent of Net Purchases for a merchandiser.

STATEMENT OF COST OF GOODS MANUFACTURED

The statement of cost of goods manufactured supports the income statement. Figure 29-1 (next page) illustrates such a statement for Lloyd Manufacturing Company. Because Cost of Goods Manufactured is incorporated into the income statement, the accountant naturally prepares the statement of cost of goods manufactured first.

Lloyd Manufacturing Company
Statement of Cost of Goods Manufactured
For year ended December 31, 19—

Work-in-Process Inventory, January 1			$ 130 0 0 0 00
Raw Materials:			
Raw Materials Inventory, January 1		$ 90 0 0 0 00	
Raw Materials Purchases (net)		230 0 0 0 00	
Cost of Raw Materials Available for Use		$ 320 0 0 0 00	
Less Raw Materials Inventory,			
December 31		100 0 0 0 00	
Cost of Raw Materials Used		$ 220 0 0 0 00	
Direct Labor		565 0 0 0 00	
Factory Overhead:			
Indirect Labor	$ 120 0 0 0 00		
Supervisory Salaries	110 0 0 0 00		
Heat, Light, and Power	42 0 0 0 00		
Depreciation Expense, Factory Equipment	32 0 0 0 00		
Depreciation Expense, Factory Building	25 0 0 0 00		
Repairs and Maintenance	24 0 0 0 00		
Factory Insurance Expired	22 0 0 0 00		
Factory Supplies Used	14 0 0 0 00		
Miscellaneous Factory Costs	16 0 0 0 00		
Total Factory Overhead		405 0 0 0 00	
Total Manufacturing Costs			1 190 0 0 0 00
Total Cost of Work-in-Process during Period			$1 320 0 0 0 00
Less Work-in-Process Inventory,			
December 31			120 0 0 0 00
Cost of Goods Manufactured			$1 200 0 0 0 00

Figure 29-1

ELEMENTS OF MANUFACTURING COSTS

No matter what type of product a manufacturer makes, the three elements that make up the cost of the goods manufactured are *raw materials used, direct labor,* and *factory overhead.*

Raw Materials Used

Raw materials are the materials that enter directly into—and become a part of—the finished product. The delivered cost of these materials is the figure one enters as "Raw Materials Used." For example, if you are manufacturing pencils, the raw materials you need are wood, lead, paint, an eraser, and a metal band. Raw materials are also called **direct materials.**

Direct Labor

Direct labor consists of the wages paid to factory employees who work—with machines or hand tools—directly on the materials, to convert them into finished products. The manufacturer debits the Direct Labor account for the gross wages of those who work directly on the raw materials. The cost of direct labor varies directly with the level of production.

Factory Overhead

Factory overhead consists of manufacturing costs (other than raw materials used and direct labor) that cannot be traced directly to products being manufactured. A manufacturer uses Factory Overhead as a controlling account. The specific titles of accounts in the factory overhead subsidiary ledger vary from company to company, with the exact accounts depending on the nature of the company and the information desired. In Figure 29-1 the accounts in the factory overhead ledger are: Indirect Labor; Supervisory Salaries; Heat, Light, and Power; Depreciation Expense, Factory Equipment; Depreciation Expense, Factory Building; Repairs and Maintenance; Factory Insurance Expired; Factory Supplies Used; and Miscellaneous Factory Costs.

Indirect labor is the cost of labor of those people who keep the plant in operation, rather than directly working on production. *Examples:* millwrights, maintenance workers, and timekeepers.

The balance of *Factory Supplies Used* reveals the cost of materials used to keep the plant in operation (oil, grease, and so on). These items are also called **indirect materials.**

Other items that may be included in Factory Overhead are: workers' compensation insurance, payroll taxes on wages of factory employees, taxes on factory building and equipment, taxes on raw materials and work-in-process inventories, patents written off, and small tools written off.

BALANCE SHEET FOR A MANUFACTURING FIRM

The ending balances of a manufacturing firm's inventory accounts appear in the Current Assets section of the balance sheet, as shown in Figure 29-2.

Lloyd Manufacturing Company
Balance Sheet
December 31, 19–

Assets			
Current Assets:			
Cash		$ 14 000 00	
Notes Receivable		50 000 00	
Accounts Receivable	$ 180 000 00		
Less Allowance for Doubtful Accounts	6 000 00	174 000 00	
Raw Materials Inventory		100 000 00	
Work-in-Process Inventory		120 000 00	
Finished Goods Inventory		250 000 00	
Prepaid Insurance		3 000 00	
Factory Supplies		2 000 00	
Total Current Assets			$ 713 000 00
Plant and Equipment:			
Factory Equipment	$ 360 000 00		
Less Accumulated Depreciation	250 000 00	$ 110 000 00	
Office Equipment	$ 62 000 00		
Less Accumulated Depreciation	45 000 00	17 000 00	
Factory Building	$ 500 000 00		
Less Accumulated Depreciation	275 000 00	225 000 00	
Land		100 000 00	
Total Plant and Equipment			452 000 00
Total Assets			$1 165 000 00
Liabilities			
Current Liabilities:			
Notes Payable		$ 40 000 00	
Accounts Payable		82 000 00	
Income Tax Payable		16 000 00	
Dividends Payable		12 000 00	
Total Current Liabilities			$ 150 000 00
Long-term Liabilities:			
Bonds Payable (due December 31, 1995)			300 000 00
Total Liabilities			$ 450 000 00
Stockholders' Equity			
Paid-in Capital:			
Common Stock, $10 par (50,000			
shares authorized, 30,000 shares issued)		$ 300 000 00	
Premium on Common Stock		100 000 00	
Total Paid-in Capital		$ 400 000 00	
Retained Earnings		315 000 00	
Total Stockholders' Equity			715 000 00
Total Liabilities and Stockholders' Equity			$1 165 000 00

Figure 29-2

WORK SHEET FOR A MANUFACTURING FIRM

You have seen three financial statements for a manufacturing firm: (1) a statement of cost of goods manufactured, (2) an income statement, and (3) a balance sheet. Since the purpose of a work sheet is to enable the accountant to prepare the necessary financial statements, it follows that the work sheet must have a set of columns for each financial statement. A manufacturer's work sheet must include extra columns for the statement of cost of goods manufactured.

Objective 2

Complete a work sheet for a manufacturing enterprise.

Let us examine the work sheet for Lloyd Manufacturing Company, shown in Figure 29-3 (pages 932–935). First notice that all accounts representing manufacturing costs in the Trial Balance columns have debit balances, just as expense accounts have debit balances. Next, look at the adjusting entries for inventories. (We are assuming that Lloyd uses a periodic-inventory system.) A manufacturer, like a merchandiser, takes two steps to adjust inventory: (1) the accountant takes off (or closes off) the beginning inventory; and (2) the accountant adds on the ending inventory. However, in manufacturing accounting, three inventories are involved: Raw Materials, Work-in-Process, and Finished Goods.

Since Raw Materials and Work-in-Process Inventory appear in the statement of cost of goods manufactured, the accountant adjusts them using the **Manufacturing Summary** account. Since Finished Goods Inventory appears in the income statement, the accountant adjusts it using the Income Summary account. Finished Goods Inventory for a manufacturing firm is equivalent to Merchandise Inventory for a merchandising firm. By T accounts, the adjusting entries are as follows.

Raw Materials Inventory			
+		−	
Bal.	90,000	(a)	90,000
(b)	100,000		

Work-in-Process Inventory			
+		−	
Bal.	130,000	(c)	130,000
(d)	120,000		

Manufacturing Summary			
(a)	90,000	(b)	100,000
(c)	130,000	(d)	120,000

Finished Goods Inventory			
+		−	
Bal.	400,000	(e)	400,000
(f)	250,000		

Income Summary			
(e)	400,000	(f)	250,000

The other adjustments are like the ones we have already seen. Notice how the figures in the Adjustments columns are transferred to the remaining columns of the work sheet. Just as the accountant transfers the figures on the Income Summary line into the Income Statement columns as separate figures, he or she also transfers the four figures on the Manu-

ACCOUNT NAME	TRIAL BALANCE DEBIT	TRIAL BALANCE CREDIT	ADJUSTMENTS DEBIT	ADJUSTMENTS CREDIT
Cash	14 0 0 0 00			
Notes Receivable	50 0 0 0 00			
Accounts Receivable	180 0 0 0 00			
Allowance for Doubtful Accounts		2 5 0 0 00		(l) 3 5 0 0 00
Raw Materials Inventory	90 0 0 0 00		(b)100 0 0 0 00	(a) 90 0 0 0 00
Work-in-Process Inventory	130 0 0 0 00		(d)120 0 0 0 00	(c)130 0 0 0 00
Finished Goods Inventory	400 0 0 0 00		(f)250 0 0 0 00	(e)400 0 0 0 00
Prepaid Insurance	25 0 0 0 00			(i) 22 0 0 0 00
Factory Supplies	16 0 0 0 00			(j) 14 0 0 0 00
Factory Equipment	360 0 0 0 00			
Accumulated Deprec., Factory Equipment		218 0 0 0 00		(g) 32 0 0 0 00
Office Equipment	62 0 0 0 00			
Accumulated Deprec., Office Equipment		40 0 0 0 00		(k) 5 0 0 0 00
Factory Building	500 0 0 0 00			
Accumulated Deprec., Factory Building		250 0 0 0 00		(h) 25 0 0 0 00
Land	100 0 0 0 00			
Notes Payable		40 0 0 0 00		
Accounts Payable		82 0 0 0 00		
Dividends Payable		12 0 0 0 00		
Bonds Payable		300 0 0 0 00		
Common Stock		300 0 0 0 00		
Premium on Common Stock		100 0 0 0 00		
Retained Earnings		214 9 0 0 00		
Sales (net)		2,000 0 0 0 00		
Raw Materials Purchases	230 0 0 0 00			
Direct Labor	565 0 0 0 00			
Indirect Labor	120 0 0 0 00			
Supervisory Salaries	110 0 0 0 00			
Heat, Light, and Power	42 0 0 0 00			
Repairs and Maintenance	24 0 0 0 00			
Miscellaneous Factory Costs	16 0 0 0 00			
Selling Expenses (control)	300 0 0 0 00			
General Expenses (control)	143 5 0 0 00		(l) 3 5 0 0 00 (k) 5 0 0 0 00	
Interest Expense	18 0 0 0 00			
Income Tax	63 9 0 0 00		(m) 16 0 0 0 00	
	3,559 4 0 0 00	3,599 4 0 0 00		

STATEMENT OF COST OF GOODS MANUFACTURED		INCOME STATEMENT		BALANCE SHEET	
DEBIT	CREDIT	DEBIT	CREDIT	DEBIT	CREDIT
				14 0 0 0 00	
				50 0 0 0 00	
				180 0 0 0 00	
					6 0 0 0 00
				100 0 0 0 00	
				120 0 0 0 00	
				250 0 0 0 00	
				3 0 0 0 00	
				2 0 0 0 00	
				360 0 0 0 00	
					250 0 0 0 00
				62 0 0 0 00	
					45 0 0 0 00
				500 0 0 0 00	
					275 0 0 0 00
				100 0 0 0 00	
					40 0 0 0 00
					82 0 0 0 00
					12 0 0 0 00
					300 0 0 0 00
					300 0 0 0 00
					100 0 0 0 00
					214 9 0 0 00
			2,000 0 0 0 00		
230 0 0 0 00					
565 0 0 0 00					
120 0 0 0 00					
110 0 0 0 00					
42 0 0 0 00					
24 0 0 0 00					
16 0 0 0 00					
		300 0 0 0 00			
		152 0 0 0 00			
		18 0 0 0 00			
		79 9 0 0 00			

Figure 29-3

(continued on pages 934–935)

ACCOUNT NAME	TRIAL BALANCE DEBIT	TRIAL BALANCE CREDIT	ADJUSTMENTS DEBIT	ADJUSTMENTS CREDIT
Manufacturing Summary			(a) 90 0 0 0 00	(b) 100 0 0 0 00
			(c) 130 0 0 0 00	(d) 120 0 0 0 00
Income Summary			(e) 400 0 0 0 00	(f) 250 0 0 0 00
Deprec. Expense, Factory Equipment			(g) 32 0 0 0 00	
Deprec. Expense, Factory Building			(h) 25 0 0 0 00	
Factory Insurance, Expired			(i) 22 0 0 0 00	
Factory Supplies Used			(j) 14 0 0 0 00	
Income Tax Payable				(m) 16 0 0 0 00
			1,207 5 0 0 00	1,207 5 0 0 00
Cost of Goods Manufactured				
Net Income After Income Tax				

facturing Summary lines into the Statement of Cost of Goods Manufactured columns as separate figures, like this.

ACCOUNT NAME	ADJUSTMENTS DEBIT	ADJUSTMENTS CREDIT	STATEMENT OF COST OF GOODS MANUFACTURED DEBIT	STATEMENT OF COST OF GOODS MANUFACTURED CREDIT	INCOME STATEMENT DEBIT	INCOME STATEMENT CREDIT
Manufacturing Summary	(a) 90 0 0 0 00	(b) 100 0 0 0 00	90 0 0 0 00	100 0 0 0 00		
	(c) 130 0 0 0 00	(d) 120 0 0 0 00	130 0 0 0 00	120 0 0 0 00		
Income Summary	(e) 400 0 0 0 00	(f) 250 0 0 0 00			400 0 0 0 00	250 0 0 0 00

On the work sheet, the accountant transfers the cost of goods manufactured ($1,200,000, the difference between the debit and credit totals in the Statement of Cost of Goods Manufactured columns) to the Income Statement Debit column as shown in the following section of Lloyd Manufacturing's work sheet. (Cost of goods manufactured can be considered to be the equivalent of Net Purchases for a merchandising firm.)

ACCOUNT NAME	STATEMENT OF COST OF GOODS MANUFACTURED DEBIT	STATEMENT OF COST OF GOODS MANUFACTURED CREDIT	INCOME STATEMENT DEBIT	INCOME STATEMENT CREDIT
	1,420 0 0 0 00	220 0 0 0 00		
Cost of Goods Manufactured		1,200 0 0 0 00	1,200 0 0 0 00	
	1,420 0 0 0 00	1,420 0 0 0 00		

Figure 29-3
(continued)

STATEMENT OF COST OF GOODS MANUFACTURED		INCOME STATEMENT		BALANCE SHEET	
DEBIT	CREDIT	DEBIT	CREDIT	DEBIT	CREDIT
90 0 0 0 00	100 0 0 0 00				
130 0 0 0 00	120 0 0 0 00				
		400 0 0 0 00	250 0 0 0 00		
32 0 0 0 00					
25 0 0 0 00					
22 0 0 0 00					
14 0 0 0 00					
					16 0 0 0 00
1,420 0 0 0 00	220 0 0 0 00				
	1,200 0 0 0 00	1,200 0 0 0 00			
1,420 0 0 0 00	1,420 0 0 0 00	2,149 9 0 0 00	2,250 0 0 0 00	1,741 0 0 0 00	1,640 9 0 0 00
		100 1 0 0 00			100 1 0 0 00
		2,250 0 0 0 00	2,250 0 0 0 00	1,741 0 0 0 00	1,741 0 0 0 00

ACCOUNTING CYCLE FOR A MANUFACTURING FIRM

In this discussion of accounting for a manufacturing firm, we have presented the financial statements first, to show you the desired end results. Because you were familiar with the statement of cost of goods manufactured, you recognized that the accountant listed each item appearing on the statement in the work sheet in the Statement of Cost of Goods Manufactured columns. Similarly, the accountant listed each item that appeared on the income statement in the Income Statement columns of the work sheet.

To fix the steps in your mind in the proper sequence, let us enumerate the steps in the manufacturer's accounting cycle.

1. Journalize the transactions.
2. Post to the ledger accounts.
3. Prepare a trial balance.
4. Determine the adjustments.
5. Complete the work sheet.
6. Prepare the financial statements.
7. Journalize and post adjusting entries.
8. Journalize and post closing entries.
9. Prepare a post-closing trial balance.

Adjusting Entries

After the manufacturer's accountant has assembled the information, he or she records the adjustments in the Adjustments columns of the work sheet, just as the accountant for a merchandising firm does. Here is the information (identified by letter) for the adjustments shown on the work sheet for the Lloyd Manufacturing Company.

Objective 3

Journalize adjusting entries for a manufacturing enterprise.

a.–b. Cost of the ending raw materials inventory, $100,000
c.–d. Cost of the ending work-in-process inventory, $120,000
e.–f. Cost of the ending finished goods inventory, $250,000
   g. Depreciation of factory equipment, $32,000
   h. Depreciation of factory building, $25,000
   i. Expired factory insurance, $22,000 (assuming the unexpired portion had already been calculated)
   j. Cost of the factory supplies inventory, $2,000
   k. Depreciation of office equipment, $5,000
   l. Estimated uncollectible accounts, $6,000
  m. Income tax, $79,900 (based on a net income before income tax of $180,000; the accountant determined this by completing the income statement columns of the work sheet without including income tax).

The accountant journalizes the adjusting entries as illustrated in Figure 29-4.

Closing Entries

Now we come to the steps one must take in making the closing entries for a manufacturer.

Objective 4

Journalize closing entries for a manufacturing enterprise.

1. Close the costs that appear in the statement of cost of goods manufactured into the Manufacturing Summary account.
2. Close the Manufacturing Summary account into the Income Summary account (by the amount of the cost of goods manufactured).
3. Close the revenue accounts into the Income Summary account.
4. Close the expense accounts into the Income Summary account.
5. Close the Income Tax account into the Income Summary account.
6. Close the Income Summary account into the Retained Earnings account (by the amount of the net income after income tax).

Figure 29-4

GENERAL JOURNAL

PAGE _____

1			*Adjusting Entries*									1
2	19– Dec.	31	Manufacturing Summary	90	0 0 0	00						2
3			Raw Materials Inventory				90	0 0 0	00		3
4											4
5		31	Raw Materials Inventory	100	0 0 0	00					5
6			Manufacturing Summary				100	0 0 0	00		6
7											7
8		31	Manufacturing Summary	130	0 0 0	00					8
9			Work-in-Process Inventory				130	0 0 0	00		9
10											10
11		31	Work-in-Process Inventory	120	0 0 0	00					11
12			Manufacturing Summary				120	0 0 0	00		12
13											13
14		31	Income Summary	400	0 0 0	00					14
15			Finished Goods Inventory				400	0 0 0	00		15
16											16
17		31	Finished Goods Inventory	250	0 0 0	00					17
18			Income Summary				250	0 0 0	00		18
19											19
20		31	Depreciation Expense, Factory								20
21			Equipment	32	0 0 0	00					21
22			Accumulated Depreciation,								22
23			Factory Equipment				32	0 0 0	00		23
24											24
25		31	Depreciation Expense, Factory								25
26			Building	25	0 0 0	00					26
27			Accumulated Depreciation,								27
28			Factory Building				25	0 0 0	00		28
29											29
30		31	Factory Insurance Expired	22	0 0 0	00					30
31			Prepaid Insurance				22	0 0 0	00		31
32											32
33		31	Factory Supplies Used	14	0 0 0	00					33
34			Factory Supplies				14	0 0 0	00		34
35											35
36		31	General Expenses (control)	5	0 0 0	00					36
37			Accumulated Depreciation,								37
38			Office Equipment				5	0 0 0	00		38
39											39
40		31	General Expenses (control)	3	5 0 0	00					40
41			Allowance for Doubtful Accounts				3	5 0 0	00		41
42											42
43		31	Income Tax	16	0 0 0	00					43
44			Income Tax Payable				16	0 0 0	00		44
45											45
46											46

On the next page are T accounts for Manufacturing Summary and Income Summary, labeled so that you can readily identify the accounts recorded.

These steps are shown in Figure 29-5 below.

Figure 29-5

GENERAL JOURNAL   PAGE _____

1			*Closing Entries*					1
2	19– Dec.	31	Manufacturing Summary	1,200 0 0 0 00				2
3			Raw Materials Purchases		230 0 0 0 00			3
4			Direct Labor		565 0 0 0 00			4
5			Indirect Labor		120 0 0 0 00			5
6			Supervisory Salaries		110 0 0 0 00			6
7			Heat, Light, and Power		42 0 0 0 00			7
8			Repairs and Maintenance		24 0 0 0 00			8
9			Miscellaneous Factory Costs		16 0 0 0 00			9
10			Depreciation Expense, Factory					10
11			Equipment		32 0 0 0 00			11
12			Depreciation Expense, Factory					12
13			Building		25 0 0 0 00			13
14			Factory Insurance, Expired		22 0 0 0 00			14
15			Factory Supplies Used		14 0 0 0 00			15
16								16
17		31	Income Summary	1,200 0 0 0 00				17
18			Manufacturing Summary		1,200 0 0 0 00			18
19								19
20		31	Sales (net)	2,000 0 0 0 00				20
21			Income Summary		2,000 0 0 0 00			21
22								22
23		31	Income Summary	470 0 0 0 00				23
24			Selling Expenses (control)		300 0 0 0 00			24
25			General Expenses (control)		152 0 0 0 00			25
26			Interest Expense		18 0 0 0 00			26
27								27
28		31	Income Summary	79 9 0 0 00				28
29			Income Tax		79 9 0 0 00			29
30								30
31		31	Income Summary	100 1 0 0 00				31
32			Retained Earnings		100 1 0 0 00			32
33								33
34								34
35								35
36								36
37								37

Manufacturing Summary

Raw Materials Inventory, Jan. 1	90,000	Raw Materials Inventory, Dec. 31	100,000
Work-in-Process Inventory, Jan. 1	130,000	Work-in-Process Inventory, Dec. 31	120,000
Raw Materials Purchases	230,000	Closing	1,200,000
Direct Labor	565,000	(To Income Summary)	
Indirect Labor	120,000		
Supervisory Salaries	110,000		
Heat, Light, and Power	42,000		
Repairs and Maintenance	24,000		
Miscellaneous Factory Costs	16,000		
Deprec. Expense, Factory Equipment	32,000		
Deprec. Expense, Factory Building	25,000		
Factory Insurance Expired	22,000		
Factory Supplies Used	14,000		
	1,420,000		1,420,000

Income Summary

Finished Goods Inventory, Jan. 1	400,000	Finished Goods Inventory, Dec. 31	250,000
(From Manufacturing Summary)	1,200,000		

DETERMINING THE VALUE OF ENDING INVENTORIES

We've been talking about the fact that a manufacturer has to record the costs of the ending inventories for (1) raw materials, (2) work in process, and (3) finished goods. The manufacturer first lists these costs in the Adjustments columns of the work sheet and then carries the figures forward into the financial statements. Let us now consider each inventory separately, because each poses a slightly different set of problems.

Raw Materials Inventory

The items that go to make up the raw materials inventory are in the same form they were in when the manufacturer bought them; nothing has been done to them yet. So the accountant first ascertains the quantities on hand and the unit costs, then determines the values of the inventories. The value of the ending inventories may be calculated by either FIFO, LIFO, or weighted-average method. One may also use the lower-of-cost-or-market rule. These alternatives involve periodic-inventory systems.

A manufacturer may choose to keep *perpetual inventories*, which provide a continuous or running balance of the firm's inventory. When a firm that uses perpetual inventories buys raw materials, it immediately debits Raw

Materials Inventory for the cost of these materials. When the materials are put into production, the manufacturer credits Raw Materials Inventory for the cost of the materials used and debits Work-in-Process. The same debiting and crediting process goes on in the Work-in-Process Inventory and the Finished Goods Inventory accounts, as these materials go through the manufacturing process. If a company keeps perpetual inventories, it verifies the balance of the account periodically by physically counting the goods on hand. Any discrepancy that exists can be handled by an adjusting entry. If there is no discrepancy, then the company does not need to make an adjusting entry involving the inventory.

Work-in-Process Inventory

How does one calculate the cost of the work-in-process inventory? We have seen that the cost of manufacturing any product consists of (1) *raw materials used*, (2) *direct labor expended*, and (3) *factory overhead*. Therefore the manufacturer keeps a record of the amount and cost of raw materials placed in production. The manufacturer also records the cost of direct labor expended on the ending work-in-process inventory.

The third item, factory overhead, consists of a group of accounts such as Heat, Light, and Power; Repairs and Maintenance; and Miscellaneous Factory Costs; to name a few. So the manufacturer cannot calculate the *exact* cost of factory overhead involved in the ending work-in-process inventory, and must therefore estimate this cost. The firm does this by using a percentage of the direct labor cost involved in the ending inventory. The reasoning here is that, since factory overhead is closely related to the level of production, and since the level of production varies directly with the amount of direct labor, the cost of factory overhead should be regarded as a percentage of direct labor. For example, Heat, Light, and Power is part of factory overhead, and varies directly with the level of production.

One may determine the percentage figure for factory overhead from the most recent statement of cost of goods manufactured. The factory overhead rate for the Lloyd Corporation is as follows.

$$\text{Factory overhead rate} = \frac{\text{Factory overhead}}{\text{Direct labor}} = \frac{\$405,000}{\$565,000} = .72 = 72\%$$

GLOSSARY

Direct labor   Wages paid to factory employees who convert the raw materials into finished products.

Direct materials   Delivered cost of raw materials used in manufacturing products.

Factory overhead All manufacturing costs except raw materials used and direct labor. Examples: heat, light, and power; repairs and maintenance; indirect labor; indirect materials.

Indirect labor That portion of work performed by workers who keep the plant in operation—such as factory maintenance workers and timekeepers—rather than workers who are directly occupied with production; considered to be part of factory overhead.

Indirect materials Factory supplies, such as oil, grease, and cleaning fluids, considered to be part of factory overhead.

Manufacturing Summary An account used to make adjustments to Raw Materials and Work-in-Process accounts; similar to Income Summary.

Raw materials Delivered cost of materials (also called *direct materials*) to be used in producing the finished goods.

QUESTIONS, EXERCISES, AND PROBLEMS

Discussion Questions

1. What inventory accounts appear in the chart of accounts of a manufacturing company?
2. Name the three major elements involved in manufacturing costs.
3. Which inventories appear in the statement of cost of goods manufactured?
4. In a work sheet, why is cost of goods manufactured entered in the Statement of Cost of Goods Manufactured Credit and the Income Statement Debit columns?
5. What is the purpose of the Manufacturing Summary account?
6. Which inventory of a manufacturing firm is handled in the same way as the merchandise inventory of a merchandising firm?
7. Name five accounts that you would consider to be factory overhead costs.

Exercises

Exercise 29-1 From the following balances, determine the cost of the raw materials used.

Raw Materials Purchases	$840,000
Raw Materials Inventory, May 31	100,000
Raw Materials Inventory, May 1	60,000

Exercise 29-2 Prepare a statement of cost of goods manufactured, using any of the following balances you need.

Raw Materials Purchases	$ 840,000
Raw Materials Inventory, May 31	100,000
Raw Materials Inventory, May 1	60,000
Work-in-Process Inventory, May 1	300,000
Finished Goods Inventory, May 31	160,000
Direct Labor	1,200,000

Work-in-Process Inventory, May 31	400,000
Factory Overhead	900,000
Finished Goods Inventory, May 1	180,000

Exercise 29-3   From the data in Exercise 29-2, determine the percentage of factory overhead to direct labor. Assume that the cost of the work in process on May 31 is $400,000, comprising raw materials of $120,000 and direct labor of $160,000. How much is the factory overhead? Verify the figure by means of the percentage of factory overhead to direct labor.

Exercise 29-4   From the following balances, determine the cost of goods manufactured.

Cost of Goods Sold	$850,000
Finished Goods Inventory, April 1	200,000
Finished Goods Inventory, April 30	150,000

Exercise 29-5   From the following, calculate the cost of the ending work-in-process inventory, which contains the following three elements.

Raw materials used	$ 90,000
Direct labor	100,000
Factory overhead (85% of direct labor)	

Exercise 29-6   The Statement of Cost of Goods Manufactured columns and the Income Statement columns of the work sheet for the Starr Manufacturing Corporation for the year ended December 31 are as follows. Starr's beginning inventory of raw materials is $20,000; its beginning inventory of work in process is $96,000. Prepare a statement of cost of goods manufactured.

ACCOUNT NAME	STATEMENT OF COST OF GOODS MANUFACTURED DEBIT	STATEMENT OF COST OF GOODS MANUFACTURED CREDIT	INCOME STATEMENT DEBIT	INCOME STATEMENT CREDIT
Sales				900 0 0 0 00
Raw Materials Purchases	160 0 0 0 00			
Direct Labor	400 0 0 0 00			
Indirect Labor	8 0 0 0 00			
Heat, Light, and Power	4 0 0 0 00			
Miscellaneous Factory Costs	2 0 0 0 00			
Selling Expenses (control)			85 0 0 0 00	
General Expenses (control)			35 0 0 0 00	
Income Tax			100 0 0 0 00	
Manufacturing Summary	20 0 0 0 00	30 0 0 0 00		
	96 0 0 0 00	100 0 0 0 00		
Income Summary			80 0 0 0 00	90 0 0 0 00
	690 0 0 0 00	130 0 0 0 00		
Cost of Goods Manufactured		560 0 0 0 00	560 0 0 0 00	
	690 0 0 0 00	690 0 0 0 00	860 0 0 0 00	990 0 0 0 00
Net Income			130 0 0 0 00	
			990 0 0 0 00	990 0 0 0 00

Exercise 29-7 From the information in Exercise 29-6, prepare an income statement for the Starr Manufacturing Corporation. Beginning inventory of finished goods is $80,000.

Exercise 29-8 From the information in Exercise 29-6, journalize the closing entries for the Starr Manufacturing Corporation.

Problem Set A

Problem 29-1A Here is the statement of cost of goods manufactured for the Denton Manufacturing Company.

Denton Manufacturing Company
Statement of Cost of Goods Manufactured
For year ended June 30, 19–

Work-in-Process Inventory, July 1			$ 160 0 0 0 00
Raw Materials:			
Raw Materials Inventory, July 1		$ 272 0 0 0 00	
Raw Materials Purchases (net)		395 0 0 0 00	
Cost of Raw Materials Available for Use		$ 667 0 0 0 00	
Less Raw Materials Inventory, June 30		260 0 0 0 00	
Cost of Raw Materials Used		$ 407 0 0 0 00	
Direct Labor		582 0 0 0 00	
Factory Overhead:			
Indirect Labor	$ 108 4 0 0 00		
Supervisory Salaries	76 1 0 0 00		
Depreciation of Factory Equipment	72 0 0 0 00		
Depreciation of Factory Building	21 8 0 0 00		
Heat, Light, and Power	18 6 0 0 00		
Repairs and Maintenance	14 4 0 0 00		
Factory Supplies Used	13 9 0 0 00		
Factory Insurance Expired	7 6 0 0 00		
Property Tax on Factory Building	7 5 0 0 00		
Miscellaneous Factory Costs	7 1 0 0 00		
Total Factory Overhead		347 4 0 0 00	
Total Manufacturing Costs			1 336 4 0 0 00
Total Cost of Work-in-Process			
during the Period			$1 496 4 0 0 00
Less Work-in-Process Inventory, June 30			175 0 0 0 00
Cost of Goods Manufactured			$1 321 4 0 0 00

Instructions

1. Journalize the adjusting entries for the Raw Materials Inventory and the Work-in-Process Inventory.
2. Journalize the closing entries for manufacturing costs.

3. Post the entries to the Manufacturing Summary account.
4. Journalize and post the entry to close the Manufacturing Summary account.

Problem 29-2A   Here is the trial balance of the Hillier Manufacturing Corporation as of December 31 of this year.

Hillier Manufacturing Corporation
Trial Balance
December 31, 19–

ACCOUNT NAME	DEBIT	CREDIT
Cash	8 7 0 0 00	
Accounts Receivable	69 4 0 0 00	
Allowance for Doubtful Accounts		2 7 0 0 00
Raw Materials Inventory	91 6 0 0 00	
Work-in-Process Inventory	142 1 0 0 00	
Finished Goods Inventory	138 4 0 0 00	
Prepaid Factory Insurance	4 2 0 0 00	
Factory Supplies	6 0 0 0 00	
Machinery	171 0 0 0 00	
Accumulated Depreciation, Machinery		86 4 0 0 00
Accounts Payable		54 9 0 0 00
Common Stock		200 0 0 0 00
Paid-in Capital in Excess of Stated Value		50 0 0 0 00
Retained Earnings		136 6 6 0 00
Sales		1 291 4 0 0 00
Raw Materials Purchases	139 9 0 0 00	
Direct Labor	421 2 8 0 00	
Indirect Labor	161 4 6 0 00	
Heat, Light, and Power	32 4 0 0 00	
Machinery Repairs	19 6 0 0 00	
Selling Expenses (control)	283 4 2 0 00	
General Expenses (control)	118 7 5 0 00	
Income Tax	13 8 5 0 00	
	1 822 0 6 0 00	1 822 0 6 0 00

You are given the following information for the adjustments.

a. Year-end inventories: raw materials, $85,400; work-in-process, $128,400; finished goods, $140,700.
b. Estimated depreciation of factory machinery, $18,500.
c. A study of the company's insurance policies shows that $3,100 of factory insurance expired during the year.
d. Allowance for Doubtful Accounts to be increased by $1,550 [debit General Expenses (control)].

e. Accrued direct labor, $720; accrued indirect labor, $240; accrued sales commissions, $280.
f. An inventory shows that $3,800 of factory supplies were used during the year.
g. Additional income tax, $11,800.

Instructions

1. Prepare a work sheet.
2. Prepare a statement of cost of goods manufactured.
3. Prepare an income statement.

Problem 29-3A Here are the Statement of Cost of Goods Manufactured and Income Statement columns in the work sheet of the Dorchester Machine Products Corporation as of December 31, the end of the fiscal year. The firm's beginning inventory of raw materials is $71,460; its beginning inventory of work in process is $126,700.

ACCOUNT NAME	STATEMENT OF COST OF GOODS MANUFACTURED DEBIT	CREDIT	INCOME STATEMENT DEBIT	CREDIT
Sales				1,508 2 4 0 00
Sales Returns and Allowances			12 6 0 0 00	
Sales Discounts			12 0 0 0 00	
Selling Expenses (control)			186 9 5 0 00	
General Expenses (control)			73 6 1 0 00	
Raw Materials Purchases	382 0 0 0 00			
Direct Labor	486 9 0 0 00			
Indirect Labor	110 8 4 0 00			
Heat, Light, and Power	27 6 2 0 00			
Factory Supervision	26 9 3 0 00			
Rent, Factory	18 0 0 0 00			
Machinery Repairs	17 9 2 0 00			
Depreciation of Machinery	17 3 8 0 00			
Factory Supplies Used	4 9 0 0 00			
Factory Insurance Expired	3 6 0 0 00			
Small Tools Written Off	1 2 4 0 00			
Miscellaneous Factory Costs	6 5 0 00			
Loss on Disposal of Equipment			8 0 0 0 00	
Interest Expense			7 6 0 0 00	
Income Tax			52 0 5 0 00	
Manufacturing Summary	71 4 6 0 00	73 8 2 0 00		
	126 7 0 0 00	132 8 4 0 00		
Income Summary			184 6 0 0 00	192 8 0 0 00
	1,296 1 4 0 00	206 6 6 0 00		
Cost of Goods Manufactured		1,089 4 8 0 00	1,089 4 8 0 00	
	1,296 1 4 0 00	1,296 1 4 0 00	1,626 8 9 0 00	1,701 0 4 0 00
Net Income after Income Tax			74 1 5 0 00	
			1,701 0 4 0 00	1,701 0 4 0 00

Instructions

1. Prepare a statement of cost of goods manufactured.
2. Prepare an income statement.
3. Journalize the adjusting entries for the inventories.
4. Journalize the closing entries.

Problem 29-4A   Here are adjusting and closing entries that appear on the books of the Seabeck Marine Products Company at the end of the fiscal year, October 31.

1			*Adjusting Entries*				1
2	19– Oct.	31	*Manufacturing Summary*	88 7 7 0 00			2
3			*Raw Materials Inventory*		88 7 7 0 00		3
4							4
5		31	*Raw Materials Inventory*	90 6 1 8 00			5
6			*Manufacturing Summary*		90 6 1 8 00		6
7							7
8		31	*Manufacturing Summary*	112 8 2 0 00			8
9			*Work-in-Process Inventory*		112 8 2 0 00		9
10							10
11		31	*Work-in-Process Inventory*	116 8 4 0 00			11
12			*Manufacturing Summary*		116 8 4 0 00		12
13							13
14			*Closing Entries*				14
15		31	*Purchases Discount*	4 2 1 0 00			15
16			*Manufacturing Summary*		4 2 1 0 00		16
17							17
18		31	*Manufacturing Summary*	794 8 7 0 00			18
19			*Raw Materials Purchases*		254 9 6 0 00		19
20			*Direct Labor*		339 4 6 0 00		20
21			*Indirect Labor*		38 4 8 0 00		21
22			*Supervision*		58 6 4 0 00		22
23			*Depreciation of Machinery*		42 0 0 0 00		23
24			*Depreciation of Factory Building*		24 0 0 0 00		24
25			*Heat, Light, and Power*		12 8 2 0 00		25
26			*Repairs and Maintenance*		9 6 8 0 00		26
27			*Property Tax, Machinery*		1 2 7 0 00		27
28			*Property Tax, Factory Building*		1 8 4 0 00		28
29			*Factory Supplies Used*		9 4 7 0 00		29
30			*Factory Insurance Expired*		1 2 0 0 00		30
31			*Miscellaneous Factory Costs*		1 0 5 0 00		31
32							32
33		31	*Income Summary*	784 7 9 2 00			33
34			*Manufacturing Summary*		784 7 9 2 00		34
35							35

Instructions

Prepare a statement of cost of goods manufactured for the year.

Problem Set B

Problem 29-1B   Here is the statement of cost of goods manufactured for the Canfield Manufacturing Company.

Canfield Manufacturing Company				
Statement of Cost of Goods Manufactured				
For year ended June 30, 19–				
Work-in-Process Inventory, July 1				$ 120 0 0 0 00
Raw Materials:				
Raw Materials Inventory, July 1		$ 250 0 0 0 00		
Raw Materials Purchases (net)		390 0 0 0 00		
Cost of Raw Materials Available for Use		$ 640 0 0 0 00		
Less Raw Materials Inventory, June 30		265 0 0 0 00		
Cost of Raw Materials Used		$ 375 0 0 0 00		
Direct Labor		600 0 0 0 00		
Factory Overhead:				
Indirect Labor	$ 110 0 0 0 00			
Supervisory Salaries	95 0 0 0 00			
Depreciation of Factory Equipment	65 0 0 0 00			
Heat, Light, and Power	19 0 0 0 00			
Depreciation of Factory Building	18 8 0 0 00			
Repairs and Maintenance	14 2 0 0 00			
Factory Supplies Used	12 0 0 0 00			
Factory Insurance Expired	8 8 0 0 00			
Property Tax on Factory Building	7 2 0 0 00			
Miscellaneous Factory Costs	6 4 0 0 00			
Total Factory Overhead		356 4 0 0 00		
Total Manufacturing Costs			1 331 4 0 0 00	
Total Cost of Work in Process				
during the Period			$ 1 451 4 0 0 00	
Less Work-in-Process Inventory, June 30			260 0 0 0 00	
Cost of Goods Manufactured			$ 1 191 4 0 0 00	

Instructions

1. Journalize the adjusting entries for the Raw Materials Inventory and the Work-in-Process Inventory.
2. Journalize the closing entries for manufacturing costs.
3. Post the entries to the Manufacturing Summary account.
4. Journalize and post the entry to close the Manufacturing Summary account.

Problem 29-2B Here is the trial balance of the Dillow Products Corporation as of December 31 of this year.

Dillow Products Corporation
Trial Balance
December 31, 19–

ACCOUNT NAME	DEBIT	CREDIT
Cash	8 4 0 0 00	
Accounts Receivable	71 6 0 0 00	
Allowance for Doubtful Accounts		2 9 0 0 00
Raw Materials Inventory	90 0 0 0 00	
Work-in-Process Inventory	142 6 0 0 00	
Finished Goods Inventory	136 4 0 0 00	
Prepaid Factory Insurance	3 6 0 0 00	
Factory Supplies	6 0 0 0 00	
Machinery	168 0 0 0 00	
Accumulated Depreciation, Machinery		84 0 0 0 00
Accounts Payable		58 6 0 0 00
Common Stock		200 0 0 0 00
Paid-in Capital in Excess of Stated Value		40 0 0 0 00
Retained Earnings		144 0 0 0 00
Sales		1 277 5 0 0 00
Raw Materials Purchases	140 0 0 0 00	
Direct Labor	419 4 0 0 00	
Indirect Labor	159 8 0 0 00	
Heat, Light, and Power	32 0 0 0 00	
Machinery Repairs	18 0 0 0 00	
Selling Expenses (control)	279 9 0 0 00	
General Expenses (control)	120 1 0 0 00	
Income Tax	11 2 0 0 00	
	1 807 0 0 0 00	1 807 0 0 0 00

You are given the following information for the adjustments.

a. Year-end inventories: raw materials, $86,000; work in process, $126,800; finished goods, $138,500.
b. Allowance for Doubtful Accounts to be increased by $1,600 [debit General Expenses (control)].
c. An inventory shows that $4,000 of factory supplies were used during the year.
d. Estimated depreciation of factory machinery, $17,500.
e. A study of the company's insurance policies shows that $2,400 of factory insurance expired during the year.
f. Accrued direct labor, $600; accrued indirect labor, $200; accrued sales commissions, $200.
g. Additional income tax, $12,400.

Instructions

1. Prepare a work sheet.
2. Prepare a statement of cost of goods manufactured.
3. Prepare an income statement.

Problem 29-3B   Here are the columns that reflect the statement of cost of goods manufactured and the income statement in the work sheet of the Howell Specialty Products Company, Inc., as of December 31, the end of the fiscal year. The company's beginning inventory of raw materials is $69,120; the beginning inventory of work in process is $124,400.

ACCOUNT NAME	STATEMENT OF COST OF GOODS MANUFACTURED DEBIT	STATEMENT OF COST OF GOODS MANUFACTURED CREDIT	INCOME STATEMENT DEBIT	INCOME STATEMENT CREDIT
Sales				1,499 9 6 0 00
Sales Returns and Allowances			12 4 0 0 00	
Sales Discounts			11 8 0 0 00	
Selling Expenses (control)			179 4 9 0 00	
General Expenses (control)			72 8 6 0 00	
Raw Materials Purchases	384 5 0 0 00			
Direct Labor	482 9 0 0 00			
Indirect Labor	110 6 2 0 00			
Heat, Light, and Power	26 9 8 0 00			
Factory Supervision	26 9 5 0 00			
Rent, Factory	16 0 0 0 00			
Machinery Repairs	15 9 0 0 00			
Depreciation of Machinery	15 8 4 0 00			
Factory Supplies Used	6 2 0 0 00			
Factory Insurance Expired	3 8 0 0 00			
Small Tools Written Off	1 2 6 0 00			
Miscellaneous Factory Costs	6 8 0 00			
Loss on Disposal of Equipment			8 6 0 0 00	
Interest Expense			6 8 0 0 00	
Income Tax			52 0 8 0 00	
Manufacturing Summary	69 1 2 0 00	71 6 0 0 00		
	124 4 0 0 00	126 4 9 0 00		
Income Summary			181 4 0 0 00	186 7 2 0 00
	1,285 1 5 0 00	198 0 9 0 00		
Cost of Goods Manufactured		1,087 0 6 0 00	1,087 0 6 0 00	
	1,285 1 5 0 00	1,285 1 5 0 00	1,612 4 9 0 00	1,686 6 8 0 00
Net Income after Income Tax			74 1 9 0 00	
			1,686 6 8 0 00	1,686 6 8 0 00

Instructions

1. Prepare a statement of cost of goods manufactured.
2. Prepare an income statement.
3. Journalize the adjusting entries for the inventories.
4. Journalize the closing entries.

Problem 29-4B Here are adjusting and closing entries on the books of Doren Sash and Door Corporation at the end of the fiscal year, October 31.

1			*Adjusting Entries*		1
2	19– Oct.	31	Manufacturing Summary	86 7 0 0 00	2
3			Raw Materials Inventory	86 7 0 0 00	3
4					4
5		31	Raw Materials Inventory	78 4 9 0 00	5
6			Manufacturing Summary	78 4 9 0 00	6
7					7
8		31	Manufacturing Summary	110 7 4 0 00	8
9			Work-in-Process Inventory	110 7 4 0 00	9
10					10
11		31	Work-in-Process Inventory	106 4 2 0 00	11
12			Manufacturing Summary	106 4 2 0 00	12
13					13
14			*Closing Entries*		14
15		31	Purchases Discount	3 8 4 0 00	15
16			Manufacturing Summary	3 8 4 0 00	16
17					17
18		31	Manufacturing Summary	954 5 3 0 00	18
19			Raw Materials Purchases	236 7 0 0 00	19
20			Direct Labor	488 9 4 0 00	20
21			Indirect Labor	48 7 4 0 00	21
22			Supervision	69 4 8 0 00	22
23			Depreciation of Machinery	50 0 0 0 00	23
24			Depreciation of Factory Building	20 0 0 0 00	24
25			Heat, Light and Power	14 2 0 0 00	25
26			Repairs and Maintenance	12 7 9 0 00	26
27			Property Tax, Machinery	1 8 5 0 00	27
28			Property Tax, Factory Building	2 2 0 0 00	28
29			Factory Supplies Used	6 8 7 0 00	29
30			Factory Insurance Expired	1 8 0 0 00	30
31			Miscellaneous Factory Costs	9 6 0 00	31
32					32
33		31	Income Summary	963 2 2 0 00	33
34			Manufacturing Summary	963 2 2 0 00	34
35					35

Instructions

Prepare a statement of cost of goods manufactured for the year.

Index